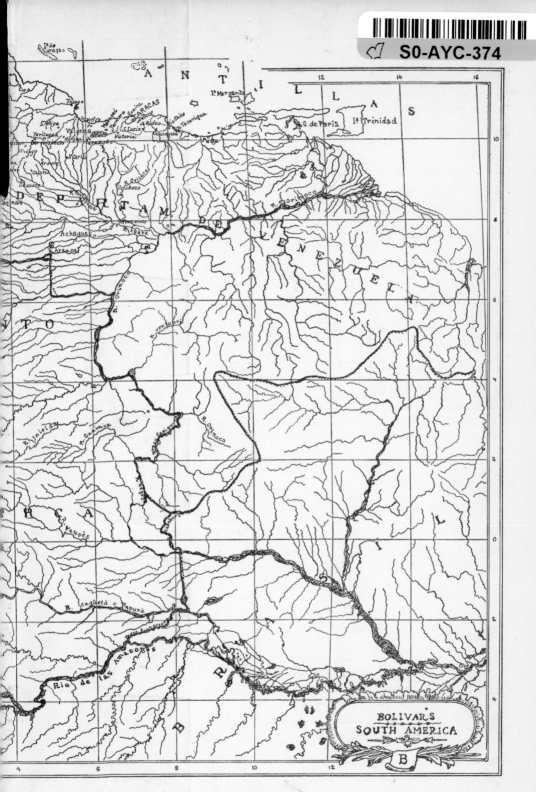

BOLIVAR'S
SOUTH AMERICA

SIMON BOLIVAR

This is a publication of

The School of Inter-American Affairs

The University of New Mexico

Inter-Americana Studies, IV

SIMON BOLIVAR

GERHARD MASUR

THE UNIVERSITY OF NEW MEXICO PRESS • ALBUQUERQUE, 1948

To the memory of
my mother
Frieda Strassmann Masur

Preface

*I*n the fall of 1935, I crossed the border into Switzerland, resolved never to return to my native Germany until the banner of the Hooked Cross had ceased to wave.

While searching for a new sphere of activity, I heard that the Colombian government was planning to invite to its country a group of German intellectuals. Waiting for the ambassador at the Colombian embassy in Geneva, my eyes fell on a portrait of Símon Bolívar.* At that time I knew as little about him as most Europeans. But I was aware at that moment that if and when I arrived in Colombia, I would be compelled to write the history of his life.

Carlyle once called Bolivar an Ulysses whose odyssey it would be rewarding to unfold, provided there were a Homer who could fashion the tale. My pretensions do not go that far. But without question it takes endurance to record Bolivar's life. Had I suspected what difficulties had first to be overcome in rounding up the material, my courage would have failed me. It was not as though there is a really satisfying biography to refer to; and the earlier works are no longer adequate. Ludwig and others like him can hardly be considered authentic or profound in their treatment. They miss what the Spanish call "ambiente," which, roughly translated, might be called milieu, or background—the study of the country, its people, and their way of life. With these Bolivar had to cope, and they contributed fundamentally to his greatness and his tragedy.

I was given the opportunity of discovering these circumstances as thoroughly as a European possibly can. But I could not foresee the almost inexhaustible amount of historical material through which I had to wade: Bolivar's letters, memorials,

* Hereafter the words *Simon* and *Bolivar* will be unaccented. All other Spanish words and proper names will carry the accents.

vii

speeches, and proclamations; official correspondence, cabinet resolutions, and instruments of government; to say nothing of diaries, memoirs, and a flood of historical exhibits, which increased from day to day.

Sometimes I felt as lost in this sea of ink as a sailor shipwrecked in the Pacific. I alternately cursed the lightheartedness with which I had embarked on this adventure and the stubbornness which bound me to it. But gradually the fog lifted and the historic landscape took shape. This was a strange assignment that I had given myself—one which made the loneliness of my exile bearable and which carried me through the darkness of the war years.

Having stated my purpose in writing the book and what led me to it, it remains for me to say why, in my opinion, no one before me undertook the task.

Although today we are in possession of the most important documents about Bolivar and the whole South American movement for independence, this material so far has been barely assimilated. There is but one way this can be achieved—by the critical, realistic methods that were developed by European historians from Thucydides to Ranke and Taine, but which have been only partially accepted in South America. Some do apply these methods, but, for most writers, history is only a part essential of the national development; fable is more important than research, legend than analysis, anecdote more interesting than interpretation. It is not my intention to criticize this attitude, inevitable in the growth of young nations. But the monuments in the public squares have such a thick patina that it is often difficult to recognize the form underneath. The figure of Bolivar developed in South America as a god for some, an evil fate for others. The passions of nationalism and political bias prevent a true appraisal of his stature. Bolivar himself says: "To judge revolutions and their leaders, we must watch them at close range and judge them at a great distance."

Never before have I been as conscious of the abyss which separates actual facts and events from what we call history. It is impossible to relate only "what really happened." The historian chooses the events which seem most important to him and welds them together to form a complete picture. His critera are not and should not be purely scientific; they should be both suggestive and artistic. Otherwise, he becomes immersed in facts and is at best a chronicler.

However, one cannot help but neglect some aspects of Bolivar's life; he may be studied from many angles: military, diplomatic, and literary, with each facet furnishing material for volumes. But the biographer should organize his facts around the core of the individual, for only in this manner can he see the integral structure from which all other aspects take their form.

Bolivar appears to me to be one of the outstanding figures of the nineteenth century and one of the great personalities of all time. There are certain principles for which he lived, and in which I myself believe: that freedom is a value in itself; that it is better to die for freedom than to live a slave; that the political organization of freedom has its expression in democracy, but that democracy must find the balance between the demands of liberty and those of stability and efficacy or anarchy will develop; that international problems must find their solution in a league of free peoples which will resist aggression with armed might and settle controversies between its members through a court of equity. This is the essence of Bolivar's political credo. Its significance for our own era seems obvious.

I am conscious of Bolivar's greatness, but I have not painted him as an infallible individual. "To history belongs neither falsehood nor exaggeration, but only truth," said the Liberator. And it is with these words in mind that I have tried to portray his life and work.—June 6, 1946

ACKNOWLEDGMENTS

The author wishes to acknowledge his indebtedness to the Rockefeller Foundation for the generous grants that enabled him during the years from 1945 to 1947 to continue in Bogotá, Caracas, Washington, and New York the research on the life of Simon Bolivar begun by him in 1941. Dr. D. H. Stevens, Professor William Berrien, and Dr. John Marshall have accompanied the progress of the book with helpful understanding. The American Committee for Emigré Scholars in New York has also been very helpful.

In addition he wishes to express his gratitude to the many individuals and institutions whose interest and coöperation were invaluable for the advance of this treatise: to the librarians of the Escuela Normal Superior in Bogotá, the Colegio de Nuestra Señora del Rosario, the Banco de la República, the Biblioteca Nacional, and the Ministerio de Relaciones Exteriores in Bogotá; to the librarians and the staffs of the Academia Nacional, the Archivo de Bolívar, and the Biblioteca Nacional in Caracas; to Mr. Lewis Hanke of the Library of Congress, and to the librarian and staff of the Pan-American Union, Washington.

Many South Americans have helped with suggestion and advice. The writer is especially indebted to Señor Vicente Lecuna of Caracas for permission to reproduce a map designed by him, for many interesting and informative conversations, and for his constant sympathy and encouragement. Thanks are also due to Messrs. Sanín Cano, Guillermo Hernandez de Alba, the late Guillermo Valencia and Raimundo Rivas, Fabio and Carlos Lozano y Lozano, and Monseñor J. V. Castro Silva, all of Bogotá, Colombia. Among many friends in Caracas, J. Nucete Sardí and Monseñor N. Navarro were most helpful.

The author is under deep obligation to Mrs. Beatrice Winokur for her altruistic efforts in translating the greater part of the German manuscript into English. Mrs. Patricia Fox prepared the first third of the copy for publication. Mrs. Helen Gaylord Knapp edited the remaining chapters; her labor and unvarying interest have been of inestimable value to the author. Dr. Dorothy Woodward, of the University of New Mexico, has rendered valuable service in checking the manuscript.

Whatever factual errors may be found are the author's own.

GERHARD MASUR

Sweet Briar, Virginia, February, 1948

Table of Contents

LIST OF ILLUSTRATIONS

ERRATA

Page 31, lines 6 and 10 from bottom, for Hippolita *read* Hipolita.
Pages 161. last line; 165. line 4; 183, line 3 from bottom, for Camillo *read* Camilo.
Page 407, line 10, for Cusco *read* Cuzco.
Page 506 Chapter Heading, for Ayachuco *read* Ayacucho.
Pages 507, 509, 511, 513, 515, 517, 519, 521, 523, 525, 527, 529, 531 running heads, for Ayachuco *read* Ayacucho.
Page 614, line 9, for become *read* became.

Part I

MAN OF AMBITION

CHAPTER 1

Background

*A*merica was not discovered. America was conquered. When the people of Europe, in their expansion across the face of the earth, conquered this continent step by step, their motives of greed, adventure, and lust for power far outweighed those of a higher nature which might have led to the discovery of America. America was conquered rather than discovered; domination preceded understanding.[1]

Is it a coincidence that Christopher Columbus never penetrated beyond the coast, deep onto American soil? It seems almost symbolic today that surrounded by blind, misunderstanding countrymen he died in despair, unaware of his own achievement.

Only in the figure of Columbus, brightly luminous among the first generation of conquerors and adventurers, pirates and gold-seekers, are there the characteristics of a discoverer. Paul Claudel compares the genius of Columbus with a mirror whose one side gleams in the light, the other showing rust and scratches. In him and surrounding him everything is mysterious, hidden under a veil which he himself fashioned and to which he clung desperately.[2] Was he Genoese, Spaniard, or Jew? Pirate, sailor, or geographer? Genius, dilettante, or swindler favored

---

1 G. Arciniegas: El sentido de los descubrimientos, en Prosistas y poetas Bogotanos. Bogatá, 1938. p. 401.
2 S. de Madariaga: Cristóbal Colón. Buenos Aires, 1940. G. Friderici: Der Charakter der Entdeckung und Eroberung Amerikas. Stuttgart, 1925. H. Vignaud: Etudes critiques sur la vie de Colon. Paris, 1905. S. Ruge: Kolumbus. Berlin, 1902. S. Morrison: Admiral of the Ocean Sea. Boston, 1942.

3

by fortune? Perhaps he was all of these, but so entangled in
an intricate knot of fate that the threads cannot be separated.
When his great hour came, we already find in him the traits
which were to constitute the final portrait: the eyes of a seeker
and the imagination of a dreamer; the forehead of a prophet
and the hands of an usurer.

His was a discovery, although differing from his own hopes
and expectations. While the lust for gold was present in him,
it was not that alone which motivated him, for there is a
definite mysticism apparent in his letters and papers. When
he reached that distant land of his dreams, he saw in it the
fulfillment of Holy Writ and the promise of the Holy Ghost,
and he believed when he reached the fresh waters of the
Orinoco that he was entering a lost Eden.[3]

But Columbus was not strong enough to win and keep a
portion of the earth. All too quickly the leadership of his
mighty undertaking passed into the hands of those seeking
personal aggrandizement. Thus America was conquered before it was discovered, enslaved before it was recognized,
ordered and ruled before it was understood. A rediscovery—
and a new outlook on this rediscovery—was necessary, and in
it Columbus' role was filled by Simon Bolivar. More than
three hundred years separated the European searcher from the
American genius—three hundred years of conquest, plunder,
and enslavement; but at last a period of growth and formation
followed, during which the forces of the country were combined and the energies united. Only at the beginning of the
nineteenth century did South America win back its identity.

Half a century after Columbus had destroyed the concepts
of the Middle Ages and established a bridgehead on American
soil, the conquerors had taken possession of the continent—
from the Río Grande to the La Plata, from the Atlantic to the
Pacific[4]—for the Crowns of Castile and Aragon.

3 A. von Humboldt: Examen critique de l'histoire de la geographie du nouveau
continent. Paris, 1836.
4 R. Levené: Historia de America. Buenos Aires, 1940. Vol. I-VII. L. Ullóa
Cisneros: Historia Universal. Edited by Institut Gallach. Vol. VI: America.

Spain contributed to the new continent its best and its worst. There were the great *condottieri,* such as Cortez; scholars, such as Jiménez de Quesada; and quarrelsome monks, such as Fernando de Luque on the one hand; with Pizarro and Benalcázar and their following of blood-and-gold-thirsty adventurers from the rank and file on the other. There were those who for one reason or another no longer wished to breathe the air of their native land—heretics, or criminals for whom life was not too important, who asked no more of it than could be contained in a brief hour of pain and pleasure. But there were also the dreamers about fabulous realms containing the castles and women promised the heroes of romantic tales. As is usual in great moments of crisis, both the good and the bad were lifted by the tide and cast together upon the new shores.

> Mis arreos son las armas,
> Mi descanso es pelear,
> Mi cama las duras peñas,
> Mi dormir siempre el velar.

What united these ill-assorted groups? Did they suffer the privations and dangers of a tropical world for a phantom of fame or for the glory of Spain? In most cases it was personal ambition which fired the conquerors. From the time of its conquest, the subjugation of South America was the work of individuals, and in most cases of young, wayward men who were lured by the spirit of adventure. The Spanish State remained aloof, watching and waiting during the early stages of the conquest of America by its sons. Although there were pacts with the expeditions' leaders and support according to their successes, the State took little active part at first.[5]

Barcelona, 1932. C. Pereyra: Historia de América Española. Madrid, 1924. R. Altamira: Historia de España y de la civilización española. Vol. IV. Barcelona, 1911. E. Gothein: Staat und Gesellschaft im Zeitalter der Gegenreformation. Munchen, 1922. L. Halphen and Ph. Sagnac: Peuples et Civilisations. Vol. VIII, IX, and X. Paris, 1929-35. R. Bigelor Merriman: The Rise of the Spanish Empire. Vol. I-IV. New York, 1936. A. Rein: Die Bedeutung der uberseeischen Ausdehnung fur das europaische Staatensystem. Hist. Zeitschr. Vol. CXXXVII.

5 J. M. Ots Capdequi: Estudios de Historia del Derecho Español en las Indias. Bogotá, 1940. p. 406. Ch. E. Chapman: Colonial Hispanic America. New York, 1933.

The traces of this attitude are indelibly engraved on the face of the developing colonial realm. The aloofness of the Spanish State explains in part the anarchy, the cruelty, and the criminal character which typifies the conquest in almost all the continent. Far removed from authority and justice, without control and command, Indian blood was shed in rivers. There was no one to call the intruders to account. So there developed from the very beginning a strain of feudal domination in the new world which was to become increasingly important in the social formation of South America.

Historians of four centuries have described the cruelty of the Spanish conquest, which it is impossible to deny in the face of the shocking testimony. Every conquest is cruel, however, and this subjugation of a strange land, an alien race, amidst untold hardships without relief, forced the Spaniards to take the policy they did. The final judgment on the Hispanization of South and Central America depends on the importance given to its colonization rather than its conquest.

It has not been rare to see a people blaze a trail with fire and sword only to succeed in dimming the remembrance of bloodshed so that yesterday's enemies become the friends of today and the brothers of tomorrow. What of Spanish colonization, then? It is the result of the sum of the conflicting forces—the Indians and the Spanish conquerors.

The world has marvelled that a handful of men so easily conquered the empires of the Aztecs and the Incas. Men have searched for the reasons and ascribed them variously to the superiority of European arms, to political disintegration, and even to the lack of vitamins in the diet of the Indians. But in the eyes of those who search more deeply, the real cause lay in the superiority of European civilization.[6]

At the time of the Spanish invasion, the Indian peoples had reached a stage in their cultural development corresponding to that of the Egyptians and Babylonians. They were in

6 I. B. S. Haldane: Es la historia un engaño? Revista de las Indias. Bogotá, 1937. No. 7. p. 22.

the period of transition from the Stone to the Metal Age. Gold and copper were in use, but iron was unknown both in war and husbandry. The political and religious organization of kingdoms and priest-castes show a similar development. Farming was primitive, and the use of the wheel was unknown. Few domestic animals were in use. Hieroglyphics and the language of knots were in common practice through Mexico and Peru. Consequently, the general economic structure restricted industry to the home, where weaving and the making of pottery, weapons, and jewelry took place.

Art, however, reached a high level of development and its barbaric splendor and daemonic genius can still be seen in the work of the Mayas and in the indestructible architecture of the Incas and Aztecs. It was, inevitably, of religious inspiration, and the priests, for whom the astronomical year was as fluid as it was for the worshippers on the Nile or the Euphrates, used it for their own purposes. The rites and cults of the Andean peoples, their idolatry and legends, possess the same mystic, awesome character as their art. Human sacrifice was the core of many of their religions, and blood was shed with an enthusiasm that was alternately childishly ecstatic and viciously cruel.[7]

In spite of the lushness of the tropical plant life, the farm implements of these primitive peoples were too inadequate to make possible a great increase in population. Estimates vary regarding the number of Indians found by the Spaniards, but certainly their number was small in proportion to their territory, and overwhelming only in comparison with that of their conquerors.

The South American Indians were forced by climatic necessity to shift their domiciles to the Andean Plateau, Mexico, Bogotá, Quito, and Cuzco. In contrast to the higher cultures

7 H. Beauchat: Manuel d'Archéologie Americaine. Paris, 1912. R. C. Markham: Los Incas del Perú. Lima, 1920. Ph. Means: Ancient civilizations of the Andes. New York, 1931. J. Acosta: Compendio histórico del Descubrimiento y Colonización de la Nueva Granada. Bogotá, 1901. H. I. Spinden: Ancient Civilizations of Mexico and Central America. New York, 1928. H. I. Spinden: A Study of Maya Art. Cambridge, 1913. S. C. Morley: The Ancient Maya. Stanford, 1946.

of Asia, which followed the courses of the large rivers, Indian civilization developed on the plateaus or cordilleras. Along the vast rivers and coastal areas of America lived the more primitive tribes. On the whole the pre-Columbus Indians were a people knowing little or nothing of seafaring, with little communication between tribes, and with practically no exchange of ideas or of material goods. It is not surprising that without ever learning much of each other, they succumbed rapidly to the iron rule of new masters with the advantage of four thousand years of intellectual and technical superiority.

The Spaniards were fully aware of this superiority. Spain entered into the era of discovery and expansion with all the impetus given her by the reconquest of territory from the Arabs. The year 1492 saw both the fall of Granada and the discovery of America. The crusader spirit which animated the expulsion of Islam was carried over to the battles and campaigns on the other side of the Atlantic and gave the undertaking the hard, proud, fanatical character of a delayed Middle Ages. The idea of a world-nation in the union of the Church, the Society of Jesus, the new mysticism of St. Theresa and San Juan de la Cruz, the new scholasticism, the romance of chivalry—all bore witness to the spirit of the Middle Ages which, in both Spain and America, outlived the span allotted to it elsewhere. This concept dominated the conquerors, even the lowliest, who dedicated themselves to the great adventure which they called the New World. And this guaranteed them the right to rule.[8]

Once vanquished and subjugated, the situation of the Indians was tragically hopeless. At best they were raw material for their Spanish masters, the clay from which to fashion the bricks of the future world-order. It was obvious that their political order, their language, their religion and customs—all would be suppressed, and they could live out only an illegitimate and subterranean existence. Whatever our sympathy for

8 Menéndez Pidal: La España del Cid. Buenos Aires, 1939. F. de Onís: Ensayo sobre el sentido de la cultura española. Madrid, 1932.

the oppressed, we must realise that this people could not have escaped the processes of western expansion.

The Spanish State and the Church were instrumental in preventing such an extermination of the Indians as had occurred in North America. The State and the Catholic Church defended the Indians against the Spaniards partly because colonial policy was predicated upon the existence of such labor-classes as could be exploited, and partly because of a sincere, Christian sense of duty. In any critical appraisal of the Spanish government's rule overseas, we must not forget that Spain was the medieval nation of modern Europe, the land without a Renaissance, and Spain's policy during the sixteenth century bore the unmistakable imprint of absolutism.[9]

It was natural that the Spanish State should permit no division of sovereignty, and did not grant an international status to its colonies. Other European nations had adopted the same attitude. But in contrast to the English settlements in North America the Spaniards denied their colonials any kind of local autonomy, and this fact became vitally important in the complex development of North and South America.[10]

The Spanish State took the constitutional formation of its possessions firmly in hand after but a short period of waiting, applying the standards which were the rule in Castile. Spain, a continental nation, was not, like Holland and Portugal, content with a coastal trading system, and soon carried out a complete penetration of its newly acquired territory.

The *Consejo de las Indias,* which had been functioning since 1511 and which sat in Madrid, assumed the authority of the King and took over the duties of the governing body as well as those of the highest tribunal, while in South America itself,

9 R. Altimira: La política de España en América. Valencia, 1921. R. Altamira: La huella de España en América. Madrid, 1924. M. Serrano y Sanz: Orígenes de la dominación Española en América. Madrid, 1918. B. Moses: The Establishment of Spanish Rule in America, New York, 1907.

10 S. A. Zavala: Las instituciones juridicas en las conquista de América. Madrid, 1935. Ots Capdequi: Instituciones sociales de la América Española durante el periodo colonial. La Plata, 1934. J. Becker: Política Española en las Indias. Madrid, 1920. Ch. H. Cunningham: The Audiencia in the Spanish Colonies. Berkeley, 1919.

governmental power was transferred from the *conquistadores* to the officials and corporate bodies designated by the Crown: viceroys, governors, commanders, and *audiencias*. The viceregal states of Mexico and Peru were patterned after Naples and Sicily, while in Quito and Bogotá, the *audiencias,* or courts of law, were copied from those of Valladolid and Granada. Venezuela and countries along the La Plata were organized into military units under the commanding general. This disposition was not final, however, and partitioning and reorganization occurred frequently.

The relative independence of these territories was not approved by the absolute monarchy, and such independence was greater than Spain's possessions in Europe obtained. Expansion, distance, and lack of regular communications made the reins of government slacker than in Europe, and it was therefore most important to delegate the authority to trustworthy and competent men. It was axiomatic that the high posts be filled exclusively with native-born Spaniards. This all-pervasive character of the Spanish administration, when examined today, represents one of the glories of its colonial control, and became the foundation of all Ibero-American culture. The organization of urban communities was of prime importance in this process of transplanting European customs to South American soil. This organization followed the Spanish pattern; there were the *alcaldes*—the mayor—and his numerous assistants, there were city councils, and also the *cabildos abiertos* or voluntary council meetings at which citizens of the community got together to discuss particularly important problems. The communities formed from the very outset a balance for the feudalism of the young aristocracy and the authoritative demands of the State government. When the hour for independence struck, it was the meetings of the free city councils which originated the impulse to revolt.[11]

11 Ots Capdequi: El regimen municipal hispano americano del periodo colonial. In Estudios, p. 136 ff. E. Schäfer: El consejo real supremo de las Indias. Vol. I. Sevilla, 1935.

It is not possible to probe too deeply into the countless details of those colonial governments. It is enough to know that the Spanish monarchy had created a rule that appeared at least to sanction order and justice. A basis for this attitude was established in 1680 by the codification of laws for America, the *Leyes de las Indias,* distinguished by its breadth and leniency.[12]

Unfortunately the established norms were not followed, or at the very least were only partially observed. The classic formula: *"Se acata, pero no se cumple"*—the law is respected but not obeyed—points the way to the chasm that was opening between ideal and reality. The contradiction between the appearance of justice and the harshness of the political and economic actuality can be grasped only through a study of the social structure of the colonial era and its domestic order. The Crown, jealous of its rights, succeeded in wresting political power from the hands of the first generation, delivering it instead to a fawning bureaucracy. It was impossible, however, to prevent the complete feudalization of the new domestic economy. The Crown saw only too well that here lay the necessary reward for all the trials and discomforts of the conquerors. Apart from the appropriation of gold, silver, and precious stones, representing only a passing phase, the decisive factor, as in every conquest, was the actual ownership of the land itself. Theoretically, according to medieval law, the land belonged to the Crown, but grants to loyal and zealous vassals was the natural result of conquest. The vast possessions created by the acquisition and development of the land caused the establishment of the *encomienda*—the backbone of colonial economy.[13] Land was apportioned as booty to the brave and the successful, but as this land would have been completely

12 J. de Solórzano y Pereyra: Política indiana. Antwerpen, 1703. A. Dempf: Christliche Staatsphilosophie in Spanien. Salzburg, 1937.

13 J. de la Peña: El tributo, sus orígenes, su implantación en Nueva España. Sevilla, 1934. S. A. Zavala: La encomienda indiana. Madrid, 1935. Amunategui: Las encomiendas de Indigenas en Chile. Santiago, 1909. L. Byrd Simpson: The Encomienda in New Spain. Berkeley, 1929. G. V. Vasquez: Doctrinas y realidades en la legislación para los Indios. México. 1940.

worthless without labor, natives were doled out to the new
owners, entrusted to them, according to royal edict, to protect
and defend, and to convert to Christianity. This ideological
definition barely concealed the economic intent of the *encomienda.* The *encomendero* was a feudal overlord who,
however, retained obligations to the King, as he had in Spain.
He did not own the land himself but was the recipient of gifts
the Indios were forced to make him, and usually only for the
length of, at most, two generations. It was natural that these
feudal masters sought to convert the land to their ownership by
graft, sale, occupation, or swindle—by fair means or by foul.
The result was the creation of the *haciendas,* the vast estates
which to this day characterize South American economy.

Thus Indian labor was indispensable, and the natives were
forced to pay their tributes with labor, the misuse and exploitation of which could not be prevented. This, added to the fact
of the Indios' laziness, caused them to sink rapidly to the level
of hopeless beasts of burden. The labor and property laws of
the period provide the best explanation for the drop in Indian
population after the conquest. However dull the Indian spirit
may have been, the memory of injustice was etched firmly on
the minds of the people and was to be a great liability to the
Spanish Crown during the revolutions that followed.

In self-defense the Spaniards have claimed that similar laws
existed before Columbus. Not only the landowners but also
high officials assumed the attitude that the social economy must
be built on the forced labor of the Indios. This forced labor
was the permanent tribute which the conquerors exacted from
their subjects for the entire three hundred years of their conquest. Moreover labor was exacted not only by landowners but
commandeered by the Crown as well for mining precious and
semi-precious metals; and the *mita,* a labor law in the mining
industry, paralleled the *encomienda* in farming. The Indios
avoided these obligations whenever possible, and frequently fled
to the cities, where they were treated a shade less brutally than

in the country. To escape the *mita* natives retreated to inaccessible and unhealthy areas and this too contributed to the drop in population.

The results of these measures are discussed heatedly to this day. Perhaps the sacrifices demanded by the Spaniards of the natives were no greater than those exacted before the conquest, but because they were imposed by strangers and invaders such sacrifices were resented more bitterly. In the heart of the Indio was stored spite, resentment, and cunning. Since the natives could not travel a straight course they sought subterfuges. Since they could not speak the truth, they resorted to lies and evasions. Thus there developed that strange psychology, which the best Hispano-American writers are still attempting to analyze—the psychology of a people who became servile but resentful, glib but dishonest, complacent but distrustful, tough and vengeful.

> O raza antigua y misteriosa,
> de impenetrable corazón,
> que sin gozar ves la alegría,
> y sin sufrir ves el dolor!
>
> Chocano.

"Oh, ancient and mysterious race of inpenetrable soul, that sees joy but cannot feel it, and sorrow but cannot suffer it." The tragic tension which characterizes the relationship of the Spaniards to the natives was not very different from that found in similar colonial dominions. The historian would violate his duty however if he did not point out the efforts that were made to improve the lot of the Indians.

A passionate war of ideas had raged in Spain since the early days of the conquest regarding the position of the Indians from the standpoint of theology and constitutional law. One side saw the Indians only as the objects of slavery, but the other, motivated by a sense of justice and compassion, acknowledged their right to at least a minimum of human privilege. The Crown knew perfectly well just how much cruelty and greed

attended the conduct of the Spaniards and in endless edicts
and prohibitions attempted to place restraint upon the uncontrollable ruling class. But the distance of royal authority from
the scene of action, and the right of the American regents to
test new laws by the results of their application, prevented in
many instances the successful execution of well-intentioned
edicts. Nevertheless the Crown was able to have the Indians
declared free men. By these measures the Crown could, at least
sporadically, stem the drop in population.

The situation regarding the theoretical freedom of the Indians is peculiar; the rights intended for them had to be bought
with injustice to others. As we write we see the honest, indignant face of Brother Bartolomé de las Casas, who became
inspired with pity for the persecuted Indios and shame for his
own compatriots. At this time the importation of Negroes
was already in progress, but it was due to his efforts that Negro
replaced Indian labor on the plantations and later also in the
mines. Research has proved that a great zeal and a revulsion
against existing conditions led him to overdo many things,
but his *History of the New World* will remain the proof of a
great social conscience which could not be silenced.[14] The
expedient, however, was almost worse than the evil itself, and
the bestial conditions under which the Negroes were brought
from Africa and the foul conditions under which they were
forced to live began a dark chapter in colonial history.[15] The
Negroes relieved the Indians wherever the mountain-reared
bodies of the latter went to pieces in the tropical sun. The
chief complaint against the policies of Las Casas is that they
heightened the already existing racial differences of the South
American world. Here, too, we meet one of the phenomena
of the continent which glides like an adder through the rubble
of colonial days. This racial difference between the peoples of
Latin American states became deeply rooted during the move-

14 B. de las Casas: Historia de las Indias. Madrid, 1927. R. Schneider: Las
Casas vor Karl V. Leipzig, 1938. C. Brandi: Karl V. Munchen, 1938. p. 148. Byrd
Simpson: *op. cit.,* pp. 1 ff.

15 Regarding the slave trade: see Sombart: Der moderne Kapitalismus. Munchen,
1928. Vol. I, 2. p. 704.

ment for independence, and it is but now very slowly disappearing.[16]

According to Cervantes, America had become the refuge of and protection for the desperate—the church of the defrauded, the asylum of murderers, a cover for gamblers, and the bait for loose women. In general it meant deception for many, a panacea for a few. But in all pulsated Spanish blood and Spanish pride. Spain forced on America its language, religion, and the laws of its government, with the Indians retaining but their lives as their own. With them, however, they soon penetrated the ranks of their numerically inferior conquerors. The Spaniards had brought over few women, and mating with the natives became a necessity. But in spite of the almost universally acknowledged increase in inter-racial unions, the fiction of the pure-blooded family was kept alive. Its members called themselves Creoles, and they were excessively proud of their origin. In addition there were the Indians of unmixed blood, the pure-blooded Negroes, and all combinations possible among these races. Alexander von Humboldt found in Mexico, as he would have found elsewhere, seven races: the *whites* born in Europe; the American-born *Creoles;* the *Mestics* of Indian and European blood; pure *Indians; mulattoes,* product of whites and Negroes; the *Zambos* with Indian and Negro blood; and the pure *Negroes.*[17] The control of such heterogeneous groups made great demands upon their rulers, and the Spaniards were far from understanding the problems involved. Their concept was quite different from that of the melting pot from which would one day emerge a unified form. Only through perpetuating the differences between races and classes did they believe that they could guarantee the complete and permanent subjugation of their colonies.[18]

16 C. Knight Jones: La transmisión y difusión de la civilización en las colonias iberoamericanas. Bogotá, 1940. p. 18. V. I. Quesada: La sociedad hispano americano bajo la dominación Española. Madrid, 1893.

17 A. V. Humboldt: Essai politique sur le royaume de la nouvelle Espagne. Paris, 1811. Vol. I. p. 76.

18 B. Moses: Social revolution of the XVIII century in South America. Annual Report of the A. H. A. 1915. pp. 163-170.

In such a society where, according to Humboldt, the social
position of a man was determined by the color of his skin, only
one point of agreement was possible, namely religion. Religion
would keep the warring elements from anarchy, and it only
could achieve this because its jurisdiction transcended earthly
distinctions of race. In colonial times everything was centered
about religious life. Since all political questions were settled
by the mother country and an American culture did not yet
exist, the unused forces tried to find their sphere of activity
here. In keeping with the Spanish mission, priests accompanied the conquerors to the Americas. Control and conversion
were synonymous.[19]

The vast organization of the Church was transplanted to
all parts of the new continent where archbishops and abbots,
following viceroys and governors in the hierarchy of the conquerors, represented the idea of imperialism to the greater glory
of God.

In addition to the secular clergy there appeared the orders
of the Franciscans, Capucins, Augustins, Dominicans, and
Jesuits, who became the spiritual pioneers among the unconquered tribes along the Orinoco and the Amazon, and who
completed here the educational projects begun by various high
prelates in many settlements. Schools were established, the
Universities of Lima and Mexico were created, and there even
began the education of the Indian population which made up
the lower classes.[20]

It is not to be expected that these establishments and the
education they disseminated expressed anything other than that
which characterized the Iberian Peninsula. The Spaniards gave
what they had to give, namely the theologically conditioned
culture of their prolonged Middle Ages, and whatever existed

19 Mecham: Church and State in Latin America. Chapel Hill, 1934. Saiz de la
Mora: La colonización Española y la Iglesia en América. Habana, 1911. L. Ayara-
garay: La Iglesia en América y la dominación Española. Buenos Aires, 1920. Desert:
L'église espagnole des Indes. Rev. Hisp. Vol. XXXIX.

20 B. Moses: Intellectual Background of the Revolution in South America. New
York, 1926. pp. 4-5. G. Hernández de Alba: Panorama de la Universidad en la
Colonia. Bogatá, 1937. G. Hernández de Alba: Cronica del Colegio Mayor de Nuestra
Señora del Rosario. Bogotá, 1938.

on the new continent in the way of intellectual life was due to
the Church. This cultural life was aristocratically exclusive—
mestics and mulattoes were kept outside—and there was no
interest in developing an intellectual class capable of devoting
itself to meeting the ever-growing needs and demands of life in
America. Literary matters were limited. The *Leyes de las Indias*
contains no less than fifteen laws controlling the printing and
sending of books to America, and both worldly and spiritual
censorship kept strict watch over this prohibition. In those
quiet colonial days little reading interrupted the stately and
snobbish rhythm of men's lives. But there was some writing,
and chronicles and geographic treatises, as well as research into
the language of the natives, can be found and are very valuable.
Garcilazo de la Vega, a descendant of the Incas, wrote *The
Conquest of Peru,* which is still a classic of that era and that
world; while in Mexico and New Granada we come across
mystic nuns who followed the precepts of St. Theresa. There
were personalities who moved into the forefront of Spanish
literature, such as Ruiz de Alarcón. The language, an incomparable bond linking all South American peoples, was cultivated
with a kind of jealous puritanism and protected from the bar-
barisms with which it was threatened by the influence of such
heterogeneous groups.[21]

Measured by permanent standards, however, there is nothing
in the literature of this period that demands inclusion in the
"eternal supply of human poetry." South American sensitivity
was then still in the formation process, but in it were the seeds
of a coming lyricism of nature and the promise of a new kind
of epic poetry.

The American spirit expressed itself less self-consciously and
more richly in art—bound closely to the Church, in fact, one
with the Church—whose character is displayed in an entirely
unique way. Colonial Baroque—its history will be written—

21 Menéndez y Pelayo: Historia de la Poesía Hispano americana. Madrid, 1913.
G. Quesada: La vida intelectual en la América Española durante los siglos XVI-XVIII.
Buenos Aires, 1917. L. A. Sánchez: Historia de la literatura Americana. Santiago,
1937.

was not especially creative in architecture, sculpture, or painting; fundamentally it followed the European example, but a
wealth of new ideas characterized its decoration. On pulpits
and chests, on shrines and altars, on drapes and crosses, on
garments and embroideries, there spreads before us a gloriously
luxurious life as intricately interwoven as the plant life of the
jungle. European ornament joins the tropical, and pineapple
and grape, the motif of the Cross and the symbol of the sun,
unite in new forms. The materials themselves tell clearly of
the origins of this art, for the walls and roofs, frames and pillars
are resplendent with gold. The crowns of religious figures contain emeralds, pearls, and amethysts, while the chests and
candelabras combine tortoise-shell, ebony, mother-of-pearl, and
silver into a new, magical whole.[22]

Their very costliness gave beauty and elegance to the innumerable feast days and holy days which interrupted the humdrum, everyday life of the colonies. The arrival of new officials,
the birthdays and deathdays of the royal family, and above all
the feast days of the Church, became the welcome excuse for
noisy festivities and costly processions, for cockfights, and
bullfights. Luxury, wastefulness, indolence, and pleasure characterized the life of the white upper classes. As revealed only
recently in papers and diaries of the day, they led the inglorious
life of drones, surrounded by a host of slaves, cut off from
contact with the rest of the world, in a climate where idleness
was desirable.[23] It is not these facts which are surprising, but
rather that these people did not degenerate more than they did.

While the lower classes were forced to do the physical work,
they too were ready at any time to imitate their masters in indolence and wastefulness. Such was life in those colonial days,
untouched for two hundred years by war or revolution—a still
life, dreamy and indolent, unthinkable for the children of the
twentieth century.

    22 G. Hernández de Alba: Teatro del Arte Colonial. Bogotá, 1938. I. G.
Navarro: La Escultura en el Ecuador. Madrid, 1928.
    23 Diario de Lima, 1640-1694. Publicado por H. Urteaga. Lima, 1917-1918.

This state of affairs continued as long as it did for several reasons; first, because invasions by new conquerors were prevented by the distance from Europe and the isolation provided by two oceans. With the exception of expeditions by English or Dutch pirates, the South Americans had no knowledge of war. Secondly, the Spanish government harshly forbade immigration of foreigners, and the Inquisition took good care that the possible ideological influence of those immigrants who did succeed in entering was successfully suppressed.

This consistent policy of isolation and detachment found its expression and its most effective weapon in the trade policy of Spain which, like most European countries, was mercantile.[24] To Spain, her colonies represented a supplementary market from which other nations were excluded. But her chief interest lay in her own enrichment through the importation of gold and silver, rather than in any industrial or economic development.[25] All competition with the mother country was forbidden the Americans, and even the individual parts of the continent could not trade with each other. American goods en route from one side of America to the other had to travel circuitously through Spanish ports, and Spanish navigation had a monopoly on trade with the colonies. Spain, however, was not sufficiently developed in industrial or maritime matters to meet all the demands arising from this trade concept. Only two flotillas a year plied between America and Europe, one to Central, the other to South America, with anything from fifteen to ninety ships in each. But even these restrictions did not make possible the conversion of the empire into a closed economic unit. The hypnotic influence of gold caused industrial production in Spain to deteriorate and the endless wars on the European continent hastened its impoverishment. Thus exports to America were reduced, and French, English, and Dutch profited by a

24 C. Haring: Commerce and Navigation between Spain and the Indies. Harvard, 1918.
25 M. I. Bonn: Spaniens Niedergang wahrend der Preisrevolution des XVI Jahrhunderts. Stuttgart, 1896. p. 109. K. Häbler: Die wirtschaftliche Blüte Spaniens und ihr Verfall. Berlin, 1888. J. J. Gervinus: Geschichts des XIX Jahrhunderts. Vol. III. Leipzig, 1858.

flourishing trade in smuggled goods. Many observers feel that
the most important reason for the decline of Spanish power lay
in this economic incompetence and inability to bind the colonies closer together. But until the symptoms developed into a
disease, those first two hundred years, between 1550 and 1750,
of domestic isolation and spiritual supervision guaranteed the
stability of the continent.

Monopolistic controls, monopolistic economy, monopolistic
culture—these epitomized the colonial government of Spain.
Little inter-province contact, no immigration, few ships, travel
only at the greatest risk, rare letters, very few books—is it any
wonder that under these conditions the Spaniards succeeded
for over two hundred years in keeping the seeds of doubt and
disintegration from America? Peace, indolence, the silence of
lazy days and longer nights, all these went to make up the
stultification that was the colonial era. The silence of the tomb,
as Schiller said? No, rather the dreamy somnolence of a child
who patiently endures a stern guardianship, with many external events and strong inner passions needed before the day
of his majority dawns.

The final period of Spanish domination is marked by reforms, rebellions, revolutionary ideas at home and great leaders
abroad, all casting their shadows across the equator. The many
influences causing the impulse towards independence, and its
prime mover, Bolivar, are important to remember.

The Middle Ages in Spain lasted until the end of the seventeenth century; Calderon's death and the end of the Hapsburg
rule marked its passing. A new period began with the Spanish
War of Succession and the advent of the Bourbons, distinguished by the Spanish attempt to catch up with a progressive
and enlightened Europe. Through the efforts of the Bourbons
the isolation of South America ended, and through their
enlightened reforms there arose the inevitable desire for independence and freedom.

Spain under the Bourbons turned her back on ancient Hapsburg tradition and identified herself with the French system

of national and foreign affairs.[26] The new rulers attempted with energy to regulate finances, stimulate farming and industry to greater effort and, in short, to transform the decadent state of the Counter Reformation into an enlightened despotism. The new dynastic relationship with France, however, brought Spain into an external conflict with an England rapidly expanding into a world power, a factor which vies in importance with the reforms of its ministers for the liberation of South America.

Charles III made tremendous efforts to raise Spain's economic potential in South America. Observers were appointed to report on the colonies, scientific studies on the use of mined ore were begun, roads were built and new industries founded. Foreigners were admitted and the inherent fallacies of the old monopolistic trade policies were recognized. The yearly flotilla system which had only filled the pockets of the Sevillian wholesalers was abolished and instead free navigation took its place, soon leading to the formation of large independent companies. Trade between Spain and her possessions mounted in ten years from 148 to 1,104 million *reales*.[27] Campomanes, Florida Blanco, and Aranda in the Spanish government, all sought to follow the advice laid down by the physiocratic school of thought, with whose indisputable success we shall concern ourselves later on. But the results did not entirely correspond with Spain's expectations, nor did she profit greatly from this advice.

For the oversevere regimentation in the last analysis prevented favorable relations with South America by the Crown and its enlightened viceroys. It was this regimentation—error of every absolutism—the exclusion of Creoles from high government office, and the system of spying that Spain was unwilling to reform. Her own system was based upon an enlightened but completely centralized despotism, and how could she therefore grant to the colonies what was denied her own people?

26 P. Zabala y Lera: España bajo los Borbones. Barcelona, 1926. R. Altamira: Hist. de la civilizacion Española. Madrid, 1935.

27 J. Mancini: Bolívar y la Emancipación de las colonias Españolas. Paris, 1930. pp. 49 ff. R. D. Hussey: The Caracas Company, 1728-1784. Harvard Hist. Studies. 1934.

The Bourbons employed vastly different methods to keep
the colonies properly subservient. To them the Counter Reformation system, depending on the interrelation of spiritual
and secular power, seemed flat and inadequate. They wanted
instead to unite all power in the hands of the governing body.
It is important to remember in this connection the expulsion
of the Jesuits in 1767 by decree of Minister Aranda, coinciding
with the general movement in Europe against the Society of
Jesus.

In the eyes of any objective observer, the expulsion of the
Jesuits from South America cannot be regarded as a constructive or a palliative measure. The loss of nearly two thousand
five hundred priests, who worked in the missions and in educational activities, did not serve to promote the development of
the American population. And as though they instinctively felt
the error of the Spanish policy, the Americans resisted the decree unanimously.[28]

This, more than any other single step taken by the Spanish
government, strengthened doubt in the wisdom of royal authority. Thousands of Jesuits, driven back to Europe from their
homes and schools, longed for their lost paradise where they
had enjoyed power and respect, and not a few of them allied
themselves with the dissenters and conspirators undermining
Spanish sovereignty at the end of the eighteenth century. The
expulsion of the Jesuits had its most telling effect in the void
left in the schools and universities and in the immediate relaxation of spiritual discipline. The American people had lost their
most loyal guardians, and the Spanish Crown some of its
staunchest defenders.

The Americans did not hesitate to increase and strengthen
their newly won freedom as much as possible, and the numerous scholars permitted by the generous Bourbons to visit and
explore the new world provided the leadership in this. We are
indebted to Jorge and Antonio Ulloa for their "secret notes"
about America. Scientific expeditions came to work in Peru

28 Blanco: Doc. Bd. I. pp. 91-103. L. A. Sánchez: *op. cit.*, pp. 134 ff.

and Chile on floral research. To New Granada went the great Mutis, discoverer of countless tropical plants, followed by La Condamine, Bompland, and the greatest of them all, Alexander von Humboldt.[29]

This scientific blooming, initiated by Europeans but passionately welcomed by Americans, is the best fruit of the attempts at reformation by the Bourbons. It marks the beginning of the second discovery which, in contrast to the first, was dedicated exclusively to South America itself. At great cost, museums were founded and high schools were built in Bogotá, Santiago, Habana, and Quito. Many restrictions were lifted regarding the importation of books, and those not entering the country legally were smuggled in. The educated Creoles attempted to reëstablish contact with European philosophy, and the names of Bacon, Descartes, Leibnitz, and Newton became familiar to them. In the work of Rousseau the South Americans found their political primer.[30]

Why, one must ask again, was Spain unsuccessful in bending these budding energies to her will? Why did the waters recede from the wheel of the machinery of state instead of making it turn? It is understandable that the first contact with liberal ideas awakened a strong antipathy to the existing regime on the part of South Americans. But a farsighted government might have succeeded in waiting out this early phase of opposition and encouraged the newly awakened intelligence through a broad program of colonial autonomy. Spain did not do this, and when finally she did attempt it, it was too late. So it is obvious that the stimulus to all Bourbon reforms stemmed from an egotistic desire to increase the fiscal income, with new regulations and plans all aimed to fill the State coffers.

A series of rebellions in the colonies, in which could be seen the prelude to the South American Revolution, were caused by

29 M. Maldonado: La obra de España en América. Maracaibo, 1928. Mutis: Homenaje del Ayuntamiento de Bogotá. 1932. G. y A. de Ulloa: Viaje histórico por la América meridional. 1752. G. y A. de Ulloa: Noticias secretes de América. London, 1826.

30 I. R. Spell: Hisp. Am. Rev. 1935. Vol. XV. p. 260.

this renewal of financial demands. Reaching far across the continent, they swelled in Peru and Colombia into mass uprisings. They differed in cause and conduct, leadership and progress. But all had the same tragic result, and in the history of the continent all bear the same name: *comuneros.*

Under the leadership of Tupac Amaru, a tribal chief boasting of the Inca blood that flowed in his veins, the Indios of Peru rebelled against new taxes and old misconduct.[31] Hated tax collectors and other officials were murdered, custom houses were stormed. Tupac Amaru, the pretender to the throne of the Incas, did not entirely repudiate his allegiance to the Spanish king, and we find among his followers both whites and mestics who were embittered by the injustices of bureaucracy. Among these was the Bishop of Cuzco. It can be understood, if not condoned, therefore, that the Spaniards, when they mastered the situation, executed Tupac in an extreme manner. After witnessing the extermination of his entire family, he was torn apart by four horses. The rebellion, while unsuccessful in its attempt to restore the Incas, at least revealed the profound and growing unrest of the masses.

Similar factors caused the revolt which broke out in New Granada in March of 1781. Demands for higher taxes were met with hails to the King and boos for the bad government on the part of the great mass of the people, with the movement growing so rapidly that the Viceroy was forced to flee to the coast.[32]

In New Granada, too, the rebels hoped for restoration of Indian rule, but the more moderate demanded preferment at least of American born for important government posts. Jose Antonio Galán and Juan Francisco de Berbeos were the leaders of the *comuneros.* The powerless government overcame the revolt by cunning and deceit. Under the good offices of the Bishop of Bogotá they promised the rebels the abolition of all new taxes and tributes, and the *comuneros,* achieving their pur-

31 B. Levin: Tupac Amaru. Buenos Aires, 1934. Blanco: Doc. Vol. I. p. 146. Tupac Amaru: 40 años de cautiverio. Lima, 1941.
32 Posada e Ibañez: Los Comuneros. Bogotá, 1905. M. Briceño: Historia de la insurreción de 1781. Bogotá, 1880. G. Arciniegas: Los comuneros. Bogatá, 1938.

pose, laid down their arms. But as soon as the Viceroy had returned safely to the capital, he ordered the renewal of all demands and the punishment of those who disobeyed. Disarmed and discouraged, the rebels were easily put down, and though Berbeos escaped, Galán was captured and hanged, his head and dismembered body exhibited as warning to all rebels. Order was restored, but in the lowest classes lay the seeds of sorrow and disappointment which blossomed forth when the time came.[33] The war against Spain was won by the sons of those so recently killed, and in Bolivar and his armies the cheated dead would arise and demand revenge. Forty-five years after the insurrection the brother of Tupac Amaru, who had survived imprisonment in Spain, wrote a touching letter to Bolivar. In it he calls himself fortunate in living to see the completion of the work begun by the *comuneros*.

The threads of historical tapestry are twisted. The Spanish wars, which called for excessive taxes and thus led to the insurrection of the *comuneros,* provoked the war for South American independence. England was waging war against a North America, which had declared its independence. What could be more natural than that support was given North America by Spain against the English? There was always hope of regaining lost territories, and when peace was declared in 1783 Spain retained Florida and Minorca. Actually, however, the losses sustained in the support of the North Americans were far greater than the territorial gains. The absolute monarchies, in approving this republican revolution, had themselves sawed through the branch on which they sat. And, in addition, Spain had presented to her overseas subjects the spectacle of aiding the revolt of foreign colonies. A blind faith in the allegiance of South America was required to believe it would not grasp this lesson. Tupac Amaru was persecuted unto death in 1781. Galán was executed in 1782, and in 1783 the United States of America won its independence. In 1789 the French Revolution broke out.

33 G. Arciniegas: Comuneros. p. 393. O'Leary: Doc. Vol. X. p. 5.

Did the South Americans know what was taking place in the world? Did they hear the ringing of the bell on July 4, 1776, and did they know of the impassioned speeches delivered to the French National Assembly? Actually, more news penetrated the walls of Spanish isolation than seems possible. The great marine companies whose ships carried trade between Europe and Venezuela not only brought in useful wares but also illegal books and newspapers. From Caracas they came to Bogotá, an intellectual center with a literary circle that discussed and recited Corneille and Racine, and a place where the pulse beat fast at the sound of verses like this:

L'injustice a la fin produit l'independence.

In Bogotá a few modest newspapers existed and soon public and private libraries were founded. From the private library of Antonio Nariño was heard the cry of French liberation, which penetrated into the heart of South America.

Antonio Nariño is one of the great figures in the history of pre-revolutionary South America.[34] He was a restless and volatile Creole who collected classic and modern works, French encyclopedias and Spanish chronicles, and he was determined to make a fortune through his clandestine enterprises. Interested in the only published newspaper, spreading the text of the Bill of Rights, he also not only obtained a report of the proceedings in the French National Assembly but he printed the report secretly in his own house. However when the publication was discovered, Nariño and ten associates were taken into custody. Among his papers were found the Triumph of Reason and eulogies on Franklin like this:

Eripuit caelo fulmen, sceptrumque tiranis!

After sentence of ten years' imprisonment and loss of property, Nariño escaped from his Cádiz jail and travelled incognito to Madrid, Paris, and London to win friends for South America's independence movement. Many years later he returned

34 Posada e Ibáñez: El precursor. Bogotá, 1903. R. Rivas: El andante caballero. Bogotá, 1926. pp. 73 ff. J. R. Vejarano: Nariño. Bogotá, 1939.

to Venezuela disguised as a priest, his role not yet played out. We meet him in many phases of the revolution.

The idea of revolution spread through countless subterranean channels to the upper Creole classes. But its nature had altered since the beginning of the eighteenth century. The fortunes of the Creoles had grown favorably through trading conditions, the profit from smuggling, and the increase in imports of colonial goods. The wealth of South America at the beginning of the war for independence was considered greater than that of the United States at the same period.[35] Like the French bourgeoisie at the outbreak of the French Revolution, the Creoles were by no means an impoverished class, but were on the contrary a flourishing group. The very economic superiority achieved served as lever to their political demands. It seemed natural to them that political self-sufficiency should follow economic self-sufficiency. Naturally, this conflicted with the Spanish will to power, and their every demand was denied. All too late did Godoy, "Prince of Peace," minister to Charles IV, grant greater concessions to the colonies at the beginning of the nineteenth century. His projects for the most part remained on paper and were finally abandoned; in his own words, "In Spain things move very slowly."[36]

But world history did not move slowly in this period of the Napoleonic wars, and Spain in its vacillation lost the last opportunity of winning over the remnants of the fast disappearing allegiance of its South American colonies. It proved a great and costly error to consider the Creoles still an effete and indolent group who spent their days in hammocks, their nights at the card table—a group consumed by disease, passion, and the dangerous heat of the tropics. The day was approaching when the Crown and the Spanish people would pay for this haughty illusion.

35 C. Pereyra: La juventud legendaria de Bolívar. Madrid, 1932. p. 270. B. Moses: Spain's declining power in South America. 1730-1806. Berkeley, 1919.

36 Mancini: pp. 222 ff. E. Benzo: La libertad de América. Madrid, 1922. Marius André: La Fin de L'Empire espagnol de l'Amerique. Paris, 1922.

CHAPTER 2

Youth

Simon Bolivar was born on July 24, 1783, in Caracas, capital of Venezuela. He was the fourth child of Don Juan Vicente Bolivar and Doña María de la Concepción de Palacios y Blanco. The Bolivar family, then one of the noblest and wealthiest among the Creole aristocracy of Caracas, had been respected and esteemed in the West Indies since the time Simon de Bolivar had settled on the island of Santo Domingo sometime between 1550 and 1560. A man of fine connections and sufficient means, De Bolivar was assigned to high government positions and when the Governor of Santo Domingo was transferred to Caracas he took De Bolivar along. Soon gaining the confidence of the Caracans, De Boliver was sent to Spain to present certain petitions on behalf of the colonies.[1] One of these petitions remains, in which Simon the Elder, as the Americans called him, requests information concerning the nobility, ancestry, and domain of his family. He received the answer on July 5, 1574, which showed that Simon de Bolivar was a nobleman whose family had lived in Basque provinces for centuries; it goes into his parentage, houses, and titles.[2]

After the family had settled in Caracas, its sons became

1 S. de Izpizua: Los vascos en América. Las ascendencia vasca del Libertador Simón Bolívar. Madrid, 1919. pp. 42-43. L. A. Sucre: Historial genealógico del Libertador. Caracas, 1930. J. Gil Fortoul: Historia constitucional de Venezuela. Berlin, 1907. p. 198. C. Pereyra: Juventud. pp. 23 ff. Simón Bolívar, el viejo. B. d. H. Caracas. Vol. X. Number 38. p. 163.

2 A. F. Ponte: Arbol genealógico del Libertador. Caracas, 1911. F. Francia: Arbol genealógico de la familia Bolívar. Caracas, 1911. J. Humbert: Les orígines et las ancestres du Liberateur. Paris, 1912.

28

active in public offices and in the courts, were devout Catholics
who made large donations to the Church and, intermarrying
with aristocratic families of the city—descendants of the conquerors—added to their Basque heritage that of Navarre and
Andalusía. San Mateo, an *encomienda* worked by the Indios,
remained in the family for two hundred years, and provided
the foundation for the family fortune. The Bolivars were appointed burgomasters and were prominent in the defense of La
Guayra. Thus we find in the ancestry of the Liberator a long,
unbroken line of respected, wealthy men and women of the
colonial aristocracy.

However, in the person of María Petronila de Ponte, who
became Juan de Bolivar's second wife at the beginning of the
eighteenth century, we find a broken thread in the genealogical
web of the Bolivar family. Her origins are not clear and thus
were unacceptable as to their racial purity in the eyes of the
Spanish. María's mother was the illegitimate child of an unknown woman found only in the birth register under the name
of María Josefa. Her father had declared somewhat unconvinc-
ingly in his will that her mother was his equal in birth. This
María Josefa was Simon Bolivar's great-great-grandmother. It
is impossible to determine from the records whether or not she
had European blood, but we must not decide at this point that
Bolivar was a mulatto. However, a study of his physiognomy
and certain character peculiarities, of which we shall speak
further on, make it appear likely that he had a slight strain of
Negro blood. In South America many people are, as the saying
goes, *café con leche*.[3]

In any case the Bolivar family derived certain advantages by
this union, and their already considerable holdings were increased by the acquisition of mines, houses, chapels, and large
properties. The Basque toughness and stamina inherited by
Bolivar became lighter, more volatile and sensuous through the
merging with tropical blood.

3 Sucre: *op. cit.,* p. 118. Pereyra: *op. cit.,* pp. 34-35. A. F. Ponte: Simón Bolívar,
Caracas, 1919. p. 226. M. S. Sánchez: Origen de Josefa María de Narvaez. B. d. H.
Caracas. Vol. XXVII. Number 106. p. 105.

Bolivar's father, born in 1726, had, as liege of his King, defended the ports of Venezuela against the British pirates, and at the age of twenty-one was appointed Caracan deputy to Spain. He spent five years at the court of Madrid, but did not estrange himself from America; and when he returned to Venezuela, richer in culture and experience, he was honored with new appointments. He successively substituted for the governor, judge, and commander of a regiment of militia whose creation was made necessary by the growing threat to the colonies by British sea power. He without question appeared to be a loyal subject of his King, but we know today that he already carried in his heart the idea of insurrection. In July, 1781, two years before Simon's birth, he signed the following letter concerning conditions in Venezuela: "We find ourselves in a shameful prison, and are treated even worse than the Negro slaves whose masters trust them more. We have no choice but to throw off this unbearable and disgraceful yoke." Bolivar sent the letter to Miranda who, he hoped, would instigate the revolution. "At the first sign from you, we are ready to follow you as our leader to the very end, and to shed the last drop of our blood in this great and honorable undertaking." It was the son, however, who was to fulfill this dream of revolt.[4]

A portrait still hangs in the house of Bolivar's birth which shows the father to be a cavalier of the eighteenth century— affected, elegant, with dark penetrating eyes of great intelligence. The resemblance between father and son is unmistakable. The father, a zestful seeker after pleasure, was a man of action, adaptable, broadminded, and independent. At the age of forty-six he married a young girl, only fourteen on the day of her marriage, who bore him four children in ten years: two daughters, María Antonia and Juana María; and two sons, Juan Vicente and the youngest, who was to immortalize the family name, Simón José Antonio de la Trinidad.[5]

4 W. S. Robertson: Life of Miranda. Chapel Hill, 1929. Vol. I, p. 28. C. Borges: La casa de Bolívar, in Antología Bolivariana. Bogotá, 1938. V. Lecuna: Historia de la casa de Bolivar. Caracas, 1924.
5 V. Lecuna: Adolescencia y juventud de Bolivar. B. d. H. Caracas. Vol. XIII. Number 52. p. 573. O'Leary: Memorias. Vol. I. p. 4. Pereyra: Juventud. p. 54.

The house where Simon Bolivar passed his early years was
spacious and luxurious, in keeping with the style of Colonial
days. It was the one story building of Andalusian origin, seen
throughout South America, with overhanging roof, crest-
emblazoned doors, and grilled windows. The simple façade
concealed the true depth of the house, in which rooms and
courtyard were symmetrically laid out. In the patio, shade-
filled by tropical plants, was centered the day and night life of
the family. Thick walls excluded the heat from without and
prevented conversations within from reaching the ear of out-
siders. In the parlor hung the family portraits, looking down
on the graceful, rococo furniture pushed against the walls, while
the silver service—the cups, bowls, plates, and platters that are
the pride of all Creole families—gleamed in the dining room.
The books in the library were mostly of a military, historical,
or religious nature—an edition of Calderón, a history of the
world, Bossuet's sermons.[6]

The four children who filled the Bolivar house with their
activities were to grow up apart. Even as young children their
differences were marked: Juana and Juan Vicente were blond
and blue-eyed, their nature gentle and docile, while María
Antonia and Simon, both dark and black-eyed, were willful,
positive, with strong personalities and a mutual understanding
that was to remain throughout their lives. As was customary
in colonial days, the children's time was spent in the care of
Negro servants. One of these, Hippolita, was Simon's nurse,
who guided his first steps and clung to him with a love and
devotion not to be forgotten by the Liberator. In a letter to one
of his sisters, many years later, Bolivar wrote: "I am sending
you a letter from my mother, Hippolita, so that you will give
her everything she wishes, and so that you will treat her as
though she were your own mother. She nourished my life. I
know no other parent than her."[7]

Simon Bolivar was orphaned early in his life. He was only
three when his father died, and the guardianship of the chil-

6 Lecuna: Papeles de Bolivar. Caracas, 1917. p. 375.
7 V. Lecuna: Cartas del Libertador. Vols. I-X. Caracas, 1929. Vol. V. p. 19.

dren, together with the management of the vast estate, were left
in the care of his mother, Doña María, and her father. Another
valuable property, left to Simon by an uncle on his mother's
side and attached to the residence in Caracas, also came under
her management.[8] Doña María led the secluded life that her
position as widow demanded. The meager information we
possess about her shows her to have been a wise and generous
woman, who, however, exercised no great influence on Simon's
education. A stronger hand than that of a highborn Creole
lady was needed to control him. Actually, since Doña María
died of tuberculosis when he was only nine, a clear line of
demarkation separates his education from the days spent in his
parents' house.[9]

Not long after his mother's death, in 1792, Simon's grandfather also died and his two sisters married, so the boy was
torn from family life and the close bonds that go with it. The
education he received, the pattern he followed, thus were not
part of his background but rather came to him from outside
influences. This possibly made him more self-reliant. Deprived
of the calming serenity of his home and thrust out into the life
of the city with its variety of turbulent impressions, the boy
quickly lost his youthful simplicity. These influences were
deeply realized by Bolivar, who wrote: "The earth of the
fatherland above all. It has fashioned our being from its substance. Our life is nothing but the essence of our poor country.
It is there that we have the witnesses to our birth, the creators
of our existence who gave us our souls by rearing us. There are
the graves of our fathers that demand security from us. Everything reminds us of our duty. Everything evokes sweet memories and gentle feelings in us. This was the stage of our
innocence, our first love, our first impressions and everything
that influenced us."

At the end of the eighteenth century Caracas was the third
largest city in South America and one of the most flourishing.

8 Lecuna: Adoloscencia. p. 446. Lecuna: Papeles. pp. 349, 379, 390.
9 Lecuna: Adolescencia. p. 454. Cartas: Vol. V. p. 20.

Built near the sea, its altitude and pleasant, summer-like climate, all contributed to make life in the city a charming one. Travellers wrote with admiration of its houses and gardens, its streets and public squares, its churches and bridges.[10]

Even if one did not have too high a regard in Caracas for education on a scientific level, there was still plenty of opportunity for a spoiled young aristocrat. Records reveal the fact that Simon was a wild lad, boisterous and more inclined to play than to study. Because of this he was, even before his mother's death, placed in the charge of a forceful tutor, José Sanz. In the house of this reputable lawyer and family counsellor Bolivar is supposed to have spent two years. It is definitely established at least that Sanz managed the Bolivar estate for several years and was frequently in the company of "Simoncito." As he described him, we see Bolivar as a lively child, always with a ready answer. Once Sanz called him a powder keg, to which Simon retorted: "Be careful, don't come near me. I might explode." At another time, when the two were riding together, Sanz on a thoroughbred and the boy on a donkey, Sanz said: "I'm afraid you'll never make a horseman." And Simon replied: "How can I become a horseman on a donkey too feeble even to carry wood?"

These anecdotes, in my opinion, are more likely to be fiction that fact. Through them all, however, runs such a similarity of opinion regarding Bolivar's character and temperament that their basic authenticity cannot be doubted.[11]

After the death of Simon's mother and grandfather, his uncle, Carlos Palacios, became his guardian, seeing to it that

10 Mancini: p. 107. F. de Segur: Mémoires et Souvenirs. Paris, 1827. Vol. I. p. 446. F. Depons: B. d. H. Caracas. Number 51 ff.
11 A. Rojas: Leyendas históricas de Venezuela. Caracas, 1891. Vol. II. p. 249. O'Leary: Memorias. Vol. I. p. 5. Pereyra: Juventud. p. 74 and Lecuna: Adolescencia, p. 446. I do not believe that it is necessary to discard these anecdotes completely. When Bolivar was already in Spain his uncle-guardian wrote the following words: "Me dices, que te quita mucho tiempo para attender a su educacion; lo creo asi; pero como quiera que tu eres un hombre que por tu constitucion te debe faltar el tiempo por mucho que lo aproveches es necesario, que no por atender a el te perjudique a tus intereses; y asi es que es preciso hablarle gordo o ponerlo en un Colegio si no se porta con aquel juicio y aplicacion que es debido como se le escribo ahora." Lecuna Adolescencia. p. 562. R. Blanco Fombona: Mocedades de Bolívar. Buenos Aires, 1942.

the boy learned the fundamentals of reading, writing, geography, and history. He received his first training at home in the manner of most children of his social caste, although Bolivar's father had cherished the hope of sending his sons to Europe for their education. But the times did not warrant this, since the European wars and the British blockade created too much of a hazard for so young a child, and Bolivar remained in Caracas. He himself wrote about his education: "My mother and my guardians did all they could to make me study. First they obtained for me excellent teachers. . . . Even if I don't know anything, I was nevertheless reared as the child of good family under Spanish rule should be."[12]

Who were these teachers? The first mentioned in Bolivar's writings was Andrés Bello, who later became a great philologist and poet, and compiled a Spanish grammar which grew to be accepted as a standard work. At this time Bello was but three years older than his pupil, and it seems a little unlikely that he was able to contribute much towards Simon's educational growth. The incorrect spelling in letters sent by Bolivar on his first trip to Europe leads us to the conclusion that either his teacher had little influence, or as a pupil he was a poor subject for theoretical instruction.[13]

The regimentation of a private school might have been salutary for a character such as Bolivar's but his uncle was too lenient to force the boy to leave home for boarding school and he therefore continued with private tutors. One man, Simón Rodríguez, had the greatest influence on Bolivar and must be regarded as his real preceptor. Rodríguez is a bizarre, even grotesque figure and his biographer was correct in naming his book *Genius or Madman?*[14] He was born in Caracas in 1771.

12 Cartas Vol. IV. p. 333. T. C. Mosquera: Memorias sobrela vida del Libertador Simón Bolívar. New York, 1853. p. 6.
13 M. L. Amunategui: Vida de Andrés Bello. Sanitago, 1882. Cartas Vol. VIII. p. 304. O'Leary: Memorias. Vol. I. p. 7. See also Homenaje a Andrés Bello. B. d. H. Caracas. Number 51. L. Duarte Level: Cuadros de la Hist. civ. y mil. d. Venezuela. Madrid, p. 214.
14 F. Lozano y Lozano: El maestro del Libertador. Paris, 1913. J. R. Wendehake: The master of Bolivar. Colon, 1930. E. Posada: El maestro del Libertador. B. d. H. Bogotá. Vol. XVI.

His name was actually Simón Carreño, but he later repudiated his father's name, sometimes even calling himself Robinson. He wanted to live like Original Man—as a part of nature. His mental equilibrium must have been disturbed at an early age. Flashes of genius and idiocy, understanding and insanity, made up the workings of that head which stares at us from portraits with the look of a lunatic able to drive normal people to distraction. He had read all the philosophy books he could get his hands on—Spinoza, Holbach, and above all Rousseau, and it was his great ambition to become the Jean-Jacques of South America. In addition he was a ladies' man, cynical, impudent, inconstant, and a gay deceiver. One could call him an Eulenspiegel of pedagogy, if it were not for the note of tragic conviction in all his dreams and fantasies. He must have realized finally that one earns little money peddling ideas and in later years supported himself by running a modest candle factory. When an old man—he reached the age of eighty—he admitted: "I, who wanted to make the world into a paradise for all, have made it into a hell for myself." Even more moving are his words: "When you can't expect anything more of life, you can expect something of death." There is no definite proof that this visionary reformer and fighter applied to Bolivar the theories of *Emile,* but he unquestionably brought Rousseau very close to the youth. Certainly the points of agreement with *Emile* are remarkable; Bolivar was an orphan, a requirement laid down by Rousseau; he was also rich, healthy, and strong. Rodríguez, who lived at this time at San Mateo with Bolivar, was able to expose him to the influence of nature and to immunize him to the influence of the outside world.[15]

In all the letters and writings of Bolivar, no author receives as much mention as Rousseau. In his confession to Simón Rodríguez, Bolivar states very clearly: "I have travelled the road you have shown me." And he goes on to say: "You have

15 J. J. Rousseau: Émile. Vol. I. pp. 17, 20, 42. Paris, 1882. M. André: Bolívar y lo Democracia. Barcelona, 1924. pp. 19-20. Simón Rodríguez: Defensa de Bolívar. Caracas, 1916. p. 12.

moulded my heart for liberty and justice—for the great and the beautiful."[16]

Rodríguez could boast of no tangible results, however, for Simon was a past master in the art of learning nothing. It was actually more training than teaching he received, but in this, at least, the teacher made for himself a place in history. He helped to fashion the great man, and what more can be asked of a pedagogue? As a matter of fact this way of Rodríguez' was most likely to reach his pupil's heart, for though Bolivar grasped quickly and memorized well, he was little concerned with his curriculum. Sensitive, frank, impatient, easily disconcerted, passionate feelings took root more readily in his soul than dry facts and philosophies. With all his unruliness, a strain of early maturity is apparent, and the youth definitely preferred the conversations of adults to the companionship of his contemporaries. Rodríguez said of himself that he did not wish to take root like a tree, and his first contact with Bolivar was not of long duration. No one can be surprised that Rodríguez, with his temperament, found himself in political difficulties which finally forced his departure from Caracas and from his pupil. The first of such incidents directed Bolivar's attention to politics. Up to that time he shared the generally accepted belief in the divine authority of the King of Spain, who was a distant deity to whom were due both loyal allegiance and blind obedience.[17] The events of 1796, however, shocked even the naive credulity of the Venezuelans. Colonial affairs had since 1796 been deeply affected by the open warfare with England, trade was interrupted by the British blockade and sales dropped, while freight and insurance rates rose. Instead of protecting American trade the Spanish Armada fought the British fleet and was roundly defeated in 1797. Trinidad was lost to the mother country and the American continent suffered considerably. A Negro riot, which had not taken on any pro-

16 O'Leary: Memorias. Vol. I. p. 6. O'Leary: Doc. Vol. IX. pp. 511 ff. Cartas Vol. IV. p. 32.

17 J. Zalamea: Infancia y adolescencia de Simón Bolívar. In Antología Bolivariana. Bogotá, 1938. p. 132.

portions, had easily been suppressed in Venezuela, but the air
was filled with revolutionary ideas.[18] People discussed the
French Revolution, events in Haiti, emancipation of the slaves,
and equal rights for Negroes. The white upper classes, watching these events very closely, saw in the uprising of the Negroes
the beginning of the end. But while this was still being discussed, a rebellion of much greater dimensions took place. The
fate of a group of Spaniards who had been accused in the
mother country of republican activities and deported to La
Guayra prison had aroused the sympathy of Venezuelans. The
prisoners were treated with great courtesy, even with deference,
in the prison, where life went on much as in Strauss' *Die
Fledermaus*. Receiving visitors, giving lectures on "the plain
and simple principles of the republican system," the prisoners,
and finally their American pupils, agreed on a plan of revolt.
First the Spaniards were to be set free and sent to the Antilles,
and then a general revolution, led by José María de España
and Manuel Gual, both respected members of Creole society,
was to break out in Venezuela.[19]

The initial part of the plan was carried out and the prisoners
escaped, but they soon forgot the help they had promised their
American friends and nothing more was heard from them.
Meanwhile revolution had broken out in Caracas, only to fail
because a premature disclosure permitted the government to
apprehend a great many of the conspirators. Among the sus-
pects was Simón Rodríguez. The upper classes among the
Creoles hastened to assure the governor of their loyalty and it
was comparatively easy to put down the uprising. The flame of
revolt had not spread far.[20] The leaders were arrested; Gual
escaped, but España was dragged by horses to the gallows and
his head and severed limbs exhibited as a warning to all.

Bolivar saw them. What were his feelings, what were his

18 Blanco: Doc. Vol. I. 230; Gil Fortoul: *op. cit.* p. 92.
19 Castro Fulgencio López: La Guayra: Casa y matriz de la Independencia.
Caracas, 1941. Blanco: Doc. Vol. I. pp. 287-88.
20 Baralt y Díaz: Resumen de la Historia de Venezuela. Brujas, 1939. Vol. I.
pp. 18-20. Blanco: Doc. Vol. I. p. 311. Lecuna: Adolescencia. p. 540.

thoughts? He had been informed of the rebel's plans and gloried in his teacher's part in the plot, betraying nothing of his knowledge of the undertaking in spite of his youth. During the treason trial, he received permission to visit the prisoners and we may assume that here his first political doubts were aroused. Rodríguez escaped conviction for lack of evidence. Since he was not greatly tempted to lose his head, he decided that it was the better part of valor to leave Venezuela, and Bolivar lost track of him for a while.[21]

Political unrest caused the government to pay more attention to the militia recently organized in Venezuela. Bolivar's father had organized a battalion, and this unit, the Militia of Aragua, young Simon Bolivar joined as a cadet at the age of fourteen. Bolivar spent a year in the militia, and though at its end he was promoted to the rank of lieutenant he can hardly have received adequate military training. It apparently gave him great pleasure to strut his uniforms. His military reports show nothing remarkable; in fact there was probably little about the youth at that time which could be called remarkable. He was alert, intelligent, elegant, and good-looking, loved dancing, riding, and swimming, excelled in everything, as did most young South Americans of his class.[22]

He had learned all he could or would in Caracas, and it seemed time to look farther afield. His uncle, Esteban Palacios, at the time living at Madrid, had influential friends at court, so the Palacios grasped at the opportunity to send Simon to Spain to make his fortune. They felt that with any luck at all he would attain money, title, and high office, but fate decided otherwise. Bolivar sailed January 19, 1799, on the *Ildefonso,* equipped with the proper letters of introduction due a young man of his position.

This was the first time that Simon Bolivar, then a pleasant and sociable lad of sixteen, had ever been on his own, and he used the occasion to throw his money away with both hands.

21 Mosquera: *op. cit.* p. 7.
22 Lecuna: Adolescencia. pp. 473, 544. Blanco: Doc. Vol. I. p. 190.

His boat stopped at Vera Cruz, giving Simon a glimpse of
Mexico, and he was able to express himself with more than
candor during an audience granted the young Creole by the
Viceroy. His audacity amazed those present when he praised
the French Revolution and even defended America's right to
independence, but it can have made little impression on the
Viceroy. Mexico was dangerous ground, having long been
threatened with political upheavals. It was unimportant if a
young jackanapes from Venezuela did speak of things he did
not understand, and the Viceroy merely dismissed him politely,
giving him fresh letters of recommendation to the Governor
of Havana.[23] But before Bolivar sailed he wrote his uncle and
guardian a letter—the first of a tremendous volume of correspondence (he later became one of the most prolific, if not the
greatest, letter writer of South America)—which was extremely
badly written and ill-composed, and described the first lap of
his journey to Europe.[24]

Simon Bolivar arrived in Spain early in the spring. His
relatives there did not question the purpose of his trip, and
agreed that the presence at court of a compatriot willing to protect fellow South Americans should certainly be exploited.
They saw immediately, however, that the youth was very
ignorant, that though he was charming to look at, he had no
culture of any kind, and that first of all it was necessary to
outfit him completely, as he had arrived in Spain without funds.
It was thought advisable to teach Simon a few languages, the
rudiments of mathematics, and dancing and duelling. We have
the itemized bills for all these expenses incurred to convert
the young provincial into a Madrid courtier.[25] From them we
see that his uncle was forced to pay more for clothes than for
books and teaching; good tailors apparently always have been
more expensive than good professors! Bolivar was prefectly
agreeable, obedient, and complacent, studied hard his own and

23 Mosquera: *op. cit.* p. 7. F. Larrazabal: Vida y correspondencia general del
Libertador Simón Bolívar. New York, 1901. p. 7. O'Leary: Memorias. Vol. I. p. 7-8.
24 Cartas Vol. I. p. 3. Lecuna: Adolescencia. pp. 552, 562.
25 Lecuna: Adolescencia. pp. 449-50, 556.

other languages and even took his mathematics lessons seriously. Early in his stay the boy lived with his uncle in the house of the South American, Mallo, but when his uncle complained that sometimes he was greatly disturbed by the boy, he was placed in the care of a great "caballero" from Caracas, the Marquis of Ustariz. It was he who first gave Bolivar a real taste for reading. According to the Liberator himself, he had in his youth read all the great poets of antiquity, all the philosophers, historians, and orators, as well as the modern classics of Spain, France, Italy, and England.²⁶ Of the ancients, Plutarch impressed him most. In any case, at this time it is certain that he read a great deal, gorging himself on ideas whose importance only dawned on him at a later date. But these studies did not occupy all his time, and his trip was never intended to be purely educational. There were more concrete and materially rewarding matters to be learned, not from books, but from life at Court.

Of all the courts of the *Ancien Regime* this was surely the most degenerate. Behind the leaden façade of Spanish ceremonials were hidden poverty and depravity. In the ten years since the outbreak of the great revolution Spanish politics had had little direction, with Charles IV weaving an uncertain course between the policies of France and England. He ran the danger of losing his mighty empire little by little, rescinding today what he had sanctioned yesterday. Farsighted men like Count Aranda had long seen the threat hanging over Spain's colonial possessions, but the Court had repudiated him as a pessimist. Charles IV, the best of men and the worst of kings, knew only the pleasures of the hunt, while the Queen controlled the state from her bedchamber. Even if one is unwilling to believe all the stories, a *Chronique Scandaleuse,* collected about Marie Luise, it is indisputable that Godoy was her lover, forced, however, to share her favors with many others. At the time of Bolivar's arrival in Madrid, the current favorite

26 Cartas Vol. IV. p. 333.

was Manuel Mallo, and it was said that when the King questioned Mallo as to the source of Mallo's money, he was told
that he was kept by a rich old woman. Bolivar was unable,
because of his lack of experience, to accept a brilliant position
offered him by Mallo, but he did live in his house at one time
and was able to observe the Queen's comings and goings, her
overseeing of kitchen matters, and her paying of the bills.[27]
At one time he even escorted her in disguise back to her own
quarters, and erotic interpretations have been woven around
this incident, which was in fact but an accidental meeting.[28]
However, these matters were not calculated to raise Bolivar's
respect for the dynasty and its monarchic form of government.
With how much religious awe the South Americans had looked
upon the idol of their Empire, which when seen at close hand
lost its glitter. Bolivar cannot have avoided such thoughts, but
they can have brought him no enlightenment or security because of his extreme youth. To him the Court provided an
enjoyable adventure.

At play he met one of his future adversaries, the Prince of
the Asturias, who would one day be King Ferdinand VII. In
the heat of a round of battledore and shuttlecock, in the
presence of the Court, Bolivar knocked his opponent's hat off
his head. The Prince waited for an apology, but none was
forthcoming, and the Queen took Bolivar's part. Later relating
this harmless incident he said: "Who would have prophesied
to Ferdinand VII that this was a sign that one day I might tear
the costliest jewel from his crown?"[29]

Officially, Bolivar belonged to the circle of Americans under
the patronage of Mallo, and he was forced to make an outward
show of respect for him, but actually their relationship was
superficial. When his uncle was suddenly arrested for some
obscure reason, Simon took the opportunity of estranging himself from Mallo, seeking instead the protection of the Marquis

27 O'Leary: Memorias. Vol. I. pp. 9-10.
28 O'Leary: *op. cit.* Larrazabal: Vol. I. p. 8. Mosquera: *op. cit.* p. 8. De Villa
Urrutia: La reina María Luisa y Bolívar. Madrid, 1927.
29 Mosquera: *op. cit.*

de Ustariz.[30] The Marquis was largely responsible for the
change of this young aristocrat into a well-read, cultivated youth
who devoted himself to his work so passionately that he was
in danger of falling ill. This is the first revelation of the passion
of Bolivar's soul which, together with an indestructible perseverance, was to lead him to victory.[31]

At the Ustariz home the boy met María Teresa, daughter of
a Caracas born nobleman, Bernardo Rodríguez de Toro, and
immediately became affianced to her. She was a girl of twenty,
not beautiful but with great charm, who attracted Bolivar by
the great gentleness of her personality and the maturity of her
character. He courted María Teresa, whom he considered a
gem of incalculable worth, with both gentleness and passion,
and she returned his love. Both the Marquis de Ustariz and
María Teresa's father gave their consent to the marriage on
condition that it be postponed because of Bolivar's youth—he
was but seventeen at the time. Since his Uncle Esteban was
still in prison, Simon sent the official announcement of his
engagement to his family in Caracas, fearing some disapproval,
as he was not of age. The letter in which he asks their consent
is a little masterpiece of diplomacy, reminiscent in some respects
of the famous courtship letter of Otto von Bismarck. Simon
wrote piously, humbly, and charmingly, reminding his uncle
of the fact that if he died without issue the vast estate which
he, Simon, had inherited on the condition he settle in Caracas,
would go over to another branch of the family. All this, though
true enough, was naturally not the real motive of the youth,
but the fact that he successfully speculated on the close family
ties of the Palacios to obtain his heart's desire reveals already
the politician in the seventeen-year-old boy.[32]

The family gave its consent, but before following the Toros
when they moved to Bilbao, he became involved in one of
those dark intrigues often preceding the fall from grace of

30 Cartas Vol. IV. p. 333.
31 O'Leary: Memorias. Vol. I. p. 10.
32 Cartas Vol. I. p. 4.

some favorite at the Court. This time it foretold the end of
Mallo, of whom the Queen had tired. Her old favorite, Godoy,
was once more in the ascendant. Before the blow actually fell,
however, Mallo's clique, to whom Bolivar at least in the eyes
of the Court belonged, felt the change of wind in the air. One
day when he was about to ride through the Puerta de Toledo,
he was stopped and handed an order from the Minister of
Finance against the excessive use of diamonds. Bolivar resisted
the search of his person with unsheathed sword—he was in
uniform—aided by friends who stepped in and succeeded in
averting a scandal. To this day the actual cause or instigator
of the incident is unknown, some believing the Queen ordered
it herself and others that it was Godoy.[33] Thus Bolivar's chances
for a great career at the Spanish court vanished—but he was
only eighteen and María Teresa meant far more to him than
Marie Luise and her favorites. Simon followed his betrothed
to Bilbao in great haste, spending many months with her there,
and towards the end of 1801 he took a short trip to France.

On his travels through the country of France, Bolivar saw
signs of the activity of Napoleon. The Peace of Amiens had
been signed and France was assured control of Europe through
her victories at Marengo and Hoehenlinden. An irreconcilable
England had for a short period, at least, acknowledged the
invincibility of Napoleon, whose own country had shown its
confidence in him by a plebiscite. We do not know what impression the state of affairs in Europe made on the young
Bolivar, whose head was probably concerned with wedding
gifts for his bride. His letters to his relatives at this time are
mostly requests for money.[34]

To Bolivar, the present was vastly more important than
dreams of an heroic future, and immediately on obtaining royal
consent he was married. According to his own confession, he
was utterly devoted to his bride and political ideas had not yet

33 O'Leary: Memorias. Vol. I. pp. 11-12. Mosquera: *op. cit.* p. 9. Pereyra:
Juventud. p. 173.
34 Cartas: Vol. I. pp. 5-8.

begun to challenge his imagination. "My head," he wrote, "was only filled with the mists of a passionate love."[35]

From Spain the couple journeyed to Caracas, arriving there around the middle of the year 1802. Though Bolivar considered himself the happiest man alive, his joy was shortlived. His wife was at first able to withstand the dangers of the tropical climate, but when a fever set in she succumbed, dying too soon to give Bolivar an heir, and he who had grown up without father or mother was again bereft. Fate apparently did not intend him for family life, allotting to him instead much loneliness for which he knew how to compensate.

Bolivar never remarried. Many years later he said to a friend: "I loved my wife dearly. Upon her death I vowed never to marry again. I have kept that vow." However, he did not remain true to the memory of María Teresa, and his short and tragic marriage was only an interlude in the midst of his full life. Indeed, it is unlikely that the gentle María Teresa would have permanently succeeded in holding this man who possessed many women and who was influenced little by any of them. In a gesture of self-dramatization, very characteristic of his temperament, which leaned to the theatrical, Bolivar once said: "I regard my wife as an emanation of that Being that gave her life. Heaven thought she belonged up there, and tore her from me. For she was not meant for this world."[36]

However great his desolation at first, it did not last. The tropical vitality and sensuality of Bolivar, who ignited at the first encounter, could not be long suppressed by the weight of a romantic oath. He knew how to bear with his loneliness and in every phase of his wanderings, through the "desert of egoism that is called life," he found an oasis and a woman willing to share it with him. In fact, cynics insist that his vow was only made in order to free him to enjoy those experiences and sensations which tempted him throughout his life.

But there was a more profound reason that impelled Bolivar

35 Peru de la Croix: Diario de Bucaramanga. Ed. by Monseñor Navarro. Caracas, 1935. pp. 226-230.
36 Mosquera: *op. cit.* p. 10.

to keep his vow. Speaking of his marriage some twenty-five years later he said: "Had I not been widowed, my life would perhaps have been different. I would not have become General Bolivar or the Liberator of South America. My wife's death led me early in my career into the road of politics." He might have lived, if we pursue his thought, at María Teresa's side in San Mateo, might have had many children and grown a cocoa plantation, and he might have been but a passive member of that great movement whose creator and leader he actually became. Bolivar knew only too well that such an existence would not have satisfied him for long. He was not born to live out a peaceful idyll, and this he realized himself, saying self-consciously: "I admit that my genius was not intended to become the Mayor of San Mateo."[37] If not that, what then?

37 D. d. B. *op. cit.*

CHAPTER 3

The Vow on Monte Sacro

On the death of Bolivar's father, the holdings left to his heirs were large and included twelve houses in Caracas and La Guayra, vast herds of cattle scattered on the wide plains of Venezuela, indigo fields in the valley of Suata, rich mines near Aroa, and San Mateo, where rum was distilled from sugar grown on the estate. In addition to his inheritance from his father, Simon controlled another estate with an income of about twenty thousand pesos. He was one of the richest men in Caracas, with the power to direct a large sphere of activity.[1]

But Bolivar always appeared indifferent to money and property. Of course he always had sufficient for his needs, but he continuously shared, donated, and wasted without thought of the future. By inclination he did not belong to that group— to which one would assign him by reason of his possessions— which considered the words "property" and "status" of paramount importance. To him money was but the means to an end and to forgetfulness after María Teresa's death. He was unable to forget her in Caracas or in the pleasant valleys of the hacienda, where everything served but to remind him of the happy days of their marriage.

Settling his affairs, he prepared to leave America again for the Old World.[2] Perhaps he was drawn back to Europe by the realization that only there could he achieve complete education

1 O'Leary: Memorias. Vol. I. p. 14.
2 Cartas: Vol. I. p. 10. Lecuna: Papeles. p. 458.

and experience, through his reading, studies, and the meeting of peoples. Or perhaps he remembered pleasures only tasted on his first trip. Both compulsions served to shape the content of the years spent in Europe during this period of his life.

He landed in Cádiz after a long and arduous voyage, hurrying on to Madrid to meet his wife's father. The grief of Bernardo Toro, who had suffered even more than Bolivar at the loss of his only daughter, served to re-awaken that of the husband. "Never," he said later, "shall I forget my meeting with Don Bernardo when I gave him the mementos from María Teresa. Son and father mingled their tears. It was a scene of sweet sorrow—for the sorrows of love are sweet."[3] But he who believes sorrows are sweet can feel neither sorrow nor love too deeply; and while Bolivar, a true pupil of Rousseau, still basked in the grief inflicted by his wife's death, he was driven forward and onward by his curiosity and urgent spirit.

In Madrid he met a group of young South Americans whom he found attractive. Like himself, they were rich, idle, and in disfavor with the Court. The hatred and sense of inferiority felt by many Creoles for the mother country was in them developing into revolutionary impulses. Perhaps Bolivar was aware of their intentions, but he was not at this time in any way a conspirator to a revolutionary movement. With his friends he was forced to leave Madrid on short notice, a temporary food shortage being used by the government as a pretext to get rid of all foreigners. Naturally, this edict was designed to affect the troublesome South Americans. Bolivar, not attempting to contest the situation, went to Paris after a short visit to Bilbao.[4]

When he had first travelled in Europe, Spain had been his destination, and there both the Court and María Teresa served to influence him. On this trip, however, the mother country was but a stop en route to France and Italy, where the major

3 Mosquera: *op. cit.* p. 10.
4 O'Leary: Memorias. Vol. I. p. 14. Larrazabal: Vol. I. p. 12. Mosquera: *op. cit.* p. 11.

and significant roles were played by his old teacher, Simón
Rodríguez, and by Madame Fanny Dervieu du Villars, whom
Bolivar had met in Bilbao on his earlier trip to Europe. At that
time he had been occupied in the wooing of María Teresa, but
now, in Paris, he remembered Fanny. Since her maiden name
of Aristiguieta could be found on the Bolivar family tree, the
two decided they were cousins, and Simon took an apartment
in her house. Fanny, who at twenty-eight was a little older
than Simon, was married to Baron Dervieu du Villars, almost
twice as old as his wife. He, as an officer in Napoleon's army,
was almost constantly away from home on foreign duty. Judging by the miniatures of Isabeau, Fanny was a charming woman
with dark, curly hair and luminous black eyes. She appeared
sentimental, proud, and sensual, a typical beauty of the period.
And Bolivar, as seen from a picture in her own collection, appears slender and well set-up in the becoming garb of the time,
with a high forehead, black hair, and magnetically bright eyes
—commanding, self-confident, volatile, and sullen.[5]

Fanny proved Bolivar's confidante in Paris. She was a warm-
hearted friend able to understand his extravagant vagaries, one
who would listen to his confession of gambling debts and who
saw him through many an embarrassing situation. But she was
also his comrade during the more serious hours when he would
confide to her his newly awakened political ideas.[6] Perhaps he
wept to her over his loss of María Teresa. In the days of
Chateaubriand and his René, Fanny was as ready to help Simon
forget unhappiness as he was inclined to allow himself to be
comforted. His confidante, she also became his mistress. How
else can we interpret her words written to him after twenty
years: "I am convinced that you loved me sincerely," and again,

5 L. A. Sucre: Bolívar y Fanny du Villars. B. d. H. Vol. XVII. Number 68.
p. 345. Lecuna: Adolescencia. pp. 655 ff. Pereyra: Juventud. p. 204. Concerning
the falsified letter from Vienna, see Lecuna, Cartas, Vol. I, p. 11, and Vol. X, p. 395.
Bolivar had never been to Vienna. The whole letter is absurd and legendary, and
it is time that it should be definitely deleted from Bolivar's biography. The same is
true for the remaining materials stemming from the same source, published by
Lecuna in Cartas, Vol. X.

6 O'Leary: Memorias. Vol. I. p. 19.

"Tell me . . . but write it in your own hand, that you are really my friend. It is the only feeling that I crave and of which I am jealous, because I have no right to claim anything more."[7] She tried to help him, and understood his reasons for wanting to appear a dandy in Paris and for competing with the French capital's men-of-the-world. But she was ambitious, both for him and for herself, dreaming of a great career and basking in the reflected glory of his coming fame. In the world of Napoleon everything was possible.

Fanny du Villars, a woman of great elegance who believed that social connections were high trumps in the game of life, kept a salon in which the society of imperial Paris met.[8] It was at her house that Bolivar met a large number of the military leaders of France, and in their train the many influential men and women who were the criteria of fashion in the capital. Eugene Beauharnais was Bolivar's rival for Madame du Villar's affections, and on one occasion it was only due to Fanny's intervention that a quarrel caused by a linguistic misunderstanding did not terminate in a duel.[9] The pride, spirit of independence, and eruptive temperament of the South American lost nothing in this galaxy of great names and glittering uniforms. He was impressed, but attempted to show his indifference by voicing his newly ripening republican opinions, and enjoyed shocking his dinner companions, members of the new regime, by his outspokenness. Not allowing for the possibility of landing on the official blacklist, he aired his views on Napoleon, whom Simon both admired and detested, and freely discussed the character of the French people in general.

Was he at that time a convinced republican? He had certainly devoured Montesquieu, Voltaire, and Rousseau; and according to his own assertion, had also read Locke, Condillac, Buffon, D'Alembert, and Helvetius. Two great thinkers of the seventeenth century fascinated him—Hobbes and Spinoza. The

7 O'Leary: Doc. Vol. XII. pp. 293 ff., 298.
8 Lecuna: Adolescencia. p. 656.
9 O'Leary: Memorias. Vol. I. pp. 16 ff. Mosquera: *op. cit.* p. 11.

independent spirit of the former and the republicanism of the
latter, both nourished by a sense of political realism, wielded a
great influence upon the thinking of the South American.[10]

The net result of all this reading was a complete satisfaction
with the enlightened ideas of the seventeenth and eighteenth
centuries, and a belief in the rights of man—in freedom, reason,
dignity, liberty, and humanity. Bolivar, a man of action, had
not put these new ways of thought to any test but rather accepted them, letting them take possession of him, and through
these ideas whatever remained of the good natured naivete of
the twenty-one-year-old was destroyed. He learned not to
accept, but to measure against the eternal ideas of reason, justice, and freedom. Bolivar became at this time, from a philosophical point of view, a rationalist, never radical or unrealistic,
but a firm believer in the great concepts which triumphed in
the revolutions of England, France, and North America. This
much is evident from any study of the vocabulary used in his
speeches, notes, letters, and pamphlets, all filled with his ideas
of independence, of the sovereignty of the people, of progress
and civilization.[11] It was only natural that he desired to have
these ideals realized in his own country, and that he compared
the status quo there to what his country might be.

It was this ideological concept that brought him into contact
with freemasonry, and he joined the American chapter in Paris,
being inducted as master. But his contempt was soon aroused
by the theatrical aspect of the lodges, and in the world in which
he lived strong forces were at work to strengthen his democratic
ideals.[12]

Among the many people whom Bolivar met in Paris, Alexander von Humboldt above all others spurred him on to greater
efforts along the liberal road. The great scientist had returned
to France in 1804 after five years in South America. With the
young Frenchman, Bompland, Humboldt had sailed down the

10 Cartas: Vol. IV. p. 333. O'Leary: Memorias. Vol. I. p. 18.
11 Pereyra: Juventud. p. 187.
12 D. d. B. p. 238. Mancini. p. 131.

Orinoco and had crossed the vast plains at the foot of the Andes. He had explored the Cordilleras and had classified the plants. He had visited in Bogotá, Quito, Lima, and Mexico. He had climbed snow-capped peaks and slept in damp foliage along the wide rivers. No effort or hazards, plagues or disease, were able to deter this man from his selfless compulsion to wrest the secrets from tropical nature. His return to Europe marked a turning point in the history of science; Napoleon honored Humboldt and Bompland by imperial decree, and all Paris echoed with their fame.[13]

Bolivar must have met the scientist in Fanny du Villars' salon, or possibly in the house on the Faubourg St. Germain. There was no lack of mutual interests. Though Bolivar was in Europe when Humboldt had landed in Venezuela, the great scientist had enjoyed the hospitality of many Caracans who were in some way connected with the young Creole. The Prussian, whom Bolivar found to be a citizen of the world, an organizer and scholar, a visionary and statesman, spoke of the immense wealth of the American continent, the fertility of its soil, the vastness of its plains, and the majesty of its streams. To the young man these were as natural as the stones in the house of his childhood, and he had given them as little thought. But he recognized from the picture painted by Humboldt the many facets and potentialities of America. In their conversation the gap between nature and history was easily bridged. Though Alexander von Humboldt had no personal reason for complaint against the Spanish government, he was nevertheless a liberal, and to him Spain remained always an instrument of despotism. He cannot have been much surprised when Bolivar said: "In truth, what a brilliant fate—that of the New World, if only its people were freed of their yoke." And Humboldt replied to the young American: "I believe that your country

13 A. von Humboldt: Voyage aux regions equinoxiales du Nouveau Continent, 1805-1832. Hamy: Lettres americaines d'Alexandre de Humboldt. Paris, 1905. N. García Samudio: El viaje de Humboldt a America. Bogotá, 1934. Boeckh and C. Ritter in Deutsche Denkreden. Munchen, 1928, and Dove, in Allgemeine Deutsche Biographie. Vol. XIII.

is ready for its independence. But I can not see the man who
is to achieve it."[14]

What sublime irony for such words to be spoken to the man
who was to carry out the great enterprise. Perhaps it was
doubt which fell, like a glowing ember, into Bolivar's soul,
and at this moment he may well have perceived the problems
which he was in the future to encounter. He certainly realized
that it was no longer possible merely to wish for America's
independence. It had to be won. Bompland's words were comforting: "Revolutions themselves bring forth great men who
are worthy of carrying them out." Unquestionably, Bolivar's
meeting with Humboldt was epochal in his life and perhaps
even responsible for his own recognition of his goal, and with
it his personal destiny.

Another influence was instrumental in making him conscious of his destiny—this young aristocrat who wasted his
money at the gaming tables and spent his nights with his
"cousin" Fanny or in the demimonde at the *Palais Royale:*
The star of Napoleon, which outshone all others, kindled an
answering flame in Bolivar's heart.

France had been turned into an hereditary empire by the
First Consul who, after his annointment by the Pope, crowned
himself and his Josephine on December 2, 1804. Bolivar had
received an invitation from the Spanish Ambassador to attend
the ceremonies in the Cathedral of Notre Dame, but he refused.[15] This event made the young republican react as violently
as Beethoven, who tore up his *Eroica* on hearing of the self-
promotion of his idol. "Since that day," said Bolivar, "I regard
him as a dishonest tyrant." And another time he said: "Since
Napoleon crowned himself, his fame seems to me like the
reflection of hell."[16] But there is some evidence that in spite
of his earlier refusal, he did attend the coronation. He had not
consented to appear among the courtiers and thus publicly seem

14 O'Leary: Memorias. Vol. I. p. 18. Larrazabal: Vol. I. p. 13. Mosquera:
op. cit. p. 12.
15 O'Leary: Memorias. Vol. I. p. 17.
16 Mosquera: *op. cit.* p. 11.

to approve what privately he despised, but that he would lock himself in his room on such a day is unthinkable. He himself relates: "I saw the coronation of Napoleon in Paris, during the last month of 1804. The gigantic show thrilled me, less by its glamor than by the love accorded the hero by this great people. This universal expression of all hearts, this free and spontaneous mass-demonstration aroused by Napoleon and his great deeds seemed to me, as he was being thus honored by more than a million men, to be the pinnacle of man's desires—the realization of man's highest ambition. I regarded the crown, which Napoleon placed on his own head, as a poor example of outmoded custom. What seemed great to me was the general acclaim and the interest which his person generated. This, I admit, made me think of my own country's enslavement, and the fame that would accrue to him who liberated it. But I was far indeed from imagining that I would be that man."[17]

This extraordinary confession reveals the attitude of young Bolivar to Napoleon, with all its contradictions and its admiration. To the young republican the coronation seemed contemptible and archaic, a betrayal of the revolutionary ideal. But the glory, the enthusiasm of the masses, the reflection of heroic deeds—all inspired him, taking possession of his thinking and inflaming his imagination. Fame was the man's deepest desire, and the adoration accorded a hero his greatest ambition. When he remembered the lack of freedom in his own country, the thought occurred to Bolivar: "What glory would descend on me, if I could become the Liberator of Venezuela!"

In the days following the coronation his soul was torn by conflicting emotions. According to his own admission, he had worshipped Napoleon as the champion of the Republic, the shining star of fame, the genius of independence. "In the past, I knew none whom I could compare with him, and the future promised to bring forth none like him."[18] But suddenly Napoleon seemed to change and become an impediment to the

17 D. d. B. pp. 226 ff.
18 O'Leary: Memorias. Vol. I. p. 15. Mosquera: *op. cit.*

generous impulses of humanity. He had shattered the pedestal
on which had stood the goddess of liberty. Who could erect
it again? In this light the coronation seemed but a melancholy
dream, and Bolivar, motivated by a fanatical love of liberty,
experienced a sudden revulsion. For him the effulgence of
Napoleon's halo changed into the dull flames of a volcano. And
what had happened to France? How was it possible that the
people of this mighty Republic, passionately hating tyranny
and thirsting for equality, could become indifferent to the loss
of hard won rights?

But on occasion such thoughts of Bolivar were interrupted
by others, in which fame seemed everything, the idea nothing.
For a second time he, while taking a trip through Italy, was
witness to a solemn ceremony in which Napoleon attempted
to conceal the failure of historic tradition from his new empire.
"All my attention was focussed on Napoleon," relates Bolivar
of this occasion, "and I saw only him among this mass of
people congregated there. My curiosity was insatiable. What
a large and glittering general staff was Napoleon's, and how
great the simplicity of his own attire! His entire retinue was
covered with gold and rich embroideries but he, alone, wore
only his shoulder-boards, a hat without device and a cloak
without trimming." But it was more than the contrast that
delighted Bolivar, who felt that he was in the presence of a
world ruler in whose person was centered the interest of an
entire continent, perhaps of humanity itself. And once again
this spectacle kindled in Bolivar the desire for fame. He compared himself with Napoleon, and was conscious of the gap
separating him from the world importance of the Emperor.
It is very revealing that he ends his description of the Milan
ceremony with the words: "I insist that I was at that time far
removed from foreseeing that I too would one day become the
object of attention—and, if you will, of curiosity of almost an
entire continent . . . one may say of the whole world."[19] How

19 D. d. B. *op. cit.* pp. 137, 198. Hiram Paulding: A sketch of Bolívar in his
Camp. New York, 1834. pp. 71-72.

much is revealed in this "I too." He could not foresee, it is true. But he desired, with every fiber of his being. Fame, fame, and yet more fame! Napoleon's career must be considered as one of the most determining factors of his youth, and it was in the France of this period that the idea of human greatness was first revealed to the South American—its laws and its destiny. The meteoric rise of the poor lieutenant of artillery who cleaned his own boots to the position of a world ruler evoked in the wealthy Venezuelan a sense of shame at his own useless existence.[20] But it was the great revolution which had made it possible for the Corsican to embark on a career without compare, while Bolivar was forced to wait until he was summoned by the movement for independence. The manner in which his name is identified with the struggle for South American freedom differed greatly from the part played by Napoleon in the French Revolution. But when he saw what a single man had been able to do in France, he became aware of his vocation. Bolivar was never tempted by Napoleon's great but dangerous example to place his *moi colosal* against or above the general weal.

Bolivar remained, as Napoleon would have put it, an ideologist or a romanticist whose soul was swept aloft on wings of freedom. As he has himself admitted, fame and freedom dominated his soul. We may add "fame *through* freedom," for he desired no other, and this is the basic chord in the tragic symphony of his life. Napoleon had changed from a passionate poet into a mathematical realist, but Bolivar remained, even throughout his most painful disillusionment and disappointment, an idealist who found it impossible to bury his hopes.

At a later period in his life Bolivar stated that he had consciously avoided open admiration for Napoleon in order that he could not be himself accused of harboring Caesarean tendencies. But actually his silence had another reason. In spite of the fact that he held Napoleon to be the top military strategist of the world, or that he considered his own genius to be

20 E. Ludwig: Bolívar y Napoleon. Rev. d. 1. Indias. August, 1939. pp. 57 ff.

closely related to that of Napoleon, he was well aware of the
one criterion which separated them. Napoleon acknowledged
above himself nothing but his star and the exigencies of life
and fate which he was unable to control. He stopped at nothing.
Bolivar, on the other hand, respected legal and ideological
structures. True, he broke through them occasionally or even
set himself above them, but he never denied their ideal
importance.

Napoleon's victories sounded loud in Bolivar's ears, but they
could not still the insistent voice of freedom in his heart.
"Freedom and fame" in 1805 became his motto. At twenty-one
he did not realize that an inexorable fate would one day demand the sacrifice of one or the other.

The credit that Bolivar did not utterly succumb to the influence of his Corsican preceptor is not due to him alone. In Paris
he had refound his old teacher Simón Rodríguez, and the
influence of this admirer of Rousseau immunized Bolivar
against the Emperor.[21] After leaving Caracas, Rodríguez went
to Jamaica and from there to the United States; true to his
great teacher he had deserted his children to work for the cause
of freedom. Later he sailed for Europe in search of new adventures. One wonders, when he met once again his old pupil,
whether he was pleased with the product of his training and
whether the old pedagogic instincts reawoke in him. This pupil,
on whom he had hoped to test the theories of *Émile,* who was
to become the free agent of a benign nature, had turned instead
into an elegant youth to whom pleasure was paramount, who
did not disdain to seek dissipation in the arms of those god-
desses whose alliances were made and broken—all within the
hour. Many years later Bolivar enjoyed perusing the list of his
amours and dreamed of a return to the Paris without which
life seemed worthless.[22] There must have been something of
the enticing quality of an Alcibiades about the youth at this

---

21 O'Leary: Memorias. Vol. I. p. 18. Pereyra: Juventud. p. 187.
22 Mosquera: *op. cit.* p. 14. Pereyra: *Juventud.* p. 191. D. d. B. *passim.* E.
Rodó: Bolívar in Antología Bolivariana. p. 259.

time, for he was frivolous, dedicated to the pursuit of happiness, wasteful, and sensation hungry, none too critical in the choice of the people and things that were to satisfy him. True, it was but a passing phase of his life, but it left an indelible mark on him, and to the end of his life he remained "a great gentleman," a Don Juan, autocratic and absolute.

His freshly discovered teacher ordered concentration against distraction, effort against pleasure, contemplation against intemperance. It was he who guided Bolivar's mind once more towards philosophy and who replaced in his hand the books of his early teaching. Many years later Bolivar wrote to Rodríguez: "You cannot imagine how deeply the books you gave me are engraved on my heart. I have not been able to omit even a single comma from these great theses which you presented to me. They have ever been before my mental eye, and I have followed them as I would an infallible leader."[23] Whence did Rodríguez take these precepts? Presumably from the *Contrat Sociale*, for he was a convinced republican, and during those months in Paris he found ample opportunity to discuss his principles with Bolivar. He never tired of setting forth arguments to counter the influence of Napoleon upon Bolivar, and this antithesis of Rousseau versus Napoleon was one of the great problems that Simon took back to South America with him after his European sojourn. The conflict was entwined in his being, but the problems of power and freedom, revolution and authority, were still unsolved within him. It is a strange coincidence that when at the crossroads of his career, twenty years later, he should receive from an admirer the copy of the *Contrat Sociale* read by Napoleon on St. Helena. The gift was of such great value to Bolivar that on his death he bequeathed it to the town of his youth, and in the symbolism of the gift is contained the story of his relation to the two figures who in Paris preordained the color of his life.[24]

Simón Rodríguez had not yet slackened his attempts to

23 Cartas: Vol. IV. p. 33.
24 Cartas: Vol. IV. p. 208.

convert Bolivar into a pupil of Rousseau. Since the atmosphere
of Paris, with its temptations and its pleasures, had affected the
health of the young man, the teacher advised a change of scene.
The two travelled to Lyon—in 1805—and then on foot across
the Savoy Alps to stop in Chambery, visiting Les Charmettes.
It was a sentimental journey in the manner of the eighteenth
century, a pilgrimage of the American Rousseau and his Émile
to the places where the Genevan had enjoyed the favors of
Madame de Warens. From Chambery the two wanderers went
on foot to Italy, and so rapidly had Bolivar's health improved
that the trip was accomplished in eleven days. From the Po
Valley they travelled to Venice, which disappointed Bolivar,
then on to Florence, which delighted him. Did Simón Rodríguez have a plan behind this journey? Did he wish to show his
pupil the mother country of occidental culture? Hardly. It
was not the urge for culture like that which brought Goethe
across the Alps, that drove the South Americans to travel
through Italy, but merely curiosity. As in the style of the time,
they were on a cavalier tour. When they reached Rome, Bolivar
once again met Alexander von Humboldt, who had come to
Italy almost at the same time to make some geological studies
of Vesuvius. And when together they beheld the wonders
of Italian nature their hearts turned once more to the desire
for the freedom and independence of the New World.[25] To
Bolivar, Rome was not the epitome of art but rather the embodiment of human nature. Historic greatness spoke to him
from the ruins and breathed from the triumphal arches and
columns, the statues and *thermae* across which his steps led
him. The Eternal City evoked in the South American the
memory of mythical and historical heroes who had breathed
this air before him, and he held vividly before him the memory
of the great men who had made Rome the mistress of the
world. His favorite haunt was the Coliseum, but contrary to

---

25 O'Leary: Doc. Vol. XII. p. 234. Cartas: Vol. III. p. 264., Vol. V. p. 212.
B. d. H. Caracas. Vol. XVI. Number 62. p. 218. For the further relations between
Humboldt and Bolivar, see also: K. H. Panhorst: Simón Bolívar und Alexander von
Humboldt. Iberoamerikanisches Archiv. April, 1930. p. 35.

the custom of his day the glory of the ruins provided no good reason for Bolivar to bed his soul on the romantic pillow of melancholy.

One day his path led him to the Monte Sacro. Rodríguez was with him. They both thought of the plebes who, when the oppression of the Roman Patricians became overwhelming, had fled to the holy mountain. And the word oppression was the keynote to turn Bolivar's mind and heart back to Venezuela. His soul became filled with reverence, and he felt impelled to express his thoughts. Sinking to his knees he vowed to Rodríguez, whose hands he clasped, that by the holy earth beneath his feet he would liberate his country.[26]

What did this vow mean, and what was its value? Was it but the upsurge of an uninhibited and then receding passion, or a conscious decision on Bolivar's part? It has been proved by history that this was a solemn promise, kept by Bolivar as he kept no other throughout his life. It was the banner thrown by him into the fortress of the enemy so that he could follow. Twenty years later he wrote to Rodríguez: "Do you remember how we went up the Monte Sacro to pledge on its holy soil the liberty of our country? Surely you have not forgotten this day of immortal glory. It was the day when my prophetic soul anticipated the hope, which we dared not yet voice."[27]

To anticipate a hope—not merely to believe in the improbable but to vow to accomplish it—this was to be the essence of his life. For Bolivar politics was the art of the impossible. That the vow made on the Monte Sacro was not merely a first impulse but the beginning of his political life is shown by the frankness with which he made known his intentions. The news of his vow spread rapidly among the Spaniards in Rome, but they mistook it for a whim, for had there not been much

26 O'Leary: Memorias. Vol. I. p. 22. Mosquera: *op. cit.* p. 14. H. Paulding: *op. cit.* A reconstruction of what Bolivar actually said is hardly possible. Forty-five years after the event took place S. Rodríguez gave a novelistic description of the famous vow which is quite obviously an imaginative invention; its historical value is nil. See: M. Uribe: El libro del Centenario. Bogotá, 1883. pp. 73 ff. Pereyra: Juventud. p. 198.

27 Cartas: Vol. IV. p. 32.

in Bolivar's bizarre youth that showed his inclinations to pose
or present a theatrical attitude? On one occasion, and in the
presence of the Spanish Ambassador, when he was presented
to the Pope, he refused to kiss the Cross on the papal sandal.
Pius VII extricated the Ambassador from his embarrassment
by holding out his ring for Bolivar to kiss. To all remon-
strances, however, the South American merely said: "The Pope
must hold the symbol of Christianity very cheap, if he wears it
on his shoes, whereas the proudest princes in Christendom
wear it in their crowns."[28]

After this short stay in Italy, Bolivar returned to Paris, where
he spoke without reservation to his friends about his new ideas.
He saw everything before him with such clarity that he was
able to confide actual plans to Fanny, who wrote to him twenty
years later: "Now everything has been accomplished according
to the plan you confided to me."[29] But his friends probably
didn't take him too seriously.[30]

Bolivar's decision to leave Europe was irrevocable, though
Fanny, who had grown extremely fond of him, was reluctant
to let him go and begged him with tears in her eyes not to
leave her. His love of fame superseded at this point in his life
all love of women, and though he gave Fanny a ring, swearing
eternal faithfulness, she could not hold him back. Actually his
love for her was cooling, and he experienced with her the
sensation he was to have in countless adventures—the satiety
of the conqueror who had achieved his desires. He had called
himself the Man of Difficulties, and this formula, originated for
politics, had its being in every facet of his soul.[31] He was
constitutionally a man of difficulties. The unconquered lured
him, but the conquered repelled him. Of the many women
who crossed his path, one only—and it was not Fanny—was
successful in never tiring him. Fanny, the confidante and friend

28 O'Leary: Memorias. Vol. I. p. 23.
29 O'Leary: Vol. XII. pp. 293 ff.
30 Lecuna: Adolescencia. p. 664.
31 Cartas: Vol. IV. p. 255. See also: F. Gonzáles: Mi Simón Bolívar. Manizalez,
1930. p. 152.

of his youth, was treated by Bolivar in later years with great coolness, and none of her many letters were answered. It is true that she, like any good Frenchwoman, had tried to capitalize somewhat on their relationship, one that Bolivar apparently wished to forget. He was no longer to be satisfied with amorous adventures.

Even if he had not grown weary of Fanny, Bolivar would at this time have returned to Venezuela, for he had received word of the insurrections in his country. Francisco de Miranda had landed in Venezuela. Bolivar wrote to a friend: "The reports we get about Miranda's expedition are a bit sad. They claim that he intends to unleash a revolt in the country which will wreak much havoc among the inhabitants of the colony. Nevertheless, I should love to be there, for my presence in the country would save me much trouble."[32] This letter was taken by some critics as an indication that Bolivar was not yet serious about the revolution. Who knows just why he wrote so cautiously? He bade Europe farewell. Having already parted from Rodríguez in Italy, he now left Napoleon's capital and boarded a ship in Hamburg late in 1806. Landing in the United States, he saw Boston, New York, Philadelphia, and Charleston, and in February of 1807 was back once more in his own country.

Like the traveler who, turning back once again before leaving his ship, thinks he glimpses behind the vast expanse of ocean the countries and peoples he has left, we shall try to sum up the consequences of this long journey.

Bolivar had been away nearly four years. On his return he was still young, only twenty-four, but the great and ever-changing impressions gathered during his travels had matured him. His education had been completed. New vistas, important for his future career, had been opened by his contacts with the centers and leaders of European culture. Bolivar had

32 Cartas: Vol. I. p. 17. We do not here agree with López de Mesa: Simón Bolívar y la cultura iberoamericana, Rev. America. Vol. I. Number 7. See also the unpublished letters in Bolivar's Archive.

long known that emancipation of the spirit would have to follow on the heels of external emancipation, that upon the
glorious days of triumph would follow the more serene days
of cultural development, and he had already offered, while
still in Paris, one half of his income to Bompland if he would
settle in Caracas. Later, when at the height of his success, he
called upon him to take over the leadership of the scientific
institute. Bolivar also kept up his connection with Alexander
von Humboldt, and they both retained that mutual admiration
freely given by one genius to another.

At the time of his return to South America, the idea of
human greatness hovered over Bolivar like a vision which he
wished to pull down to the earth so that he could wrap himself
in its glowing colors. At first it was but a dream, and he was
not enough of a Don Quixote to believe that the hour of liberation would sound the moment he set foot on American soil.
He had to wait, to experiment. We shall leave him at this
point to review the great events sweeping the American
colonies along in a flood of revolutionary uprisings, a flood
which was not to abate until America was freed of Spanish
domination.

CHAPTER 4

Francisco de Miranda and the

Policies of the Great Powers

The history of South American independence, if it is evaluated as the accomplishment of a few exceptional men, will appear as a tragedy composed of catastrophes and triumphs, of fame and ingratitude. But if it is regarded instead as the achievement of the people, it appears to be an epic in which the national will is set against all the obstacles of nature and tradition. Each of these points of view is inadequate, however, if in them the South American Revolution is not set into the framework of world history. Without a familiarity with the fabric of international politics, the fight for freedom waged by the American republics must forever remain unintelligible. Even the mightiest will becomes impotent against the constellation of world history. That is how we look upon Bolivar's achievement today, and in order to do it justice we must remember the over-all conditions which made the achievement possible.

The structure of the Spanish colonial empire has already been described, and it remains to explain the external position of the empire in the complex game of international diplomacy during the period preceding liberation of the South American continent.

Historically the eighteenth century is marked by the conflict between two imperialisms—the British and the French—and the struggle of these two nations for the upper hand in Europe and abroad began with the expansionist policy of Louis XIV

and ended with the downfall of Napoleon. British ambition
for world supremacy, challenging that of the French in secular
combat, finally triumphed on the high seas and upon the
battlefields of Europe.

The Peace of Utrecht, a compromise between the two
powers, brought the War of the Spanish Succession to an end
in 1714, with France retaining her hold on the European continent and the Spanish crown worn by a Bourbon. England,
on the other hand, made secure her colonial possessions in
North America, around the Hudson Bay, Newfoundland, and
Nova Scotia. Spain was eliminated as a great power. Her
colonial possessions remained untouched, but most of her
Italian territories were relinquished and Gibraltar was lost to
England.

Thus the conflict took on a global aspect, with two power
groups ranged against each other: France, bound to Spain by
ties of family, versus England. According to Mephistopheles,
war, trade, and piracy form an inseparable triumvirate, and the
colonial imperialism of the eighteenth century cannot be better
described. By virtue of her naval supremacy Britain was best
able to put this system to most efficient use. Ever since the
foundering of the Spanish Armada, English naval heroes—
half robbers, half conquerors—had dreamed of the possibilities
in the Spanish colonies, and the Hawkins, the Drakes, the
Raleighs, and the Morgans regarded them, as they did every
other part of the earth, as divinely ordained for England. South
America, and its possibilities for conquest, was already in their
minds.[1]

On the whole, however, British expeditions were more of a
nuisance than a threat to the Spanish crown.[2] Whenever a
foothold was gained at American ports, the Spaniards always
succeeded in repulsing the enemy, as in the memorable siege
of Cartagena in 1741. At this time claims were actually heard

1 W. Spence Robertson: Francisco de Miranda y la revolución de la América
española. Bogotá, 1918. p. 1.
2 C. H. Haring: Historia de los Bucaneros en las Indias orientales. Paris, 1939.

proclaiming that Britain's policy was not one of conquest, but rather one of liberating South America from its Spanish yoke in order to open the continent to British trade, though British diplomacy was not yet ready for this concept.[3]

When the thirteen colonies rose against England and declared their independence, the hour of reckoning seemed at hand. Helped by France and Spain, the rebels were successful, and the loss of the important North American possessions was as damaging and bitter to England at this time as had been the loss of Canada to France twenty years before. But the loss of the North American states resulted in consequences other than those hoped for by Britain's enemies. Far from dealing the death blow to British imperialism, a change was merely effected in British colonial policy.

The Declaration of Independence of the United States originated in a dispute over taxes between the mother country and her colonies. This was the first symptom of the collapse of monopolistic trade forced by European nations upon their colonies. Within that system trade was of major importance. Colonies meant trade—the more colonies the larger the trade, and the greater the trade the more income for the mother country. When this imperialistic structure collapsed and a vital part of colonial income was lost, British statesmen were given the opportunity of measuring the usefulness of their overseas possessions. At the same time there was beginning in England that momentous revolution that converted the country into the foremost industrial nation, a fact that was to have far-reaching universal repercussions.

But this industrial revolution called for a complete change in colonial policy, for instead of commerce, industry was declared the source of national wealth. Instead of a mercantile system which excluded competition on the part of other nations, the new policy sanctioned the peaceful acquisition of markets abroad for British industry. This acquisition of foreign markets became from then on as important as the gaining of new terri-

3 Robertson: Miranda. p. 5.

tory, and under this new system, commerce was but the means for finding markets for home industries.

Such a concept was predicated on the idea that the old mercantile methods would disappear also from non-British colonies, as only thus could the new markets be acquired. So it followed that when countries resisted, as did the Spanish colonies, the last resort was conquest or revolution. Once again England came into conflict with Spain in the western hemisphere, whether or not England had intended to liberate or win the continent.

What were the reactions of South Americans to these possible plans of Great Britain? Among those who were dissatisfied with Spanish domination in Central and South America and therefore looked toward Britain were the expelled Jesuits, who conspired with Protestant England to cause the downfall of Spain in South America, thus avenging their wrongs. British merchants and seamen reported the plans existing among the Jesuits to liberate the continent, and they recommended attacking the Spanish colonies in Mexico by means of expeditions. From Mexico itself voices were heard, declaring the country ripe for revolution.[4]

Envoys appeared in England from other parts of the world to gain support for an uprising in the Spanish colonies. Among these groups were men who came to London from New Granada after the failure of the revolt of 1781, men who called themselves representatives of the *comuneros*.[5] Others were concerned with the secession of the southern territories—Chile, Peru, and Patagonia.

Most of these projects originated between 1779 and 1784, the duration of the war between Britain and Spain. But apparently the English statesmen did not trust the South American envoys too much, placing them in a catgory of possibilities.

It was the tremendous achievement of one man to have

4 J. M. Aguilar: Aportaciones a la biografía de Miranda. Pub. d. Centro d. estud. amer. en Sevilla, 1919. Vol. I. p. 40.
5 Briceño: Comuneros. p. 231. Mancini: p. 45.

perceived at this time that South American freedom might be attained through negotiation with and support by the great powers. This man, recognizing the necessity of interesting the European nations in the fate of the South American continent, and realizing the importance of taking advantage of the ever changing game of diplomacy and war, threw himself into this vast undertaking with an energy far surpassing the powers of those who had attempted previously to effect a solution of the South American problem. He is the first great figure of the revolution, and his name is Francisco de Miranda.[6]

He was born in Caracas on March 28, 1750. While his mother was a Caracan, his father, Sebastian de Miranda, came from the Canary Islands to Caracas, where he devoted himself to trade and was highly thought of by the Spanish authorities. To the intense annoyance of the Creoles, he was appointed Captain of the Militia. In an atmosphere, therefore, of jealousy and hatred Francisco spent his childhood. His education was the best his family could afford, but it is difficult to evaluate the intellectual training he received in South America, though his keen spiritual alertness and interest in the cultural and political life surrounding him make it possible to assume that his mind was awakened at an early age.[7]

We do not know the reasons which prompted Miranda to go to Spain and seek admission into the army. Ambition must have been strong within him, as well as a determined concentration upon his own ego. Observation of himself and his world—of people and his surroundings—a premonition of future problems and an awareness of his own gifts led him to keep a diary from the time he sailed for Spain throughout his

6 Archivo del general Miranda. Ed. by V. Dávila. Caracas, 1930. Vols. I-XV. Marques de Rojas: El general Miranda. Paris, 1884. R. Becerra: La vida de Francisco de Miranda. Caracas, 1896. 2 vols. C. Parra Pérez: Miranda et la revolution francaise. Paris, 1925. W. S. Robertson: The Life of Miranda. Chapel Hill, 1929. 2 vols. J. R. Vejarano: La vida fabulosa de Miranda. Rev. America. Vol. III. Numbers 3, 4, 5. 1945.

7 G. Nucete Sardi: Aventura y tragedia de don Francisco de Miranda. Caracas, 1935. Robertson: Life. Vol. I. pp. 4-5. Blanco: Doc. Vol. I. p. 80. Rojas: op. cit. p. 176.

life.[8] In Madrid, where he arrived with considerable means and
letters of recommendation to the Court, he studied mathematics,
languages, and the military arts, knowing that great deeds are
not the product of accident but rather of talents methodically
trained. Such an excessive desire for knowledge doubtless
made him suspect in the eyes of the Inquisition, so that even
in those early days he was sowing the seeds of future conflicts.
His military career, which was to develop into a succession of
glorious misfortunes, began the following year, when he bought
himself a captaincy for 40,000 *pesetas*.

The daily routine of army life did not suffice, however;
Miranda was overwhelmed with restlessness, an eagerness for
heroism, and the desire to see and to learn. He studied the
military science of the day; he visited the fortifications of
Gibraltar; he attempted a transfer from the army to the navy;
altogether he marshalled all his resources to no avail, and
merely succeeded in finding trouble for himself. In 1777 he
was arrested, his indictment reading "neglect of military duty."
Miranda blamed the Inquisition.[9]

He lived his arrest down, however, and in 1780 was sent
to Cuba and the Antilles as adjutant to a high officer with
whom he had become friendly in Spain, Juan Manuel de
Cagigal, a native American with great confidence in Miranda.

The Spanish expedition was directed—it was at the time
of the North American revolution—against British Caribbean
possessions. Miranda, with the rank of lieutenant-colonel under
De Cagigal, received the orders for which he had wished, and
in taking part in the conquest of Pensacola he saw as much
action as he had hoped for in his dreams. In August, 1781,
he was given the delicate assignment of treating with the Governor of Jamaica on the exchange of prisoners, though the
real purpose of his mission was to acquire in Jamaica ships
much needed by the Spaniards. Since open purchase was out
of the question, Miranda was forced to resort to smuggling,

8 V. Dávila: Biografía de Francisco de Miranda. Caracas, 1933. p. 11.
9 Arch. Miranda. Vol. V. pp. 140 ff.

and also used the opportunity to do some spying on his own. Altogether this undertaking to which he was committed by his superior officer was of a clandestine, not to say shady, nature. Whether Miranda was careful with the means put at his disposal is hard to say, though it is certain he was always most cautious in financial affairs of his own! But the Cuban authorities thought it advisable to examine Miranda's activities, and though De Cagigal attempted to protect him, he was unsuccessful. The Minister for India disagreed with arrangements made by Miranda, and, objecting to the methods by which Miranda had purchased two ships, demanded his discharge from the service. His career in the services gives a picture of that confused atmosphere of hatred, jealousy, and suspicion which hung like a thundercloud over the American colonies. Miranda escaped arrest by royal decree only with great difficulty, and with the help of friends succeeded in leaving Havana for the United States in June, 1783.[10]

Thus, in disgrace, Miranda left the Spanish service, accused of conspiracy, with government agents charged with his apprehension. It marked the turning point in his career. He felt, as he said, "as innocent as Socrates," and sixteen years later, after a careful study of all the facts, the Supreme Court of Spain, the *Consejo de las Indias,* agreed with him and pronounced him innocent.[11]

The suspicions against him were aroused by the very talents that made him outstanding—he was restless and volatile, he read extensively and made notes, he did not wish to suffocate in the monotony of the service. Instead of allowing such unusual qualities full play, the Spanish government tried to destroy them, but succeeded only in arousing his resentment and hatred. His genius sought outlet in the destruction of Spanish possessions, for Miranda conceived the idea of liberating his own country and with it the entire South American

10 Arch. Miranda. Vol. I. p. 141. Dávila: *op. cit.* p. 12. Parra Pérez: *op. cit.* p. 14. Robertson: Life. Vol. I. pp. 27 ff.
11 Robertson: Life. Vol. I. pp. 32-33.

continent. In a letter written to the Spanish monarch in 1785, Miranda requested release from the army because he felt at a disadvantage owing to his American birth, and because he was tired of fighting powerful enemies. Asking to be reimbursed for the money used to buy his captaincy, he vowed to use it for the education of American youth: his compatriots could better understand the current situation and could in the future conduct themselves with more self-confidence; so that they could learn to control the noble passions then agitating American youth![12] This was the challenge flung at an empire by a single man.

Miranda became rebel and adventurer from this time on, and his aim was to gain partisans and supporters for the liberation of South America. He began in the United States, where he gave himself ample opportunity to study this youngest of the great powers, its military techniques, its political and economic aims and characteristics; and above all, its great men: Washington, Thomas Paine, Hamilton, and the rest.[13]

Hounded constantly by Spanish agents, Miranda went to London in 1785 with the aim of becoming acquainted with Europe—to win important men for his cause, to search into the soul of the old world, to learn from it the lesson for his own future. While in England he met British aristocracy as a group for the first time, but soon felt the urge to continue on his way. He travelled to Germany, where he was present at the maneuvers of Frederick the Great's famous army at Potsdam. He visited Vienna and inspected the Imperial troops in Hungary. He met Hadyn and attended his concerts, and in Italy he made contact with expelled Jesuits. He travelled through the Balkans to Constantinople and thence across the Black Sea to Russia, where he was introduced to Potemkin and the great of the Russian Court. He finally met the Empress Catherine, who showered him with her favors—legend has it

12 Arch. Miranda. Vol. V. pp. 148-49. Dávila: *op. cit.* p. 14.
13 Dávila: *op. cit.* p. 13. Parra Pérez: *op. cit.* p. 16. The Diary of Francisco de Miranda; tour of the United States, 1783-1784. ed. by W. S. Robertson. New York, 1928.

that he was her lover—a gift of a thousand gold guilders, the privilege of wearing the Russian uniform, and letters of introduction to diplomats and other representatives of Russia abroad. From Russia, Miranda visited Sweden, and then on to Norway. He stayed everywhere long enough to study the people and the conditions under which they lived, but he tarried nowhere long enough to take root. Wherever he went he found men intelligent enough to listen to him and women to love him, for he had an extraordinary faculty for making friends, for working his way into society.[14]

Miranda was tall, robust, and athletic, and of ruddy complexion. He had good teeth of which he took great care, a strongly modelled nose, and searching, fiery eyes. His profile expressed willfulness, intelligence, and energy to the point of stubbornness. Altogether his appearance was impressive. Always ready to endure any privations demanded of him by circumstance, he had the manners of a great gentleman, and no one ever saw him look slovenly. Even in the most tragic moments of his life he was able to shave and dress as carefully as though he were about to pay a call. He was persuasive in gay and serious company both, and it was hard to resist his arguments because he was at the same time passionate and detached. These characteristics were enhanced by his considerable knowledge, careful observation, and a remarkable facility in languages, for he was equally at home in English, French, and Spanish, while he read German, Portuguese, Greek, and Latin. Many people who met him felt that he was the most unusual person they had ever known.

His intelligence was quick, his energy inexhaustible, his imagination lively, and his curiosity insatiable. But he also had many human failings. He had many manias, such as the one for emulating Roman antiquity in word and gesture. He was vain, preferring to talk about himself, to listen to no one but himself, and the success he had with so many blinded him to his limitations. Impulsive, opinionated, authoritarian, and

14 Parra Pérez: *op. cit.* p. 20. Dávila: *op. cit.* p. 15.

aggressive, he never deviated from an opinion once formed and brooked no arguments, announcing his own point of view with an air of infallibility.

It would be naive to judge Miranda by bourgeois standards. His was a personality which identified itself with great causes; and, like others of a similar nature, he believed that whatever suited his purpose was right. Whatever was advantageous to him also served the greater cause, and he saw no difference between his own, personal profit and the pursuit of a great idea. Thus many of his actions appear in a dubious light, in which it is hard to distinguish where revolutionary idealism ends and selfish interest begins. It was his indefatigable energy and his obsessed belief in victory that raised him and his efforts above all hazards. His words to young O'Higgins, the future liberator of Chile, shed some light on his mind's purposefulness. "Never admit that despair or discouragement ever possessed your soul. Strengthen yourself in the conviction that not a single day can pass without some incident which will bring you encouraging thoughts about the dignity and judgment of man."[15] Something of the greatness of Kant and of Schiller lives in these words.

In the vernacular of his time, Miranda was a dilettante in his determined desire for experience. But he was never confused. On the contrary, everything he did breathed the methodical and careful calculation of his rationalistic training. Perhaps in it lay his weakness. Possibly he planned too much.

After his travels Miranda returned to England which was the natural center for all anti-Spanish movements. He soon found the opportunity of divulging his plans to the British government.

In 1790 Spain and England were in conflict over the right to Notkasund. This peninsula, lying close to the coast of what is now British Columbia and the island of the same name, served the British as a fur trading post. The Spanish based their claims on an uncertain title which became valid only

15 Parra Pérez: *op. cit.* pp. 58 ff. Robertson: Life. Vol. I. p. 201.

under the force of arms, but the great statesman, William Pitt, who was then guiding the destinies of his country, never considered relinquishing Notkasund to Spain. He brusquely demanded indemnity from the Spanish government and began to arm.[16] In this situation, which foreshadowed a lengthy war with Spain, Miranda presented his great project and was granted an audience by Pitt. He requested that their conversation be recorded, and it took place on March 5, 1790.

Miranda envisioned a vast, independent realm extending from the Mississippi to Cape Horn, bounded on the west by the Pacific, on the east by the Atlantic. In the South American interior it was to extend to Guiana and Brazil. In his mind's eye Miranda placed at the head of this an hereditary emperor— to be called Inca—and as a law-giving body two chambers, a senate and a house of representatives, to be elected for five years. Included in his plan also were *ediles, questores,* and *censors.* The whole was aimed at a blending of North American and British principles. This South American empire was to be purely continental, and its products exclusively agricultural. That was the bait which Miranda offered to England. As a reward for British help in the establishment of the empire, these vast territories were to be opened to British trade.[17]

When Spain favored an amicable settlement of the Notkasund quarrel, Pitt thus winning a complete victory, Miranda was beaten. The British statesman had only committed himself to help Miranda in case of war. But the South American was far from discouraged. There were even richer possibilities for a revolutionary. Agreeing with Coriolanus that "there is a world elsewhere," he left the British Isles to offer his services to the French Revolution.

France had been in the throes of a mighty upheaval for the last three years, and already the revolutionary parties of the Gironde and the Jacobins threatened the thousand-year-old

16 Manning: Notka Sound Controversy. American Hist. Assn. Report, 1905. p. 369.
17 Robertson: Life. Vol. I. p. 104.

monarchy. It was natural for Miranda to hope and believe that
this movement might extend to the Spanish kingdom. His
ambition in France was identical to that in England—the liberation of his own country—but he realized that he had to change
somewhat his ideological argument. In England he had supported the constitutional monarchy; in France he became a
republican and revolutionist. Since the Gironde was the leading party, he joined its ranks, and after March, 1792, was to be
seen in the company of Brissot, Gensonné, and Pétion. His
decision to enter the French service cost him the favor of the
Czarina and caused an estrangement with England.[18]

Miranda hoped to play an important role politically as well
as militarily. He went to the front on September 10, and was
later promoted to brigadier-general and offered the command
of an expedition to Santo Domingo. At this time French politicians were considering a simultaneous attack on Hispano-
America, not for the purpose of liberation but rather to open
it to European trade and to divide it as booty among the European powers. Miranda heard of these plans, and the possibility
that all his hopes might come to nothing nearly broke his
heart.[19] He did not lose patience, however, and presented to
the French revolutionists the same plan he had laid before Pitt;
the ministers agreed upon it provided the North American
Union would also participate. Since such participation did not
materialize, Miranda's plan foundered again, and he himself
decided to remain in the army.[20]

It is not possible here to follow him through all the stages
of his military career. It is enough to state that his position
became precarious following the decapitation of Louis XVI
and the ambiguous attitude of Dumouriez in the early months
of 1793. Miranda was recalled to Paris and thrown into prison.
Accused before a revolutionary tribunal in May, 1793, he defended himself passionately, succeeded in refuting all accusa-

18 Parra Pérez: op. cit. pp. 18-19. Rojas: op. cit. pp. 270 ff.
19 Parra Pérez: op. cit. p. 38. C. A. Villanueva: Napoleón y la Independencia de
América. Paris, 1911. p. 64.
20 Parra Pérez: op. cit. p. 49. Dávila: op. cit. p. 23.

tions and gained complete acquital. Political circumstances now prevented his return to the army, and he, who had been called the sword of the Gironde, was incriminated in its downfall. He was rearrested in July, 1793, and incarcerated until the beginning of 1795. Determined not to mount the gallows, he had provided himself with poison if the situation should come to the worst.

But his life curve had not reached its end, for he was freed. Even then he did not dream of leaving the country. Enjoying the favors of Delphine de Custine, one of France's most beautiful women, he devoted himself to the development of a political program.[21] At this time Miranda's life was as active as it was remarkable. Without a regular income, he was nevertheless able to dress elegantly, to give banquets, and to surround himself with the important men of the day. Nobody knows where he obtained his money, but the impression that he was an adventurer was heightened by the many romantic entanglements in which he found himself — entanglements which always contained a political flavor. Bonaparte, whom he met at this period, saw in him a Don Quixote, but Bonaparte also recognized the holy zeal burning in his soul.[22]

With France and Spain in a state of war, Miranda could still dream of achieving his ambition, the liberation of South America. But Spain concluded a pact with France following the Peace of Basle, and this, to the revolutionist, again meant a step backward. Disguised by his mistress, Miranda fled first to Calais, then on to London to seek haven in free England and to renew his relationship with Pitt.

In the period which followed he did not allow himself to forget the higher destiny which had brought him into the French Army; and he never broke connections with the conspirators who worked for the same ends in both the Old World

21 Dávila: *op. cit.* p. 28. Parra Pérez: *op. cit.* pp. 295 ff. Robertson: Life. Vol. I. pp. 144-45. Delphine de Custine, Belle Amie de Miranda. Lettres inedites publiées par C. Parra Pérez. Paris, 1927.
22 Duchesse d'Abrantés: Memoires. Vol. I. p. 329. Paris. Parra Pérez: *op. cit.* p. 321. Dávila: *op. cit.* p. 28.

and the New. Under his leadership secret organizations were formed in the cities and provinces of South America, while meetings took place regularly in Paris, attended by Peruvians, Chileans, Cubans, and representatives of New Granada. Several of the most important revolutionaries, such as Nariño and Cortes Madariaga, travelled across the European continent, but much effort was aimed at keeping the conspiracy an impenetrable secret.

Shortly before Miranda left France for London a plan was agreed upon—in December, 1797—signed by Miranda and four others: Pablo de Olavide, Pedro José Caro, José del Pozo y Sucre, and Manuel José Salas, all representatives of South America. The first declaration of the document was the right of Hispano-Americans to freedom. Mutual trade pacts were made among the twenty colonies to be liberated; and, with amazing foresightedness, the two canals near Panama and Nicaragua were envisaged.

Miranda, who retained command of all military action, was requested to furnish the necessary means in England and to influence Great Britain and the United States to provide some twenty thousand men. England's reward was to be the opening of markets in South America and the Antilles, while the United States was to have Florida and Louisiana. Finally, a free South America was to enter into a coalition agreement for defense with both these powers.[23] Miranda, immediately on arrival in England, sent messages to various sections of South America, treated with the Ambassador of the United States; and, most important of all, renewed relationship with William Pitt.[24]

In the last analysis, however, both governments, British and American, held the problem of revolutionizing the Spanish colonies as too dangerous, unless they were forced into it.

23 Becerra: *op. cit.* Vol. I. pp. 54-61. Pereyra: Juventud. p. 230. Robertson: Life. Vol. I. p. 167. R. Caillet Bois: Miranda y los orígenes de la Independencia. B. d. H. Caracas. Vol. XII. Number 47. p. 321.
24 Robertson: Life. Vol. I. p. 171. See Documentos relativos a las actividades revolucionarios de Miranda. B. d. H. Caracas. Vol. IX, Number 35.

Though the British government did not renounce the idea completely, the plan was only to be considered as a last resort. Once again Miranda received a setback. Moreover he was not permitted to leave the country. He was suspect, and too valuable to be allowed out of sight.

It is strange that at a moment when Miranda had almost forgotten to wish for it, he should receive reinstatement. The *Consejo de las Indias* finally acquitted him, and a return to Spanish service was once again open. But this was unthinkable on the part of Miranda, for it was the very indictment which had forced him to deviate from the usual path and had made him into a rebel. He now found it impossible to reverse himself.[25]

Instead he threw himself tirelessly into the subterranean world of politics, working to undermine relations with Spain and to place in the best possible light the revolutionizing of South America. His chances were naturally greatly influenced by the ups and downs of power politics. His native resilience and toughness permitted him to emerge from each crisis, and he always found new friends—naval officers, adventurers, merchants, statesmen—who supported his ambitious projects. Now and then he despaired of his work in England and called the country shortsighted, perfidious. Sometimes he complained of the treatment he received, but through it all he remained on British soil, living on English money and in contact with the country's politicians.

Miranda's plans for action received new impetus with the return of Pitt as Prime Minister and with the declaration of war against Napoleon. And when Spain declared war on England in October, 1804, the moment seemed to have arrived. From all sides the British government was begged to relinquish its role of coquettish hesitation.[26]

But again British politics dictated delay, for the threat of a

25 Robertson: Miranda. p. 189. See also Doc. B. d. H. Caracas. Vol. IX, Number 34. p. 55.
26 Robertson: Life. Vol. I. p. 256.

Napoleonic invasion hung over the country, making any division of forces impossible.

In the face of this new defeat a disillusioned, but not discouraged, Miranda left British soil after seven years. He arrived in the United States at the end of 1805. He took with him £6,000 in currency, given him by Vansittart, Chancellor of the Exchequer, and permission to raise an equal amount. It is not known whether he actually came to some sort of terms with the British government, who perhaps promised him support if he should succeed in persuading North America to attack the Spanish colonies. Such an attack was not too unlikely, since the United States seemed definitely interested in Florida and Texas.

It was into this atmosphere, charged with political tension, that Miranda plunged when he landed in New York in November, 1805. While there was no lack of old friends and supporters of his revolutionary ideas, the available military aid was too meager to serve his needs. Miranda's discussions with the government were unfruitful. In them he bared his hopes and the data on which his plans were based, putting his cards on the table with complete lack of circumlocution. But President Jefferson and his Secretary of State, Madison, promised him no active participation whatever. Somehow in this, Miranda, an incurable optimist, saw a silent promise of support, and meanwhile talked of his great plans to other friends. At the end of the year he began to prepare seriously for an armed attack upon the South American mainland, pawning his valuable library in London to enable him to chart ships, recruit volunteers, and buy war materials. He wished all activities and preparations to remain secret. When, on February 2, 1806, the *Leander,* a ship of two hundred tons, took to the high seas with Santo Domingo its objective, secrecy was maintained as to the real purpose of the trip.[27] Even the unhappy soldiers aboard did not suspect what lay ahead.

But in spite of Miranda's precautions the Spanish govern-

27 Robertson: Life. Vol. I. p. 299.

ment, through its ambassador in Washington, got wind of his plans. He was continually under watch by spies and much information about him was gathered and passed on to the colonial officials.[28]

In the meantime Miranda was nearing his goal. Attempting to organize his slight military strength as best he could, he swore his soldiers in among the peoples of South America, hoisting the flag of his new empire—yellow, blue and red. In an audacious attempt to link the idea of independence with that of the discovery of the continent, he called the country Colombia.[29] Miranda had previously received assurance from his North American friends that other ships would join his in Santo Domingo. Waiting in vain for a month, he was forced to acknowledge that he had been deserted. During this time he had only been able to enlarge his forces by two small ships. His fighting force, with which he was to land on the coast of Venezuela, consisted of exactly 180 men—not a large number with which to remove a province from Spanish domination. While the Spaniards did not, by any means, maintain a great army in South America, they could still stand up to Miranda's little band. It appeared that he considered his mere presence sufficient to cause Spanish imperialism to crumble to the dust.

If Miranda's actions were humanly understandable, they were militarily inexcusable. His enforced sojourn in Santo Domingo enabled Spanish officials in Venezuela to make more than adequate preparations. When he set out to land in Puerto Cabello, Venezuela's chief port, the post was alerted. The coast patrol followed the tiny fleet for some time, and it was extremely easy to paralyze attempts at landing. The two smaller ships were attacked first, and though the men aboard defended themselves, they were taken prisoner and the ships scuttled. Miranda, fleeing on the *Leander,* was only able to escape pursuit by throwing the entire artillery overboard.[30]

28 Robertson: Life. Vol. I. p. 296.
29 Robertson: Life. Vol. I. p. 303. Mancini: pp. 203 ff.
30 Robertson: Life. Vol. I. pp. 306-7. B. d. H. Caracas. Vol. X. Number 37. p. 42.

The unhappy prisoners, victims of their own ignorance regarding the true purpose of the expedition, were condemned
to prisons, fortresses, or death. The Spanish would have liked
to deal thus with Miranda, but even they could not hang a
man who had escaped their hands, so they had to satisfy themselves with the burning of the flag, the proclamation, and the
picture of Miranda, who was declared an enemy of God and the
King.

It is not surprising that Miranda lost the crew's confidence.
The dilatoriness of his preparations, the military stupidity of
his plans, his weakness at the crucial moment of action—all
these were symptoms which made his qualities of leadership in
a revolution most questionable. This was not his first failure
with men under his command, nor was it his last. One wonders whether he possessed all talents save that of knowing how
to put them to good use.

With his companions Miranda wandered among the British
Antilles, landing first at Trinidad, then at Barbados. It was
an invincible quality in the man that no failure could shake
him or rob him of the courage to try his luck again. In Barbados he made contact with the Admiral of the British fleet in
those waters, Cochrane, who was destined to become one of
the great figures in the history of South American independence. The Admiral was convinced of the necessity of opening
new markets for British trade, since European ones were closed
by the Continental blockage. To him the Spanish colonies of
the South American continent seemed eminently suitable for
that purpose, and independently he came to an agreement with
Miranda, promising the protection of the British fleet during
the continuation of his project.[31]

Miranda was, therefore, able to dare a second attempt which
promised to be more successful than the first. On August 1,
1806, he landed troops in Coro, Venezuela, under the aegis of
the British fleet and routed the Spanish garrison there. Once
again the Colombian flag was raised and a proclamation sent

31 Robertson: Life. Vol. I. pp. 312-13.

out to the South Americans. But no one answered the call. Strangely enough, he had appeared only when military action was over. When he landed with about six hundred men he entered an ugly, deserted city from which the population had fled. His call for freedom found no echo.

Spanish authorities had not been idle, and they were fully aware of the danger of an attack upon a territory containing a large number of Negro slaves, with no lack of unrest and discontent. Venezuela's governor at that time, Manuel de Guevara y Vasconcelos, was an inordinately capable man with a great sense of realism in his appraisal of the situation, and he knew that it was vital for him to have the support of the civilian population. He did not stop at military preparations, but succeeded in convincing the province's civilians that it was necessary to repulse Miranda with all the means at their command. In this way the words of the rebel found no response in the hearts of his compatriots, and he remained to them a pirate, a traitor in British employ who would sell them out to England. Since British support depended solely on Cochrane's decision, Miranda's position became increasingly difficult, and he was faced with the choice of remaining in Venezuela without the protection of the British fleet or retaining this protection and retiring from the scene. He chose to leave Venezuela once more, returning to Trinidad, and by the fall of 1807 it was clear that his revolutionary plans had once again miscarried.[32]

During this same period a similar coup was attempted in the southern part of the continent by Captain Popham, a friend of Miranda's, who attacked Buenos Aires in June, 1806, with a few ships and a small armed force. Popham appeared successful and the city was taken.

Contrary to all expectation, the British soon lost this easily won territory, and Buenos Aires was won back to the Spanish after three days of fighting by Jacques de Liniers, a French nobleman in the service of Spain. The people had never for one moment placed their approval on the British occupation.

32 Robertson: Life. Vol. I. pp. 318-19.

The words of an Argentinian patriot spoken some time later: "We want the old masters or none," expressed exactly the attitude of the colonial population towards Spain and attempts on the part of other European countries to gain a foothold on the South American continent.[33]

Thus a century of European colonial policy ended with the failure of Miranda and the unsuccessful attack on Buenos Aires. Four powers still competed—Spain, Portugal, England, and the United States. While Spain sought desperately to defend her possessions, England and the United States were attempting to expand theirs at the expense of this erstwhile Catholic world power. And none of these nations was directly interested in the liberation of South American territories from Spanish or Portuguese domination.

Was the Hispano-American population actually ready to revolt at this time? Colonial society, looked at as a whole, had remained true to the ancient concepts of loyalty and devotion to King, mother country, and Church. But while its effect could not immediately be detected, Miranda's expedition did have some influence on the American peoples. South America had successfully defended itself against attacks from without and had done so minus the help of Spain; this immeasurably heightened the self-confidence of the Creoles. And in this undesired and unintentional autonomy lay the seed of future revolutionary development. This seed required a particular soil in which to grow. But at this time it was impossible to realize that the day was near on which South Americans from the Rio Grande to Cape Horn would be forced to decide whether they wanted "the old masters or none."

33 Sassenay: Napoleon I et la fondation de la Republique Argentine. Paris, 1892. R. Levene: H. d. A. Vol. V. *passim*. Mancini: *op. cit.* p. 220. Robertson: Life. Vol. I. p. 322. Webster: Vol. I. pp. 8-9.

CHAPTER 5

The Dawn of Revolution

$\mathcal{M}$iranda lives in the memory of the South American peoples as the "precursor," the vanguard of a greater man, a voice calling in the desert. His life story is but a prologue to the drama of South American freedom. His plans, his efforts, and in the end even his failure were but rivulets emptying into the lifestream of the real hero, Simon Bolivar.

At the time of Bolivar's return to his native country in 1807, Miranda's collapse was obvious. Obvious, also, was the loyalty of the colonial peoples who had been unwilling to remain passive in the face of British expansion and who refused to exchange Spanish for British domination with docility. We must not be misled, however, by the failure of the attack on Venezuela into misjudging the temper of the Creoles at this time. How many of them watched with sullen, helpless rage the terrible action taken against Miranda's troops? How many with hatred in their hearts were present at the burning of his portrait and the other symbols of a better future? The naiveté of his plans, their bad organization and execution, robbed Miranda from the start of all chances for success, but there can be little doubt that a greater part of the population, the Creole youth in particular, sided with him.

Bolivar counted among these. Although he was aware that the hour for action had not yet arrived and that Miranda had pushed ahead precipitously in response to false information, the revolutionary impulses in him, which had been strength-

ened by his European trip, could not be paralyzed by a tactical
error such as Miranda had committed.[1] In the years following
Bolivar's return we find him in a dual role. In the eyes of the
world at large, and of the Spanish spies in particular, he posed
as the rich landowner occupied only with the supervision of
his lands and the administration of his vast estates. As a matter
of fact, Bolivar *was* greatly interested in indigo planting, and
he planned to connect and irrigate the various parts of his
estate. It was necessary for the successful carrying out of this
project to obtain the permission of his neighbors, and between
Bolivar and one of these, Antonio Nicolás Briceño—known as
"the devil"—a quarrel arose which only terminated in a criminal action. Bolivar was forced to defend himself against Briceño's slaves, armed with knives and firearms and ordered to
intercept Bolivar's work. Following these acts of violence,
long lists of complaints were lodged with the authorities.[2]

But this visible and respectable side of his life served to
conceal the plans of the conspirators—*conspirators* because Bolivar knew that he was not alone, that there were many sharing
his republican ideas and revolutionary ambitions. There was
his brother Juan Vicente, the family of the Marquis de Toro,
relatives of his deceased wife, as well as his uncle José Félix
Ribas, and Tomás and Mariano Montilla, whom he had known
in Paris. In addition to the many others, there was his old
teacher, Andrés Bello, now promoted to the post of secretary of
the Governor of Venezuela.[3]

The members of this group made up the *jeunesse dorée* of
Caracas. Their gatherings had the character one would expect.
Bolivar gave brilliant affairs, sometimes having tables set up
for gambling or engaging in heated discussions. He told about
his travels or listened to Bello's translations of Tacitus, Virgil,
and Voltaire. Bolivar's opinions and tastes were greatly respected among his friends, and Bello did not object to the

1 Mosquera: *op. cit.* p. 14. Larrazabal: Vol. I. p. 19.
2 Lecuna: Adolescencia. p. 586.
3 J. D. Díaz: Recuerdos de la rebelión de Caracas. Madrid, 1829. p. 13.

criticisms of his versions of Voltaire or to Bolivar's praise of his Virgil.[4] These literary meetings served Bolivar perfectly as a smoke screen, and in them he could air his high flown political ideas. Not that he could at this time have been thinking of revolutionary action. On the contrary, action seemed hopeless to him, and he felt that caution was mandatory. But here were gathered together a group of men whose influence on the progress of the independence movement was to become decisive.[5] Serious purpose was concealed behind this façade of seeming wastrels and aesthetes, and a secret organization was founded. The question arose as to who would lead the revolt, and Juan Vicente proposed his brother. But though his courage was undoubted, no one considered Simon capable of such an assignment; they did not attribute to him the necessary qualities of leadership. Before his companions would give him their confidence, he had to prove himself in desperate and urgent situations. If a movement of real importance was to stem from these meetings—half literary, half revolutionary— a change was needed in the political atmosphere. Such a movement could never arise merely from the somnolent still life of those Colonial times.

Bolivar had recognized on his return that the great adventure of the revolution could only commence when the Goddess of Possibility was favorably inclined. At this moment the occasion seemed at hand, and it was Napoleon who had created it. Here, as everywhere else, his mighty will forced itself upon a way of life which had been in progress for hundreds of years. Napoleon was, as Hegel said, the "secretary of the World-Spirit," thinking only of himself and the enlarging of his own powers, but a man who nevertheless served world history in the impetus he gave to the progress of freedom.

Napoleon stood at this time at the zenith of his political and military power. He had laid Austria low, destroyed Prussia, and brought Russia at least to her knees. He had founded

4 Larrazabal: Vol. I. p. 41. Amunategui: *op. cit.* p. 61.
5 Lecuna: Adolescencia. p. 616.

the System of Tilsit, the most mature evidence of his statesmanship. His aim was the organization of Europe—*La France será
le Monde*—and this expression of his ambition to rule the world
seemed near to realization. The other continental powers were
forced to the position of second rate nations. Thus it was an
easy matter for Napoleon to offer the conceited Czar a share
in the rule, and the consequent agreement with Russia brought
peace to the European continent. This peace permitted Napoleon to devote himself exclusively to the blockade of England.
Since Nelson's victory at Trafalgar, the hope of conquering
Britain by invasion had been destroyed, and therefore as a last
resort was born the idea of a continental blockade. Napoleon
believed that he could force British capitulation in the shortest
possible time by closing to her all European ports, thus upset-
ting her balance of trade. In order to achieve this successfully,
Europe had to be transformed into a closed economic bloc
which no British goods could penetrate. There were still places,
however, which were not completely under French control—
in particular the Iberian peninsula, composed of Spain and
Portugal.[6]

Napoleon acted quickly, as was his habit, beginning with
a Portugal that had for centuries been a British vassal state. In
November, 1807, Junot attacked Portugal and Napoleon declared the throne lost to the House of Braganza. The royal
family was able to save itself by fleeing to Brazil on a British
ship. Portugal occupied, it remained to deal with Spain.

We remember from the account of Bolivar's youth that
Spain at this time had been reduced to a great degree of moral
degeneracy. Godoy, the Queen's powerful lover, still ruled the
Court and the Cabinet. In 1808, when Napoleon turned his
attention to the problem of Spain, the very existence of the
Minister gave him the excuse he needed for intervention.[7] His
wish was to incorporate Spain within the continental system,

6 C. Oman: History of the Peninsular War. Oxford, 1902. La Fuente y Valera:
Historia general de España. Barcelona, 1922. Vols. XVI and XVII.
7 A. Savine: L'Abdication de Bayonne. Paris, 1884. J. R. Vejarano: El Zarpazo
Napoleónico contra España. Rev. d. Indias. August, 1945.

and it seemed inevitable that a dependable regent should occupy the Spanish throne. The everlasting dissension within the Madrid palace permitted Napoleon to dicker with all parties. Ferdinand, the successor to the throne and well-beloved by the people, had in 1807 unsuccessfully attempted to seize the government; and the King, or rather the Queen and Godoy, had turned to Napoleon to settle the matter. The Emperor managed to put them off and instead under different pretexts began infiltrating his troops into the country. He expected at this point that the royal family would flee like the Braganzas, but matters happened otherwise. The Spanish people, believing that the French army was on their territory for the purpose of raising Ferdinand to the throne, revolted against the ruling monarch and his minister. By the revolt of Aranjuez they forced Charles IV to abdicate in Ferdinand's favor. Napoleon, however, was not satisfied, and he lured the young king to Bayonne, in French territory. Here the other actors in this tragi-comedy foregathered: Charles IV, Marie-Luise, and Godoy; and because of their utter defenselessness, Napoleon succeeded in achieving just what he wished, a renunciation of the Spanish throne. The inept and ineffectual Bourbons abdicated on May 5, 1808, and Napoleon summoned his brother, Joseph, to claim their inheritance. This, perhaps the greatest crime of his life, was, as Talleyrand said, more than a crime. It was an act of stupidity.[8]

The Spaniards, in indignation over their betrayal and disappointment, became uncontrollable. They organized guerrilla warfare against Napoleon's army, and throughout the country they created *juntas provinciales*—autonomous representation of districts—in opposition to Napoleon's rule. The agreement of Bayonne was declared invalid, and all Spain proclaimed Ferdinand as rightful king. On September 25, 1808, a *junta suprema*, or national assembly, convened and declared a state of war with France. A pact was made with England, and the revolt of national forces against the Napoleonic Empire had begun.

8. La Fuente: *op. cit.* Vol. XVI. p. 243.

What response did this course of events evoke in South
America? The unconquerably aggressive will of Bonaparte
would not have permitted them to remain passive even if the
colonies had wished to disassociate themselves from the events
in Europe. His grasping, far-reaching spirit, which fed on
dreams, had never relinquished the idea of an empire overseas.
After the sea victory of Nelson, East India and Egypt appeared
unattainable, but with the conquest of Spain it was now possible to acquire the empire of Charles V without bloodshed.
In one stroke the damage done to France overseas would in
this way be vitiated and a highly prized jewel snatched from
under the very nose of France's rival, Great Britain. Napoleon
therefore sent capable, dependable men to the capitals of South
America to inform the citizens of the latest events in Europe
and to influence public opinion in favor of the new master. The
Emperor appointed viceroys and governors as though the continent were already his.[9]

Venezuela was in complete ignorance of the state of affairs
in Europe. Juan de Casas, who as governor had ruled Caracas
since 1807, was not a strong personality like his predecessor,
and was little equipped in times of stress to hold the rudder
firmly in his hands. The first news reached Venezuela around
the middle of 1808, when the British government in Trinidad
sent the governor a detailed report of everything that had
occurred in Spain. This news seemed so incredible to the colonial officials that they declared it an invention of British perfidy.[10]

Proof was not long in arriving, however, for on July 15,
1808, a French ship entered the port of La Guayra with Napoleon's delegates to Venezuela on board.[11] When the Governor received the French officials, he heard to his horror that
the King of Spain was named Joseph Bonaparte. The impression created by this piece of news is indescribable. The Spanish

9 C. Parra Pérez: Bayona y la política de Napoleón en América. Caracas, 1939.
pp. 5, 12.
    10 See the important book by J. R. Vejarano: Los orígines de la Independencia
Suramericana. Bogotá, 1925. p. 18.
    11 O'Leary: Memorias. Vol. I. p. 58. Larrazabal. Vol. I. p. 39. P. de Urquina-
ona: Memorias. Biblioteca Ayacucho. Vol. XIV. Madrid, 1917. p. 18.

colonial officials believed that lightning had struck at their very feet and that the earth had opened. To which of the two monarchs did they owe allegiance? The legitimate ruler was Ferdinand VII, but he had abdicated and was a prisoner. The new monarch was in power, but he was an illegitimate usurper, to whom the American people were in no way bound.

While the officials were vacillating, the people of Venezuela made their decision. In the ten days that had passed since the first news had come from Trinidad, public opinion had turned against Napoleon. Two separate parties were formed and agreed on one point—the complete rejection of the usurper and his claims on America. Demonstrators, excited and angry, gathered beneath the governor's windows shouting "Long live our King" over and over again. A delegation was sent to the Governor demanding that Ferdinand VII be proclaimed King.[12] This was promised for the following day, but the aroused populace would brook no delay, and that very evening the ceremony took place, with Ferdinand's picture exhibited in the city hall. The people took a passionate part in all proceedings, and would not have needed much suggestion before seizing the French emissaries, who were at last forced to realize that their mission had failed. A British frigate had arrived at this moment at La Guayra, and there was little for them to do but flee to their ship under cover of darkness.[13]

The situation in Caracas was being repeated, with slight variations, in the other capitals of the Spanish colonies. Wherever the French delegates showed themselves they were turned away and expelled. In Mexico, Buenos Aires, Montevideo, and La Paz, obedience was refused Napoleon, and Ferdinand VII was declared the rightful ruler. As in Spain, so also in America, he became *El Deseado,* the Desired.

The French soon realized that there was no hope of winning the favor of the people and stopped sending their agents.

12 Vejarano: Orígenes. p. 19.
13 See Capitán Beaver's letter to Sir. A. Cochrane, Larrazabal. Vol. I. p. 39. Blanco: Doc. Vol. II. pp. 161-163.

Instead, South America received the messengers of the Spanish
National Assembly, who reported on the glorious war being
waged by Spaniards for the sake of liberty. They were enthusi-
astically received. Celebrations were held in their honor, masses
were said in the churches, and the cities were illuminated. In
their hats or belts the people wore the Spanish colors with the
inscription: "Let us die or triumph for our King." The women
donated their jewels, and millions of gold pesos were collected
in a few days for the cause of Ferdinand VII. When it was
learned that guerrillas had forced the French to capitulate near
Baylén, the patriotic fervor of Spain spread to South America.[14]

Colonial authorities had followed the impulse of the population unwillingly and hesitantly. It seemed as though the
majority of them were more inclined towards the new Napoleonic dynasty. In any case, they insisted on the principle
that the colonies must, no matter what dynasty ruled in Madrid,
form an integral part of the monarchy.

In order to fulfill their aims, the excited masses had renewed
the old form of city government, the *cabildo abierto*. They
wished to create a form of local representation patterned after
the mother country. They respected the official representatives
of Spain at first, but they also demanded the recognition of
their own native talent. Within the totality of the Spanish empire they demanded for America the rights of the mother
country, and it became apparent that the movement would not
be long in leaving behind the old forms of colonial government.
A new day was dawning in the life of South America. Spain
herself was aware that she would have to comply with demands
for constitutional representation on the part of the colonies.[15]
Henceforth, says a Spanish proclamation, the vast and valuable
regions of America are no longer colonies or plantations, but
an integral part of the Spanish monarchy. However, the Spaniards were ungenerous in granting that which they had declared

14 R. Lévene: H. d. A. Vols. V and VI, *passim*. Clerc: Capitulation de Baylen.
Paris, 1903. Parra Pérez: Historia de la primera República de Venezuela. Caracas,
1939. Vol. I. p. 214.
15 La Fuente: *op. cit.* Vol. XVII. p. 7. Blanco: Doc. Vol. II. pp. 230, 231, 235.

indispensable, and whereas thirty-six delegates were assigned to the twelve million Spaniards, only twelve were to suffice the fifteen million South Americans.[16] It was evident that a strong fermentation was taking place within the Spanish Empire on both sides of the Atlantic, and it was obvious that conditions would never again correspond to those in existence before Napoleon had imperilled the very life of Spain.

There were, as we have already mentioned, two revolutionary factions in Venezuela, one of which was led by Captain Matos, a violent and rebellious man utterly incapable of concealing his feelings. But his very directness became his nemesis, and the colonial officials found it very easy to prosecute him.[17]

The action taken by the other faction, which had clustered around Simon Bolivar, was much more far-reaching. The conspirators met in secret conclave at Bolivar's El Palmito estate on the banks of the La Guayra River. They were defiant youths who wished, as a Spanish writer remarked, to learn the art of rebellion at first hand.[18] They surrounded their meetings with an aura of mystery, gathered in the small hours of the day and extended their discussions far into the night. What were they plotting, and were they really thinking of destroying the existing order? Not yet, perhaps, but they did feel that events had placed them at the cross roads. The proclamation declaring Ferdinand VII as their King could only have been the first impulse necessary to put into motion the lethargic colonial masses. The next step was to be the granting of autonomous representation according to the pattern set by Spain herself. Perhaps these young revolutionaries, pushing ever harder in their demands, did not actually visualize their goal. But there was one man who did, and he had fiercely awaited this moment for three decades.

Miranda returned to London following his failure in attacking Venezuela. On July 20, 1808, he wrote a letter from Eng-

16 Mancini: p. 257. Larrazabal: Vol. I. p. 44.
17 Vejarano: Orígenes. pp. 11 ff. Lecuna: Adolescencia. p. 614. Lecuna: La Conspiración de Matos. B. d. H. Caracas. Vol. XV. Number 56. p. 387.
18 Díaz: *op. cit.* p. 9.

land to the city council of Caracas in which he exhorted its members to take the rule of the provinces into their own hands without further hesitation.[19] He considered it essential that the affairs of America be separated from those of Spain, and he asked that a diplomatic mission be sent to London to treat with the British regarding the security and future of the New World. It was much easier at this point to give advice than to execute it, for the authorities had decided to proceed firmly against all efforts towards autonomy.

Bolivar was also feeling the will of officialdom at this time. His house was watched, his actions suspect, and finally the son of the governor was dispatched to warn him. He was advised not to receive guests or hold parties, and through it all he played the innocent. "I am desperate," he declared, "and only wish I could get rid of those uninvited guests of whom I am thoroughly sick. I call no one, and am innocent of any slander." So that he would not be connected with any movement, he promised to retire to his country estate, and most of the other conspirators followed his example. Thus the two early revolutionary moves were unsuccessful, the leaders scattered or under arrest.[20]

However, the patriots did not wish to relinquish that which they had so nearly won, and there began at this time a two-year struggle between the liberal Creoles and the Spanish authorities. In Caracas the idea of establishing an autonomous government was reanimated, and hundreds of important men met together. This was conspiracy in the broad light of day. In November, 1808, the notables of Caracas made a most impressive statement.[21] These men, while reaffirming their loyalty to the King and the Holy Faith, demanded the right to call an assembly, which together with the authorities, was to exercise the highest authority in the country until the King's return to the throne of his fathers. The government answered by arresting the

19 Robertson: Miranda. pp. 277, 284. Antepara: South American Emancipation. London, 1810.
20 Lecuna: Adolescencia. p. 617.
21 Larrazabal: *op. cit.* Vol. I. p. 41. Blanco: Doc. Vol. II. pp. 179-80.

author of the declaration. Bolivar was not among its signers, for the document was not worded as he wished. His plans went further, and he aimed at something more than a compromise between the old rule and the new. Here the greatness and the tragedy of his statesmanlike temperament are revealed for the first time. He wanted, wherever he functioned, if not to rule, at least to lead. When he could not command he felt superfluous.[22] He was far too big a man to be regimented, and it was already his aim to lead the revolution. In him the Spaniards saw a young man of "indomitable pride and unlimited ambition." He was both indomitable and ambitious, and he had tired of the role of a conspirator who never achieved palpable results. It frustrated him to know that no one considered him capable of leading the coming revolution. The political program that he had refused to sign he considered preposterous in its meekness, inconsistency, and ambiguity. What possible value to Venezuela lay in this demand for autonomous representation and proclamation of loyalty to Ferdinand? Bolivar considered himself a republican: what was the King to him, or he to the King? Ferdinand had no power, being but a prisoner of Napoleon, who had marched victoriously into Madrid. The representatives of the Spanish provinces were no longer able to meet, and the very existence of the National Assembly was threatened by the disintegration of Spanish forces at Ocaña and Alba de Tormes. Bolivar gained courage from what he saw in Europe to proceed with his fight for freedom, and in 1809 he publicly joined the movement for American independence.[23] What commenced as an uprising against the Napoleonic usurpation ended with a revolution against Spanish domination.

In May of the same year a new governor, Field Marshal Vicente de Emparán, had come to Venezuela, and he was considered both conciliatory and affable. As in all revolutionary epochs, however, his conciliatory tendencies were attributed to

22 Vejarano: Orígenes. p. 95.
23 O'Leary: Memorias. Vol. I. p. 24. Lecuna: Adolescencia. pp. 617-21.

weakness. Bolivar had thrown all caution to the winds, and accompanied by his friends and relatives, wandered through the streets provoking Spanish officers. At a banquet attended by the Governor, he drank to the freedom of Venezuela and all America. The Spanish authorities tried by gentle means to bring him to reason—what they considered reason, of course —and invited Bolivar and others sharing his views to a discussion in which high ranking officials explained the dangers inherent in a conspiracy. Bolivar listened in silence until they had finished, and then told them that while all that they were saying was true, he and his companions had declared war on Spain and could not withdraw.[24]

The government was really in a tragic dilemma. Was it possible to preserve its authority and at the same time win the good will of the colonials? The problem was the more insoluble owing to Napoleon's uninterrupted wooing of the Americans. He duplicated the offer of Spain to give the colonies a voice in the General Assembly, and what is more he announced that he would grant complete independence to the Hispano-American countries if they would close their ports to British trade.[25]

American events dovetail again and again with events in Europe, whence of course they originated. The further French forces pushed into the Iberian Peninsula, the closer came the day when the shadow of Spain's independence would vanish, and the goal of converting the South American subject states into free, independent countries appeared more attainable. That was the credo of the American liberals: "Since the monarchy is dissolved and Spain is lost, we find ourselves in the same position as do adult sons after their father's death. Each son insists on his own rights. He furnishes his own house, and rules it himself." Revolution was the logical outcome of such a state of affairs.[26]

24 J. F. Heredia: Memorias. Biblioteca Ayacucho. Vol. XI. Madrid. p. 163. Torres Lanza: Vol. II. p. 92.
25 Parra Pérez: Bayona. p. 14. La Fuente: *op. cit.* Vol. XVI. p. 312.
26 Mancini: p. 268.

We have seen with what audacity the Venezuelans were already rallying around Simon Bolivar, and now they turned from the mere expression of their feelings to the actual organization of the revolution.

At the same time as the appointment of the new governor, a new inspector of the militia had also been named; he was Fernando Rodríguez de Toro, Bolivar's brother-in-law. Through him the patriots were able to learn of every military order on the part of the government. The rebels planned the staging of a riot with the help of the grenadiers of Aragua, whose barracks became the headquarters of the conspirators. The date of the uprising was set for April 1, 1810, but the Governor, Emparán, was able to abort the plan by the arrest of a few of the hot heads and the banishment of others to their estates. Among these was Bolivar, who retired to the country.[27]

However, the authority of the state was greatly weakened, and but a few days following the discovery of this plot Bolivar returned to Caracas and was able to remain unmolested.

At the request of the mother country, the Spanish authorities had done their utmost to keep the Americans in the dark regarding the true state of affairs in Europe, and ships arriving in American ports were searched carefully for letters and newspapers. But the news that the French had conquered Andalusía and taken Cádiz had leaked through. It was said that the *Junta Central* had been disbanded, and a regency-council composed of five members had taken over the government. This news was corroborated on April 17, when a ship arrived in La Guayra with two representatives of this regency-council (to whom the National Assembly had delegated its rights) on board. They had been sent to America to procure the approval of the regency-council. Bolivar, after meeting the newcomers and having learned what he could from them, declared that he and his followers were forced to establish representation in Caracas for self-government owing to the vacillation in the

27 Larrazabal: Vol. I. p. 48. Urquinaona: *op. cit.* pp. 26-27. Pereyra: Juventud. p. 267.

mother county on the part of the supreme council, which had been unsuccessful in acquiring a permanent form.[28] The revolutionists were unwilling to acknowledge the regency-council and wanted to use the dissolution of the *Junta Central* as an excuse for establishing the government they desired. While the patriots were thus deciding upon extreme measures, the Governor lost his head. He posted announcements of the recent events throughout the streets, and the masses learned the exact state of affairs in Spain. Nothing could have been more welcome to the rebels.

On April 18, the details of the revolt were finally determined upon by the conspirators who, Simon and Juan Vicente Bolivar among them, met throughout the night. Every one of them realized that the moment had arrived in which to enforce independent representation in Caracas; but while the conservatives were still discussing compromise with the authorities, extremists such as Bolivar demanded the impeachment and banishment of the Spaniards. He was aware of what it would mean to draw the masses into an uprising.

Thus dawned April 19, 1810. It was Maundy Thursday. The city was already swarming with groups of excited citizens.[29] Towards seven o'clock the City Council met in the customary manner to take part in public services, and when they had assembled they sent for the Governor, who accepted the invitation. On the way he found the public square filled with the masses, and in the town hall itself he found himself confronting men whose fighting spirit he had once attempted unsuccessfully to dampen. Hardly had he taken his place when they demanded he establish a representative body in Caracas, since the situation in the mother country and the dissolution

28 D. Arias Argáez: El Canónigo don José Cortés y Madariaga. Bogotá, 1938. p. 41. With regard to Bolivar's participation there exist two contradictory statements. Larrazabal, Vol. I. p. 48 affirms Bolivar's participation. O'Leary: Memorias, Vol. I. p. 24 denies it. We side with Larrazabal whose statement is also strengthened by Díaz, p. 14.

29 Larrazabal: Vol. I. p. 49. Urquinaona: *op. cit.* pp. 31 ff. Blanco: Doc. Vol. II. pp. 377, 380, 391. Parra Pérez: Primera República. Vol. I. p. 267. Baralt: Vol. I. p. 48.

of the highest tribunal permitted of no delay or hesitation. Emparán was offered the chairmanship of such a body, but he delayed his decision, telling them that he would tackle this difficult problem after the church services and that in any case it was unwise to make hasty decisions without knowing the exact situation in Spain. Following his answer he left the Chamber to go to the cathedral opposite the court house. He had almost reached the threshold of the cathedral when one of the patriots caught him by the arm and ordered him to return to the Council chamber. The rebels realized that the matter had to be settled at once, before the services began. Frightened and surprised, the Governor agreed to return to the meeting, where two deputies of the people explained to him their plan for the representation of Caracas. Already he was made to feel he was no longer the ruler of the country.

Emparán, in his confusion, offered no protest and was on the point of accepting the proposal when the chamber was thrown into an uproar by the entry of Canon Cortés Madariaga. A descendant of the great Cortez and born in Santiago, Chile, Cortés Madariaga had made contact with Miranda during his travels in Europe and had dedicated himself to the fight for South American independence. Knowing how to conceal his political opinions very skillfully and never taking part in the secret meetings, he was later appointed Canon of Caracas.

On the eve of April 19 he had stepped out of his reserve and had promised his support to the conspirators, and at the Council meeting the next day he declared himself the representative of the clergy. He described in the gloomiest colors the situation in Spain, demanded the establishment of self rule, and ended by demanding the expulsion of Emparán on the grounds that the people hated him.[30]

The Governor went out on the balcony to ask the masses if they were satisfied with his rule and to hear their true reaction. Madariaga, standing behind him, exhorted the crowd

30 Arias Argáez: *op. cit.* p. 45 ff. Díaz: *op. cit.* p. 17. M. Torrente: Historia de la Revolución Hispano americana. Madrid, 1829. Vol. I. p. 134.

with words and gestures to such a degree that finally the cry broke: "We don't want him. We don't want him." The Governor, his pride deeply wounded, retired from the balcony saying: "Well, I don't want it either."[31]

With this sentence, which was immediately read into the minutes of the meeting, the Governor of Venezuela gave up his administration and abdicated his position. The *Junta de Caracas* was solemnly constituted and Emparán's power declared null and void. With all due honors he was escorted to La Guayra, where he embarked for the United States. The revolution had triumphed.

To put it more exactly, the revolution had won its first victory. April 19, 1810, marked not only the overthrow of a weak official by accidental removal, but also the triumph of a revolutionary group who for three years had fought and undermined the Spanish regime. That this regime was ripe for collapse is proved by the rapid succession of events occurring in other South American capitals.

A *pro tempore* assembly was constituted in Buenos Aires on May 25, 1810, and on July 20 the viceroy was overthrown in Bogotá, capital of New Granada. Chile and Mexico followed this example and after a bloody struggle Ecuador also fell in line. In less than six months—from April to September—by far the greatest part of South America had torn itself loose from the mother country and declared its independence. As though by prearrangement, the revolution had blossomed almost simultaneously in all capitals.[32] Only the Kingdom of Peru remained untouched and unaffected.

It had throughout been a small group of determined men who pushed things to a head. These men did not belong, as the Spaniards noted with astonishment, to the needy or enslaved among the populace, with nothing to lose and everything to gain in chaos.[33] On the contrary, they were those who

31 Larrazabal: Vol. I. p. 52. Blanco: Doc. Vol. II. p. 391.
32 Blanco: Doc. Vol. II. pp. 450 ff., 519 ff., 549, 573, 590 ff., 639. E. Posada: El veinte de Julio. Bogotá, 1914.
33 Díaz: *op. cit.* p. 21.

had everything to lose—the owners of vast estates, scions of ancient families, men who had distinguished themselves in the service of Spain. It was these men, and not the mass of the population, who had been the decisive factor in the victory of the revolution. This aristocratic character of the independence movement is of the greatest significance. It was the Creole upper classes who had snatched the reins of government from the hands of the Spanish overlords, and the people, whether colored or of mixed blood, did not at the outset take any part in the uprising.

Creole aristocracy wished to establish self rule on an American continent free of the Spanish yoke. They could not possibly have realized that the rebellion which they had set in motion would result in a generation of bloodshed, sacrifice, and ruin. Their revolution was not, as had been the case in North America and France, the result of long, ideological preparation. They had adopted the programs of these two great uprisings without asking whether the conditions under which they had taken place and been successful were compatible with South America. Thus nothing vital was added to the revolutionary ideology of mankind.

Only *Liberté*, of the three great battle cries of the French Revolution, interested the South Americans. *Egalité* and *Fraternité* were hardly ever mentioned. Their concept was harder to achieve than in a Europe, where no racial differences existed. Liberty—that was the demand which in 1810 was heard in all the capitals of the Spanish colonies, and for them liberty meant national independence. All were aware *of* what they would be free, but in the intoxication of the victory and following unrest of the first few months no one asked *for* what they would be free. In this honeymoon of the revolution no one questioned what gifts lay at the bottom of Pandora's box.

Representative government of the province of Caracas was established a week after the victory of the revolution. Moderate elements had prevailed, however, and the left wing, which included Bolivar among its adherents, found itself practically excluded. Bolivar was known as radical and nationalistic, and neither his ideas nor his procedure met with the approval of the new government. The cautious gentlemen of the *Junta de Caracas* still suffered the delusion that they might come to terms with the King of Spain. The patriots of Caracas soon learned from reality that thoughts live closely together, while material things conflict in space. Was it possible for Caracans to influence other Venezuelan provinces with their convictions? They were successful in some instances, but not in others: the emissaries from Caracas were received with scorn in Coro, a district in western Venezuela, while in Maracaibo they were imprisoned and later sent to Puerto Rico as prisoners of the State.[34] It became apparent to the patriots of Caracas that the revolution could not proceed through its own momentum, but would require the aid of the great powers if it were to succeed. It is possible that, faced with this situation, they remembered the advice of Miranda to send a mission to London. In any case this was done, and the government of Caracas entrusted the leadership in this important assignment to young Simon Bolivar.[35]

34 Blanco: Doc. Vol. II. pp. 411, 434, 436. Mancini: *op. cit.* p. 313.
35 Misiones de Juan Vicente Bolívar y Telesforo Orea a Washington. B. d. H. Caracas. Vol. XVIII. Number 72. pp. 711 ff. Larrazabal: Vol. I. p. 55. C. A. Villanueva: Fernando VII y los Nuevos Estados. Paris, 1911. p. 3.

CHAPTER 6

A Mission to London

Until this time Bolivar had been one among many. He had belonged to the group of active patriots, but merely as one of the group. We must not imagine that he was the leader of the revolution, though he had wished to fill that role. The uprising had so far produced no one personality fit to lead. The sending of Bolivar to London marked the beginning of a great career, one of the greatest, actually, in the realm of political and military achievement. He was promoted to Colonel of Militia, perhaps because the government wanted to invest this young envoy on his trip to London with a little additional prestige. Since he was really too radical for the old gentlemen in Caracas, he owed his appointment as envoy to his own offer to pay expenses. He knew just what he was about when he put all the means at his command to ensure his successful entry into politics.[1]

The record of Bolivar's appointment on June 6, 1810, names him as leader of the mission, with Luis López Méndez as second in command, and with Bolivar's teacher, Andrés Bello, as secretary. The letter sent by the Caracan government to the British Foreign Minister, as well as the records of the time, present the preservation of trade relations between the two countries as the reason for the mission.[2] The three Venezuelan

1 O'Leary: *op. cit.* p. 25. Marques de Rojas: Simón Bolívar. Paris, 1883.
2 O'Leary: Memorias. Vol. I. p. 28. Blanco: Doc. Vol. II. p. 514. Misión de Bolívar y López Méndez a Londres. B. d. H. Caracas. Vol. 18. No. 72, and B. d. H. Caracas. Vol. 21. No. 81.

envoys were to report in England on the revolutionary changes which had taken place in their country and to ask the protection of Great Britain. The Caracan delegation was instructed to emphasize from the beginning to end the importance of the preservation of the Spanish monarchy and the importance of future action within the framework of the monarchy's laws. In its private instructions for the indoctrination of its envoys the government had composed questionnaires, following the same lines of thought, which provided solutions for every conceivable problem posed in England.[3]

The political accent of these documents is placed on the concept of Great Britain acting as guardian of the South American peoples, and it was intended to organize the liberation and independence of the Hispano-Americans under the leadership of that nation which had first made legal freedom a reality on her own soil and who was fighting the current tyranny of Napoleon.[4]

The delegation set sail for London during the early part of June aboard a British ship. On July 10 it arrived in Portsmouth. What success could Bolivar expect, and what would England's attitude be toward the problem of South American independence?[5] After the failure of the attack on Caracas and Buenos Aires, British statesmen had reëxamined their plans concerning the Western Hemisphere. Foreign Minister Castlereagh considered it his duty to convince his Cabinet that it would be a hopeless undertaking to conquer these vast territories against the will of the people. He believed that while searching for a scheme to liberate the continent, England should never present herself as more than auxiliary and protector.[6] In this way she could satisfactorily achieve her objectives, which were not primarily conquest of territories, but the control of trade and of the precious metals—the gold and silver mines

3 Mancini: p. 307. See also: B. d. H. Caracas. Vol. XVIII. p. 675.
4 Pereyra: Juventud. p. 310.
5 Rojas: Bolívar. p. 13. G. Hernández de Alba: La misión de Bolívar en Londres. Rev. d. Colegio d. Nuestra Señora d. Rosario. Bogotá, 1934. p. 312 ff.
6 Webster: op. cit. Vol. I. pp. 8-9. Mancini: p. 312.

in particular—of the Spanish colonies. In the hands of the
British government the control of this wealth would serve to
finance the titanic struggle against Napoleon. Actually, motivated by these reasons, England was more interested in Mexico
than in Venezuela and the lands of the La Plata.[7]

Napoleon's attack on the Iberian Peninsula changed the
situation completely; and Spain, in the throes of an uprising,
became an ally of Great Britain. Spanish soldiers fought side
by side with English troops for the liberty of the Iberian peoples. On January 9, 1809, the British government made a treaty
with Spain in which it pledged itself to support the Spanish
nation against French tyranny with all the means at its disposal, and at the same time acknowledged Ferdinand as the
sole legitimate king.

In spite of these publicly announced objectives, British
diplomacy still harbored the old compulsion to break the
monopoly of Spanish trade policy and to open new markets
to British industry in South America. While the British government disapproved of her Antilles officials' support of the
revolution in South America and was completely willing to fulfill its obligations towards the Spanish ally in good faith, it was
felt necessary for British trade to expand. The Spanish Empire,
therefore, had to be prepared to accept British goods. Only
thus could the costly help given to Spain be repaid. When the
Venezuelan delegates arrived in Portsmouth in July, 1810, the
British position towards Spain improved visibly.

July 11, the day following his arrival, Simon Bolivar dispatched a letter to the Marquis of Wellesley, who had succeeded
Castlereagh as Foreign Minister. In it he announced his arrival
and requested the necessary pass. Two days later the Marquis
sent a note to his brother, Sir Henry, then ambassador to the
regency-council in Cádiz, instructing him regarding the proper
exploitation of Bolivar's arrival for British purposes.[8] The gov-

7 Webster: *op. cit.* Vol. I. pp. 10-11.
8 Mancini: pp. 312 ff.

ernment hoped to intimidate the regency-council and make it tractable to British commercial policy by the use of the Venezuelan delegation. While on the surface England assumed this role of neutral agent between the Spanish mother country and her American colonies, actually she was following the course of self-interest with calculating deliberateness.

On receiving the requested passes, the delegation left Portsmouth, arrived in London on July 12, and established themselves at Morin's Hotel. Wellesley had indicated that he would receive them at any time. Since it was considered improper to receive them at the Foreign Office, as they were not the authorized ministers of a recognized state, he suggested that they come to his home, Apsley House.

The conference was opened by the British Foreign Minister with the critical remark that in considering the action taken by Venezuelan patriots as unwise, they had concluded erroneously that Spain's cause was lost. It was important to him, he stated, to know whether they had merely demanded the cessation of certain malpractices in Caracas, or whether they were determined to declare their independence and bring about an actual break with Spain.[9]

Boliver answered Wellesley with an account of the events which culminated in the revolution of April 19. He described the suspicions and espionage to which the Caracans were subjected owing to their patriotic attitude, and the final explosion set off by the establishment of the regency-council. At this time, he said, it had been decided to separate from the Spanish government and to declare as arbitrary all her regulations and decisions.

Wellesley realized immediately that this was tantamout to a declaration of independence. England's best interests would not permit him to sanction such a separatist movement within

9 Minuta de la sesión tenida el 16. de julio, etc. Published in Rev. Bolivariana. Vol. XI. Numbers 20-21. Bogotá by E. Posada. Dr. Posada allowed me to examine the manuscript of the "minuta." They are written on English paper made in 1809, and are without any doubt authentic. They were probably taken down by Bello or López.

the dominion of an ally, still less support it, and he made this clear to Bolivar without circumlocution. Bolivar, who refused to consider his mission lost, begged the Marquis to learn from his credentials of the real spirit animating the Caracas government.

Bolivar handed his credentials to the Marquis, but added to them the instructions which had been so carefully worked out in Caracas. Thus Bolivar, schooled little or not at all in any kind of diplomatic protocol, began his career with this incredible blunder.[10] He had hurried to the conference without making any preparations regarding what he wished or was permitted to say. Perhaps he had not even read his instructions, since his political ideas were utterly at variance with those of the circumspect politicians in Caracas.

Wellesley listened to the Venezuelan with cold attention, and when he had finished, the British diplomat remarked that the ideas just presented conflicted with the documents in his hand. Did not these credentials speak of a council meeting in Venezuela in the name of Ferdinand VII, for the purpose of protecting his rights? The instructions expressly forbade the delegates to touch the subject of Venezuelan independence. These were the facts, and the realistic minister did not hesitate to lead the passionate South American back into the world of stark actualities.

The discussions, conducted in French, circled for two hours around the constitutional attitude adopted by the Caracans and the political implications which might result. Bolivar emphasized the desire of Venezuela to adhere to Spain and the Empire. Such a statement held little meaning in the light of Bolivar's previous remarks, and Wellesley said as much.

The Minister, however, did not wish to discourage the South Americans completely; he therefore assured Bolivar that he realized that it was important to find a basis for mutual understanding. Bolivar, suspecting a trap, countered that he would be unable to enter into any negotiations predicated on recogni-

10 Amunategui: *op. cit.* pp. 87-93.

tion of the regency-council. The independence of Venezuela
would influence favorably the war fought by Spain against
France, with Great Britain reaping the benefits. Her trade
would increase and her prestige throughout the whole American continent would be immeasurably enhanced if her protection was granted to Caracas. Any attempt to force Venezuela
back under the Spanish yoke was doomed to failure at the
outset, with no result possible other than the loss of America
not only to Spain but to England as well.

Wellesley complimented Bolivar, telling him that he admired the passion with which he presented his country's cause.
Bolivar answered, with ready wit, that the Marquis demonstrated even greater passion for the cause of Spain, and the
atmosphere of the conference, changing at this moment, became
lighter and more friendly. The Minister promised to have the
petition which had been handed to him translated at once,
so that it could be presented before the King. Wellesley also
requested another visit from the delegation.

The first meeting did not result in total failure. Though
Bolivar realized that England could not agree to the separation
of the colonies from the mother country,[11] he recognized that he
was at least able to direct the attention of the British government to the great movement now ripening on the other side
of the ocean. He did not exaggerate when he wrote to his
government: "Despite everything that has been done to discourage us, the suggestions of the Venezuelans have been taken
up by Lord Wellesley, and given all the fairness and courtesy
which we could expect."[12] The second conference followed
on July 19, during which Wellesley again attempted to force
the Venezuelans to recognize the regency-council as the government of the Spanish Empire. But Bolivar remained adamant. He repeated his country's plea for support, so that Venezuela could defend itself against French aggression, and finally
he appealed for Great Britain's intervention so that an armed

11 Amunategui: *op. cit.* p. 90.
12 B. d. H. Caracas. Vol. XXI. No. 81. p. 48. Pereyra: Juventud. pp. 305-6.

conflict between his country and Spain could be avoided. To this Wellesley agreed, on condition that Venezuela would continue aiding Spain in her struggle against Napoleon with all the means at her command. England could not sanction the establishment of an independent Venezuela, but it was neither her duty nor to her interest to condemn those steps already taken by the Caracans.[13] It was decided that the delegation was to present its wishes programmatically defined in a note, which, when it was executed, evinced considerable astuteness. Bolivar agreed to more of the British demands than he liked to admit, but in so doing he hoped to lay the foundation for future discussions with the Foreign Minister.[14] He forgot, however, that Wellesley was adept at dealing with both sides, and that his conversations with Bolivar were useful in the breaking down of Spanish resistance to England's commercial policies.

The Duke of Alburquerque and Admiral Apodaca, Spanish emissaries in London, were informed of Wellesley's reception of the Venezuelans; in fact they had even been invited to attend. They preferred, however, to report their displeasure directly to Cádiz, and their attitude reacted on Wellesley. Although he received Bolivar again on August 4, he felt it necessary a few days later to set down in a memorandum the procedure and purpose of the discussions with the representatives of the South American revolution.[15] This memorandum was intended for both sides, and it reflected a characteristic picture of British duplicity.

Another note was dispatched to Bolivar on August 9 in which England answered the petition of the rebellious colonies. Three vital points were contained in this communication. First, Her Britannic Majesty's government promised the province of Venezuela the protection of the fleet against their common enemy, France. Second, England recommended to the colony

13 Minuta: Rev. Boliv. Vol. XI. Numbers 20-21.
14 B. d. H. Caracas. Vol. XVIII. p. 680. Pereyra: Juventud. p. 305. Mancini: p. 317.
15 B. d. H. Caracas. Vol. XVIII. p. 685.

an immediate reconciliation with the mother country, and to this end proffered her good offices. Finally, England advised that Venezuela preserve friendly relations as well as trade with Spain, so that the help so badly needed at this time would be available.[16]

Bolivar and the other envoys acknowledged receipt of the note and made but one comment. They declared they could only subscribe to the suggestion of the British government if they did not include recognition of the regency-council. With this memorandum the exchange of notes between the young emissary, Bolivar, and the representatives of the British government ended.[17]

Neither Spain nor Venezuela gained anything from Bolivar's mission, but England did. The regency-council in Cádiz, confronted with the danger that Great Britain might deal directly with the rebels, permitted trade between England and the American colonies, but limited this permission to the duration of the war. Later, however, the British Foreign Minister challenged that the right to trade with South America had been settled at that time. The year 1810 began a new era in the relations between South America and Great Britain. To assure this, British diplomacy had made good use of Bolivar.[18]

Spain demanded, on the other hand, that England break off relations with the rebellious colonies if a reconciliation between the regency-council and Venezuela had not been achieved by a specified date. This Great Britain was unwilling to fulfill. The Spaniards, acting on their own, declared the Venezuelans rebels and laid down a blockade of the mainland coast.

What were the results of Bolivar's mission from the point of view of Venezuela? In the light of what he had wished to accomplish, neither success nor failure. Too distant from the war and events in Europe, he had not taken into account the resistance which blocked the way to British intervention on

16 B. d. H. Caracas. Vol. XVIII. p. 681. O'Leary: Memorias. Vol. I. p. 33.
17 B. d. H. Caracas. Vol. XVIII. p. 688. Pereyra: Juventud. p. 309.
18 Webster: op. cit. Vol. I. pp. 9-10.

behalf of the colonies. He had not made it clear to himself that England's first objective was the overthrow of Napoleon in Europe, and he had underestimated the value of her alliance with Spain. Considering these circumstances, Bolivar might well have been satisfied with his reception by the British Minister. As he himself stated in a report sent home to Caracas: "The Minister's conduct could not have been more favorable, as things stand. The sponsors of the regency-council have conspired and done whatever they could against us. They have considerable influence."

Bolivar could scarcely have realized how much his presence contributed to the opening of South American ports to British trade. But one thing he understood. England was the only great European power for whom South American independence was desirable. Through her commercial interests, she had become deeply involved in the fate of the continent. This fact was the more important because in England's hand lay the key to freedom, and only with the help of the British fleet could greater fighting forces be sent from Europe to South America.

Confronted by these difficulties, Bolivar began to understand the inestimable importance of the British position, and England became for him the great power upon whose good will the fate of South America depended. He never tired of wooing her favor and her good will. "Only England, Mistress of the Sea, can defend us against the united forces of European reactions."[19] His admiration even extended to England's internal policies, and he spent many of his leisure hours studying parliamentary institutions and public life and procedure. It was at this time that Bolivar reached the decision to enforce the recognition of legally established freedom, insofar as the differences in customs, climate, and circumstances would allow.[20]

But we must not picture the Bolivar of 1810 as too much the pupil of Montesquieu, spending his nights reading parlia-

19 Webster: *op. cit.* pp. 11-12.
20 O'Leary: Memorias. Vol. I. p. 34.

mentary reports. He was a young man of elegance, and he was once again enjoying his sojourn in a European capital. His arrival had created a sensation in social London, where he and his companions were greeted as envoys of an entire hemisphere, envoys whose presence might betoken innumerable possibilities. For the benefit of his British listeners Bolivar conjured up a magnificent panorama of America's future. He told them that the various colonies planned to set themselves up as individual states, but hoped ultimately for a federation which would include them all.[21] Bolivar propounded here for the first time the Pan-American idea. Fifteen years later he was to bring this plan to fruition.

In the England of this period, political connections immediately became social, and social contacts drew in turn political benefits. Bolivar met the Duke of Gloucester and the Earl of Mornington, brother of Admiral Cochrane. He attended affairs of high society; and, as he had once in Paris, those of the demimonde.

We know of only one instance when Bolivar later referred to this time spent in London, and it is astonishing that his memory concerned an involvement with a woman. Since she did not understand Spanish and Bolivar spoke scarcely any English, their meeting resulted in a peculiar misunderstanding. The girl, mistaking him for a homosexual, created a great disturbance; and when Bolivar thought to quiet her with a few banknotes, her rage increased and she fed them to the fire. The future liberator of South America could see no way out, and finally fled from the house in deep humiliation. Perhaps this incident in London contributed to Bolivar's preference for Paris.[22]

During his London stay a remarkable portrait of Bolivar was painted by Charles Gil. Bolivar dressed for the portrait, as he had seven years earlier in Paris, in a high, standing collar and black silk cravat, the mode of the elegant world. His

21 B. d. H. Caracas. Vol. XVIII. p. 682.
22 D. d. B. pp. 214-215.

face, in comparison with the earlier portrayal, is more serious, his hair somewhat smoother and receding more from his high, arched forehead. Beneath his handsome brows his dark eyes are wide, searching, and questioning.

Bolivar is shown in the portrait wearing a medal suspended from a silken cord around his neck. On close examination its inscription may be deciphered, and it reads: "There is no country without freedom."[23] This had been Miranda's motto, and Bolviar had learned it from him in London. In fact, one of the most important events of his London trip was his meeting with Miranda, and it was of great consequence in the success of the American revolution. Included in Bolivar's instructions for his London trip was a section dealing with Miranda, stating that he had spoken against rights and principles which the Caracan government wished to defend. If the delegates met with General Miranda in London, they were to remember these facts without, however, disregarding the political opinions of their compatriot. In this is the key to the florid language of the instructions. The Caracan government, its position being what it was, could not enter into an open agreement with Miranda, but it empowered its delegates to listen to his opinions and therefore was actually permitting them to associate with him.

After the failure of his undertaking in 1806, Miranda had returned to England, where he drew a pension from the government. During this period, he tried to influence the course of the revolution in South America through letters and through the public papers. When his countrymen arrived in London, he hastened to get in touch with them. Bolivar himself wasted no time in visiting Miranda at his house on Grafton Square.[24]

Their discussions concerned primarily Miranda's possible return to Venezuela and his assumption of the leadership of the revolution. The two men mapped far-reaching plans, and Bolivar went even further than his instructions warranted when

23 Mancini: p. 315.
24 B. d. H. Caracas. Vol. XVIII. p. 703. O'Leary: Memorias. Vol. I. p. 34. Mancini: p. 321. Robertson: Life. Vol. II. p. 84.

he ordered Miranda to return to his country. This sort of initiative was characteristic of Bolivar's unique temperament. He was a rebel. Bolivar appeared everywhere in the company of the "famous General Miranda"—at the theater, in the public places; and the London papers reported the fact. In his turn, Miranda gave a tea at which he introduced Bolivar to his friends, and it was there that Bolivar met Wilberforce, leader of the anti-slavery movement, and Lancaster, pioneer of a new type of pedagogy.

The bonds that were thus forged between the old conspirator and the young revolutionary were the expression of their deep agreement. But it was an agreement of program, not of temperament, for the characters of the two were diametrically opposed. Miranda had become an adventurer. Like a gambler who stubbornly waits until the wheel of chance hits his number, he had risked everything in the cause of revolution. Now his chance had come.

Bolivar, on the other hand, was no adventurer. He was generous, disinterested, and bent on sacrificing everything, even himself, to the idea to which he was dedicated. While Miranda identified the cause with his own person, Bolivar identified himself with the cause. Bolivar grew with difficulties. They made Miranda small. Bolivar had a genius for the moment and a talent for decision, while Miranda was indecisive in the face of great problems. Out of this antithesis grew a relationship which was to end in tragedy. In London they did not suspect this, however, and were united in their judgment of political events and in their hopes for the future of South America.

It is possible to find the announcement of their agreement in a newspaper article appearing on December 5, 1810, in the *Morning Chronicle*. Bolivar, who pretends his article is a note from Cádiz discussing the effects of the Venezuelan blockade, writes: "The day is not far off, when Venezuelans will be convinced that their restraint and their desire to preserve friendly relations with the mother country have brought them neither the respect nor the gratitude to which they are entitled. Then

they will at last hoist the flag of freedom and declare war on
Spain. Nor will they forget to invite the other peoples of South
America to join with them."[25]

While Bolivar expressed in this way his great ambitions for
South American liberty and unity, Miranda prepared for his
return. On August 3 he sent a letter to the government of
Venezuela announcing his decision to live once more in his
own country. The letter commenced with an enthusiastic statement regarding the April 19 uprising and went on to describe
Bolivar's activities in London in bright colors, ending with a
plea for permission to return.[26] At the same time he was nego-
tiating with the British for an exit permit.

His decision to depart was most unwelcome to the British,
who, though they actually were unable to prevent his departure,
suspected that his arrival in Venezuela would cause great unrest which might react unfavorably on Spain and the course
of the war. The government, therefore, attempted to postpone
at least the leaving of Miranda. Bolivar was notified on September 16 that the *Sapphire,* a ship put at his disposal by the
British Admiralty, was ready to leave. Seeing no reason to
prevent his sailing, Bolivar left England on September 21. He
was never to return to Europe.

Miranda, as an enemy of Spain, was not permitted to travel
on a British warship, and therefore could not voyage with Bolivar to South America. Seeing through the ruse of the British,
he made plans to leave without their permission. Once again
he left the country which had sheltered him, against the will
of its government, and sailed for Venezuela early in October.

Thus Bolivar's mission to London came to an end. Its consequences for international diplomacy were negligible, and this
was characteristic of the whole course of the South American
revolution. In contrast to the French Revolution, there was no
release of international complications. All that was necessary
was the favorable alignment of a foreign policy which would

25 Larrazabal: Vol. I. p. 56.
26 Blanco: Doc. Vol. II. p. 580. Robertson: Life. Vol. II. p. 88.

leave Spain and the other European powers little time or strength to intervene. Of the tangible results of the London mission, Miranda's return, instigated by Bolivar, was the most important.

CHAPTER 7

The Declaration of Independence

*B*olivar returned to a country in ferment. States do not spring, Minerva-wise, full-grown from Jupiter's brow. They are born of travail, and Venezuela was indeed suffering the birth pangs. Bolivar was deeply disappointed that nothing decisive had been achieved during his six-months' absence.

The young community which was no longer a colony but not yet an independent republic, began its career with a series of important measures. Freedom of trade was established with neutral and friendly nations, and duties hindering exports were abolished.[1] Bolivar approved of the removal of the *alcabala*—a sales tax on vital necessities and articles in daily use—and he was in agreement regarding the lifting of the tribute exacted from the Indios for hundreds of years. He also joined the Patriotic Society formed to improve the farming and industry of the country.[2]

The decisions on the part of the Venezuelan politicians regarding these matters, however generous and far-seeing they were, did little towards the solution of major problems such as safeguarding the state from within and provision for its maintenance from outside forces. Both these problems were inextricably intertwined.

The Caracan government believed that its justification for self-rule was derived from the traditional attitude of the Span-

1 Baralt: *op. cit.* Vol. I. p. 52.
2 Parra Pérez: Primera República. Vol. I. p. 281.

115

ish people. The government made known these principles
through a number of solemn declarations, and arrogated to the
Americans the privilege of deciding their own political compe-
tence. The regency-council in Spain had already been informed
that the Caracan government could not recognize either the
council's authority or its legitimacy, but at the same time Venezuela offered a refuge for Spaniards driven from Europe, and
even pledged participation in the war against France.[3] These
suggestions were met with a definite and frigid refusal by the
regency-council, as Bolivar had expected. He realized that the
Spaniards, believing their obligations to the colonies fulfilled,
were unable or unwilling to face the fact that their superannuated imperialism was on the point of collapse. Bolivar read
to the Americans an appeal contained in one of the manifestos
of the regency-council: "From this moment on you may consider yourselves raised to the dignity of a free people. You are
no longer that which you had been, enslaved under a yoke that
was the more oppressive because you were so far from the
center of power, treated with indifference, pursued by greed
and destroyed by ignorance."[4] That this proclamation constituted a fearful accusation against the Spanish nation did not
apparently occur to the regency-council, who instead regarded
the colonies' refusal of the proffered hand as a sign of ingratitude. In this brusque fashion did they condemn the independence movement and brand the Venezuelans as rebels. A
blockade was imposed on the American mainland under the
command of a royal commissar in Puerto Rico, Antonio
Ignacio de Cortabarria, who was expected to lead a rebellious
Caracas back into the fold.[5]

Bolivar had urged his countrymen to reply to the blockade
by a declaration of war against Spain while he was still in
London. Not surprised by the uncomprehending attitude of the
regency-council, he was, however, bitterly disappointed by the
hesitation of the Caracan government. The confidence which

3 Blanco: Doc. Vol. II. pp. 419-422.
4 Baralt: *op. cit.* Vol. I. p. 56. Blanco: Doc. Vol. III. p. 403.
5 Blanco: Doc. Vol. III. p. 8. Baralt: *op. cit.* Vol. I. p. 56.

impelled Spain to refuse so definitely the colonies' demands was not based upon trust in her own powers. Humbled, vanquished, without ships, without an army and without money, Spain could not by herself expect to win back her American possessions. But in each of her overseas colonies she could rely upon strong forces desiring the continuation of Spanish rule. The fight for American independence, therefore, resolved itself into a conflict between the Creoles who wanted to cling to the mother country and those who had abjured it forever.

There were three provinces in particular in Venezuela which decided in favor of reaction: Coro, Maracaibo, and Guyana, who saw their highest authority in the regency-council. In these three provinces the news of the blockade imposed on Venezuela was celebrated by illuminations of the cities and *Te Deums* in the churches.[6] This celebration was less for love of Spain than for hatred of the capital, Caracas. For the first time in the history of the South American revolution we see the rivalry between the cities, the provinces, and the countries of the continent. This hatred was to become as influencing as it was fateful.

The position of Caracas was certainly difficult, threatened as it was by enemies within and by the blockade without. The ascendancy of Spain in the Caribbean was strengthened by the bond between the royalist Americans and the outer world, especially in Puerto Rico, the Gibraltar of the Antilles. Without a fleet the independents could take no action against the Spanish authorities in Puerto Rico, so the only possible course of action remaining was the subjugation by armed force of the separatist provinces—Coro, Maracaibo, and Guyana. If this method proved successful, the Americans hoped to rebuild the territorial unity of the mainland and to sever the dangerous bonds becoming strongly woven between the Spanish Antilles and the royalist provinces.

Caracas began the action by gaining control of the regions of Trujillo and Mérida, both belonging administratively to Maracaibo. This step had a twofold significance: the provinces

6 Baralt: Vol. I. p. 59. Mancini: p. 328.

of Coro and Maracaibo were divided from each other and thus
contact was cut off between them; and Caracas was able to set
up close relations with her new neighbor, New Granada.[7]

Nevertheless, Coro and Maracaibo remained a source of
infection for the young state, and their governors, Miyares and
Ceballos, called up the militia and incited the resistance of the
population against Caracas. They obviously planned to meet
force with force. In Caracas the necessity was realized of attacking the provinces before they were able to march upon the
capital, and preparations were made for the overthrow of the
rebel states. The Marquis of Toro was placed in charge of the
Caracan troops. He was one of Bolivar's closest friends, a man
of the world, an excellent host, but perhaps a man who did not
take warfare too seriously. This was the first act of aggression
on the part of a free Venezuela, and the Marquis proved himself loath to shed the blood of fellow Venezuelans. He marched
against Coro with some three thousand men at the end of
November, 1810. Although his adversary was numerically inferior and poorly equipped, the Marquis was forced to retire
in great disorder and with heavy losses.[8]

An uprising in the region of the capital itself increased the
complications confronting the Caracan government following
the Marquis' defeat. Intrigues and plots were uncovered at
every turn. A movement on the part of army officers, in col-
laboration with Puerto Rican Spanish factions to overthrow the
Venezuelan government was easily quelled, but here again the
patriots avoided extreme measures, fearful of staining the banner of the revolution with the blood of their compatriots. This
very mildness became an accusation against the government on
the part of the lower classes, and new and dangerous elements
were added to the complexes of the South American revolution
—class conflict and racial antagonism. Until now the movement for independence was inspired by the representatives of

7 Blanco: Doc. Vol. III. p. 31. E. Posada: Nuestro primer tratado. B. d. H.
Bogotá. Vol. III. No. 26.
    8 Baralt: Vol. I. pp. 62-63.

the colonial aristocracy—the Creoles—who wished to drive out the Spanish exploiters while retaining their own class privileges. Naturally, those of a different social order were at variance with this, particularly the *pardos,* descendants of white and slave races.

Some Creoles, however, Bolivar among them, disagreed with the government's softness. His uncle, José Félix Ribas, demanded sharper measures and drastic punishment for all enemies of freedom, and he tried to include the ignorant masses of the people in his way of thinking.[9] The government, distrusting Ribas as it did Bolivar, banished him and his brothers.

In general terms this was the situation when Bolivar returned to Venezuela, deeply dissatisfied with the weak and vacillating policy adopted by the government. He reported on his mission, but he was determined not to work with the government. His own program embraced a declaration of independence and the defense of freedom at any price. He felt, too, that the revolution required stronger personalities to guide it to success.

Bolivar expected a great deal from Miranda's coming, and since he himself had returned to Venezuela a few days earlier, he took advantage of this time to smooth out the opposition to Miranda's return on the part of his compatriots who did not hold Miranda in great esteem.[10] Many of them believed him to be in the pay of the British, and that he was using his revolutionary program as a smoke screen in his plan to turn over countries of Spanish tongue and Catholic religion to Protestant Albion. Bolivar, who was responsible for Miranda's return, may well have known how to spike this unfavorable attitude. Public opinion changed in Miranda's favor, and the government, which had tried to prevent his landing, was forced by public pressure to grant permission for his arrival in Caracas on December 12, 1810.[11]

9 G. V. González: Vida de J. F. Ribas. Madrid. pp. 34-35 ff. Baralt: Vol. I. p. 61.
10 Robertson: Life. Vol. II. pp. 92-93. Rojas: Bolívar. pp. 32-33.
11 Robertson: Life. Vol. II. p. 93.

Miranda was greeted with a great ovation when he arrived at the port of La Guayra, showing himself to the masses in the theatrical manner which he loved. A true veteran of the revolutionary idea, he wore the uniform of a French general of 1793—blue tunic decorated with the colors of the Republic, white trousers, shiny black boots, long sword, and the two cornered hat.

Miranda's arrival in Venezuela instigated a change in the direction of the revolution. Bolivar, with whom he stayed, praised him to his friends as the man of the hour. Against him were ranged the high officials of the government, the aristocrats who feared his influence, and the wealthy old families who regarded him as the "son of that merchant from the Canaries." They were forced, nevertheless, to bow to the trend of public opinion in favor of Miranda, and he was appointed Lieutenant General.[12]

Around Miranda, whose person exuded self-confidence and faith, were gathered all who demanded an energetic and goal-conscious policy for the country. At sixty, he was serious, dignified, pompous, and incredibly articulate. He knew how to win support. He had been persecuted by the Inquisition. He had fought the battles of the French Revolution. He had sat at table with Napoleon. Pitt had conferred with him. For those who saw only what they wished to see, Miranda's failures faded into insignificance in the face of such a background.

Bolivar was one of these. He closed his eyes to the obvious shortcomings of the older man, blinding himself to the presumption which saw good in nothing, overlooking the fault-finding mania of a man whose whole life had been a series of failures, but who still boasted of knowing and doing better than other men. During Miranda's forty-year absence from Venezuela, he had not only become a stranger to his compatriots, but had forgotten how backward and primitive was life in the Spanish colonies. He allowed himself to speak disdainfully of their weaknesses, and he forgot that these weak-

12 Amunategui: *op. cit.* p. 98. Díaz: *op. cit.* pp. 30-31 and Baralt: Vol. I. p. 64.

nesses were but the product of an era that only time could change.[13]

The establishment of a law-making body was the great problem in local politics at the moment. Thirty-one delegates, the names of the best Creole families among them, met in Congress on March 2, 1811, in Caracas. Almost all belonged to the liberal party, and at the same time were representatives of the Creole upper classes. No radical decision could be expected from them. Since the country still preserved the fiction of loyalty to the monarch, the Congress called itself the Council for the Preservation of the Rights of the American Federation of Venezuela and Don Ferdinand. In a solemn ceremony they vowed to defend the rights of their fatherland and those of Ferdinand VII.[14]

The Society for the Improvement of Economics, created in August, 1810, became the focal point of political debate on the part of the radical element, who formed a new center through this organization, less for decisions than for political agitation. Bolivar supported them, having fallen out with the government men, and decided to make this organization the springboard of his revolutionary career in Caracas. Meetings of this patriotic group, held mostly at night, were attended not only by radical young aristocrats, but also by men of the people and even by some women. In this group was crystallized the idea of complete independence for Venezuela. The popularity of the organization grew rapidly, and the authorities could do little. There were, therefore, two congresses meeting at this time— the National Assembly and the club of patriots who felt it was their duty to criticize what was being done or what, in their opinion, was being left undone.[15]

Miranda succeeded in becoming president of the Patriotic Society. Possessing the instincts of a demagogue and the experi-

13 Robertson: Life. Vol. II. p. 100. Parra Pérez: Primera República. Vol. II. p. 14.
14 Blanco: Doc. Vol. III. p. 27. Gil Fortoul: Hist. Vol. I. p. 199. Parra Pérez: Primera República. Vol. II. p. 5.
15 Baralt: Vol. I. p. 74. Austria: Bosquejo de la Historia militar de Venezuela. Caracas, 1855. pp. 40 ff. Parra Pérez: Primera República. Vol. II. p. 15.

ence of a revolutionist, he used the Society to put pressure on
the legitimate parliament as once the Jacobin clubs had en-
enslaved the French National Assembly. His supporters—
Miranda's men, they were called—showered vituperation upon
the Spaniards and their work in South America. To achieve
their aim of independence they turned not only against their
Spanish overseers but also against the American aristocrats still
bent on compromise.

On April 19, the anniversary of the revolution of 1810, two
parades were held in Caracas and the image of Ferdinand VII
was destroyed amid cries of opprobrium against the Spanish
tyranny. Even the press expressed itself against the ignoble
interregnum existing in Venezuela. "Today," wrote the *Patriot
of Venezuela* on April 19, 1811, "is the anniversary of our
revolution. . . . May the first year of independence and freedom now begin."[16]

Nothing could arrest the national movement, despite all the
caution exercised by Parliament. Parliament was forced to summon a committee meeting at the beginning of June to confer
on possible means of securing the independence and sovereignty
of the country. This resulted in a demand by the committee
for a declaration of rights, abolition of torture, and freedom of
the press.

On July 1 the Bill of Rights was solemnly accepted, and on
July 3 the topic of independence was the only subject discussed
in Congress.[17] No decision was reached that day. The same
night the Patriotic Society met to discuss the accusation against
it: the charge of injuring national unity by attempting to oust
the present Congress. Bolivar, in the first great political speech
of his life, denied the charge.[18]

"There are not two congresses," he said. "How could they
encourage dissension, they who, above all others, know the

16 Eloy G. González: Al margen de la Epopeya. Caracas, 1906. pp. 8-9. Parra
Pérez: Primera República. Vol. II. p. 22.
17 El Libro Nacional de los Venezolanos. Actas del Congreso constituyente en
1811. Caracas, 1911. pp. 42, 43, 44, 45.
18 V. Lecuna: Proclamas y Discursos del Libertador. Caracas, 1939. p. 3.

necessity of harmony? What we want is to make unity effective. . . . To relax in the arm of lethargy and to sleep was but a weakness yesterday. It is treason today. In the National Assembly they discuss what is to be decided. And what do they say? That we should begin with a confederation! As if we were not all united against foreign rule! That we should await the effects of Spanish policy. What concern is it of ours, whether Spain sells her slaves to Bonaparte or keeps them for herself, since we are determined to be free? These doubts are the tragic consequences of the old fetters. That the great plan should be made with deliberation . . . are not three hundred years of deliberation enough? Do they want three hundred more?" Bolivar stated that the Society of Patriots respected the Congress, and that the Congress in turn should listen to the Society, the center of revolutionary impetus. "Let us lay the cornerstone of American freedom without fear," he ended. "To hesitate is to perish."

In these words live the future statesman. He addressed his listeners like a general addressing troops before battle. Short, incisive, impressive, his words had the power of unalterable decision. As it was with all great political leaders—Caesar, Frederick, Napoleon, Bismarck—the word was at Bolivar's absolute command. He was not only the greatest fighter of his continent, but one of its greatest orators.

Bolivar's suggestions adopted, the Society of Patriots sent a delegation to Congress presenting demands. On July 4, thirty-five years after the United States had declared their independence, the Assembly received these demands and discussed in secret session the vital question of independence. The Patriots, who considered the United States as a model for their political organization, wanted to declare their country's independence that very day. But Congress still hesitated. The next day, following a stormy session, Congress voted, with but one voice dissenting, in favor of a declaration of independence for Venezuela.[19]

Churchbells were rung in Caracas to proclaim to the people

19 Parra Pérez: Primera República. Vol. II. pp. 50-51. Libro. Nac. p. 90.

that a new era of their history was beginning. The solemn
words *Confederación Americana de Venezuela* heralded the
proclamation. The colors of the new flag, which Miranda had
brought to Venezuela, were to be yellow, blue, red; and on
July 14—Bastille Day—the colors were paraded through the
streets of the city. The secession from Spain was solemnly celebrated in the presence of the Archbishop and the head of the
legislative body, and on July 30 a manifesto giving an account
of the recent events in Venezuela was published to the world.[20]

The rule of America, stated this document, belonged not to
the Spaniards, but to those conquerors who had built it up with
their labors and their efforts, who had united with the native
born, and who were themselves born on American soil.
Through the veil of revolutionary terminology, obviously borrowed from France, were visible the true origins of South
America's revolution. The men who proclaimed it and brought
it to fruition were the owners of vast fortunes who enjoyed
positions of influence. These men were without doubt sincere
in their humanitarian ideals and in their criticisms of the
Bourbon dynasty, but the mightiest upsurge came from other
sources.[21]

Venezuela, no longer wishing to be the vassal of a European state, had broken with the Spanish Crown and the Spanish
nation. The country was proud to have shown this example of
a people able to declare their independence without the horrors
of anarchy or the crimes of revolutionary passions. Events,
however, were only too soon to give the lie to this roseate
optimism.[22]

Not all members of the Creole aristocracy viewed the revolution as intended primarily to preserve the sovereignty of their
class. Bolivar, in giving the final impetus to the Declaration of
Independence in his speech on July 3, was not moved either by
selfish desires or narrow interests. He was imbued rather with

20 Libro. Nac. pp. 128, 133.
21 Pereyra: Juventud. p. 270.
22 Blanco: Doc. Vol. III. pp. 189-206. Parra Pérez: Primera República. Vol. II.
pp. 53 ff.

the great ideal of freedom and national independence. Not allowing himself a moment's rest, he took part in everything that went on—he spoke, he worked, he persuaded, he inspired —all with the impatience that characterized his nature.[23]

Bolivar was the first to bring the idea of freedom within the narrow circle of his own estates. Breaking utterly with tradition, he freed his slaves,[24] as did the Toros, Montillas, the Ustariz, and Ayalas.

Venezuela was the first of the Spanish possessions to declare her independence. Neither the richest nor the largest of the provinces, it nevertheless set the example for breaking with Spain's overseas rule when, on April 19, 1810, it led the way by constituting itself a free and independent nation.

What element made it possible for Venezuela, out of all parts of the Spanish domain, to grasp the banner of liberty? That it was Venezuela that took the decisive step towards the liberation of Hispano-America cannot be explained by economic or political reasons, or by ideological or geographic influences. There is but one answer. It was the greatest and most puzzling influence of historic life that was responsible— the existence of a particular generation of men, with one man, Bolivar, outstanding—the *human* factor.

23 O'Leary: Memorias. Vol. I. p. 25. Larrazabal: Vol. I. p. 76.
24 Larrazabal: Vol. I. p. 77.

CHAPTER 8

The First Republic

Venezuela's position had been clarified by the Declaration of Independence. A statement of political plans should have followed, but much was still to be achieved before this was possible. During the days when Congress was engaged in the vital discussions regarding independence, certain indications made apparent to the leaders of the revolution the fact that not all their dreams of glory would be fulfilled.

The First Republic of South America was attacked on all sides by antithetical groups who, nevertheless, all claimed to be monarchists bent on preserving hereditary rule. First it was the Spaniards then living in Venezuela, who with the Capucin monks, incited unrest in the provinces, but they were put down without great difficulty.[1] An attempted uprising within the capital itself was followed by more disastrous results. The republican government, unbusinesslike and inexperienced as it was, had squandered the public funds and was now forced to make certain regulations which confounded and dismayed merchants and businessmen. Many of these had come to South America from the Canary Islands, and they desired the restoration of Spanish rule.[2]

The parades that were held in the capital on July 11 resembled theatrical pageants, and perhaps they were only

---

1 Parra Pérez: Primera República. Vol. II. p. 57.
2 Baralt: Vol. I. p. 90. See also: F. X. Yanes: Relación Documentada de los Principales Sucesos Ocurridos en Venezuela. Caracas, 1943. Parra Pérez: Primera República. Vol. II. p. 59. Robertson: Life. Vol. II. pp. 125, 134-35.

intended to make the revolution appear ridiculous. In the midst of the throngs rode a group of sixty men from the Canaries, mounted on mules and accoutred in tin helmets. They cheered the King, hailed the Virgin Mary, and anathemized the traitors. They were, of course, arrested and sixteen or seventeen of them executed a few days later. Since the revolutionary leaders did not hesitate to maintain the barbaric customs of earlier days, the heads of the victims were exhibited on poles at the city gates.[3] The Patriots believed that they owed it to their newly won independence to shed this blood, but it only produced a sea of blood and tears: the tragic epic of the American war for independence, which was begun by brothers, was carried out brother against brother. The incident of July 11 was symbolic. Two days later word came of an uprising in Valencia, an important city some two hundred kilometers west of Caracas. This revolt showed most clearly the confusion of purposes in which Venezuela found herself. Here the leaders of the loyalist reaction were native Venezuelans, and the defenders of the Republic, Spaniards.[4]

The government was given extraordinary powers by Congress to put down the Valencia uprising, and at first the Marquis of Toro, in spite of the defeat suffered the year before at Coro, was put in command of the army. But he was not any more successful on this occasion, and the command was turned over to Miranda. After waiting seven months, Miranda received the appointment he felt was his due, and he made the government understand that a man of his importance could not be overlooked with impunity. Where, he demanded, were the forces that a general of his position should command without loss of dignity or reputation? But he agreed finally to lower himself to the extent of accepting the command of the punitive expedition on condition that Bolivar had no part in it.[5]

3 Díaz: *op. cit.* p. 34. Heredia: Memorias. pp. 45-46. Urquinaona: *op. cit.* p. 62.
4 Urquinaona: *op. cit.* p. 52. M. Palacio Fajardo: Memoire pour servir a l'Histoire de la Revolution de Caracas. Paris, 1817. Blanco: Doc. Vol. III. p. 160.
5 O'Leary: Memorias. Vol. I. p. 47. Briceño Méndez: Apuntes para la vida del General Bolívar. Caracas, 1933. Larrazabal: Vol. I. p. 97. Mosquera: *op. cit.* p. 17.

What had estranged the two men so completely within the space of a few short weeks? It is a difficult question to answer. At the end of July, 1811, Bolivar had suffered a tragic loss in the death of his brother, Juan Vicente, who had been shipwrecked while on a government mission to Washington to buy arms and ammunition. No private woes, however, could now restrain Bolivar, in whom the demon of the statesman had already grown strong, and his personal life was swept along in the maelstrom of the revolution.

His role thus far in the great drama had been restricted to giving others their cue, but now he was consumed by the desire to take the stage himself. As Lieutenant Colonel of the Militia he had hoped to distinguish himself in the attack on Venezuela, and Miranda's conditions must have been like a slap in the face. It seems likely that what divided the two men was the problem of Spaniards living in America. Bolivar was all for having them expelled in short order, while Miranda, himself the son of a Spaniard, supported their right to remain. Actually, the expulsion of the Spaniards, who were for the most part merchants, might have been disastrous for the already weakened economy of the country and Miranda was in the right, while Bolivar wished to apply radical tactics without foreseeing the consequences.[6] This lack of foresight was characteristic of his early phase as politician and soldier, a characteristic only overcome through bitter experience.

The estrangement between Miranda and Bolivar had yet another cause. Miranda distrusted the Creole aristocracy, while Bolivar was its representative. Miranda possessed a cool, methodical mind matured in the cold and sober atmosphere of the eighteenth century, but Bolivar was a young, passionate romantic, a true son of the nineteenth century. Miranda detested Bolivar's theatrical manner and inclination to show off, although he himself was afflicted with the same disease. On one occasion, during a parade, Miranda observed an officer stepping out of formation to address the troops in stentorian tones. It

6 O'Leary: Memorias. Vol. I. p. 46.

was Bolivar, and Miranda could not conceal his displeasure. This was not the spirit that created disciplined forces, and he called Bolivar a "dangerous youth."[7] But it was not only this contempt of the mature man for the neophyte and military dilettante which was working within Miranda, but also fear of the younger man's coming greatness; and envy on the part of the adventurer for the man of genius. For his part Bolivar saw in Miranda a rival whose abilities he was beginning to doubt but who was barring his way to power. And beyond all political differences, tensions existed between the *precursor* and the *libertador* that emanated not from the realm of ideas, but from the fires of passion.

Since Bolivar's command, the Militia of Aragua, was a part of the army sent to Valencia, he complained to the government about Miranda's injustice. He declared that his exclusion could only be explained on personal grounds and stated that only if a courtmartial defended Miranda would he subject himself to such humiliation. The government agreed with Bolivar and asked Miranda to withdraw his condition, but the request was refused, Miranda being unwilling to entrust even the most insignificant assignment to Bolivar. A crisis was averted when the Marquis de Toro named Bolivar as his adjutant, but the enmity between the two men remained.

Miranda marched on Valencia, July 19. In the first attack, when all possible forces were used, Bolivar fought with great distinction. General Miranda was forced to retire to reorganize his forces, having suffered too great losses both in men and munitions. In his report to Caracas, he mentioned the name of Bolivar among those officers having earned the gratitude of the nation.[8] Fifteen days later Miranda made another determined attempt on Valencia. This time he lay systematic siege to the city, cut off the water and food supplies, and by the middle of August, Valencia capitulated. To inform the government in Caracas of his success Miranda sent both his own

7 Yanes: Relación. Vol. I. p. 5. Austria: *op. cit.* p. 83.
8 O'Leary: Memorias. Vol. I. p. 47. Larrazabal: Vol. I. p. 97.

adjutant and Lieutenant-Colonel Bolivar, who had distinguished himself once again. Bolivar's prestige as a warrior and his influence in the army were established and were impossible to vitiate by future failures.[9]

While Miranda acknowledged Bolivar's soldierly prowess, the breach between them had not entirely healed. Bolivar was of the opinion that clemency was out of the question for the leaders of the conspiracy and advised that they be liquidated. Moreover, he wished to extend punitive expeditions to other provinces loyal to the Crown and therefore against the revolution. The sword, once drawn, could only now be sheathed when all its purposes were accomplished. Bolivar felt strongly that nothing was to be gained by half measures serving only to irritate but not to remove the enemies of the Republic. Miranda was more inclined to a policy of leniency. Miranda's weak leadership convinced Bolivar at this time that the man's capabilities were very limited. But the important thing was the successful continuation of the campaign.

The fall of Valencia made possible the overthrow of Coro and Maracaibo. However, the fine points of strategy were obscure to the inexperienced politicians of Caracas, who wasted their time and energy upon fruitless debates.[10] At this time all attention was focused on the wording of the Constitution—it was consistent with the spirit of the times to place constitutional problems above all others—and the basic question was this: what form of government should bind together the various sections of the country, and what should the relationship of these sections be to Caracas, the heart and soul of the revolutionary movement? Parliament was divided into two factions: centralists and federalists.[11]

Miranda and Bolivar, mistrusting the political abilities of their compatriots, supported an authoritarian principle. Realizing that time was necessary to make Venezuelans politically

9 O'Leary: Memorias. Vol. I. p. 47.
10 Parra Pérez: Prima República. Vol. II. p. 117.
11 Gil Fortoul: Hist. p. 157. Heredia: Memorias. p. 43.

mature and that a long training period was necessary, Miranda devised a plan of rule by a central government.

Most politicians saw in the Federal Constitution of the United States the realization of their own political ideals. Even Bolivar felt this way, yet he was unwilling to apply it to Venezuela, for here there were no states to unite but only administrative bodies. The masses of the population, indolent, fanatic, could not have been controlled by the flexible link of a federation. Stronger bonds stemming from a central government were necessary here. But in the Venezuelan Congress the supporters of a state federation outnumbered those few who, like Miranda and Bolivar, recognized the need of a federal union. The Constitution of the Federated States of Venezuela was signed December 21, 1811, by thirty-seven representatives. It displayed an admixture of American and French influences, but while the influx of French ideas made itself felt more by the vocabulary and erection of humanitarian postulates, the North American influence was actually the determining factor in the structure of the first Venezuelan Republic.[12]

Whole sections of the North American Constitution were used *verbatim*. In one respect, however, the Venezuelan Constitution differed from its northern counterpart, and not to its advantage. The strength of the North American Constitution lies in the President's position, but the Venezuelans wanted to delegate executive power to a committee of three, who were to alternate as president. In this way the executive was immeasurably weakened. It had already been agreed that the provinces would be granted a liberal autonomy, and costly and complicated rules were established for their administration. The young Republic was ushered into life with the seal of doom on its brow.

The Federated States of Venezuela was made up of seven states, each with the right to create its own constitution. Thus at a time when only unity could protect the country against chaos

12 Yanes: Relación. Vol. I. p. 18. Parra Pérez: Primera República. Vol. II. p. 131.

and ruin, its forces were aroused only to be dissipated. No high ideological tendencies which might have characterized in principle the Constitution challenged these disadvantages. It is true that the abolition of rank and privilege was anticipated, and also the idea of confederation, based on principles of friendship and unity, was held out to the sister nations of the continent. But as long as the pressing problems of governmental organization remained unsolved, these ideals remained ineffectual.

This represented Miranda's opinion, and when the Constitution was adopted in December, 1811, he felt that he owed it both to himself and to his compatriots to utter a protest. "I believe that in the present Constitution, power is improperly balanced. . . . Instead of uniting, it will divide us at the cost of our security." Bolivar, in spite of the tension separating him at this time from Miranda, also avowed these ideas. Whether he obtained them directly from Miranda or whether they originated within himself is not clear. Miranda's influence on him was without doubt profound.

Both men were aware that centrifugal forces had gained the upper hand throughout the Spanish Empire. The great units fell apart, province separated from province, cities rose up against their neighbors. The leap from a three-hundred-year-old vassalage to complete independence was too great. South America had first to grow up to earn its freedom. The projectile strength of the separatist trends was heightened by the economic and social consequences of the revolution.

The first year of independence had gone well, for the Patriots had found three million pesos in the royal treasury when they took over on April 19, 1810. This money soon went, however, and the enemies of the Republic were quick to accuse the government of wasting public funds on balls, celebrations, new officials, and pensions.[13] Actually the young state had been in need of vast sums for the army and munitions and was caught unprepared in that it had made no plans to overcome

13 Yanes: Relación. Vol. I. p. 14. Urquinaona. *op. cit.* p. 47. Díaz: *op. cit.* p. 26. Baralt: Vol. I. p. 93.

possible future difficulties. In a matter of months the entire savings of the Colonial era had been consumed, and new sources of supply were impossible to find.[14] The economic situation was desperate. Trade with foreign countries was almost entirely cut off by the Spanish blockade. The prices of cocoa and coffee, the two most important articles of export, had dropped sharply, and the revenues from taxes and duties were cut in the same way. Towards the end of August, 1811, the fiscal problems had so increased that wages of state employees were reduced by half. The government seized upon a remedy which served only to make the situation worse—the distribution of paper money, first one, then two million pesos in value. With the consequent inflation conditions deteriorated. The notes found no takers. The provinces preferred to hoard their products rather than sell them for worthless currency. Prices rose sharply. The troops grumbled and officers received their pay irregularly. The people were hungry. Severe penalties were set to prevent gold and silver from dropping out of circulation and property was confiscated. In spite of these measures the government only succeeded in embittering the merchants and encouraging smuggling. Forged paper currency was circulated in quantity. Discontent was universal, and the people were unable to understand the reasons for restrictive measures which past governments had never imposed.

During three decades Venezuela had enjoyed great prosperity. Suddenly, with the success of the independence movement, came the utter collapse of economic health. It is understandable, therefore, that the masses felt great resentment. The young Republic thus began its career under its new constitution beneath an ill-omened star.

Valencia, the same rebellious city only recently overthrown, had been chosen as the federal capital, and there Congress met on March 16, 1812. The early optimism had vanished and a feeling of an approaching crisis was alive in many of the delegates. Conviction that the young Republic could not long

14 Parra Pérez: Primera República. Vol. II. p. 109.

endure was general.[15] Only ten days after Congress convened the collapse came.

As on the day two years before when the patriots had overthrown the Spanish regime, it was Maunday Thursday, March 26. The tropical sky above Caracas was clear and brilliant, but an oppressive silence appeared foreboding. Toward four o'clock in the afternoon the heat became unbearable. A few drops of rain fell, though no cloud was visible. Suddenly the earth trembled. Houses and churches crashed earthward. Once again the town echoed with the cries of wounded and the noise of falling buildings. Silence followed on the heels of the clamor —a silence more terrifying than what had preceded. The people saw in this catastrophe a sign of God's anger at the events of the last two years, and ran from their houses crying: "Mercy! King Ferdinand!" Among the ruins and desolation priests and monks preached to the masses; and the frantic populace deserted the banner of freedom, cursing the atheists who forced them to betray their King.[16]

When the first news of the disaster reached him, Bolivar ran coatless into the street. Dagger in hand he went everywhere, doing what he could to dig the wounded out from beneath the rubble. Suddenly he came face to face with José Domingo Díaz, Spaniard and ardent monarchist. He felt immediately that Díaz regarded the earthquake as a judgment of God, and called out to him: "If nature oppose us, we shall fight it. And we shall force it to our will."[17] This was proof of his heroism, high-flown but invincible. He was ready to fight anything, even the elements of nature.

Bolivar came upon a great crowd gathered in the public square listening to the harangue of a monk. When he interrupted, the fanatic called down celestial vengeance upon him should he persist in interfering. Bolivar, spurred on by supporters among the crowd, drew his sword and pulled the monk

15 Heredia: Memorias. p. 51.
16 O'Leary: Memorias. Vol. I. pp. 49-50. Larrazabal: Vol. I. p. 108. Heredia: Memorias. pp. 65-66. Urquinaona. *op. cit.* p. 90.
17 Díaz: *op. cit.* pp. 38-39.

down from his improvised pulpit. He was determined to kill him if necessary. Some soldiers who were at hand helped Bolivar disperse the excited crowd, and he then continued his tireless efforts to help.[18] He suggested burning the houses beneath whose rubble the dead were buried, as a precaution against epidemics, but no matter what action he took, neither he nor any other could prevent the independence movement from receiving the blame for the frightful consequences of the earthquake. The devastation was impossible to imagine—in Caracas alone the number of dead was estimated at ten thousand. The earthquake of March 26, 1812, ushered in the physical and moral collapse of the First Republic of Venezuela.

The clergy exploited to the utmost the disaster in favor of the Spanish cause, and the masses succumbed to religious hysteria. Some publicly confessed their sins on bended knee, asking pardon of their God and King. In vain did the government attempt to calm the populace. In vain it issued manifestoes describing the catastrophe as a phenomenon of nature. Too long had the people been trained in superstition.[19] The movement for independence suffered irreparable reverses. Swift action was imperative to stop the growth of reaction on Venezuelan soil, and Congress gave the government dictatorial powers.

The monarchist counterthrust, in spite of the general discontent, was long in coming. Spanish reaction might have manifested itself sooner had not the loyal provinces of Coro and Maracaibo been stripped of all supplies. The entire garrisons of both cities numbered hardly more than a thousand men, and only a part of these were equipped with firearms, the remainder with lances and spears. They were ill-clad, some almost naked, and dying of hunger.[20] The clergy, however, was unreservedly devoted to their cause, and even the native

18 O'Leary: Memorias. Vol. I. p. 50.
19 Parra Pérez: Primera República. Vol. II. p. 213. Gil Fortoul: Hist. p. 182. Pereyra: Juventud. p. 392. Key Ayala: Apuntes sobre el Terremoto de 1812; El Cojo Ilustrado, Vol. XXI. p. 158. Caracas.
20 Urquinaona: *op. cit.* p. 66.

leaders in these provinces agreed with the Spaniards. But because of their sentiments and in spite of prevalent conditions,
Miyares, the governor of Maracaibo, decided to establish a small
expeditionary force of some five hundred men under the command of Domingo Monteverde, then captain of a frigate. Born
in the Canaries, this officer was daring, aggressive, and unscru-
pulous, and had already distinguished himself in service.

Any attack launched from the two loyal provinces, situated
as they were on the western edge of Venezuelan territory, had
to aim eastward in order to conquer the capital of Caracas.
The geographic formation of the country was characterized by
the mountain chain of the Andes in the north and northwest,
lying parallel to the ocean, and by the wide plateau of the
Orinoco in the south. Thus any attack from the sea was
impeded by the natural barrier of the Andes. However, there
was hope that the Monarchists could conquer their enemies by
pushing forward on land from the west to Caracas. The following subjection of the plains would be easy. Monteverde,
opening his campaign in March, 1812, moved quickly eastward,
and by the end of a week had conquered the entire region of
the Siquisique.[21] Setting in motion uprisings in all areas that
he overran, Monteverde took Carora with ease on March 23
and marched on to Barquisimeto, where a superior republican
force was stationed.

Congress still debated the constitutionality of any plan to
send an army against Monteverde. As Miranda had long recognized and openly advocated the necessity of preparing against
such a Spanish counterattack to the revolution, it seemed
mandatory to hand him the dictatorship of the country. On
April 23, a full month since Monteverde had begun his march,
Miranda was appointed Commander-in-Chief of the Army of
the Federated States of Venezuela, given unlimited powers
with no purpose other than the salvation of the state and its
independence.[22]

21 Heredia: Memorias. pp. 220 ff. Restrepo: H. d. R. C. Vol. II. p. 58. Gil
Fortoul: Hist. p. 181.
22 Robertson: Life. Vol. II. p. 150.

Already, where skirmishes had taken place among Patriots and Monarchists in certain sections, whole troop divisions had gone over to the Spaniards, the cavalry in particular proving most undependable. This betrayal of closed units who changed over to Monteverde during his encounters was instrumental in the achievement of a succession of easy victories. He was supported by the peasants who longed for an end of Republican misrule. After taking Barquisimeto, which had been reduced to rubble by the earthquake, Monteverde pushed on towards Valencia. Priests, hastening to meet him along the way, gave assurance that the people were eagerly awaiting his arrival as their saviour.[23]

Miranda, meanwhile, making military law the only valid one, attempted to raise an army for the Republic. On April 30 three hastily organized divisions under his command moved on the enemy. However the brave, but inefficient officer assigned to the defense of Valencia evacuated the city hastily in the face of obvious hostility on the part of its population. It is worth speculation as to Bolivar's success had he been given this command to defend Valencia. But Miranda had destined Bolivar for another mission, assigning him to the defense of Puerto Cabello, Venezuela's most important port.[24] The orders were accepted as a military duty, but Bolivar would have preferred a command more in keeping with his will to action. He believed, and his belief was human, that his appointment originated in Miranda's distrust of the Creole's military ability, and that the Commander-in-Chief intended keeping him as far as possible from active combat. Many years later Bolivar remarked to Marshal Sucre, in a similar situation: "Fame consists in being great and useful."[25] Miranda could justify his decision, even if his jealousy was responsible for holding Bolivar far from military activity. Puerto Cabello, in addition to being a most vital port, was one of the few fortresses of the Republic now directly threatened by the enemy. But Bolivar as-

23 O'Leary: Memorias. Vol. I. pp. 54 ff.
24 O'Leary: Memorias. Vol. I. p. 55.
25 Cartas: Vol. IV. p. 180. Austria: *op. cit.* p. 128.

sumed his post convinced that his dignity had been impugned. When Monteverde entered Valencia, he had already made himself Commander-in-Chief of all royalist troops. He was himself astonished at the ease of his victories, and had visions of being hailed in Valencia as a Messiah. He was too much the officer, however, not to realize that he was entering a critical situation. He in fact begged urgently for reinforcements, expecting a counterattack by Miranda's superior forces. Realizing the importance of Valencia, he determined to defend himself there with all the forces at his command. He wrote to this effect to the Governor of Coro, informing him that the fall of Valencia would be catastrophic to the monarchist cause.[26]

Faced with an enemy whose troops were numerically weaker and no better equipped than his own, Miranda saw two possibilities open to him. He could attack with his superior forces Monteverde's weak army in Valencia, or he could threaten them from the rear by attacking Coro, the Royalist port. No action was taken, however, not even the perfectly feasible prevention of reinforcements going to the help of Monteverde.[27]

In these days Miranda's attention seemed exclusively directed to the organization of his army according to superannuated tactical principles. He expected success through discipline and drills, according to the ideas of a past era, and thought more of exhausting than actively besieging the enemy. He had learned nothing from Napoleon's strategy of extermination. It was this over-cautious attitude, this obsession to make his command into a smoothly organized force, that gave Monteverde the time necessary to regroup his army. Miranda's wish to build a well-trained fighting force was certainly natural, but the moment's urgency demanded rather the destruction of the enemy. Everything, in fact, depended upon the speed of his decision. Every hour that was wasted meant losses and death, while each day spent in anticipating the foe was a gain. Mi-

26 Austria: op. cit. pp. 130 ff. Pereyra: Juventud. pp. 399, 413. Blanco: Doc. Vol. IV. p. 21.
27 Robertson: Life. Vol. II. p. 152. Parra Pérez: Primera República. Vol. II. pp. 234-36.

randa accomplished nothing but an increase in the number of his deserters. It simply was not possible to develop these South American troops into a European army overnight.

Miranda was skeptical of the fighting spirit of his people; in this lay his principal fear. He withdrew, therefore, to what he considered a strategic point where he could fortify his position and at the same time defend the capital against any attack. He hoped in this way to delay Monteverde, and ultimately, if slowly, to destroy him. At this time the action of the enemy army was temporarily delayed.

Meanwhile, in the plains to the south of Miranda's position, rebellion was breaking out against the Republic. Royalist troops, commanded by Captain Antonañzas, pushed steadily forward in a series of small engagements, all without exception successful. Villages were burned, republican soldiers beheaded, and entire civilian populations murdered. Thus began the horrible chain of crimes whose bloody links stretched to the end of the war for independence.[28]

The enemy pushed towards Caracas in ever closer circles, and the city's supply lines were already seriously threatened. In the face of continuous failure the Patriots were seized with profound agitation.

Miranda seemed impervious to the dangers threatening the very existence of the Republic. Remaining inactive, he did not attempt to defend the fertile plains, but restricted himself solely to a defensive action. He fortified his position, which he considered unassailable. He did enter the field of politics, motivated by the belief that, like Napoleon, he had to succeed in all fields of the national life. But the aging man had long lost any ability he may have possessed to undertake the dual role of field marshal and statesman; and instead of restricting his energies to the solution of the most urgent problem, he dissipated them. In other words, he was more active with pen than sword and remained what he had been for thirty

28 Llamozas: Acontecimientos Políticos de Calabozo. B. d. H. Caracas. Vol. IV. 1921. No. 16.

years—the plotter and conspirator rather than the man of action.[29]

Monteverde, on the other hand, was never still. Convinced that a frontal attack on his enemy's position entailed too many sacrifices, he planned to attempt encirclement of the republican column which rested beside a lake extending from Valencia to Victoria (the second largest city on the road to Caracas). He decided to flank Miranda to the north and to the south, and his maneuver was entirely successful. His enemy was thus forced to evacuate a position he had considered impregnable.[30]

Miranda retired to Victoria on June 17, first burning his large store of supplies and ammunition. His technique of exhaustion had failed and his line of fortifications proved worthless, while irreplaceable supplies had been senselessly sacrificed.

Throwing Miranda back on Victoria, Monteverde followed close on his heels, early renewing his attack on the republican lines. This time Miranda was able to repulse him; but unable to take advantage of his victory, he allowed the fruits of victory to slip through his fingers. He remained deaf to the pleas of his officers for swift pursuit of the enemy. Instead of taking the offensive at long last, the troops returned to their positions. It was the last chance to save the first Republic of South America from destruction, and Miranda, by not taking it, lost both his country and his reputation as a soldier.[31]

That a conspiracy against the General should be born in these days, for the first time, is only too natural. In fact, his own officers wished to make him a prisoner and appoint a new Commander-in-Chief. When Miranda, away for a few days in Caracas, heard of the plot, his rage was monumental. Militarily the plot had little effect, and Miranda remained passive, handling all protests presented him with the superiority peculiar

29 Austria: *op. cit.* p. 135. Blanco: Doc. Vol. III. p. 728. Robertson: Life. Vol. II. pp. 154-55. Pereyra: Juventud. p. 419.
30 See the description by Yanes: Relación. Vol. I. pp. 40 ff. Baralt: Vol. I. pp. 116 ff. Austria: *op. cit.* p. 141. O'Leary: Memorias. Vol. I. p. 58.
31 O'Leary: Memorias. Vol. I. p. 58. Austria: *op. cit.* pp. 147-48.

to him. His behavior was similar to that of the Austrian general who reprimanded Napoleon for winning a victory through the wrong method.

The correctness of the officers wishing to appoint a more inspired commander is proved and demonstrated by the fact that at this time Monteverde was seriously considering retiring his troops from their advanced position, since no further help was expected and the lines of retreat were exposed to flanking attacks. After consultations with his staff, however, he merely halted, and his confidence in Miranda's incompetence was fully justified.[32]

Simon Bolivar had reluctantly undertaken the defense of the most important Republican seaport, Puerto Cabello. Its possession by the Republic was vital for two reasons: in the first place its principal fort, San Felipe, held a large number of political prisoners, among them many powerful and wealthy men active in the counter-revolutionary movement; in the second place the greater part of the supply of arms and ammunition held by the state was stored in the fort. Bolivar had early called attention to the danger of keeping prisoners of such importance and influence in so threatened a place.[33] By the end of May, with a few advanced positions around the fortress already lost, he seriously feared for the safety of the port. Believing that a forward thrust proved always most successful, he suggested to Miranda that an offensive be directed against Maracaibo with the hope of cutting off Monteverde's retreat. But the plan found no favor with Miranda.[34]

For some time a contact had been operating between treasonous factions of the troops and the wealthy political prisoners. Open rebellion broke out on June 30 when the royal flag

32 Larrazabal: Vol. I. p. 117. Becerra: Miranda. Vol. II. p. 221. H. Poudenx and Mayer: Memoire pour servir a l'Histoire de la Revolution de Caracas. Paris, 1815. p. 79.
33 O'Leary: Memorias. Vol. I. p. 50. Parra Pérez: Primera República. Vol. II. p. 293.
34 Until the present time historical research has not been able to establish definitely whether Bolivar or Miranda was responsible for keeping the dangerous prisoners in the threatened fortress. See: Robertson: Life. Vol. II. p. 164.

was hoisted on the fort by a Lieutenant Francesco Fernando Vinoni, who led the insurgents and seized the fort with its prize of prisoners, arms, and artillery. Bolivar was at his quarters in the city proper when this news was brought to him around noon. His position was desperate, for he was without ammunition and with but a few troops remaining. The city suffered heavily under shell fire, but Bolivar, still attempting the impossible, offered amnesty to the rebellious troops if they would give themselves up. But their advantage was only too obvious, and the bombardment continued, lasting throughout the night. At three o'clock in the morning Bolivar sent a laconic message to Miranda: "My General, an officer unworthy of his Venezuelan name, has seized the prisoners at Fort San Felipe and is making a night attack upon the city. If Your Excellency does not attack at once from the rear, the city is lost. Meanwhile I shall hold it as long as I can."[35]

Possibly Miranda received this letter too late to render help to a situation already hopeless. In any case he took no action to save Puerto Cabello. The bombardment became so fierce the next day that the population began to flee the city, and of the troops remaining Bolivar lost a further 120 men. Those who stayed were filled with fear, seeing their fate sealed. The small garrison, having fought to the very last a force ten times superior, surrendered on July 6. Bolivar fled by ship to La Guayra with seven other officers, having great trouble in escaping arrest.[36]

The Declaration of Independence of Venezuela was celebrated in Miranda's camp on July 5. That night the General received Bolivar's note announcing the loss of Fort San Felipe, and he informed his staff: *"Venezuela est blessée au coeur."* Having become, as an old man, more theatrical and pedantic than ever, he continued: "That is the way of the world. A little while ago we thought that all was secure. Yesterday Monteverde had neither weapons nor ammunition. Today he has

35 Cartas: Vol. I. p. 24 of July 1, 1812. V. Dávila: Investigaciones históricas. Caracas, 1923. p. 46: La traición de Puerta Cabello.
36 O'Leary: Memorias. Vol. I. p. 59. Larrazabal: Vol. I. p. 118.

both in abundance. I am told to attack the enemy. But he already has everything in his hands. Tomorrow we shall see what happens."

To Bolivar he sent a cryptic reply: "From your report of the first inst. I am informed of the extraordinary events that have taken place in San Felipe. Such things teach us to know men. I impatiently await more news from you. Tomorrow I shall write to you in detail."[37] What do the words mean: "Teach us to know men?" Certainly Bolivar had committed a military blunder when he left the prisoners in a fort storing all his arms. He can be criticized in addition for allowing such a conspiracy to take him by surprise. But the responsibility for the loss of the campaign itself does not fall on Bolivar but on his General, Miranda. For even at this hour there might still have been time for one final attempt. The advantage gained by Monteverde with his capture of Puerto Cabello could have been vitiated had an attack been directed on his rear guard before he had had time to regroup.

Bolivar was fully conscious of his responsibility, and this consciousness was almost too much for him to bear. He had exhausted all his forces in the defense of Puerto Cabello, but the fact remained that he had lost it. He assumed entire responsibility for the defeat and allowed no shadow to fall on the officers who had served under him. Writing to Miranda from Caracas on July 12, he said that he felt incapable of taking command and wished to be subservient to the lowest of his officers.[38] Bolivar never quite forgot this first defeat, and when in 1819, following the Battle of Boyacá, Vinoni fell into his hands as a prisoner of war, Bolivar hanged him as a traitor.

The majority of historians attach great importance to the loss of Puerto Cabello, feeling that the capitulation of the city sealed the doom of the First Republic. Unquestionably the possession of the port was of vital importance in the defense of Venezuela, but it would be assuming too much to claim

37 Blanco: Doc. Vol. III. p. 759. Parra Pérez: Primera República. Vol. II. p. 298.
38 Cartas: Vol. I. p. 24 of July 12, 1812. Austria: op. cit. p. 146.

that its loss was the decisive event of the campaign of 1812. Nevertheless, subsequent events or lack of them made it develop thus, for the Commander-in-Chief did not dare risk all in such a difficult situation. Under the circumstances Miranda had nothing to fear and much to hope—since all appeared lost, he could only win. However a decision for action was too much to expect from a man at the end of his strength.

Only he with the faith to move mountains could cherish any hope of victory for independence. Most of the western regions had been taken by Monteverde, and those provinces not yet in his hands were in a state of disintegration, while the areas in the east, which should have been supplying Caracas with food and reinforcements, were seething beneath uncontrolled rebellion. The counter-revolution had triumphed. Even in the capital, factions engaged continually in hand-to-hand scuffles with the authorities. Anarchy was rife. Miranda watched from the sidelines as his army disintegrated. Whole groups—up to a hundred men with arms and ammunition—deserted. Officers mutinied, then fought alongside the enemy. Miranda, faced with resigning, and thus possibly saving the cause of revolution, or with surrendering to the enemy for better or worse, chose the latter. The military situation was desperate, and the economic conditions of the country hopeless. At best Venezuela could expect a long-drawn-out civil war from which the lower classes, the mestizos and Negroes, would be the beneficiaries. Miranda had, a long time before, made the statement that he would prefer his country to remain another hundred years beneath Spanish oppression that be transformed into an arena for crime. He capitulated.[39]

Above all it must be remembered that the nature of the man was that of an adventurer who took himself more seriously than he did an assignment entrusted him. It was himself that he wished to save. Perhaps he even hoped that Great Britain might someday allow him to occupy the position now barred him by fate. He believed that Spain would enlist England's

39 Parra Pérez: Primera República. Vol. II. p. 357.

aid in pacifying and solving the problems of her American colonies.[40]

It is not too easy to decipher the motives which prompted the General to capitulate. Exhausted, humiliated, defeated, he abandoned this adventure as he had so many others in his life. On July 12, 1812, he delivered to a war council his explanation for signing an armistice with Monteverde. He had already sent his emissary the day before to the camp of the enemy. He flattered himself on being able to deal with the opposing general on an equal footing, but privately he was willing, from the very outset, to accept any and all conditions. During lengthy negotiations, during the time when proposals and counter-proposals were exchanged between the two headquarters, Miranda left Victoria for La Guayra in order to charter a ship to ensure his flight. Here was proof inconvertible that he had relinquished the cause of the Republic for his own.

The entire country was left at the mercy of Monteverde under the conditions of surrender. Only the inhabitants of territories not yet conquered were protected from persecution and expropriation. Those of the colored population that might be of some use to the conquerors were promised indulgence and the abolition of degrading laws under which they had lived in colonial days. Apart from these exceptions, Venezuelans were to be governed by the rules and regulations to be established by the Spanish Parliament for all of South America. This was the most that the Marquis de Casa León, Miranda's confidential aide, could hope to achieve. While Monteverde was willing to allow a respite of eight days for the evacuation of regions not yet occupied by him, he demanded ratification of the treaty as a whole within forty-eight hours. Miranda was willing to accept this too, concerned as he was only with his own fate.[41]

40 Blanco: Doc. Vol. III. pp. 760-61. Robertson: Life. Vol. II. p. 173. Pereyra: Juventud. p. 464.

41 Urquinaona: *op. cit.* p. 142. Baralt: Vol. I. p. 123. Yanez: Relación. Vol. I. p. 48. Díaz: *op. cit.* p. 45. Larrazabal: Vol. I. pp. 125 ff. Blanco: Doc. Vol. IV. pp. 9, 10.

Two separate sources testify that at this time Miranda was concerned with making himself financially secure. One report states that he accepted eleven thousand ounces of gold offered him by the Spaniards, while the other dealt with a check drawn in his favor by his friend, the Marquis de Casa León. Whether true or not, these dealings do not sound implausible, though it cannot be said that Miranda sold out his country to the Spaniards. He did unquestionably have his eye cocked for the main chance.[42]

Having arrived in Caracas on July 26, Miranda made his report to the City Council on the surrender, without, however, specifying at all the manner in which it had occurred. The thought of his flight possessed him. His papers and belongings had already been sent to La Guayra where the *Sapphire*—the ship on which Bolivar had returned from London—lay at anchor. Miranda himself arrived at the port on July 30, and besides the twenty-two thousand pesos given him out of the state treasury, he took along one thousand ounces of gold. The captain of the *Sapphire* begged him to board the ship immediately, but the General, in preferring to spend the night in La Guayra, signed his own death warrant.

After the fall of Puerto Cabello, Bolivar had fled first to La Guayra and then to Caracas, profoundly depressed by the disgrace that had befallen him. He sent a lengthy report to Miranda on the course of the tragic events, a report which gave further proof of his honesty and modesty. By the time news of the surrender reached him, Monteverde's troops had already pushed to within three miles of Caracas. Bolivar, accompanied by a number of other officers, fled to La Guayra on July 30. His indignation against Miranda was boundless. No one knew the conditions of the armistice. When Miranda met for the last time with the leaders of the Patriots at dinner, on July 30, he was pressed for an explanation. But they received answers not only irate but insulting. The report circulating that the

42 Urquinaona: p. 159. Rojas: Miranda. p. 699. Parra Pérez: Primera República. Vol. II. p. 368.

General had ordered no one to leave the port other than himself increased the anger at the secrecy surrounding the capitulation. Information concerning the large sums of money stowed aboard the *Sapphire* soon leaked out, and it became evident without further room for doubt, that Miranda had first sold his country down the river and was now preparing to betray those officers willing to continue the fight. Had Miranda believed in the sincerity of the Spaniards and expected the stipulated conditions would be fulfilled, he would have found no reason to flee. And if he did not believe this, he was obviously a traitor.

When Miranda had withdrawn from the company of his dinner companions, the officers proceeded to hold consultation. In addition to Bolivar, there were taking part in this war council the Commandant of La Guayra, Las Casas; Miguel Peña the political delegate; and six or seven high ranking officers. The decision was taken to place Miranda under arrest. Some wished merely to enforce his remaining in the country, while others, Bolivar among them, wished to shoot him as a traitor. The patriots entered Miranda's room before dawn. He thought at first they came to wake him, but on discovering their purpose, asked them to wait. In a few moments he appeared fully dressed and completely composed. His imperturbability never left him, and when Bolivar harshly announced him to be under arrest he did not deign to reply. He took a lantern from the hand of one of his aides, and holding it up to the faces of the conspirators, accused them instead: "Noise, noise, and more noise! That is all these people can make!" He uttered no further word and was brought in silence to Fort San Carlos.[43]

Whatever plans the Patriots may have made, Monteverde left them no time for execution. By July 31 he had already sent an emissary to La Guayra demanding the port's closing and insisting that the non-fulfillment of this order would entail cancellation of all previous pacts. In his desire to win the favor of the conqueror, Las Casas, the commandant, followed the

43 In regard to Miranda's imprisonment see Yanes: Relación. Vol. I. p. 52. Baralt: Vol. I. p. 124. O'Leary: Memorias. Vol. I. p. 74. Larrazabal: Vol. I. p. 125. Heredia: Memorias. pp. 76-78. Robertson: Life. Vol. II. pp. 180-81.

order, and the Venezuelan flag flying on the fort was replaced by the Spanish colors. Miranda was handed over to the Spaniards.

Little in Bolivar's life gave his critics as much food for discussion as his attitude and conduct towards Miranda. Had a man who himself had suffered defeat, whose miscalculations caused the loss of Puerto Cabello, any right to sit in judgment? Had not this man also left his country three times during the fateful years between 1814 and 1818? Bolivar would have answered thus: "I, too, was unhappy as a soldier. But I never surrendered. Never did money or possessions mean anything to me. Never have I lowered the flag of victory." More than his military ineptitude Bolivar resented in Miranda the atmosphere of secrecy and treason with which he surrounded himself. Bolivar was actually proud of his action against Miranda and boasted of it. Napoleon, questioned on St. Helena on the death of the Duke of Enghien, stated that he would do the same thing again under the same circumstances.[44] There is yet another reason for the tragic ending of the relationship between the two men—perhaps the most cogent. Miranda had at no time been willing to make personal sacrifices, and whether corruptible or not, had not achieved anything it is possible to construe as great in terms of history. Miranda had remained throughout his life a freebooter for whom nothing was as important as his own person. Miranda failed because his personal ambitions were greater than his abilities.

The conquering Spaniards were uninterested in the causes of the Patriots' anger against Miranda. They saw in him the originator of the movement for independence, and therefore they seized him. He remained in the fortress at La Guayra until 1814, when he was taken to the Prison of Four Towers in Cádiz. He died there on July 16, 1816.

Monteverde, under the flimsiest of pretexts, broke all agreements made with Miranda. Large numbers of the leaders of the independence movement were arrested on August 1, and

44 See the letter of Adjutant B. H. Wilson in O'Leary: Memorias. Vol. I. p. 75.

there began a period of persecution and proscription of all those who had fought for freedom. Eight of the most important, "eight monsters, the origin and root of all evil and trouble" as Monteverde called them, were placed in chains and sent to Cádiz.[45]

By some miracle Bolivar managed to escape arrest. He had fled in disguise from La Guayra under cover of dusk on July 31. He entered Caracas unrecognized and stayed hidden for a while in the house of the Marquis de Casas León. Since he neither wished to give himself up nor was inclined to pass the rest of his life rotting in a Spanish jail, he asked his friend, the Basque Francisco Iturbe, to intervene on his behalf. As a friend of Monteverde's, Iturbe was able to ask for a pass to enable Bolivar to leave Venezuela. Monteverde was at first disinclined to let Bolivar go, knowing that he had been proved a true patriot in his defense of Puerto Cabello, where he had told his soldiers that it was better to die than to return to slavery. But Iturbe, renewing his pleas, offered himself as guarantee, and seeing Monteverde beginning to weaken, he brought to him Simon Bolivar who he introduced with these words: "Here is the commander of Puerto Cabello for whom I have offered my bond. If punishment is visited on him, I shall suffer for it. My life stands for his." Monteverde replied, "Very well," and still looking at Bolivar, said to his secretary: "This gentleman is to be issued a pass as reward for the service he rendered the King by the arrest of Miranda."[46] Bolivar had until now remained silent, but at the implied contempt in the Spaniard's words was moved to answer with boldness: "I had Miranda arrested to punish him for betraying his country, not to serve the King." At this Monteverde regretted his decision and cancelled the pass. Only Iturbe's persistent importunities were responsible for the final issuance of the pass and Bolivar's escape. That he was able to leave is somewhat surprising, since

45 Yanes: Relación. Vol. I. p. 56. Parra Pérez: Primera República. Vol. II. pp. 420 ff.
46 O'Leary: Memorias. Vol. I. p. 80. Larrazabal: Vol. I. 1.157. Gil Fortoul: Hist. 1.189. See also Bolivar's letter to his sister: Cartas: Vol. V. p. 19. Torres Lanza: Vol. III. p. 208.

his conduct during this time was more theatrical than wise: he was given to offering confessions no one wished to hear, to put on acts no one wished to see. Bolivar never forgot the person who had made his flight possible. Nine years later, when at a meeting of the Congress of Greater Colombia in Cucuta it was voted to confiscate all property of emigrated Spaniards, the property of Francisco Iturbe was affected. Bolivar, who was then President of Greater Colombia, appealed to Congress in a letter describing what had happened in 1812: "Could I forget such generosity? Can Colombia penalize such a man, without being ungrateful? If Francisco Iturbe's property is to be confiscated, I offer my own in its place, just as he once offered his life for mine. And if the sovereign Congress wishes to show him leniency, I shall be the one rewarded."[47]

Monteverde, who might have restrained the genuis of the South American revolution, rejected the historical moment. Spain could never recapture this lost opportunity. Indeed it is said that when in later months Bolivar's name was mentioned, Governor Monteverde blanched.

After procuring his pass, Bolivar dined with two friends, giving the impression that he was about to sail for England to volunteer in the British Army. Actually his only thought was to take up action against Spain on another front.[48] On August 21 he went to La Guayra, boarding the first ship planning to leave the port. But the ship's papers were not in order and at Curaçao the customs officials impounded his luggage and all his belongings. Material misfortune, however, never troubled Bolivar much: "Since the brave and honest man must be impervious to the strokes of fate, I have armed myself with endurance, and I can minimize the shafts that fate hurls at me. Only my conscience rules my heart. That is serene and nothing can disturb it. What then does it matter, whether I have or do not have material things? No man dies of need on this earth."[49]

Bolivar remained in Curaçao only as long as necessary to

47 Cartas: Vol. II. pp. 385-86.
48 O'Leary: Memorias. Vol. I. p. 82. See Lecuna's introduction to Yanes' work.
49 Cartas: Vol. I. pp. 29-30. September 19, 1812.

discover the means of proceeding to Cartagena, the principal
port of New Granada. He was successful in borrowing money
and left the island accompanied by a small group of officers
emigrating like himself. He arrived in Cartagena in the middle
of November.

When this new chapter in the life of Simon Bolivar began,
he was thirty years old. The Republic of Venezuela had lasted
but one year. On looking back, that year must have appeared
to Bolivar like a veritable chain of mistakes and failures, with
his own actions bearing the mark of error and guilt. Bolivar
was not the type of genius who, like Napoleon and Alexander,
dazzled the world with talents in full bloom. He had to learn
each step along the way, in everything he undertook, and nothing equalled the school of training into which he was forced
by the events of 1812. But here we see his real greatness, for
each defeat found him ready to reëxamine his ideas, to confess
mistakes, and to begin the hazardous course all over again. His
is the genius of the mountain climber. The catastrophe of the
First Republic neither exhausted nor discouraged him. With-
standing the first shock, the anger and resentment, his regret
and defiance turned into motivating forces. He had two tasks:
to grasp the experience of the past, and to take up the fight once
again. For he knew well that only war could restore that which
had been lost to him—"the honor of Venezuela."

Part II

MAN OF FREEDOM

CHAPTER 9

El Manifesto de Cartagena

The adversary Bolivar had challenged in a fight to the death was a force not to be despised. Spanish colonialism was still very much entrenched. A flexible constitution had been drawn up by Spanish liberals in 1812, a constitution which seemed to open a way towards reconciliation with the rebellious colonies. Such reconciliation was strongly supported by an England ever intent upon promoting negotiations between the mother country and her Latin American colonies.[1] It is true that the Iberian Peninsula was almost entirely occupied by Napoleon's armies, but it was the end of 1812—and the fall of the despot was imminent. In America the situation was such that hereditary rule was assured swift victory over rebels.[2]

Cuba and Puerto Rico had always remained loyal to Spain. The rebellion in Ecuador appeared crushed. Venezuela had been reconquered. In Mexico the independence movement, after a glorious beginning, had faltered and stopped completely. The viceregal kingdom of Peru, as yet unstirred by thoughts of freedom, was of course on the side of the mother country, and her provinces might well serve Spain as a base in stamping out rebellion in Chile, Bolivia, and the regions of the La Plata.[3]

Bolivar had turned to New Granada,* where power was

1 Mancini: *op. cit.* p. 401. Blanco: Doc. Vol. III. p. 621.
2 Levene: H. d. A. Vol. VI. pp. 79-86, 155-175: Vol. VII. pp. 3-45 ff., 145 ff.
3 Levene: H. d. A. Vol. V. pp. 30-104. Mitre: San Martín. Vol. I. *passim.*
E. Ravignani: Historia constitucional de la Argentina. Buenos Aires, 1926-27.
* The term "New Granada" as used hereafter refers to the area now included in the Republic of Colombia. This designation is used to avoid a possible confusion between the Republic of Colombia and the Greater Colombian Republic established by Bolivar in 1819.

still in the hands of the independents. The Liberals were triumphant in the interior, but federalist and centralist factions fought each other with such passion that this large and important region was on the verge of civil war.[4] Many provinces, those along the Atlantic seaboard in particular, had not acknowledged the revolution. Cities such as Cartagena, while remaining true to the ideal of liberty, had nevertheless risen up against Bogotá, the capital, declaring their own complete independence. Universal anarchy had in fact overwhelmed the country. Even the smallest of communities became intoxicated with the concept of sovereignty.[5]

Bolivar was far from discouraged by this scene of disintegration. On the contrary he based his calculations and his hopes upon the fact that a state threatened by such dangers would need his services. The independent government of Cartagena was headed by young Manuel Rodríguez Torices, and he showed himself eager to befriend Bolivar and the number of friends of compatriots who had accompanied Bolivar to Cartagena. President Torices realized that only swift military action could save this artificially created state, and when Bolivar arrived in November, Torices hastened to enroll him in the army of Cartagena.

Bolivar's future, however, could no longer be circumscribed by his profession as a soldier. To go off to the wars with other Venezuelan officers would be the measure of valor; but to plot the liberation of South America as a whole—this was the measure of greatness. In a pamphlet describing Miranda's surrender and the atrocities of Monteverde, Bolivar expressed the feelings of his companions when he stated: "Is there an American worthy of the name, who would not cry 'Death to all Spaniards!' when he beheld the destruction of so many victims in Venezuela? No, and No again!"[6]

Bolivar realized that the mere continuation of the fight was

4 Restrepo: H. d. R. C. Vol. I. pp. 109 ff. Henao y Arrubla: Historia de Colombia. Bogotá, 1929.
5 J. de la Vega: La Federación en Colombia, 1810-1912. Madrid.
6 Proclamas: p. 4.

insufficient. The future of New Granada, more, the future of all South America, depended on the independence of Venezuela. The catastrophic collapse of his fatherland marked the turning-point in Bolivar's life. As Hegel said, it was the nocturnal fastness of his being, through which he forced himself to a realization of his true purpose.

Bolivar as the hero of South America was born in Cartagena in the year 1812. No longer was he the hot headed conspirator nor the fanatic Jacobin of earlier years. He had learned from his failures. The months spent on the hot, arid coast of Curaçao and the weeks wasted in the tropical heat of Cartagena wrought a change in the man. And in Cartagena where the gigantic walls, the massive forts, and the Palace of the Inquisition spoke all too eloquently of the oppressor he hoped to overthrow, Bolivar found the much needed words of hope.

We see a totally new person in the Bolivar who, both proud and modest, addressed the people of New Granada as his fellow citizens. This appeal, a document now famous, begins: "I have, as a son of unhappy Caracas, miraculously escaped from its political and material destruction, and am here to serve the banner of freedom."[7] In continuing, Bolivar held that the terrible plight of Venezuela must serve as an example to all America in the reëxamination of the present position and in the rectification of the lack of unity, solidarity, and energy of its governments. The Bolivar who thus raised his voice was in no way the same as the man who emerged humiliated and beaten from the collapse of the First Republic. Several months of enforced solitude had served to mature him. Searching, he had found the causes for his country's downfall in its history. His voice was heard, clear, and persuasive, on a continent which listened for the first time to the call of its leader.

To Bolivar the primary cause for the destruction of the Republic lay in its false tolerance. Its officials had not consulted those works from which they might learn the science of

---

7 Memoria dirigida a los ciudadanos de la Nueva Granada por un Caraqueño. Cartas: Vol. I. pp. 35 ff.

government, but rather books compiled by good natured vision-
aries who had conjured up ephemeral states ruled under political perfection. Instead of leaders, Venezuela had philosophers;
instead of laws, philanthropy; dialectics in place of policy;
and sophists in place of soldiers. General disintegration proved
the result. Crimes against the state went unpunished, the Spaniards were forgiven time and time again for their never ending
conspiracies and disregard for public welfare. Criminal leniency
contributed more than anything else to the destruction of the
political power of the Republic, a republic not yet fully established. This same fallacious doctrine had prevented the formation of an army of experienced soldiers. In their place had
been a poorly disciplined militia whose pay not only exhausted
the state treasury, but also destroyed the national economy
because peasants were removed from their regular occupation.
Understanding that situation with all its ramifications, Bolivar
also thought clearly concerning the political economy of
Venezuela—the squandering of public funds, the creation of
superfluous offices, and finally the distribution of paper money.
This last had so disturbed the sense of possession of the ruling,
moneyed classes, that they welcomed the commandant of the
Spanish troops and expected him to liberate them from conditions they regarded as worse than slavery.

Bolivar was persuaded that the system of government itself,
in its acceptance of a federal constitution which broke social
contracts and consigned the nation to anarchy, provided the
most potent reason for the fall of the First Republic. In the
Federated States of Venezuela each province was independent
and each city demanded the right to govern itself as it saw fit.
It is impossible to determine whether Bolivar was conscious of
the need for a centralized government before he presented the
Manifesto of Cartagena. But from that day on, in any case, he
made known his demand for the State's security in all of his
speeches and announcements. "Our compatriots," he said, "are
not yet capable of exercising their legal rights. They lack those
virtues which distinguish the true republican. Moreover, what

country on earth can afford a weak and intricate system of government such as a federation of states, where different factions quarrel within and war threatens from without?" Bolivar, like every really great statesman, was a realist: "Government must accommodate itself to circumstances, to the era, and to the men that comprise it. If these are adjusted and flourishing, government must be mild and protective. But when they are dangerous and confused, government must prove to be formidable and ruthless without regard to law or constitution, until peace is established. I believe that our enemies will have all the advantage as long as we do not unify our American government. We shall be inextricably caught in the web of civil war, and be shamefully beaten by that little horde of bandits which pollutes our country. That is the fundamental cause of Venezuela's misfortune."

"Not the Spaniards, but our own disunity has led us back into slavery. A strong government could have changed everything. It would even have been able to master the moral confusion which ensued after the earthquake. With it, Venezuela would today be free."

Even after the passing of a full century these words on the tragic history of the First Republic remain both astute and penetrating. This description of Venezuela's woes is only the prelude, however, to the true purposes that animated the publication of *el Manifiesto de Cartagena*. New Granada had seen her neighbor, Venezuela, perish and understood the necessity of liberating Venezuela for the sake of her own safety. As the first measure towards this end Bolivar proposed the conquest of Caracas. On the surface this appears a plan that would prove costly, and possibly hopeless. Actually, it was a vital move in the ensuring of the safety of New Granada and America as a whole. If rebellion in the provinces of Coro had led to the fall of Caracas, could not the destruction of Venezuela lead to the total subjugation of America? Spain, ruling the coastal regions of Venezuela, was in a position to send troops and munitions there under the command of French officers and easily accomplish the penetration of all of South America. Venezuela, therefore, was a bridgehead to the possible reconquest of the colonies. And here, as so many times in his life, Bolivar was the prophet of events to come.

The only defense, he felt, against this great danger, lay in the swift recovery of all lost territories. The forces of the revolution must go over to the offensive and give battle. "Under no circumstances," Bolivar exhorted his friends, "must we remain on the defensive." Prospects for a victorious campaign are good, the situation of the enemy critical, his soldiers undependable and scattered among the larger cities. An attack from the west could, without developing into a battle, reach as far as Caracas. If we attack Venezuela, thousands of brave Patriots will join our ranks.

"Let us hasten to break the chains of those victims who languish in prison and await rescue at your hands. Do not mock their confidence and trust. Do not be unfeeling towards the sorrows of your brethren. Go, quickly, to avenge the dead, to give life to the dying, relief to the oppressed, and freedom to all."

The *Manifiesto de Cartagena* takes its place among the great documents of statesmanship. With it begins in Bolivar's life a series of far-reaching pronouncements that are proof of his political thinking and his spellbinding rhetoric. And with it also begins his career as a spiritual leader, tragically determined to give unity and endurance to South American independence.

Bolivar, addressing his words to the South American continent, was fully aware of the existing chaotic conditions. A gremlin of disunity had taken possession of the colonial realm —down to the smallest village. What seemed to work in one community was out of the question for its neighbor. Disintegration was increased by the striving personal ambitions of corrupt politicians.[8]

Bolivar, alone among the Patriots, was able to admit to himself that to all intents and purposes the entire population

8 C. Jane: Libertad y Despotismo en América. Buenos Aires, 1942. p. 35.

was without any political training, and that South America possessed no such tradition of self government as that enjoyed by its great neighbor to the north. But this knowledge did not deter him. Confronted by the existing political dissolution, he wished to awaken once more the ideal of a free nation. But to him the continental concept was even more important. Bolivar lived and breathed in terms of a whole hemisphere, while other men of the Revolution looked only within their own limited horizon—their particular province or country. His struggles were not directed solely towards the overthrow of Spain. He had also to win over his compatriots to his entire concept—independent states forged together by unity into a continent, the continent of South America.

Bolivar's appeals to the people of New Granada, whom he addressed as Colombians for the first time, were meaningful in yet another sense, showing as they do the vast dimensions of the world historic problem assumed by him. In his task was implicit not only the strengthening of political ideas and the forming of nations, but above all the assumption of responsibility for military leadership.

Bolivar's immediate objective was the reconquest of Venezuela; but to gain the necessary support for this, he had first to fight for the renegade province of Santa Marta, a region of prime importance to the future of Colombia.

A supreme council of the independents had been formed in New Granada on July 20, 1810, but shortly thereafter the territory had been divided by the centralist and federalist factions.[9] Cundinamarca, the most important of the provinces, with Bogotá its capital, was in favor of a central government and in 1811 approved its own constitution. But the other provinces were unwilling to subordinate themselves to the leadership of Bogotá. Their delegates, meeting in a counter congress, founded the Federation of New Granada Provinces, its capital Tunja. Camillo Torres, passionate defender of the federal idea,

9 Restrepo: H. d. R. C. Vol. I. p. 173. Blanco: Doc. Vol. II. pp. 563, 565, 661, 665, 683.

was elected first President of the Federation, while Antonio
Nariño, a champion of human rights and a convinced centralist, headed the government at Bogotá.

Bolivar, faced as he was by three governments to deal with,
begged all of them to aid him in his undertaking to liberate
Venezuela.[10]

The situation in New Granada was further complicated by
the fact that the Spaniards had gained a foothold in the country.
They had taken the valleys forming the border between Colombia and Venezuela; and, more serious than this, were advancing
along the Magdalena River. This majestic water is the main
artery of Colombia today, and it was doubly important in an
era when airplanes and railroads were unknown. The Spaniards, having reached the lower levels of the river below Santa
Marta, had cut Cartagena off completely from any contact with
the interior.

The government of Cartagena commissioned Pierre Labatut, a French captain who had fought in the army of the
Venezuelan patriots, to lead the advance against the Spaniards.
Bolivar was placed under his command. He saw clearly that
the situation of Cartagena was critical, open as it was to encirclement from both flanks—from Panama and from Santa
Marta. To him, the only hope of resistance lay in attack. To
the man planning the liberation first of Venezuela, then of
South America as a whole, Cartagena was no more than a
strategic base along the way.[11]

Bolivar was charged by Labatut with the defense of Barrancas, a small community on the left bank of the Magdalena.
He was to remain here and not to take action without orders.
Bolivar, however, was not one to temporize when his judgment
and his conscience both told him that salvation lay in swift
action, that delay could only react unfavorably on the villages
and towns situated on the river bank. He realized that it was

10 Blanco: Doc. Vol. II. p. 697; Vol. III. pp. 279, 357, 662-63, 676-77, 712.
Restrepo: H. d. R. C. Vol. I. p. 195.
11 O'Leary: Memorias. Vol. I. p. 85. Larrazabal: Vol. I. p. 154. Cartas: Vol.
I. p. 31. Rivas Vicuña: Las Guerras de Bolívar. Bogotá, 1934. Vol. I. p. 89.

vital in the rallying and organization of all forces for the river to be open to traffic. His plan, therefore, was to clear the Spanish militia from the river and to reëstablish traffic.

Bolivar had arrived in Barrancas on December 21, 1812. A few days later he had organized a small but tightly knit fighting unit of two hundred men, and with them set out upstream on ten rafts that had been hurriedly thrown together. On December 23 he reached Tenerife, and when the Spanish garrison quartered there refused his command to surrender, he attacked. The defenders fled, leaving valuable ships and supplies which enabled Bolivar to increase his small flotilla. On Christmas Eve he consigned the inhabitants to the Constitution of Cartagena and continued his march.[12]

He reached Mompox on December 27. His troops were joined by the young men of the town; and Bolivar, accompanied now by a force of five hundred, pushed on upstream, taking ships, guns, and munitions in a series of minor engagements. "I was born in Caracas," Bolivar said later, "but my fame was born in Mompox." In truth after but fifteen days of action, he was able to inform the sovereign Congress of New Granada that the river was free of Spaniards as far as Ocaña.[13] Cartagena was no longer separated from its hinterland.

Bolivar made his headquarters in Ocaña, having already pushed on from the banks of the river towards the mountains that extended eastwards to Venezuela. But before he could carry out his great plan, he was forced to await word from Cartagena as to whether his daring intentions were sanctioned. Although he had done the government of Cartagena a great service, he was not sure whether it would support him, since in acting contrary to Labatut's orders he had defied military law. In fact, his commander was demanding Bolivar's conviction by courts martial. But it was obvious that the help Bolivar had given Cartagena in crisis was more important than stand-

12 Proclamas: p. 22. See also V. Lecuna: La Campaña admirable. B. d. H. Caracas. Vol. XXVII. No. 106. p. 124.
13 O'Leary: Doc. Vol. XIII. p. 133.

ing upon the points of formal discipline, and the President of
the city had come to his defense.

Nothing, says the proverb, succeeds like success. But four
months had passed since Bolivar was forced into flight from
his own country, beaten and impoverished. Already his iron
will was triumphant over difficulties. He dealt simultaneously
with three governments, depending on nothing but the esteem
in which he was held and on the confidence his genius breathed
into everyone coming into contact with him. Now, leader of
an army that had at first been created in his phantasy, head of
a state still only existing in his own imagination, this man so
recently a fugitive was now an ally.[14]

New Granada, divided into separate republics without a
unified command and almost without military strength, now
felt the pressure of Spanish arms. A force of one thousand men
commanded by Ramon Correa was pushing from the east on
the borders of Colombia. Correa, overcoming the opposing
Patriots, occupied Cúcuta, today capital of Santander province.
It would have been an easy matter to push forward from this
point—either to the south or to the north where Bolivar was
stationed at Ocaña. In the south Patriotic troops under the
command of Colonel Manuel del Castillo, who felt he was
unequipped to resist the Spaniards, were trying to make a
stand on the way to Bogotá and Tunja. Colonel Del Castillo,
appealed to Bolivar for assistance.[15]

Bolivar, glad to help, told him that he would first have to
obtain permission from the President of Cartagena. He unhesitatingly told his new allies that he considered their stupid
constitution and senseless civil war responsible for the dangers
to which Colombia was now exposed. Nevertheless, he was
determined to give aid to the allied provinces, since only thus
could he hope eventually to advance upon Venezuela.[16] Upon

14 Rivas Vicuña: *op. cit.* p. 89. E. Posada: Colombia, Provincias Unidas de la
Nueva Granada. 1811-1816. Bogotá, 1924.
15 O'Leary: Doc. Vol. XIII. pp. 135-36.
16 O'Leary: Doc. Vol. XIII. pp. 136-38. E. Posada: La Patria Boba. Bogotá,
1902.

receiving permission from Cartagena to extend his operations to the regions of the Confederacy, he saw that his road lay first in the liberation of Cúcuta—and then on to Venezuela.

Camillo Torres, the President of the Confederacy, was well disposed towards Bolivar. He had sensed the future greatness of the man in the words and deeds of the young Colonel, and although never approving of Bolivar's centralist beliefs, he was nevertheless convinced that in his person the independence movement was identified. The friendship between these two men was particularly gratifying to Bolivar, surrounded as he was in his lifetime with ingratitude, enmity, and hatreds. "Understanding spoke to understanding" here.[17]

Torres was perfectly willing to support Bolivar's plans, but could only do so after the Spaniards were driven off Colombian soil. And this Bolivar was determined to accomplish. "My advance guard," he wrote on February 8, "moves on the enemy's position tomorrow." Bolivar followed them a week later. The Spaniards had settled in the hills overlooking the fertile valleys of Cúcuta, and Bolivar determined to drive them from this position in the shortest possible time. Cúcuta bordered on Venezuela.

Only a reader familiar with these regions can imagine the conditions which confronted Bolivar as, after leaving the hot town of Ocaña, he wound his way through the impassable canyons of the Cordilleras, on mule tracks that rose steeply from the plains of the Magdalena River. A false move meant certain death in the abyss below; the ground was damp and slippery, the temperature dropping sharply with the ascent. There were no settlements in these regions other than an occasional hut housing a barely existing Indian family. The soldiers Bolivar led through this difficult terrain were children of the tropics, poorly conditioned to withstand the privations of long marches through cold mountain altitudes. But Bolivar swept them along with him in his vigor and enthusiasm, subjugating both men

17 Gervinus: *op. cit.* Vol. III. Chap. V. *passim.* Restrepo: H. d. R. C. Vol. II. p. 133. "Los tres Torres." B. d. H. Bogotá. Vol. III.

and circumstances. When a stream blocked his path, he himself crossed it countless times in a single, frail boat until every man and all the supplies were safely on the further side.[18]

He reached the hills surrounding Cúcuta on the morning of February 28. The struggle was neither long nor particularly bloody, since the Spaniards retreated when the patriots, their ammunition exhausted, attacked with bayonets. One cannot call this action led by Bolivar great, but nevertheless its moral effect was incalculable. Within two weeks he had vitiated entirely any danger of a Spanish invasion of Colombia. Considerable money had fallen into his hands which enabled him to pay his men adequately, and therefore to discipline them. And most important of all, he had reached the borders of Venezuela. This fact he chose to stress in his first proclamation to his newly organized, newly tested army "In less than two months, you have completed two campaigns and begun a third which starts here and will end in the land of my birth. Venezuela has arisen anew!"[19]

Bolivar at this point was promoted by Torres from the rank of Colonel to that of Brigadier General in the army of the Confederacy, and on him were conferred all the civil rights of those states.[20] Everything that had been accomplished during these two months had in effect been due to Bolivar. To Bolivar, always thinking in terms of countries and hemispheres, Cúcuta, like Cartagena, was but a base from which freedom for America could be won. He now had before him the task of convincing those who controlled the fate of New Granada. For Bolivar, fame was no longer enough. He needed power.

Bolivar sent in one report after another, each with a new date line, in his attempts to sway the vacillating politicians.[21] Perhaps Torres was willing to give Bolivar complete freedom of action, but his personal enthusiasm was tempered by narrow

18 O'Leary: Memorias. Vol. I. pp. 103-104.
19 Proclamas: pp. 27-29.
20 O'Leary: Doc. Vol. XIII. p. 160. Restrepo: H. d. R. C. Vol. I. p. 200.
Larrazabal: Vol. I. p. 162.
21 O'Leary: Doc. Vol. XIII. pp. 156-59.

minded officials unwilling to put the weak forces of their country to the task of liberating a sister nation. Their arguments appeared weighted by the fact that the commander of the New Granada troops, Colonel Castillo, had expressed himself firmly opposed to Bolivar's policies.[22]

Castillo made no attempt to conceal his jealousy and antagonism, quarrelling incessantly about rank and prestige, impeding Bolivar whenever possible. He even took his complaints to Congress, and plotted against Bolivar's "mad undertaking."

Bolivar on his side did not wish to push the quarrel to a head and tried to iron out their differences in a letter to Castillo in which he addressed him as a friend and offered him the top command—willing, it seemed, to step down and thus keep harmony within the ranks of the army. This was the first time that he had attempted to serve an idea through personal sacrifice. He continued such offers of self-sacrifice until his death; sometimes he meant them sincerely, sometimes they were but a political expedient, sometimes the result of fatigue, and sometimes even an attempt to embarrass his opponent.[23] In any case he had no luck with Castillo, and finally there was a complete break between the two men. The government refused Bolivar's offer of resignation and, on the contrary, named him Commander-in-Chief of all the troops in the north.

Thus empowered, Bolivar ordered Castillo to attack the Spaniards. After considerable delay the order was carried out. Castillo overcame the Spaniards, but handed in his resignation immediately following, because, he said, the reconquest of Venezuela was against his moral principles. His example was ominous, and the rebellion spread throughout the division. Everything hung in the balance. Bolivar rushed to his troops and received from them an impression that was more than suspicious. Even his officers supported Castillo. When ordered by his commander to march, one of the officers refused to obey.

22 O'Leary: Doc. Vol. XIII. pp. 163-65. Restrepo: H. d. R. C. Vol. I. p. 201. Blonco: Doc. Vol. IV. p. 546.
23 Cartas: Vol. I. p. 51. E. Ludwig: Bolívar. Buenos Aires, 1940. p. 133.

In a stern voice admitting of no argument Bolivar answered
him: "March! Either you shoot me, or, by God, I'll shoot
you." The man obeyed. That first mutinous officer fought on
at Bolivar's side for many years. First his friend, then his rival,
and finally his bitterest foe, the officer never forgot the insult.
He was self-contained, secretive, and vengeful, and his name
was Francisco de Paula Santander.[24]

As Bolivar won the upper hand with the army, so he also
finally convinced the government. He reiterated again and
again the dangers arising if an attack on Venezuela was not
carried out, and described to them how such an attack might be
made. Once again he offered to step down from his command
and attempt this on his own, supported only by volunteers.[25]
Step by step, one by one, he finally succeeded in calming the
fears of Colombian politicians. Always playing one against
another, first a soldier, then a diplomat, he succeeded after two
months of waiting and dickering in receiving a small satisfaction. He was granted permission to occupy the Venezuelan
border provinces of Trujillo and Mérida. Bolivar's reply to this
was characteristic. They offered him a finger, so he took the
whole hand. He admitted with frankness his intention of
marching on Caracas. He ended his letter to the government
with provocative audacity: "I shall receive the answer to this in
Trujillo." The letter was dated May 8, 1813. On May 10 he
swore allegiance to the government of the Confederacy, and
a few days later he entered Venezuela.[26]

Eight months had passed since his flight from Caracas.
Already he had made good the defeat of Puerto Cabello, had
beaten the Spaniards, and had created an army that obeyed his
commands. The steep ascent that followed his downfall was
not all jubilation, however. And the man who had first hoisted

24 O'Leary: Memorias. Vol. I. p. 123. In regard to the conflict with Castillo
see: O'Leary: Doc. Vol. XIII. pp. 182, 184, 188, 191. Archiv Santander. Bogotá, 1913.
Vol. I. p. 175.
25 Cartas: Vol. I. p. 49. Cartas: Vol. IX. p. 417.
26 O'Leary: Doc. Vol. XIII. pp. 209, 220. C. Torres: Documentos Históricos.
Bogotá, 1898. G. Masur: Suramérica vista desde afuera. Rev. Feminina. Medellín,
1933, pp. 151 ff.

like a banner his continental ideas in the *Manifiesto de Cartagena,* was to realize at this time the frightful fatigue of the
voyage that was the price of reaching his goal.

Two factors stood in his way: man as an instrument, and
nature as an element. The hemisphere itself, far more than the
armies of Spain, seemed to delay the achievement of independence. Bolivar was just beginning to grasp what it meant
to have untrained human material in the midst of nature
unconquered.

The conflict with Castillo was the first of the human difficulties that were to continue to impede his path. There were
officers who envied his fame, politicians who resented his authority and hoped to wrest his power from him. The brothers-
in-arms of yesterday became today's enemies, while those who
had allied themselves with him were only too likely to turn
traitors. In all his undertakings Bolivar had to reckon with
such factors as the narrowmindedness of the regionalists, the
quarrelsomeness of the separatists, the inferiority sense of other
races, the untamability of the anarchists, plus the lack of understanding, the demands, and the follies of them all. These were
the human qualities of a people too young to be obedient, too
varied to be stable.

As the wildness of the South American was still uninhibited,
so was nature in that country still utterly untamed. What contrasts it presented—from the beneficent heat of coastal lands,
across the humid heat of the river valleys, to the snow-covered
crests of the Andes. The tropical nature of the continent knows
no transitions, and everything is full of crass contrasts. There
were times of drought, when the earth seemed to spew flames,
alternating with the rainy seasons when rivers overflowed their
banks to sweep villages and entire settlements along in their
flood. Only he who has seen the Magdalena, the Orinoco, the
Amazon, at such times, can appreciate their vast majesty. Burning heat and fever in a hot country—cold, damp, fog on the
plateau; and in between the Bush, the forest primeval, untrod-
den and impenetrable, choked by its luxuriant flora. Decay

and rebirth intermingled. Concealed within was the animal world of snakes, spiders, tarantulae, mosquitoes, and scorpions; the wild game of the forests, the tiger and puma. On the river banks were the reptiles, the crocodiles and alligators—all an endless and deadly threat to man. Few are the places in northern South America blessed with any sort of a temperate climate. To reach such a climate it is necessary to ascend thousands of feet above sea level: through canyons, up trails that mules find almost impossible to scale, across heights of towards four thousand metres.

Behind the mountain chain of the Andes with its broad valleys and gorges lie the plains, as sweeping and open as the sea. But these are uninhabitable, save for those able to brave the privations of the monotonous life of the Llanos and who lead an animal existence caring for the huge cattle herds and who are consumed by yellow fever and malaria.

With this Bolivar had to deal. No other military commander had, up to this time, to contend with such privation and hardship; no other confronted such endless denials of nature with such affirmation of genius. Bolivar had set as his goal the liberation of America. Only he could accomplish this—he, the son of this majestic and cruel earth. Here was the "Man of Difficulties." World history has need of such men to face and overcome the obstacles avoided by the weak.

CHAPTER 10

The Liberator

*A*top the lonely crests of the Andes the condor makes his nest. After him is named the chief province of Colombia—Cundinamarca, the Land of the Eagle. And as the condor swoops upon his prey, so Bolivar now came swooping down to tear Venezuela from the grasp of the enemy.

Anyone who today attempts to consider Bolivar's prospects in that first great campaign must agree, with his opponents, that it was a foolhardy undertaking. Once again he was confronted with Monteverde, whose fighting forces, far superior to his own, were set up in two lines, one to the west and one to the east, from the borders of New Granada all the way to Caracas.[1] Each of the Spanish divisions consisted of some two thousand soldiers; and it was possible to shift their units from one line to another depending upon Bolivar's movements.

It was between these two lines that Bolivar saw a possible route of attack. Against the superior number of Spanish forces, Bolivar's numbered but 650 soldiers at the most.[2] But though his supplies were low, his weapons poor, his human element was excellent, consisting chiefly of Colombians, with a sprinkling of Venezuelan officers. Bolivar was in command, with Urdaneta as chief-of-staff. This was an officer of excellent bearing with an implicit sense of duty. Utterly dependable and

1 Rivas Vicuña: Vol. I. pp. 106 ff.
2 V. Lecuna: La Guerra a Muerte. B. d. H. Caracas. Vols. XVII and XVIII. O'Leary: Doc. Vol. XIII. p. 255.

devoted to Bolivar; Urdaneta had written his commander: "General, if it takes two men to liberate the fatherland, I am ready to follow you."[3] Girardot, a perfect example of Colombian patriotism, commanded the advance guard, while the rear guard was under José Félix Ribas, Bolivar's uncle.

It was necessary to resort to many different expedients in order to overcome the numerical superiority of the enemy. One of these was the vanquishing of enemy divisions one at a time, and for this Bolivar employed the elements of surprise, speed of action, and the swift exploitation of every advantage. Bolivar was inspired not only by his own blind faith in his ability and in the rightness of his cause, but also by the general dissatisfaction of a people who, having overcome their fear of a collapse, were horrified by the cruel despotism of Monteverde's regime. "Another earthquake," the outbreak of open rebellion against the Spaniards, was in sight. Bolivar saw that it was expedient to exploit to the full this unrest in favor of the republican cause.[4]

His plans were dictated by circumstances. His first task was to overcome Monteverde's western line, which he broke through in the direction of Mérida, towards the northeast; the whole province rose up to rally at his side. The Spanish leader relinquished his position with hardly a struggle. Bolivar entered Mérida on May 23, 1813, and was hailed as a liberator. "Our forces," he proclaimed to its citizens, "did not come to lay down the law to you—still less do they want to persecute the noble Americans. They have come to defend you against your enemies, the Spaniards of Europe."[5]

Meanwhile Bolivar's advance guard had chased the Spaniards to a different position towards Trujillo. With the winning of their second engagement, Trujillo too was free. Bolivar, who had managed to double the size of his little army during the three weeks spent in Mérida, entered the capital of the

3 O'Leary: Memorias. Vol. I. p. 122. R. Urdaneta: Memorias. Madrid, 1916. N. Urdaneta: Bolívar y Urdaneta. Caracas, 1941.
4 Cartas: Vol. I. pp. 47, 49. Lecuna: Campaña admirable. p. 177.
5 Proclamas: p. 30.

second border province in triumph on June 14. He had already
carried out the minimum program assigned to him by the
Tunja Congress. But as his own plans reached much further
afield, he left to Girardot the necessary follow up action and
set about marching across the borders of Trujillo towards
Caracas.

The operation of such a campaign could in no way be compared to the methodical planning and conduct of European
warfare. Bolivar was spurred by the ideal of hemispheric independence, and his purposes were indeed revolutionary, the
means he was forced to use unheard of. The problems of
organization and general strategy vanished before moral questions which crowded in on him and seemed more pressing.

Bolivar had grown up in the eighteenth century of humanitarian ideas, and this had become the hereditary possession of
his political train of thought. After the revolution had come
the counter revolution of Monteverde with its wake of inhuman
cruelties, slaughter of civilians, mass plunder, and finally the
many crimes following Miranda's surrender. Monteverde had,
as a matter of fact, himself written to the Spanish Regency-
Council that Caracas and other provinces loyal to the cause of
independence should be treated according to the "Law of Conquest." This meant the law of terror, confiscation of property,
despotism—all of which resulted in the death of thousands.[6]
Spaniards knew of no way to extinguish the flames of revolution other than by shedding the blood of Americans.
One of their officers wrote in 1812: "The plague that spreads
among them is thus being wiped out, and the army no longer
needs to waste its time in supervision."[7]

The old law that vengeance begets vengeance was working
here. Among the Venezuelans that had fled to Cartagena was
the passionate Antonio Briceño, called The Devil by his own
compatriots, and with whom Bolivar had quarreled violently

6 Blanco: Doc. Vol. IV. p. 623. O'Leary: Memorias. Vol. I. p. 106. Larrazabal:
Vol. I. pp. 144 ff. Baralt: Vol. I. p. 114. Parra Pérez: Primera República. Vol. II.
p. 420.
7 Blanco: Doc. Vol. IV. p. 627. Yanes: Relación. Vol. I. p. 153.

several years before. This irresponsible soldier started his own
personal war of revenge against the Spaniards and informed
his troops that their rank was to depend upon the number of
Spaniards produced. He who could show twenty Spanish heads
would be made ensign, he with thirty a lieutenant, and he
with fifty a captain.[8] Briceño himself succeeded in decapitating
two Spaniards during his first engagement. His army was
mown down, however, and he himself captured with seven of
his men. The Spaniards did not hesitate to shoot him as a
criminal.

Bolivar had considered this boastfulness of Briceño's a
method of terrorizing the enemy. But when he received the
heads of the two Spaniards from Briceño, accompanied by a
note written in blood, he was horrified and parted company
with him. In fact, he reported the insane intentions of this
man in a letter to Congress, since they struck him as both
unmilitary and unpolitic.[9] At the end of May, Bolivar had
promised indulgence to all deserters, prisoners, and scattered
troops of the enemy; but a week later he released the dread
proclamation calling for death to all enemies of American
independence.[10]

"Those henchmen," Bolivar announced in this document,
"who call themselves our enemies, have broken international
law." He remembered only too well the executions in Quito
and La Paz, the slaughter of thousands in Mexico, and the
living dead in the prisons of Puerto Cabello and La Guayra.
"But these victims shall be avenged, these henchmen exterminated. Our revenge shall equal the cruelties of the Spaniards,
for our forebearance is exhausted. Since our oppressors force
us into this deadly war, they will vanish from the face of America. And our soil will be cleansed of the monsters that sully it.

8 J. V. González: op. cit. p. 68.
9 O'Leary: Memorias. Vol. I. p. 124. O'Leary: Doc. Vol. XIII. p. 236.
10 O'Leary: Doc. Vol. XIII. pp. 246-47. Restrepo: H. d. R. C. Vol. II. p. 138.
See also V. Dávila: Investigaciones. pp. 5 ff. According to Dávila the first to begin
the war of extinction against the Spaniards was Francisco Espejo. He was followed
by Briceño. Bolivar, at least, limited the cruel and inhuman warfare to the enemies
of the republic.

Our hatred knows no bounds, and this is a war to the death."

In a solemn proclamation issued some while later, Bolivar offered the Spaniards one last chance for clemency. If they joined the Army of Independence or supported civilians that were on the right side, they would eventually be pardoned. In other words, those Spaniards who would serve the new state would be regarded as Americans—but all others, even those who were merely indifferent, would be wiped out. Bolivar, on the other hand, offered exemption from punishment to all Americans, whether they were traitors or deserters. "Spaniards and Canary Islanders," so ends the proclamation, "be prepared for certain death, even if you are merely indifferent.[11] Americans, you shall live, even if you are guilty." Was it personal cruelty that motivated Bolivar in the taking of this tremendous step—a man who but a few short days before had condemned as insane Briceño's barbarities? Bolivar did occasionally speak harsh words and commit acts of violence, but in a world where unbridled passion proved the rule, there is little proof of any action on his part attesting to sadistic pleasure in power.[12] It was rather the Spanish policy of extermination and the wicked cruelty practiced by Spain's soldiers that impelled him. An inevitable wake of theft, plunder, rape, and death followed any overcoming of revolt by the Spaniards, and Bolivar's decision was born of his desire for retaliation. The Spaniards, in their disregard for the life of innocent men, had brought on their own shoulders the blood now being shed. Bolivar could only follow up and bring his fight to a successful conclusion if he used the self-same weapons—he had to meet terror with terror.

This declaration of war to the death was, he thought, gratifying to the American soul. This war of independence was not only an international war between the mother country and her colonies. It was also a civil war and a race war, waged by Spaniards against their American born brothers, the Creoles, among whom there fermented, in sullen semi-consciousness,

11 O'Leary: Doc. Vol. XIII. pp. 251 ff.
12 M. A. Vila: El sentido jurídico penal en el Libertador, in El Heraldo, Caracas, March 3, 1941.

the dissatisfactions of the great mass of the colored races. Both sides sued for Creole support. The overwhelming majority of the people hardly suspected, at least in the beginning, the meaning of the bloody events in which they were involved. The concept of independence was alive at that time only among a small section of the upper class. The Spaniards prodded the masses, urging them to revenge themselves upon the Creoles, and the Creoles in turn incited the masses against the Europeans. Bolivar, in his decision to fight the war to a bitter end, had as his chief aim the dividing of the monarchist front into Spaniards on one side and Americans on the other. With his promise of immunity to Americans, he hoped to draw many over to his side. Many years later he remembered and wrote of the violent methods he had been forced to employ in his struggle to bring America into being. "To win four insurgents, who helped to liberate us, it was necessary to declare this war-to-the-death."[13] If it was not posssible to stir the dull, inert masses by ideas, he would appeal to their passions. *Acheronta movebo.*

"I decided to wage this *war to the death,* to take from the tyrants the matchless advantage their system of destruction had given them."[14]

This can explain Bolivar's actions, but they still can not be condoned. It was perhaps the Spaniards who conjured up this anarchistic situation; nevertheless it was outrageous to put oneself beyond all ethical and legal concepts. But in the lives of most great architects of state it is possible to find deeds where political will has outstepped the limits of right and decency: Richelieu, Cromwell, Frederick the Great, Napoleon, Bismarck all found it impossible to maintain an ethical balance. Only a narrow line divides actions dictated by necessity and actions which spring from arbitrariness. It will never be known whether Frederick's breaking of treaties or Napoleon's shooting of the prisoners in Haifa were acts of expediency or of personal unscrupulousness.

13 Cartas: Vol. II. p. 113. Lecuna: Guerra. Vol. XVIII. p. 19.
14 Cartas: Vol. I. p. 63.

Was this war to the death necessary, and did American independence depend upon it? Was the price Bolivar was forced to pay worthy of the objective? He was trying to achieve the restoration of the spiritual unity of America, but the result was the spread of destruction. If the Spaniards had aimed at the wiping out of the Creoles, it would have been Bolivar's duty to save them. Bolivar's actions have been condemned by many historians on this basis.[15]

However, there are arguments to explain Bolivar's decision. When his decree was published in 1813, Napoleon's rule was nearing its end and Spain was again in process of becoming an independent nation. With Church support Venezuela could well become the bridgehead for the reconquest of the colonies. This was the danger that Bolivar had recognized. He believed it was necessary to sacrifice his country to the cause of freedom, and he assumed the responsibility of a long and cruel conflict in which the only law was the law of destruction. Even if Spain's strength had not been shattered at this time on the violence of Venezuelan resistance, the fight for independence could only have continued longer and would not been any less cruel. Bolivar's decision, therefore, has some justification. As Ranke said: "Only absolute ideas can survive in the history of the world."

In judging Bolivar's policies we must remember that independence did not come to the people of South America as a gift from heaven. It arose rather from the bodies of hundreds of thousands whose blood had flowed into and contributed to the very vitals of democracy.[16]

With the liberation of the border provinces of Trujillo and Mérida, Bolivar's mission was ended. All further steps could only be undertaken after the careful consideration and consent on the part of the congressional committee assigned to this

15 Among the historians who have condemned Bolivar are Gil Fortoul, Mitre, and Cantú. See also C. Lozano y Lozano: Bolívar Maquiavélico. Antología Bolivariana. Bogotá, 1938.
16 C. Pereyra: Bolívar y Washington. Madrid, 1915. pp. 65, 101.

particular campaign of Bolivar's.[17] Fortunately, however, the committee did not put in an appearance. Bolivar had already attempted to convince the apprehensive politicians of the necessity of continuing his march—that after this occupation of the border lands the descent upon Caracas would be no more than a promenade. He was, however, unsuccessful, and was ordered to stay where he was.

Bolivar realized that if he obeyed orders both he and his troops would be lost, and Venezuela would be forever enslaved. He wrote to the congressional committee: "More than ever, we must act with speed and force. If we remain passive, or take one step backward, all will be lost and I will be responsible for nothing. Please note that all troops of New Granada, no matter under whose command, have already suffered many setbacks, and that only the army in which I have the honor to serve has suffered no losses. Fortune has willed to crown our efforts, and has decided to protect us. Let us not waste her benevolence."[18] For the second time in his short military career Bolivar determined to make his own decisions, even if they went over the heads of the officials.

Bolivar had rolled back Monteverde's first line and had pushed the enemy troops back towards the northwest. The chief danger now threatened from the second enemy line, whose striking power was centered in Barinas. In the operations that followed, both armies engaged in encircling movements that crossed like duelling sabres. Barinas, lying in the plains at the foot of the Andes, was Bolivar's goal. He did not take the direct route, but turned north to attack the enemy's rear as he descended from the Cordilleras. Monteverde, too, had ordered a rear attack upon Bolivar, hoping in this way to cut off his communication lines. But the Patriots who had the advantage of waging war in friendly country, learned beforehand of the enemy plans, and were thus able to vitiate them. Near Niquitao, Bolivar's rear guard, commanded by Ribas, was able to overcome a numerically superior enemy force, and the

17 O'Leary: Doc. Vol. XIII. pp. 237, 250. Yanes: Relaciónes. Vol. I. p. 110.
18 O'Leary: Doc. Vol. XIII. p. 271. O'Leary: Memorias. Vol. I. p. 132.

four hundred prisoners taken were immediately drafted into the army of the Independents.[19]

Bolivar himself had pushed on meanwhile towards Guanare. Following the steep and perilous trails along the mountain cliffs, he reached the hot and fertile plains. The Spanish commander at Barinas took his arrival to indicate the defeat of Monteverde's second line, and he fled towards the southwest, leaving all arms and supplies in the city. Bolivar occupied Barinas on July 6.[20] He found 200,000 pesos in the treasury of the tabacco administration, and was thus enabled to pay the back wages of his small army, which had in this short time tripled its size. Since Bolivar's means were limited, he ordered all revenues of the liberated provinces sent directly to headquarters, commanding also that no official was to receive pay during the campaign. Fortunately for the officials, however, the end was near.

Bolivar had dared to brave the web of the enemy's positions without allowing it to ensnare him, and his advance appeared irresistible. He had prevented the consolidation of enemy units, had beaten and pushed back their two wings, and now averted any threat of a flanking movement. Monteverde, himself, stood alone now between Bolivar and his objective—the entrance of the capital.

Bolivar faced an enemy formation in the form of a triangle, and once again had to overcome the Spaniards before they could consolidate their position.[21] He planned to advance in two columns—one to the west, commanded by Ribas, and the other to the east under his own command. The divisions were to meet in San Carlos and march together on Caracas.

Ribas found his way blocked by the united Spanish troops and was forced to make two bayonet attacks before he could split the enemy formation and disperse the Spaniards. He took possession of the cannons, munitions, and baggage, while his

19 R. Urdaneta: *op. cit.* p. 7. O'Leary: Doc. Vol. XIII. pp. 265, 286-87. Rivas Vicuña: Vol. I. p. 130.
20 O'Leary: Doc. Vol. XIII. pp. 286, 288, 292, 297. O'Leary: Memorias. Vol. I. p. 136. Proclamas: p. 37.
21 R. Urdaneta: *op. cit.* p. 9. Restrepo: H. d. R. C. Vol. II. p. 156. Rourke: *op. cit.* p. 101.

cavalry chased the fleeing enemy, whose leaders managed to escape to Puerto Cabello. He had accomplished an extraordinary feat, and his victories gave shining proof of military genius and the greatest courage and fighting ability. All that he accomplished, however, had been planned by Bolivar. The success of the campaign as a whole—*campaña admirable*—is due to both men.

Thanks to Ribas' successes Bolivar was able to step up his march on San Carlos, where the two forces met on July 28. On examining his troops Bolivar noted that they had now quadrupled; volunteers, deserters, and prisoners had effected this remarkable increase and the army now totaled 2,500 men.

Only twelve hundred Spanish troops blocked Bolivar's way to Caracas, and their discouragement was so great that their commander decided to retire to Valencia. Bolivar, for his part, wished to force the Spaniards into battle, and while the enemy retired in formation, making a slow but orderly retreat, Bolivar swung his cavalry to encircle their left flank and his infantry to attack their center. This was the first large scale battle under his own command and the fight lasted the whole day.

Bolivar felt it was necessary to block the enemy's retreat to Valencia and to do this he resorted to a rash expedient—albeit one highly characteristic of South American warfare. On each of two hundred selected horses he mounted two men, the rider and an infantryman, and this little band was sent to cut off the enemy. In the dark of night this coup was completely successful, and while the Spaniards found their road blocked, Bolivar himself attacked their center and flanks. In a few moments all resistance was broken and the enemy dispersed.[22] Almost all officers, the army commander among them, fell in the fight, while the soldiers were taken prisoner and went over to the republican ranks. Only a few were able to flee. The Battle of Taguanes was Bolivar's first great victory.

Monteverde was on his way to the front when he heard

22 R. Urdaneta: *op. cit.* p. 13. Larrazabal: Vol. I. p. 191. O'Leary: Memorias. Vol. I. p. 139. O'Leary: Doc. Vol. XIII. p. 321.

news of the defeat. He turned immediately and fled to Puerto Cabello, the only city offering possible prospect of prolonging resistance to Bolivar. Delegating pursuit of Monteverde to Girardot, Bolivar marched into Valencia on August 2 amid the jubilation of the inhabitants. He met with no further resistance and on August 4 was in Victoria, where he was met by a delegation from Caracas offering him submission. The campaign had been concluded.[23]

Among the men coming to Bolivar to sue for peace were two whom he knew: The Marquis de Casas León, in whose house Bolivar had hidden, and Iturbe, who had vouched for him with Monteverde. They were received with great politeness and found it easy to reach an agreement. Bolivar granted amnesty, cancelling all that had happened in the past, and as conditions he demanded the surrender of the city and province of Caracas and the port of La Guayra; he gave those not wishing to remain in an independent Venezuela the opportunity to leave. He refused at this time to reëstablish, as he was requested, the liberal Spanish Constitution of 1812, and announced that a form of government more compatible with the circumstances would be instituted. In his letter to the representative of Monteverde, Bolivar demanded ratification of the treaty within twenty-four hours and he added: "The noble Americans disregard the insults and give the enemy a rare example of their leniency and moderation. Those very enemies who had violated international law and had broken their most sacred covenants. This armistice will be strictly enforced, to the disgrace of the infamous Monteverde and the glory of the American name."[24]

Writing to Camilo Torres, Bolivar said: "Here your Excellency has the fulfillment of my promise to liberate my country. We have undertaken no battle during the past three months which we could not have won." On August 6 Bolivar entered Caracas.

Nine months had gone by since he had driven the Spaniards

23 Lecuna: Guerra. Vol. XVII. p. 368. O'Leary: Doc. Vol. XIII. p. 324.
24 O'Leary: Doc. Vol. XIII. p. 327. Mitre: San Martín. Vol. III. p. 344.

from the Magdalena River, and but three since he had set out
to liberate Venezuela. During this period, standing trial by fire
both as politician and soldier, he had organized the administration and breathed new faith into the people, who were won
over by his great and resounding proclamations. For him
Napoleon had not lived in vain, and like a stream of lava the
speeches, manifestos, and declarations flowed from his volcanic
temperament. He addressed everyone, the politician and the
soldier, the rich as well as the victims of the civil war. For this
man, yet but thirty years of age, nothing had any meaning or
reality other than the achievement of his goal. "These are the
emotions which must animate every republican who has neither
parents nor sons but only freedom and his country."[25]

Bolivar also took Napoleon as his model in war and remembered as examples the battles of Novi and Marengo. Bolivar
had never attended military school, and as a commander in the
field he was as autodidactic as he was in his role as statesman.
He was forced to learn in the field what belonged to the career
of a soldier, and circumstances not infrequently compelled him
to improvise. In a country split by the Andes, almost utterly
lacking in roads, he had marched twelve hundred kilometers. He had fought and won six battles, with an army
only on loan to him, in a campaign that can be favorably compared to any daring feat of war in Europe. By the genius of
Bolivar the Spanish rule was restricted once again to Coro and
Maracaibo, as it was before 1812 and the conquest of Monteverde. Governor Monteverde was now immured in Puerto
Cabello along with six thousand adherents to the Spanish
regime who feared Bolivar's revenge.

The republican leader has been criticized for turning aside
to Caracas instead of continuing to attack Puerto Cabello, where
it would have been easy to wipe out the remaining Spanish
resistance, as the port was unprepared for a state of siege. He
devoted himself instead, his critics say, to the enjoyment of
power and thus lost his opportunity to winning a more com-

25 Cartas: Vol. I. p. 53.

plete victory. Undeniably, Bolivar possessed a flair for the theatrical, and the idea of marching into Caracas in the role of conquering hero flattered and appealed to him. It was only human for him to enjoy the taste of his victory cup after the privations of the past year.

But it was not sentimental motives alone that impelled him to go to Caracas.[26] He had become convinced, by the deep-seated animosity between Republicans and Monarchists which divided Venezuela into two irreconcilable camps, that it was of the greatest necessity to create a center of government. This could only be in Caracas. Only there could Bolivar find maintenance for his army, for in this country only the capital was capable of bearing the burden of quartering a large number of troops. There was real and constant danger that without essential supplies the army that had been gathered so speedily would disintegrate at the same rate. Further, Bolivar's best troops were not Venezuelans but had been put at his disposal by Colombia, and the neighboring government had soon to be freed of this burden.

Actually, the danger of Spanish reaction in Venezuela would not have been averted even if Bolivar had taken Puerto Cabello, since Coro and Maracaibo were intact and still in the hands of the Monarchists. The troops that Bolivar had not destroyed completely but only dispersed reformed again on the plains. The capital appeared the logical point to resist them —from there the forces of the Patriots could burst forth to destroy what remained of Spanish rule.

In addition to his military reasons, Bolivar had very definite political motives for settling in Caracas. In the course of his plans for the liberation of his country from the west, a group of men, fired by the same objective and under the leadership of Mariño had arisen in the east, and they too had had their successes. "I am afraid," Bolivar wrote to Camillo Torres, "that our illustrious brothers-in-arms in Cumaná and Barcelona will liberate our capital before we can share that glory with them.

26 Rivas Vicuña: Vol. I. p. 138. Lecuna: Campaña admirable. p. 166.

But we shall fly, and I hope no liberator will tread the ruins
of Caracas before me." [27] In this last phrase lies an honesty
rarely shown by statesmen. Bolivar, from the earliest days of
the revolution, had wished to lead it. He wanted to liberate
his country without sharing any of the glory. It was not only
fame he coveted, but power. Today the liberator of his country,
tomorrow its ruler—the glory of the *libertador* and the power
of a dictator, that was his dream for the future. This campaign
of 1813, which had developed Bolivar from a fugitive into the
saviour of his country, saw the beginning of the myth created
around the person of Simon Bolivar by the South American
people. And ever since that time he has been *The Liberator*.

27 Larrazabal: Vol. I. p. 188.

CHAPTER 11

The Dictator

*B*olivar entered Caracas at the head of his troops on August 7, 1813. The entire city had turned out to welcome him and from all sides he heard their cries: "Long live our Liberator! Long live New Granada! Long live Venezuela!" From the midst of the excited, enthusiastic crowd stepped a group of young girls, dressed in white and with flowers in their arms, who rushed up to the youthful general, seizing the reins of his horse. Bolivar dismounted and from their hands received the victor's crown. Bells rang out the victory, guns shot salvos into the air, bands played hymns to fatherland and victory, while the populace strewed flowers in the path of the army. Bolivar's friends threw themselves into his arms. After the dreary silence imposed on Caracas by Monteverde's despotism, the jubilation now filling the streets was indescribable. The persecuted dared to leave their hiding places, the prisoners returned to life, and everything possessed the quality of a dream.[1]

After his entrance into the city, Bolivar wrote to the Commission in New Granada: "When my soul has recovered from the emotion of seeing my country liberated, and from the many attentions which have distracted me, and from the host of my

1 Lecuna: Guerra. Vol. XVII. p. 374. Entrada triunfal del general Bolívar en Caracas. Gazeta de Caracas. No. 1. The statement that Bolivar made his entrance into Caracas on a gilded chariot drawn by twelve girls from the city's aristocracy, is an invention of du Coudray Holstein: Memoires, London, 1830. p. 151. It is difficult to understand how Mancini, and later Rourke, could have accepted such a lie on its face value.

185

fellow-citizens who are congratulating themselves and me on the resurrection of the Republic, I shall speak more explicitly about many things which now demand our attention."[2] On that same day he proclaimed to the people of Caracas the goal of his victory—the reëstablishment of liberty.[3]

No one expected Bolivar to return to the methods of government responsible for the downfall of the First Republic. He had, however, promised his protectors in Colombia that he would reconstruct the Federal Constitution in Venezuela. Circumstances and his own political thinking made him unable to keep such a promise.

Fearing reprisals on the part of the victors, the Spaniards had left no sort of government within the capital. Bolivar's first step was to see that public safety was guarded. He then faced the problem of creating a new form of government, as well as that of gathering his forces for the final and conclusive destruction of Spanish military power. For the enemy was still abroad in the land.

Bolivar announced first to his fellow citizens the urgent necessity of political reforms, and he called a meeting of respected and experienced men to discuss those forms of government that seemed possible under these conditions.[4] The Liberator himself declared that he wished for no other assignment than the leading of his soldiers to whatever location the salvation of his country demanded. But nothing, he added, would deflect him from his first and only ambition, that of serving the cause of freedom and the glory of Venezuela.

Ustariz, who had been ordered by Bolivar to draw up an outline for the constitution, suggested that the law-making and executive powers be given over to the commander of the army. Under his leadership the officials were to decide what problems were to concern government and national economy.

As far as foreign policy was concerned, Ustariz laid em-

2 O'Leary: Doc. Vol. XIII. p. 334.
3 Proclamas: pp. 41, 44, 48. Yanes: Relación. Vol. I. pp. 110 ff.
4 Proclamas: p. 47.

phasis on as close unity as possible between Venezuela and New Granada. His was the project of a dictatorship, with few restrictions in regard to powers, controlled only by mandate and necessitated by circumstances.[5] In this project Bolivar found corroboration for his own plans: "During the civil war and internal revolution, our administration must be reduced to the simplest denominator. From it we derive strength and speed," he wrote to Camilo Torres. "When the soil of Venezuela is free of the enemy, and my mission is ended, the representatives will meet and choose a president of all the states. This meeting will arrange the union with New Granada, if that has not been accomplished by that time." The letter ends with a grandiose anticipation of his future career: "It will then be my fate to lead our invincible soldiers against the enemies of American independence." [6]

Bolivar assumed the role of dictator, and named three men most loyal to him as secretaries of state for the administration of all public affairs: for finance and policy he named twenty-two-year-old Muñoz Tebar, whom he had known since the days of the Patriotic Society; as Minister of War he named Tomás Montilla, a leader of the revolution from the beginning; and as Minister of the Interior, Rafael Diego Mérida. A special post was created later for the control of public revenue, and this was entrusted to a brother of General Ribas. To him Bolivar gave the top command of the province and the capital of Caracas.

The interim government was thus created within a very short time, founded upon military prestige. To give this prestige a boost, as it were, it was important and necessary to wrest from the hands of the Spaniards a weapon that they had used to hoodwink the ignorant and fanatic masses, to turn them against the cause of freedom—the Church. The Archbishop of Caracas had, in a pastoral letter, attempted to persuade Americans to give acknowledgment only to the Monarchist govern-

5 O'Leary: Doc. Vol. XIII. pp. 343 ff. Plan del Gobierno provisional para Venezuela. Lecuna: Guerra. Vol. XVII. pp. 427, 440. Rivas Vicuña: Vol. I. p. 147.
6 O'Leary: Doc. Vol. XIII. p. 361.

ment. Bolivar demanded that he retract these words in another
pastoral letter, going as far in his request as to threaten the
Archbishop's life if he did not immediately obey.[7]

Bolivar, however, was well aware that he would also have
to penetrate through to the lower clergy, whose influence from
pulpit and confessional was both unpredictable and uncontrollable. "This is not the time," he wrote to the Archbishop,
"to mock the laws of the government. The entire weight of the
law will fall upon those who break it." And he ordered all
priests to explain the principles of independence to their con-
gregations not less than once weekly.[8]

The attempt to win over the clergy to the side of the Patriots by force or persuasion was part of Bolivar's effort to create
a public opinion that reflected the ideals of the American Revolution. Throughout his life his task was to breathe a soul into
the clay of American existence, and his many proclamations
and appeals must be judged in this light. They were not born
primarily of a wish for a show or self glorification, but rather
had the purpose of instilling into the apathetic masses a national conscience and a continental consciousness. Bolivar
alone could do this. Bolivar alone could snatch them from their
day-dreaming and guide them into an active life.

His plan is revealed to us in yet another aspect, that of his
struggle against the federal idea. "We would spoil all our efforts and waste all our sacrifices," he told the Federalists, "if
we returned to the complicated forms of government which
caused our ruination. How can small, poor, and impotent lo-
calities demand sovereignty? Never has the division of power
created governments and caused them to endure. Only the
concentration of power invites respect, and I have liberated
Venezuela in order to create such a system."[9]

Bolivar's attention, however, was not solely directed towards
Venezuela, but to America and the world at large. While striving to create faith in ultimate victory among the amorphous

7 O'Leary: Doc. Vol. XIII. p. 351.
8 Cartas: Vol. I. p. 58.
9 Cartas: Vol. I. p. 72.

and ignorant masses, he was attempting also to win the confidence of other nations. He invited foreigners to settle in Venezuela. In a letter to the British Governor of Curaçao concerning the spirit of the American revolution, he contrasted this spirit to the one animating the Spaniards aiming solely at the enslavement of an entire people. Finally, he addressed himself to all the peoples of the earth.[10] So much for the ideological and sentimental part of the great work initiated by Simon Bolivar. But in order to endure and not follow in the footsteps of the ill-fated First Republic, the Second Republic needed stern and practical measures.

In the eyes of many of his compatriots, Bolivar's legal claim to rule lay in the triumph of his "blitzkrieg," which had put half of the country at his feet within three months. His strength had its basis in his army. Enthusiasm is the bloom of a single day, the world over, and this was particularly the case in South America, where exultation and depression followed each other in rapid succession. Bolivar, on entering the city of Caracas, won the hearts of his fellow citizens. He felt that his first task was to weld the army into a dependable, cohesive unit that nothing could threaten. But here the will of the dictator was confronted with obstacles that Bolivar struggled in vain to overcome. Venezuela was hardly able to support a standing army. Her cities had been destroyed, her land depopulated, foreign trade was paralyzed, and internal commerce almost non-existent. As state revenues dwindled, expenditures mounted. It was indisputably necessary to find a new source for bolstering the economy—an economy able to support the continuation of the war against the Spaniards. Bolivar extended his dictatorship, therefore, to take in the national economy.

While taxes set during colonial days were still in force, the entire fiscal system had been destroyed by the confusion surrounding the revolution. The tobacco tax alone gave promise of greater returns; it was organized in the form of a state monopoly. Trade in contraband had, however, taken on such pro-

10 O'Leary: Doc. Vol. XIII. pp. 365, 379.

portion that among the earliest of Bolivar's measures was one directed against such malpractices.[11] A death sentence was imposed on all guilty of tax evasion or secret dealings, and their property was to be confiscated by the state.

Bolivar had already appealed to the patriotism of his fellow citizens by asking for voluntary contributions. Those unable to comply were to donate objects of military value, while those who could do neither were requested to enter the services of the Republic without pay, content only to have their names inscribed in the great book of the Fatherland's glory. State employees were to share their salaries with the soldiers who were under the heaviest burden.[12] It is easy to see that Bolivar had learned much from the French Revolution. His aim was to control the entire nation—its people and their resources. His will was totalitarian.

Nevertheless, these measures were not sufficient to cover the army's expenses. But Bolivar's creative spirit was able to find a new expedient, and in October, 1813, he linked income taxes directly to the budget of the army. All property owners and store owners were to pay to the State the cost of supporting at least one soldier. Not even the clergy was exempt from this tax, which was payable in advance. The results of these measures were considerable, and it is worthy of mention that many Venezuelans paid twice and even three times the amount demanded by the law.[13]

Six days following Bolivar's entry into Caracas, he ordered an administrative reform that complimented his economic policy. Bolivar stated that every official held his post only to serve the state, not to attract attention by ostentation nor to obtain special privileges. He attacked vehemently that social disease, in South America called *empleomanía,* the mania to become employed by the State. "A crowd of candidates surround the public officials, and rob them of time needed to

11 Lecuna: Guerra. Vol. XVII. p. 387. O'Leary: Doc. Vol. XIII. p. 358.
12 O'Leary: Doc. Vol. XIII. pp. 335 ff.
13 O'Leary: Doc. Vol. XIII. p. 400. Lecuna: Guerra. Vol. XVII. p. 420.

organize the government. . . . But there is no lack of good men, who are satisfied with the bare necessities of life. I shall make use of these, to stimulate all branches of the administration." Thus did Bolivar succeed in reducing by one-half the administration's expenditures.[14]

No matter how greatly his plans were determined by economic necessity, the idea of liberty remained Bolivar's highest ideal. He who took up this fight was not a mercenary, and Bolivar found his reward in a sphere where money had little value. His great model, Napoleon, had created the Legion of Honor, and Bolivar emulated Napoleon by the formation of the Order of the Liberators of Venezuela for those able to claim title to that honor by virtue of a long succession of victories. The emblem of the order was a seven pointed star, symbol of the Venezuelan provinces; and among the first to receive it were Ribas, Urdaneta, and Girardot.[15]

This name—Order of Liberators—possessed a double meaning politically, for it was as Libertador that the inhabitants of Mérida had greeted Bolivar in May of 1813. He, who was now Commander-in-Chief of the army and Dictator of his country, preferred this title to all others. In creating the Order of the Liberators he appeared to put his companions in arms on an equal footing with himself, thus catering to their sensibilities and their vanity.

Eager as he was to maintain the democracy of the battlefield and the brotherhood of death, he was almost forced to assume in the hierarchy the position due him. When the country's leaders assembled in Caracas in mid-October to discuss the drafting of the constitution, their first act was to approve Bolivar's self-chosen rank. They named him Liberator of Venezuela.[16]

Bolivar called these same men together a few weeks later to report to them on his progress. They met in the Church of St. Francis, together with the high ecclesiastics, the representatives

14 O'Leary: Doc. Vol. XIII. p. 340. Lecuna: Guerra. Vol. XVII. pp. 365, 419.
15 O'Leary: Doc. Vol. XIII. p. 402.
16 O'Leary: Doc. Vol. XIII. p. 395. According to T. Febres Cordero, Archivo de Historia y Variedades, Vol. I, p. 288, 1930, Bolivar had already been greeted as Liberator when he made his entrance into Mérida.

of the University and other academic professions. Bolivar, accompanied by officers and men of his staff, read his report on the activities of the government, and this report was approved. He then asked to be relieved of his post as Dictator.[17]

"Fellow-citizens," read the most vital part of his speech, "I have come to put the control of the law into your hands. I have come with the intention of preserving your sacred rights. . . . A successful soldier does not earn the right to command in his native country. He is not the judge of the laws or of the government. He is the defender of its liberty. His honor must be one with that of the state, and his pride must be satisfied if he has worked for the happiness of his country. . . . I beg you to relieve me of a burden that is too great for my strength."

Bolivar played this role of selfless Republican remarkably well. Others, he said, were better fitted to rule Venezuela, and he seemed reluctant to accede to the will of the assembly. He only agreed to retain this highest of authority until the worst dangers to the State had passed.

If we fail to hear the real tone of sincerity in these assurances, we would be guilty of misjudging this great and lofty soul. Bolivar spoke in real sincerity to his fellow citizens when he said: "Flee from this country where one man holds all the power, it is a land of slaves" and when he said: "You call me Liberator of the Republic, I shall never be its oppressor. . . ." In his heart he was still the pupil of Rousseau and the successor of Napoleon. True, he wished for power and glory and was convinced of his ability to rule. But he also wished to serve the ideals to which he had dedicated his life. This duality had been present in his soul since his youth. All his life he was to try to overcome it. Again and again he was to assume power in the state as a matter of course only to reject it as a temptation. Again and again he was to resign only to allow himself to be persuaded to take again the helm of the ship of state. "My emotions are in terrible conflict with my authority," he stated.

17 O'Leary: Doc. Vol. XIII. p. 410. Acta popular, celebrado en Caracas el día 2 de Enero de 1814. See also B. d. H. Caracas. Vol. V. No. 18. p. 365.

"Fellow-citizens, believe me, this sacrifice is more painful than the loss of my life would be." And as though he felt some might have guessed at this inner conflict that throughout his life existed in his soul, he went on: "I beg you, do not believe that my moderation is meant to deceive you. . . . I swear to you that I am sincere in what I say. I am no Sulla who brings grief and bloodshed to his country. But I shall imitate the Dictator of Rome in one respect . . . in the selflessness with which he renounced all power and returned to private life."

Bolivar remained the Dictator, but no one can doubt that this was the only possible solution at the time. Judgment of his deeds cannot falter. Finding chaos, he did what was necessary to give it form. Realizing that hesitation would mean destruction, as it had three years earlier, he labored impetuously, despotically, and irresistibly. His dictatorship spared neither public conscience nor wealth, but it was nevertheless a dictatorship of training—intended to mature a people that was immature. His dictatorship should not be compared to or confused with the abuse of power that characterizes the totalitarian tyrants of our own day.

During those first weeks his conduct aroused much admiration, but although he was the center of a series of celebrations dedicated to pleasure and adventure, he was unremittingly active. He made decisions, he organized, he dictated letter after letter, manifesto followed manifesto, decree issued upon decree. This thirty-year-old man who had in but a few months changed from a fugitive to the ruler of his country, had an ear for all and a heart for the underprivileged. During the first days of his rule, he found time to send the following message to the governor of Barinas: "Whatever you can do for this woman would express the gratitude of a heart that, like my own, cannot forget her who nursed him like a mother. It was she who held me on her lap during the first months of my life. Is there any need for higher recommendation for him who knows how to love and be grateful, as I do?"[18]

18 Cartas: Vol. I. p. 60.

Bolivar was Dictator of Venezuela. But in reality he was but half a dictator, master only of territories conquered by him in the western part of the country. What was taking place in the eastern regions?

Bolivar had suggested, in his speech to the Assembly, that General Santiago Mariño be given his command. Why did the Liberator select Mariño; on what accomplishments did he base his estimates of the soldier? When Monteverde took Caracas in August, 1812, the eastern provinces of Venezuela had fallen to him without a struggle. He had appointed as commander Francisco Cerveris, a man whose one ambition was the extermination to the last man of all Creoles. "Not one who falls into my hands shall escape."[19] he wrote to Monteverde. Nevertheless, a small group of Patriots had eluded him successfully—a group of young men whose names live in the history of Venezuelan independence: Francisco Bermúdez, bold, energetic, and uncontrollable; Manuel Piar, a mulatto from Curaçao, ambitious, brave, and violent; and above all, Santiago Mariño, born on the island Margarita and related to some of the finest families in the east. Unafraid, no more than twenty-four years of age, he was full of high aspirations and was a born leader; he was, however, vain and inclined to the theatrical.[20]

Mariño had fled to British Trinidad, but he was ill-received there and treated as a rebel. However, he considered this name of rebel an honorable title in his determination to liberate Venezuela. The audacity of his plan was no less than that of Bolivar, perhaps even greater, since he was not backed by the support of a friendly government. Mariño was only able to gather around him forty-five men, and their equipment consisted of five old guns. The group elected Mariño their leader and signed a declaration obligating themselves to land in Venezuela and restore the dignity of the nation: they would live or die for the glory of their cause.[21]

19 Blanco: Doc. Vol. IV. p. 623.
20 O'Leary: Memorias. Vol. I. p. 148. La guerra de Independencia en la Provincia de Cumaná. B. d. H. Caracas. Vol. XVII. No. 65. p. 25.
21 Blanco: Doc. Vol. IV. p. 752. Yanes: Relación. Vol. I. p. 104. See Mariño' Proclamation in Lecuna: Campaña admirable. p. 183.

This declaration was signed on January 11, 1813, and the next day Mariño and his companions landed on the coast of their native land. After they successfully attacked a small point in the port of Paria, the natives joined them and the Spaniards fled. Mariño increased his forces and his arms and forced the Spanish commander to retire. Monteverde, beginning to fear for the fate of the province of Cumaná, sent five hundred men under Zuazola, a Basque and one of the most bloodthirsty leaders of the Spanish counter-revolution. But the patriots had by this time entrenched themselves; reports of Zuazola's barbarities served but to fortify their courage. Finally, Monteverde himself attempted to attack them from the sea, but he was unsuccessful, barely escaping capture and allowing rich booty and much military equipment to fall into Mariño's hands. His flight resembled a rout. Almost simultaneously with the surrender of the west to Bolivar, the eastern areas of Venezuela lay open to Mariño's attack. He received reinforcements from the sea, collected a small flotilla, and took Cumaná on August 2. All that was left to the Spaniards in the east was the port of Barcelona under command of Field Marshal Cajigal, and he was completely discouraged by the news of the double victory of the revolution in the east and west. He fled to Guayana, leaving only one hundred men behind with instructions to commence guerrilla tactics against the Patriots. This group was led by José Tomás Boves and Francisco Morales, commander of the Legion of Hell. Mariño occupied Barcelona on August 19 and appointed himself dictator of the east. His representative was Manuel Piar.

Mariño was exceptionally young and most susceptible to flattery. His friends were not slow to serve him the nectar which he craved, and his government was more personal in character, more military than political. No one could question his fearlessness, but a penetrating intelligence was not his. He had promised to liberate Venezuela, and he now began to fulfill this promise in the grand manner. However his progress was impeded by jealousy of his rival, for Mariño was not inclined

to come to any kind of understanding with Bolivar. Bolivar,
as we know, was not free of envy himself. But he realized that
now that his goal was achieved, now that he had entered
Caracas as liberator, it was doubly important to reach an agreement with Mariño. Bolivar was better able to judge the situation at this point than was his young rival. The war was not
over. Though the Spaniards were dispersed, they were not
annihilated. In the future the advantage would lie with which-
ever of the opposing forces was first able to gather his host
together.

Bolivar attempted to woo Mariño. "The individual and
collective security of these states depends on our working together," Bolivar wrote him. "Foreign and domestic enemies
are ready to attack them. Treachery, deceit, folly—all are in
motion to subjugate us once again."[22] He placed emphasis on
the fact that they must aim at the creation of an administration
for the entire country, and that to this end both armies should
join forces. But Mariño would not agree to this, proposing
a partitioning of Venezuela into eastern and western blocs.
Bolivar attempted to convince him that this would only succeed in forming two separate states unable to survive alone
with the result of making the name of Venezuela a laughing-
stock. "Divided, we will be weaker and less respected by both
our enemies and the neutral countries. Unification under a
single government would strengthen us and make us produc-
tive for all."[23]

Bolivar, soldier and politician, possessed a great gift for
dealing with people, and he knew how to get at men through
their weaknesses. He tried, therefore, to bolster his political
reasoning by *argumentum ad hominem*. He had long since
been aware that Mariño's attitude was caused by his vanity,
that he belonged to those men for whom the semblance of
power is as great, if not greater, than its actuality. Bolivar,
therefore, flattered him with the prospect of becoming presi-

22 O'Leary: Doc. Vol. XIII. p. 388.
23 Cartas: Vol. I. pp. 85 ff., 88.

dent of the new state. But he spoke to deaf ears and was
forced to accept the partition of Venezuela. This lack of success in reaching agreement with Mariño was of great hindrance
to Bolivar's plans for the future. Whereas he had thought to
win him over as an ally, he realized that he now had a bordering state that was barely neutral. Mariño's refusal to Bolivar's
proposals for unification meant that the Liberator was forced
to overcome singlehanded the monarchist reaction.[24]

The existence in Venezuela of people of Spanish origin presented Bolivar with a double problem—that of military danger,
and of political threat to the Republic. This problem had to
be met and overcome. Following Mariño's refusal to coöperate,
Bolivar allowed the Spaniards to feel the full weight of hatred
by the Republicans. He felt weakened, and he therefore fortified his dictatorship. There no longer was any question of
forbearance; Spaniards were incarcerated in the prisons of La
Guayra and a rigid control was imposed upon them. By these
measures Bolivar hoped to obviate all threat of an uprising.

Bolivar also resorted to more machiavellian methods. He
created a spy system with his own agents forging contacts with
dissenters. He planned not only to ferret out enemies of the
State, but also to convict them of conspiracy—an ancient trick
used by all chiefs of police, from Walsingham to Fouché and
Heinrich Himmler. Bolivar succeeded in catching some in his
trap, for on September 21 some sixty Europeans and Americans
were put to death.[25]

Bolivar was driven to such extreme measures not only by
the internal political threat but also by the existing military
situation. After the fall of Caracas, the position of the Monarchists appeared at first hopeless, controlling as they did but a
very narrow coastal strip. This strip, however, possessed three
ports through which help could come from the mother country, from the Antilles, or from Central America. In addition,
the Spaniards occupied the only fortress in a country other-

24 Restrepo: H. d. R. C. Vol. II. p. 173. Rivas Vicuña. Vol. I. p. 160.
25 O'Leary: Doc. Vol. XIII. p. 357. J. V. Gonzales: op. cit. pp. 105, 110.

wise utterly lacking in fortification. Bolivar was well aware that the key to every future action lay in Puerto Cabello.

He had actually begun to lay siege to Puerto Cabello prior to his successful entry into Caracas, and at the same time he had sent one division to the west to check the troops stationed in Coro. He even thought to build against possible attack from the plains. His whole military position, therefore, was in the form of a wide circle whose focal point was Caracas.[26] His most urgent problem, however, remained the capture of Puerto Cabello.

Immediately after his triumph, Bolivar had hoped to force Monteverde to capitulate. He used anarchistic warfare as an excuse to draw out the negotiations.[27] But he was mistaken in his evaluation of Monteverde's character, for the Spaniard answered him with all the pride of his nation that there could be no dealings with rebels. Bolivar, alternating between threats and promises, still tried to reach some understanding. He proposed an exchange of prisoners, threatening that if this were not accepted he would eradicate all Spaniards from the soil of Venezuela. Still Monteverde remained adamant. At the beginning of September, Bolivar was still confident regarding the outcome of the war, considering the fall of Puerto Cabello imminent and assured. But during the course of the same month, fate turned the tide in the Spaniards' favor. Bolivar was unable to achieve any decisive action over the defenders of the fortress.

Word had come early in September that a large convoy from Spain was on its way to aid Monteverde, and the republican forces determined to capture it. The fleet comprised numerous warships and thirteen transports. Ribas, commander of Caracas, in his attempt to seize the expedition caused the royal flag to be hoisted on the forts of La Guayra and, taking Spanish officers from their prisons, forced them to act out the role of envoys. The ships were nearing the port and the ruse seemed about

26 Rivas Vicuña: Vol. I. p. 161.
27 Lecuna: Guerra. Vol. XVII. pp. 379, 433, 435. Blanco: Doc. Vol. IV. p. 725. Larrazabal: Vol. I. pp. 198 ff. R. Urdaneta: *op. cit.* p. 21.

to succeed. But the Spaniards became suspicious too early, and the convoy was able to escape to Puerto Cabello.[28]

This timely arrival of twelve hundred well-disciplined and well-equipped troops gave a considerable advantage to Monteverde, and Bolivar found himself forced to give up his siege. For his part, Monteverde renewed the tactics he had employed successfully the year before against Miranda. Pushing out from Puerto Cabello, he attempted to crush the enemy. But the patriots threw themselves on him with fury and defeated him at Barbula on September 30, driving him back behind the walls of Puerto Cabello. Wounded, the Spanish commander was forced to yield his command and the war passed over him.

The victory at Barbula cost Bolivar one of his best officers, the young Colombian, Girardot, who had fallen in battle. While hoisting the republican standard over the enemy's position, a bullet struck him in the forehead. Bolivar ordered national mourning for a month and ordered the name of Girardot inscribed as benefactor of the country in all the communities of Venezuela. His heart was taken to Caracas for burial in the Cathedral. While his remains were being sent to Colombia, Bolivar himself took the heart of the young hero to the capital. In solemn procession the army marched across the silent city. The soldiers had laid down their arms, and each man carried a flaming torch as sign of mourning. Following a requiem mass in the Cathedral, the heart of Girardot was placed in a golden urn and buried in a crypt. In a letter to the young man's father Bolivar expressed the impression he wished to create with all these honors he had accorded his comrade: "His memory will live in the hearts of all Americans as long as national honor is the law of their lives and as long as lasting glory can attract noble hearts."[29]

Lasting glory—this is what Bolivar himself wished. He had

28 Lecuna: Guerra. Vol. XVII. pp. 416-17. R. Urdaneta: *op. cit.* p. 22. Larrazabal: Vol. I. p. 216. Baralt: Vol. I. pp. 192-93. Yanes: Relación. Vol. I. p. 124.

29 Lecuna: Guerra. Vol. XVII. p. 445. N. E. Navarro: El corazón de Girardot. B. d. H. Caracas. Vol. XII. Nos. 46, 47. Cartas: Vol. I, p. 68.

thought it already achieved, but it now threatened to vanish. Once more the life of the Second Republic, begun so gloriously, was seriously endangered. The masses vacillated from one side to the other, and the pressure of deprivations constantly imposed upon them weighed more heavily than the more ephemeral intoxication of victory. The people were accustomed to obeying the Spaniards, and with each new reverse of the Republic they were more inclined to return to their colonial form of government. It became increasingly apparent that the hope of peace was merely an illusion. While Bolivar stood in the center of the country, the Spanish army had wedged itself between Venezuela and Colombia so that contact between the sister republics was disrupted. Heavy clouds darkened the horizon, and from the valleys of the Orinoco was approaching a mighty storm. A new phase of the revolution was beginning —the uprising in the Plains.

CHAPTER 12

Rebellion in the Plains

*I*t would indeed be a vain undertaking to describe what now occurred in chronological order; the picture would remain incomprehensible. There were battles that decided nothing; armies that were destroyed one day to rise again the next. Military movements fluctuated hither and yon, like a wave, from the cliffs of the Andes through the vast plains to the shore of the Atlantic. And wherever this wave struck it buried beneath its waters all life—destroying the villages, ruining property,— whole cities were annihilated or deserted by their terrified inhabitants. There were endless and indescribable atrocities— rape, murder, church theft, and the torture of prisoners.

Who were the victims, who the henchmen? Was it Spaniards who hoped to wipe out the Americans, or Venezuelans turning on their erstwhile masters? If the fronts had been more sharply defined, the recounting of events that took place during these months would be an easier task. Iberians fought Iberians, Venezuelans stood against Venezuelans—an inextricable tangle of impulses, greed, and demands. An apocalyptic vision of hunger, death, and disease. In South America's history this period is known as *la guerra a muerte*—the war to extinction. It has often been described in anecdotal and picturesque detail.

What explains this prolonged outburst of human and sub-human passions that hurled an entire country into tears and bloodshed? We have seen the host of problems that crowded

201

Bolivar after his initial victory. He had reconquered his native land. But in spite of the measures imposed upon it by its Dictator, the country was unsatisfied. His victory had resulted more from the element of surprise, the swiftness of his attacks, than from the actual superiority of his forces.[1] It became too evident, following his victory, how small his fighting forces really were, how inadequate was their support, how poor their weapons.

The enemies of South American independence were able to benefit by the opportune international situation. Coincidental with Bolivar's march to Caracas, Napoleon found himself surrounded by allied armies in the Central European area. The French left the Iberian Peninsula and Spain found her hands free to begin the subjugation of her rebellious colonies. As it had been in the early days of the revolution, news from the Old World caused far-reaching repercussions in the Western Hemisphere. The Spaniards and their partisans in Venezuela gained new hope and were convinced that if they could only hold out until the land of their origin sent help, the victory would be theirs. Meanwhile, they seized upon every means, even the most desperate, to prevent the fall of the bastions of monarchy into the hands of the rebels.

Under these circumstances the military situation was acute and was deteriorating for the rebels. Bolivar's inability to create a new army with rapidity prevented him from exploiting his earlier successes. He lacked money, he lacked weapons, and he lacked manpower. Only in a few cities—Mérida, Trujillo, and Caracas—did he find the response he sought. The great majority of the population, at first indifferent to the independence movement, became later actually antagonistic. They were unable to believe that this little band of Republicans could hold out against powerful Spain. Here a new element enters which was to become of vital importance.

Hitherto the revolt against Spain had been a movement of urban forces, and the conflict of the first four years had been

1 Lecuna: Guerra. Vol. XVIII. p. 250.

for the cities. Caracas, Valencia, Victoria, Coro, Maracaibo, and Puerto Cabello—these names stood as milestones of victory and defeat. But now came an unheard-of development—country-wide revolution. It set fire to the Plains, and the rural population rose up, the Plains rose up, but not to support the Revolution. On the contrary. Under Spanish leadership these fresh energies were thrown into the scale on the side of hereditary rule. War to extinction was only a program when declared by Bolivar on June 8, 1813. It became a reality when carried out by the inhabitants of the Plains.

A tragic day dawned, and at its close the Second Republic lay buried under the rubble of cities, raped by barbaric forces rampant in the land. In order to explain satisfactorily the eruption of these forces with which no one had thought to reckon and which no one had foretold, we must examine the source of their being. Only a sociological account can explain the phenomenon of this war to the death.

There are two vital characteristics in the geographic organization of South America. In the west, along the Pacific coast, the corrugated Andean chain rises to a height of seven thousand meters. To the east stretch the vast plains of the valleys of the Orinoco, the Amazon, and the La Plata. The valley of the Amazon is covered by a dense, impenetrable jungle, but the valleys of the La Plata and the Orinoco possess a different character. The Pampas and the Llanos are limitless grass steppes unbroken by trees. Here are the greatest pastures in the world, where grasses grow to the height of man—so that the beasts are lost within them.

Descending from the highlands of the Andes into these plains, one sees a picture to plumb the depths of the soul. Emerging from the mountains, one finds a land as mighty as the ocean, endless as the desert, in which man all but vanishes. There is hardly an elevation in sight, just a hill here and there covered over with bushes. The great rivers of the Orinoco, Meta, Apure, and Arauca turn in the rainy seasons into lakes which flood the valleys and become regions of malignant fevers.

In the dry season a deadly sun singes the earth and dupes the lonely rider with an illusion of farms and shade trees. To live here men need a sixth sense—a capacity for orientation and a toughness of resistance developed only by an implacable urge and will to survive.[2]

Long before the arrival of the Spanish conqueror there lived in the Plains of Venezuela Indian tribes that belonged for the most part to the Caribbean races. Warlike and savage by nature, they were cannibals—some from necessity, some by religion. The Spanish conquest of the Llanos was ill-equipped to break the utter wildness of these people. However, there slowly emerged some semblance of order and property and this, as throughout South America of colonial days, took the form of the *encomienda*.[3] These tremendous estates, almost the size of provinces, served for the most part to pasture cattle. The people who lived on them were of a different mould than the Indians of the mountain regions. They lived by cattle raising, hunting, and fishing, and only occasionally were they able to build up small areas of land on which to grow fruit and vegetables. Their chief food was meat, usually cooked over an open fire or, when circumstances demanded, ridden soft under the saddle and eaten raw. Otherwise they knew only bananas, yuccas, and sugar cane. They caught and broke wild horses and guarded diligently their herds of cattle. They castrated the bulls, and alongside their own animals led themselves an almost animal existence.[4]

Their natural instincts were developed to a sharp awareness by the dangers threatening them constantly—tigers, pumas, snakes, alligators; above all was the dread *caribe,* a fish, able to smell blood at a great distance, capable of turning any living thing it catches into a skeleton within a few minutes—this was

2 Rodó: *op. cit.* p. 270. A sociological analysis of the "Llanero" is still lacking. The best description, to my knowledge, is to be found in A. Páez: Autobiografía. Caracas, 1888, and in Rómulo Gallego's novels, such as *Doña Barbara* and *Cantaclaro.*
3 J. Gumilla: El Orinoco Ilustrado. Madrid, 1741. J. Rivero: Historia de las Misiones de los Llanos de Casanare y de los Ríos Orinoco y Meta. Escrita en 1736. Bogotá, 1883. Fray Pedro Simón: Noticias Historiales. Bogotá, 1882.
4 Baralt: Vol. I. p. 194.

the world against which the Llaneros had to defend themselves; and their hazardous lives—the endless marches and
endless rides—gave them strength, toughness, and an amazing
mobility. Their needs were few. In addition to the tools of
their trade, the lasso and the lance, they valued only a few
objects. Clothing was made almost superfluous by the scorch-
ing climate and the constant danger of floods, but even had
they desired it, the poverty of the Llaneros would have kept
them from acquiring any. Their huts were poor; a cowhide
or the bare floor served as bed and the trunk of a tree a table.
This rural proletariat was scattered throughout the Spanish
colonial dominion at the end of the eighteenth century. In
Argentina they were known as Gauchos, and in Venezuela
they were called Llaneros.[5]

No breath of officialdom reached them, for the larger cities
were far away. There were no schools, and so they were unaware
of the simplest facts. Even religion scarcely touched them. In
the Plains they knew neither communities nor churches. Spiritual care was delegated to the missions, and there, as everywhere
else, the larger orders dominated. The hearts of these semi-
savages, however, were unreceptive to the teachings of evangel-
ism. The remnants of a primitive and magical religion of
former days continued among them: they cured the sick by
magic, conjured the dead, and cursed the herds of their enemies
with secret incantations. They were familiar with the plants
that make one able to see the future and those that becloud the
mind, and they administered love potions and powerful mixtures able to kill or strike insane.

Into what category of man does this group fit? They were
at once shepherds, hunters, and fishermen. Not shepherds,
however, similar to the men of the Swiss Alps; rather to the
Bedouins whom Mohammed led against the cultures of the Old
World, or to the Mongols of Khengis Khan. They were
nomads. In their search for pasture land they wandered from
plain to plain, across many rivers, and only halted when they

5 Rodó: *op. cit.* p. 272.

met resistance. Other races mingled with them, and they possessed the endurance of Indians, the sensuality and good nature of the Negroes, and the strength and urge for conquest of the Spaniards. With this went the instinct for independence natural to all primitive peoples. They were so inured to danger that they sought it out. They gambled, drank, and loved cockfights and bullfights. Their diversions were monotonous and bloody.[6]

> Sobre la yerba la palma
> Sobre la palma los cielos
> Sobre mi caballo yo
> y sobre yo mi sombrero.[7]

> (Above the grass, the palm-tree
> Above the palm-tree the sky
> Above my horse am I
> And over me my hat.)

When the eastern part of Venezuela was defeated by Mariño in the summer of 1813, the greater part of the Spanish troops, with their officers, had been pushed to Guayana. But two officers remained—Tomás Boves and Francisco Morales. Boves was born in the Asturias and from his early youth had served on ships plying a dangerous contraband trade between the mother country and Venezuela. Involved in a lawsuit in 1808, he was sentenced to eight years imprisonment, but his employers in Puerto Cabello succeeded in having his sentence changed to exile. These circumstances led Boves first to the Llanos, where he lived by buying up cattle in the valleys to sell in the cities.[8]

At the outbreak of the revolution he enlisted in the patriot army. However, he was not trusted and was insulted and once more thrown into prison. He was set free by Monteverde's troops in 1812, and he left his jail consumed with a gnawing

---

6 E. Blanco: Venezuela heróica. Caracas, 1935. V. M. Ovales: El Llanero. Caracas, 1905. Rivas Vicuña: *op. cit.* Vol. I. p. 227.

7 Mancini: p. 499.

8 J. V. Gonzáles: Ribas. p. 134. O'Leary: Memorias. Vol. I. p. 172. Baralt: Vol. I. p. 184. L. Bermúdez de Castro: Boves. Madrid, 1934. p. 96. A. Valdivieso Montaño: Boves, Caracas, 1931.

hatred of the Republicans. He vowed vengeance. And he wrote the story of that revenge in blood and flames upon the face of a horrified Venezuela.

Boves was short and stocky, with broad shoulders and a back from which rose a tremendous head. His brow was broad and his deep-set eyes were a dull blue. His hair and beard were red. He was taciturn, cold, bloodthirsty, indefatigable, mobile, cunning, and treacherous. Half hero, half smuggler, Boves was of the tribe of Pizarro and Cortés—an evil genius. He would be subject to no one and laughed in scorn when the Spaniards made him a colonel. He demanded absolute and blind obedience. Pillage interested him little, but he enjoyed cruelty for its own sake, and he reveled in the power that grew in his hands into tyranny.[9]

Morales, his companion, was born in the Canary Islands. Like Boves, he was bold and sadistic, but also greedy; and he followed his leader as a jackal follows a jaguar. In the autumn of 1813 these two villains succeeded in mobilizing the Llaneros for the Spanish cause.

How did they attract the energies of this rural population? In the first place, the people of the Plains were less antagonistic to the Spaniards than the inhabitants of the cities. Living in freedom, unrestricted by laws, they had not yet felt the pressure of colonial officialdom. When Boves declared the slaves and underprivileged to be free, masters on many estates were killed by their thieving slaves or by robber bands.[10] And mulattoes, mestices, and Negroes, able for the first time in their lives to do as they liked, went over to Boves. He had an easy time with them. They were the beggar-proletariat of Venezuela, and most of them owned only a pair of trousers and a hat. If one has seen the poverty of the Llaneros in the present day, following a full century of industrial development, it is not difficult to understand how it was in 1813. Even the wealthy families in those days considered clothing a luxury that was handed down

9 Relación del General P. Briceño Méndez in O'Leary: Memorias. Vol. I. p. 174. Blanco: Doc. Vol. V. pp. 92, 171, 173, 177, 201.
10 Lecuna: Guerra. Vol. XVII. pp. 335, 417, 418.

from one generation to the next. Only the prospect of loot—a prospect enticingly held out by Boves—could enlist these poor souls for war service.

Among the horsemen enlisted to fight against the Patriots was a Negro who later changed over to fight under the banner of freedom. Asked why he fought on the side of the Spaniards, he replied that it had been his ambition to get shirts for his brothers and himself. His ambition satisfied, he felt that the war must be over.[11]

Allowed to steal and plunder, these poor devils became obligated to the service of Her Catholic Majesty. Who set in motion this drive for independence? The rich gentlemen of the cities. And who kept it in motion? Again, the rich gentlemen of the cities. It was only too obvious that amid this anarchy and lawlessness the "have-nots" would in time turn against the "haves." And as the men of property were apparently in sympathy with the revolution, it was simple to make the "have-nots" turn against them and follow the banner of the monarchy. Those who had nothing wished for something. This was the underlying motive of the uprising in the Plains. It was an easy matter to sweep the people of the Llanos into battle, for they were born fighters; instead of animals they now hunted men. Thus a huge host gathered. Slaves but yesterday, they were the henchmen of today: a fantastic group, grotesque, without uniforms, without rank or order, a herd rather than a host. But for this very reason they were better qualified to arouse terror along their path—The Legion of Hell.[12]

Why were these untrained fighters such a danger to the Second Republic? Bolivar was forced to recruit in the towns, but these were being sucked dry. In addition, the urban population was ignorant of the trade of war and it was necessary to train the soldiers. Boves, able to draw from sources hitherto scarcely tapped, had little to teach his men; the Llaneros knew

11 Páez: Autobiografía. p. 265. L. Vallenilla Lanz: La Guerra de Nuestra Independencia fué una Guerra Civil. Caracas, 1912. L. Vallenilla Lanz: Disgregación e Integración, Caracas, 1930. Vol. I. p. 169.
12 Lecuna: Guerra. Vol. XVIII. pp. 150, 161, 363, 364.

already everything that was expected of them. Fighting was their trade. Bolivar had to pay and equip his soldiers and was thereby tied to the norm of a regulated administration. And however much he resorted to dictatorial measures, in his own mind he was still subservient to the law. But Boves knew no such inhibitions. His people had fewer needs than those in the cities, and since theirs was the law of plunder and loot, they were able to acquire easily anything they might need. Nor did Boves have the problem of equipment, for most of the plains-men had their own horses, and those without horses broke foals and mules to their use. If they had saddles, they used them; but if not, they simply rode bareback. Their weapons, which they always carried with them, consisted of lassos with projec-tiles, knives, and spears. When they lacked spears, they took the gratings from windows and used them instead, and all the Llaneros were trained in the use of lassos.[13]

The question of arming his men became a serious question for Bolivar. There were no arms factories in his country and he was forced to buy from other countries. This became in-creasingly hopeless with each day that followed Napoleon's defeat. England had officially forbidden any trade in arms, and the United States had adopted a policy towards Spain which Bolivar termed "arithmetical." Hoping to acquire the Florida Peninsula from Spain by peaceful means, the United States refused to sell arms to the rebels.[14] There was an occasional concern willing to deal in contraband, but the conditions were oppressive and degrading. It was impossible to manufacture arms in a country without industrial preparation, though Boli-var did order the manufacture of gunpowder and bullets.[15] There remained only one step for Bolivar—to buy up all the weapons he could lay his hands on, and this immediately. Merchant ships coming to Venezuela were permitted to carry thirty to forty guns with which to defend themselves against

13 Lecuna: Guerra. Vol. XVIII. p. 150.
14 A. Whitacker: The United States and the Independence of Latin America. Baltimore, 1941.
15 Lecuna: Guerra. Vol. XVIII. pp. 101, 289.

attack by pirates, and from these Bolivar was able to obtain at least a part of the arms he required. But it was clear that recruiting was greatly hindered by these conditions. This lack of guns became, in the course of the year 1814, one of the decisive factors in the collapse of the movement for independence.[16] Boves' armies were not dependent upon any importation of arms, and in addition, as an army consisting chiefly of cavalry, it was tactically superior to the Republicans.

Artillery, as a weapon, played no very important role in the South American war of independence. On the whole, we find in this struggle mostly cavalry and infantry action, and the infantry, on which the Republicans depended, had burdens making it definitely inferior to the cavalry. The climate and the vastness of the territory were all favorable to the cavalry. Movements were less restricted by the tropical sun, and when the rainy season turned the roads into slimy swamps, horsemen were able to progress easily, while footsoldiers required many days. The slowness of their movement exposed them also to mosquitoes and the dangers of tropical fevers. And when it came to fighting, the cavalry again had the advantage, as the antiquated guns of the infantry required six complicated motions to load. When the cavalry attacked, the first salvo might catch the vanguard of the riders, but so much time was lost while the guns reloaded that the cavalry could reach into the enemy positions. In close contact the cavalry was vastly superior to the infantry and was able to rend it asunder.

Apart from the element of technical superiority, there was another element which developed in the fight for independence with the entry of the horsemen from the Plains, and this was the human aspect. Used to bloody diversions, the Llaneros impressed their seal upon the conflict. They murdered for pleasure, tortured for pastime. None of these dehumanized soldiers was able to surpass the leader himself in imagination and originality of torture.[17]

16 Lecuna: Guerra. Vol. XVII. p. 365.
17 R. Blanco Fombona: La Guerra a muerte, in El Constitutional de Caracas, December 1906, January 1907.

Boves looked on calmly while his soldiers dismembered men and children who had sought refuge in the churches, even on the steps of the altar. It was considered customary to cut off the ears of citizens in hostile cities. Others had the skin torn from their feet and were then forced to walk on glass splinters. Young people suspected by Boves of inciting to revolt were undressed in the market place and kept bound to posts until they perished of hunger and thirst.[18] Sacrifice did not move Boves, and even his own word was not sacred to him. Once a father and son were brought into his camp, and the son offered to take all the punishment for his father. Boves promised to spare the father if the son was able to have his ears and nose cut off without screaming. The lad somehow suffered the disfigurement according to the condition, but Boves regretted his promise and ordered them both killed.[19]

There is one among the countless stories still abounding in Venezuela that has a positively Dantesque character. In one of the cities which he took, Boves invited the ladies to a midnight ball. A dim lamp illumined the hall and melancholy music was played. Gradually the Creole women appeared, pale, tear-stained, and exhausted. None had dared refuse the invitation, for each hoped to achieve indulgence for her family. They danced with their husbands' enemies, the murderers of their sons, the despoilers of their homes. When they returned from the ball, they learned that Boves had meanwhile ordered their husbands shot.[20]

The suffering and martyrdom of those years remains forever in the memory of the Latin American peoples. Even if these memories are based only upon anecdotal truths, the despair that emanates from them is impossible to mistake.

Bolivar could only meet the type of warfare employed by Boves with similar actions. No more pardons were granted in battle. Whoever fell into the hands of the enemy met certain

18 O'Leary: Memorias. Vol. I. p. 174.
19 Mancini: pp. 535 ff. Heredia: Memorias. p. 131. O'Leary: Memorias. Vol. I. p. 188.
20 O'Leary: Memorias. Vol. I. pp. 209-10. González: Ribas. p. 175.

death. The war for extinction that was set in motion by the
Legion of Hell held a political meaning for its leaders. It aimed
at the destruction of the Republicans and the subjugation of the
population by terror.

The atmosphere of a rule of terror is contagious. Finally
the persecuted lose their fears and themselves turn into persecutors; they have nothing more to lose, nothing more to hope
for. This is what took place in Venezuela. When General
Ribas witnessed the cruelties of 1814, he took the following
oath: "The terrors I have had to witness make me shudder and
fill me with a deadly hatred of the Spaniards. I swear to leave
no means unturned to wipe them out."[21]

Bolivar had declared the war to extinction as a retaliatory
measure. He hoped thereby to split the Spaniards and Americans into two enemy camps. But the weapon was torn from his
hands. Venezuelans fought against their own people with the
same fanaticism—country against city, slaves against their
masters. There could be no armistice, no mercy. Not until this
time had the revolution changed its nature into a civil war in
the fullest sense of the word.

As the Spaniards among the Patriots became fanatical in
their wish to attack the rule of their motherland at its very
roots, the confusion of fronts became even greater. Among
those officers acquired by Bolivar in his successful campaign of
May, 1813, was the Spaniard, Campo Elías, who had left his
family to join the Patriots. He distinguished himself in all
engagements, fighting his own flesh and blood with cruel
determination. To all questions regarding the reasons for his
hostility he replied that he intended to kill all Spaniards and
finally himself, so that no Spaniard remained. No one has
solved the riddle of this hatred.[22] But this case is not unique.
Perhaps in the depths of the Spanish soul there lies a Cain-like
emotion of fraternal hatred that rises to the surface in times of
crisis.

21 González: Ribas. p. 176.
22 Baralt: Vol. I. pp. 198, 218.

One is reminded, in looking back over the history of this war for independence, of a painting by Leonardo, *The Battle of Anghiari*. Horses lashing out at each other, riders engaged in a death struggle, all intertwined in a tortuous knot. This was the fate breaking over Venezuela with the rebellion of the Plains in 1813. And this was the situation confronting Bolivar. He dispatched troops, won battles only to lose them, conquered provinces and relinquished them. But all held little meaning when compared to the only battle able to insure the freedom of his country. Three months after his victorious entry into Caracas, Bolivar began to feel that the greatest conflict of all still lay ahead—the battle for the soul of Venezuela.

CHAPTER 13

1814

A year of battles, but admitting of no comparison with wars of other ages, other regions of the world. It all seems very small when viewed from the point of view of the number of combatants. Napoleon and his enemies, both were able at that time to raise armies exceeding a quarter of a million men, but in South America it was only a question of a few thousand. Seen, however, in the light of the size of the theater of war, the whole is gigantic.

In the Old World, military campaigns could be compared to games of chess. Roads and boundaries, rivers and seasons, munitions and fortresses, all had a value that the commanders in the field learned to evaluate in the course of centuries. But in South America there existed no tradition of military science regarding the meaning of positions, of cities, that Bolivar might have studied. The officers, including Bolivar himself, were but dilettantes. Bolivar was forced to improvise. The boundless Plains, the Andes, the expanse of ocean—all offered his adversary a refuge wherein to recuperate after defeat, to regroup his forces, to fight again. And in these refuges lay the possibility of strategy for Bolivar, but by the time he had learned how to take advantage of them many years of strife had already passed. And his battles during those years resembled not so much the considered moves of a chess player as the headlong sallies of a gambler.

Bolivar's strategy was governed by his geography, the center

214

of which was the province of Caracas. The capital was the operational base, and the secondary towns, such as Victoria and Valencia, were the indispensable points of support.[1] In the course of his rapid advance from Colombia to Venezuela, he had been able to purge the enemy from territory crossed by his troops. But to the right and left of this corridor were left groups loyal to the Crown, and these groups lost no time in reassembling.

His strategy determined, therefore, by the law of the "inner line," Bolivar had to defend not only the province of Caracas but also the hinterland on which it depended for supplies. His major problem at this time was to keep the enemy forces scattered, but in order to face the dangers threatening him from all sides, he was forced to throw his troops from one part of his territory to another. To plug one gap he had to open another, and he himself took the responsibility for the correct action at the crucial moment. This was no war of static fronts nor of premeditated movements. Pushing forward here, giving way there, Bolivar was attempting to obviate the greatest dangers and ultimately rout the enemy. Thus the events of the year 1813-1814 bore an unsettled and unfathomable character. The real meaning of the countless skirmishes and engagements lies in the desperate effort on Bolivar's part to hold firm this inner line and its communications and to prevent the enemy from consolidating.

The fate of Puerto Cabello still in the balance, Bolivar turned his attention to the Plains where two Spanish units, independent of each other, were carrying on the war against the Republic. The unit operating in the east was commanded by Boves, the other by a Spaniard from the Canaries named Yanes. Both divisions marched upon the province of Caracas.[2] The Patriots, under the leadership of Campo Elías, defeated Boves near Mos-

---

1 Austria: *op. cit.* pp. 246 ff. Rivas Vicuña: Vol. I. p. 140. For a good account of the small number of fighting forces on both sides and the countless skirmishes and battles, see Batallas de la Independencia. B. d. H. Bogotá. Vol. XIV. p. 669.

2. Lecuna: Guerra. Vol. XVIII. p. 254. J. F. Blanco: Bosquejo histórico, B. d. H. Caracas. Vol. V. No. 17. p. 531.

quiteros on October 14, and the Spaniard escaped with a few countrymen.[3] What began as a battle ended a slaughter, for the Republicans gave no quarter. In Calabozo, the capital of the region supplying Caracas, one fourth of the population was mowed down for not taking arms against Boves!

But no sooner was the enemy repulsed on the Plains than another rose up, this time in the west. The Spanish Governor, Ceballos, was advancing towards the east from the province of Coro. The confronting armies met near Barquisimeto. With victory in the hands of the Republicans, the order came to retreat, throwing Bolivar's infantry into a panic. No one knows who gave this order.[4] The first regiment to surrender was stripped of its medals, rank, and standards, by order of Bolivar, thus losing its name and honor. He took this drastic step upon the realization that defeat had come through psychological rather than military reasons. He did, however, permit the regiment to win back lost honors upon the field of battle. But the fact that a false signal was able to demoralize an entire army, showed Bolivar how flimsy were the bonds holding together the Republican soldiers. This defeat, the first Bolivar had suffered in a year and a half, gave new impetus to the Spanish cause.

As the Patriot troops streamed back to Valencia, the Third Spanish Army division besieged in Puerto Cabello attempted to exploit this advantage by attacking in the direction of that town. Ribas, for whom the word "impossible" did not exist, was called upon by Bolivar for support, and he gathered together five hundred men, mostly students, and two hundred cavalry. These increased Bolivar's troops to two thousand and with this small and inexperienced force he unhesitatingly sought out the enemy. It took him three days of uninterrupted attack to defeat them, as the Spaniards had entrenched themselves. Pushing their way into the Spanish rifle pits, the students routed old and battle-tested soldiers. The result was of

3 O'Leary: Doc. Vol. XIII. p. 387. Larrazabal: Vol. I. p. 234.
4 R. Urdaneta: Memorias. pp. 27, 31. O'Leary: Memorias. Vol. I. p. 175. Larrazabal: Vol. I. p. 235. Baralt: Vol. I. p. 202.

the greatest importance, for Valencia remained in the hands of the Patriots, and the Spaniards were confined once more within Puerto Cabello.[5]

Bolivar, as he was proving at this time, had the gift of making swift decisions, and his plan of action proved forceful. It was necessary to defeat the enemy before the garrison at Puerto Cabello was able to rally and at the same time prevent the two units of Yanes and Ceballos from joining, so that he could defeat them one at a time. He was not entirely successful, for he was unable to prevent the enemy from joining forces, and the Llaneros, commanded by Yanes, united with Ceballos in Araure during the early part of December. Their combined strength amounted to five thousand men, while Bolivar's army numbered three thousand. In spite of the numerical disparity Bolivar decided to attack, and marched before dawn on December 5. However, his advance guard fell into a trap and was wiped out. The patriot army pushed forward in spite of this early setback, singing songs of freedom. In their center marched that nameless battalion with no weapons other than knives and sticks. They overran the enemy artillery, causing the infantry to retreat. But the Llaneros attacked, and the balance tipped in favor of the Monarchists.

During the battle Bolivar remained among his men. He was not like Napoleon, in the rear guard of the fighting, cold and imperturbable and surrounded by his staff. He was more like Frederick the Great, pulled hither and yon as his temperament dictated. And the moment that his luck turned against him, he himself led the cavalry attack against the Llaneros. The resulting clash was violent, but the Patriots were able to gain the upper hand again. It was Bolivar's personal entry into the battle that had decided matters. The pursuit lasted into the night, and no one, not even those who surrendered, was given mercy. Bolivar, who had been in the saddle since two o'clock in the morning, himself directed the annihilation.[6]

5 Lecuna: Guerra. Vol. XVIII. p. 254. Baralt: Vol. I. p. 203.
6 For the battle of Araure, see O'Leary: Doc. Vol. XIII. pp. 407-8. O'Leary: Memorias. Vol. I. p. 176. Urdaneta: Memorias. p. 34. Heredia: Memorias. p. 230. Lecuna: Batalla de Araure B. d. H. Caracas. Vol. XXVII. No. 108. p. 374.

With this engagement the Republicans gained a respite and
were able to catch breath for the next round. On the morning of
December 6 Bolivar called upon the "nameless" regiment. "Soldiers," he addressed them, "your courage has won you a name
on the field of battle . . . while the bullets were still flying
and as I saw you fight to win, I named you the Regiment of
the Araure Victory."[7]

Indeed, the Republican Army had fought well. Even the
Spanish officers, in admitting that the conduct of the rebels in
courage and coolness was worthy of the best European armies,
paid them tribute. The Republicans had saved themselves, it is
true, but in the negative sense of averting an imminent danger
rather than in the positive sense of defeating the enemy once
and for all. No one saw this more clearly than Bolivar. On
December 16 he wrote: "If we have finally been able to defeat
Ceballos and Yanes, it was by an extraordinary effort, such as
we are not always able to put forth. So that we could unify the
forces which we led to Araure, we had to leave all the rest of the
region unprotected and exposed to the greatest danger. The
enemy did not exploit his advantage at this time. But he will
at least have perceived his mistake, and will proceed with
greater energy and better leadership in the future."[8] In this
objective statement Bolivar revealed the difficulties of his position. His forces were numerically too small to oppose the
enemy on all fronts with equal strength. Each victory achieved
over the Spaniards was a miracle, made possible only through
the gathering together of all available men and material at one
point. But it was questionable how long these tactics of risking
all on one move could be maintained. Bolivar, at the beginning
of 1814, was in the position of a tightrope walker whose every
accurate step enabled him to stay aloft, but whose one false step
meant death and destruction.

Immediately following this victory Bolivar made every effort to build up to the limit the slender war potential of the

7 Proclamas: p. 79.
8 Cartas: Vol. I. p. 89. of December 16, 1813.

Republic. Appealing to the army, he said: "Our arms have avenged Venezuela. The great army that tried to enslave us lies beaten on the battlefield. But we cannot rest. New glory awaits us. And when the soil of our country is entirely free we shall sally forth to overcome the Spaniards wherever they try to rule in America. And we shall drive them into the sea. Liberty shall live by the protection of our swords."[9] This was Bolivar, warrior and visionary, hero and prophet. But a short while ago surrounded by the enemy, himself barely escaping destruction, he was still able to look beyond the confines of Venezuela. And his goal remained the freedom of the whole continent.

There were, however, matters of greater urgency, and Bolivar returned to the capital. During the battle of Araure, Caracas had been completely emptied of troops, and now Bolivar, to preclude the possibility of a sudden attack that might be similarly successful, ordered the immediate construction of fortifications. Each day the problem of transportation became more difficult. The introduction to military tactics of large bodies of cavalry had diminished the supply of horses and mules. Plunder and theft spread throughout Caracas, and in order to combat this a national guard was organized. Bolivar improved the hospital system. He bought arms at every opportunity and made every attempt to speed up production of gunpowder and bullets. Precious metals were disappearing from circulation, and the financial problem required immediate solution. Many people paid their taxes in goods, some even producing slaves in order to pay their debts. Money famine was universal. Smiths working in army factories were willing to continue work at half pay, but the money was insufficient even for this. Bolivar requisitioned all precious metals, and soon even the silver vessels of the churches and monasteries were confiscated and melted down. This extreme procedure was justified by the urgent need of the State, but the population, rebellious under

9 Larrazabal: Vol. I. pp. 245-46.

any circumstances, was made more restive and obstinate by
these measures.[10]

Bolivar left no stone unturned in his attempts to win over
his people. Two days after Araure he published a proclamation
to the Venezuelans, promising them tolerance and leniency if
they would submit to the laws of the Republic. In January,
1814, he extended a pardon to those reporting voluntarily to
the authorities, with or without arms, and strict instructions
were sent to military and civil authorities to put an end to
arbitrary shootings.[11]

At this time Bolivar gave Richard Wellesley an exact account
of his position. "The weakness . . . or more correctly the non-
existence of our position forced me to be on the battlefield and
at the head of the government at the same time. I had to raise,
and then lead, all our forces. Thus you see me, of necessity, at
the same time head of the State and Commander-in-Chief of
the Army."[12] This letter to Wellesley was a stone in the mosaic
of the foreign policy Bolivar was trying to establish. No matter
how greatly he was irked by his military responsibility or
troubled by his growing anxiety over internal policies, he never
forgot that Venezuela was but a part of the continent of America. And to liberate the continent implied the creation of a
place in the world for Venezuela.

Bolivar sent a delegation to London to achieve, as he had
attempted to achieve four years before, the recognition of Venezuela. Again he held out the prospects of a monopoly to British
trade, in exchange for a loan, weapons, and the protection of
the coast by the British fleet.[13]

Bolivar made a similar attempt to enlist the sympathy of
the sister republic, and his representatives in Washington were
to emphasize the Pan-American theme. If the delegates were
unable to achieve their primary purpose—namely, international
recognition—they could at least urge an intensification of ship-

10 Lecuna: Guerra. Vol. XVIII. pp. 30, 35, 41, 45, 79, 80, 84, 96, 98, 368, 383.
11 Proclamas: pp. 79-81.
12 Cartas: Vol. I. p. 92.
13 See the Instructions in O'Leary: Doc. Vol. XIII. pp. 459 ff.

ping. Greater shipping would bring vital necessities, arms, and improved trade relations, all of which would sooner or later force recognition.[14] Bolivar's impetuous will raced far ahead of snail-paced reality. However, it was certain that the day which saw Bolivar in possession of money, men, and weapons, and of a fleet to protect the coast-line and to assure supplies, would see the winning of his greatest gamble.

In the year 1814 this was no more than a dream, and Bolivar was forced to deal with conditions as they were. Following the victory at Araure, his program comprised these points: (1) the capture of Puerto Cabello; (2) defense of the western border; (3) destruction of the armies on the Plains. And the first step towards its realization lay in the unity of Venezuela, the joining of east and west. It was imperative that Bolivar conclude some sort of understanding with Mariño, who had turned deaf ears to his constant plea for support from the east. This division of the country into two military dictatorships sealed its fate. In order to assure the victory at Araure, Bolivar had been forced to remove his republican troops from the Plains, and Boves was not slow to take advantage. He defeated the Patriots at La Puerta on February 2, and once again it was the superiority of his cavalry that brought him success.[15]

Only two months after Araure the very existence of the Republicans was in the balance, for Boves was advancing on the capital from the Plains. Once again Bolivar begged Mariño to attack Boves' rear. Meanwhile, Bolivar tightened his own position in order to keep the center intact.

The defeat at La Puerta saw tragic results in the interior. We have seen Bolivar's vacillations when faced with the problem of Spaniards in Venezuela. Having declared a war to the death, he then turned round and offered the hand of reconciliation. He threw the Spaniards into prison and then attempted to exchange them with the enemy. Because the very existence of prisoners constituted a threat to internal security, he resorted to

14 Lecuna: Guerra. Vol. XVIII. p. 321.
15 O'Leary: Doc. Vol. XIII. p. 432. Blanco: Doc. Vol. V. pp. 34 ff. Larrazabal: Vol. I. p. 276. Baralt: Vol. I. p. 226.

the device of exiling them to North America aboard neutral ships. At the time of this decision he learned of the fall of La Puerta. The Republic was in danger. If the eight hundred or more prisoners within La Guayra could contact the enemy, Caracas was in danger of a fate similar to that of Puerto Cabello two years before. Bolivar therefore ordered the execution of all prisoners. There were no exceptions—not even patients in the hospitals were spared, and the order was carried out in a most cruel manner.[16]

This decision, most monstrous and conceivable only during times of revolution, was not defensible even when looked at in this light. Bolivar realized fully the horror of his acts, and he addressed a manifesto to the world trying to justify himself. As his first reason he referred to the atrocities committed by Boves and his men and considered his own actions in the nature of reprisal. But the real reason lay in his fear of conspiracy between the prisoners and the Spanish Army. Bolivar insisted that such plots existed.[17] He was able to find no means of thwarting them other than eliminating the eight hundred men, who constituted a fifth column within the Republic.

I do not attempt to exonerate Bolivar. He had no wish to shirk the responsibility that rested upon him. In a world recognizing only the law of vengeance, he had little choice. All around him lawlessness existed, and it was impossible for him alone to control his actions according to the norm. Terror, therefore, ruled both camps.

Bolivar's will to resist was indestructible. Only four days after the defeat at La Puerta, Ribas hurled himself at the army of the Plains and forced it to retreat. But though the worst was averted for the time being, the situation remained critical. Republican reserves of man power and materiel were almost exhausted, but reinforcements streamed constantly into the monarchist camps.

Bolivar was forced to gather all his forces at one point in

16 Lecuna: Guerra. Vol. XVIII. pp. 19 ff. O'Leary: Doc. Vol. XIII. p. 433.
17 Cartas: Vol. I. pp. 97, 107-8. O'Leary: Memorias. Vol. I. p. 192.

order to defend the vital cities of Valencia and Caracas. For
this he chose San Mateo, since the terrain there was unfavorable
to the enemy's cavalry attacks. Bolivar knew San Mateo only
too well. He had spent many peaceful days in the valleys of
Aragua on the estate where, thirteen years ago, he had dreamed
the brief dream of his marriage. But memories lacked reality
in face of the bloody struggles that lay ahead.

For more than a month Bolivar defended the positions of
San Mateo against an enemy whose cavalry surpassed his in
number at least ten fold. The first big clash came on February
28, following a number of short encounters. Boves was wounded
and his troops pushed back. Bolivar, however, suffered considerable losses, and two of his best officers were killed, one of
them the Spaniard-hating Campo Elías. Bolivar hoped to force
a decision before Boves recovered, but he was too weak to take
the offensive. He instead attempted to lure the enemy from its
hiding place so that the cavalry could be mowed down by his
artillery. The Llaneros did not fall into this trap. But by March
24 Boves was able to take command again, and he too tried
to force the issue. Mariño, after his unforgivable delay, decided
to join the fight. Since Boves feared his attack from the rear, he
ordered his men to attack Bolivar's positions on March 25.[18]

He turned first against the Patriots' left wing, situated
around the sugar cane mill at San Mateo. In this building a
a weak garrison defended Bolivar's supplies and munitions.
When the enemy troops approached at dawn, the Republicans
knew their doom was sealed. They were commanded by a
Colombian, Ricaurte, who gathered his men inside the mill.
He saw that escape would be out of the question. In order to
prevent the fall of the precious supplies into the hands of the
enemy, he caused the mill, with his men and himself inside,
to be blown up.[19]

18 Baralt: Vol. I. pp. 240, 248. Lecuna: Guerra. Vol. XVIII. p. 263.
19 In "Diario de Bucaramanga" p. 373, we find a statement made by Bolívar in
1828, that Ricaurte died in a less dramatic way, and that he, Bolivar, himself
invented the Ricaurte myth in order to strengthen the war effort of the Colombians.
This and similar outbursts of Bolivar in his last years must be considered as biased
by his aversion to the liberal Colombians who were fighting him at this time. The

Ricaurte's heroism bolstered the courage of the Patriots. However, this action was not decisive as far as the battle was concerned, and Boves' cavalry hurled themselves again and again against the center and right wing of the Republican infantry. During part of the battle, which lasted throughout the day, Bolivar and his men were surrounded by enemy cavalry, but his artillery prevented the Llaneros from approaching his positions. Vantage points changed hands several times, till, towards five in the afternoon, the patriots reformed their battle line and Boves was forced to retreat back to the launching point of his attack. For the third time that month the Republican army had escaped annihilation.[20]

It was, of course, questionable whether Bolivar could keep this up. The monarchist leaders were attempting to unite and strike the revolution mortally, once and for all. Bolivar in his turn was attempting to keep them apart with every resource under his command and to defeat them individually. He was never successful in destroying them entirely. Towards the middle of May he was in Valencia faced by an opposing army of five thousand men under Cajigal. The adversaries entrenched themselves in order to resist enemy attacks from secured positions, Bolivar considering himself too weak to take the offensive, and Cajigal waiting to join forces with Boves. Two weeks passed with only outpost skirmishes. Bolivar finally decided to risk everything, for he realized that each day of delay only brought closer the Legion of Hell. He forced the issue on May 28, on the Plains of Carabobo. Fortune was kind to him, and the Royal Army was trounced, its forces split asunder.

Another victory, yes, another delay—for the Second Republic was really bleeding to death. Losses were severe, so severe that Bolivar dared not reveal them. With the passing of each day the lack of weapons grew more serious. The soldiers'

majority of the historians accept Ricaurte's self-sacrifice as authentic. See, L. Orjuela: Ricaurte y sus impugnadores ante la critica. Bogotá, 1922.

20 Blanco: Doc. Vol. V. p. 97. Urdaneta: Memorias. p. 74. Larrazabal: Vol. I. p. 311. O'Leary: Memorias. Vol. I. p. 202. Lecuna: Guerra. Vol. XVIII. pp. 267, 337, 340.

equipment was pitifully meager; many were well-nigh naked. If Bolivar had led a well-equipped army, he might possibly have sought out the enemy following the victory of Carabobo. But he could not under these conditions. To make matters worse the rainy season had begun and the rivers were swollen, the fields turned into swamps.

Bolivar returned to Caracas. But if he hoped to give the Republic a blood transfusion out of the veins of the most loyal of its cities, he was to be bitterly disappointed. For lethargy had followed the tremendous efforts of the past year during which internal unrest and external threats had alternated without pause. Caracas had given her utmost, and who could blame the people now that they were becoming faint hearted. The Bourbons had just returned to the throne of Spain, and it seemed inevitable that reaction was to triumph over the hopes of free peoples. When Bolivar demanded renewed efforts from his fellow citizens he was met with an apathy that resulted from hunger, poverty, sorrow, and despair. But he was not defeated. A warrior yesterday, today he seized his pen in order to convince his brothers that the Allies' triumph over Napoleon would not be to Spain's advantage. Sooner or later, he maintained, Great Britain would become the defender and ally of American independence.[21] A marvelous prophesy, but one that convinced no one. England was far away, but Boves was at the gates.

Once again Bolivar was in the position of being forced to risk everything. Having left Caracas, he took command on the morning of June 15, of the army that lay near La Puerta. The same day he clashed with Boves. Both armies were of more or less equal strength, about three thousand men. After exhorting his troops to victory, Boves ordered his infantry to advance on Bolivar's center and his cavalry to ride against both flanks of the enemy. His operation was entirely successful, and in a battle lasting two and a half hours Bolivar's army was completely routed. Artillery, munitions, and the whole line of Patriots fell in Boves' hands. At Bolivar's side fell his Secretary

21 See Bolívar's Artical in Lecuna: Guerra. Vol. XVIII. p. 350.

of State, Muñoz, and four colonels with him. The Liberator, dagger in hand, was able to escape. Bermúdez threw his costly robe to the Llaneros and fled while they were fighting over the booty. Colonel Jalón, who was captured, was invited to dine with Boves, and in his presence the conquering Spaniard ordered him shot following the meal.[22]

Boves, thinking he would find Bolivar in Valencia, marched on the city. With each day his army increased in size, men joining him both from fear and out of loyalty to the cause of hereditary rule. Valencia capitulated on July 11.

Complete panic seized Caracas in the midst of this general collapse. No one knew what to do, and Bolivar's authority was challenged. Supplies became scarcer, and Republicans who had fled from the interior into the capital were forced to sleep in the churches because there were not enough houses to shelter them. Slowly the enemy troops marched on Caracas, but so great was the discouragement of the people that no attempts were made to impede the enemy's progress.

On July 6 Bolivar decided to evacuate Caracas and withdraw to the eastern section of Venezuela. With him went twenty thousand people, only a few of whom would ever again see their homes. Four thousand inhabitants, preferring to await death in their own houses, remained behind in the city.

And death came to them. But according to Boves, death was too good for the Republicans, and he permitted rape, torture, and mutilations. Age did not protect the innocent, nor was any place sacred. Pyramids of skulls lined the route of the Llaneros. Those merely suspected of being Patriots were branded, like common criminals, with a P on their forehead.[23]

Those who could, emigrated to save themselves. It was not the first time, for since the early days of the war the civilian population had been driven from place to place. There wandered behind Bolivar a caravan of misery. Almost destitute of

---

22 O'Leary: Memorias. Vol. I. p. 204. Larrazabal: Vol. I. p. 314. Baralt: Vol. I. p. 270. Heredia: Memorias. p. 261. Lecuna: Guerra. Vol. XVIII. pp. 270, 363, 364.
23 Lecuna: Guerra. Vol. XVIII. pp. 161, 379, 402, 573.

supplies, lacking in horses or mules, with only the hope of saving their lives left them, women, old men, and children trudged over the difficult paths along the coast. Those who followed Bolivar were for the most part members of the Creole aristocracy. Unaccustomed to go on foot even to church, they were now forced to march through swamps and across swollen streams, since it was the rainy season. They were attacked by mosquitos and consumed by fevers. Barcelona, their goal, was almost four hundred kilometers away. Following Bolivar's example, those on horseback took women and children up behind them. Thus the cavalcade plodded on for twenty days. It was a pilgrimage of despair. Mariño had assured them that the east would hold, and for this reason they headed in that direction.[24]

But on arriving in Barcelona, Bolivar found that things had changed materially for the worse. The people had become rebellious, the supplies exhausted, the coffers empty. Though Bolivar swiftly drafted as many men as he could, these, added to those he had led from Caracas, scarcely numbered twenty-five hundred. Boves meanwhile had dispatched the greater part of his entire army to the east and turned his command over to his representative, Morales.

The clash that followed between Morales' fighting forces and the small Republican army came only a few days after Bolivar had entered Barcelona. But Bolivar was unable to control the plan of battle, and this was symptomatic of the anarchy existing in the Patriots' camp. The catastrophe was hastened by the numerical superiority of the Spaniards. This battle, at Aragua, was one of the bloodiest of the entire war, and as always, the civilian population, too, was involved. Almost four thousand men died in this battle. Morales was forced by the putrefaction of the corpses to leave Aragua the following day. With this defeat was sealed the fate of the east, and this region,

24 G. González: Historia de Venezuela. Vol. II. Caracas, 1930. pp. 102-3. Baralt: Vol. I. p. 277. O'Leary: Memorias. Vol. I. p. 206. Rourke: *op. cit.* p. 129. Blanco: Venezuela heróica. Caracas, 1883. p. 183.

too, was lost to the cause of freedom.[25] The black flag with its death head, given to his troops by Boves, flew above the Venezuelan tricolor.

Bolivar had escaped. But there was no rest for him. Everyone set himself up as leader, and seemed unwilling to recognize Bolivar as commander-in-chief. The unhappy refugees who had hoped to stay in Barcelona were forced to drag themselves onward, with Cumaná as their next stop. Some were able to escape by sea, many died. Mothers killed their children. Bolivar did everything he could to ameliorate their suffering, but he was powerless. He arrived in Cumaná with two hundred men, and it was obvious that he could not make a stand here either. A council of war was called, with Ribas, Bolivar, Piar, and Bermúdez taking part, and a decision was reached to retreat to Guiria or to Margarita Island, where they might obtain reinforcements from the British Antilles. Bolivar wrote immediately to his friends in Trinidad and Barbados. As long as breath remained in him, the revolution was alive.

But now he was alone. His army was routed, and around him were men of the east who had always mistrusted his fame and his position. Even the few old friends he retained began to doubt him.

Before the retreat from Caracas, Bolivar had managed to salvage twenty-four chests of church silver and gems, and from the proceeds of their sale he intended to buy munitions from the British colonies. He had entrusted the chests to an officer and sent them ahead to Cumaná, but when it was decided to evacuate this town also, Mariño ordered the silver to be taken to one of his ships and sent on to the next point of resistance.

Bolivar arrived in Cumaná at dusk on August 25, and a new war council was held while he was still eating his evening meal. Word came that the little fleet had sailed, and treason was feared, since Bianchi, in command and Mariño's man, was little better than a pirate and had been led to the Republican camp through the prospect of booty. In order to save the state treasure

25 Larrazabal: Vol. I. p. 327. O'Leary: Memorias. Vol. I. p. 207.

Bolivar and Mariño went aboard and demanded the immediate surrender of the chests. Bianchi proposed a division. During the discussion the ship continued its course towards Margarita Island, where Bolivar was finally able to force the Italian captain to come to an agreement, and obtained the greater part of the silver, and several ships.[26]

But those Patriots who had remained behind were seized during this time with confusion and emotional turbulence, mistaking Bolivar's intentions. He had fled, therefore he was a traitor; and, worse, a thief who had stolen money belonging to the Republic. There followed an outburst of political hysteria not unrare during moments of crisis, in a time of upheaval. The leaders of this doubting group were Ribas, who had taken command of the troops, and Piar, Mariño's chief-of-staff. Piar was unquestionably courageous, but undependable, and his attitude was not surprising. But Ribas? Did he lose his head and allow himself to be persuaded by Piar? It is impossible to be sure. But it is certain that these two men, both of whom had risen to positions of power in the Republic, now threatened the leadership of Bolivar and Mariño. And on October 2 these men outlawed Bolivar.

A few days later the Liberator returned to Carupano with the money and salvaged ships, but no one believed his explanation for his actions. Ribas would not admit that in Bolivar's return a refutation of their accusations was implicit. Instead he seized the money and munitions and, treating Bolivar as a coward and a deserter, arrested him and demanded his promise not to escape. Now Bolivar was in a position to realize the injustice and humiliation suffered by Miranda two years before. But he was no Miranda, and since the power of his oratory had not deserted him, he managed to convince the officers guarding him of their mistake in holding him. Two days later he was set free.[27]

There was no time to lose if Bolivar hoped to save himself,

26 Lecuna: Guerra. Vol. XVIII. p. 488. See also B. d. H. Caracas. Vol. XIII. No. 49. p. 13. Cartas: Vol. I. p. 102. Baralt: Vol. I. p. 282.
27 Lecuna: Guerra. Vol. XVIII. p. 494.

and on September 7 the vanquished and proscribed leader made
this appeal to his fellow citizens:

"I have been chosen by fate to break your chains. But I have
also been the tool which fate used to complete your misfortune.
It was Venezuela's destiny that her citizens did not wish for
freedom." He expressed his intention of reporting his activities
to the Congress of New Granada, and planned to return to
liberate the country with the help of his Colombian brothers,
if Venezuelans had not already liberated themselves by that
time. Liberty or death—that was his watchword and would
remain so. No earthly force could move him from it. "Never
has liberty been enslaved by tyranny. Do not compare your
material forces with those of the enemy. Spirit cannot be compared with matter. You are human beings, they are beasts.
You are free, they are slaves. Fight, and you shall win. For
God grants victory to perseverance."[28] The next day Bolivar
boarded ship and headed for Cartagena, as he had done two
years ago. Mariño and forty-two men accompanied him.

He was leaving his country in ruins. With his usual clarity
of thought Bolivar was able to perceive that Venezuela herself
had prevented her own independence. Those who, with Ribas
and Piar, ascribed the fall of the Second Republic to human
failure were tragically in error, and only too soon was the country to realize her mistake. Boves moved up to the east, taking
command, and Republicans were slaughtered by the thousand.
Some, like the fourteen-year old sister of Marshal Sucre who
jumped from her balcony, preferred to take their own lives.[29]

The detailed account of these battles does not belong in a
biography of Simon Bolivar. In general, however, Ribas held
out until the year's end, when on December 5, exactly one year
after the battle of Araure, he was overcome at Urica. But one
consolation was granted the Republicans for this final destruction of their forces—the death of Boves by the thrust of a spear.
For many days Ribas wandered through the Plains until he

28 Proclamas: p. 111.
29 Lecuna: Guerra. Vol. XVIII. pp. 569, 572, 585.

was recognized at last by a slave and betrayed. Following his execution, his head, still in the Phrygian cap he had worn as a symbol of liberty, was exhibited in an iron cage. Twenty-one members of his family had died in as many months. Now, at the beginning of 1815, Venezuela was once again a possession of Spain. The uprising in the Plains had accomplished all that Boves had hoped, and the country was once again enslaved at the price of its destruction. An account of the condition of Venezuela at this time was made by the Spaniard, José Manuel Oropesa: "It is no longer a province. Settlements of one thousand souls have shrunk . . . some to just a few hundred . . . some to even less. The villages are ruined. Whole families have vanished, their only crime that of owning property from which they were able to live honorably. In the towns there is neither corn nor fruit. From the churches, everything, even the Holy of Holies, has been stolen."

It was the great, wealthy families who wished to terminate their allegiance to Spain that caused Venezuela to enter the movement for independence. But the dream of these aristocrats, who believed they could liberate the country without losing their privileged position, was dissipated, and the majority of the Creole families was wiped out. Their wealth vanished. The seeds of the revolution had blossomed in terrible fashion, their stalks strangling the delicate blooms of colonial society. This—the result of the year 1814—was beyond the confusing drama of battles, of victories and defeats, of anarchy and crimes.

Spain had won the round. Already the sails of her great fleet could be seen at the horizon, a fleet bearing an army sent by the mother country to subjugate the rebellious colonies once and for all. Yet the concept of national liberty was not dead, even though silenced by the terror of a barbaric regime. Boves was dead, but Bolivar lived. Colonial society, first to take up the banner of independence, no longer existed, but on the battlefields of the years to come a new group was to arise, the foundation of South American democracy. And it was in the nature of things that only one man could lead this group, a man who, borne down by the collapse of today, still harbors in his heart the inextinguishable vision of tomorrow.

Fourteen years later Bolivar remarked that he had never earned greater laurels than during this dreadful year, 1814. "This unbelievable and pitiful campaign in which, despite so many and repeated catastrophes, the glory of the defeated could not be dimmed. For everything was lost—but not honor."[30]

30 D. d. B. p. 382.

CHAPTER 14

Long Live the Chains!

*I*n flight once again! But Bolivar was given a hero's welcome when he arrived in Cartagena on September 19, 1814, after ten days at sea. Only a few months before, the state had conferred on him an honorary citizenship, at which time Bolivar had replied that the sons of Caracas and Cartagena were members of the same family.[1] And now he was welcomed like a brother, everyone fully aware of the great movement he had set in motion. No one blamed him for being unable to carry it through successfully at this time. Frustrated, deposed, outlawed by his own people, Bolivar had never for a moment lost faith in his star. He had said to Mariño on the voyage to Cartagena: "There can be no victory over liberty. Those who rule today in Venezuela will be humbled and ousted tomorrow." According to Mariño, Bolivar "could have convinced stones of the necessity of his victory."[2]

The plan Bolivar had in mind when he arrived in Cartagena resembled in some ways that of 1812. Once again he hoped to win back Venezuela with the help of Colombia. But he was able to see the situation more clearly now. Cartagena alone was not strong enough to liberate his country. Only the Congress of the Allied Provinces could give him the help he needed. He sent a report immediately upon arrival to the president of the Congress on the events that had destroyed Venezuela, and

1 Proclamas: p. 108. Blanco: Doc. Vol. V. pp. 87-88.
2 Larrazabal: Vol. I. p. 341. Baralt: Vol. I. p. 315.

233

he announced his intention of appearing before the Parliament.
Early in October he sailed up the Magdalena River with Tunja
as his objective. On reaching the city of Ocaña, he heard that
his army in Venezuela had not been utterly destroyed. Urdaneta had succeeded in fighting through to Colombian soil with
his division. In this fragment Bolivar saw the nucleus of a new
army. Misfortune, he told his soldiers, is the school of heroes.
His watchword remained: Liberator—or dead.[3]

But at the same time Bolivar heard of a misunderstanding
that had arisen between the Venezuelans and the Colombians
that might easily jeopardize everything. "Our country is America," he told his men. "Our enemies are the Spaniards. Our
goal independence and liberty!" The army acknowledged the
authority of its leader once again and followed him on his
march into the heart of the country.[4]

He arrived at Tunja, the seat of the Congress, on November
22. Camilo Torres was no longer head of the government, but
he had been made President of the Parliament and he still had
influence. Hearing of Bolivar's arrival, Torres sent him one of
his best horses and a costly saddle as a present. The signal honor
paid to Bolivar in this action can only be estimated by those
knowing the love which the South American, even in this
mechanical age, attaches to his horses. But Bolivar did not
accept the gift until he had made his report to Congress, before
whom he appeared with his friend at his side. Reporting on
the rise and fall of the Second Republic, he asked that his deeds
be examined carefully and judged impartially. Camilo Torres
kept faith with Bolivar. "General," he said, "your country is
not dead, so long as your sword lives. Parliament will give you
protection, for it is satisfied with your conduct. You were unfortunate as a soldier. But you are a great man."[5] This tribute
on the part of Torres was for Bolivar the man.

Bolivar's aim was unalterable: freedom for America. And

3 Proclamas: p. 116. O'Leary: Doc. Vol. XIII. p. 573.
4 Proclamas: p. 117. Cartas: Vol. I. p. 103. Urdaneta: Memorias. pp. 96-97.
Larrazabal: Vol. I. p. 343.
5 Larrazabal: Vol. I. pp. 343-44.

the primary condition for this was the restoration of Venezuela's independence. What possibilities were the neighboring
countries able to offer Bolivar towards the realization of this
great ideal?

The once viceroyal kingdom of New Granada was as yet
but a loosely bound union of states, and its very existence was
threatened by Spanish forces to the north. Within, unproduc-
tive quarrels among the various members of the union had a
disruptive effect. But it was understood by even the most
deluded of these states that the elements contributing to Venezuela's misfortunes yesterday could tomorrow bring about
Colombia's nemesis. It was only possible for America to gain
its freedom if its component parts would put their ideal of
freedom before any other consideration. If Colombia, therefore,
was now to become the springboard for Bolivar's new campaign, it was essential to assure the internal unity of the country.
And this was the purpose guiding his actions for the next six
months. Here was no mercenary, who changed masters and
waged war for war's sake. If he used his command of the
Colombian union to subordinate the rebellious provinces to the
central government, he did so because he realized it was the
eleventh hour. It was not by accident that Spain had defeated
Venezuela. At the end of 1814 Spain was in a position to
draw the utmost benefits from this victory.

The heir to Spain had returned to his throne as Ferdinand
VII, after the collapse of Napoleonic rule. On his journey to
Madrid the King was the object of such excessive jubilation
that he believed he could do anything he wished. The Servile
Party sponsoring Spain's return to its decadent absolutism had
been opposed by the Liberal Party responsible for the Constitution of Cádiz. Ferdinand rescinded this Constitution immediately and imprisoned thirty of the leading liberal representatives.
In the wake of this brutal and shortsighted attitude, certain
outmoded tools of reaction appeared, namely censorship, the
Inquisition, and even torture. But the Spanish people accepted
this return to the old form of existence without a protest and

reacted to the royal renunciation of the constitution with a
"Vivan las cadenas—Long live the chains!" The people appeared willing to follow the idolized monarch to any lengths.

America could only expect of him the restoration of royal
rule under the most ruthless application of force. In November,
1814, the King decided to send over an expeditionary force
with the subjugation of America its aim. But Bolivar, when he
accepted appointment as Captain-General of the Colombian
State-Federation, had little knowledge of these intentions.[6] He
did foresee that the South American continent would only too
soon feel the full impact of Spanish might. For this reason he
attempted to unite the provinces of New Granada before the
Spanish forces landed on its shores. Once again he was able
to accomplish the impossible with his rhetoric, and the government showed its belief in him by presenting him with an army
for the continuation of the war. With the fire of his personality
he was able to penetrate the mists of indifference.

Bolivar's first task was the defeat of the rebellious province
of Cundinamarca, with Bogotá, its capital. But this part of the
country was strange to him and it seemed as though he were
more of a hindrance than a help towards political unity. In
addition to this he was known as the Man of Terror, persecutor
of the clergy and murderer of prisoners. The Archbishop of
Bogotá had excommunicated him, and political officials even
made requests to the Spaniards for help against him. Bolivar
tried everything in his power to put an end to the civil war.
He spared Spanish prisoners and promised not to wage the war
of extinction in Colombia, offering to let the rebels go unpunished. Was it possible for his critics to believe that he was
dazzled by the idea of becoming Dictator of Colombia? He
who wished to carry the banner of independence to Lima?
Thus, ten years before his expedition to Peru, did Bolivar reveal
to the Colombians this highest ambition of his strategic political

6 O'Leary: Doc. Vol. XIII. pp. 539, 540. Restrepo: H. d. R. C. Vol. I. p. 265.
Lecuna: Documentos inéditos: El Libertador en Nueva Granada, 1814-15. B. d. H.
Caracas. Vol. XIX. No. 73. p. 21.

planning. However, no argument of his could prevail upon them.[7]

In a swift advance from Tunja to Bogotá, Bolivar took possession of the greater part of the province of Cundinamarca and on December 9 he stood before the gates of the capital. Bogotá attempted to defend itself, but after a battle lasting two days, it was forced to capitulate.[8] Bolivar reported his success to the government in Tunja; the richest province in the country had been forced into the federation, and the fertile highlands were united once again. On December 12 Bolivar entered for the first time that city called by Alexander von Humboldt the Athens of South America. Bogotá lay in the shadow of gigantic mountain cliffs that formed its protection. It was to become the stage for the more tragic events of Bolivar's life. But of course he did not realize this at that time and attacked the problems facing him with his customary tireless energy. He granted the inhabitants the full security of their civilian freedom. The Church lifted its ban against him, and he attended the *Te Deum,* the ceremony celebrated in the Cathedral for the restoration of national unity.[9]

He was Captain-General of Colombia. And if this was not to remain an empty title, it would be necessary for him to erect an instrument of power capable of welding this loose political unity in such a way that the Spaniards could be effectively resisted. Bolivar summoned all deserters back to the colors and exhorted all Colombians to rise up against Spanish tyranny. He demanded sacrifices, donations. "War," he said, "is the epitome of all evil. But tyranny is the substance of all war."[10] This adjuration was not intended to be taken only from the ideological viewpoint, and it resulted in a campaign which placed the entire Colombian region in a condition for resistance. A small army was sent south to the borders of Ecuador, while

7 Cartas: Vol. I. pp. 107, 110, 112, 113. Proclamas: pp. 118-9. O'Leary: Doc. Vol. XIII. pp. 556-7. Blanco: Doc. Vol. V. p. 191.
8 Restrepo: H. d. R. C. Vol. I. p. 292. O'Leary: Doc. Vol. XIII. pp. 554-66. Groot: Historia civil y eclesiástica de la Nueva Granada. Bogotá. 1898. Vol. III. p. 334.
9 O'Leary: Doc. Vol. XIII. pp. 579, 588, 589. Proclamas: p. 119.
10 Proclamas: pp. 121, 123. O'Leary: Doc. Vol. XIII. p. 590.

Urdaneta was charged with the defense of the eastern boundary near Venezuela. Bolivar chose the most difficult assignment of all for himself, that of the liberation of the coastal region from Spain. The only point on the Colombian coast that the royalists had been able to hold was Santa Marta. Bolivar was aware of the necessity of driving the Spaniards from this bridgehead so that it could not be useful to an overseas expeditionary corps.

Without delay, therefore, he made preparations for his campaign against Santa Marta, drafting new recruits and raising arms and munitions—these were the technical problems facing him. The political aspect was more difficult. Cartagena, for three years an independent state, was the focal point of independence in the coastal regions of Colombia. Without the political and military help of this port, Bolivar could hope to accomplish little against Santa Marta. Up until now Bolivar had been assured of the good will of Cartagena, but when his first requests for help went unheeded, he began to realize that there were forces at work that intended to impede his political unification of Colombia. The conflict among Colombians took on the character of the Hydra of Hercules. Bolivar chopped off one head, but seven new ones grew up in its place.[11]

During the campaign of 1813 Bolivar had come into contact with Colonel Castillo. He, a sworn enemy of the Liberator, had left the army that then marched against Venezuela. At this time he was in command of the fighting forces of Cartagena, and hardly had he learned of Bolivar's plans when he published a pamphlet against Bolivar challenging his ability to lead and even questioning his personal courage. Bolivar felt that his hopes were vanishing before his eyes and realized that relief could come only from the federal authorities. He turned, therefore, to Camilo Torres. The government supported Bolivar's request, and in order to separate Castillo from his command in Cartagena made the latter Brigadier General with membership on the highest council of war.[12]

11 O'Leary: Doc. Vol. XIV. p. 33. Cartas: Vol. I. p. 119. Blanco: Doc. Vol. V. p. 215. Rivas Vicuña: Vol. II. p. 32.
12 Cartas: Vol. I. pp. 122, 124. O'Leary: Doc. Vol. XIV. pp. 42, 45, 49.

Everything seemed prepared, and Bolivar left the plateau of Bogotá on January 29, 1814, and began the descent into the Magdalena Valley. In the beginning the campaign promised success. Bolivar was able with a few telling blows to rout the Spaniards who had pushed up from the coast deep into the valley. Ocaña, then Mompox, were liberated, and Bolivar determined to pursue his adversary until he was pushed into the sea. He was, however, overlooking his political enemies, who in Cartagena had united with his personal foes. Hate, revenge, and anarchistic stupidity were the driving forces motivating this group of men, who accused Bolivar of causing the collapse of Venezuela, charged him with cruelty and the desire to drive Colombians from their homes, their land. Castillo, of course, was the originator of these charges, but other one-time friends of Bolivar had joined him. Once again a condition of civil war prevailed. A council of war was held in Cartagena which relieved Bolivar of all authority and demanded his removal.[13] For his part Bolivar was prepared to make any personal sacrifice to avoid civil war and achieve the unity daily becoming more urgent. He remained in Mompox for over a month, writing letter after letter, sending delegates to Cartagena offering his resignation as Commander in Chief—anything, in fact, to prevent any delay of the most vital operation of all, securing the safety of the Atlantic coast.[14]

Castillo continued to do his utmost to ruin Bolivar's plans. He sent his officials instructions to disobey the Liberator and even removed troops and supplies from his hands. Deciding on one last desperate attempt, Bolivar arranged a personal meeting with Castillo, since his emissaries had not been able to win over his rival, a meeting where he could put to use his own powers of persuasion. Bolivar arrived at the assignation, but Castillo had regretted his promise and did not appear.[15] All following attempts were hopeless. Bolivar realized that his generosity

13 O'Leary: Doc. Vol. XIV. p. 70. Blanco: Vol. V. p. 238. Lecuna: B. d. H. Caracas. Vol. XIX. pp. 36-37.
14 Cartas: Vol I. pp. 129, 131, 132, 136.
15 O'Leary: Memorias. Vol. I. p. 253. O'Leary: Doc. Vol. XIV. pp. 137-40.

must appear ridiculous to an enemy moved only by hatred and resentment. And of course there was no lack of advisers trying to persuade the Liberator to settle the score with his enemy once and for all.

The situation was desperate. Bolivar's stay in Mompox had used up all his resources. A smallpox and fever epidemic raging along the swampy river bank had decimated his army to half its size. It seemed impossible to drive the Spaniards from Santa Marta with only one thousand men. Perhaps he should hurl his forces at Cartagena and compel the rebels to respect his authority? His statesmanship compelled him to decide to attack the Spaniards, but his temperament gained the ascendency and he seized the other alternative, one that meant civil war.[16]

He captured the forward positions of Cartagena's line of defense, and on March 23 he was in Turbaco, four miles from the center of the city. He had not given up completely the hope of breaking resistance with persuasion, and to this end he sent one of his officers into the city to negotiate. But he was maligned and threatened as an outlaw by the mob incited by Castillo. Manifestos were published against Bolivar, and men suspected of being his friends were arrested. Bolivar, therefore, moved on to the siege, and this action was too soon proved to be beyond his strength. The city was the most strongly fortified point in all South America. The Spaniards had spent vast sums in building great forts and walls ten meters high and sixteen meters wide, and it seemed that the Spanish monarchs had wanted them to be visible to the naked eye from the Escurial! Bolivar had little prospect for success without artillery. The hostile inhabitants had poisoned the wells outside the walls by throwing animal carcasses into them. Below the enemy cannons Bolivar's army lay thirsty and infected. The position was not an enviable one, and the Liberator's heart was torn. He knew only too well that victories in civil war are always dearly

16 Larrazabal: Vol. I. pp. 356-57. O'Leary: Memorias: Vol. I. p. 254. O'Leary: Doc. Vol. XIV. pp. 139, 141, 148. D. d. B. p. 366. Lecuna: B. d. H. Caracas. Vol. XIV. p. 82. G. Porras Troconis: Gesta Bolivariana. Caracas, 1935. p. 77.

bought, bringing glory to no one.[17] He felt ready to renounce all, and on March 25 he made known to his officers his desire to resign his command. He was not permitted to do so, but he continued to beg the government in Bogotá to relieve him of his duties, as he felt nearer to mounting the scaffold than to serving out his command.[18] No notice of this was taken, however, and days, weeks, and months went by with only fruitless discussions and unimportant skirmishes. And during this period reports were coming in confirming Bolivar's pessimistic suspicions.

While his forces were being squandered in a senseless civil war, the Monarchists were meeting with successes in the Magdalena Valley. Were his personal enemies really so blind that they could not see the flames already licking at the foundations of their own houses? Bolivar's new attempts to make peace met with disappointments. He wrote finally to the Commissioner of Cartagena: "If New Granada does not wish, or is not able, to become free, is it not possible at least for us to reach an agreement so that those who prefer freedom above all else may go to other countries there to die as free men? I am one of these. If I am not permitted to attack Santa Marta . . . my friends and I will leave."[19] But one day followed the next, with Bolivar tortured as one evil tiding followed another. The Spanish expeditionary force landed in Venezuela and on April 29 Barranquilla fell to the Spaniards. The Republicans thus lost the lower course of the Magdalena River and Castillo's insanity had opened the gates of Colombia to the enemy.

What was Bolivar to do? If it were true, as his enemies insisted, that he had prevented unity, surely there was nothing left but to sacrifice himself? He called his war council together and announced his decision, and on May 7 he left his comrades and New Granada. "The renunciation of my top command," he wrote to the Government, "the sacrifice of my reputation and my fortune . . . is no strain . . . I shall no longer be a

17 D. d. B. p. 366.
18 Cartas: Vol. I. p. 141.
19 O'Leary: Memorias. Vol. I. p. 262.

general. I shall live far from my friends and compatriots. I shall not die for my country. But I shall have done it a new service by giving it peace through my absence. . . . For my services I ask no better reward than that my mistakes be forgiven me."[20] On May 8 Bolivar left the mainland and accompanied by a few of his friends, sailed aboard an English man o' war bound for Jamaica.

The despair of these days was perhaps more painful than Capurano, for now it was not the Spaniards who had defeated him. Greed, revenge, and hate had caused his failure. Before he was forced to flee, but now he had exiled himself. Bolivar, who had preached unity to the Americans as no one had ever done before, was used as the pretext for the present rift. It was of little comfort that he could say to himself that he was innocent. And in actuality, was he able to do this? The rightness of his intended coercion of Cartagena is questionable. He himself stated later that it might have been wiser to occupy the valley of the Magdalena River, rather than to attack the city. But his egotism, his passionate temperament, his firm belief that a revolution would open all gates to him, his overpowering desire to enter the city in triumph as he had entered Bogotá—all had led him into this erroneous path.[21]

We can add nothing to this self-criticism, though we can ask whether he might not have remained in the country following his failure before Cartagena and continued to fight from the interior. But the discovery that he was looked upon as an interloper by the Colombians was a devastating one. If he was to fight again, it would have to be in Venezuela. There was an additional factor governing his decision for self-banishment. In his life as a statesman his failure at Cartagena had brought about a crisis. It was necessary for him to get over the resulting disillusionment concerning himself and his enemies. Exile, therefore, with its promise of healing, seemed desirable to him at this time.

20 Cartas: Vol. I. p. 143.
21 D. d. B. p. 366.

It was May 11 when the coast of the American mainland
vanished from view. On that same day Pablo Morillo, the Spanish general in command of the expeditionary force, entered
Caracas at the head of the greatest army ever sent by Spain to
America. The fleet that bore it across the ocean was made up
of eighteen warships and forty transports. The army itself consisted of six infantry and two cavalry regiments and was well
equipped with artillery. All in all the army numbered almost
eleven thousand men, all seasoned soldiers of the Napoleonic
battles of Bailén and Victoria. Their commander had personified the great national movement of the Spanish people against
their oppressor and had been lauded for his fearlessness by
Wellington.[22]

Of obscure parentage, Morillo had fled his home at the age
of thirteen to join the Marines. From a simple private he rose
to the rank of general. Ruthless, blindly devoted to his King,
he was not without generosity when he felt it possible to give
his impulses free rein. To him had been entrusted the mission
of the pacification of America. His official title was *pacificador,*
and his powers were unlimited. His instructions were to proceed with caution, with goodwill, and to proclaim a general
amnesty.

But Morillo was too foreign in this atmosphere of a colonial
world to accomplish this successfully. His good intentions soon
atrophied. Following a brief period during which he tried to
reach an understanding with his subjects, he returned to the old
Spanish principles of rule and submission.

The expedition, which had left Cádiz in February, 1815,
was to make the lands of the La Plata its first stop. The Spaniards, however, were able to realize that the strategic point for
a successful defeat of the colonies lay to the north—a point that
Bolivar had tirelessly hammered into the heads of his fellow
citizens. First Venezuela, then Colombia, and then Ecuador
were to be subdued. Peru was securely dominated by Spain,

22 Pablo Morillo: Memoires. Paris, 1826. Rodríguez Villa: Biografía de Pablo
Morillo. Madrid, 1908-10. 4 Vols. R. Sevilla: Memorias de un oficial del ejército
español. Madrid Biblioteca Ayacucho.

and Morillo intended to cross the Andes there and put down the revolution in Argentina from the rear.

At the time of his arrival in Venezuela, this great country had already been won back for the Spaniards. Only the tiny Margarita Island still espoused the cause of independence, led by Arismendi. But even this last stronghold, small as it was, was forced to capitulate upon sight of the approaching armada. Morillo extended pardon to the Republicans, inviting Arismendi to dine with him. One man alone was unwilling to demean himself to the conqueror—Bermúdez. He managed to escape on a cutter that passed between the big ships of the Spanish fleet, and as he sailed by he shrieked insults at the enemy.

Morillo entered Caracas on May 11, and here, too, he declared an amnesty. But it was not possible to accomplish a return to the old form of colonial government by a mere stroke of the pen. Fortunes had vanished, estates had changed hands, thousands had emigrated. Many from the colored section of the population had been advanced to important positions and had become used to them. No matter how much Morillo attempted to turn back the wheel of time, it became evident that it was impossible. If Spain had agreed to regard the amnesty as the beginning of an era of self-government, she might have been able to hold on to her colonies. But neither the King nor the Camarilla in Madrid was gifted with sufficient vision for this, and the concept was beyond Morillo's depth also.

Making the necessary military preparations to secure Venezuela, Morillo stationed garrisons and organized his army. His next aim was the pacification of Colombia, and in July, 1815, he landed in Santa Marta, which had become the provisional capital of the viceregal kingdom. At the same time he sent Morales by land to lay siege to Cartagena, and not much later he took command himself.

Cartagena was now to pay the price for its stubbornness. And it paid dearly. Too late were the necessary measures taken to prepare for the siege. The city was cut off completely from the interior, and for 106 days the city of Cartagena demonstrated its heroism and an unbelievable spirit for self-sacrifice. The population was well aware that there was no prospect at all of winning. The Spaniards had superiority of weapons. Time was in their favor, also pestilence and famine. People died of exhaustion in the streets or beneath the rubble of crumbling houses. But no one mentioned surrender. At last by November, when every horse, mule, dog, and cat had been consumed, an evacuation of the population by sea was attempted. Small boats tried to reach the open sea, scuttling between ships of the enemy fleet. But a wind blew them back to shore and most of them capsized. Only a few inhabitants escaped with their lives.[23]

Morillo occupied the city on December 6, 1815. According to his own report, the most horrible sights greeted the conquerors. "The streets were littered with corpses which polluted the air. And the greatest part of the population had literally died of starvation." The few that had survived were living skeletons, clinging to the walls in order not to fall. For twenty-two days they had eaten nothing but water-soaked leather. Morillo was willing to spare them, but his adjutant, Morales, killed them unmercifully with truncheons or bayonets. The prisons of the Inquisition were crammed with the heroes of this resistance. And after perfunctory trials they were hanged. Among those losing their lives in this fashion was Colonel Castillo, who had been deposed during the siege. Now he paid his debt.

Cartagena conquered, the subjugation of Colombia was easy. Morillo advanced his troops upon Bogotá from several directions. Once the town was occupied there began an openly proclaimed reign of terror. Hundreds of Colombians were put to death, including many leaders of the independence movement: Camilo Torres, Rodríguez Torizes, Lozano. The Inquisition flourished. All printed matter with the slightest liberal

23 Camilo Delgado: Historio del sitio de Cartagena. Cartegena, 1916. Lecuna: B. d. H. Caracas. Vol. XIX. p. 85. Restrepo: H. d. R. C. Vol. I. p. 377. Larrazabal: Vol. I. p. 380.

taint was publicly burned. The rulers worked on the principle that only books in Spanish or Latin escaped suspicion. Anyone able to read and write was regarded as a rebel. This, according to Morillo, was the best way to stem the revolutionary tide.[24]

From Central America to Chile the Restoration had triumphed. And only in Argentina was the Army of the Revolution able to hold firm.

But at this point in history, terrain was to come to the help of the Independents—the vastness of the country, the immeasureableness of the Plains, and the insurmountable mountains. Not all leaders had fallen under the Spanish sword. Mariño, Bermúdez, Santander, Urdaneta, and Piar had been able to save themselves. Some remained in hiding, others secretly commenced the organization of resistance. And from the British Antilles, far from the mainland, burned the torch of independence, sending its rays out like a lighthouse piercing the night of oppression. Bolivar lived.

24 Blanco: Doc. Vol. V. p. 342. Rivas Vicuña: Vol. II. pp. 53 ff. G. Hernández de Alba: Recuerdos de la Reconquista. Bogotá, 1935.

CHAPTER 15

The Letter From Jamaica

$\mathcal{B}$olivar was in his thirty-second year. His forehead was high, narrow, and already furrowed. His brows arched thickly above bright and searching eyes—windows which revealed the soul of a man forever swayed by his emotions. His nose was long and curved, the cheekbones high, the cheeks sunken as a result of hardships and privations. His mouth was strong and sensual; his teeth, of which he took great care, were beautiful. His hair, black and slightly curly, had early begun to turn gray. He was not tall but was well proportioned and extremely agile, with a broad chest and slender body and legs. His small hands and feet, beautifully formed, might well have caused a woman's envy. His complexion was dark and deeply tanned by the tropical sun. His facial expression altered with unbelievable rapidity, giving the impression of a constantly changing personality as he came under the influence of hope, anger, grief, happiness.[1] The physical portrait of Bolivar conforms to the admixtures of his blood and reveals particularly the Spanish, or rather, the Basque aristocrat whose progeny, native to the tropics, had been somewhat modified by nature and environment. A man like

1 M. S. Sánchez: La Iconografía del Libertador. Caracas, 1916. We are indebted to the European officers and diplomats who met Bolivar for the most vivid descriptions of his personality. I. Miller: Memorias, Spanish edition, Madrid, 1910. F. Burdet O'connor: Memorias sobre la Independencia Americana. Biblioteca Ayacucho. Madrid. pp. 106-107. G. Cochrane: Journal of a Residence and Travels in Colombia. London, 1825. Campaigns and Cruises in Venezuela. London, 1832. Vol. I-III. G. Hippesley: Narrative of the Expedition to the Rivers Orinoco and Apure. London, 1819. pp. 382 ff. Blanco Fombona: Bolívar pintado por sí mismo. Paris-Buenos Aires, 1913. J. A. Cova: El Superhombre. Caracas, 1940.

Bolivar was possible only in the tropics. He was fashioned of American clay, and he animated it by the breath of his own spirit.[2]

At the outbreak of the Revolution, Bolivar was classed among the richest noblemen of the Spanish Empire. When he arrived in Jamaica in May, 1815, he was as poor as any one of his former slaves. The little he had been able to take with him was soon gone, and after a short time he became dependent on the generosity of his friends. "I have," he wrote, "not one peso."[3] Probably there has been no other man of action in the history of the world to whom money meant so little. Even his enemies and slanderers admitted this.[4] His generosity was boundless. Without hesitation he gave not only all he possessed, but frequently went into debt to help others. Whenever a needy case appealed to him, he responded with ungrudging liberality. He would sell his belongings, dispense with his salary, empty his purse to the last penny.[5] In spite of the change in his own fortunes, Bolivar remained the innate gentleman. He could bear hunger and misery, but he could also appreciate the luxuries of life. He enjoyed good food and drink, preferring champagnes and Graves. He was, however, moderate in the use of liquor, despised drunkenness, and enjoyed dinners more for the company than for the food.

His dress recalled the time when he had played the dandy in Paris. Without being extravagant, he was always neatly and meticulously attired. He bathed several times a day and used large quantities of eau de Cologne. He was patrician in appearance and manner, a man of perfect deportment and winning personality.[6]

His relationship with women bound him most closely with this era of adventure and indulgence. Bolivar's life without its

2 Rodó: *op. cit.* p. 268. See also: Simón Bolívar: Libertador de la América del Sur. Madrid, 1914. Martínez: Bolívar íntimo. Paris-Buenos Aires.

3 Cartas: Vol. I. p. 222.

4 Ducoudray Holstein: Memorias. Vol. II. p. 238.

5 Cartas: Vol. II. p. 349. J. D. Monsalve: Estudios sobre el Libertador. Bogotá, 1930. p. 15. Cortes Vargas: Magnanimidad de Bolívar. B. d. H. Bogotá. Vol. XXIV. p. 498.

6 C. Hispano: Libro de Oro del Libertador. Paris, 1925.

erotic associations with women is inconceivable. To work he had to love, or rather he had to make love, for Bolivar never really loved any woman. He needed women, but not as companions who would converse with him and give him advice. In his voluminous correspondence his letters to women take up small space, and even in these the reader finds nothing that is in any way comparable to the love letters of Bismarck or Disraeli. Nevertheless, women were indispensable to Bolivar. His sensual nature, made more intense by an hereditary disposition to tuberculosis, struck sparks at the sight of every pretty face. Yet he was rarely the slave of his amorous experiences. With but a single exception, the many women whose paths he crossed left no mark on him. Their beauty, their grace, their devotion were necessary to him. In their fleeting and passionate embraces he found relaxation and forgetfulness. Because of them he loved to dance. Bolivar was an excellent dancer, and wherever he turned up a ball would be given. After days of work and marching, which were strenuous enough to exhaust the strongest man, he would dance for five and six hours on end. He called dancing the poetry of motion.[7] At these affairs he was all grace and charm, completely captivating. His personality was adorned by a garland of amorous adventures woven of as many victories as any field marshal could boast. The women to whom Bolivar gave himself, or who gave themselves to him, are scarcely more than names to us. Fanny du Villars, Josefina Núñez, Manuelita Madroño, Luisa Crober, Isabel Soublette, Janette Hart, and the many others whose names we do not even know—in Bogotá, in Popayán, in Quito, in Guayaquil, in Lima, in Potosí—unmindful of their background and of the conventions, they followed Bolivar to camp or palace. And Catholic society of South America overlooked these affairs. At no time did Bolivar live alone or without women, but it is difficult to tell whether he ever had a deep or spiritual relationship with

7 Ducoudray Holstein: Memorias. Vol. I. p. 308. V. Dávila: Bolívar galante e intellectual. México, 1942. L. Correa: Viaje Stendhaliano; tres ensayos sobre la psicología amorosa del Libertador. Caracas, 1940. L. A. Cuervo: Apuntes historiales. Bogotá, 1925. D. Carbonell: Escuelas de Historia en América. Buenos Aires, 1943. pp. 218 ff.

them. His existence seems to have been too stormy to have permitted of real communion with others. *"Une promesse de bonheur,"* that is what they all were to him. Real happiness, his real happiness, came to him from other sources. One is obliged to believe that glory alone was enough to satisfy his desires, and that his amours were merely the ornament that decorated his life.[8]

Yet it was not purely the sensual imperative that drove him to women, like Napoleon's famous command "A woman." It was the desire to conquer, indication of his Spanish heritage, for Bolivar's relation to women was that of a Don Juan. It would be idle to set up any theories as to whether the erotic impulse was one of the requisites of his genius. History bears witness to many instances where great works have been born of an overwhelming desire for happiness on the part of sensual beings. And yet again it testifies to others which have not conformed to this rule. In the summation of Bolivar's personality his erotic drive cannot be overlooked, for this aspect of his being is tied up with all the others. The suavity of the man-of-the-world, the glamor of the lover, are both visible and effective in his political and military conduct. His heroism was neither mythical nor monumental. Bolivar personified, as Rodó said, *una elegancia heroica*—an heroic elegance. Bolivar was free of pose, yet he loved the theatrical gesture, "the plastic form of heroism and fame." It was as natural to him as it was necessary to the growth of South America, which realized itself for the first time in its leader and felt itself reflected in him.[9]

In a man thus constituted inspiration is everything. Bolivar had done great things as organizer, but administration was not his element. He was not a man of methodical calculations or planned reckoning like Richelieu or Pitt. He was a man of intuition and creative improvisation. He spoke much and well. He had the gift of conversation to a high degree. His past was always with him. With a few strokes he could sketch the char-

8 C. Hispano: Historia secreta de Bolívar. Bogotá, 1944. E. Naranjo: Bolívar y Jeanette Hart. El Tiempo de Bogotá of September 2, 1944.
9 Rodó: *op. cit.* p. 259.

acters of the men he met, and he was able quickly to evaluate the abilities of his friends and coworkers. He knew how to be persuasive and how to inspire confidence. He could not, however, tolerate contradiction, and like most of the great of the world, he enjoyed any tribute to his genius. He expected to have his opinions respected and his intentions understood. He was irked by refusals, and when he felt he was misinterpreted he was angered and saddened at the same time.[10] He was irascible and showed it. His temper changed sharply from one extreme to the other, but he never held a grudge nor did he conceal a desire for vengeance for later release. Bolivar was always willing to forgive his enemies, and he hated to have rumor or gossip brought to him. He was loyal to his friends and entirely honorable. He would not permit anyone to speak ill of another in his presence. He trusted his friends and fortified this trust with gratitude that did not forget kindnesses even after decades. "Friendship is my passion," he said of himself.[11] He never ceased being what Spaniards and South Americans call a *caballero*. An Englishman, who met Bolivar later, called him "the gentleman of Colombia."

His temperament found outlet in constant activity. When he was not fighting, he made plans; when he was not making plans, he dictated; when he was not dictating, he read—books, newspapers, reports, letters.[12] His restless energies did not permit repose. Lying in his hammock or pacing rapidly up and down like a beast of prey, he listened to his secretaries and aides as they read reports and memoranda to him. He announced his decisions at once. He dictated to three scribes at the same time and complained at their inability to keep up with him. Even when he was interrupted during dictation, he could pick up the thread of his thought at once and could end the sentence without error or pause. He made it a principle to answer every letter, every request, no matter how lowly the writer. An extra-

10 O'Leary: Memorias. Vol. I. p. 488. Miller: Memorias. Vol. II. p. 294. D. d. B. pp. 215, 244, 334. Cartas: Vol. IV. p. 277.
11 Cartas: Vol. I. p. 262.
12 O'Leary: Memorias: Vol. I. p. 488.

ordinary memory made this easy for him.[13] The restlessness
of his spirit often made him impatient with others less gifted
with whom he was forced to work. He was sarcastic to them,
though not to make them feel his own superiority. Like Frederick the Great and Napoleon, he was inclined to make too great
demands on co-workers.

Although Bolivar, like many another, had to suffer the
tragic loneliness of genius, he was never alone. Nor did he crave
solitude; he felt alone in the midst of a crowd. His thoughts
clarified while he rode, or danced, or chatted—even, indeed,
under a hail of bullets.[14] He required constant motion and
companionship, for his imagination was very active and he
needed someone to whom he could throw the ball. He generally
preserved a formless kind of etiquette in all his contacts, but he
frequently broke through the barriers of convention. Once,
when he was already President of Greater Colombia, he received
a British officer while entirely naked. At banquets he would
get up on the table to propose a toast.[15] What he said on these
occasions and the way he said it were always memorable. Even
his cooler Anglo-Saxon observers thought that his impromptu
speeches could be printed without editing. On one day he responded to seventeen different addresses, one after another, and
always with a different turn of speech and style.

The innermost recesses of his soul were filled with emotional
unrest, with an intuitive urge to action and a prophetic vision.
There was but one way to cure this unrest and to realize this
vision—to wage war. Bolivar was equipped for war.

Bolivar was born for the war in South America, where man's
will must triumph over time and space. He was skillful in the
use of arms and was an excellent horseman.[16] On arising in
the morning, and he was an early riser, he would inspect his
stables. Whether he was in the country or in town, he rode out

13 O'Leary: Memorias. Vol. I. p. 489.
14 D. d. B. p. 153.
15 Miller: Memorias. Vol. II. pp. 294-225.
16 Restrepo: H. d. R. C. Vol. III. p. 607. O'Leary: Memorias. Vol. I. p. 487.
E. López Contreras: Bolívar, Conductor de tropas. Caracas, 1930. W. Dietrich:
Simón Bolívar. Hamburg, 1934.

several times a day. He could have taken his place as a horse-man among the Llaneros, and the Llaneros admitted it. They called him *"culo de hierro"*—iron ass. Never before or since has a general covered so much territory on horseback as did Bolivar. His tough Basque fibre, the iron determination of the Spanish conqueror, triumphed over every difficulty. "When nature op-poses us, we shall fight to conquer her."

Five or six hours of sleep, in his hammock or wrapped in his cloak on the bare earth, sufficed him. His sleep was as light as an animal's. A life of ceaseless danger had sharpened his instinct for self-preservation. There were times when only this gift saved him from his enemies. An existence under the most primitive conditions had also quickened his other senses. Sight and hearing functioned with the precision of the hunter.

What the Spaniards call *hombría,* and what is equal to Machiavelli's *virtú,* Bolivar typified as a warrior. He made a place for himself in the army because of his vital authority.

The South American revolution was not primarily an ideo-logical movement, as was the English, the North American, or the French. It did not even develop any original ideas in the course of events. But it did create a human phenomenon which to this day determines life among the South American people. This human phenomenon is the *caudillo*—a leader of the masses, a soldier and politician at the same time, borne along by the will of the people, but guiding and dominating that will.

The caudillo has impressed his seal upon all Latin-American people from Argentina to Mexico. He has formed their consti-tutional life. In him is personified the ideal of presidential democracy.[17]

The caudillo as a social phenomenon is explained by the rift which existed between the indolent and ignorant mass of Indo-Americans and the small groups of the revolutionary élite. Bolivar was more than a caudillo; he was a continental figure. But in becoming one he could not skip over the stage of the caudillo. The South American movement for independence

17 Andre Siegfried: L'Amerique Latine. Paris, 1934. p. 94.

shows in its two focal points, Venezuela and Argentina, a duality of form and character.[18] It existed in the cities as a revolution of ideas and spread to the country as a release of passions. Caracas and Buenos Aires, the Llanos and Pampas, together created South American independence. Led by the caudillo, the barbaric democracy of the steppes flowed into the oligarchic movement in the cities and helped to achieve freedom. In Argentina the two currents diverge in their representatives. The cities produced highly trained soldiers like San Martín or Belgrano; the Pampas produced a gaucho like Artigas. In Bolivar's person both types were united. He was the representative of the urban patrician officer, diplomat, and statesman. But when the situation called for it he was a Llanero, wild and as uncontrollable as a Bedouin.

A few events of his life which might appear like the caprices of a madman are given here as evidence of this duality.[19] One day he was bathing in the Orinoco with his officers. One officer boasted that he could swim better than Bolivar. The Liberator, thereupon, chose a goal and declared that with both hands tied he could get there ahead of his officer. His hands were bound and he jumped into the stream. He reached his goal, but only with great difficulty and at some distance behind his officer. However, his men took this as an example of his indomitable will, whose watchword was, "Never give up."

At another time he saw his aide, Ybarra, jump over his horse's head from behind. Bolivar said that this was nothing remarkable. He took a dive, but failed. His vanity was wounded and he made another attempt only to fall on his horse's neck. Finally at the third trial he was successful. "I admit," he said later, "that I did a stupid thing, but at the time I did not want to have anyone excel me in agility, nor did I want anyone to boast that he could do anything of which I was not capable."[20]

In the spiritual sense of the word Bolivar was more warrior than soldier or strategist, and it is this which characterizes his

18 Rodó: *op. cit.* p. 268.
19 D. d. B. p. 185.
20 D. d. B. p. 363.

activities during the fourteen years of the war for independence. He had not systematically studied the art of war as did Frederick or Napoleon. He was no born strategist like Hannibal, Alexander, or Gustavus Adolphus. He was a born fighter. At the moment of action he was unrestrained, violent, and often hasty. Páez, the leader of the Llaneros and himself a man of daring, said of Bolivar that he often jeopardized his successes with his foolhardy advances.[21] In contrast to the coolheaded San Martín, Bolivar was more fighter than strategist. In his early days his ardor and exuberance sometimes brought him victory, as in the brilliant campaign of 1813. Sometimes, however, they swept him into the abyss.

"I am the son of war," he said of himself, and at another time, "War is my element—danger, my glory." Technically speaking, officers like Morillo were at first his superiors, and it was only after 1817, when he began systematically to emulate Napoleon, that he became a strategist. Yet he always remained a man of warlike impulses, of stormy inspirations. Fortunately for him and for South America, he was able to find men who served his intuitions as filters and who promoted his gifted improvisations.

Who knows whether a more highly trained officer could have accomplished as much with the barbarous human material at hand and under such chaotic conditions. The exigency creates the man to solve it. Bolivar built his army out of nothing. A minimum of men and weapons was adequate for him to keep the fight going. Bolivar had yet another characteristic of the warrior, one which became decisive for the victory of the revolution. He never admitted defeat, but he was, as Morillo said, more terrible in defeat than in victory.[22] He was a very Antheus in his downfall, drawing from each experience new strength for his next ascent. "One learns the art of victory from one's defeat," confessed Bolivar . . . a highly personal remark, and one applicable to but few great generals.[23]

21 Páez: Autobiografía. p. 174.
22 O'Leary: Memorias. Vol. I. p. 488.
23 Rodó: *op. cit.* p. 262.

In Bolivar's unshakable belief in freedom, and in himself
as its chosen instrument, lies the explanation of this rare ability
to emerge stronger from each misfortune. This is the Arche-
medic point from which he pulls out a whole world by its roots.
Bolivar would not have understood Cromwell's remark: "He
gets furthest who does not know where he is going." Bolivar
knew exactly where he was going, and he was sure that he
would get there. He could not be shaken from this belief by
any momentary circumstance of time or of failure. The darker
the situation seemed, the more clearly he saw the stars shine.
Once, during the struggle of 1817, when he had barely escaped
from a Spanish ambush, he began in the middle of the night to
speak of his plans. "I shall liberate New Granada and create
a Greater Colombia. I shall carry the banner of liberty to Lima
and Potosí." In the tropical night his voice sounded like the call
of a prophet, thrilling and unreal. His officers thought he had
lost his reason.[24] Seven years later, on his way to Lima to fulfill
these prophecies, ill, exhausted, and surrounded by his enemies,
he was asked, "What are you going to do now?" "Triumph!"
replied Bolivar.[25]

Bolivar belonged to that group of negatively strategic gen-
iuses, like William of Orange and Coligny, who, often defeated,
emerge more indomitable after each new encounter. Bolivar
was different from these two great Protestant leaders, however,
in his attitude toward religion. The Calvinists of the sixteenth
century found in their faith the strength to resist, while Bolivar
was indifferent to all religion. Philosophical confessions and
religious expression are extremely rare in his letters and discussions. They are rare because these were problems that did not
interest him and whose solution he did not credit to the human
spirit.[26] He had gone through the school of the eighteenth century. Voltaire was one of his favorite authors. Bolivar was
skeptical and an agnostic, if, indeed, he ever thought of religion

24 Blanco: Doc. Vol. V. p. 643.
25 Blanco: Doc. Vol. IX. p. 343.
26 D. Carbonell: Psicopatología de Bolívar. Paris, 1916. Porras Troconis: *op. cit.*
p. 214. C. Hispano: Bolívar y la posteridad. Bogotá, 1930.

at all. He could say with Faust, "The Beyond troubles me little. If you smash this world into fragments, the next one will endure."

He wrote to Sucre, "Of all sure things the surest one is doubt." He was not superstitious like Bismarck, nor did he, like Wallenstein, believe in prophecy. Superstition and prophecy alike were to him either an aberration or the indication of a mood. If he allowed a friend to question him about his metaphysical opinions, his answers were materialistic and skeptical.[27]

Bolivar's world was uniformly Catholic. He was obliged to consider this fact if he wanted to make South America independent. Freedom as he saw it was not freedom of religion or conscience. The Catholic Church had for three centuries held the monopoly of religion in South America, and it was to Bolivar's interest not to irritate it with attacks, but to win it over to the cause of independence. He tried to gain the confidence of the papal princes. He proved to them that they had nothing to fear from free republics, that they had more to hope for from these free republics than from the Spanish monarchy. He retained the form of the religious oath and called upon Providence and the Almighty in his speeches and exhortations. He attended mass and services, for Bolivar knew that the people expected this conformity from him.[28] Bolivar's relation to the church and to religion was a respectful outward acknowledgement of their form and importance, coupled with an inner indifference to everything that concerned dogmatism and the mystical. He believed only in ideas, and in them he found the strength to begin his work anew after each failure. As the Cuban, Jose Martí, said, Bolivar believed in the heavens, in the stars, in the gods, in the god of Colombia, in the genius of America, and in his own destiny. This was his religion, and he knocked at the gates of glory with a sword.[29]

27 D. d. B. p. 389.
28 Mary Watters: Bolivar and the Church. The Cath. Hist. Rev. Vol. XXI. 1935-36. pp. 312 ff. P. Leturia: La acción diplomática de Bolívar ante Pío VII. Madrid, 1925. P. Leturia: Bolívar y León XII. Caracas, 1931. N. E. Navarro: La política religiosa del Libertador. Caracas, 1933. Monsalve: Estudios, pp. 87 ff.
29 J. Martí: Obras completas. Madrid, 1929. Vol. VII. p. 138.

So now in Jamaica, robbed of his sword, he again turned to
ideas. He dared not rest, for either with pen or with sword
the independence of South America must be won.

Bolivar had been given a friendly welcome when he arrived
in Jamaica in May, 1815. The Governor of the island, the Duke
of Manchester, who had invited him to dine, saw a man whom
exhaustion had emaciated, yet in whom the conviction of the
coming of independence to South America was stronger than
ever, and he marvelled. The flame had consumed the oil, he
said of Bolivar.[30] On the whole, the rich merchants of the island
were against the revolution, but the person of the Liberator
inspired sympathy and admiration in them.[31] With the few
companions who had come with him, Bolivar lived in seclusion.
"I have nothing," he wrote to a woman friend. "The little that
I brought with me I have divided among my companions. But
I have a heart that does not fear the strokes of fate."[32] A generous Englishman, Maxwell Hyslop, assured him that he would
always help him out, but only when Bolivar had no further
hope of getting money from the continent did he accept the
offer. Money problems were the least of his worries. He had
other and more serious difficulties to face.

Bolivar shared his room with several refugees. Whether
because the space was too small or because his landlady annoyed
him, he looked for other quarters and found two rooms that
he liked in the house of a French woman. He arranged with
her to have his luggage and books sent over on the very next
day and started to leave the house. Just then there occurred one
of those tropical cloudbursts, and the Liberator decided to spend
the night in his new quarters. This incident saved his life. The
Spaniards, who were well aware that the cause of independence
was not dead as long as Bolivar remained alive, had bribed one
of his black servants, an erstwhile slave named Pío, to murder
him. Pío thought Bolivar was in his hammock, but a friend,
Félix Amestoy, was sleeping there in his stead. The Negro

30 Larrazabal: Vol. I. p. 388.
31 O'Leary: Memorias. Vol. I. p. 290.
32 Cartas: Vol. I. p. 154. Lecuna: Papeles. Vol. I. p. 11.

could not see in the dark and killed Amestoy with a thrust of his dagger. He was apprehended and confessed his crime, but refused to reveal the originator of the plot. Pío was executed, but we know today that it was Morillo who had given the order to kill Bolivar.[33]

From their point of view the Spaniards were right. Bolivar was just as fatal to Spanish rule with his pen as with his sword. Half of his influence was attributable to the word, his power in the word.[34] His friends, his detractors, his enemies, all felt the magnetism that emanated from him whether he spoke or whether he wrote.

Bolivar had the temperament of an artist, a sensitivity to beauty, an almost religious penetration into the nature that surrounded him, and a receptivity for the perfected form. He had educated his taste on his great models: Rousseau, Napoleon, Chateaubriand. They all influenced him, but when he wrote he yielded to the impact of his passions or the force of his thoughts. His words then came from some deep impulse within him. This unusual quality made Bolivar the most outstanding Spanish writer of his day. He became the liberator of thought in South America.

Bolivar was not like one of those gifted men who concentrate on giving expression to one faculty only, like Flaubert or Charles XII. He more nearly resembles those versatile personalities like Leonardo and Michelangelo, like Caesar and Goethe —an exemplification of the universal man. He possessed passion and grandeur of thought, perception and intuition, phantasy and swiftness of decision. Like every true genius Bolivar was a combination of traits which seem mutually exclusive . . . *coincidencia oppositorum*—a marriage of opposites. He was a poet and a soldier, a thinker and a statesman.

Napoleon is said to have written his poems with his dagger on the field of battle. Bolivar wrote his poems down on paper

33 Larrazabal: Vol. I. pp. 407-8. O'Leary: Memorias. Vol. I. p. 311. O'Leary: Doc. Vol. XV. p. 28. D. d. B. p. 174. Lecuna: B. d. H. Caracas. Vol. XIX. p. 315.
34 Blanco Fombona: Simón Bolívar. Madrid, 1914. p. 311.

in moments of leisure. But this fact has little significance in
estimating his poetic nature. He had the soul of a poet.[35] His
one inspiration in word and deed was the freedom of America.
He pursued this ideal as Don Quixote pursued the ideal of
knighthood, and disappointment and defeat frightened him
just as little as they did Don Quixote.[36] The idea of freedom
made him a prophet, as it made him an orator, an actor, a
thinker.

One could study his life through his speeches and proclamations. They are without doubt the most inspiring that have
ever been addressed to the people of South America. But they
bear the character of his era. They show the influence of the
French Revolution. In them Bolivar is the actor who wants to
enthrall the masses and to draw the attention of the world to
America.[37]

In his letters and memoirs he was entirely himself, poet and
soldier at the same time, spontaneous, articulate, colorful, sometimes confidential and melancholy, sometimes grandiose and
convincing. He was master of the word and had a rare gift for
metaphor. He poured his inspiration into unforgettable form,
for in these documents Bolivar is all Bolivar.

But we would misunderstand the man if we called him a
political writer. The word was always a tool for him, the
means to an end as was war, and indispensable where the
inhabitants call their part of the world *continente de la palabra,*
the continent of the word.

In exile the word served him as a means of propaganda and
appeal. Once again he tried to convince the British that they
would benefit by unrestricted trade with a free America. He
received answers to his attempts and from these grew one of
the most noteworthy testimonies to his political thinking—the
Letter from Jamaica.[38] From the day he had landed on the

---

35 O'Leary: Memorias. Vol. II. p. 33. J. M. Samper: Bolívar. Bogotá, 1879.
R. Blanco Fombona: El pensamiento vivo de Bolívar. Buenos Aires, 1942.
    36 G. Valencia: in Antología Bolivariana. pp. 21 ff.
    37 C. Hernández: El estilo de Bolívar. Bogotá, 1945. J. Nucete Sardi: El
Escritor y Civilizador Simón Bolívar. Caracas, 1930.
    38 Cartas: Vol. I. p. 181.

island his mind had never ceased working on his big idea. An accidental impulse sufficed to crystallize it.

The question that was put to Bolivar concerned the future of the South American peoples. Was there a man well enough acquainted with conditions to express himself on the subject? In Bolivar's opinion not even Alexander von Humboldt was qualified to answer. Yet Bolivar had done nothing but ponder this question during his enforced idleness in Jamaica. While he was agitatedly swinging in his hammock or pacing up and down in his room, he tried to penetrate the veil that covered the face of time.

The analysis of Bolivar's famous Letter from Jamaica may help to clarify his political position. The revolution had failed. Spain had won. If Morillo acted quickly and effectively Spanish rule could be reëstablished in the New World.[39] Was there any future for a free America? This was the first point that Bolivar considered. In his opinion the fate of South America had been decided. He wrote, "The bonds that united us to Spain have been severed. The hatred which the Iberian Peninsula inspired in us is greater than the ocean which separates us. The war of extermination has done its work. Two camps oppose each other." America had liberated itself and Spain was vainly trying to enslave it again. America had fought with courage and desperation, and history knows of only a few cases when desperation has not finally attained a victory. The fact that the Spaniards had won the upper hand in some places was no cause for discouragement as far as Bolivar was concerned. The New World was determined to defend itself. "A people that loves freedom will in the end be free," he said.[40]

And so, as though he stood on the highest mountain of the Andes and measured the world with his eyes, Bolivar unfolded a panorama of the American Revolution. He began in the south, in the regions of the La Plata, where independence had triumphed. Chile was still in the conflict. Just as the Chilean

39 Cartas: Vol. I. p. 146.
40 Cartas: Vol. I. p. 184.

Indians, the Araucanians, had once repulsed the Spaniards, so would they again. Peru was the most submissive of all the South American countries, but not even this part of the colonial dominion lived in peace, and it would not permanently be able to resist the maelstrom of the revolution. New Granada, the heart of America, might be threatened, but it would not submit. Venezuela had been conquered by the Spanish at the price of its destruction. And so it went, right up to Mexico, Puerto Rico, and Cuba. Sixteen million people would defend their right to freedom.

Could Spain hope to reconquer America without a fleet, without money, without soldiers? And could Spain, a country without industries or an economic surplus, without arts or science of politics supply America with the vital necessities of life? Even if Spain could have subdued America at this time, the same demands and the same problems would have arisen again in twenty years.

The liberation of Latin America was to change international policies from the ground up. Bolivar's far-sightedness recognized the creation of a new era in the international relations of the peoples of the world. South American independence was to become a vital element in the coming world. The free nations which here were formed were to establish a balance of power which would encircle the globe. South America, said Bolivar, is no longer the soil for experimentation. On the other hand, the European nations, if they would support independence, would find sure markets for their goods. Here, too Bolivar's prescience is notable. Up to the days of the Second World War, South America was one of the most important markets for European industry.

But who understood Bolivar in those days? He spoke to a world that had not yet comprehended these possibilities. Ignorance and indifference had to be overcome, and only that man who had himself suffered and helped to shape the destinies of South America could arouse the sympathies of humanity. The interests of a whole continent centered in Bolivar. For him

America rose on the crest of history's wave like a new Atlantis. "We are," he said proudly, "a macrocosm of the human race. We are a world apart, confined within two oceans, young in art and science, but old as human society. We are neither Indians nor Europeans, yet we are a part of each." What form would America assume after the collapse of Spanish rule? he asked. Would it emerge as an entity from this catastrophe? Would it be a monarchy or a republic? These were the intrinsic problems of America's future which Bolivar tried to solve.

Could South America become one republic? Were its peoples capable of fulfilling the obligations which such a super-state would impose? The people of the Western Hemisphere had for centuries led only a passive existence. "We were," Bolivar confessed, "but one step beneath slavery. That is why it is so hard for us to accept freedom. In everything that concerned public affairs, we were left in perpetual infancy. Under the Spanish system most Americans were bonded for slavery, but all Americans were bonded for the consumption of foreign goods. In all that concerned government or the administration of the state we were outside the world." It is not difficult to conclude from this statement that America was not ready to separate from the mother country when the time came to take this step. "The South Americans have blundered through the centuries as the blind blunder among colors. They were on the stage of action, but they were blindfolded. They neither saw nor heard." Now, they were obliged to play the roles of lawgivers, officials, diplomats, and to play these roles extemporaneously.[41]

Thus Bolivar continued the criticism which he had begun three years earlier in his Manifesto of Cartagena. His Letter is a constructive critique of South American conditions, and one can see how, step by step, his political thinking had developed.[42] Having once adopted the ideologies of the French Revolution, he completed his break with the absolute traditions

41 Cartas: Vol. I. p. 207.
42 C. Parra Pérez: Bolívar, Contribución al estudio de sus ideas políticas. Paris, 1928. J. D. Monsalve: El ideal político del Libertador. Bogotá, 1916. Belaunde: *op. cit.* p. 163. F. González: *op. cit.* p. 172.

of Spain. At that time he was a Jacobin in word and thought.
After the downfall of the First Republic, he proclaimed the
necessity of a strong and unified government of the South
American states. In his Letter from Jamiaca he held firmly to
this idea. "As long as our fellow citizens do not acquire the
talents and virtues which distinguish our brothers to the north,
a radical democratic system, far from being good for us, will
bring ruin upon us. Unfortunately, we do not possess these
traits. . . . We are ruled by corruption, which must be accepted
under the rule of a country which has distinguished itself by
inflexibility, ambition, vengefulness and greed." Bolivar repeated Montesquieu's famous sentence—"It is harder to free a
nation from slavery than to enslave a free nation."

The South Americans had expressed their willingness to
possess liberal institutions, but would they be capable of solving
the problems that such possession incurred? Was it possible
that a nation just out of bondage could fly into the realm of
liberty without having its Icarian wings melt, without falling
to destruction? The creation of one free republic in South
America was impossible and therefore not even desirable. Even
less satisfactory was the idea of a single monarchy. What solution could the future hold for these problems?

Inasmuch as the Spanish colonies would not be able to
emerge from the revolution as a state, Bolivar had to propose
individual solutions for the problems of internal politics and for
interstate relations. "The American states need the efforts of
paternal governments to heal the wounds and scars made by
despotism and war." Bolivar remained a centralist. He considered as indispensable the guardianship of a strong government, with principles of unity, stability and efficiency.

Bolivar's republic would, therefore, be a conservative one,
based on the leadership of strong men and the moral élite. He
wanted unity *and* liberty, but unity was more important to him
than internal political freedom, for unity was the prerequisite
for all the achievements of independence. Unity and liberty
were the guiding stars of the nations arising in the nineteenth

century. Liberal statesmen like Cavour stressed the primary principle of liberty. Conservatives like Bismarck and Bolivar stressed the principles of unity.[43]

Bolivar, however, did not wish to renounce liberty, and this conflict in his ideological thinking was both an expression of his personal predilections and of the situation on the continent. America felt as one, but nature, with its river and mountain barriers, seemed regionalistic. Democracy demanded a relaxation of strict colonial rule, but the need of the hour demanded a centralized and stabilized government. Democracy proclaimed the equality of all men, but racial differences permitted only a slow and gradual realization of this principle.

In the case of Bolivar himself, was he not torn between the ambition to rule and the desire to have only the glory of the liberator? He strove for a dictatorship, yet abhorred it at the same time. Out of a desire to resolve this inner conflict he grew to be the thinker of the Revolution. He sought a constitution for America which would give form to its manifold and diverse elements. An Anglo-Saxon realism within him combined with the French radicalism of Rousseau. "Inasmuch as it is not possible to take the best and most successful features from the republics and the monarchies, let us at least avoid falling into anarchistic demagogy or tyrannical despotism." It was Bolivar's desire to reconcile the idea of sovereignty of the people with the principle of authority. "Democracy on his lips; aristocracy in his heart," said his enemies. Liberty without license; authority without abuse, said Bolivar. It was his aim to harmonize the technical democracy of the masses with the hierarchical principles of leadership. Our age has more understanding of this ideal than did the nineteenth century. Bolivar himself called this constitution a copy of the British form of government with the important difference that it had no king. Executive power rested in the hands of a president who was to be elected for life.

---

43 C. Lozano y Lozano: Bolívar Macquiavélico. p. 73. See also F. Meinecke: Weltburgertum und Nationalstaat. Munchen, 1913.

This solution might seem to be inspired by Bolivar's personal ambition; actually it expressed his desire for stability.

Bolivar conceived a law-making body consisting of two chambers. He had in mind an hereditary senate comparable with the House of Lords in England, but since there was no resident nobility in South America, the senate was to be composed of the wealthy families of the upper Creole classes. The second chamber was to be freely elected. The vote was to be conditioned, like its British model, on a minimum of property. Such a setup would combine the advantages of constitutional forms without sharing their weaknesses. Bolivar knew that not all the American states would accept his constitutional ideas. He believed that Colombia—that is, Venezuela and New Granada together—would be the first to adopt it.

Bolivar also predicted the fate of the other South American nations. His prophecy of what would happen in Mexico and Central America, in Peru, Chile, and Argentina, was incredibly accurate. "In 1815," writes F. García Calderón, "while America was still under Spanish domination Bolivar was not only prophesying the immediate conflicts, but he envisioned a century's development of ten nations."[44]

The fact emerges that Bolivar was not thinking in terms of creating a great South American state. Although he wrote: "Nobody desires more keenly than I to create the greatest of all nations of the world here in South America. Great, not so much by expansion and wealth, as by freedom and its glories," yet he could not convince himself that the New World could be governed as one republic, even less as one monarchy. A single government which could do this would have to have god-like gifts. Bolivar's decision here was the result of his clear insight into the historic and racial reality of South America, for even the Spanish empire had never been a unified whole. It had existed for three centuries as a federation of empire units. The colonies did not form a chain, but rather a many-pointed star whose center was the Spanish crown.

44 F. García Calderón: Simón Bolívar, in Antología Bolivariana. p. 252.

The movement for independence had broken up this center. The federation was dispersed. Nations and nationalities had crystallized, and they could not again be compressed within an artificial form. When Bolivar later undertook to form a superstate in the region of the Andes, he had to recognize how prophetically in his Letter from Jamaica he had perceived the impossibility of such an undertaking.

In Europe, too, people had begun to discuss the problem of South America's future. The Archbishop of Malines, Msgr. de Pradt, had developed a plan whereby fifteen or seventeen monarchies were to be established in South America. Bolivar also thought that seventeen free and independent nations would arise in South America, but he repudiated any monarchistic form.[45] Bolivar considered the republican system more durable than the monarchistic. Freedom is not imperialistic. Whenever republics proceed to make conquests, even in forcing a liberal form of government on other nations, they are in danger of degenerating. Bolivar's program was the creation of seventeen free republics.

Although his realism prevented him from wishing for the impossible and from thinking of South America as a sovereign entity, he could not lay aside his continental point of view. At the end of the Letter Bolivar strikes the chord of American solidarity. "It is a lofty idea to risk the attempt to make a single nation of the New World, with a single bond to hold all its parts together. Because they have one religion, one language, similar customs, they should logically have one government. . . . But this cannot be, for extremes of climate, differing conditions, opposing interests, and variations of characteristics divide America."

His reason told Bolivar that the dream of American unity could not be fulfilled at this time, but his heart would not allow him to relinquish the dream. "How ineffable it would be if the Isthmus of Panama should become for America what the

45 See also, Laura Bornholdt: The Abbé de Pradt and the Monroe Doctrine. Hisp. Am. Hist. Rev. May, 1944. p. 201.

Straits of Corinth were for the Greeks. May God grant that we can some day enjoy the good fortune of opening a congress of representatives of the republics, kingdoms, and empires that will discuss peace and war with the rest of the nations of the world." Ten years later he called the first Pan-American Congress together, and from that time on the idea of American solidarity has never waned. Simon Bolivar was the torch-bearer for the whole continent. He had also foreseen the role that America would take after Europe's self-destruction. "Then science and art, which were born in the Orient and shed light over Europe will fly to a free Colombia which will offer them a haven of refuge."

But South America was not yet free. What did she need in order to wipe out the Spaniards and create a free form of government? America was divided, forsaken by all the nations, isolated in the midst of the universe, without diplomatic connections and without military help. "But if we are strong the world shall see that, under the aegis of some free nation who shall help us, we shall develop the virtues and qualities that lead to glory. Then we shall begin the solemn crusade for salvation that South America is destined for."

This is the end of the Letter from Jamaica. His last words clearly indicate that the letter was meant for England. It is hard to say whether any tangible success followed this incomparable document. We feel sure that this new idea of the balance of power reached Canning's ear and that ten years later it inspired his famous pronouncement that the creation of the New World was necessary for the equilibration of the Old.

The letter may also have made an impression on the adventurers, soldiers, and fighters who soon came across the Atlantic. On the whole, however, it died away unheard. Its significance lies not in its immediate effect, but in its attitude toward the facts of American existence and in its vision of America's future, Jamaica, which had once been the scene of Columbus' trials and disappointments, became the locale of the rediscovery of America by an American.[46]

46 Parra Pérez: Bolívar. pp. 56, 44. O'Leary: Memorias. Vol. I. p. 289.

Bolivar had already tried to interest the British in intervention in behalf of the revolution. The Antilles had been a refuge
for the Independents; here they sought safety and an arsenal
for weapons. Bolivar tried to explain to the British that they
could profit a great deal with but little effort. Twenty or thirty
thousand guns, a loan of one million English pounds, fifteen or
twenty-five warships, munitions and a few volunteers, were all
that was required. As a reward the British government was to
get the provinces of Panama and Nicaragua. England should
then build canals connecting the Atlantic and Pacific Oceans.
Such a step would bring these countries into the center of world
trade and would assure England's commercial superiority for
all time.[47]

It would seem that these proposals were not taken seriously
in London. A few weeks later Bolivar appealed to Richard
Wellesley in an attempt to persuade him that the political balance of the world and the interests of Great Britain demanded
the liberation of South America. "If I had a single ray of hope,"
he wrote at that time, "that America could win through alone,
nobody would have desired more than I to serve my country
without the humiliation of having to beg the support of a foreign power. But this hope has gone. I came to beg for help.
I shall go to London to find it. If necessary I should go to the
ends of the earth."[48]

He wrote other letters. He bombarded the newspapers with
justifications for the revolution. Between times he appealed to
Camilo Torres. But everyone seemed to have forsaken him.
England had other worries in the summer of 1815. Napoleon
had fled from Elba. English foreign policy, headed by Castlereagh, was making approaches to the Holy Alliance. Bolivar
was not even allowed to buy weapons in Jamaica, and his despair grew with each day as he heard of Morillo's successes.
There were times when he came close to committing suicide.
Death seemed preferable to a life of dishonor and torment.[49]

47 Cartas: Vol. I. pp. 147-48.
48 Cartas: Vol. I. pp. 152, 217. Webster: The Foreign Policy of Castlereagh.
London, 1925.
49 Cartas: Vol. I. pp. 220, 150. Blanco: Doc. Vol. V. p. 365.

At the beginning of December an invitation to resume his top command came to him from Cartagena, which was still defending itself against Morillo. The idea of revenge for its own sake was foreign to Bolivar. He felt incapable of hatred where Colombia's interests were at stake. "I love America's liberty more than my own honor. To gain it I have shirked no sacrifice."[50] But what would his sacrifices avail under these circumstances? Was not the situation the same as that which had led to his self-exile? Could his presence in Cartagena prevent its downfall?

In spite of everything he was ready by the middle of December to return. He could no longer stand the inactive existence of his exile. On Demember 18 he left for Cartagena, and sailed the ocean for days to escape the Spanish blockade. While on the high seas he heard the news that Cartagena had fallen. Where should he go now? The next free state in the region of the Antilles was Haiti. Bolivar changed his course, and on December 27, 1815, he arrived at Aux Cayes.

50 O'Leary: Memorias. Vol. I. p. 313. See, Cartas inéditas de Bolívar. B. d. H. Bogotá. Vol. XXVIII. p. 754.

CHAPTER 16

From Cliff to Cliff

*B*y 1815 Haiti and the United States were the only countries in the Western Hemisphere where republican ideas had prevailed. The population of Haiti, consisting almost entirely of half-breeds and Negroes, allied the island more with Central and South America than with North America. A French colony until the outbreak of the great Revolution, it had realized the ideals of freedom and equality in its own fashion. When Bolivar arrived in Aux Cayes, Alexander Pétion was president of the Republic.

Pétion was forty-six years old at that time, and his appearance betrayed the fact that he was a half-breed. His father was French and his mother was a Negress from that caste on which the impact of colonial exploitation weighed most heavily. Pétion had learned to be a blacksmith, but had later enlisted in the French army, and in 1789 had contributed his efforts to the uprising of the island. Still later he spent long years in France, and only returned to Haiti in 1802. In 1807 Pétion became President of the Republic. Twice again he was elected and in 1816 he became President for life. The Haitians recognized him as their liberator.[1] Bolivar reached Port au Prince on January 1, and was received by the President on the following day.[2]

1 Blanco: Doc. Vol. V. p. 412. D. Bellegarde: Petion et Bolivar. Rev. de l'Amerique Latine. Paris, December 1924. F. Dalencour: A. Petion devant l'Humanité. Port au Prince, 1929.
2 Cartas: Vol. I. p. 223. Lecuna: La Expedition de los Cayos. B. d. H. Caracas. Vol. XIX. No. 75. p. 317.

Two great exponents of American life thus stood face to face. Pétion, a slave by descent, had risen to the position he now held by his own efforts. He was all dignity and understanding. He loved merit and believed in earning it. The two men quickly understood each other. They were united by the same ideals and a belief in the dignity of man. Pétion saw, as did Camilo Torres a year earlier, that the liberty of the continent was embodied in the person of Simon Bolivar. Pétion now added something new to his accomplishments as patriot and statesman. He became Bolivar's protector.

In the numerous discussions between these two men during the early days of 1816, Bolivar gave Pétion a brief summary of the state of the revolution. Cartagena had fallen and the Spaniards were pushing on in Colombia. Nevertheless, Bolivar vowed that he would liberate Venezuela and the continent. He asked Pétion for the means that had been refused him in Jamaica—money, arms, ammunition, ships, and food. His plan appeared both mad and hopeless, but Bolivar knew, as usual, how to make the impossible seem possible. He convinced Pétion. The President promised to help with all the means at his command, but he made one condition. Bolivar was to promise to free the slaves in all the states that he should liberate.[3] Bolivar gave his promise without hesitation. Years before he had set his own slaves free, and he had long since outgrown any class-conscious thinking. His perspective encompassed an entire hemisphere. With this agreement for the emancipation of the slaves Pétion and Bolivar achieved world historic significance. Before Abraham Lincoln had raised his voice in the Anglo-Saxon world these two men on a little island in the Caribbean proclaimed the application of the principles of liberty and equality to an anonymous host of slaves.[4]

Bolivar wanted to give credit for the decrees that were to free the slaves to President Pétion, thereby raising a monument to the humane character of Haiti's President, but Pétion did not

3 Cartas: Vol. I. p. 225.
4 J. S. Rodríguez: La abolición de las Esclavitud en Venezuela. B. d. H. Caracas. Vol. XX. p. 393. A. N. Whitehead: Adventures of Ideas. Cambridge, 1939. p. 29.

want to be mentioned.[5] He wrote to Bolivar, "You know my sentiments for the cause whose defense you have undertaken and my personal feelings for you. You must be permeated with the knowledge of how keenly I wish that all who suffer under the yoke of slavery be freed."[6] Haiti was, however, in a difficult position. Half of the island was still a Spanish colony, and Pétion had also to consider the United States. It was understandable that he should prefer to work behind the scenes. He did not need personal acclaim. For these reasons all instructions concerning Bolivar went out to the ports and to the officials in the form of secret orders. Pétion put arms and ammunition at Bolivar's disposal. He permitted him to recruit sailors, but he also took care that these decisions were so worded that they could not endanger the independence of his little state. Even the money with which the expedition was to be financed could not be paid out of the state treasury. A wealthy English merchant, Robert Sutherland, a friend and admirer of Bolivar's, undertook to make the payments in order to veil their ultimate purpose.[7]

Next to Sutherland the most important figure among Bolivar's friends and supporters was Luis Brion. Brion was a well-to-do merchant from Curaçao who had put his fortune at the disposal of South American independence. Half pirate and half entrepreneur, he belonged to that class of reckless traders who, in times of crisis, find wasteful outlets for their gambling instincts and their love of adventure. In Jamaica, Bolivar had already called him the first of his protectors and the freest of men. In Haiti his participation in the cause of the revolution became of the greatest importance. Brion had chartered a small fleet on whose aid depended the success of every expedition to the mainland. His entry brought about a complete change in revolutionary strategy. When Brion died in 1821, Bolivar wrote,

5 Cartas: Vol. I. pp. 223, 225.
6 Blanco: Doc. Vol. V. pp. 399-402.
7 O'Leary: Doc. Vol. XV. pp. 46-68. L. A. Cuervo: Bolívar y Pétion. Bogotá, 1937. p. 18.

"Admiral Brion has a shrine of gratitude in every Colombian heart."[8]

During the first days of his stay in Port au Prince, Bolivar turned to Brion for help in uniting the different factions. He believed that together they could plan a constructive attack against the mainland.[9] What were these factions? What, indeed, was the human material with which Bolivar expected to win his battles?

A number of Venezuelan officers had sought refuge in Haiti with Bolivar. Hordes of persecuted politicians and soldiers arrived daily from Cartagena. They had preferred to flee on small ships rather than face certain death at the hands of the Spanish. Under the Frenchman, Louis Aury, a flotilla which had fought for Cartagena, also arrived in Haiti. Pétion took care that these unfortunates did not go hungry. Bolivar undertook to organize them both politically and militarily.

Bolivar returned from the capital to Aux Cayes with a letter from the President which opened to him all the sources of help in the province. His task was now to prepare the attack upon the mainland. He named his general staff at once. Any attack upon the Spanish regime in South America, however, was as much a political as a military act. Bolivar called a meeting at which the new government of Venezuela was to be outlined. Seated at this meeting were the most influential men of the Revolution: Mariño, Bermúdez, Piar, Leandro Palacios, Brion, Aury; the Scotsman, MacGregor; the Frenchman, du Coudray; Holstein, and Zea.[10]

Bolivar opened this "parliament" of the dispossessed with an address. The end in view, he stated, was the liberation of the mainland. He did not conceal the dangers of the expedition from his colleagues, but he proclaimed his implicit faith in the ultimate triumph of freedom. He declared that the prerequisite of victory was the creation of a government with unrestricted

8 Cartas: Vol. I. pp. 169, 170. Vol. II. pp. 416-17.
9 Cartas: Vol. I. p. 223.
10 Larrazabal: Vol. I. p. 412. Lecuna: Los Cayos. Vol. XIX. p. 325.

powers. A single man should administer the government. It was Bolivar's old plan of a dictatorship in time of need.

The assembly did not accept him without some resistance. Aury proposed the formation of a triumvirate. Bolivar replied that, though there was nothing about his own person to suggest that he was the man most capable of being the dictator, he would never consent to a division of power which might easily endanger the success of any military undertaking. Brion put an end to the passionate debate. He offered the services of his fleet on condition that Bolivar be named undisputed leader of the expedition. And thus it was agreed.[11]

But resistance to Bolivar's leadership was not broken by this decision. Petty rivalries among the leaders, which in years past had impeded the progress of the Revolution, broke out anew. Bolivar was accused of incompetence and cowardice. He was challenged to a duel. Finally Bermúdez and Aury joined to prevent his departure. As the day for Bolivar's leave-taking approached, Aury ordered the schooner *La Constitución* for himself and declared that he would attack Mexico unaided.[12] Bolivar appealed to the authorities of the country—first to the Governor, and finally to the President himself. Pétion then gave another proof of his political sagacity. He realized that any disunity among the refugees was bound to harm the cause of freedom. He sharply forbade the attack on Mexico and reaffirmed his faith in Bolivar, saying that anyone who did not wish to follow his leadership would be obliged to remain at the port of Haiti. *La Constitución* was returned to Bolivar so that not one moment of this world historic hour should be lost.[13]

Thus protected against rebellion in his own camp, Bolivar named Mariño as his representative. Brion became the first Admiral of the Republic, and Zea the chief administrator. The insurgents had withdrawn from the army. The moment of departure had come. Once again Bolivar went back to the

11 O'Leary: Memorias. Vol. I. p. 340. Blanco: Doc. Vol. V. p. 399: Historial del senador Marion: La primera Expedición de Bolívar.
12 Larrazabal: Vol. I. p. 417. For the conflict with Bermúdez see, Bolívar's letter of August 7, 1816. B. d. H. Caracas. Vol. XVI. No. 62. p. 84.
13 Larrazabal: Vol. I. pp. 417-18.

capital to bid Pétion farewell. With tears in his eyes the older man said, *"Que le bon Dieu vous benisse dans toutes vos entreprises."* The other officials of Haiti were enchanted by the tact and courtesy which the Liberator had shown under such trying circumstances. *"Il a eté d'une courtoisie remarquable dans cette circonstance."* Bolivar had needed three months to re-create an army. On March 31, 1816, the little fleet left the waters of Santo Domingo and sailed in the direction of Venezuela.[14]

In all, Bolivar's expeditionary force numbered scarcely 250 men, the majority of whom were officers. To many the voyage seemed like a sea voyage with Don Quixote, and there were grave doubts concerning the success of such a foolhardy undertaking. Bolivar took arms for six thousand men. He also took a printing press, for he hoped to arouse the enslaved population with leaflets. The ships were small and none too numerous: six schooners and one sloop comprised the whole fleet, hardly more than one thousand tons in all.[15]

Bolivar had to skirt around the warships that lay off Puerto Rico. He found time and opportunity, however, to take aboard the woman of his heart, Josefina Machado. This affair delayed the trip considerably. For a run which usually occupied a period of ten days, Brion was obliged to take thirty-two. On May 2 the Patriots reached Venezuelan waters.

The fleet headed for Margarita Island, which lies off the east coast. In a brief encounter with the Spanish ships which blockaded the island the Patriots were victorious and two warships were captured. On May 3 Bolivar dropped anchor in the little port of the island. Here began the third epoch of the Republic. Not conquest but reconstruction, announced Bolivar, should build a free Venezuela. This was his program: unification of the people, creation of a central government, and the convening of a congress. The mistakes of the past had to be avoided. The Venezuelans could not be free men and slaves at the same time.[16]

14 O'Leary: Doc. Vol. XV. p. 52. Lecuna: Los Cayos. Vol. XIX. p. 332.
15 Rivas Vicuña: Vol. II. p. 127. Ducoudray Holstein: Vol. I. p. 308. See also, B. d. H. Caracas. Vol. IV. p. 354. Lecuna: Los Cayos. Vol. XIX. pp. 315, 421.
16 Proclamas: pp. 146, 147. Cartas: Vol. I. p. 228.

The Third Republic still lay in the distant future. Before it could be resurrected, Venezuela had to shake off the Spanish yoke. How did Bolivar intend to accomplish this? What were his plans of operation? When he had left Haiti with a vision of speedy victory, he had promised the governor of Aux Cayes that he would send him horses of the finest breed as soon as he should get possession of Angostura and Guayana.[17]

Angostura and Guayana, however, meant the Orinoco. That mighty river was the gateway not only to Venezuela, but to great stretches of territory beyond. Navigable far upstream, one could reach New Granada by way of this great artery. The vast plains of the Orinoco, with their horses and cattle, could easily nourish a whole army. Tropical fruits could be brought down the river to the Atlantic coast and there be exchanged for arms and ammunition. An army operating in the region of the Orinoco could not be defeated without a fleet, nor could it defend itself without the protection of a fleet.

Bolivar had succeeded in slipping through the Spanish patrols. At what point did he hope to break through the safety belt of Spanish fortifications? On what did he base his plan for an attack on the regions of the Orinoco?

In eastern Venezuela the revolution still smoldered. Dispersed troops from the beaten army of the Second Republic had fled into the plains. New leaders had been found to lead these indomitable men once more against the Spaniards, with no other hope than to keep the war going. For the time being there was little expectation of defeating the enemy. Bolivar wanted to get to the Orinoco because the Patriot guerrillas were quartered there. He may have known little about them, but he could bring them weapons and increase his army with them. Margarita Island was to be only his springboard for an attack on the mainland. The little island had surrendered to Morillo in 1815 when he promised a general amnesty. But the policy of conciliation did not last long. In September, 1815, Arismendi, the political and military leader of the Margaritans,

17 Blanco: Doc. Vol. V. p. 403.

escaped the Spanish grasp and loosed the uprising anew. The war was carried on with great cruelty by both sides. Arismendi had instigated the killing of prisoners in Caracas in 1814. His wife and small son had remained in the hands of the Spaniards, and the Monarchists threatened to kill them in reprisal. Arismendi, however, remained obdurate, and when Bolivar arrived, he promptly acknowledged the Liberator as the supreme commander.

In Margarita a meeting was called at once to confirm the resolutions of Haiti. Bolivar could henceforth proceed with some semblance of legality. The Spaniards withdrew in surprise from the capital of the island and retired to a small fort. But here they held firm. Bolivar demanded their surrender and solemnly promised on his part to end the war to extinction forever. The Spaniards refused his offer. They denied any guilt for the frightful conduct of the war and declared their intention of resisting Bolivar's siege. After several fruitless attempts, the Liberator admitted that he would only be wasting time if he were to devote himself personally to this offensive. Arismendi could hold the Monarchists in check while Bolivar crossed over to the mainland to find supplies and men.[18]

Bolivar sailed in the direction of the continent on May 26 with a fleet that consisted of eleven units. He reached Carúpano in six days. A successful landing was made with the guns of the warships covering the operation. The first troops under Soublette and Piar reached the soil of their homeland, and the Spanish commander was routed with all his force. A sizeable booty remained in the hands of the Patriots.

Bolivar's first concern was for the army. He quickly raised a small force of recruits. The regiments bore the old, glorious names of Girardot, Araure, Cumaná. Bolivar sent the generals, Mariño and Piar, to the port of Guiria to arm the population and to find recruits for the main camp. Success now depended on his being able to keep his soldiers supplied, and the British

18 Cartas: Vol. I. p. 231. O'Leary: Memorias. Vol. I. p. 343. Larrazabal: Vol. I. p. 428.

islands of Trinidad and Barbados were natural depots for an invasion of the mainland. Trinidad controlled the eastern coastal area down to the mouth of the Orinoco. But the British authorities met the Patriots with cool animosity. Bolivar appealed to the governors of both islands and asked for recognition of his fleet, which flew the Venezuelan flag. For the rest he had the old bait ready for the English, which he expected them to swallow sooner or later. "Our relations with Great Britain will always be the same . . . always friendly and advantageous to British trade."[19] During these weeks he also redeemed his promise to Pétion. He freed the slaves. Of course Bolivar made one condition. Every eligible man between the ages of fourteen and sixty would have to enter the army; those who refused to do this would remain slaves as would their entire families. The effect of this revolutionary measure was far removed from Bolivar's expectations; only a few hundred joined his army. The majority followed the Spanish flag.[20]

In general, Bolivar's position was difficult and became more so with each day. There was a price of ten thousand pesos on his head; the people were hostile; supplies were scarce. The Spanish were again pushing on toward Carúpano. Bolivar could only check them with his artillery; he had lost all mobility. He had hoped that Mariño and Piar would send help, but in this he was disappointed. Perhaps they were unable to do so; perhaps they simply did not wish to.[21] Whatever the cause, Bolivar remained alone. The belt of Spanish encirclement grew tighter and tighter, and the Spanish fleet threatened to cut off his retreat by sea. Bolivar had to act quickly if he wanted to escape the trap. He tried his old method of defeating the enemy before they could concentrate their forces. He wanted to attack the Spanish fleet, and then, after its defeat, hurl his forces at Cumaná. But here, too, his tools failed him. The sailors on the ships were not experienced seamen. They had no real interest in the movement for independence. Only

19 O'Leary: Doc. Vol. XV. pp. 75-78.
20 Proclamas: pp. 147-49. Cartas: Vol. I. p. 241.
21 Cartas: Vol. I. pp. 238, 239, 243, 244.

their hope for booty had induced them to follow Bolivar. Hitherto, these pirates had not been able to pocket anything worthwhile, and their discontent was increased by the poor food aboard their ships.[22] They laughed at Bolivar's solemn promises, and when he announced his plan to attack the Spanish ships, they refused to fight. There was nothing left for Bolivar to do but to give in and renounce the attack.[23]

It would seem that the failure of the fleet had a disastrous effect on his original intentions. Wherever he attacked he needed the support of Brion and his ships. On these rested all his hopes for the invasion. If worst came to worst, they were the instruments of his rescue. With their help he could again seek refuge in the Antilles. Relying on the fleet, he had planned to attack the Spanish lines at the Orinoco; and this was exactly what the enemy expected.[24]

To his misfortune, Bolivar gave up his original intention. He abandoned his attack on the Orinoco line, and decided to carry the fight into the heart of Venezuela instead. Caracas now became his goal. He resolved to evacuate Carúpano and to sail on with his troops. In a letter to Arismendi he confessed that it was more the force of circumstance than his own desire which induced him to do this thing. And as though he were aware of the suicidal character of his new plan, he added, "If my luck forsakes me, I can lose no more than my life. It is always great to attempt the heroic."[25] With a thousand men and all that he possessed in the way of arms and ammunition he went aboard.

His destination was Ocumare, a little town between La Guayra and Puerto Cabello. Bolivar thought he could take Caracas within eight days and he wanted then to return to the east. From the very beginning chances were against him. He expected more active support from the population of the west

22 O'Leary: Doc. Vol. XV. pp. 82-83. Cartas: Vol. I. p. 240. See, the Proclamation to the Fleet; Blanco: Doc. Vol. V. p. 420.
23 Blanco: Doc. Vol. V. p. 455. Rivas Vicuña: Vol. II. p. 158.
24 Rodríguez Villa: Vol. III. p. 134.
25 Cartas: Vol. I. p. 244. Lecuna: Los Cayos. Vol. XIX. pp. 460 ff.

than he had found in the east. But this advantage would be counteracted by the great masses of Spanish troops and the greater vigilance with which the Spanish defended their most important dominion.[26]

The fleet arrived in Ocumare on July 6. The Spanish commander retired. Bolivar sent the greater part of his troops under Soublette against Maracay. He wanted to raise another army himself consisting of friends and Patriots, but he had not reckoned with the Spanish. Bolivar had as little following in the west as he had had in the east. The governor of Caracas had been astute enough to vitiate Bolivar's propaganda in advance.[27]

Morillo had given Morales, the Man of Terror, command of Venezuela. Morales attacked Soublette on June 13, and after a battle that lasted three and a half hours, the Independents were beaten. Soublette feared the superiority of his adversary and retreated in orderly fashion. Bolivar, who had hurried to his aid, had come too late to prevent the defeat of his soldiers. When Morales resumed pursuit the next day and marched on Ocumare, he found the town and port deserted. Littered all over the beach were the Patriots' supplies: one thousand guns, sixty thousand bullets, flint, and spears—in short, everything that Pétion had given Bolivar for his expedition. "The band of criminals who already believed themselves the masters of Venezuela, has vanished like smoke," said Morales triumphantly. What had happened?[28]

From the very outset, Bolivar had failed to recognize the hopelessness of his undertaking. The reports he had received concerning the strength and movements of the Spaniards had been false. He thought he had the whole coast to himself, and that it would be an easy matter to take Puerto Cabello or Caracas, and so he had permitted his whole transport section to disembark. Then something totally unexpected happened. The fleet refused to remain outside Ocumare, ostensibly because

26 Rodríguez Villa: Vol. III. p. 149.
27 Proclamas: p. 151. Cartas: Vol. I. p. 247. O'Leary: Memorias: Vol. I. pp. 346 ff. Lecuna: Los Cayos. Vol. XX. p. 14.
28 Rodríguez Villa: Vol. III. pp. 82-83. Rivas Vicuña: Vol. II. p. 170.

of lack of supplies. Actually, the reason was that the pirates had filled the ships with tropical fruits in Ocumare which they wanted to sell at a profit in Curaçao, and Brion himself steered the greater part of the fleet to that port. Only three of the smaller ships remained. Bolivar's expedition thereby lost its mobility. He was forced to divide his troops, so that supplies which had been guarded by the fleet would not remain unprotected.[29]

This was the situation on the morning of July 14. When the troops that had been beaten by Morales streamed back to Ocumare, everything was in utter confusion. Two matters had to be settled: what was to be done with the army, and what was to be done with the irreplaceable supplies? Morales was at the Patriots' heels. A council of war was held, and it became obvious to all that the three little ships would never suffice to carry the army across the sea to safety. The officers were determined not to sail; they did not want to desert their men. They thought they could fight through the Spanish lines and then find their way to the plains where they would join small bands of guerrillas who fought there. They did not, however, want Bolivar to go with them, for the hazards of this plan were tremendous. If Bolivar could save himself, there would still be hope some day of liberating the fatherland. The conference took place in Bolivar's quarters. The officers begged him to sail, but Bolivar would not hear of it. He sent his heavy luggage to the port and prepared a small box so that he could join the army on its march.[30]

There was still another problem that needed solving, that of salvaging the equipment. Bolivar decided to take care of shipping the supplies himself. He hurried to the port and found himself in the midst of indescribable confusion. The day was ending, and in the lowering dusk Bolivar saw that the beaches were filled with men and women who were trying to save themselves. All about them lay strewn the costly war materiel that

29 O'Leary: Memorias. Vol. I. pp. 349 ff.
30 See Soublette's report in O'Leary: Memorias. Vol. I. p. 351.

the sailors could not or would not take aboard. It will never be entirely clear what now happened. One of the main witnesses of these events, General Soublette, has left us these ambiguous words: "Into these events came love . . . Marc Antony, unmindful of the danger in which he found himself, lost valuable time at Cleopatra's side." We know that Bolivar was never without a woman even in his war camps. Very likely he met his friend, Pepita, or another, in the port of Ocumare. Whether he was busy trying to rescue her, and thus, as Soublette says, lost valuable time, or whether she begged him to take her with him, will never be known.[31] One thing is certain: in the midst of all the confusion, news reached Bolivar that Morales had already taken Ocumare. The report was false, but in the general panic no one thought of checking. Bolivar and his men jumped into a cutter; and, as its anchor lifted, reached the very last ship to sail.[32]

Meanwhile, in Ocumare the officers waited in vain for Bolivar's return. They had received no orders; only the news of his flight reached them. They were now forced, on their own responsibility, to begin their march to the interior, but they were unable to salvage their precious supplies. These remained on the beaches where a victorious Morales gathered them up the next day.

No event in Bolivar's life became the object of so much bitter criticism as the catastrophe of Ocumare. Bolivar himself later thought of it as something utterly incompatible with his military career. When he planned during the last months of his life to have an account written of his deeds, he said, "I never took a step during the war which one could call cowardly." But it was highly characteristic of him that he mentioned the night of Ocumare as the only instance which could be used to contradict his statement.[33] Even his own reports of these events vary. Immediately after his flight he assured his friends that his

31 See Brion to Arismendi in Blanco: Doc. Vol. V. p. 456.
32 O'Leary: Memorias. Vol. I. pp. 349 ff.
33 Cartas: Vol. IX. pp. 241 ff.

concern for the supplies forced him to abandon Ocumare.[34]
In later years he said that his aide had betrayed him with a false
report, and that he had been about to kill himself when a friend
pulled him into one of the boats at the last moment. Bolivar
never admitted that the fatal occurrence had been caused by his
interest in a woman, but the implication of Soublette's report
is not made less significant.

From a military point of view, Bolivar's conduct on that
night was inexcusable. The expedition was his responsibility
and his own inspiration. It is unforgivable that, after the collapse, Bolivar deserted his army without even saving the vital
equipment. It was the failure of the general rather than of
the man, a failure of self-possession and clearheadedness, more
than a lack of courage. It was not the first occurrence of this
kind in Bolivar's life, nor the last. Other generals and statesmen have had such moments of weakness. Frederick the Great
at Mollwitz, Napoleon on the eighteenth Brumaire, Richelieu
many times in his career. And Bolivar was a son of the tropics,
a genius of the moment, for evil as well as for good.

The small fleet that left the port of Ocumare consisted of
two merchant ships and one warship. In vain did Bolivar try
to persuade the captain to make for the nearby coastal harbor
of Choroni so that he could rejoin his troops. The captain
refused and headed for the little island of Bonaire near Curaçao.[35] Bolivar ordered the warship to fire on the merchantmen,
but the latter had too great an advantage. All that Bolivar could
do to save the weapons was to follow the merchantmen. In
Bonaire, Bolivar met Brion who, thanks to his position, was
able to settle the quarrels with the pirates. Bolivar convinced
the Admiral of the necessity of making contact with the troops
which had stayed behind on the mainland. The following day
he sailed back to the coast with Brion, but they found all the
ports occupied by the enemy, and they learned through spies
that the Republican troops had marched on to the interior.[36]

34 Cartas: Vol. I. p. 250.
35 O'Leary: Memorias. Vol. I. p. 353. Larrazabal: Vol. I. p. 433. Lecuna: Los
Cayos. Vol. XX. pp. 20-21.
36 Cartas: Vol. I. p. 250. O'Leary: Memorias. Vol. I. p. 353.

Bolivar's position was desperate. Depressed by his own failure, without money or supplies, he did not know where to turn. He could not stay in Bonaire, and Curaçao was closed to the "rebels." He lacked food enough for a sea voyage to the east coast. Finally he conceived the foolhardy idea of landing on another of the Spanish isles, there to plunder what he needed. He selected a little island near Puerto Rico for his venture, but on the way there his schooner ran aground. A passing Spanish vessel sent its captain aboard to examine the ship's papers, whereupon Bolivar had him seized. When the captain learned that he had fallen into Bolivar's hands, he fell on his knees and begged for his life. Bolivar promised to spare it if he would give the ladies who were aboard and who were the cause of so much confusion, safe conduct to St. Thomas. The captain swore that he would do this, and Bolivar's ship was made ready to sail, supplied with food, and once again went out to sea.[37]

The incident sounds as though it were taken from a novel of adventure; and, as a matter of fact, Bolivar's life during those weeks did, indeed, resemble that of a buccaneer. The Caribbean Sea, brilliant stage of the great sea robbers, Drake and Morgan, now beheld South America's Liberator driven from port to port, from island to island. But at last he found a minimum of supplies and food, and with these he was willing to hazard the crossing to the east coast and Guiria. But if he thought to end his wandering there, he was to be bitterly disappointed.

A month had passed since the catastrophe of Ocumare, and the leaders of the independence movement in Guiria had long before been informed of it. All put the blame on Bolivar. General Mariño, who was in Guiria, had, from the beginning of the revolution, pre-empted the highest rank for himself. Bermúdez, whom Bolivar had excluded from the expedition in Haiti, whom, indeed, he had forbidden even to set foot upon Venezuelan soil, was also there. Both men thought the time had come for them to square their accounts with Bolivar. From

37 O'Leary: Memorias. Vol. I. p. 354. For a criticism of O'Leary's report see, Lecuna: Los Cayos. Vol. XX. p. 28.

the moment of his landing they denied his right to give orders, and heated altercations arose.[38] Bermúdez and Mariño called Bolivar a deserter and a traitor and declared him dismissed. Bolivar accused them of being insurgents. Both sides seized arms, and only the efforts of a few coolheaded men prevented an open fight. The army was split. One part still acknowledged Bolivar's authority; the other followed Mariño and Bermúdez.[39] Bolivar realized that this situation left no alternative but civil war. For the third time in two years his own companions had stabbed him in the back. In 1814 it was Ribas; in 1815, Castillo; now it was Mariño and Bermúdez. He would do again what he had done in other years; if his presence caused a division among the Patriots, he would again go into exile.[40]

After six days he prepared to leave Guiria. But the hatred of his adversaries was so great that they did not even approve of this decision. Bermúdez was determined to capture Bolivar and pursued him, dagger in hand, down to the port. Bolivar was obliged to fight his way to the ship with his sword. He had hoped that at least a few of his troops would follow him in order that he might attempt an invasion at another point on the east coast. Under the circumstances he could not contemplate such an undertaking, so he steered his course to Margarita Island. Here, however, the Spanish fleet barred his way. He changed his destination and sailed toward the small port of Jakmal. For three days his ship ran through a terrific storm, and in the end he fled to Port au Prince, which he had left six months before. For the second time he had to ask Pétion for help.

Pétion had remained a devoted friend. He had an instinctive confidence that the Liberator would not fail a second time and again offered his help. Bolivar, nevertheless, felt bitterly humiliated. "When a man is unhappy," he wrote then, "he is always in the wrong. It is not surprising that I, too, am subject

38 O'Leary: Memorias. Vol. I. p. 355. Larrazabal: Vol. I. p. 432.
39 Lecuna: Los Cayos. Vol. XX. p. 29.
40 Larrazabal: Vol. I. p. 438.

to this universal law."[41] He planned a manifesto which was to describe recent events and the extent of his responsibility for them. He did not descend, however, into introspective contemplation. All was not lost. Important points had been won on the coast. Now it was just a question of raising new funds for a second expedition which would bring about the final liberation of Venezuela. "This time we shall deliver the final blow."[42]

There were signs in Haiti that confirmed the passing of Spanish rule in South America. Bolivar met the Spaniard, Javier Mina, who had fought for the freedom of Americans in Mexico. He heard from Jamaica that one of the oldest pioneers of the revolution, Canon Cortés Madariaga, had sought refuge there. Without further delay Bolivar invited him to coöperate in the reëstablishment of political order in Venezuela.[43] Meanwhile, he asked Pétion, who had just been elected president of Haiti for life, for his support. For his own return to Venezuela Bolivar needed Brion's fleet, and Brion had just sailed to the United States to seek war materiel and support. The ensuing delay, however, proved to be to Bolivar's advantage. In the Patriot camp on the mainland there had been a reaction in favor of the Liberator. The maltreatment and opprobrium to which he had been subjected in Guiria were well known. The more thoughtful men felt this to be only an increase in the misfortune and confusion which afflicted the country. Those officers who had not participated in the uprising did not want to acknowledge any other leader. In October, 1816, a war council with Piar as chairman again called Bolivar to assume top command.[44] The inhabitants of Margarita Island and Arismendi supported this demand. The Colombian, Francisco Antonio Zea, was sent to Haiti as spokesman for the Patriots.

Bolivar did not hesitate. If they needed him he was ready. He waited only for Brion's arrival and then took leave of his

41 Cartas: Vol. I. p. 252. Cuervo: *op. cit.* p. 24. See also Cartas del Libertador. B. d. H. Caracas. Vol. XXV. No. 97. p. 38.
42 Cartas: Vol. I. p. 253.
43 Cartas: Vol. I. p. 256.
44 B. Tavera Acosta: Historia de Carúpano. Caracas, 1930. p. 200. Blanco: Doc. Vol. V. pp. 492-93.

Haitian friends. On December 21, 1816, he once more set sail for Venezuela.

That he forgave did not necessarily mean that he had forgotten. His axiom that "the art of victory is only learned through defeat" was valid in helping to dissipate the gloom of the year 1816. The experiences of this year of wanderings and misadventures were both military and political. The debacle of Ocumare had taught Bolivar that any attack on the north coast of Venezuela would come close to military suicide. The capture of Caracas could be only the end, never the beginning, of any victorious campaign. The east coast, on the other hand, was less guarded and easier to reach. To penetrate Venezuela from the east he had to take the line of the Orinoco and to strengthen his forces there.

Organization was the second great lesson of these months, and it was political in character. Bolivar's failure in 1816 was attributable not alone to military factors; it was first of all politically conditioned. His defeats in Carúpano, Ocumare and the disgrace of Guiria, had their origin in the general disintegration in the camps of the Patriots. Anarchy in the army, anarchy among the leaders, anarchy in the fleet—these were the characteristics of the situation. Each man, impelled by private motives, whether for glory, for ambition, or for greed, acted on his own initiative, and each man was against the other. If Venezuela wanted to be free, it was imperative that a central government be set up and a central authority recognized. "Weapons destroy tyrants in vain," wrote Bolivar at the end of 1816, "unless we create a political order which can make good the damages of the revolution. The military system is a system of force, and force does not create governments."[45] This opinion contains Bolivar's program for the period ahead.

The revolution could succeed only if it recognized one man as its personification, if it promised to follow him and would put its highest authority in his hands. That he, Bolivar, was qualified to fill this role he never doubted, despite all his set-

45 Cartas: Vol. I. p. 257.

backs. There were men in Venezuela at this very hour who had performed greater deeds than he, but he was the only one whose personality included understanding and military ability, the only one who could set up a government, form a nation, and call an entire hemisphere to life. Despite all his weaknesses and failures, he was the genius of the South American revolution. The problem that was presented to him was a twofold one: to liberate America he had to defeat Spain; to defeat Spain he had to bend the Americans to his will. Would he find the means of creating form out of chaos?

CHAPTER 17

Piar and Páez

At Margarita Island, toward the end of December, 1816, Bolivar once again set his foot upon the soil of Venezuela. But he did not remain here long, for the way to the mainland was open. Great events had taken place while he had for the second time sought refuge in Haiti.[1] The rebellion had continued on Margarita Island for the whole year, nor had Bolivar's rivals—Mariño, Bermúdez, and Piar—remained idle. They had succeeded in forcing the peninsula of Paría, which protrudes from the east coast, into their power. From this point of vantage they had harassed the Royalist troops in the province of Cumaná. The small expeditionary corps which Bolivar had left behind when he fled from Ocumare had thrown the plans of the colonial rulers completely into the discard.[2]

Before he had gone down to the port, the Liberator had outlined the steps he would take to free the small army from encirclement.[3] When he had failed to return, his officers decided to carry out the plan without him. They chose the Scotsman, MacGregor, as commandant. He was one of those European adventurers who had volunteered to serve the revolution. Hitherto he had not held any position, but had proved himself to be a strong and cold-blooded character. Only two

1 Larrazabal: Vol. I. pp. 447-48. O'Leary: Memorias. Vol. I. p. 364.
2 Lecuna: Campaña de Barcelona. B. d. H. Caracas. Vol. XX. No. 78. p. 193.
3 O'Leary: Doc. Vol. XV. pp. 85-92.

weaknesses were apparent in him—an unquenchable thirst and a strong aversion to water.[4]

The plan of operations was as bold as it was desperate. Rescue was possible only if the troops could make contact with other groups of Independents. To this end they made their way through the Spanish lines toward the southeast. The march of this small band, which lasted more than sixty days, sounds like an adventure story. First the Patriots crossed the Cordilleras which, lying inland, separate the valleys from the sea. Along the roads on their way down they found the corpses of forty citizens who had been executed because they were suspected of sympathizing with the revolution. The troops realized what they would face if they fell into Spanish hands. Carefully skirting the Spanish garrisons, MacGregor defeated single units who opposed him. He tried to reach the plains of the province of Barcelona, and fortunately, his intrepid men found guides who were familiar with the country. It was the rainy season, the rivers were swollen, and the plains flooded; nevertheless, the troops covered 750 kilometers in a month. The most surprising fact was that MacGregor's army doubled in size during the march. His troops had numbered scarcely six hundred men when they had started out. His slight losses were more than compensated by the two hundred Indians and six hundred riders who joined him.

With this enlarged division he dared to make the attack on the capital of the province of Barcelona. Luck played into his hands. The Spaniards were defeated and lost over six hundred men. MacGregor occupied Barcelona on September 13 and captured a rich booty. In Barcelona the methodical Scot reorganized his army and asked other units to join him, for he was well aware that the main struggle was still ahead. His most dangerous adversary was Morales, who had pursued him and who was now approaching Barcelona. Among all the Patriot leaders, General Piar was the man who most clearly

4 O'Leary: Memorias. Vol. I. p. 357. Baralt: Vol. I. p. 335. L. A. Cuervo: Notas Históricas. Bogotá, 1929. pp. 170 ff. Rafter: Memoirs of G. MacGregor. London, 1820.

realized the seriousness of the situation. He finished his missions in Cumaná and hurried to Barcelona. Three days later came the clash with Morales in the Pláins of Juncal. The Republicans were numerically inferior to the Spaniards, but they were fortified and encouraged by their triumphs of the past weeks. Morales was beaten and fled to the west with heavy losses. Thus ended the year 1816 with the balance in favor of the Americans.[5]

Bolivar heard of the rescue of his troops when he arrived in Barcelona. He did not exaggerate when he called them "the bravest of the brave." At about the same time he heard that bands of guerrilla fighters had gathered in the west in the direction of New Granada, on the slopes of the Andes. Their leader was an unknown youth, Antonio Páez. Bolivar's faith was boundless. He ordered the fighters of Ocumare to liberate the Orinoco and then to march on to Bogotá and to Peru. "Our fate demands that we go to the borders of America. Let the world look at us in admiration, as much for our defeats as for our heroism."[6]

Bolivar, however, was no longer merely a visionary. The experiences of the past year had made him more mature and more circumspect. He did not wish to be the leader of the Braves of Ocumare; instead he called them his brothers. He courted Mariño as though nothing had happened between them. He tried to convince the refugees that they should return to Venezuela.[7] He made an effort to have Venezuela recognized abroad, and appointed agents in London. What was more revealing, however, was his admission that he could not always meet all the conflicting obligations his compatriots put upon him. Again he demanded the convening of a national assembly which should receive his reports and take all final authority into its own hands.[8]

All this was sincere and deceitful at the same time. Bolivar's

5 Blanco: Doc. Vol. V. p. 481. Rivas Vicuña: Vol. II. p. 198.
6. Cartas: Vol. I. pp. 258-9.
7 Cartas: Vol. I. p. 259. B. d. H. Caracas. Vol. XVI. No. 62. p. 185. See, Lecuna: Campaña d. Barcelona. op. cit.
8 Proclamas: p. 151.

words contained a new political concept which he wanted to impose on his country—the creation of an absolute authority which would be responsible for the conduct of the revolution. Bolivar was not so certain of his procedure when it came to taking his first military steps. To liberate Venezuela he was obliged to take an offensive position, and here he hesitated between two possibilities. He summoned the soldiers to liberate Guayana in order that he might set up permanent headquarters on the Orinoco. But first he had to defend Barcelona, where he had stored all his supplies. So he undertook a diversionary maneuver. He wanted to make the Spaniards believe that he thought seriously of taking Caracas. He tried to deceive them with proclamations, which he dated from the interior of the country. He scarcely hoped that his attack would succeed, and he wanted to go to Caracas only when he should no longer encounter resistance on the way. He made the attempt with only seven hundred men of whom four hundred were new recruits. The Spaniards held their positions. Bolivar lost the battle at Clarines, withdrew to Barcelona, and immediately changed his strategy.[9] Nothing more could be gained by isolated engagements that had no plan or cohesion. He must first collect all available units. Where vast distances hindered his progress, communications had to be established and a detailed plan agreed upon.

The day after his defeat at Clarines, Bolivar sent Arismendi to present his plan for a concerted attack to young Páez, the commander of the troops in the west.[10] Bolivar also wrote to the other Patriot leaders, especially Piar. He summoned Piar to join him in Barcelona as soon as possible.[11] The concentrated attack on the Spanish forces was to be made gradually. In the first place, it was important to protect the eastern coastal regions of Venezuela, because only in this way could the outside lines

9 O'Leary: Memorias. Vol. I. p. 370. Restrepo: H. d. R. C. Vol. II. pp. 373 ff. Mitre: San Martín. Vol. III. p. 454. Rivas Vicuña: Vol. II. p. 244. Lecuna: Campaña de Barcelona. Vol. XX. p. 198.

10 O'Leary: Doc. Vol. XV. pp. 114-17. Blanco: Doc. Vol. V. pp. 570-71.

11 Blanco: Doc. Vol. V. pp. 572-73. Lecuna: Campaña de Barcelona. Vol. XX. p. 200.

of communication, on which his supplies depended, be kept intact. Bolivar hoped to collect an army of ten thousand men in Barcelona and then proceed to the interior. At this point he no longer thought of Caracas. His destination was the plains of the Orinoco; if he could take them the Spaniards would be obliged to confine themselves within Caracas or to hunt the Patriots in the vast plains. As a matter of fact, whoever had the plains as hinterland and the Orinoco as base, was invincible. Sooner or later he would be the master of Venezuela. This was Bolivar's great strategic concept of the War for Independence, and shows his insight into the geo-political character of Venezuela. If the coast should be taken by the enemy, Bolivar could retire to the Cordilleras; if the Cordilleras were lost, he could flee to the plains where the rivers and swamps would afford him protection. As a last refuge there remained the primeval forests into which the soldiers of northern regions could not penetrate.[12]

Bolivar's plans, however, were only patchwork, and once again the anarchistic element of the movement refused to follow him. General Piar, together with MacGregor, had liberated Barcelona, and had united fifteen hundred men under his banner, not an inconsiderable number in view of the small size of the armies which fought in the South American revolution. Piar then made the surprising decision to go with them to the Orinoco and to subdue the province of Guayana.[13]

This decision of Piar's was one of the most fateful in the entire War for Independence. It gave direction to all future operations; it pointed the road to victory.

Piar, however, did not originate this plan of action, and his march to the Orinoco was no more than an ingenious improvisation.[14] He lacked certain indispensable equipment, especially ships, to maintain communications in this vast region. He was

---

12 Páez: Autobiografía. p. 23.
13 Blanco: Doc. Vol. V. pp. 490, 492, 495. O'Leary: Doc. Vol. XV. p. 114. O'Leary: Memorias. Vol. I. p. 367.
14 The first to attempt an attack on the Orinoco was Bermúdez. See his letter dated March 1, 1815, in B. d. H. Caracas. Vol. XVI. No. 61. p. 1.

unable to take any decisive step against the Spaniards. And at the Orinoco only that man who had a fleet at his disposal could accomplish anything. When Bolivar's summons to appear at the assembly arrived in January, 1817, he refused to heed it. Piar wanted to stay where he was, and instead of hastening to the aid of the Liberator, he waited for Bolivar and his fleet to come to the Orinoco.

Piar's refusal had little effect on Bolivar's action in Barcelona. He could not give up the city because all his supplies were stored there and the future depended on them.[15] But Bolivar's troops numbered only six hundred men, and they were equipped for the most part with bows and arrows; in other words, they were Indians whom Bolivar had hurriedly recruited. On the other hand, the Spaniards were slowly moving on Barcelona with almost four thousand men. In face of Piar's failure Bolivar had to depend on the other leaders, especially on Mariño, who was operating in adjacent Cumaná. He urgently begged him to relieve Barcelona, but before Mariño could arrive the Spaniards were already within gunshot range.

Bolivar had all his supplies taken to the monastery of St. Francis, put up fortifications, and entrenched himself. He called this place of defense a fortress, but in reality it was an emergency building and not a very durable one. Barcelona, itself, he gave up.[16] The Spaniards entered the city on February 8 and found it deserted, but when they heard that Mariño was approaching and would cut off their retreat, they evacuated Barcelona at once. Bolivar, who had been forced to retreat to the monastery, celebrated his action as a victory.[17]

General Bermúdez, who six months earlier had treated Bolivar as a traitor and a coward and had threatened him with his drawn sword, accompanied Mariño's soldiers as they entered Barcelona. Bolivar knew how to treat his compatriots. He was aware that hardly any of them could resist the effect of a well-

15 O'Leary: Doc. Vol. XV. pp. 118, 119, 122, 138, 146. Urdaneta: Memorias. p. 107.
16 Cartas: Vol. I. p. 260.
17 Larrazabal: Vol. I. p. 456. O'Leary: Doc. Vol. XV. pp. 166-67.

enacted theatrical scene. He rode out to meet Bermúdez and
said in greeting, "I come to embrace the liberator of the Liberator." Bermúdez had not expected such generosity and could
find no words with which to answer Bolivar. Finally he broke
the silence with a cry of embarrassment: "Long live free
America!"[18]

Mariño and Bolivar had joined forces, but the Spaniards still
had numerical superiority. Bolivar's position continued to be
extremely critical. He could not resist a combined attack by
land and sea. The incompetence of the enemy, whose top command was disunited within itself, saved him. While February
went by with small skirmishes, the sea-ways remained open.
Brion brought up powder and flint, and the equipment of the
army grew better each day; even horses and cattle were procured. Meanwhile, Bolivar worked on the great idea of unity.
He wanted to put an end to the chaotic regime of the gang
leaders and generals and to create an orderly administration
on which the Republic could be based.[19] There were two ways
to do this, by persuasion or by subjugation. In February, 1817,
Bolivar tried the way of persuasion once more. He had become
reconciled with Mariño and Bermúdez, and they had confirmed
him in his position as commander-in-chief of the independence movement. How sincere they were . . . who could tell?
Bolivar himself probably did not overestimate the value of
their assurances, but he was faced with momentous decisions.
His departure for the interior of the country had been definitely
decided upon, and the appearance of harmony between him
and the men of secondary rank was better than an open break.

With each day that passed Bolivar was more convinced that
the reconstruction of Venezuela would have to begin at the
only place where there was any prospect of a lasting gain,
namely, at the Orinoco and in the plains of Guayana.[20] Therefore, he decided to have everything shipped to Margarita that
he could not take along with him on his march to the interior.

18 Larrazabal: Vol. I. p. 458.
19 O'Leary: Doc. Vol. XV. pp. 172-73.
20 Cartas: Vol. I. p. 262.

The island was to serve the Republicans both as a refuge and as an arsenal. He was willing to give up Barcelona but the officials of the city were not. They offered to defend the city with a single battalion, and at length Bolivar gave in to them. He left a garrison, which could withdraw to the monastery of St. Francis in an emergency. From a military standpoint it was a mistake for Bolivar to split his forces, but this was not a war that could be fought according to technical rules. It was most important to win the hearts of the people for the cause of independence; and he, therefore, consigned Barcelona to the care of Mariño, who had been given the task of defending the east coast.[21]

On March 21 Bolivar set out for the Orinoco, but the situation was so uncertain that he left his army on the plain of Barcelona so that he could first examine the possibilities of this campaign. Only fifteen officers went with him. On the second day he managed to escape a Spanish attack only by a ruse. The Spaniards were lying in wait for him. Bolivar saw them, and, as though an entire army were behind him, gave orders for an attack. The Monarchists were intimidated and retired. Indeed, who could believe that the commander-in-chief would be so foolhardy as to undertake a reconnaissance trip to the Orinoco with only fifteen men? Miraculously, Bolivar slipped through the enemy net and reached the Orinoco on the third of April. He crossed the river by night accompanied only by his secretary. He had scarcely reached the shore and comparative safety when a Spanish patrol boat came on the scene and commandeered the canoe in which Bolivar had made the crossing. The next day he met Piar.[22]

So far Piar had not been any too successful in his assignments. He had been unable to take the fortress of Angostura, his first objective. His chief difficulty had been the lack of ships. The enemy, on the other hand, could sail up and down the river observing every move of the Republicans, and thus

21 O'Leary: Memorias. Vol. I. pp. 373-74.
22 Larrazabal: Vol. I. p. 460.

kept control of the stream. Thus Piar had been forced to leave
the enemy at his back and to penetrate deeper into the province
of Guayana. He had more luck with this move. His objectives
now were "the missions." These were the areas which in colonial
days had been assigned to the Capucin monks for cultivation.
They had founded no less than nineteen stations in which lived
about seven thousand Indians. The Capucins were the highest,
and indeed, the only, authority for the natives. As they were all
of Spanish origin, they were antagonistic to the revolution and
influenced their wards in this feeling. These areas in the wilder-
ness of Guayana were the most respectable and the best cultivated. Their possession was vital to both parties, for here both
could find what they needed to supply their armies. Piar subdued the missions and imprisoned the monks. The Republicans
now had an easy task with the more pliable natives.

The conference between Bolivar and Piar was long and
included all the military and political problems of the situation.
Piar vowed to acknowledge the authority of Bolivar, an oath
which carried very little weight in those days.[23] The most important result of their meeting was of a military nature. Piar
gave Bolivar final assurance that Guayana was a land of promise
for the Republicans. Bolivar saw his plans confirmed. He
commissioned Piar to attack the enemy in Angostura and immediately returned to lead his army to the south. He crossed
the Orinoco again on April 6, and in eleven days he met his
army on the plain of Barcelona.[24] But it was not the army he
had hoped to find. While Bolivar rode out to the Orinoco, the
Spaniards had hurled themselves at Barcelona, had captured
and then destroyed it. Mariño had not turned a hand to help
the city. He hated to serve under Bolivar. He was a son of the
east and believed that leadership in this theatre belonged to him,
both by nature and by destiny. A few of the officers abetted
him in his senseless ambition. The troops were split up; rumors
ran about that Bolivar had been murdered and that affairs

23 B. Tavera Acosta: Anales de Guayana. 2 Vols. Ciudad Bolívar. 1913. Vol. I.
p. 277. Restrepo: H. d. R. C. Vol. II. p. 384.
24 Lecuna: Campaña de Guayana. B. d. H. Caracas. Vol. XX. No. 80. p. 426.

were in a chaotic condition. Finally Arismendi and Bermúdez broke with Mariño. They awaited the Liberator in the plains with some five hundred men. On learning of the circumstances, Bolivar became terribly enraged. "How long," he cried, "will Mariño continue to harm our cause with his greed for power? Does he not realize the injury he does to the country with this lust which nothing will satisfy?"[25]

But this was not the moment to complain or to square accounts. That hour would come. Bolivar took command and set out for the Orinoco. On April 24, he reached the northern shore of the river with his men. The soldiers began to cross the stream in canoes, an operation which took three days. And now they had to blaze their trail through the jungle, which, at the Orinoco, is as thick as a wall. The supplies were exhausted; the torment caused by mosquitoes was unbearable. A few soldiers ate roots and died. Finally the officers' horses were slaughtered to feed the troops. After four endless days they came upon the supplies that Piar had sent. On May 2, the two armies joined in the vicinity of Angostura.[26]

On Bolivar's staff were Arismendi, Soublette, and Bermúdez. Bolivar's prestige among the soldiers was undisputed, but Piar's position was also secure. Bolivar confirmed Piar's rank; he was to remain commanding general of the army of Venezuela, while Bolivar, *el jefe supremo,* would continue to be the highest authority on questions of war and policy. Seen from an objective point of view, this struggle for titles and glory in a Republic which existed only in the hearts of a few thousand men may appear petty and ridiculous, but behind this display of human vanities and weaknesses was concealed the great problem of consolidating a formative state, of applying military discipline and civil order—in a word, of overcoming the era of anarchy.

The campaign which now began had as its goal the conquest of Guayana. Two factors were responsible for Bolivar's

25 Urdaneta: Memorias. p. 111. Restrepo: H. d. R. C. Vol. II. p. 385.
26 O'Leary: Memorias. Vol. I. pp. 382-83. O'Leary: Doc. Vol. XV. p. 249. Tavera: *op. cit.* p. 223.

success in this gigantic undertaking: In the first place, his
pre-vision enabled him to calculate all the chances of victory,
and in the second place, the mistakes committed by his enemy,
Morillo, were of great advantage to him. These considerations
made the year 1817 the turning point in the South American
War for Independence. When Bolivar landed in Venezuela in
1816, Morillo had felt very sure of himself. At that time he
was in New Granada, the subjugation of which had just been
completed.[27] The troops left behind in Venezuela had been,
he thought, sufficient to check a horde of ill-equipped rebels.
Nevertheless, they had not been able to dislodge the Independents in the east. Morillo had been forced to stay in western
Venezuela to fight the soldiers of young Páez. Now, however,
in less than a year, the situation had changed so much in favor
of the Patriots that Morillo wrote in 1817: "I left Venezuela
with sufficient troops to keep its territories intact. . . . This is not
the same place."[28] He still believed that the best way to resist
the revolution was the complete annihilation of its supporters.
But such axioms were no longer effective in 1817; and, instead,
acted as a boomerang wherever he met men who were on their
own part intent on wiping out the Europeans. And worse was
yet to come. Morillo now committed his most grievous mistakes as a general. He knew exactly how important the lands of
the Orinoco were, yet when he heard that this region was
threatened, he made no move to defend it, merely sending some
auxiliary troops to Fort Angostura. He wanted to go to eastern
Venezuela, where he thought he would find the leaders of the
revolution.[29]

Morillo also wanted to descend on Margarita Island to cut
off the Patriots' lines of reinforcement. He did not realize that
Bolivar, the genius of the independence movement, was already
preparing to march to the Orinoco. One thing more happened
to paralyze Morillo. He was a European and never quite able
to orient himself to tropical warfare with all its wildness and

27 Rivas Vicuña: Vol. II. p. 248.
28 Rivas Vicuña: *ibid*.
29 Rodríguez Villa: Vol. III. p. 372.

barbarity. He always remained the methodical soldier of the
Old World who expected to count on the regular arrival of supplies, efficient transport, and systematic movement. He mistrusted the undisciplined native troops; he wanted to fight with
experienced and seasoned soldiers. A new Spanish expeditionary corps was on the way, and Morillo wanted to await its
arrival in order that he might use this force to purge the east.
The march to the Orinoco seemed to him to be a very perilous
undertaking.[30]

Morillo acted accordingly. He tried ruthlessly to extinguish
the freedom of the east. The confiscation of property, the
exiling of liberal families, the execution of leaders, made up his
program. He thought he could ignore Bolivar and his plans.
He considered the summons of the Liberator the bravado of
defeat. In reality it was he who let the prize slip through his
fingers, he who grasped at shadows. The mistakes of Morillo
gave Bolivar the opportunity to carry out his great plan.

Good news awaited Bolivar when, at the beginning of May,
he joined Piar at the Orinoco. On April 12 near San Felix,
Piar had defeated the reinforcements Morillo had sent to Angostura. The Royalists had lost over one thousand men and their
commander had barely escaped capture.[31] But Piar had not
been able to make any headway against the Spanish fortifications on the Orinoco. The enemy moved freely up and down
the majestic river. So long as it was not taken, possession of
the province could not be gained. If Bolivar could liberate the
Orinoco, he could win the vast territory along the river.[32] But
here, as always, he had more than a mere strategic problem.
He had to fight on two fronts, an outer one and an inner one.

In addition, there was Piar. Would he be satisfied to have
another man complete the work he had begun? Bolivar gave
him command of the missions districts. These areas were the
depots for troop supplies and their possession was vitally impor-

30 Rodríguez Villa: Vol. III. p. 394. Rivas Vicuña: Vol. II. p. 265.
31 O'Leary: Memorias. Vol. I. p. 377. Larrazabal: Vol. I. p. 469. O'Leary:
Doc. Vol. XV. pp. 153 ff., 198 ff. Blanco: Doc. Vol. V. pp. 618-20, 633.
32 Cartas: Vol. I. p. 263.

tant, but conditions there were involved. Even in prison the Capucin monks had constituted a threat, and Bolivar had ordered them sent deep into the interior. Through a misunderstanding which has never been clearly explained, they were shot. There were twenty-two Brothers, and the memory of this atrocity is still a blot on the Republican conduct of the war.[33]

Piar went into the interior of Guayana with a special task in mind, but there were others from whom Bolivar might expect resistance. His first objective was the Orinoco, but he could not take the Orinoco with troops alone; he needed ships. However, the fleet was under the command of Brion, and Brion did not come to the mouth of the Orinoco because he was simultaneously conspiring with Mariño against Bolivar.

Mariño thought the time was propitious to take the leadership of the revolution into his own hands. Bolivar was far away, and it seemed expedient to use this opportunity to pollute the waters. On May 8, in Cariaco, a small spot on the east coast, a few men who called themselves the representatives of the nation banded together and took over all the power.[34] Among them were some real friends of Bolivar's, like Brion and Zea. One can only conjecture how Mariño managed to deceive them. He told some that Bolivar had approved his plans; others he assured that the Liberator had perished in Guayana. The conclusions arrived at in this badly played farce are not worth mentioning here. The government was to be carried on by a governing board into which Bolivar was also elected. They planned, in this way, to outvote him. Mariño took command of the army and left the fleet to Brion. But the theatrical coup of Cariaco fell far short of its desired effect. The people either continued to resist or were indifferent. The edicts of the fake government found no echo. Bolivar listened coldly to the decisions. He would not acknowledge the pseudo congress, and even less did he heed its instructions. Instead he took counter measures. He sought out those who were favor-

33 O'Leary: Memorias. Vol. I. p. 376. Blanco: Doc. Vol. V. p. 646. Tavera: *op. cit.* Vol. I. p. 257. Lecuna: Campaña de Guayana. Vol. XX. p. 431.
34 Blanco: Doc. Vol. V. p. 640. O'Leary: Doc. Vol. XV. pp. 228, 250.

ably disposed to him, dismissed Mariño, and sent loyal officers
to the east. The disaster they had planned for Bolivar fell instead upon the traitors. The better officers gave up Mariño and
set out for Guayana to serve under Bolivar. Urdaneta was
among them, as was also Colonel Antonio José de Sucre, whose
profile in the mirror of historical events appears here for the
first time.[35]

But the occurrences at Cariaco had a symptomatic significance which lifted them above the rank of the ordinary. Three
times in the course of a year had Mariño tried to create a palace
revolution, and three times had he betrayed Bolivar. Unfortunately, the mass of the Patriots was too disloyal or too stupid to
stop this idiotic race for power among the seconds in command.
Bolivar had to take this task upon himself, not only for his own
sake, but because the future of America was at stake. The campaign in Guayana had to end in a victory over the external as
well as the internal enemy or South American liberty was lost
for another generation.

So Bolivar had a three-fold problem to solve: he had to rout
the Spaniards, recreate the unity of his forces, and establish a
government. But he was sure of his cause. "If I have thus far
been moderate," he wrote, "it was from wisdom, not weakness.
Never believe that the intrigues are so great that they can
destroy us. My position has never been better . . . Three thousand men do my bidding, and continue to do what I command.
. . . We are neither in Constantinople nor in Haiti. Here
there are neither tyrants nor anarchy, nor will there be as long
as I live and can wield my sword."[36]

Bolivar did not waste time while he was waiting to hear
whether Brion would sail to the mouth of the Orinoco with his
fleet. He commissioned General Arismendi to supervise the
construction of the lighter vessels.[37] His plan of campaign
also became clarified during those days. Two fortified places

---

35 Cartas: Vol. I. p. 281. Blanco: Doc. Vol. V. p. 661. O'Leary: Doc. Vol. XV.
p. 259.
36 Cartas: Vol. I. pp. 276-77.
37 O'Leary: Memorias. Vol. I. p. 383.

controlled the Orinoco. Upstream it was Angostura, which thus far had resisted every attack, and downstream it was the city of Guayana, called Old Guayana. Bolivar wanted to starve out the former and take the latter.

After almost two months had passed, Brion appeared. He brought eight ships and five smaller boats. With the number that Bolivar had built, it was a river fleet that could counterbalance the Spaniards. Brion sailed upstream. By night he slipped between the guns of Old Guayana and awaited the Liberator in one of the countless tributaries of the Orinoco. Bolivar had already sent his boats ahead, and he now set out to greet Brion. Only the high staff officers accompanied him: Soublette, Arismendi, and the adjutants. The Spaniards had observed that the Liberator was leaving his army and sent out a division to capture him. They cut off his return, and there was nothing for him to do but to jump into one of the small ponds and stay hidden until the enemy should give up the search. At this moment he made up his mind to kill himself rather than fall into Spanish hands.[38]

That night, while the others were still overcome with terror, Bolivar suddenly began to speak. "I shall liberate New Granada and then Ecuador. I shall go to Peru and hoist the flag of resurrection on the turrets of Potosí." To his companions these words sounded like the delirious ravings of a feverish mind.[39] But Bolivar was never more sane than in those days. To protect the fleet he had a small fort erected, before which the ships could safely ride at anchor. In only a few days the results of his decision became apparent. Angostura, starved and polluted by disease, could no longer hold out, and on July 17 the Spanish general decided to evacuate. The garrison, and with it the bishop, the chapter of the church, and fourteen hundred inhabitants sought refuge on the Spanish ships. This wretched remnant sailed down the river in thirty boats. Only a few survived. Many fell into Brion's hands; others lost their way among the countless tributaries; still others died of hunger.

38 O'Leary: Memorias. Vol. I. p. 400. Larrazabal: Vol. I. p. 478.
39 Blanco: Doc. Vol. V. p. 643.

On the following day, Bolivar occupied the city, and with its fall the fate of Old Guayana also was sealed. Bolivar had repeatedly ordered the fortress to surrender. What was it that held them to the colors of an ungrateful and dull-witted King? Instead of subjecting themselves to the rule of one man, they should, under Bolivar, become a free people who would be tomorrow on a par with the Spaniards.[40] Hunger, in this case, had more influence than persuasive words. Guayana was entirely cut off without the slightest hope of reinforcements or replacements. On August 3, the Spaniards gave up the fight. The fall of Old Guayana precipitated the collapse of the whole province and the great river of Venezuela was now rid of the Spaniards.[41]

Within three months Bolivar had achieved his goal. He was master of the Orinoco. A rich area was at his disposal. He could now replenish his supplies, and barter for arms and ammunition with foreign countries. Toward the east he had contact with the coast and with Margarita Island. Toward the west he made contact with the riders fighting in the plains at the Apure. Five years of ceaseless struggle, five years of exile, of loneliness, and of wandering, ended here. The program he had projected in Haiti was fulfilled. In the war for independence of the Netherlands, the Calvinists had said, "Victory began at Alkmar." For the South American revolution, victory began at Guayana.

Bolivar had triumphed over his external enemy. He was now militarily and morally strong enough to set about creating an inner front. The two tasks that remained were to overcome anarchy and to create a legal authority. They were inextricably intertwined. The control of the inner dispersive forces was established during one of the most dramatic events of the revolution. Bolivar's opponent was General Manuel Piar.[42] Piar had not been born in Venezuela. His father was Venezuelan,

40 Proclamas: p. 159.
41 O'Leary: Memorias. Vol. I. p. 401. Larrazabal: Vol. I. p. 480. Cartas de Santander. Caracas, 1942. Vol. I. p. 3.
42 Proclamas: p. 160. Blanco: Doc. Vol. VI. p. 105. E. Restrepo Tirado: El General Piar. B. d. H. Bogotá. Vol. X. p. 113.

but his mother was a Negress from Curaçao. He often boasted
of his European origin and claimed that he was the son of a
prince. Sometimes he acted as leader of the Negroes—depending on the situation and the time. He had come to the mainland early in his career, and since the outbreak of the war had
fought on the side of the revolution. He was a talented officer
familiar with all the elements of tropical warfare, but uncontrollable and wild. Ambitious, with a penchant for intrigue
and the theatrical, he lacked self-control and tact. He was
rebellious toward his superiors, gruff to his inferiors, and he
knew no other dictate for his conduct than his will. Amid the
confusion he had risen to the rank of general. No one can
refuse to credit him with having planned the campaign on the
Orinoco. But it was Bolivar who carried out the scheme.

When Bolivar stepped into the theatre of war that Piar
considered his most private domain, the conflict became acute.
The cause was the usual one, a contest for rank and superiority.[43]
There was also the importance of the mission area to be considered. A minister from Caracas, one Blanco, had been
entrusted with the mission area's supervision. Piar took this
appointment as an encroachment on his rights and sabotaged
all of Blanco's provisions. Bolivar was indignant at this insubordination, but he had good reason to overlook it while the
campaign was on. He begged Blanco to put himself voluntarily
under Piar and wrote to him, "Dear friend, I beg you to suffer
in silence, as we all are doing for the sake of our fatherland."[44]
He wrote to Piar in the same vein. Conciliatory, almost, in
tone, he assured him that everything would be done to satisfy
his demands. Then came the news of the creation of an independent government in Cariaco. Piar took up the idea at once.
He, too, now acted as the defender of the democratic freedom
of the people. Bolivar sent one of his closest collaborators to
Piar to learn the latter's intentions. Piar explained that his
plans were not directed against Bolivar's authority. Mariño
had said the same thing.

43 Blanco: Doc. Vol. V. pp. 661-66. Vol. VI. p. 109. O'Leary: Doc. Vol. XV.
pp. 261-63.
44 Cartas: Vol. I. p. 264.

But it became clearer with each day that Piar was bent on rebellion. He continued to complain about Blanco, and although the latter graced his position with dignity, Bolivar dismissed him in order to pacify Piar.[45] But Piar was no longer to be controlled; his rage now turned on Arismendi. Piar accused him of stealing horses and mules, and of using his position to increase his personal fortune. Bolivar cleared up this misunderstanding. He wrote to Piar, "I prefer a fight with the Spaniards to a conflict among the patriots. If we are divided, if we succumb to anarchy and destroy each other . . . then Spain will triumph. . . . Please do not insist on leaving your post. If you were at the head I would not desert you, just as I shall not desert him who tomorrow will be in my place . . . no matter who it is, as long he has justice and right on his side and his country needs him."[46] But Piar was deaf to all pleas. The further the campaign moved on to the Orinoco, and the clearer it became that Bolivar was winning ground against the Spaniards, the more obdurate Piar became. In the end he did precisely what Bolivar had begged him not to do. Pleading ill health, he asked to be relieved of his post. Bolivar granted his request, and Piar received a pass which enabled him to move freely in the area of the Republic, or, if he wished, to go abroad. This was the state of affairs on June 30.[47]

Up to this moment Bolivar was ready for any settlement which would leave his authority unquestioned. But he owed it to himself and to his country to eliminate intrigue, and he felt strong enough to do this. "Here," he wrote, "that man commands who can, not he who would."[48] It was in those days that he must have decided to put an end to the appeasement of men in high places. Venezuela was not Constantinople, where such appeasement was a recognized procedure. Bolivar knew, moreover, that Piar was, in many respects, more dangerous than Mariño or Bermúdez. He was, for instance, a better soldier.

45 Cartas: Vol. I. p. 275.
46 Cartas: Vol. I. p. 278.
47 Blanco: Doc. Vol. V. p. 676.
48 Cartas: Vol. I. p. 292.

After Angostura had fallen, General Bermúdez informed
Bolivar that two officers had told him that Piar had plans for
an insurrection. Bolivar sent for Piar to come to headquarters
and ordered him to be arrested if he did not heed the summons.
Piar evaded Bolivar's grasp and fled, and his flight was an admission of guilt.[49] It chanced to coincide with Bolivar's triumph
over the city of Guayana. The Liberator reorganized the army,
assembled the generals, and had his own position confirmed.
It was obvious that the tide had turned. The commander was
about to carry out a long thought out plan. Every direction
he gave during those weeks was intended to strengthen the
unity of the army. Unity in government was bound to follow.

Piar had fled to the eastern provinces. There was cause
to fear that he would unite with Mariño, but what made him
even more dangerous was his hatred for the white race. He
insisted that he was a victim of the white caste. A mulatto,
a child of the people, he had fallen a prey to the greed for
power characteristic of the Creole aristocracy. Piar had been
received in the east by Mariño. It was no simple problem to
track him down in this vast area, but Bolivar's directions were
unmistakable. On September 27, a division of horsemen chanced
upon Piar in the province of Maturin. He was surrounded by
troops, and when he was told of the orders for his arrest, he
threatened to meet force with force. General Sedeño, who
commanded the Bolivian riders, turned to Piar's soldiers and
asked them whether they would acknowledge Bolivar's authority. They answered with a cheer for the Liberator. Piar saw
that he had lost and acted like a bull chased by the Llaneros.
He lowered his head, hesitated for a moment, and then fled
to the nearest woods. But he could not escape Sedeño's horsemen. During the night of October 2, he was brought to headquarters in Angostura. He demanded to see Bolivar, but his
request was refused. Instead the war council convened at once.
The indictment was desertion, insurrection, and treason. In

49 Cartas: Vol. I. p. 310. O'Leary: Memorias. Vol. I. pp. 422-23. O'Leary:
Doc. Vol. XV. pp. 351 ff., 421.

selecting the judges, Bolivar tried to preserve the appearance of impartiality. He himself did not prejudice the case, nor was this necessary. Piar's crimes were verified by all witnesses. The verdict of the war council was demotion and death.[50]

The sentence was submitted to Bolivar. He objected to the demotion, but confirmed the verdict of guilt with its penalty of death by shooting. Even those in his confidence had not expected this. They reminded him of Piar's accomplishments in a vain hope of ameliorating the sentence. They feared an uprising of the officers or mutiny among the men on the day of execution. But Bolivar was adamant and ordered the sentence carried out. Piar received the news in prison and listened to the pronouncement in silence. When he heard, however, that Bolivar had approved the sentence, he ripped off his shirt and fell to the floor in a convulsion. Regaining consciousness, he tried to convince himself that Bolivar only wanted to humiliate him, and that he would not dare to have him shot. Piar continued to entertain this delusion until, on October 16 at five o'clock in the afternoon, he was led to the place of execution.[51] Bolivar had ordered that the execution take place in public, and this was done. Piar saluted the flag, begged the soldiers to aim true, and died like a man. Many of his companions-at-arms hid inside the houses. Bolivar, himself, was moved. But all bowed to the inevitable. Piar's tragedy became Bolivar's triumph.

Immediately thereafter the Liberator made two appeals, one to the citizens of Venezuela, the other to the soldiers. One need not look to them for any considered judgment regarding Piar as man and soldier. They are a product of a moment of the greatest passion and were intended for propaganda purposes.[52]

Historians of Bolivar are not unanimous in their opinions concerning the execution of Piar. Bolivar is accused of being motivated by racial hatred, by greed for power, even of envy

50 O'Leary: Doc. Vol. XV. p. 422. Restrepo: H. d. R. C. Vol. II. p. 424.
51 Proclamas: pp. 160, 170.
52 N. Sañudo: Estudios sobre la vida de Bolívar. Pasto, 1925, and Tavera: *op. cit.* Vol. I. p. 243 deny Piar's guilt.

of a possible rival.[53] But none of these accusations is plausible. Piar was guilty of rebellion. No one has been able to contest this fact. What remains is the human and the political aspect of the drama. Piar was one of the most fearless of patriots, his achievements were great and important. But if Bolivar is to be accused of forgetting these, one must remember that he did his utmost to hold Piar to his promises. It was Piar's tragedy that he did not understand that the time for gang war was over. He had overestimated his own powers and underestimated Bolivar's. Bolivar had more than power on his side; he also had reason. He possessed a great continental vision and a program for its realization. Piar had nothing but his own personal desires. From the outbreak of the War for Independence, discord and chaos had been liberty's nemesis. Each year the rivalries and jealousies of seconds in command had deflected Bolivar's course or cancelled out his plans. Now, in 1817, a lasting gain was made for the first time, with the conquest of Guayana. However, great problems had still to be resolved.

It was necessary to tame the human element of the revolution if liberty was to find a home in South America. As always in times of revolution, men of strong will had been tossed up by the wave of events. But greed, vanity, ambition, licentiousness, and despotism appeared with them. These men were but one step removed from criminals, but they were indispensable as long as the war lasted. If they were to serve the cause of American freedom, however, they would have to submit to the law. In 1817, after five years of fruitless effort, the law was, finally, Bolivar's will. It was force that spoke, and these wild hirelings recognized the voice. The shots that were fired on October 16 in Angostura re-echoed in Venezuela. For this reason Bolivar never had any pangs of conscience about the execution of Piar. "The death of General Piar," he said eleven years later, "was a political necessity which saved the country. The rebels were disturbed and frightened by him. . . . Mariño and his congress in Cariaco were disarmed. All came under

53 D. d. B. pp. 315 ff.

my command. My authority was established, and civil war and the enslavement of the country were avoided. Never was there a death more useful, more politic, and at the same time more deserved." "General Mariño," Bolivar added, "also deserved to die. But he was not so dangerous; in his case policy could give way to humanity." It is questionable whether Mariño was less dangerous than Piar. But Piar, a mulatto and a foreigner, was a better victim to Bolivar's assumption of authority. No political repercussions were to be feared from his death.

After Piar's execution, Mariño's counter-government collapsed like a pricked balloon.[54] His congress, born amid so much clamor, had found no recognition. On the other hand, the men sent out by Bolivar had achieved their objective in the east. They, like their leader, exercised both military and civil authority.[55] Inasmuch as the home provinces of Mariño were gradually joining Bolivar, he could now afford to show some leniency, and the voluntary submission of Mariño would be of greater value to him than the exercise of implacable justice. This may not have been juristic, but it was a well-considered political move. Bolivar was never a Cato, for whom the execution of principles was above the good of the state. To bring Mariño into line, young Colonel Sucre, himself a son of the east, was sent to the coast. His task was to persuade the men to acknowledge Bolivar's authority. In this way Mariño would be isolated and brought to his knees; he should then be spared and treated with honor. If Mariño submitted he would be harmless, and, as Bolivar wrote, "To lessen an evil is already to do good."[56] Mariño tried to protest and complained that he had been stripped of his command. Bolivar replied firmly and coolly, explaining that from now on Bermúdez would command the division of Cumaná and that everything would be left in his hands. Mariño was to come to Angostura and swear allegiance to the government of the Republic. In return, Bolivar offered to forget his sins. *"Soyons amis!"* did not fail to make an im-

54 Cartas: Vol. I. p. 309. O'Leary: Doc. Vol. XV. pp. 316-323, 327, 332, 425-26.
55 Cartas: Vol. I. p. 318.
56 O'Leary: Doc. Vol. XV. pp. 454-57. Blanco: Doc. Vol. VI. p. 156.

pression. Mariño realized that he had overplayed his hand and gave up.[57]

Thus the external enemy was defeated and the internal one tamed and made temporarily harmless. Bolivar's front was centered in the province of Guayana, with headquarters in Angostura. His right wing included the regions of the Venezuelan coast. For the protection of his left wing, in the direction of New Granada, other forces were required. Here, too, Bolivar had planned in advance. With no means other than persuasion, he had won over the men in the west. Actually, it was a single man to whom Bolivar had turned and upon whose approval everything depended—Páez.

The appearance of this man in the South American movement for independence was, in truth, an extraordinary phenomenon; in him the special quality of the continent, the elemental forces of earth, came into being. Antonio José Páez was seven years younger than Bolivar. He was born in July, 1790, in Barinas. He has recounted his life in a colorful book which gives a clear picture of the hard, untamed life in the steppes of South America.[58]

His father was a petty official in the administration of a tobacco monopoly, and the family was in poor circumstances. Antonio was the eighth son. He grew up in a little spot on the slopes of the Cordilleras and reports that he was sent to the local school. God alone knows what he learned there. When he was fifteen, he shot a man in self-defense and fled to the plains. The territories of the Llanos were vast pasture-lands which the owners visited once a year. They left the business of supervision to the overseers, who had unlimited power over beast and man, the animals being by far the more important of the two. Páez came to such a farm and had the misfortune to have as his superior a gigantic Negro, who took especial pleasure in tormenting him. Páez was white. His eyes had the indeterminate color of a beast of prey. His hair was brown and slightly wavy,

57 Blanco: Doc. Vol. VI. p. 188.
58 Páez: Autobiografía. A. P. Carranza: El General Páez. Buenos Aires, 1924.

his nose straight, his nostrils wide. Everything betrayed his European heritage. The Negro hated him for this. He made him ride unsaddled stallions; he ordered him to lead the cattle through rushing streams, and in the evening young Antonio was forced to wash the Negro's feet and swing him in his hammock until he fell asleep. Páez suffered the most intense humiliations and in this school learned to be a man of the plains. Raised amid privations, inured to rain, sun, and vermin, unfamiliar with the comforts of urban life, he developed the stoicism of a Bedouin. He was destined to become the leader of the riders of the plains. He lived the life of these shepherds. Even when he became a general, he had not learned the use of knife and fork.[59]

Páez loved the bloody games of the Llaneros and he understood their greed, for he had once been as poor as they, and he let them plunder and rob to their hearts' content. When he became president of the Republic, he still pursued the same course. His intelligence was limited, but his physical strength was tremendous and he could tame the most violent of the Llaneros. They called him Uncle Antonio, and he chatted with them and took part in their games. His courage was of a peculiar sort. In his contacts with people he was wary and suspicious, especially when he had to deal with persons whose culture was superior to his, but in battle he was as bloodthirsty as a tiger.[60] Danger was unknown to him, for, like Nelson, he had never felt fear. Battle called forth a kind of blood intoxication, and he boasted of having killed more than seventy men with his own hand. His lust for murder was so overpowering that it often induced an epileptic fit. Covered with blood and foaming at the lips, he would fall off his horse in the middle of a fight.[61] If these attacks left him defenseless, as often happened, he was in danger of being trampled underfoot. Among those who were devoted to him was a huge Negro who had once fought with the Spaniards in the hope of gaining a rich

59 Páez: *op. cit.* p. 178. L. A. Cuervo: Notas históricas. p. 170.
60 O'Leary: Memorias. Vol. I. p. 441.
61 Páez: *op. cit.* p. 185.

booty and who later had gone over to the Republicans. He was called the First Negro and carried a tremendous knife so large that no one else could wield it. His chief assignment was to protect Uncle Antonio. He took the place of a whole bodyguard. When his master fell off his horse, stiff and glassy-eyed, the big Negro picked him up and carried him away. Other men, too, often rescued Páez. His people went through fire and water for him. He was their commander, but first he was their comrade, and he had the grace of a born leader.

Páez could neither read nor write during the first year of the war. The simplest concepts of tactics were unknown to him. It would be a mistake, however, to believe that he fought at random. He had strategic ideas which no one had taught him, which were instinctive, the expression of American nature in all its wildness. Páez was the first to understand the possibilities of space and the necessity of carrying the war to where no European could inflict a decisive defeat—in the plains, on the banks of the mighty rivers, on the edge of the impenetrable jungle. What, for Bolivar, was the result of careful planning or the knowledge gained in defeat, was known to Páez instinctively. He chose the plains as his battlefields, recognizing, as does the wild animal, the element best suited to him. He was for the cause of freedom because nature in South America was free, and his own untrammeled nature answered its appeal. He was unsurpassed as a guerrilla fighter; he understood the importance of cavalry. He fought the Spanish bayonet with his lance, and he fought the disciplined troops of the Spanish with the frenzied strength of his riders. He overcame artillery with the swiftness of his movements. Expeditions on horseback which were endurance tests for European soldiers were regarded by him as a normal day's work.[62]

Thus Páez became one of the most important figures of the war. He mastered the tactics of tropical warfare, a type of conflict which can be compared only to desert fighting. During the rainy season, Páez could distinguish between the countless

62 Páez: Autobiografía. pp. 66, 125-26.

streams as no other; during the season of drought he alone could find the water sources. He marched at night, both to save his men and to conceal from enemy view the heavy clouds of dust raised by his horsemen. He oriented himself by the stars. His movements had the speed of mechanized war, and he sometimes covered a hundred kilometers a day. His fame grew, and some of the Llaneros who had hitherto fought under Boves went over to his side. Since booty was their main interest, this was a practical step, because the Monarchists were again, after 1814, the ruling class, and booty of any value could be acquired only by fighting them. Páez allowed his soldiers to plunder; he thought it kept them in good spirits, and it eased the task of supplying the army. The cattle taken from the enemy were driven far into the plains and were used to feed his own men.

With such support he was a power, but a power at first only for guerrilla warfare. He emulated the great European cavalry generals and made sudden daring attacks. But he lacked the discipline of a Seidlitz or a Murat. As he said himself, he felt no responsibility to anyone when it came to a matter of life or honor. The area to which he retired was the border-region of Venezuela and Colombia. Officers of both nations met here and endeavored to create a government. However, quarrels soon arose over various matters, notably the choice of location for future action and the selection of a leader. The council of officers answered the latter question by naming the New Granadian, Santander, as commander-in-chief. The horsemen of Páez were determined to have Uncle Antonio, and Páez became commander-in-chief of the west in September, 1816.[63]

He began now to spread guerrilla war, first to the lands of the Arauca River, later to the plains of the Apure, which rises in the Orinoco. Speed, surprise, and attack were everything. Since Páez was almost always numerically inferior, he resorted to subterfuge. At one time, he ordered his men to frighten some of the horses and then drive them into the Spanish camp. At

63 Urdaneta: Memorias. p. 101. Páez: *op. cit.* p. 118.

the height of the confusion, he attacked. At another time he
had the grass of the steppes, which burns like tinder, lighted all
around the Spanish encampments. His attacks were like the
rides of the Bedouins. The horsemen were hurled forward
without unity or formation, then they streamed back and attacked again until the enemy succumbed. In one battle Páez
rode no less than fourteen attacks. In this way he won brilliant
victories over the hitherto undefeated soldiers of Morillo. The
Spanish general was forced to admit that these men were not
so negligible as the ministers in Madrid wanted to believe.[64]

The full value of Páez' victories can be realized only when
one considers the location of the areas in which he operated.[65]
He was the leader of an undisciplined horde of riders, which
waged war on its own account; but if he united with Bolivar,
he would become terrifying, for if there was agreement between
him and the Liberator, the independence movement would
control an area from the mouth of the Orinoco to the slopes of
the Andes. It was a vital part of Bolivar's program to bring
the young leader under his control.

Bolivar sent out a delegation to demand Páez's fealty to him
as his commander. They readily came to terms and Páez decided to put his army under Bolivar. The riders protested, but
Páez was adamant and swore his allegiance in the presence of
the army chaplain. The Llaneros followed Uncle Antonio's
example.[66] In a letter to Bolivar, Páez affirmed this act of discipline. Bolivar thanked him, and with the suavity and wisdom
that characterized his correspondence, he addressed Páez as
his equal. He approved the latter's plans and in turn informed
him of his own. Then he carefully drew in his reins. He asked
for a regular report on the strength of the troops and sent war
materiel and technical directions.[67]

---

64 Rodríguez: Villa: Vol. III. p. 360.
65 Cunningham Graham: Páez. London, 1929. pp. 99 ff., 120 ff. For Páez'
tactics, see, Lecuna: La Guerra de la Independencia en los Llanos. B. d. H. Caracas.
Vol. VI. No. 21. p. 1017.
66 O'Leary: Memorias. Vol. I. p. 382. Páez: op. cit. pp. 168-69. Blanco: Doc.
Vol. VI. p. 33.
67 O'Leary: Doc. Vol. XV. pp. 324-26, 445-47, 460. Blanco: Doc. Vol. VI. p. 61.

After Piar had been executed and Mariño made harmless, Bolivar told Páez that he planned to take his own army to the Apure and join Páez there. Páez became seriously ill, however, and the plan was delayed. Bolivar sent him a physician, and, in case of emergency, a substitute. After various other postponements the two men finally met. They were the most important figures of the revolution in the northern part of the continent. Bolivar had great nervous energy; Páez had strength. Bolivar was generous and extravagant; Páez was careful and greedy. Bolivar was loyal; Páez was inconstant. Both were ambitious—the one because the idea of American liberty was always before his eyes, the other because of a lust for power. Bolivar was not without vanity, but Páez was vain through and through.[68]

When these men met on January 30, 1818, they embraced in South American fashion. Páez scrutinized the man and his horse, but he found nothing to criticize. Here was a man whom one could follow, because he had everything of which any Llanero could boast and something more. Páez, with his dull shepherd's soul, could not articulate this certain something, but he recognized genius and knew that he could follow its light as he followed the stars on lonesome nights on the plains. The front was stabilized, and from a horde of guerrilla fighters an army was raised which swept from the Atlantic to the Andes. The new organization required closer coördination.

As long as the territorial extent of the Republic changed from day to day and could be increased or decreased by whole provinces, the state demanded the services of an active and efficient army. Bolivar had regrouped his units even during the campaign.[69] Dependable men were charged with the command of the various divisions and internal discipline was strengthened by the introduction of court-martial.[70] The maintenance of the army had been greatly facilitated by the conquest of the Ori-

68 P. M. Arcaya: Bolívar y Páez. Caracas, 1917.
69 Urdaneta: Memorias. p. 124. Lecuna: Creación del Estado. B. d. H. Caracas. Vol. XXI. No. 82. p. 113.
70 O'Leary: Doc. Vol. XV. p. 264.

noco. "We possess a vast area on the banks of the Orinoco,
Apure, Meta, and Arauca. We own cattle and horses."[71] This
unminted wealth must be converted into money and goods.
"The conquest of the Orinoco," wrote Bolivar, "opens a breach
in all the provinces of the mainland."[72]

Besides horses, mules, and cattle, the rich mission area had
to produce coffee, fruits, and hides. Bolivar invited the merchants to bring arms, ammunition, and uniforms to the
Orinoco; in exchange they received tropical products. When
one reads Bolivar's letters of those months, one is obliged to
smile at the way Bolivar concerned himself with cows for the
Admiral, or soap and salt for a certain division. But this
attitude shows the greatest characteristic of his world historic
aspect. He knew how to create something out of nothing. The
economic and political organization of colonial days was wiped
out or had never existed in these sections of the primeval forest.
In a country lacking administration or tradition, he had to
establish a minimum of order and well-being to insure the
continuance of the war. He built hospitals; he sent to England
for a printing press. He tried to get the most out of the conquered provinces within a few weeks, but he did not become a
scourge, and amid the greatest efforts he forbade anyone to
mistreat the native Indians.[73] The time for a war to extinction
was past. Bolivar thought in terms of the new state which was
being formed in South America, where the races could live in
amity side by side. He thought in terms of equality and
reconstruction.

The property of all those Americans who had left the
country was confiscated. Spanish estates were, of course, also
appropriated. The reason for this measure is clear. The
Revolutionaries could not be blind to economic interests, and
after their years of sacrifice, the Patriots needed to be assured
of rehabilitation. The confiscated properties were divided
among the generals, officers, and men, according to their

71 Cartas: Vol. I. p. 291.
72 Cartas: Vol. I. p. 297.
73 Cartas: Vol. I. p. 302.

merits.[74] Thus Bolivar killed two birds with one stone. He attached the army of the covetous to the cause of the Republic, and he lightened his financial obligations. It was now, as always, sometimes even impossible to pay the army. Bolivar was consistent in his attitude toward life and in his manner of living. The privations he suffered in company with his officers and soldiers can hardly be estimated. For everyone Bolivar's word was law: "From the head of the state down to the last soldier, no one in Venezuela has more than one room and one meal a day."[75]

He was now, in truth, head of the state. "A king on his throne," he wrote at that time, "can have no greater anxieties or problems than I, so great is the confusion and lack of organization in which we find ourselves. Everything still remains to be done."[76] To create the state Bolivar did only as much as was necessary to achieve a minimum of civil order. More than that would have deflected attention from the main objective, namely, winning the war, and might have burdened the final form of the state with innumerable mortgages. Caracas, the city of his love, was unattainable, so Angostura, today called the City of Bolivar, was chosen as capital. Thus the nomad Republic took form. The internal problems of states' rights and state sovereignty were thornier.

One may remember Mariño's plans and the objections which Piar raised to Bolivar's position of power. Both men had criticized mixing political and military authority. Bolivar was willing to concede everything to civil liberty if the great goal of a free America was not endangered. The first thing he did was to order the reëstablishment of independent courts.[77] The municipal government was created on a legal basis. Legal protection was offered to trade and to river navigation.

For the time being, a parliament was out of the question. So was a national assembly, and Bolivar resorted to the expedient

74 O'Leary: Doc. Vol. XV. pp. 335-37, 437-38.
75 Cartas: Vol. I. p. 318.
76 Cartas: Vol. I. p. 297.
77 O'Leary: Doc. Vol. XV. pp. 328, 332, 464.

of a state council. It was to have the right to propose laws; its judgments were to be heard and heeded, but its powers were only advisory, not definitive. It was a halfway measure between a state council and a ministerial cabinet.[78] Bolivar convened this body on November 1, 1817, with an address in which he gave an outline of the formative state. This State Council was to have all authority in case of his death, but as long as Bolivar lived he was not to be deflected from his position of absolute rule. At the first opportunity he made the State Council realize that no one besides himself, the "Libertador y jefe supremo" had the right to pass judgment.[79] Thus was the new state created—merely an emergency state in the beginning. The law-giving power was hardly more than a screen; the courts were of uncertain structure, and executive power towered above all. Bolivar wrote at once to London and Buenos Aires to put his state before the eyes of the world. What he had announced to the Venezuelans in May, 1816, had become a reality. On the banks of the Orinoco, the Third Republic was born. In a brilliant campaign he had wrested one of South America's four great arteries from the Spaniards. He was thirty-four years old, at the height of his intellectual development, in full possession of his manly and human energies. His reserves seemed inexhaustible, his zest for work unlimited. His power was unrestricted. He had tamed anarchy, and chaos lay behind him. The year 1817, representing a decisive change in the life of the Liberator, became also the turning point in the history of South American independence. "There are events in any war which, without being too effective, are yet so powerful that they bring about a decision."[80] With these words Bolivar described the importance of the campaign of 1817. From this point the road leads on, not in a straight line, not unswervingly, but mounting constantly to the complete liberation of his world. Here occurs the great caesura in the story of Simon Bolivar's life.

78 Blanco: Doc. Vol. VI. p. 151.
79 Proclamas: p. 177. O'Leary: Doc. Vol. XV. p. 507.
80 Cartas: Vol. I. p. 297.

Part III

MAN OF GLORY

CHAPTER 18

Foreign Legion

Even the great leaders of history are indebted to their enemies. Their accomplishments could never have been realized without the mistakes of their adversaries. Just so Bolivar owed his creative opportunities to the blunders of his enemy, Morillo. While Bolivar was becoming undisputed head of the revolution, while he was taking Guayana from the Spaniards, liquidating his rivals, founding the Third Republic, and conceiving the plan to join with Páez at the Orinoco, Morillo was dissipating his time.[1] He considered Páez and his hordes more dangerous than Bolivar, but he could not destroy Páez. The combats to which Morillo challenged Páez, cost more than they gained for the Spanish cause. In the end, he realized that he would have to abandon the attack on this barbaric enemy unless he were willing to lose the whole eastern part of Venezuela. But instead of striking now at Bolivar, he attacked Margarita Island.[2] As great as this mistake was, it was not entirely without justification. Morillo's position was untenable without contact with the mother country. His reserves and his supplies came across the Atlantic, and he was afraid that the revolutionary pirates might cut through his main artery from Margarita. A Spanish convoy of twenty-two ships was on the way, and Morillo hoped to unite with this new expeditionary corps. He

1 Blanco: Doc. Vol. VI. pp. 5 ff. Baralt: Vol. I. pp. 375, 377. Rivas Vicuña: Vol. II. p. 256.
2 Blanco: Doc. Vol. VI. p. 13. Baralt: Vol. I. p. 389. Yanes: Relación. Vol. II. p. 22.

then would have ships at his disposal and could expect a speedy defeat of Margarita.[3] In the middle of July, 1817, Morillo attempted an invasion. It is said that a personal hatred of Arismendi, the leader of the island inhabitants, impelled him, and it is a matter of fact that the two generals despised each other like true Homeric heroes. Murderer, traitor, and scoundrel were the mildest of the invectives they hurled at each other. But even in an age of loud-speakers, battles are not won with words.[4] This was even more true in those days. The island episode was a bitter disappointment to Morillo. An army of only four hundred men fought the Spaniards for every foot of the unfruitful and steaming soil.[5]

The Republicans withdrew to the interior, leaving small divisions on the coast that made life a hell for the Spaniards. Morillo paid for his early successes with heavy losses. The three thousand soldiers of his army were not enough. He asked for reinforcements from the mainland, especially for men of the tropics who were less susceptible to malaria, typhoid, and yellow fever than were the Europeans.[6] His attempt to take the capital failed. He thought he could starve out the island, but the natives continued to fight from every nook and corner. Cacti and acacias formed dense copses on the stony island, through which only the natives could find their way. From these ambushes came the deadly bullets. After a month, Morillo had to admit that he was in danger of paying too dearly for possession of the island, for during the time he had spent in this disastrous adventure, Bolivar had become master of Guayana. The news from Caracas was also bad. The Governor felt insecure because the Patriots were again on the march, and he begged Morillo for help.

This turn of events was not entirely unwelcome to Morillo. It served as a pretext, without endangering his prestige, for

3 O'Leary: Memorias. Vol. I. p. 406.
4 F. J. Yanes: Memorial sobre Margarita. B. d. H. Caracas. Vol. XXII. No. 86. p. 216. R. de los Rios: Importancia de laisla de Margarita, según testimonio de Moxo y Morillo. B. d. H. Caracas. Vol. II. p. 261.
5 Yanes: Relación. Vol. II. p. 23.
6 O'Leary: Memorias. Vol. I. p. 409.

withdrawing from the island campaign, which had taken on the nature of a dead-end expedition. After a month of fruitless effort, he ordered the island evacuated and arrived in Caracas at the beginning of September.[7] The only trophies he brought with him were seven hundred diseased men. In the over-all picture of the South American revolution, Morillo's excursion to Margarita was one of the most costly mistakes of the Spanish command.[8] Morillo played the wrong card at the most critical moment and thus hastened the collapse of colonial rule.

It is part of the Spanish character that acknowledgement of defeat comes either too late or not at all. Back on the mainland, Morillo thought he could divide the royal forces in such a way that he could with certainty destroy the heads of the revolutionary hydra. Belatedly he decided to send an army under General La Torre to the Orinoco to check Bolivar's movements. Morillo himself wanted to go back to the Apure to prevent Páez from breaking through to Bolivar's army.[9]

As a matter of fact, Páez' break-through had been precisely what Bolivar had planned, but Bolivar was not ready with his preparations and wanted to confine himself for the next few weeks to defensive action. So he sent a division to meet the Spaniards to protect him from any surprise attacks. Its commandant, Zaraza, had strict instructions to restrict himself to defense and evasion. This order was either misunderstood or not carried out for other reasons; possibly Zaraza wanted to earn his own laurels; possibly the orders were incorrectly relayed. Suffice it to say that on December 2 he came to one of the vast pasture lands, called La Hogaza, where he met La Torre. Spaniards and Americans were equally strong, but Spanish tactics proved to be better. The Republican cavalry was surrounded; the infantry was defenseless and was mowed down; officers, men, transport, arms—all were lost. When the battle was over, the pampas grass rose in flames; the ammuni-

7 O'Leary: Memorias. Vol. I. p. 414. Díaz: *op. cit.* p. 212. Yanes: Relación. Vol. II. pp. 25-26.
8 Rivas Vicuña: Vol. II. pp. 298-99.
9 O'Leary: Memorias. Vol. I. p. 419.

tion exploded and killed the wounded who lay on the ground.[10]

Bolivar's plans were ruined by the defeat of December 2. But it is one of the distinguishing traits of his genius that he always had some improvisation with which to meet each new situation. He had his scattered troops rounded up. To counteract the loss of men, he declared a state of siege and called every man between the ages of fourteen and sixty to the colors.[11] Horses and cattle were brought in and weapons were mended. Angostura seemed more like a factory than a city during those days. After three weeks the equipment was patched up for better or for worse, and Quixote could set out on new adventures. Bolivar announced his plan of campaign for 1818 to his officers.

The Spanish victory near La Hogaza, said Bolivar, was a result of the hazards of fate; he might also have added that it was a result of disobedience and lack of discipline. To prevent Páez from suffering the same fate, Bolivar ordered him to postpone any decisive action, to keep on the alert, and not to allow himself to be surprised.[12]

The plan for the movements of the army was also changed. Instead of telling Páez to come down the Orinoco, Bolivar arranged to go to meet him. At the beginning of January, Bolivar began his march of over three hundred miles. Twice it was necessary to cross the Orinoco, as well as the Caura and the Arauca, with their thundering falls.[13] In the wide fields of the plains, Bolivar was able to pick up a few scattered troops, so that he now had about three thousand men with him when he met Páez on January 30, 1818. One must not think of them as well-equipped soldiers. The riders were armed only with lances. A few of the foot soldiers had firearms; the rest had

10 Blanco: Vol. VI. pp. 180-81. O'Leary: Doc. Vol. XV. pp. 485-90. O'Leary: Memorias. Vol. I. p. 437. See also La Torre's statement in Lecuna: Creación d. Estado. Vol. XXI. p. 227.

11 Proclamas: p. 180. Cartas: Vol. I. p. 321.

12 Blanco: Doc. Vol. VI. p. 199. O'Leary: Doc. Vol. XV. pp. 512-18. Lecuna: Creación d. Estado. Vol. XXI. p. 149.

13 Blanco: Doc. Vol. VI. pp. 242, 243, 250. O'Leary: Doc. Vol. XV. p. 540. Lecuna: Campaña de 1818. B. d. H. Caracas. Vol. XXI. No. 84. p. 341.

bows and arrows. With Páez' Llaneros the army of the Third Republic numbered about four thousand men.

The plains of the Orinoco had been incorporated in the state. The regions of the Apure had now to be made safe from any further war action. This great river, together with the Orinoco, formed the line which had to serve Bolivar as rear guard defense. At the confluence of the Apure and the Apurito there is a place called San Fernando, which the Spaniards had fortified and had manned with troops. Bolivar wanted to cross the stream near this fort. The time was ten o'clock in the morning of February 5. Despite Bolivar's explicit instructions, the little fleet of river barges which had accompanied him on his march was not to be found. The Liberator became impatient, for not a single canoe was to be seen far or near in which the troops could be taken across the river. He consulted Páez, who said, "There are our ships!" On the opposite shore was a gun ship under the Spanish flag, and a number of sloops manned by Spaniards. Páez ordered fifty of his best riders to overpower them. Lances in hand and clutching their horses' manes, these centaurs swam across the raging river, routed the Spanish garrison, and confiscated the ships.[14]

Bolivar crossed the Apure and moved on toward San Fernando, where he began his siege. As the river was in Bolivar's hands, he knew that the fort was cut off from all supplies, so he left a small part of his army there—enough to starve out the Spaniards—and then turned northward. His next destination was Calabozo, capital of the plains that supplied Caracas.[15]

The unexpected, said Foch, is the law of war. In the tropical war of the nineteenth century surprise was most important. The tremendous distances, the lack of roads, the sparse population; and, finally, the absence of all organized reports from military heads, made it impossible for both the Spaniards and the Republicans to follow the movements of their enemy's

14 The descriptions of this extraordinary event differ from one another in certain details. See, O'Leary: Memorias. Vol. I. p. 443. Larrazabal: Vol. I. p. 514. Páez: Autobiografía. pp. 175-76. Briefe aus Colombien. Leipzig, 1822. p. 105.

15 O'Leary: Memorias. Vol. I. p. 443. O'Leary: Doc. Vol. XV. pp. 560, 563-66.

armies. Morillo had said after La Hogaza, "A victorious Bolivar goes a way that can be reasoned out, but a defeated Bolivar is more active and more terrible than ever, and no one can tell where he will break out." He was, therefore, prepared for further conflicts.[16] But he thought Bolivar was still in Angostura. He only learned on February 7 of the Liberator's astonishing march to the Apure. In the opinion of the Spaniards this march of over 865 kilometers was one of Bolivar's most brilliant accomplishments.[17]

Morillo heard of the march on Calabozo and began to go to the aid of the city. Bolivar attacked him not far from the town. The victory of the Republicans was complete. The only thing Morillo saved from this defeat was a part of his infantry. With this remnant of his forces, he retired to Calabozo.[18] On the next day Bolivar offered to terminate the war to extinction. To reinforce his words he suggested an exchange of prisoners. Morillo did not even deign to reply. Despite this affront, the Liberator was determined from then on to respect the laws of humanity, and he forbade the killing of prisoners.[19]

If Bolivar had but recently surprised Morillo, the latter paid him back in his own coin. Morillo took over the reconnaissance service and observed that the American cavalry performed its duties only perfunctorily. So he dared, in the dark of night, to flee from Calabozo. Even without horses he succeeded in escaping Bolivar's riders. The responsibility for Morillo's escape rested with one of those who was second in command. Thus the victory of February 12 turned into a stalemate. Negligence and a lack of discipline among the Republican officers became more noticeable with each day.

Bolivar began to pursue the enemy. There were a number of engagements, but Morillo always managed to escape. However, like the fox who has extricated himself from the trap,

16 Larrazabal: Vol. I. p. 509.
17 M. Torrente: Hist. d. l. Revolución Hispano-Americana. Madrid, 1830. Vol. II. p. 443. Lecuna: Campaña de 1818. Vol. XXI. p. 350.
18 O'Leary: Memorias. Vol. I. p. 446. Larrazabal: Vol. I. p. 515. O'Leary: Doc. Vol. XV. p. 569.
19 Cartas: Vol. II. p. 3. O'Leary: Memorias. Vol. I. p. 451.

he did not elude his pursuers unscathed; a handful of prisoners often remained. Nevertheless, the general, with the greater part of his army, finally reached Valencia, where he was able to reinforce his exhausted troops.[20]

A reckoning of the first two months of 1818 shows a balance in favor of Bolivar. He had not been able to force any decisions, but Morillo was obliged to cede to him large parts of the hinterland of Caracas. Bolivar thought he was again master of Venezuela—at least he wanted others to believe this. Again the fanfare of his proclamations rang out. He spoke to the people of the plains, to the Americans who had served the cause of Spain, to the settlers and peasants who had just been liberated. He promised pardon to the guilty; he promised indemnity and declared all slaves emancipated.[21]

Nevertheless, Bolivar's offensive was not to go beyond the point it had reached at the end of February. Strategically viewed, it halted in a kind of no man's land. Morillo had sought refuge on the slopes of the Cordilleras where Bolivar's cavalry collapsed. Bolivar's infantry also was worn out by the long marches over hundreds of kilometers. The Liberator had two choices: he could fall back on Calabozo and set up his winter quarters there, or he could move forward to a point from which he would have a chance to push through to Valencia or Caracas.[22] The second of the two solutions was more in character. It was positive; it promised decisions. But Bolivar ran aground on the objections of his officers, especially those of Páez.

The wild shepherds of the Apure followed reluctantly into regions where they were not at home. They resented the more rigid discipline and stricter service of Bolivar's command. They felt more like his allies than a part of his army. National independence did not mean much to them, but personal liberty meant everything. Páez knew his people. To prevent his

20 Rodríguez Villa: Vol. III. p. 504. O'Leary: Doc. Vol. XV. p. 580.
21 Proclamas: pp. 182, 183, 185, 186.
22 O'Leary: Memorias. Vol. I. p. 452. Larrazabal: Vol. I. p. 516. O'Leary: Doc. Vol. XV. p. 558.

men from disbanding, he proposed withdrawing to the Apure.
He wanted, he said, to help with the siege of San Fernando.
This plan was without sense because the army that lay before
San Fernando was strong enough to maintain the siege. But
Páez was a despot and accustomed to having his own way.
Even before this he and Bolivar had had some violent quarrels.
His concept of war was diametrically opposed to Bolivar's.
Páez wanted to wear the Spanish out with constant blows;
Bolivar wanted to destroy them. Páez was a nomad; Bolivar
was a fighter. But the Liberator could not do without Páez'
support and he did not have the power to bend this man to his
will nor to the authority of the state. Bolivar's position resembled that of a medieval prince who depended on the
approval of his vassals.[23] Thus he sacrificed his military acumen
and was tricked into a compromise with Páez. Together they
led the army back to Calabozo. Here Páez and his men left
Bolivar and hastened to the siege of San Fernando. Bolivar
soon had the questionable satisfaction of seeing his pessimism
justified. This was not an army that could be put up in winter
quarters with any confidence that discipline would be maintained. During the marches and battles the officers were able
to keep a measure of control over the raw troops, but in a city
like Calabozo they scattered like dust in the wind. "With deep
sorrow," wrote Bolivar to Páez, "I find my worst fears confirmed. . . . The army has almost disbanded."[24] And who
could blame the poor devils if they did not like a service that
forced them to go half naked, gave them scarcely enough to
eat, and furnished them with no pay. The fault lay with Páez.

However, Bolivar could not long endure inactivity. He
called his war council together, and the majority of his officers
agreed that they would have to seek out the enemy. In order
to do so the Republicans had to push themselves between two
enemy divisions that had their centers in Caracas and Valencia.

---

23 Larrazabal: Vol. I. p. 516. Páez: Autobiografía. pp. 125-26. Lecuna: Campaña de 1818. Vol. XXI. pp. 354-55. J. Estrada Monsalve: Bolívar. Bogotá, 1944.
p. 135.
24 O'Leary: Doc. Vol. XV. p. 600. O'Leary: Memorias. Vol. I. p. 454.

Herein lay the greatest hazard of the new undertaking. Bolivar wanted to defeat first one and then later the other. But the Spaniards gave him no choice. Bolivar suddenly found himself between two fires.[25]

The encounter took place at a small town called El Semen, on March 25. The battle was long and costly; the outcome was uncertain. Bolivar rode with his staff from one line to the other and encouraged his troops. Finally, the tide of battle turned because Morillo was able to throw fresh reserves into the fight at the last moment. Bolivar lost the battle of El Semen. On his flight through the pass of La Puerta over one thousand were killed. The entire infantry and every bit of Bolivar's war materiel were lost, and all of his papers fell into the enemy's hands. Four of his top ranking officers were wounded. The Spanish losses were also great. Morillo was so severely wounded by a spear that had penetrated his abdomen that he was obliged to relinquish his command. Further pursuit was out of the question. Bolivar owed his salvation to these circumstances. But the battle of El Semen precluded any hope of victory for the campaign of 1818.

The locale of Bolivar's defeat was again the territory near La Puerta which had proved disastrous for him in 1814. The King advanced Morillo's rank, and he became the Marquis de la Puerta. The Spaniards thought Bolivar's career was ended, that he could never recover from this blow.[26] But the conflict continued. To the amazement of the Spaniards, there was nothing that could break this man's self-confidence and tenacity.

Bolivar continued the fight for one and a half months. He raised recruits; he fetched the convalescents from the hospitals; he sent to Angostura for weapons; he sought to lure the enemy from the hills into the plains; he made sporadic attacks. Blind to all danger and unmindful of his own fate, he flung himself

25 Lecuna: Campaña de 1818. Vol. XXI. p. 377. O'Leary: Doc. Vol. XVI. p. 7. O'Leary: Memorias. Vol. I. p. 459.
26 Blanco: Doc. Vol. VI. p. 351. Rodríguez Villa: Vol. III. pp. 522-23. O'Leary: Doc. Vol. XVI. pp. 13-17. O'Leary: Doc. Vol. VI. p. 360.

at the enemy like a tiger, and it was as a tiger that the Spaniards strove to trap him.[27] On April 16 Bolivar pitched his camp on a pasture called "The Corner of the Bulls"—*el rincón de los toros*. The Spaniards were at his heels and were lucky enough to take a prisoner who betrayed the password of the Republicans for the coming night.

The Spanish captain, Renovales, with a division of forty men, set out for the Patriot camp with the single intention of killing Bolivar. They met Santander, gave him the password, and under the assumption that they were a Republican patrol, were led within the lines. When they asked to see Bolivar, Santander pointed to his hammock. Just what occurred from this point on is uncertain. Perhaps Bolivar had a premonition of danger and flung himself to the ground; perhaps he had already left his bed. Whatever the case the assassin's bullets missed their mark and Bolivar got away. In his own words, it was the night that saved him. The ensuing confusion was terrific. Bolivar had thrown away his uniform and helmet so as not to be recognized by the Spaniards, and the men thought he had been killed. Riders flew by him. He begged them to take him along, but, failing to recognize their leader, they refused. Meanwhile the Spaniards believed that Renovales' ruse had succeeded, and they stormed the camp. Bolivar finally found a horse and was able to save himself, but the greater part of his officers were captured and his entire infantry was wiped out. The Liberator slipped out to Calabozo with only a handful of men.[28] The Spaniards had the feeling that Fate had protected Bolivar. Morillo, like Nelson, might have said that "the Devil's spawn have the Devil's luck." But Bolivar was at the end of his strength. His army was routed, he himself near the breaking point. A few days after the attack at the Corner of the Bulls, he was brought down with a fever appar-

27 Cartas: Vol. II. pp. 30-31.
28 The reports of this event are necessarily contradictory. I have tried to reconstruct the affair according to the most trustworthy testimonies. O'Leary: Memorias. Vol. I. pp. 465 ff. Larrazabal: Vol. I. p. 529. Páez: *op. cit.* pp. 200-01. D. d. B. pp. 179 ff. Santander: Cartas. Vol. II. p. 6. Lecuna: Campaña de 1818. Vol. XXI. pp. 392, 457 ff.

ently occasioned by his general state of exhaustion. In May, 1818, he sought refuge in San Fernando. Condemned to a month of inactivity, he learned with great concern that the other armies of the Republic had fared just as badly. Nothing had been accomplished in the east and Páez had been thrown back into the plains of the Apure at the conclusion of a bloody battle. It was the end of the campaign of 1818.[29]

Bolivar was obliged to admit that he had failed again. He could now do no more than maintain a defensive position and keep the guerrilla war going. He sailed down the Apure and the Orinoco to Angostura, where he remained from June until December. On the surface he appeared to be immersed in administrative assignments. Actually, however, Bolivar was devoting himself to the difficult task of preparing a new attack. What mistakes had he made? How had the Spaniards repulsed his offensive? The Republic was just where it had been at the beginning of the year, and the Spaniards still held all the important cities. No one could drive the Republicans out of the plains, but Bolivar was forced to admit that he could never reach Caracas from the Orinoco. His army was powerless to fight successfully in the hills which formed the entrance to the city. He had to revise his strategic concepts. There must be another way to drive out the Spaniards. If a frontal attack was impossible, he would have to seize the enemy's flank.[30]

But Bolivar had learned still another lesson. His army was not equal to the seasoned Spanish regiments of Valencia, Burgos, and Asturias. It was not so much a question of equipment as of techniques and fighting tactics. "Successes that the enemy achieve," wrote Bolivar, "and advantages that their cavalry have over ours depend on their tactics." The Spaniards attacked in closed squadrons and were likewise able to hold firmly against counterattack.[31] But it was not only the Republicans' cavalry that was inferior; it was also their infantry. Bolivar's foot sol-

29 Cartas: Vol. II. p. 5. O'Leary: Doc. Vol. XVI. pp. 42, 44.
30 Cartas: Vol. II. p. 7. Lecuna: La Guerra en 1818. B. d. H. Caracas. Vol. XXII. No. 88. p. 66.
31 Cartas: Vol. II. pp. 30-31.

diers consisted of boys between fourteen and twenty years of age who had scarcely learned the use of firearms. On the other hand, the Spanish fought, as Páez expressed it, *"culo contra culo,"* unmindful of the dead and wounded, and they fought with the cold-bloodedness of seasoned troops.

Bolivar had to find a way of counterbalancing this lack of strength on his side. To bring his troops to the level of the European soldiers, as Miranda had once wanted to do, would have entailed years of drill. Bolivar thought of another way. He imported trained soldiers. With this act Europe's participation in the liberation of South America began. One might compare the situation to the part played by France in the North American Revolution. But no Lafayette mustered these soldiers; they came because Bolivar called them.[32]

The idea of letting Europe, especially Great Britain, coöperate actively in the creation of a free world may have occurred to Bolivar as early as 1810. After the tragic events of Ocumare, however, he pursued this policy with great urgency. The European officers of his staff suggested forming a foreign legion, and Bolivar decided to do this. He ordered his old friend, López Méndez, who since 1810 had been London agent of the Venezuelan Republic, to raise money, arms, and men with which to float the grounded ship of state.

This appeal to Great Britain to participate in America's fight for freedom fell into an atmosphere of economic depression which followed upon twenty years of war. Countless men were without work. From Ireland alone, thousands emigrated because they could no longer earn their bread at home. The British army was gradually being reduced to peace time strength. Over thirty thousand men had been discharged and these found no place in the already failing economic system. Here was a reservoir from which Bolivar could replenish his

32 L. Cuervo Marquez: Participación de la Gran Bretaña y de los Estados Unidos en la Independencia. Bogotá, 1935. A. Hasbrouck: Foreign Legionaries in the Liberation of Spanish South America. New York, 1928. M. A. Galan: La Legion Britanica. Bogotá. In addition to Lecuna's collection of Bolivar's letters important material may be found in: A. de la Rosa: Firmas del ciclo heroico. Lima, 1938.

exhausted battalions. His appeal for volunteers was supported
by the British press. The embassy in Grafton Street soon overflowed with applicants: officers on half-pay, adventurers, seekers
after gold, intrigants, romantics, and revolutionaries.[33]

Bolivar offered them the following conditions: all officers
were automatically to be promoted in rank at the time of joining the American army; the pay was to be the same as in the
British army; upon landing in South America, they were to
be reimbursed for the cost of the trip; those wounded in battle
were to be compensated. A few men tried immediately to
organize the affair on a grand scale. Colonels Hippesley, Campbell, Wilson, English, Skenne, Elson, and the Hanoverians,
Streowitz and Uslar, formed regiments and brigades. The uniforms were of great importance to them. There were the red
outfits of the hussars with their blue lapels, and the green outfits
with scarlet lapels. Some wore the uniform of the royal artillery. All the colonels tried to outdo each other. Field and
parade equipment were ordered suitable for the Buckingham
Palace Guard, instead of for mercenaries in the jungles of the
Orinoco.[34]

British merchants had stored large supplies of arms, uniforms, and equipment of all sorts which they had been unable
to unload on a European market. They were glad of this opportunity to sell to South America. López Méndez was, of course,
in no position to offer cash and simply gave promissory notes.
Occasionally, when the bills were overdue, he was obliged to
exchange his home for a cell in the debtors' prison. But that did
not bother him; the expedition was on the march.

The encounter of the Europeans with the tropical world was
both violent and painful. On both sides the first effect was
disappointment. The Legionnaires had dreamed of a land flowing with milk and honey, where gold and emeralds were found
in the streets. They found instead a city of clay barracks and
shingled houses. Immediately beyond these was the jungle.

33 A. Hasbrouck: pp. 29, 30, 34, 35, 37.
34 Cuervo: Participación. p. 351. O'Leary: Doc. Vol. XVI. p. 9.

Malaria, small-pox, and yellow fever were rampant. When they did not get the pay they expected, the Legionnaires refused to swear allegiance to the Republic. They were face to face with strangers whose language they did not understand and who did not know theirs. They complained about bad treatment and about hardships which were unavoidable at the equator. Food was scarce and indigestible for European stomachs. There were only corn, bananas, and beef—and what beef! There was no thought of bread, and too often there was no salt. The deaths increased alarmingly, and no one seemed to feel any concern. In the tropics human life means very little, and after eight years of murderous war, no Republican shed any tears over the loss of a stranger.

The elegant uniforms literally fell to pieces. Soon even the officers had to go barefoot or in *alpargatas,* American sandals made of hemp strands. Captain Thompson, who had managed to salvage a pair of boots, was ashamed to be better off than his comrades and threw them into the Orinoco. Colonel Rooke appeared at a dinner that Bolivar gave clad in a coat without collar or shirt. Bolivar ordered his boy to fetch one of his shirts, but Bolivar owned only two himself and the other one was in the wash.[35]

Since the British continued to be without pay, they were forced to sell their equipment. Páez conducted a lengthy correspondence with Bolivar about the purchase of uniforms.[36] He outfitted his bodyguard with English tunics, which made a strange contrast with the ragged Llaneros. Bolivar bought a cloak and a helmet with plumes. General Manrique had so many uniforms that he could appear in a different one every day. What seemed most bitter to the British was the fact that, having no pay, they were expected to loot. All of this deeply offended the British.

The Republicans also had complaints to register. The presumption, the lack of good will, and the alcoholism of the

35 Hasbrouck: pp. 88, 92-93, 96.
36 Cartas: Vol. II. p. 68.

Legionnaires exceeded their worst apprehensions. The foreign soldiers drank until they lay in the streets in a stupor and the city looked like a battlefield. Difficulties arose at the very first attempt to induct the British into the army. Bolivar did his best, but his best availed very little in the face of the arrogance and intrigue among these new officers. Two of them, Colonel Hippesley and Colonel Wilson, made names for themselves, the one by his presumptuousness, the other by his treason.[37] Hippesley had been assigned to Páez and demanded the rank of Brigadier General for himself. When he was refused, he returned to Angostura and asked for his release. Bolivar promised to fulfill all his commitments, but he refused to be intimidated by any report that might be made to the British government. "If the actions of the Venezuelan government do not count in England, the same is true of the British government in Venezuela." Hippesley returned to England and devoted himself to the task of slandering Bolivar.[38] The case of Wilson was more serious. He, too, had been sent to Páez and arrived in San Fernando in May, 1818. Here he soon learned of the latent rivalry between Bolivar and the leader of the Llaneros. He assumed the role of commander of the British troops, collected a group of drunken officers, and declared, amid general cheers for Páez, that he no longer wished to serve under Bolivar. The drunkards then looted all the supplies. On the next day Wilson held a parade, after which he solemnly proclaimed Páez as chief of the army.[39] At first Páez felt flattered, but after thinking the matter over he changed his attitude. He sent Wilson to Bolivar, in Angostura, with a protocol of what had happened. Bolivar knew what he must do. Wilson's guilt was indisputable, and he was thrown into prison in Guayana. He managed to escape, however, and returned to England. Much later Bolivar heard that Wilson had

37 Cartas: Vol. II. pp. 4-5. Cuervo: Participación. p. 362.
38 Blanco: Doc. Vol. VI. pp. 381, 387. Cartas: Vol. II. pp. 12, 13, 14, 22, 24, 26. Hasbrouck: pp. 72-74. See also, Hippesley: *op. cit.*
39 Páez: Autobiografía. p. 110. Hasbrouck: p. 74. O'Leary: Memorias: Vol. I. p. 484.

been an agent provocateur, whom the Spanish government had sent over to make trouble.[40]

Such an effort to create confusion was hardly necessary. There was plenty of trouble, and great events were necessary to clear it up. Bolivar made up his mind to deal with Páez later, and he determined to continue the experiment of the Foreign Legion in spite of these episodes. He did not agree with Urdaneta, who said he preferred ten battles to one march with the British Legionnaires. On the contrary, Bolivar urged López Méndez to raise more money in London and to send over more men and munitions. Soon after, an Irish regiment under General d'Evereux arrived, also composed mostly of revolutionaries, adventurers, and men out of work. But of all the Europeans who came in response to Bolivar's appeals, the Germans seem to have been the best.[41] These were Hanoverians who had fought under Wellington.

Spaniards, too, who despised their King's despotism, joined Bolivar. They were doubly welcome to him because they spoke the same language and because they justified the uprising of South America to the world. French, Italian, and Polish officers also came, but the heart of the Legion remained English. Bolivar realized from the very beginning that the difficulties would be only transitory. They were the typical manifestations of every European emigration into the tropics—the childhood illnesses of the assimilation process. The incompetent, the bad, the greedy, and the ambitious were screened out, as were also the weak and the fractious who could not or would not acclimate themselves to the demands of a new life. When the period of unrest and complaints and accusations was over, however, a second phase began—the adjustment of the Foreign Legion to the vicissitudes of tropical warfare and their preparation for the final showdown.[42]

40 Cuervo: Participación. p. 366. O'Leary: Doc. Vol. XVI. pp. 57-58. De la Rosa: Firmas. p. 138. Lecuna: La Guerra en 1818. Vol. XXII. p. 744.
41 Cartas: Vol. II. p. 59. Hasbrouck: pp. 171, 183, 184. Kienzl: Bolívar. Berlin, 1935. pp. 173 ff. Dietrich: op. cit. p. 151.
42 Cartas: Vol. II. p. 9.

Not all the officers were like Hippesley or Wilson. Bolivar found some excellent co-workers among them: like Colonel Rooke; like Fergusson, indeed, who actually gave up his life for Bolivar; like O'Leary, who became one of his closest confidants; like Peru de la Croix, to whom he opened his heart as he did to no other.

The Legionnaires were grouped into regiments. To the first Hussars, Bolivar gave the following device, "Always faithful to the highest authority." Along with the purely English, German, and Irish battalions, Bolivar now began to form mixed troop bodies. In these mixed units the experienced European soldier trained his inexperienced American brothers-in-arms; and in his turn the white man learned to endure the hardships that were natural to the Indians and mulattoes. From these units Bolivar could get tactically trained bodies and thus resist the technical superiority of the Spaniards. He instructed his generals to strengthen these regiments especially, "so that the Creoles would mix with the British and receive the same discipline, and their cavalry learn maneuvers according to the rules of tactics. All were to receive British uniforms."[43]

The army with which Bolivar was to fight the battles of Boyacá and Junín grew slowly. The outcome of the war would be determined not so much by the number of Legionnaires as by their military value. Nevertheless, in the face of the small number of troops that was scattered over the continent to fight for American freedom, numbers also played an important role. The four thousand Europeans who had come to Bolivar as fighters became a vital element in the melting pot of the American future.[44] Bolivar was fully aware of this. He said once that it was not he, but López Méndez, who was the real liberator of South America, for it was López Méndez who sent over the British Legion.[45]

So much for the immediate importance of the British

43 Cartas: Vol. II. p. 58. O'Leary: Doc. Vol. XVI. p. 104.
44 Hasbrouck: pp. 390 ff.
45 Cuervo: Participación. pp. 391-92.

Legion in the military picture. It had a more intrinsic meaning
for Bolivar. At a time when no one could yet think of international recognition for the free states of South America, the
participation of European volunteers gave these states an
historic meaning. The prestige lent to Bolivar's world by the
British Legion was like that of Lafayette's to Washington's
world.

Soon great and familiar names followed the anonymous
troops. An Ypsilanti wanted to join Bolivar's army; a Sobieski,
nephew of the Polish hero of liberty, Kosciuszko, asked to
become his aide; Daniel O'Connell sent him his son. Wellington spoke of the Liberator as a great general. Bolivar enjoyed
not only the first rays of fame; he understood the ideological
meaning of these signs. He asked one of his British friends to
take over the role of chief of propaganda and to feed public
opinion in Great Britain with news about Venezuela.[46] While
he was in Angostura preparing his campaign for the coming
year, he was concerned with giving the world a picture of the
real motives that animated the South American Revolution.
Among the many things which had come to the Orinoco on
the transports of the Foreign Legion was a printing press. On
it Bolivar ran off the first newspaper of the Third Republic—
the *Orinoco Post*.

In Caracas at the same time appeared a counter-revolutionary
paper, *La Gazeta de Caracas*. Its editor in chief, J. D. Díaz,
was His Catholic Majesty's royal liar and story teller. With real
or forged documents, with calumny, hatred, and fanaticism,
this paper wooed the people of the Caribbean. It was Bolivar's
aim to combat Díaz' influence. Thus the *Orinoco Post* became
a fighting and a propaganda sheet. In a country which did not
yet have the bad habit of reading, a daily paper had neither a
public nor a staff of journalists. Even if there had been both,
there would still have been a lack of money and paper. Bolivar
confined himself to a weekly issue, which appeared every Sat-
urday and which also served as the official government bulletin.

46 Cartas: Vol. II. pp. 14, 21. Blanco: Doc. Vol. VI. p. 611.

It was, as Bolivar said, a remarkable thing that the paper of a free people could appear in the vast solitudes of the Orinoco.[47] Zea, the New Granadian, became the editor. He was a friend of Nariño and had worked with Mutis on his botanical expedition. Later he became director of the Botanical Gardens in Madrid, then deputy in Bayonne, and finally champion of freedom in his country and his hemisphere. For two years now he had followed Bolivar's star. The best pages of the paper, however, were not those that Zea wrote. They were the appeals and speeches of the Liberator, himself, which were published therein.

In the autumn of 1818, Bolivar's faith in victory was greater than ever.[48] He might have been called a man possessed, because reality seemed to refute him. The Spaniards were successful on all fronts. Bolivar was defeated, and his second in command never ceased trying to conspire against him. But his confidence originated not in the wild dreams of the fanatic, but in the farsightedness of the prophet. The Spaniards might temporarily be successful. Bolivar knew they were winning themselves to death. Time worked against them. The tie with the Holy Alliance had not benefited Ferdinand VII. The despotism of the Spanish King was becoming unendurable to the nation.

British opinion now favored South America. Still more important, however, was the change in America itself. President Monroe had mentioned the South American independence movement for the first time in his message of February 12, 1817. Monroe considered it neither a revolution nor yet an ordinary uprising, but a civil war between two factions that had equal rights.[49]

Events of the greatest importance had occurred in the south of the continent at the same time. The provinces of La Plata

47 Blanco: Doc. Vol. VI. p. 403. Restrepo: H. d. R. C. Vol. II. p. 470. L. Correa: El Correo del Orinoco. B. d. H. Caracas. Vol. XXII. No. 88. p. 639.

48 Cartas: Vol. II. p. 33. O'Leary: Memorias. Vol. I. p. 473. O'Leary: Doc. Vol. XVI. p. 69.

49 Ch. Griffin: La opinión pública norteamericana y la Independencia. B. d. H. Caracas. Vol. XXIV. No. 93. pp. 7 ff.

had been the first to win their independence. The commander in chief of the Argentinian army, General San Martín, had undertaken to drive the Spaniards out of Chile and Peru. For two years he had been quietly working on the creation of a new army. Then, in one of the most daring campaigns of history, he had crossed the Andes and liberated Chile. In 1818, Bolivar received from the Argentinian chief of government, Pueyreydon, the first announcement of American solidarity. Bolivar reiterated Venezuela's purpose of staking everything on freedom. "Our sacrifices are our triumphs," he wrote.

But he went further. He foresaw the creation of an American union of states which would allow the New World to take its place beside the Old, great and worthy. "The fatherland of all Americans must be one."[50] This explains the fact that the mere rumor of European intervention in favor of a peaceful settlement caused in him the greatest possible fury. Venezuela would enter into no negotiations with Spain before its complete independence should be acknowledged. It would deal with Spain only as an equal.[51]

Bolivar could justify this audacious attitude. New hope was dawning on the American horizon. Bolivar received reports which convinced him that the future of Venezuela and New Granada would be decided simultaneously and soon. Morillo was obliged to withdraw a part of his troops from New Granada in order to assert himself against Bolivar and had been unable to prevent a new fire of patriotic uprisings from forming at the foot of the Andes. Guerrilla bands were already penetrating into Colombia.

Bolivar had more detailed reports in August, 1818, concerning the state of affairs and decided to organize an expedition to liberate the sister country. He did not yet plan to force the final issue of the war in New Granada. He merely wanted to lure the enemy from Venezuela by barring the rich supplies which came from New Granada.

50 Cartas: Vol. II. p. 19. Proclamas: p. 187.
51 Cartas: Vol. II. pp. 90-91. Proclamas: p. 196. Lecuna: Guerra en 1818. Vol. XXII. pp. 845 ff.

After some hesitation, he named Colonel Santander commander in this new theatre of war, assigned a general staff to him, and equipped him as completely as the limitation of his own purse would permit.[52] Then he summoned the people to an uprising. He reminded them of the glorious days of their common battles. As they had left in 1813 to liberate Venezuela, so he, Bolivar, came today to give them back their independence. "Before a year has passed the altars of liberty will have a new site in Colombia. Colombians, the Day of America has dawned!"[53]

52 Cartas: Vol. II. pp. 51, 54. O'Leary: Doc. Vol. XVI. p. 85.
53 Proclamas: p. 189. Cartas: Santander. Vol. I. p. 4. O'Leary: Memorias. Vol. I. pp. 472 ff.

CHAPTER 19

The Congress of Angostura

*A*merica's day had dawned. But only the watcher high on the battlements could see that the sky was slowly beginning to clear. The year 1818 had been, to use Bolivar's own words, a failure, a mixture of victories and defeats like the dreadful campaign of 1814.[1] Then, Bolivar had been forced to leave his country. Now he entrenched himself in Angostura, there to await the reorganization of the army. The fusion of Europeans and Americans, the reorientation of the officers, the procurement of new equipment—all these required time, at least a year's time.

On the other hand, the war had to be kept going: first, because Bolivar's troops began to desert as soon as they were quartered in towns and villages; second, because each respite also gave the enemy time to catch its breath; and third, because the world must be convinced that South America's independence was on the march. The operations of the next few months were necessarily tentative and inconclusive. They rippled the surface of the water, but they did not lead events into new channels.

Bolivar now approved Páez' guerrilla tactics. It was the warfare suitable to the period of transition in which Bolivar could afford to risk nothing.[2] In the east, as in the west, he had to confine himself to harassing the enemy. A strategy of exhaustion took the place of the strategy of annihilation. In

1 D. d. B. p. 179.
2 O'Leary: Doc. Vol. XVI. pp. 53, 171.

344

order not to be overrun by Morillo, who had remained in the west, Bolivar conceived a new plan. He wanted to meet Páez again at the Apure and to anticipate Morillo's moves.[3]

Accordingly, for the second time in six months he made the long voyage from the Orinoco to the Apure. On December 21, 1818, a whole convoy of river boats left Angostura, and on January 16 he met Páez. The Llaneros greeted him with cheers. It was the first time that Bolivar and Páez had seen each other since before the rebellion of Colonel Wilson. Bolivar knew that the spark of revolt still smoldered in the army, and he was determined to extinguish it. He explained to Páez that any resistance to him personally was bound to harm the Republic, and that he would sacrifice anything and anybody to establish his authority. It was obvious that this innuendo was directed at Piar. Páez agreed with his point of view and assured him that he, Páez, was quite without any plan of revolt.[4] Bolivar was satisfied. He named Páez Division General, and put the entire cavalry under his command.

What Bolivar and Páez had discussed was not revealed to the army. At the parade Bolivar told the Llaneros, "Your lances and your deserts liberate you from the tyrants. Who can harness infinity? Prepare yourselves for the fight. . . . Brave General Páez will lead you to victory."[5] While he was still occupied with reorganizing the army, letters reached him announcing the arrival of fresh British troops in Angostura.[6] Bolivar cut short the march he had scarcely begun against Morillo. He had never been too serious about it, and he saw the possibility of completing the creation of a trained army. All the generals received instructions to make their soldiers ready for field service, and rewards were offered for special accomplishments in drilling.[7]

Bolivar wanted to organize the British himself, but there

3 Cartas: Vol. II. p. 93.
4 Larrazabal: Vol. I. p. 545. Baralt: Vol. I. p. 434. O'Leary: Doc. Vol. XVI. p. 199 ff.
5 Larrazabal: Vol. I. p. 545.
6 O'Leary: Doc. Vol. XVI. pp. 212, 213.
7 O'Leary: Doc. Vol. XVI. pp. 177, 212, 213. Cartas: Vol. II. pp. 102-03.

were still other reasons which demanded his presence in
Angostura. The first parliament was to convene there on February 15. The enforced leisure to which he had been condemned
since May, 1818, had given him time to prepare for this event.
There had been no parliament in Venezuela since 1812, and
Bolivar had been accused of disregarding the voice of the nation.
He was told to subordinate his powers to a legal body, and he
complied by instituting the State Council. But the scaffold he
had erected in 1817 had been only an emergency measure, and
it had to be gradually replaced by a more secure construction.
The army could liberate Venezuela from the Spaniards, but
with this its functions were completed; it did not enter into the
life of the state as a contributing factor. Bolivar was no Caesar,
and the phrase *"exercitus facit imperatorem"* did not apply to
him. So he conceived the bold idea of calling a parliament into
being. More than half of the national soil was still under
Spanish domination. Free elections were impossible, and yet
such popular representation would be very important. Hitherto,
independence had been the work of separate heroic individuals.
With the meeting of a parliament, the homeless Republic would
become stabilized and the decisions of statehood would have
a legal basis.[8]

Bolivar turned to the State Council and explained his plan.
To win was not enough. One had to be free under the protection of a free law.[9] He asked the Council to work out the
necessary technical measures.

Bolivar set sail from the Apure to meet the delegates who
were to come to Angostura. Slowly the ship glided down the
river. The heat was unbearable. Swarms of birds arose from
the jungle and swept like clouds across the sky. Tigers, jaguars,
tapirs, and other big game came out of the bush and went to
the river to drink. The passing ships scarcely disturbed them.
Hundreds of crocodiles lay buried in the slime; hordes of insects surrounded the ship. The nights were calm and clear,

8 Proclamas: p. 193. Libro del Centenario de Angostura. 1919.
9 Proclamas: pp. 191, 192. O'Leary: Doc. Vol. XVI. pp. 113-159. Blanco: Doc.
Vol. VI. pp. 470 ff., 478. Cartas: Vol. II. pp. 100 ff.

and the moon was large and beautiful. Monkeys and birds screamed in the nearby forests. Bolivar was unaware of all this. Swinging in his hammock or walking up and down the verge of the river when the boats stopped to allow the crews to rest, he evolved the future constitution. One hand on the collar of his uniform, the other at his chin, he dictated to his secretary the greatest speech of his life.[10]

Those who study Bolivar as soldier might find in him certain resemblances to Attila and Ghenghis Khan. What raised him above the riders of the steppes, however, was the image of a free state that he carried in his heart and which he now planned to reveal to his people for the first time. There was one distinguishing characteristic of Bolivar's actions and ambitions which he shared with no other genius of history; this was a tropical exuberance, a dionysian enthusiasm generally lacking in statesmen. But had there ever been such a situation? Who else could have conjured up a state without tradition, without laws, without norms? Never has the idea of a state come to light under such circumstances.

Angostura is a little town like dozens of others in South America. It is situated on the south bank of the Orinoco, which is here "only" about two miles wide. At that time it had about six thousand inhabitants. The streets ran parallel to the river; the houses were one-storied and all alike. On the square were the cathedral and government building, the court house and the barracks. Parliament was to meet in the large hall of the municipal building. The elections had been difficult. Ten years of destruction had swept away all semblance of order; not even the baptismal records of the community had survived.[11] Bolivar counted on thirty-five delegates, but only twenty-six came. They represented the provinces of Caracas, Barcelona, Cumaná, Barinas, Guayana, and Margarita. Bolivar expected the New Granadian representatives later.

10 O'Leary: Memorias. Vol. I. p. 492.
11 Gil Fortoul: Hist. pp. 271-72. For details of the franchise, see, Blanco: Doc. Vol. VI. p. 485.

The day of the opening, February 15, was celebrated with salvos. The city had been festively illuminated the night before. The clergy and a sprinkling of foreigners who lived in Angostura were invited to the opening session. The people crowded the doorways. At eleven o'clock in the morning, Bolivar, accompanied by his staff and heralded by a three-gun salute, entered the hall. The meeting was opened, and after the observance of parliamentary formalities, Bolivar took the stand.[12] He brought a manuscript to the desk and read it in his rough and slightly coarse voice. Any fatigue that might have attended the procedure was entirely dissipated by the passion in his voice, the expression of his face, and the eloquence of his gestures. His listeners were breathlessly attentive.

The speech of Angostura is not an oration, but a message. It is a message from the commander-in-chief to his co-fighters, and as such it is personal and dramatic. Again, it is a message from the President to the Congress of a future republic, and as such it is objective and provocative. These two aspects of Bolivar's address emerge separately and positively. "The first day of my peace will be the last day of my power" was the promise with which Bolivar summoned the Congress.[13] In this manner he confessed his decision to subordinate himself to the law.

"Lucky the citizen," begins his message, "who, under the protection of arms, calls on national sovereignty to exercise its unrestricted will. I count myself among those men favored by providence, for I have united the representatives of the people in this Parliament, and I return to it the supreme power which had been given to me. Only the most urgent necessity brought me to the point of taking over the onerous and dangerous responsibilities of the dictator. Now I can once again breathe freely. The era during which I guided the destinies of Venezuela was not only full of political storms and bloody battles;

12 Larrazabal: Vol. I. p. 549. Blanco: Doc. Vol. VI. p. 584. Baralt: Vol. I. p. 438. Congreso de Angostura: Libro de Actas. Publicado por R. Cortazar y L. A. Cuervo. Bogotá, 1921.
13 Proclamas: p. 196.

it marked the ascendancy of chaos, the overflowing of a hellish stream, which flooded Venezuela. What could a man, and particularly a man like myself, do to stem the tide? I could do neither good nor evil. Invincible forces guided the course of events. To ascribe them to me is to give me an importance I do not deserve."[14]

Bolivar had the sagacity to know that even the greatest man can do nothing other than what historic destiny dictates for the world. It was no exhibition of false modesty for him to say, "If you want to know the true originators of the events, ask the annals of Spain and America, . . . examine our character and the bitterness of our enemies." Nevertheless, he knew that he owed an accounting to Congress. He offered his deeds to the scrutiny of Parliament.

This gesture of the selfless Republican was necessary, even if it convinced no one. Since Jamaica, Bolivar had advocated presidency for life, and he was convinced that such a position was due him. But it was essential that he should play the role of Brutus in Angostura, and that he should speak of the dangers which arise from the unrestricted exercise of power by one and the same man. "He becomes accustomed to command, the people become accustomed to obey. Usurpation and tyranny are the results." The fatherland, Bolivar went on to say, had other and more deserving sons who could rule it. Before he had begun to work on his original plan, the creation of the state, he formally renounced his power. Then he began his analysis of Venezuelan politics.

One of Bolivar's greatest inspirations, the result of his daily contact with reality, was that he did not interpret the state as an empty vessel, but as a living and mobile accompaniment to society. The Republic was the result of the revolution. The revolution, however, was the result of Spanish domination. Like Schleiermacher, Bolivar felt that the mistakes of the state were the mistakes of public opinion. After the overthrow of

14 Proclamas: pp. 203 ff. Bolivar's first draft was later edited by M. Palacio Fajardo because Bolivar's Spanish was not always correct. See also, Gil Fortoul: Hist. p. 274.

the Spanish colonial dominion, America resembled the Old World after the fall of the Roman Empire.

We are familiar with Bolivar's ideas on slavery in South America from his Jamaica letter. He repeated these ideas in Angostura in almost the self same words. The Spanish Empire imposed a despotism on Americans that was more disastrous than that of the oriental monarchies, for the Turks, Persians, and Chinese are at least ruled by their own kind. But America was condemned to passive slavery by Spain because it was ruled by foreigners. Slavery is the daughter of darkness. "An ignorant people is the tool of its own destruction." And Venezuela was an ignorant people when it entered the revolution. But the ignorant are like children. They take imagination for reality; they confuse revenge with justice; they take treason for patriotism and license for true liberty. "Liberty," said Bolivar, recalling Rousseau's words, "is a food that is hard to digest."[15]

It was necessary to express all this, not only because Bolivar addressed himself to people who were inexperienced in the art of writing a constitution, but because he spoke to a generation whose sense of proportion had been beclouded by ten years of chaos. The citizens of the future Republic had first to be strengthened and trained before they could digest the heavy food of freedom. They were like the men of Plato, who lived bound in a cave. The glory of the sun confused and dazzled them. "Lawgivers," cried Bolivar to the delegates in Angostura, "weigh your conclusions. Do not forget that you must lay the foundations for a formative state." This consciousness of thinking and working for a nation that is in the act of coming to life is peculiar to Bolivar. No other statesman of his world felt as he did. The few who, like him, pondered the problems of the American constitutions were satisfied to array the body of the young nation in the rigid forms of the Old World. . . . in ready-made constitutions which did not fit the growing countries.

15 Proclamas: p. 207. See M. Briceño Iragory: Discurso de Angostura. B. d. H. Caracas. Vol. XXVIII. No. 112.

Bolivar was an American, not only in his outward semblance, but in his consciousness. He had seen that he could
not spare his hemisphere the pangs of birth. He wanted to
give his growing people a foundation on which it could build
the pyramids of its existence to the height nature had destined.
It was a grandiose but a tragic undertaking, and anyone who is
familiar with South America must admit that it has not ended
to this day. These people are still seeking a basis for their future
greatness.

We have said that Bolivar knew his country must bear its
birth pains, but he also knew that growth can be guided and
determined. He reminded Venezuela's lawgivers of the examples of history. These all seemed to prove that it was easier
for humanity to bear the burdens of despotism than to keep
the balance of liberty. Many nations have shaken off the bonds
of oppression; few have tasted the rare moments of liberty.
He spoke not only for his own time but for ours when he said,
"Not only the governments . . . but the people themselves
conjure up despotism."

Where did these reflections lead? Bolivar's skeptical thoughts
about the ability of people to use their freedom ended in a criticism of the first constitution of Venezuela. From a purely legal
point of view, the Constitution of 1811 was still in force. Could
Congress just go back to the fundamentals laid down eight
years ago? Bolivar feared that his enemies would make this
attempt. He knew the weakness of the federal idea. The supporters of a federation of states referred to the great example
of North America. Bolivar thought it a miracle that a federation of North America could exist at all. He pointed out that
there, too, new developments would occur. But whatever the
fate of the United States, they could never serve as a model,
because the conditions in North and South America were not
the same. Did not Montesquieu prove that laws must conform
to the spirit of the nation in which they are in force, and that
the soil, climate, and expansion of territories influence the con-

stitution? This, said Bolivar, is the book of laws we must consult—and not the Washington constitution.

But the Constitution of 1811 had gone even beyond that of North America. "We were," confessed Bolivar, "not prepared to live in this state, which would have called for a republic of saints. Our moral conditions did not conform to the political ones." One important factor hindered the realization of absolute democracy in Venezuela—the human factor. Democracy is based on the postulate of equality. But can there be equality in a world where the inhabitants shut each other out . . . where there are six or seven races, where men are classified according to the color of their skins? The demands of equality conflict in South America with racial reality. No one could believe that the Liberator wanted to perpetuate racial differences on this continent in the form of a caste system. On the contrary, he demanded that the law and humanity set aside the barriers which nature herself had erected. But politics could not go beyond the existing differences with eyes blindfolded.

Such differences demanded a sure will and exceedingly great tact in the leadership of a society whose complicated structure confuses itself, and divides and disintegrates at the slightest change, said Bolivar. No sociologist could have better defined the condition of internal politics in South America. These were new and unheard-of truths for South American ears. Everyone knew the facts, but no one wanted to hear them. Bolivar hid his astute conclusions under a cloak of restrained eloquence. In this way they might more easily reach his public, who were of all shades of skin. Up to this point his speech had been retrospective and critical. He had weighed the accomplishments of the past and found them wanting. Now he moved on to the new structure.

Three virtues characterize the complete state: a maximum of happiness, a maximum of social security, and a maximum of political stability. It was the duty of Congress to find the magic formula which expressed these three desiderata in laws. The South American Revolution was a fight for freedom. Every nation which emerged from it had, therefore, to be a free state. "The government of Venezuela was republican and must be republican. Its basis must be the sovereignty of the people, a division of power, civil liberty, abolition of slavery, and the extermination of monarchy and its privileges."[16] This had been the program of all democrats since 1793. But Bolivar was neither a Danton nor a Robespierre, and his concepts of state were closer to those of Napoleon than to the men of the Terror. As soon as he had proclaimed as the unassailable heritage of the future state these fundamental rights of a democratic republic, he began to describe them more specifically. The acceptance of democratic principles did not in the least mean the establishment of absolute democracy. Absolute democracy, said Bolivar, has throughout all human history foundered on the weakness of governments. The pure rule of law is impossible. Nations consist of people and need people . . . capable, patriotic, well-informed men are the ones who create a republic.

It was the old cry which he had raised immediately after the fall of Miranda and which can best be transcribed into the English maxim, "Men, not measures." The work of a government consists not in form and not in mechanism, but in the conforming to its folk character, for which it is being created.

We have already taken note in the Jamaica letter of how Bolivar's political "storm and stress" began to clear up under the influence of Anglo-Saxon positivism. At Angostura he praised the British form of government as the great example which Venezuela should copy. He became more and more the pupil of Montesquieu. Like this master, Bolivar found that the British body of law combined the greatest amount of political well-being with the greatest number of human rights. The most important way in which Bolivar wished to shape the Venezuelan Constitution like that of the British was in regard to the structure of its law giving body. The Constitution of 1811 provided for a House of Representatives and a Senate. Bolivar approved the House. What he had to say about it

16 Proclamas: p. 215.

stamps him as a democrat. But he was an hierarchic and authoritarian democrat who wished to balance the freely elected representatives with hereditary senators. In place of an elected Senate, he wanted an upper house consisting of hereditary members.

It is clear that Bolivar wanted, with this measure, to put a stop to the vacillations of the masses. He believed in the nation, but he did not believe in the masses. The sovereignty of the people, he once wrote, cannot be unlimited, because justice is its basis and complete usefulness its goal. "Most people fail to recognize their own true interests. . . . The individual fights with the mass; the mass fights with authority. . . . In every government there must be one neutral body, which stands on the side of the attacked and disarms the attacker."[17] This duty devolved upon the hereditary Senate. Bolivar wanted the first Senate to be elected by Congress. He gave them to understand that men who had distinguished themselves in the cause for independence deserved a place in this body. He wanted to establish a sort of school for leaders of the future generations in which the sons of the senators were to be trained for the difficult tasks that lay ahead.

This manner of assembling the hereditary Senate was taken in part from Plato's State, and in considerable part from the Catholic church. Bolivar's ideas approximate those of Napoleon and anticipate something of the fascist system. He defended himself against the accusation of wanting to create a new nobility by saying that the dignity of the senator was no title, but a position for which the aspirants had to prepare themselves.

Though Bolivar did not wish to create a new nobility, he did think of creating an elite class, which would, in the course of time, develop a new American patriciate. Herein lies the weakness of Bolivar's thinking. This Senate was irreconcilable with democratic principles. A still more serious consideration was the lack of any quality in the Latin-American people on which such an institution could be based. In South America there had been no development of a blood aristocracy, because

17 Proclamas: p. 219. Estrada Monsalve: *op. cit.* p. 155.

it was to Spain's interest to prevent the formation of any such nobility. Nevertheless, an upper class had grown up in the colonies, rich, family-conscious, and exclusive. It had assumed leadership in all the countries south of the Rio Grande. But it could never turn into a closed blood aristocracy, because that would have been contrary to its own principles. It had achieved political power as leader of a democratic movement. It had thrown off the feudal absolutism of Spain. It was the result of racial mixtures which the Iberians scorned. The Creole elite could feel like nobility, but it could never function as such.[18]

Today, after more than a century, South America is still ruled by this elite. It was said of France that it was ruled by two hundred families. In South America there are about four hundred ruling families. They comprise an oligarchy based on tradition, wealth, possessions, or capitalistic interests. Its leadership is anonymous and discreet. It does not appear in state documents and the law ignores it. The jockey club and the country club are more important for their power than Parliament. According to democratic ideology all men are equal, and the arrogance of the rich families is suffered by Indians, Negroes, mestizos, and mulattoes as long as they are assured by Parliament and the newspapers, on the radio and on the street, that all men have equal rights, and that, as Anatole France would say, even the rich are forbidden to sleep in hallways. One must be familiar with South American society to understand why Bolivar's hereditary Senate was a mistake. His plan for an American upper house was like the idea of importing basalt to build banks for the river beds of the Amazon or the Orinoco. His idea of an hereditary Senate conflicted with one of the basic principles of democracy—the selection of the best qualified. Democracy can tolerate neither schools for leaders nor the creation of orders. Bolivar's Senate would have prevented fresh energies from emerging. His proposal was rejected throughout the South American nations.

If, in the foregoing plan, Bolivar misunderstood Venezuela's

18 In regard to the problem of elites in South America, see, J. M. Samper: Ensayo sobre las revoluciones politicas. Paris, 1861. p. 173. P. M. Arcaya: Clases sociales de la Colonia, in Sociología Venezolana. Madrid.

possibilities, he did show extraordinary perception in the next chapter of the Constitution. He now turned to the administrative department and demanded a president into whose hands all national power would be placed. This president would not be responsible, but his ministers would be responsible to Congress and the courts. It was said that Bolivar wanted kings for South America with the title of president.[19] As a matter of fact, he believed that the administrative power within the Republic was more important than the law making power. Therefore, he demanded more power for the head of the Republic than was granted a constitutional king. It was his ideal of a presidential democracy. It is that form which, under many guises, has survived to this day in South America, because it conforms to the sociological structure of the continent.

The description which Bolivar gave of future presidents reflects the conflicts he had already won. The president, he said, is an isolated individual in the middle of society. His duty is to control the people's urge to anarchy. He must supervise the judges and the administration to prevent the abuse of law. He is the man who alone must resist the attack of opinions and special interests and social passions. He is torn between the desire to rule and the desire to avoid being ruled. He is a prize fighter who challenges a whole company of prize fighters. The bitter experience of the years in which, as president of Greater Colombia, he fought anarchy singlehanded should have confirmed these words.

Yet one must not think that he wanted to take the responsibility of the constitution upon himself as the only capable man. The leadership of the state by great men is a necessity and was never more so than in South America, where maturity was reached after decades of crises. Bolivar never tired of hammering into the lawmakers the fact that only a strong presidential hand could protect the government from sinking into incompetence and abuse. He wanted a democracy, but a stable

19 Proclamas: p. 222. Estrada Monsalve: p. 146. I. B. Alberdi: in Simón Bolívar. Madrid, 1914. p. 180.

democracy. Without these elements the Republic of Venezuela would be no more than an experiment which would inevitably sink into tumult and chaos. Bolivar demanded a powerful president. But he was careful in Angostura not even to mention the idea of life term presidency. He knew that such a suggestion would be construed as personal greed for power.[20]

But Bolivar not only provided for the three traditional powers; he planned a fourth. His ideas on the subject were deep and lofty. A nation was for him not the sum of its people. It was a unit animated by a national spirit. Only such a national will to unity could create a lasting government, for he tuned the different strings of the political orchestra harmonically. It was not enough to create the state; society, too, had to be formed. Social freedom had to guarantee political freedom. Only a society that feels free and wants to feel free will aspire to be a free state.

Venezuelan society, however, was a long way from loving liberty. "The Venezuelans love their country," said Bolivar, "but they do not love its laws." Therefore, society seemed condemned to go down in confusion in a war of all against all. Here the fourth power was to enter the picture. It was to be responsible for moral training. Bolivar wanted to create an ethical Aeropag—a community comparable to the censors of the Roman Republic. It was not only to supervise the training of children; it was to cleanse the Republic of all corruption, to combat egoism, despondency, and lethargy. Bolivar's ambition to set up a court of morals was born of a horror at the decadence and degeneration into which the people had sunk during the ten years of the civil war. Miranda, before him, had once expressed the same idea. We meet similar thoughts in Plato and Rousseau. But like the hereditary Senate, Bolivar's court of morals was also impracticable.[21]

Had South America shaken off the Spanish Inquisition only

20 Proclamas: p. 225. Most historians have overlooked the fact that at Angostura Bolivar did not even mention the life-time presidency.
21 See Bolivar's letter to G. White: Cartas: Vol. II. pp. 177-78. Parra Pérez: Bolívar. p. 82.

to establish a new one? Bolivar wanted his morals court to be
a consulting body, but we know from the history of Geneva,
from the annals of Anglo-Saxon puritanism, and from the
French Revolution, that the opinions handed down by such a
council are written in human blood. And where were the men
on whom Bolivar could have put such a tremendous responsibility? War and persecution had decimated the intellectual
nobility of America. Bolivar could not have named fifty men
in 1819 who had the moral energy to carry out his plan. Only
time and patient training could make good in generations what
Spanish rule and the dehumanization of war had ruined. Bolivar had to content himself with this. For the rest he had to
leave the problem of morals and controls to the church and
the Aeropag of old ladies who to this day sit in judgment on
morals and tradition in South America and who are sometimes
more terrible than the Spanish Inquisition itself.

These were the fundamentals that Bolivar showed the lawmakers as he would show them a plan on a drawing board.
"Let us not attempt the impossible," he cried. "If we rise too
high in the sphere of liberty we shall again fall into the abyss
of tyranny. Unity, Unity, Unity—that must ever be our
motto." [22]

An indivisible Venezuela with a central government was
Bolivar's plea. It was urgent and it was vital—a conservative
republic, the plan of a man who feared anarchy and who mistrusted the instincts of the masses. It was the product of observation and reading, realistic and chimerical at the same time.
Montesquieu and Plato, Machiavelli and Rousseau were the
godfathers of his ideas. He retained the integral thought of
his Angostura speech to the end of his life. Among the great
political documents of Bolivar, it is the best balanced; his style
is solemn and stern, the sequence of ideas compact and master-
ful. In it he kept a happy balance between the authoritarian
and the democratic tenets. [23] We shall see later to what extent
his message was accepted by the delegates.

22 Proclamas: p. 225.
23 Belaunde: Bolívar and the political thought of the Spanish American Revolu-

Bolivar could not leave the stage without promising Congress to give an exact picture of his political and military activities. But he did not want to bury the impressions of the first hour in details. The ministers would do their duty, but there were two laws the defense of which he undertook himself: the abolition of slavery, and the compensation of the Patriots for their losses and sufferings. Congress might rescind all other decrees; these two constituted a debt of honor which the movement for independence owed to posterity.[24]

Bolivar ended his message with a view to the impending decision. He mentioned that a defeated Spain had asked help from the European powers. But Venezuela would refuse all foreign interference. It would defend its individuality, not only against Spain, but against the whole world.

Finally he conjured up the ideal of a greater Colombian State, which would result from the union of Venezuela with New Granada. In the heart of the world a new republic was being born which would serve humanity as bond and focal point. Its gold and its silver, its medicinal plants, its treasure, would go out in all directions. Colombia would put the majesty of the New World before the eyes of the Old.[25]

His speech over, he put down the manuscript and addressed the lawmakers. "Gentlemen, begin your tasks. I have completed mine." Bolivar's speech struck the men in Angostura like a blow to the heart. The cheers for Venezuela mingled with the thunder of applause. It was a scene of enthusiasm and ecstasy such as can occur only in the tropics. When Bolivar had read his outline for the new constitution, he asked for the election of a new president so that he could hand over his duties to him. Francisco Antonia Zea was provisionally chosen and Bolivar swore him into office. Then Bolivar turned to his officers. He and the generals of his staff were at the moment only simple citizens. Congress would confirm them in rank

---

tion. Baltimore, 1938. pp. 186-87. Parra Pérez: Bolívar. pp. 70 ff. Monsalve: Estudios. pp. 105 ff. C. Lozano: *op. cit.* pp. 83-86.

24 Proclamas: pp. 232-33.
25 Proclamas: pp. 234-35.

or repudiate them. To strengthen his own subordination to
Parliament, he went up to Zea and handed him his marshal's
baton, symbol of command. It was a theatrical gesture, such as
Bolivar and his countrymen loved.[26] But this gesture was needed
to satisfy such rebels as Mariño and Páez. Of course, Bolivar was
unconditionally confirmed in rank—he remained the ruler
and the highest authority in Venezuela. Bolivar explained that
he could not accept this power and asked permission to leave
the meeting. On February 16 Congress elected him President
of the Republic. Bolivar insisted that he lacked the gifts of
an administrator and that his only wish was to share the dangers and honors of war with his army. Congress insisted on his
acceptance, and finally Bolivar gave in. He organized the cabinet and named secretaries for the departments of Finance, War,
and the Interior. It was characteristic that the formative Republic did not yet need a minister for foreign affairs. Provisional
President Zea was elected Vice-President. He was to take Bolivar's place in his absence.[27]

The Congress of Angostura meant more than a victorious
campaign in Bolivar's life. It was a triple victory. It secured
Bolivar's personal status; it silenced his enemies; it presented
the Republic to the world as an independent state. Bolivar was
no longer a rebel leader who assumed top command on his own
initiative, nor was he merely a general or a dictator. He was
the President of a new nation. He retained all his former power,
but it was veiled in the cloak of the law. At last he outranked
all his rivals. After February 20, 1819, he was no longer dependent on their whims and caprices. Who could still reproach him
with the execution of Piar? "I left all my opponents buried
behind me in the Congress of Angostura."[28]

No one saw through his game. Colonel Hamilton, who was
present at the meeting, wrote to the Duke of Sussex, "General

26 Larrazabal: Vol. I. p. 560. O'Leary: Memorias. Vol. I. p. 517. Blanco:
Doc. Vol. VI. p. 598.
27 Proclamas: p. 236. Blanco: Doc. Vol. VI. pp. 600 ff. Congreso de Angostura,
Libro de Actas. pp. 6, 7, 8. O'Leary: Doc. Vol. XVI. p. 258.
28 Cartas: Vol. III. p. 201 of May 30, 1823.

Bolivar gave a proof of his modesty and his patriotism such as cannot be found in the history of any country."[29] He called the meeting at Angostura a decisive blow against the Spanish government. And this was, in fact, the last triumph that Bolivar had in Angostura. A Parliament had been formed that gave news of a young nation that had political talents and was growing in experience. Bolivar's ideological flight had brought the Republic to such a height that astonished contemporaries became aware of the nation for the first time.

The year 1819 was a year of reaction for Europe. Bolivar had made no attempt at making himself agreeable to the princes of the Holy Alliance. He had made no concessions to monarchy. But his praise of Great Britain, the conservative tenor of his thoughts, showed wiser politicians that he was no tyrant, nor murderer, nor Jacobin. Thus his speech at Angostura became an appeal to the world to show justice to South America. With it, Bolivar not only reëstablished the constitutional life of Venezuela, but paved the way for recognition of his Republic by foreign powers.[30]

He required two weeks for this extraordinary task. Bolivar set out again on February 27 to join the army at the Apure.

29 Blanco: Doc. Vol. VI. p. 712. Larrazabal: Vol. I. p. 564.
30 Some letters to Bolívar. Hisp. Am. Hist. Rev. May 1944. pp. 277 ff. Gil Fortoul: Hist. p. 274. O'Leary: Doc. Vol. XII. p. 302. G. A. Sherwell: Simón Bolívar. Washington, 1921. p. 119. Hamilton's letters in Arch. Bolívar, Section-J. de F. Martin. Vol. VIII.

The Liberation of New Granada

In October, 1818, Bolivar had promised, "The enemy will be attacked simultaneously on all fronts."[1] But this assurance entailed military efforts which the exhausted Republic could scarcely put forth. Bolivar limited this far-reaching program when he went to join the army. He left a small force under Mariño which undertook to guard Angostura, but the glorious name, Army of the East, deceived no one. It was a division made up of recruits and convalescents, numbering about one thousand men. One could not expect too much of them.[2]

Bolivar put greater hope on a transport of British troops due to arrive in Margarita at any moment. Urdaneta was to receive this reinforcement and to increase it with five hundred natives. Bolivar's plan was to hurl this new army at the opposite coast. Caracas was to be their objective. No one, least of all Bolivar, who had so often tried in vain to win back his native city, believed that Urdaneta would be successful. As a matter of fact, Bolivar tried to deceive Morillo and to lure him first eastward and then northward in order to disperse the royal fighting forces.[3]

The Spanish general had united seven thousand men of all military classes in Calabozo at the entrance to the plains. He knew that he could break Bolivar's resistance only by driving

1 Proclamas: p. 192.
2 O'Leary: Memorias. Vol. I. p. 526. O'Leary: Doc. Vol. XVI. p. 265.
3 Urdaneta: Memorias. pp. 158-59. O'Leary: Memorias. Vol. I. p. 526. O'Leary: Doc. Vol. XVI. pp. 250, 252.

362

him out of the Llanos.[4] He had to go to the Orinoco and the Apure to force him into battle.

While Bolivar was still in Angostura, Morillo had moved to the south and had crossed the Apure without any opposition from the Independents. Páez had taken his stand behind the Arauca River, the second largest waterway crossing the plains from west to east. Like the Apure, it flows into the Orinoco.[5] The stream is 250 meters wide at the point where Páez took his stand and the banks are steep. Nevertheless, Morillo, in his pursuit of Páez, succeeded in crossing the river. The Patriots hindered him as little there as they did at the Apure. Morillo wanted to force a showdown, but it was to the Patriots' interest to prevent it. They wanted to avoid battle, and to inveigle the Spaniards deeper and deeper into the plains, for it was there that everything conspired against the Europeans. Bolivar reached his army about this time, in the early days of March. Although defensive action was contrary to his nature, he had to admit that the tactics of exhaustion promised the greater benefits.[6]

Now began a curious war. Bolivar's horsemen lured the Spaniards into the swamplands from which only natives could extricate themselves. The enemy sank into the slime with both horse and equipment.[7] The Republican infantry, which was not yet equal to that of the Spaniards, was quartered on the alluvial soil of the islands formed by the great tropical streams. Here they were safe and had water and the beef cattle which had been sent on beforehand. Whenever Bolivar's riders withdrew, they set fire to the pampas grass so that the Spanish cavalry could not graze. The few farms were set ablaze, and horses and cattle were driven off. The Spaniards, who had invented guerrilla warfare, found their master in Bolivar. Morillo was a fearless soldier who was not daunted by any hardships, but he saw in a very few weeks that self-denial and sacrifice were

4 Blanco: Doc. Vol. VI. p. 631. See Lecuna: La Guerra en 1819. B. d. H. Caracas. Vol. XXIII. No. 89. pp. 36 ff.
5 O'Leary: Memorias. Vol. I. p. 527. O'Leary: Doc. Vol. XVI. p. 265.
6 O'Leary: Doc. Vol. XVI. pp. 259, 270, 272.
7 O'Leary: Memorias. Vol. I. p. 529. O'Leary: Doc. Vol. XI. pp. 507-8.

useless. Bolivar deluded him and then disappeared like the mirage which confuses the exhausted rider in the desert.

Morillo went back to the Apure, where the general conditions were more favorable. Now it was Bolivar's turn to take up the chase. Encounters took place with varying degrees of success for both parties.[8] In one of these engagements, Páez accomplished a coup which is remembered in South America to this day. Bolivar had ordered a reconnaissance of the enemy lines on the other side of the Apurito. Páez selected one hundred and fifty of his best riders and with them swam across the river. Reaching the shore, he divided them into small groups and let them ride against the Spanish position with slack reins. Morillo heard the calls of the Llaneros and saw the dust kicked up on all sides. He thought the whole Patriot army had crossed the river and was delighted that he could finally take Bolivar's measure. He had his army take battle formation and rode toward the Llaneros at the head of the cavalry. Páez turned and lured the Royalists farther and farther away from their army, only to turn again and fall upon them, driving them back to their point of departure, where only their infantry fire saved them from total destruction. The encounter took place at Queseras del Medio on April 2. The Spaniards lost four hundred men; the Patriots lost six.[9]

Bolivar celebrated the victory with lofty words. In his proclamation to the army he said, "What you have done is only a prelude to what you can do. Prepare for battle and count on victory. You will win it with the points of your lances and bayonets."[10] The meaning of such small skirmishes lay in the fact that they fanned the fighting spirit of the troops and gave them a sense of superiority over the Spaniards. Also, such encounters bolstered confidence in Bolivar's leadership. So the war went on, surging between the great rivers. It consisted only in attacks, skirmishes, harassments. The Republicans now

8 O'Leary: Doc. Vol. XVI. p. 286. Torrente: *op. cit.* Vol. II. p. 519.
9 Páez: Campañas de Apure. B. d. H. Caracas. No. 21. p. 1192. O'Leary: Doc. Vol. XVI. p. 293. O'Leary: Memorias. Vol. I. pp. 533-34. Dávila: Investigaciones. p. 185. Lecuna: Guerra en 1819. Vol. XXIII. p. 50.
10 Proclamas: p. 237.

had to suffer the consequences of their own tactics! They had themselves destroyed the grass and the sparse settlements. Wherever they went, they found nothing but the barren soil. It was summer, the dry season, and a merciless sun seared the earth from morning till night. No tree gave shade; the brooks ran dry; rations were meager and consisted almost entirely of beef. At night officers and men slept on the bare ground. Disease and vermin heightened these discomforts. Bolivar asked nothing for himself beyond what he could give the common soldier, and faith in him grew from day to day. By one of those intuitions which defy analysis, they were all convinced that his luck had turned for the better and that his star was in the ascendant.[11]

But if the Patriots had to accept hardships in this campaign, matters were still worse for the Monarchists. They were less familiar with the country, and the people were hostile. Wherever they went they found almost no inhabitants who could give help of any description; there were only "old dogs that were too lame to accompany the Republicans." Finally Morillo gave up. The rainy season was near and he felt that he could not ask for further exertions from his weary men, so he moved into permanent quarters behind the Apure. He had lost many weeks and had won no marked advantage. The results of the first months of 1819 are described in a letter of Bolivar's: "Our defense was fatal for Morillo, because he lost almost half of his army in the marches and countermarches and skirmishes. I would have made a frontal attack and challenged him to open battle, but I had to suppress my desire and avoid the issue because I was obliged to listen to all the repeated advice of our friends who did not wish to risk the fate of the Republic in one engagement. . . . In everything I am advised to take the attitude of Fabius, and this to my sorrow. For, unfortunately, my character is very different from that of the Roman general. He was cautious; I am impetuous."[12]

11 O'Leary: Memorias. Vol. I. p. 538.
12 Cartas: Vol. II. pp. 107-08, of April 4, 1819.

The puma, the American lion, stalks its prey sometimes for days through the jungle. Silently he follows, awaiting the moment of attack. Thus Bolivar lay in wait determined to fall on the enemy's flank. His plans fluctuated; he was still uncertain about the fate of Urdaneta and the British expeditionary corps. He expected fresh supplies from Angostura, but first of all he had to know which way Morillo would turn. He wanted to prevent the fight from being carried to the east, so he suggested to Páez that he, Páez, penetrate into the province of Barinas to tie the Spaniards down in the west.[13] None of these plans was carried out, for none was entirely thought through. They were mental attempts to clear the fog behind which the Spaniards lay hidden. The solution came suddenly and from another source. On May 14, Bolivar received a message from General Santander, who reported the success of the Patriots in the plains of Casanare, and suddenly Bolivar saw a light. It was a moment of crystallization in which one of the most daring ideas of history was born.[14]

The plains of Casanare were the only sections of New Granada that had resisted the Spanish Restoration. Seen geographically, they form a part of the American pampas. With the same width of land, vast rivers, sparse trees, they go over into the Llanos of the Orinoco and the Arauca. When Morillo subdued New Granada with an iron fist in 1816, the best and manliest of the Patriots had fled to Casanare and had here survived the terror. The Spaniards had sent troops to put out the flames of rebellion in this place of refuge, but all their efforts had been in vain. The Patriots had become one with the vastness, and the vastness was unconquerable.[15]

Two years passed. The mountain region suffered in silence, but Casanare, in the plains, breathed the air of freedom. The Spanish viceroy, who was again in residence in Bogotá, feared

13 O'Leary: Doc. Vol. XVI. pp. 344, 362. Lecuna: Guerra en 1819. pp. 66-68.
14 O'Leary: Memorias. Vol. I. p. 540. O'Leary: Doc. Vol. XVI. pp. 360-62. Cartas Santander: Vol. I. pp. 23-24.
15 Plinio A. Medina: Campañas de Casanare, 1816-19. Bogotá, 1916. F. P. Santander: Apuntamientos para las memorias de Colombia y de la Nueva Granada. Bogotá, 1838. N. González Ch.: Estudio cronológico de la Independencia. Paris, 1879.

that the Patriots would push into the highlands, and he had the gorges occupied by strong garrisons.[16] But he could not drive the Independents out of the plains. Bolivar had assigned the organization of Casanare to Santander, who had fulfilled the mission in exemplary fashion. He could boast of having created administrative order in the midst of chaos. He challenged the Spaniards in a proclamation, secret copies of which reached Bogotá and were passed from hand to hand among the Patriots.[17]

Viceroy Samanó was no longer willing to watch these antics of Santander and sent one of his best officers to put an end to them. Santander, however, following Bolivar's instructions, harassed the enemy, but refused to engage in a battle which might prove disastrous to him. Meanwhile the rainy season set in, and the Spaniards felt first discouraged and then hopeless in their desert surroundings. Forced to admit once more that the "Robbers of Casanare" were invincible, they began to retreat. By the end of April the plains were again free. When Santander forwarded this information to Bolivar,[18] his decision was immediate. He wanted to liberate the Colombian highlands, for he felt that the key to victory lay in New Granada. In Bolivar's geopolitical and geostrategical thinking Venezuela and New Granada had always been one. Twice the sister nation had offered a refuge to the homeless Liberator, and in Jamaica he had spoken of New Granada as the heart of America. Less than a year before he had prophesied that the year 1819 would bring freedom to the Colombians. The time had now come to fulfill this prophecy and to wrest the heart of America from the Spaniards. He knew that once he had control of the highlands, he would be able to roll back the enemy position to the north and to the south, toward Panama and Venezuela, and also toward Ecuador and Peru. From there

16 A. Obando: Autobiografía. B. d. H. Bogotá. Vol. VIII. p. 596. L. Vallenilla Lanz: Centenario de Boyacá. Caracas, 1919. O'Leary: Doc. Vol. XVI. p. 200.
17 Cartas Santander: Vol. I. p. 5. Arch. Santander: Vol. II. pp. 68, 87. O'Leary: Doc. Vol. XVI. p. 286.
18 Libro de órdenes militares del General Santander en las Campañas de 1819. B. d. H. Bogotá. Vol. XXVIII. p. 1089.

he could make contact with Chile and Argentina and thus achieve his dearest ambition, the freedom of the continent.[19]

Bolivar first considered the advantages of such a campaign. It would have an element of surprise, for if he set out now for New Granada, Morillo would never suspect his plan. Because of the rainy season, the roads were almost impassible and all information was delayed for weeks. Morillo would receive no reports, or if he did, he would place no credence in them, since a bold and audacious move like the crossing of the Andes at that time of the year would never occur to him. Moreover, the Spanish army in New Granada would not be prepared, and Bolivar would also be fighting in friendly territory and in a country that, though oppressed, was not destroyed as was Venezuela. But Bolivar did not conceal the hazards from himself. The risk of such a march during the rainy season was great—how great he did not even guess at the time. If he left, taking with him the best part of the army, no one could predict what might happen to Venezuela. Let us consider Bolivar's problem. His daily correspondence made him aware that he could not depend on any of his generals. Urdaneta quarreled with Arismendi; Mariño fought with Bermúdez. One officer would assume a rank to which he was not entitled; another would countermand orders that came from above. Would such men be able to defend the Republic against Morillo? Was he not betting too much on one card? But, thought Bolivar, God is great. Perhaps Morillo would learn only when he got into his winter quarters just what had happened and then it would be too late for him to attack Guayana and the Orinoco. Perhaps Páez would be able to tie the Spaniard down and make him believe that the whole army was still in Venezuela. Páez and his riders constituted another hazard. Which of them would go with Bolivar, and could he feel confident of their support?

19 Proclamas: p. 190. One of the first to suggest the conquest of New Granada was J. F. Blanco: Doc. Vol. VI. p. 646. However, not only the concept but also its execution in 1819 must be credited exclusively to Bolivar. Páez, on one side, and Santander on the other have claimed to be responsible for the conquest of New Granada, but their contentions are without basis.

Bolivar carried the bold plan of invasion in his head for several days and then suddenly decided to act. First he consulted Páez. He described the hazards of remaining inactive in the plains during the rainy season. The army might desert or die of fever. Then he conjured up the conquest of New Granada in glowing colors. He did not expect Páez to take part in it, since his task would be to keep Morillo busy. At a given time he was to attack the valley of Cucutá and cut the Spanish lines of communication.[20] Páez listened to all of this in silence and finally agreed. He did not dare oppose Bolivar, for, to use his own words, the eyes of the Liberator were irresistable. Whether he was really convinced or whether he was merely glad to be rid of his great rival, knowing him to be engaged in a dangerous adventure, is a question. Enough that he agreed. From the others Bolivar expected no opposition.

On May 23 he called a war council to explain to the generals who were to accompany him his plans for the conquest of New Granada.[21] Their decision was reached in a poor hut on the banks of the Apure. The poverty of the country was so great after ten years of war that there were neither chairs nor table in the place. The officers sat on the skulls of dead oxen which the sun had bleached and the rains had washed white. The gathering was as picturesque as the surroundings. All the officers were young. None had reached forty. The first seat next to the Liberator was occupied by the chief of staff, Carlos Soublette. He was just past thirty and in every way represented Venezuelan aristocracy. Slender, tall, with impeccable manners and a facility for words, he had succeeded because of his ambition and methodical gifts.

Anzoátegui, commander of the infantry, was born in eastern Venezuela. He, too, was only twenty-nine years old, but for ten years he had fought for the cause of freedom. His fearlessness won the hearts of his comrades. As for his character, it was scarcely such as to win him many friends. He was always dis-

20 Páez: Autobiografía. pp. 136-37, 175. O'Leary: Doc. Vol. XVI. pp. 356-57.
21 O'Leary: Memorias. Vol. I. p. 543.

gruntled, and there was no situation that pleased him or which he did not criticize. He was a born nagger and pest and was, moreover, filled with a passionate hatred of certain other men on the staff. But he was completely devoted to the Liberator.[22]

Colonel Rooke, under whose command Bolivar had placed the British Legionnaires, was the antithesis of Anzoátegui. He was pleased with himself and the world and found everything wonderful. His optimism knew no bounds. To him the climate of the plains seemed most healthful; his soldiers were the best in the world as long as they lived, and when they died he found that they should have died long before. Wherever he was, he thought he had heaven in his hands. He had an exemplary temperament for a soldier and fighter, and as he lived, so he died. These were the leading personalities among the eleven officers whom Bolivar had called together. He explained the campaign to them, and then asked, "Do you want to go along?" The first to answer was Rooke. "General," he said, "with you I shall go wherever you wish, if necessary down to Cape Horn."[23] The other officers also declared their willingness to do his bidding. Only one refused.

But this voice did not carry much weight. Bolivar's ideas had won. Everything now depended on their execution. The first condition was secrecy. The troops were not to know where they were being led nor what they were about to do. Because of the great number of deserters, an ill-advised word might spoil everything. Bolivar was so careful that he did not reveal all the details of the campaign even to the war council. But after the idea was accepted in all its fundamentals, he worked with the speed that was characteristic of him. Santander was instructed to begin his operations against New Granada. He, too, was ordered to make all his preparations in the strictest secrecy.[24]

22 O'Leary: Memorias. Vol. I. p. 555. F. Lozano y Lozano: Anzoátegui B. d. H. Bogotá. Vol. XII. p. 548.
23 Larrazabal: Vol. I. p. 579.
24 O'Leary: Doc. Vol. XVI. p. 364. Arch. Santander: Vol. II. p. 131. O'Leary: Doc. Vol. XVI. pp. 371-74, 389. Restrepo: H. d. R. C. Vol. II. p. 506.

Bolivar confined his preparations to the most necessary things, such as procuring arms and ammunition, horses and cattle. He had already ordered all boats to be collected. They were vital, because the plains were like lakes in the rainy season. The precautionary Santander was worried for fear the troops could not cross the mountains without boots and woolen blankets, but no one knew where to find woolens and leather shoes.[25]

Toward the end of May the army set out. Bolivar found less resistance among the troops than he had expected. Most of his men were glad they had something to do again. They were young, unconcerned about their lives and used to hardships. Many women went with them. These "juanas," as they are called, served as nurses and camp followers. Their vocabulary did not always conform to the rules of the Royal Academy of Madrid, but they were as brave as the men, and when necessary, they even bore arms.[26]

The army did not head for Cucutá as Bolivar had made his people believe, but toward the plains of Casanare. On June 11 Bolivar met Santander. This officer was one of the youngest generals in the army. He was not more than twenty-seven years old, of medium height, and with a tendency to corpulence which detracted somewhat from his appearance. His face was stern and determined and without a trace of humor or kindliness. His hair was straight and brown, and he wore it in the fashion of the day, in straight strands that reached to the collar of his unform. Like Bolivar he belonged to Creole aristocracy, but a slight trace of Indian blood was apparent. His amber eyes, shaded by long lashes, lay deep in their sockets and were penetrating and secretive.[27]

Bolivar ordered a three-day rest and used it to arrange his troops. He took command himself, while Soublette remained chief of staff. The advance guard was assigned to Santander,

25 Cartas Santander: Vol. I. pp. 12-13.
26 O'Leary: Memorias. Vol. I. p. 547.
27 Cartas Santander: Vol. I. pp. 23, 29, 41. O'Leary: Memorias. Vol. I. p. 473, 553. M. Grillo: El hombre de las leyes. Bogotá, 1940. P. Gómez: Santander. Bucaramanga, 1940. G. Camacho Montoya: Santander. Bogotá, 1940. M. J. Forero: Santander. Bogotá, 1940. L. E. Pachero: La Familia de Santander. Cucutá, 1940.

who, as a native New Granadian familiar with the terrain, was
a logical choice for leader, especially since his men were also
New Granadians. It is difficult to give an exact picture of the
size of this army, since numbers and reports vary. In all prob-
ability Bolivar's army, counting all reserves, was about three
thousand strong; twenty-three hundred were infantry, and
seven hundred cavalry.[28]

Their way led through the plains, but they were no longer
plains. Rivers had turned to lakes; through the once dry beds
of brooks flowed rushing streams; the land between was swamp
and morass, and cloudbursts poured unremittingly upon the
steaming earth. Swarms of mosquitoes whirled over the waters
and harassed the army. The troops had little clothing to protect
them, and in the torrential rains it would have availed them
little. Many soldiers did not even own trousers, but went about
in a *guayuco,* an apron that just covered the loins. Whatever
was available in uniforms was used to keep the arms and ammunition dry. "For seven days," asserts O'Leary, "we marched
in water up to our waists."[29] Settlements in the plains of Casanare were sparse, and only occasionally did they come upon a
village. The most difficult task was crossing the rivers. Bolivar's
boats were insufficient so he had others made of cowhide sewn
together. In these the guns and powder and those soldiers who
could not swim were taken across.

The Liberator was always in the midst of his men. After
a long march he was usually busy caring for horses and mules
or helping to unload the canoes. On its march from Venezuela
to New Granada, the army crossed the Arauca, Lipa, Ele, Cravo
del Norte, Tame, Casanare, Ariporo, Nuchia, ten navigable
rivers, besides brooks, swamps, and lakes. Many mules and
horses were drowned; half of the cattle was already lost.[30]

28 M. Paris: Campaña del Ejército Libertador Colombiano en 1819. Bogotá,
1919. p. 26. P. J. Dousdebes: Trayectoria Militar de Santander. Bogotá, 1940. H.
Bingham: The Journal of an Expedition across Venezuela and Colombia. New Haven,
1909.
29 O'Leary: Memorias. Vol. I. p. 552. Cartas Santander: Vol. I. p. 54. Rivas
Vicuña: Vol. IV. p. 6.
30 O'Leary: Doc. Vol. XVI. pp. 401-02. Cortes Vargas: De Arauca a Nuchia,
Campaña libertadora de 1819. Bogotá, 1919.

Bolivar did his best to invent remedies, but he had neither the engineers nor the tools. Moreover, any loss of materiel was better than a loss of time. Already there were days on which the troops had nothing to eat, but the frugality of the Llaneros enabled them to survive all vicissitudes. When Bolivar approached the foothills of the Cordilleras at the end of June, he wrote to Páez, "The operations of the army have thus far been confined to marching through friendly territories. After we had successfully crossed the Arauca and all the navigable streams from there to the Pore, I thought that the most important obstacle of our undertaking had been overcome. But in the face of the new hazards which arise each day and double at every step, I almost despair of ending it. Only a constancy which is above every trial, and our determination not to give up a plan that found universal approval, have permitted me to conquer these paths."[31]

Bolivar was not mistaken. The conquest of this region, which according to Santander was more like a small sea than firm ground, was not the greatest of the problems. From June 22 on the army met an obstacle which seemed insurmountable. Mighty and inaccessible, the chain of the Andes loomed before their eyes. The few trails had been washed away by the rains. The Andes were considered impassable at this time of the year. Moreover, the material handicaps were not the only ones, nor even the greatest. Psychological resistance arose which was harder to combat.

Bolivar's army consisted almost entirely of men of the hot earth. They had never dreamed that anything like these mountains even existed, and their wonder grew with every step they took. With each crest they reached they thought the climb was over, and that ahead lay a land comparable with their own. But instead of the plains which they expected, there were new abysses and new and higher ascents. Rock upon rock the summits ranged into the heavens, their highest points lost in mist and clouds. Primitive man feels helpless in sudden changes in

31 O'Leary: Doc. Vol. XVI. pp. 404-06. Santander Cartas: Vol. I. p. 55.

his surroundings. All his forces are natural forces, and only
with spiritual and moral energies can he measure up to the
demands of new forms of existence. These intrepid shepherds
who swam rushing streams, fought tigers and alligators, became timid in the face of an overpowering nature.

With each new ascent the temperature dropped. The senses
lost their alertness, the body its mobility. Horses that could
run unshod through the Llanos fell on the slippery paths.
Their feed did not agree with them and they died in droves.
The animals carrying the guns and ammunition collapsed and
blocked the way for those that followed. Rain came down in
torrents and the cold water caused a kind of dysentery for many
soldiers. After four days of marching through the mountains,
almost all the vehicles became useless. The beef cattle died,
and everything seemed to conspire to cause Bolivar's plan
to fail. The Venezuelans became fractious. What did they care
about New Granada and these Godforsaken mountains? But
Bolivar was inflexible. Again and again he succeeded in stirring
up the troops. He told them of the fame that awaited them, of
the plenty that would be theirs once they reached the highlands.
The soldiers believed him and marched on.[32] The enemy was
finally encountered on June 27. The third division of His
Catholic Majesty was stationed in New Granada, and Morillo
had assigned command of this division to young Colonel
Barreiro.[33]

Morillo considered two points of New Granada strategically
vital: the capital, Bogotá, and the port of Cartagena. Accordingly, the troops were dispersed over the extended mountain
regions. Bogotá could be conquered only from the plains. The
Andes, rising here to a height of five thousand meters, were
its natural defenses. In this location, Barreiro had disposed his
five thousand troops. He had, however, made three mistakes in
his calculations. Instead of concentrating his forces in the most
important places, he had scattered them over a long-drawn-out

32 O'Leary: Memorias. Vol. I. p. 561.
33 Rodríguez Villa: Vol. III. p. 499. Restrepo: H. d. R. C. Vol. II. p. 596.

line. Moreover, he did not understand how to organize an intelligence service which could report the movements of an invasion army, so he was obliged to grope in the dark to ascertain where the enemy break-through would occur.

The third mistake lay in his choice of headquarters. Barreiro had stationed himself at Tunja, capital of the province of Boyacá. But Tunja was many miles from the front. If he had chosen, instead, a small town in the vicinity of the pass as his headquarters, the campaign might have had very different results.[34] The number of his soldiers and equipment and arms was much superior to that of the Patriots, and his position on the top of the mountains was invincible. A far smaller army should have been sufficient to repel the ascending enemy.

The first encounter showed the mettle of the Patriots. Santander's advance guard met a Spanish troop of three hundred men near Paya. The Monarchists had occupied a fortified position and the Patriots stormed it and drove them out. From a psychological point of view, this opening success was of great importance. The mood of the army, lowered by effort and exhaustion, became more confident. It was the inspired moment to call the people of the country to take part in the fight for freedom. Bolivar issued his first proclamation on New Granadian soil. "You are Patriots; you are just. You will turn against the Spaniards those weapons which were given you in order that you might become your own henchmen."[35] After the first encounter, Bolivar was entirely optimistic. Although he heard that Páez had again failed him, he wrote to the general of the Llaneros, "I shall be in Boyacá in eight days."

Before the last and most difficult part of the way could be negotiated, he again called his generals together. Knowing that a few of his compatriots disapproved of his plan, Bolivar played the two nationalities against each other in order to spur them on to their higher tasks. He led them to believe that he now desired to retreat. The Granadians naturally protested and de-

34 Paris: *op. cit.* pp. 88-89.
35 Proclamas: pp. 238-39. Arch. Santander: Vol. II. p. 163.

clared that they would carry on the war on their own initiative. The Venezuelans felt guilty and asserted that they were capable of any effort the others could make. Bolivar's diplomacy had won a new victory, and the campaign went on.[36]

The Spaniards had withdrawn at one point to a position that blocked the only road considered passable in the rainy season. Bolivar was determined to continue his surprise tactics. Following the advice of Santander, he chose the high pass of Pisba as a crossing place. Here, from the crest of the Andes, he could descend into the fertile plains of New Granada. In the minds of the Spaniards this feat approached the impossible. They considered the heights of Pisba as insurmountable, and for this reason the Patriots were not confronted by enemy defenses. On July 4 Bolivar arrived at the foot of this pass, which rises to a height of three thousand meters.[37] The trail was gutted by the rains and was slippery. At some places huge masses of stone had tumbled down and blocked the way, and trees, felled during the bad weather, lay across the trail. The few remaining horses died the first day. It was impossible to carry anything except the guns, and the soldiers were obliged to throw away their four-day rations. The descending darkness brought apprehension and dismay. Rain and hail, falling constantly, extinguished the feeble flames of the camp fires. An icy wind blew, and the scantily-clad troops froze to the marrow. On the next day they crossed the mountain pass, but hundreds fell by the way and died of exhaustion. Discipline had vanished; women in the throes of labor brought on by fatigue and exertion delayed progress; officers left their units; the exhausted men had to be beaten to keep them from falling asleep. With one hundred men on the mountain pass of Pisba the Spaniards could have prevented the liberation of New Granada. Men in groups of ten and twenty stumbled down the trail.

Bolivar had hastened ahead, and he welcomed his prostrated

36 Restrepo: H. d. R. C. Vol. II. p. 530. Obando: *op. cit.* p. 601. Medina: *op. cit.* p. 60. Santander: Apuntamientos. p. 14. González: Santander. Bogotá, 1940. p. 331.

37 Geografía económica de Colombia: Vol. III. Bogotá, 1936.

troops with the assurance that the worst was now behind them.
But this group of desperate men needed no encouragement.
Looking back at the mountains lying above them in the brown
mist, they knew there was no choice. They must win or die.
No Spanish bayonet could be more terrible than their recent
experience.[38] In spite of their courageous attitude, however,
it still would have been an easy matter to have annihilated the
Patriots. So far, only two-thirds of the army had crossed the
Andes. The rear guard with the British Legionnaires was far
behind. Fortunately, the Spaniards were unaware of their
enemy's whereabouts. This secret crossing of the Andes made
it possible for Bolivar to grant his army a short respite.[39]

The first place the Patriots reached was called Socha. It lies
five hundred meters below the pass, and the chain of mountains protects it from the icy winds. Its people plant corn,
wheat, and potatoes. After the wastes of the pass, poor little
Socha seemed like an oasis to the soldiers. They were welcomed
by the population and given tobacco, bread, and chicha, a native
beverage brewed from corn. Bolivar saw that his hopes had
not betrayed him. He was now fighting on friendly soil. With
the help of these oppressed people the losses sustained by the
army in their conflict with nature were gradually replaced. Bolivar lost no time in building up his army. The soldiers, scattered
during the climb up the Pisba, were picked up and brought
back to their units. A great part of their equipment lay in the
defile, and Bolivar sent peasants out to gather it up. All this
activity went on while the enemy was only a few days' march
distant, but the friendliness of the population made it easy for
Bolivar to set up a spy system. He asked every peasant to give
a glowing description of the Patriot army. They were to act,
he said, as though the Heavenly Host had come Himself to
conquer New Granada.[40]

When at last Rooke and Soublette joined the army, Bolivar

38 O'Leary: Memorias. Vol. I. p. 564.
39 O'Leary: Doc. Vol. XVI. p. 413. Cartas Santander: Vol. I. pp. 56-57.
40 O'Leary: Memorias. Vol. I. p. 569. O'Leary: Doc. Vol. XVI. p. 420.

welcomed them with open arms. Rooke still found everything
wonderful. According to him, the crossing of the Pisba was
just a pleasant walk. Bolivar invited him to a breakfast consisting of roast meat, bread, and chocolate, and Rooke asserted
that this was the best breakfast he had ever eaten. Meanwhile,
the eternally disgruntled Anzoátegui arrived and announced
that one-fourth of the British Legion had died on the march.
Rooke, who was still busy with his chocolate, looked up and
said, "It is true, but they deserved no better. Their conduct was
miserable, and the Legion has only profited by their deaths."
Even Bolivar was obliged to smile at this rejoinder. With men
like this he could not fail.

The Spaniards began slowly to recuperate from their surprise at learning of Bolivar's presence in Boyacá. Barreiro had
set up quarters near the enemy line and with sixteen hundred
men had occupied an unassailable position on a rock mound
that controlled the river Gameza. Bolivar was afraid that
Barreiro had sent to Bogotá for reinforcements and gave orders
to take the Spanish position. His men crossed the Gameza
under enemy crossfire, but tried in vain to make a successful
attack. Barreiro's fortifications were only too good. The Spanish general saw with scorn how Bolivar's ragged troops stormed
ahead: These beggars should never rob him of New Granada.[41]

On July 15 Bolivar again called a war council. He confessed
that it had been his original plan to force an entrance into the
valley of Sogamoso in a frontal attack. As the enemy strong-
holds proved impregnable, the only alternative was to flank
Barreiro. Bolivar proposed swinging off to the southwest, crossing the Chicamocha, and then penetrating into the valley of
Santa Rosa. The strength of the army would only increase
thereby, as Patriots would come to him from all sides. The plan
was approved and carried out at once. The crossing of the river
was successful, and the further the Republicans pushed forward,
the better they were received.

41 O'Leary: Doc. Vol. XVI. pp. 411-13. Paris: *op. cit.* p. 105. M. A. López:
Recuerdos Históricos. Bogotá, 1889. p. 9. Dousdebes: *op. cit.* pp. 248-51.

After a four-day march, Bolivar had improved his strategic position materially. The enemy was outflanked, and Bolivar controlled the valley of the Sogamoso. Barreiro withdrew, fearing that his way to the capital would be cut off. Bolivar was now quite certain of success. He sent small divisions into the neighboring provinces to arouse the people.[42] On July 24 the whole army of liberation was assembled on the left bank of the Sogamoso. The Spaniards stood on the opposite bank.[43] Both Monarchists and Patriots lay in positions that were well adapted for defense. But Bolivar did not care about defense, for Barreiro could get reinforcements from the interior in a day. Bolivar decided to deceive the enemy. He crossed the Sogamoso with the intention either of attacking the Spaniards from behind or of drawing them out of their positions. Barreiro was informed of the Patriots' movements and set out to frustrate them. At twelve o'clock Spaniards and Americans met. Bolivar was not in an advantageous position; his one wing was crowded by the swamp, *el Pantano de Vargas,* which gave its name to the battle. The Monarchists occupied the surrounding hills and according to all the rules of war had the advantage. The six hours of the battle's duration passed in attack and counterattack, with the possession of the mountain chain as objective. An attempt by Santander to take the hills failed. The Royalists drove him down and threatened to surround Bolivar's left wing. At that moment everything seemed lost. Bolivar threw the British Legion into the fight and they took the hills with fixed bayonets, but Barreiro made another counterattack and drove them off. Finally the Llaneros turned the scales. Bolivar called to their leader, "Save the fatherland!" In an instant the riders fell upon the enemy. It was almost inconceivable that the cavalry could attack on this rugged terrain, but the horsemanship of these men was unique. The infantry followed the example of the cavalry and attacked again. Finally, darkness put an end to the fighting.

42 Restrepo: H. d. R. C. Vol. II. pp. 533-37. Cartas Santander: Vol. I. p. 62.
43 Paris: *op. cit.* p. 111. O'Leary: Doc. Vol. XVI. p. 421.

Seen as a single action, the battle at the Pantano de Vargas
must be considered inconclusive, but in the sum total of the campaign, it was the event that brought about the turn of affairs.
The report that Barreiro sent to the viceroy already betrayed
which way victory would lie. "The annihilation of the Republicans," wrote the Spaniard, "appeared inevitable. Not one
seemed able to escape destruction. But despair gave them un-
equalled courage. Infantry and cavalry rose from the swamps
where we had thrown them and began to climb the heights in
a real frenzy. . . . Our infantry could not resist them."[44]
Nothing had changed in the position of the two armies, but
while Barreiro remained where he was as though paralyzed and
in fear of making a move before help came from Bogotá,
Bolivar's strength increased.

His losses had been heavy. The most painful was the death
of Colonel Rooke. During an attack by his Legion, a bullet
had shattered his arm. It had to be amputated, and he bore
the operation with fortitude. When the doctor, an Irishman,
had finished, Rooke exclaimed, "Give me the arm. Have you
ever seen such a beautiful arm?" The doctor smiled, but Rooke
insisted. Finally he held the arm up high, and cried, *"Viva la
patria!"* "Which country?" they asked him. "The one which
will hold my grave." Three days later he was dead.[45]

In general, the infantry had suffered most. Bolivar decided
on a daring step. He put the whole region under martial law
and ordered a draft of all able-bodied men. The Indians, who
were used to obedience, came to headquarters and offered their
services. They appeared with flat felt hats on their black hair,
their *ruanas,* or woolen shawls, hanging from their shoulders.
They were no soldiers, and it cost some effort to train them in
the use of firearms. Usually they closed their eyes and turned
their heads away when they pulled the trigger, a practice more
dangerous for their comrades than for their enemies. But it

44 O'Leary: Memorias. Vol. I. p. 571. Blanco: Doc. Vol. VII. pp. 7-8. Arch.
Santander: Vol. II. p. 219.
45 O'Leary: Memorias. Vol. I. pp. 555-56. Blanco: Doc. Vol. VI. p. 719.
Hasbrouck: pp. 202-03.

was these same men with whom the Liberator later fought the battles of Carabobo and Bombona. In all there came about eight hundred men.[46]

On August 3 Bolivar again crossed the Sogamoso and forced Barreiro to evacuate the little town of Paipa. He pretended to establish his quarters here and to put his army in prepared positions. But after dark he countermanded the order. Stealthily he led the army out of Paipa. The Patriots marched throughout the night, but they did not take the main road. Instead they pushed over an out-of-the-way path toward the west. On the afternoon of the following day they reached their destination, the capital of the province. Bolivar entered Tunja on August 5, and was greeted by the people as their saviour. All the equipment of the garrison was taken. More important than this acquisition was the change in his strategic position. Bolivar had cut off Barreiro's contact with Bogotá. For the third time he had succeeded in seizing his enemy's flank. Barreiro learned of the capture of Tunja on the morning of August 6, and he was enough of a soldier to realize that the fate of the whole country was now at stake. He had no other thought than to escape from the trap and keep his line of retreat open. Since Bolivar kept the main route occupied, Barreiro took the way over the mountains. Both armies fought with reversed fronts. On August 7 Barreiro continued his retreat. It was clear that he wanted to reëstablish contact with the interior. Bolivar, seeing through the enemy's tactics, gave orders to hinder his movements and if possible to force him into battle.[47] On August 7 at two o'clock in the afternoon the encounter took place. The situation was now the opposite of what it had been at the beginning of the campaign. Barreiro's men were tired from their long marches, were poorly fed, and had lost their reserves. Bolivar's soldiers were rested and sure of success. Barreiro was on the point of crossing the bridge of Boyacá. Possession of the bridge meant control of the road

46 O'Leary: Doc. Vol. XVI. p. 426. Cartas Santander: Vol. I. p. 63.
47 O'Leary: Doc. Vol. XVI. p. 428.

back to Bogotá, for here the route controlled by Bolivar and
the side roads on which Barreiro marched converged. As Barreiro's advance guard approached the bridge, it was suddenly
attacked by the Patriot riders. They were believed to be reconnaissance troops and Barreiro's advance guard opened fire
to free the way for the march of the Spanish forces. But now
Bolivar's entire fighting force loomed up on the surrounding
hills.[48] Some of the Spaniards were able to cross the bridge,
but the mass stayed a mile away on the other bank. Barreiro's
one thought was to bring the rest of his army across the bridge,
but the Americans knew how to thwart this. The battle that
now developed consisted really of two separate engagements.
Santander fought for possession of the bridge. Anzoátegui was
one kilometer away on the mountain slopes with the main part
of the Patriot army. Bolivar arrived on the battlefield only
after the engagement was well under way. Here, too, the tide
was turned by the Llaneros, who rode around the right wing
of the Royalists. The Spanish infantry withdrew and the
artillery was mowed down. The Spanish advance guard, which
had thus far held out at the bridge, surrendered when it saw
that the battle was lost. Of the three thousand men of the
Royal army, sixteen hundred were taken prisoner. Among
them were Barreiro and his staff. The entire equipment of the
Spaniards fell into the hands of the Patriots. Bolivar himself
pursued the remainder of the fleeing army.[49]

The campaign for the liberation of New Granada ended

48 Paris: op. cit. p. 123. Restrepo: H. d. R. C. Vol. II. p. 533. Academia Nac.
d. Historia, Contribución en el Centenario de la Batalla de Boyacá. Bogotá, 1919.
49 Blanco: Doc. Vol. VII. pp. 9-10. Two controversies, one historical, the other
topographical, arose from the battle of Boyacá. The officers of the Colombian General
Staff, like Paris and Vargas, believe that the main fight took place on the northern
bank of the Boyacá River, and that only the Spanish vanguard had reached the southern bank. Restrepo: op. cit. p. 537, and E. Prieto: Repertorio Boyacense. Vol. V.
No. 43, think the whole battle was actually fought on the southern bank. A survey
of the battlefield makes the first thesis more probable. The second question concerns
Bolivar. E. Otero d' Costa, El Tiempo de Bogotá, February 24, 1936, has launched
the idea that Bolivar did not participate in the battle. The documents concerning the
affair are not very detailed, perhaps because it was taken for granted that the commander-in-chief was present. Bolivar's participation is confirmed, however, by the
English officer, T. E. Wright: B. d. H. Caracas. Vol. XX. No. 79. p. 305. See also,
Lecuna: Rev. Bol. Sept. Oct. 1936. Bogotá.

with the encounter at Boyacá. In South America they still speak
of the Battle of Boyacá and celebrate it on August 7. Neither
in respect to the duration of time nor in respect to the number
of casualties can this event be called a battle. It lasted for only
two hours, and the Republicans lost only thirteen dead. But it
was the last move in a brilliant game—check and counter-
check. It was, as Lenin would have said, a blow to a cripple.

Bolivar now went toward his last goal, possession of the
capital. The Spanish authorities gave up everything as lost.
Viceroy Samanó, who had just published a high-sounding
bulletin about the defeat of the Republicans, fled from Santa
Fe de Bogotá on the morning of August 9.[50] He disguised
himself as an Indian, wore a *ruana* and a red oilcloth hat, and
thus escaped to the Magdalena River. The other high Spanish
officials followed his example. They fled the city head over
heels. Many went on foot, but anything seemed preferable to
exposing themselves to Republican vengeance. Bolivar, on the
other hand, had handled the captured Spanish officers with
dignity. After the battle he invited them to his table and
assured them that they could have confidence in the justice
of the Patriots. Only one man was punished. Among the Spaniards was a certain Vinoni, who in 1812 had played an important role in the treason of Puerto Cabello. Bolivar recognized
him, and the memory of the most shameful moment of his
military career arose in him. He had the man hanged on the
battlefield.[51]

Otherwise the Liberator of New Granada desired neither
vengeance nor retaliation. Bolivar entered Bogotá on August
10, and, much to the astonishment of the inhabitants, dismounted in front of the Palace of the Viceroy. On the following
day Santander arrived with the greater part of the army. As
Bolivar rode through the city the amazed masses cheered him.
One of those busybodies who are never absent and who have
an unclouded joy in hearing themselves speak, pushed forward

50 Groot: *op. cit.* Vol. IV. Appendix 3.
51 O'Leary: Memorias. Vol. I. p. 575.

and favored Bolivar with a speech. He compared the Liberator with all the heroes of history; they were but pale shadows in comparison with Bolivar. The General answered him with a few words, "Great and noble speaker," he said, "I am not the hero you have painted. Emulate him and I shall admire you." The Liberator made a lifelong enemy; his name, Vicente Azuero.[52]

But what were words in the face of the army's accomplishments? In seventy-five days, Bolivar had completed his task and liberated New Granada. One might compare the campaign with Hannibal's crossing of the Alps. But Hannibal had prepared his plans by long years of effort, and the tropics made sterner demands on men than did the mild Mediterranean. In 1817 San Martín crossed the Andes in the south of the continent, but he, too, had been able to train his army for two years for this assignment. In Bolivar's campaign everything was done by improvisation, and the inexhaustibility of his genius found a remedy for every situation.

Considered as a strategic achievement, the campaign of 1819 was extraordinary. Undoubtedly Bolivar learned from Napoleon. The three maxims of Napoleon had become his own: destruction of the enemy army, capture of the capital, conquest of the country. The single actions of 1819 cannot be represented as great battles, but the over-all plan was great. Inasmuch as Bolivar knew that he was inferior to his opponents in numbers and equipment, he had to operate so that surprise and deceit outweighed these weaknesses. The campaign of 1819 is the history of three strategems. Each of them brought the Spaniards closer to destruction, until at length on August 7 they fell into the trap like startled beasts.

The small armies that fought for American freedom in 1819 might mislead us into minimizing their achievements. The modern world is accustomed to armies with a personnel of millions. But historic accomplishment does not rest upon the number of men involved. Robert Clive won an empire with

52 Blanco: Doc. Vol. VII. p. 16.

a handful of men. However, the British in India only destroyed one form of rule in order to establish another; Bolivar
conjured up an era of freedom on his continent. This year of
1819 lifted a hemisphere out of its chains. After endless efforts
he brought to reality what he had written in 1815: "The weak
man needs a long fight in order to win. The strong one delivers
a blow and an empire vanishes."

CHAPTER 21 ═══════════════════════════

The Great Colombian Republic

On a single day Bolivar destroys the fruits of a five-year campaign, and in one battle wins back all that we have gained in countless engagements," exclaimed Morillo when he heard of the defeat of the Spanish army at Boyacá.[1]

Bolivar was now faced, first of all, with the creation of the state begun at Angostura. From February to August, 1819, he had been a general only; now it was time to remember that he was also President of the Republic. He announced his program for a Republic of Greater Colombia to be formed by a union of New Granada and Venezuela.[2]

The devastation of war had hardly touched New Granada. The hatred of the Spaniards had turned only against the intellectual and moral elite of this country; five hundred of its best men had died, but it had been to Morillo's interest that this territory be protected for use as a supply depot while he fought in a devastated Venezuela. During three long years of oppression the people of New Granada had learned to cherish the blessings of freedom, which in other times they had taken too much for granted. They had recovered from the initial sufferings and tribulations of the revolution. The age that had loosed a civil war for constitutional principles, the time of *patria boba,* the foolish fatherland, was over. While the process of development from adolescence to maturity in Venezuela had been accompanied by bloody efforts and nameless sacrifices, the

1 Rodríguez Villa: Vol. IV. p. 49.
2 Cartas: Vol. II. p. 110.

386

normal life of the New Granadians had changed but little. They continued to follow their peaceful pursuits; they drank chocolate, snuffed tobacco, attended mass, and did not vary the ironical character of their conversation, a trait for which they were well known. Few of their towns had suffered. A small textile industry flourished in Socorro; in Antioquía the mines continued to produce ore. A source of money, which Montecuculli has said is the soul of war, was found by Bolivar in New Granada. After practicing for years an economy based on barter, he now controlled over a million pesos, and he determined to squeeze all he could out of the country. Freedom had its price, and he knew that men, willing or not, would pay it.[3]

Wages of civil employees were cut in half. The property of Spaniards who had adhered to the King's cause, as well as that of the Americans who had emigrated when the Republican legions approached, was confiscated. Bolivar demanded that the clergy pay its tithe into the state treasury and made it clear that he also expected voluntary contributions from them.[4] The cautious Santander advised him to proceed with care. He felt that the Spanish tax imposts had outraged the country more than the shooting of five hundred innocent victims. But Bolivar had a different concept of man and his destiny. He replied to Santander, "To carry out an undertaking without help, it is necessary to take stringent measures, even if they are harsh. Remember what arbitrary means I had to use to achieve the few successes which have saved us. Experience has taught me that one must demand much to get little." And again, "We cannot pay old debts, nor dare we do so, for this is the creation of a new republic, not the resurrection of the old. This is no longer the 'foolish fatherland,' but the land of Americans."[5]

Money, arms, and men were what he needed, and, tossed up on a new wave of enthusiasm, many offered their services and gave active help. Bolivar demanded even more. He again wanted to unite independence with freedom and brought

3 Cartas: Vol. II. p. 110.
4 O'Leary: Doc. Vol. XVI. pp. 435, 453, 460.
5 Cartas: Vol. II. pp. 112, 113. Cartas: Vol. II. p. 115, of November 8, 1819.

forward the plan of building new army units with emancipated slaves. In exchange for two years of service the slaves were to be granted complete freedom. Santander accepted the idea reluctantly. His point of view was that of the propertied classes, who saw the slave, not as a human being, but as a mere chattel, and who were unwilling to relinquish their ancient rights over the colored races. Bolivar was more generous and farseeing. A new race of men, the American race, was to emerge from the crucible of war. Bolivar felt it to be utterly illogical that men of European blood should be sacrificed in order that colored men might be free to enjoy independence on the American continent. He wrote to Santander with this thought in mind. "Is there a better or more just way to achieve freedom than to fight for it? Is it just that free men should die to free the slaves? Is it not significant for these bondsmen to win their rights on the battlefield? And is it not of some value that their threatening number may be materially reduced by strong and legal methods? In Venezuela we saw the free population die and only the enslaved live. I do not know whether this is politic, but unless we make use of the slaves of Cundinamarca, the same thing will happen again. I repeat, therefore . . . my earlier instructions."[6]

The execution of these orders could be carried out only if the country was militarily occupied and properly administered. The first of these two considerations was the most immediate. Even before August 7, Bolivar had sent small divisions to the border provinces of Pamplona and Socorro, which connect Venezuela with New Granada. The bottleneck of Cucutá, where there is a mountain pass between the two countries, was all that the Spaniards now held in this section. In the west the conquest of the province of Antioquía became an easy matter. It had been entrusted to young Colonel Córdoba, one of the most audacious talents of the Republican army. The Republicans pushed beyond Antioquía into the primeval forests of

6 Cartas: Vol. II. pp. 151-52, 180. O'Leary: Doc. Vol. XVII. pp. 169-70. J. M. Rivas Groot: Páginas de la Historia de Colombia. Bogotá, 1909.

Choco on the edge of the Pacific Ocean. The province of Neiva, source of the Magdalena River, was also taken without difficulty. All these lands were rich in cattle, wheat, potatoes, tobacco, and in some gold and silver.

Thus the Spaniards had almost entirely relinquished New Granada. The Viceroy had fled to Cartagena, and the Monarchists could maintain their stand only in the border regions. One center of Iberian resistance lay on the Atlantic coast, a second in Cucutá, and a third in the southern part of the country toward Ecuador. That part of the Spanish army not occupied with the Atlantic coast or Cucutá had turned toward this third section and here they made contact with the Spanish garrisons of Quito and Lima. Even the clergy of the south had rallied to the King. The bishop of Popayán called Bolivar a traitor and excommunicated every man who fought for the cause of freedom. But the Republican army pushed constantly southward. The fertile and beautiful valley of the Cauca opened before them. They took Popayán, cradle of patriotic idealism and home of Camilo Torres and Caldas. But the highlands that connect Ecuador with Columbia remained in the hands of the Monarchists, and it was obvious that the struggle for these provinces would be long and hard. This fact affected the completeness of Bolivar's victory but little. Two months after the battle of Boyacá, nine provinces of the viceregal dominion were liberated.

Almost one million men were at Bolivar's disposal, as well as a vast territory divided by three Cordilleras. And now the political problem arose. Bolivar's plans were simple. At the head of every province he placed a military governor in whose hands lay everything that affected the safety of the cause. The governor's aid was a civil servant called the political governor in charge of internal affairs. Bolivar allowed the municipal constitution to remain as the Spaniards had written it. The towns had proved themselves to be the backbone of the independence movement during this entire period; accordingly, the Spanish tax system remained in force for the time being. We know that it was anything but adequate, but at a time when it was necessary to get a maximum of revenue into the state coffers, every change was bound to reduce the income. Bolivar saw to it that Patriots gradually replaced the Spanish officials, but he was unable to prevent embezzlement and waste of public funds.[7] "Everyone," he wrote, "is an enemy of public funds, some because they are rogues, and others because they are honest. . . . When once we are safe, they can all pay or they can all steal for aught I care. Storms are less dangerous in a port."[8]

Only the most indispensable courts were established. Bolivar left local jurisprudence to the mayors and judges, as had been provided by Spanish law. He created an appellate court, and continued the already existing upper court with its seat in Bogotá.[9] He did not neglect the question of education, "the safest basis for the freedom of men." The Republic undertook the instruction of orphans and the needy whose fathers had fallen in battle. This whole task, the work of a few weeks, attests to Bolivar's sense of realism. He planned to merge Venezuela and New Granada into the Greater Colombian Republic, but he wisely refrained from trying to equalize the administration of the two countries. He knew that each administration should conform to the peculiarities of its own peoples.

Bolivar was a highly talented organizer as far as large-scale planning was concerned, but he was not a man for ordinary trivia. Work at his desk, he confessed, was martyrdom for him. But even if he had been willing to sacrifice himself in this way, more important matters would have kept him from burying himself under the piles of papers on his desk. Bolivar needed a representative in Bogotá, so he instituted the office of Vice-President for New Granada, and appointed General Francisco de Paula Santander to the post. This turned out to be one of the most momentous decisions of his life. Santander's military record had been, as we have noted, both impressive and import-

7 O'Leary: Doc. Vol. XVI, pp. 434, 458. Restrepo: H. d. R. C. Vol. II. pp. 542, 549. Blanco: Doc. Vol. VII. p. 59.
8 Cartas: Vol. II. p. 121.
9 O'Leary: Doc. Vol. XVI. pp. 462-63.

ant, and in recognition of this Bolivar had made him division general.[10] But Santander was not a born soldier nor a trained officer. Revolutionary events had forced him into these roles. Actually, Santander was a jurist. Born in Villa del Rosario near Cucutá in 1792, he belonged to the Hidalgo caste. His native town on the border between Venezuela and New Granada became a fateful influence on his thinking and feeling. Santander was a man of the border, like Barrès and Poincaré in France, the kind of man who clearly reflects the good and evil qualities of his country.[11] He spent thirteen years in his father's house and was then sent to Bogotá to the famous school of San Bartolomé. Here he was under the tutelage of his uncle, Canon Nicolás Omaña. The strict discipline of priestly regulations became a further component of his life. He was a good student, industrious and conscientious, and so he remained throughout his life. He continued his training in Bogotá, studying law and winning a scholarship because of his ability in this subject. Bolivar once wrote to him, "You are the Man of Law," and this pronouncement indeed described Santander. In the dark chambers of San Bartolomé, with its cloistered atmosphere, Santander drenched his soul in that science which so often "finds reason turning to rubbish and virtue to vexation." He became the Man of Law.[12]

Then came the revolution and swept the twenty-year-old lad, who had just completed his studies, into the maelstrom of anarchy. His career as a soldier was not always felicitous. It would be ridiculous to deny Santander's personal courage, for he had no imperative to fling himself into the front line of the Republican fighting force and to fight on when everything seemed lost. It must be admitted that Santander lacked that physical prowess which alone could occasion respect among the wild fighters of the plains. To Páez' riders he

10 O'Leary: Doc. Vol. XVI. p. 456. Archive Santander: Vol. II. p. 251.
11 Archive Santander: Vol. II. p. 403. Pachero: *op. cit.* F. González: Santander. p. 47.
12 L. A. Cuervo: La Juventud de Santander. Bogotá, 1936. L. García Ortiz: Estudios Históricos. Bogotá, 1938. Arch. Santander: Vol. I. pp. 1-2.

seemed remote and intellectual. They refused to obey his
orders and he suffered many rebuffs and humiliations. These
he swallowed, but was thereby merely strengthened in his
resentment against the Venezuelans.[13]

Santander's potentialities were realized only after his path
had led him to Bolivar in 1817 and after he had by slow steps
regained that confidence which he had all but lost in 1813.
Bolivar saw wherein Santander's capacities lay and how they
could best be used. Santander had accomplished extraordinary
feats in the battles of Boyacá, but Anzoátegui and Soublette
were his superiors as officers. On the other hand, no one could
surpass him at a desk. He was an indefatigable worker; he saw
all the details of an undertaking; he wrote letters all day long,
reports, orders, laws. It was quite fitting that Bolivar should
call him to the vice-presidency.

There are those who claim that Bolivar thereby sharpened
the dagger that was later to cut him to the heart. These are
idle surmises and overlook the complications of historical events.
Bolivar's friendship with Santander was one of those tragic
relationships which always exist among great men. Their paths
seem to have united after the first divergence, but the vagaries
of man's fate do not have the constancy of those heavenly bodies
commonly said to guide his destiny. Santander was the center
of his own universe. It was not likely that he would be content
to become a lesser star in the American constellation; neither
his character nor his historic heritage fitted him for such a
role. The slow estrangement between the two men belongs
to another chapter. At this time Santander was Bolivar's logical
choice.

It is difficult to love the man, Santander, but one cannot
refuse to acknowledge his achievement. He was admittedly
cruel; by his orders prisoners of war whom he had personally
invited to his table were shot in cold blood. He even attended
the executions and relished them. When a certain Monarchist
leader was captured, he wrote, "They are bringing me the

13 Urdaneta: Memorias. p. 103.

famous Segovia from Neiva. I shall celebrate with him in the public square."[14] But although he constantly indulged himself in such cruelties, he always expected Bolivar to cover up for him. He feared responsibility, and he did his utmost to appear blameless. The spirit of a law meant nothing to him so long as the letter was carried out. He did not seek justice, perhaps not even right. Written orders and their execution were his only commandments.

He had many friends and he did not misuse them, but from his letters the reader gets a sense of cold calculation in his dealings with people. He gave no proof that he ever loved anyone more than himself and his power. He did love money. In contrast to Bolivar's extravagance, Santander displayed frugality and thrift. A prospect of drawing more pay delighted him out of all proportion, and in his will he mentioned even the smallest amounts owed to him, and directed that they be collected after his death.[15] A glance at his profile is all that is needed to show what he really was—noble features clouded by passion, furrowed brows, sullen eyes, compressed lips, a face that repels as its attracts. But one must not forget this attraction nor underestimate its power, because it was significant.

It was actually Santander who made Bolivar's future successes possible. Colombian historians call him the "organizer of victory." He called on the clergy, soldiers, merchants, and farmers to coöperate. When he assumed the vice-presidency, he said, "I swear that New Granada will never again be struck from the list of free peoples."[16] And he kept his oath. He laid the foundations for a legal government and paved the way for a democratic era in Colombia. He belonged among those spirits who led the revolution out of chaos and into legal control. This was no slight accomplishment in the midst of a world of lawlessness and dissolution.[17]

14 Cartas Santander: Vol. I. p. 78. See, García Ortiz: *op. cit.* p. 157.
15 Santander's will in B. d. H. Bogotá. Vol. IV. p. 161. García Ortiz: *op. cit.*
16 Arch. Santander: Vol. II. p. 292.
17 S. Camacho Soldán: Escritos varios. Bogotá, 1893. Vol. II. p. 522. Bolívar y Santander: Correspondencia; 1819-20. Bogotá, 1940.

During the first years Santander carried out Bolivar's orders faithfully. Occasionally he was obliged to slow matters down. He was naturally more cautious than Bolivar. The old and the fanatic received his consideration, and he sighed when Bolivar seemed to ask too much of him and his country. On the whole, however, he did what was asked of him, and Bolivar was satisfied. In the six years succeeding Santander's appointment, it was he to whom the Liberator addressed most of his letters, and these show a note of confidence and frankness that cannot be ignored. Bolivar was not, however, blind to Santander's weaknesses. He was aware of his greed for money; he knew Santander did not always act openly.[18] But Bolivar's criticisms remained benevolent. As long as he had a faithful co-worker in the man, he could afford to overlook the weak spots in his character. Bolivar erred, however, in gauging Santander's significant limitations; he thought he could sweep Santander along into the full stream of his own profound belief in continental freedom and solidarity. Here it was that Santander failed him. His horizons never reached beyond the skyline of New Granada. This defect in Santander was scarcely noticeable in 1819, and Bolivar trusted him implicitly. When he accorded him leadership in political affairs, he said to the New Granadians, "In Santander I leave you a second Bolivar."[19] This compliment was not addressed to Santander as statesman, but to Santander as the representative of the people whose favor Bolivar was trying to win. His first thought now was to unite New Granada and Venezuela. "The union of New Granada and Venezuela is the burning desire of all intelligent citizens and of all foreigners who love the cause of America and defend it."[20]

The Liberator addressed this appeal to the New Granadians before he rejoined the army. The people were unwilling to let him depart before they had expressed their gratitude, and on September 18 a celebration in honor of the victory at Boyacá

18 Cartas: Vol. II. pp. 138-170.
19 Cartas: Vol. II. p. 121. O'Leary: Doc. Vol. XVI. pp. 86-87.
20 Proclamas: p. 240.

took place. Bolivar rode through the city in a solemn procession followed by his army and all the officials. Triumphal arches of Roman design had been erected; banners and rugs hung from the windows; flowers were strewn along his path. The procession halted in front of the cathedral, and here Bolivar and his committee attended the *Te Deum*. Grandstands had been erected in the great square before the cathedral. Six statues representing the virtues of the Dictator were displayed; twenty white-clad maidens sang a hymn to his glory, and one of them whose father had been decapitated by the Spaniards, handed him a wreath of laurel.[21] From the sublime to the ridiculous is but one step, and Bolivar has been criticized for lending himself to these excesses of enthusiasm. It is indeed difficult to find satisfaction in South American hero worship. It seems superficial and hollow, and we must also admit that Bolivar himself was not lacking either in egotism or vanity. He enjoyed his victories and was elated when the people extolled him to the skies.

As always Bolivar knew how to exploit any demonstration to his genius. He took part in the celebrations, playing up to the national vanities because he wanted to win the people over to his ideals. Moreover, the celebration of September 18 was a farewell.

Among Bolivar's last official acts in Bogotá before he left for the army was the transcription of a letter to the escaped viceroy. Bolivar had long intended to wipe out the terrible memories of the war-to-extinction. With this in mind he offered Samanó an exchange of prisoners. He agreed to release Colonel Barreiro and his officers if the Spaniards would reciprocate with a like gesture. But Samanó did not deign to reply, and Barreiro was left to his tragic fate.[22]

Bolivar prepared to return to Venezuela. His presence was needed in Angostura because he could establish the Colombian Republic only through Congress. Various military problems

21 Groot: *op. cit.* Vol. IV. p. 276.
22 O'Leary: Memorias. Vol. I. p. 582. O'Leary: Doc. Vol. XVI. p. 455. Restrepo: H. d. R. C. Vol. II. p. 550

also demanded his attention. It was imperative both that New Granada be made secure and that Venezuela be liberated. After the battle of Boyacá, Bolivar had addressed his soldiers: "From the Orinoco to the sources of the Magdalena in the Andes, you have wrested fourteen provinces from the legions of tyrants. Soldiers, you will spread freedom from north to south on this continent."[23] He now set out to realize this risky promise.

The imminent threat to Colombia came from Cucutá in the northeast. Morillo had sent La Torre to the Colombian border, and after August 7 Bolivar opposed him with a small force and was successful in checking him. Meanwhile, Morillo remained inactive in Venezuela. The rainy season continued, and Morillo did not dare to set his army in motion. He did not underestimate the effect of Bolivar's victory, but for that very reason he wanted to avoid facing him for the time being. A new expeditionary corps soon to sail from Spain was promised to him. Its arrival would again make the Royal forces superior to those of Bolivar, and the hour of reckoning would be his. This prospect kept Morillo from taking any action against Bolivar. Again he played the Liberator's game, but he committed a two-fold error not only because his hopes on the expeditionary force failed him, but because he completely overestimated Bolivar's strength. The Republican army was still in a pitiable state. In the rugged mountain areas the cavalry, Bolivar's main weapon, was of little use, but the infantry was invaluable. The army needed guns and fresh tactical training to operate in this unfamiliar terrain.[24]

Bolivar needed time and more time, and it was this that Morillo's waiting policy granted him. Bolivar's march through the provinces was a march of triumph. "All along the way masses of enthusiastic people slowed my progress . . . flowers, eulogies, wreaths placed on my head by beautiful maidens, celebrations, and a thousand evidences of approval were the least of the gifts I received. The greatest and those dearest

23 Proclamas: p. 239.
24 Cartas Santander: Vol. I. p. 108.

to my heart were the tears mingled with joy which flowed over me, and the embraces of the multitude which often threatened to suffocate me."[25] Bolivar managed to achieve by acclaim what might otherwise have been gained by force alone. "From this province I think I shall get twenty thousand pesos." Such is the refrain that appears in all his letters.[26] Nothing escaped Bolivar's notice. A poverty-stricken convent was endowed with the income from the liquor tax; a priest who had adhered to the Spanish cause was removed from office and forced to pay the ten-thousand-pesos fine. All state revenues were first sent to headquarters. The governors were responsible to him, and were deposed if they did not measure up to his demands. They would sigh, but they would procure what the Liberator wanted. Thus, in all the villages and towns through which he went, the President left a trail of respect and admiration.[27]

La Torre made a new attempt to attack New Granada at the end of October, but Bolivar was convinced that he constituted no real threat in that place. An army under Urdaneta stationed at the border, called the Army of the North, undertook the defense of New Granada.

With the rest of his forces Bolivar turned off to Venezuela. After long weeks during which he was without any news from Guayana, he had received a stack of letters on November 13. "This most important correspondence induced me to go to Venezuela . . . to prevent civil war from spreading . . . La Torre's forces do not make it worthwhile for me to stay here and defeat them . . . but the intrigues of Mariño and Arismendi require my full attention."[28]

Once again Bolivar sailed down the Apure and the Orinoco. In order to hasten his journey he left his staff behind and proceeded almost alone to Angostura, arriving finally on December 11.[29]

25 Cartas: Vol. II. p. 111.
26 Cartas: Vol. II. p. 112.
27 O'Leary: Doc. Vol. XVI. pp. 507-08.
28 Cartas: Vol. II. p. 118.
29 O'Leary: Doc. Vol. XVI. p. 536.

The Third Republic which Bolivar had created in the plains of the Orinoco was a tottering structure. Its gleaming superstructure rested on supports made of tropical material, and, like bamboo stalks, they teetered in the breeze. Bolivar had given over the leadership in political affairs to Antonio Zea, an experienced and cultivated man who had proven his loyalty to liberty and to Bolivar. But Bolivar had overestimated Zea's political acumen. Zea was not the man to steer the ship of state through stormy weather. He was a good parliamentarian, but with all the weaknesses that characterize the type. Clever, vain, well able to express himself, in fact, a brilliant speaker who intoxicated himself with his own words, he nevertheless was lacking when deeds were necessary.[30] The men of the Angostura Parliament suffered from what might be called the complex of the front line fighter. They scorned anyone who had not killed at least one Spaniard, and Zea had never seen the face of the enemy.[31] Hardly had Bolivar left Angostura in February, 1819, when the wild elements began to turn on each other. Congress fell apart like iron filings from which the magnet has been withdrawn. As in earlier years, the quarrel began among the military leaders. Before his march to the west Bolivar had demanded that Arismendi support the expedition to the east coast with all available means, and had ordered him to strengthen Urdaneta's troops by five hundred men. Arismendi explained that the people of Margarita Island were not suited for this assignment and had refused to carry out the order.

Zea ordered a draft, and hostilities ensued which Arismendi was accused of having instigated. He was charged with having disregarded the authority of the state, was condemned and brought to prison in Angostura. This was a dubious step for Zea to take in regard to both time and circumstance, for Arismendi was considered a martyr and a hero of the revolution throughout the East.[32] In addition, Zea unwisely irritated

30 R. Botero: Zea. Bogotá, 1945.
31 Larrazabal: Vol. I. p. 599.
32 Larrazabal: Vol. I. p. 600. Restrepo: H. d. R. C. Vol. II. p. 557. O'Leary: Doc. Vol. XVI. pp. 441, 446. Lecuna: Guerra en 1819. pp. 102-14.

Mariño by relieving him of his command. We know Mariño's talent for intrigue. He came to Angostura, made Congress the scene of his complaints, and joined the numerous followers of Arismendi. The immediate object of Mariño's attacks was Zea. But the Vice-President was, after all, only Bolivar's representative. The Parliament members now began to speak quite openly against the Liberator. They accused him of desertion, of having left the country without the permission of Congress. Rumor supported the charges. The report spread that the Spaniards were about to attack Angostura. Bolivar, they said, had taken the army away and left Guayana defenseless. Panic seized the inhabitants of the city. There were other rumors that the Liberator had been defeated and he himself captured. Finally Mariño's and Arismendi's partisans said quite openly, "Let us get used, once and for all, to disregarding Bolivar. Then we shall be rid of his guardianship."[33]

The meetings of Congress became stormier with each day that passed. The ministers defended Bolivar, but Zea made no attempt to control the situation. The mob on the stands joined in the debates. Zea realized that his resignation was the only solution. On September 14 Arismendi was elected Vice-President and brought in triumph from prison to Congress. He assumed office and named Mariño Commander-in-Chief of the Army of the East.

The horizon of the rebels became clouded for the first time when the news of Bolivar's victory at Boyacá arrived. They had thought the Liberator was still far away, detained by problems of the New Granadian campaigns. Suddenly on December 11 he appeared in Angostura. None of his enemies was prepared for the President's return. Mariño was with the army, and Arismendi was on a tour of inspection.[34]

Bolivar came as a friend. If he felt any bitterness or disappointment, he gave no indication of it. He saw Zea and assured him of his confidence. He also received Arismendi's friends

33 Larrazabal: Vol. I. p. 601. Baralt: Vol. I. pp. 473 ff.
34 Lecuna: La Guerra en 1819. Vol. XXIII. No. 19. B. d. H. Caracas. p. 335. Blanco: Doc. Vol. VII. p. 139.

quite as though nothing unusual had occurred. Bolivar needed
the Congress and based his plans on his knowledge of his
compatriots' psychology. If he spared them the humiliation
of this, their latest betrayal, they would be more amenable to
his wishes. So he acted as if he were blind to all that had happened behind his back. His analysis of the situation proved
correct.[35]

Three days later, on December 14, Bolivar appeared in Parliament. The President gave him his chair, and Bolivar, greeting the delegates with a deep bow, began his address. This
speech consists of a crowded report on the campaign of 1819.
In it he gives all the credit of the Republican successes to the
army and the people of New Granada, and he added that New
Granada's only desire was to unite its provinces with Venezuela. "The union of New Granada and Venezuela is the goal
that I set for myself even in my earliest fighting days. It is
the desire of all the citizens of both countries, and would give
the assurance of South American freedom. Legislators, the
time has come to guarantee our Republic a sound and firm
basis. It is the duty of your wisdom to make this decision and
to lay down the principles of the treaty upon which this great
Republic will be founded. Announce this to the world, and
my services will be amply rewarded."[36]

When Bolivar had finished, Zea arose. He praised the deeds
of the President. Genius, he asserted, would receive the reward
for which it had asked. The new Republic was to include not
only New Granada and Venezuela but Ecuador also. Other
speakers followed. Those who had but yesterday cried, "Cru-
cify," were the first to shout, "Hosannah."[37] Bolivar answered
every speaker. When, finally, a committee for the study of
the foundations of the future Republic was named, Bolivar
rose, again made a profound obeisance to Congress, and retired.

Arismendi had meanwhile returned to Angostura. He saw

35 Larrazabal: Vol. I. p. 607. O'Leary: Doc. Vol. XVI. pp. 563-69.
36 Proclamas: pp. 244-45.
37 Congreso de Angostura. Libro de Actas. pp. 240 ff. Arch. Santander. Vol.
III. p. 373.

that his game was lost and resigned his position as Vice-President. Bolivar maintained his composure and spoke to Arismendi in his customary manner. Three days later the statute that was to announce to the world the creation of a new Republic, *la república de Colombia,* was completed.

The new state consisted of three departments which today correspond to the republics of Ecuador, Colombia, and Venezuela. Each department had its own capital: Quito, Bogotá, and Caracas respectively. A federal capital, called Bolivar, was to be founded, and Congress was to select its site. The executive branch lay in the hands of the president of the Republic, and in his absence, was to be assigned to the vice-president. Both were to be elected by the existing Congress. Besides the president and the vice-president of the central government, there was a separate governor and administration for each province. The governors were also given the title of vice-president.[38]

On January 1, 1821, a new congress was to convene in Cucutá. This body, the first Congress of Colombia, was to decide on the final form of the constitution. On the morning of December 17, Parliament accepted the new covenant. An extraordinary session, which Bolivar attended, met in the afternoon. He read the document in a solemn voice, kissed the parchment, and then signed it. All the delegates followed suit. Then Zea arose and announced, "The Republic of Colombia has been founded!"[39] Immediately thereafter they proceeded with the election of a president. None other than Bolivar could head the new state, and Parliament unanimously voted him the presidency. His representative had to be a Granadian, and the choice fell upon Zea. That Bolivar could put Zea's name through for a second time proved the completeness of his triumph.

Thus the Liberator ended a year of successes with one last triumph, which was perhaps the most important of his career. A future national greatness which could be materialized only

38 O'Leary: Doc. Vol. XVII. pp. 5, 7, 8.
39 Larrazabal: Vol. I. p. 614.

in the nascent Colombian Republic swept before his eyes. "In ten years of conflict and unbelievable effort," he wrote to Santander, "in ten years of suffering which almost surpassed human endurance, we have learned to know the indifference with which all Europe and even our brothers to the north have watched our extermination. One of the reasons for this indifference was the multiplicity of sovereignty. The lack of unity and consolidation, the lack of understanding and harmony, above all the lack of material, is the true cause for the failing interest which our neighbors and the Europeans have shown in our fate." The new Republic had resources and would give foreigners confidence, he added. It would find allies and with them establish freedom for all time. Colombia would have an importance which Venezuela and New Granada could never have achieved singly.[40]

The publication of the statutes was received with great enthusiasm in the towns and communities. Bolivar set out for Bogotá, where he would again put through the new idea of state, but his advent was anticipated. Santander called a meeting of dignitaries which voted unanimously for the law. Bolivar's gratitude knew no bounds.[41]

The new Republic was the fruit of Bolivar's own mind. Many years before, Miranda had coined the name of Colombia, but the embodiment of the idea was Bolivar's personal achievement. "The ambition of my life was the creation of a free and independent Republic of Colombia. . . . I have achieved it. Bless the God of Colombia."[42]

It is not surprising to find that Bolivar's attitude became more free and unrestrained after such successes. The tone of his letters changed. He remained a master in the art of the individual appeal. To Páez he wrote simply and objectively; to Santander, logically and precisely. But his tone of command became more intense, and his word became the epitome of law

40 Cartas: Vol. II. pp. 125 ff.
41 Arch. Santander: Vol. IV. p. 118. Restrepo: H. d. R. C. Vol. III. pp. 18 ff.
42 Proclamas: pp. 248-49.

to them. His sentences rose to a staccato pitch, and his irony emerged with greater facility. He defined an ecclesiastical address as "a flood of words over a desert of thought." Nor was Bolivar any longer the fanatical fighter of 1813-14. He arranged to have prisoners treated in a humane fashion. The same Spaniards before whom a whole continent trembled but yesterday now seemed to him too insignificant to fight. Was he the man to attack an enemy that lay ruined and bleeding to death?[43] Bolivar was never more quixotic than when he wrote these words, but it was not gallantry alone that prompted him. As a statesman he felt the deep wisdom of Virgil's *"parcere subjectis."* He wanted to spare the defeated because he needed them, because the new fatherland needed them. It was also imperative that the defeated native Monarchists be reconciled. If all parties acknowledged the new law, equal justice should be meted out to them. "Utmost harshness is needed for all evil doers, be they Monarchists or Patriots, for the Republic gains as much from the destruction of a good Royalist as from the death of a bad citizen. Crime is equally hateful in all parties and to be condemned. Let justice triumph and freedom will win."[44]

This was the credo of the new Republic, but only a few understood it. The majority of the Patriots could not see the State for the parties. Each envisioned his own group as the State, and Bolivar was obliged to fight this egoism. He had to breathe reason, will, and conscience into the fatherland he had conjured up. The basic statute was intended to bind the provinces together, but the bonds were of paper and would give under strain. So in the midst of military plans, diplomatic efforts, and administrative work of all kinds, Bolivar began to organize the country. "We have done much, but more remains to be done." How difficult the generation of a spirit of state unity could prove to be, only he knew. Had not his own comrades attacked him from the rear? But Bolivar refused to be

43 Cartas: Vol. II. p. 157. See also, Rourke: *op. cit.* p. 230.
44 Cartas: Vol. II. p. 140.

confused by what he considered minor issues, and he remained
loyal to the policies of conciliation. He sent Arismendi to the
army, where his energies would find their natural outlet. Mariño was to go to the west, where his prestige was slighter and
would not constitute a threat to Bolivar. Only a sigh betrayed
the Liberator's thoughts. "I still do not know what to do with
this man (Mariño)." [45]

He wrote these words of uncertainty to Santander, whom he
trusted most at that time, but Santander, too, furnished him
with many perplexities. Bolivar had no more than left Bogotá
in the fall of 1819, when Santander ordered the execution of
thirty-eight Spanish officers and their leader, Barreiro. They
were brought to the public square in chains and there shot in
the back. Santander watched the executions from the door of
the government palace, but his pleasure in the gory spectacle
was impaired by Barreiro's manly and dignified conduct. Santander asserted that the officers had constituted a fifth column
within the Republic, but he failed to produce any proofs of
his assertion, and the only reason that can be assigned for his
deed is a desire for revenge. There is little doubt that the thirty-
nine officers died in memory of the unavenged blood of Torres,
Caldas, and the many innocent men whom the Spaniards
had murdered. Santander later added to the ignominy of his
act by asking Bolivar to condone the affair. This Bolivar could
not do, but he was obliged reluctantly to accept the accomplished fact. He considered Santander's action a grave error
fraught with possible danger to the international prestige of
Colombia. As a matter of fact, the cold-blooded executions
were judged very harshly abroad. [46]

Even before the new political edifice was completed, it
showed cracks. Rivalries arose between Venezuelans and Granadians. For the time being they were trifles, but they pointed
to danger zones in the coming developments. Bolivar was

45 Cartas: Vol. II. p. 128. O'Leary: Doc. Vol. XVII. p. 13.
46 Cartas Santander: Vol. I. pp. 82, 84-85. O'Leary: Memorias. Vol. I. p. 585.
O'Leary: Doc. Vol. XVI. p. 515.

PLATE I

SIMON BOLIVAR

PLATE II

THE FORTRESS OF SAN FELIPE, IN CARTAGENA

desperate. "The misunderstandings which arise out of the union which I tried to establish make me suffer the tortures of the damned. The only reason which prompted me to propose the creation of Greater Colombia was the thought of forever dissipating the causes of hatred, disunity, and disintegration. What a disappointment if these are now multiplying instead."[47]

For the first time there appears a suggestion of melancholy and pessimism in his mind. Just as a beautiful woman, at the height of her loveliness feels the dread of approaching age, so this year of triumph, in Bolivar's eyes, presaged the dangers of collapse. A tragic sense of failure began to overshadow his imagination. "I am determined," he wrote in November, 1819, "to bid farewell to Venezuela next summer and to go to Chile, Buenos Aires, or Lima, to die . . . for wherever I go there is disunity and disorder. Soon it will be death. What devilish people we have here."[48] And again . . . "If we triumph, I have decided to follow Sulla's example, and Colombians will doubtless thank me for their freedom, as the Romans once thanked Sulla. If we are beaten there will be no country and no courts. And if I die I shall be paying with my life."[49] And yet again, "I convince myself more and more that neither liberty, nor laws, nor the best instruction, can make us into decent people . . . even less into Republicans or real patriots. My friend, in our veins flows no blood, but evil mingled with terror and fear."[50]

This America, his America, was it not the cask of the Danaids into which he poured his best efforts only to find them drained away before culmination? It is easy to understand the moving confession found in his letters of that year: "Since I first went from here (Cucutá) to Caracas, I was firmly decided to give up my powers on the day when my country should be free. . . . This decision has been ever more urgent during the course of time and events, and grows in geometric proportions

47 Cartas: Vol. II. p. 192.
48 Cartas: Vol. II. p. 119.
49 Cartas: Vol. II. p. 144.
50 Cartas: Vol. II. p. 186.

with each day. I have many times told some of my friends
that I was at sea and sought a haven of refuge to which I could
go. Peace will be my refuge, my fame, my compensation, my
hope, my fortune . . . in short everything that is worth while
in this world. I have already proclaimed it to Venezuela that
the first day of freedom would be the last day of my rule.
Nothing can change this decision. If there is no other way left
to me but flight, then flight shall be my salvation."[51] There can
be no doubt as to the sincerity of this outburst, for these words
were not written in a public document or as part of a parliamentary speech, but in a private letter. Yes, Bolivar wanted
to renounce his power. He wanted sincerely to serve freedom.
He wanted, when he had done his duty, perhaps to become free
himself, in order to live, to find a port, far from all storms,
where he could conjure up that idyllic time in which he began
his life. This was the goal for which he strove, but could he
have believed seriously that he was still master of his own life?
No matter how profoundly he desired tranquillity, he was to
learn that fate is inexorable. The day of peace had not yet
come. The Spaniards still occupied large parts of Venezuela,
and the royal banner still waved over Caracas, Quito, and Lima.

51 Cartas: Vol. II. p. 192.

CHAPTER 22

Armistice

$\mathcal{M}$aturity implies more than man's knowledge of his own capacities and how to use them. It unites gifts of character and mind. What was a multiplicity of aptitudes in youth becomes unity of effort in man. In Bolivar the qualities of statesman and general are now felicitously merged. The president is more the conqueror; the general more the diplomat.

Intent on reaching a goal whose remoteness and loftiness were known only to him, he tried more than ever to win the coöperation of that generation which had initiated the movement to liberate South America. Quito, Lima, Cusco, Potosí, would remain beyond reach if he could not find a staff of helpers and coöperators to carry out his orders. Bolivar could draw up plans; he could influence and guide, but he could not do all the work alone. He was now obliged to seek among the enemies of yesterday and the friends of tomorrow someone who could assist him.

Between the Atlantic and Pacific oceans a great republic had come into being. It must be presented to the powers of the Old World and to the United States in a worthy manner. It was no longer enough to publicize it in weekly issues of the *Orinoco Post*. Diplomatic representation was imperative. But whom could Bolivar send to the United States and to Europe? Who knew the customs and languages of the Old World? Bolivar considered Zea. He knew that Zea was too weak to represent him effectively in the home government, so he wel-

comed the opportunity of sending him out into the world as
the first ambassador of the Republic of Colombia.[1] Zea's assignment was carefully defined. He was to establish credit for
Colombia in London, the stock exchange of the world, and to
build faith in Colombia's solvency. Besides this, he was to prepare for the international recognition of the Republic in the
United States, England, and France.[2]

Zea's mission was not an unqualified success. He had been
amply supplied with money, but he squandered it thoughtlessly.
He regarded the state finances as his private purse in which he
could permit his friends and companions to share, and he paid
scant attention to Bolivar's orders for weapons and materiel.
He gathered all Colombia's creditors together in London and
began to transact affairs in a very highhanded manner. He
assured the group that he considered it beneath an ambassador's
dignity to check bills and payments. Such a procedure, he said,
would be unworthy of his country and Bolivar's prestige. He
acknowledged all demands with a grandiose gesture. "My
country will pay everything it owes regardless of the origin of
the debt." Quite naturally he was taken advantage of and made
to acknowledge many fictitious debts.[3]

Bolivar, who counted every peso to keep the war going, was
desperate over Zea's delusions of grandeur. Nor was Zea entirely happy in the field of diplomacy. He was by no means
unshakable in his Republican convictions. Weak, and inclined
to compromise, he suggested all kinds of expedients and subterfuges. He proposed that the Spanish King should recognize
the independence of the South American states. In return the
states should unite in a federation headed by Ferdinand VII.
The project was, of course, impossible on every count. A violent "Never" from the Liberator shattered this dream.[4]

Zea's failure in the diplomatic field is a clear example of the

1 Cartas: Vol. II. p. 127.
2 Cartas: Vol. II. p. 129. Blanco: Doc. Vol. VIII. p. 345. Larrazabal: Vol.
II. p. 45.
3 Larrazabal: Vol. II. p. 45.
4 Cartas: Vol. II. p. 387. O'Leary: Doc. Vol. XVIII. p. 481. Larrazabal: Vol.
II. p. 47.

difficulties which confronted Bolivar in the task of political organization. Not all the men whom Bolivar sought were failures, however. Santander continued to hold his own, and with the appointment of Sucre, Bolivar made a fortunate choice. The young general was just twenty-five years old at this time. Two years earlier Bolivar had entrusted him with a delicate mission which he had carried out successfully. When, in December, 1819, Bolivar had sailed down the Orinoco to Angostura, he had met a small boat. "Who goes there?" he asked. "General Sucre," was the reply. "There is no General Sucre!" he rejoined indignantly, for he knew nothing of the appointment made by Zea in his absence. Sucre assured Bolivar that he had never dreamed of assuming the title without the Liberator's consent, and Bolivar, mollified by his words, confirmed his rank. From this time on they had been the best of friends. Now he entrusted Sucre with the important business of buying weapons.[5]

Since the victory of Boyacá, the state had had cash and was no longer restricted to the complicated barter system. Nevertheless, it was forbidden by international law to sell arms to rebels, and therefore this commission demanded a reticent, tactful man of absolute dependability and personal integrity. Sucre proved himself. He succeeded in buying from four to six thousand guns in the Antilles and in bringing them to Angostura. From there he took them up the Orinoco, the Apure, and the Meta as far as New Granada.[6]

Another instance of Bolivar's ability to win men is to be found in the case of Mariano Montilla. In 1815 Montilla had belonged to that group which had refused to let the Liberator enter Cartagena. Bolivar and Montilla met for the second time in exile in Haiti. Now, in 1819, they met in Angostura, where Montilla had gone in company with Urdaneta. Montilla feared that Bolivar would hold the old grudge against him, and was

5 Cartas: Vol. II. p. 132. O'Leary: Doc. Vol. XVII. p. 31. O'Leary: Memorias. Vol. II. p. 67.
6 Cartas: Vol. II. pp. 139, 174-5, 181, 182, 211, 232.

shy and embarrassed. But Bolivar appeared urbane and quite
forgetful of the past. He embraced Montilla and invited him
to his house. In tears they promised each other to let bygones
be bygones. Bolivar asked Montilla to join his staff. His persuasiveness was irresistible and he won in Montilla a friend for
life and a dependable co-worker until the time of his death.
Montilla was sent at once to Margarita Island to receive a
transport of Irish troops.[7]

Bolivar was in Angostura during only two weeks of December, 1819, and at Christmas time he was ready to set out again.
He who in misfortune had been impetuous and violent, became
more considerate and restrained with each new success. His
plans for 1820 depended on many and complicated factors. First,
he was obliged to consider Morillo. The Spaniard was still on
the alert and watched Bolivar like a hawk. But Bolivar also
watched his enemy intently. Who would make the first move?[8]

Bolivar was faced now with the immediate military and
strategic problem. Should the Republic attack in Venezuela, in
New Granada, or in Ecuador? He was also obliged to decide
whether he could depend with more certainty on the infantry or the cavalry. His letters reveal a great deal of uncertainty
on all these matters. He thought of liberating Venezuela, but
this idea seemed too hazardous.[9] He also considered an attack
on the Atlantic coast of New Granada. In addition, he had to
bear in mind the march to the south and the liberation of Quito.
Finally caution won out. "The enemy," he wrote to Santander,
"must be divided, for divided we can destroy him without
risking the fate of Colombia in a general and perhaps fatal
battle. Discipline is the soul of these enemy troops just as courage is ours, but it is clear that the former is more useful in battle
than mere courage. It is possible that this delay is wise; it could
also be disastrous, for the fortunes of war are unpredictable. I

7 Larrazabal: Vol. I. p. 613. See, Bolivar's letters to Montilla, in Cartas: Vols.
I to IX. D. d. B. p. 342.
    8 Restrepo: H. d. R. C. Vol. III. p. 12. L. Duarte Level: Cuadros de la Historia
militar y civil de Venezuela. Madrid, 1918. p. 352.
    9 Cartas: Vol. II. p. 123.

now hold the fate of eighteen liberated provinces in my hands and dare not risk a game of chance."[10]

Repeatedly he felt the urge to do something definite, but a feeling of responsibility restrained him. "In the end I decided to remain on the defensive in Venezuela and to take the offensive in New Granada."[11] These words give us the plan of campaign for 1820. Bolivar wanted to refrain from any grand scale action, but since action was necessary, even if it was only for the purpose of concealing weakness from the enemy, Bolivar decided on a restricted strategy in the New Granadian territory. The center of Colombia was secure; the problem was merely the liberation of the Atlantic coast. The conquest of the provinces of Cartagena, Santa Marta, and Maracaibo constituted, therefore, the modest program for 1820.

Montilla was to take the Irish from Margarita Island to the north coast of Colombia and attempt an invasion by sea. Bolivar himself wanted to go from Cucutá into the valley of the Magdalena, thus liberating the river to its mouth.[12]

Bolivar had decided on this limited program because he hoped in the course of the year to increase his army by ten thousand men and, above all, because his intuition told him not to risk anything at this time. The presiding genius that guides and influences great men in their decisions restrained his arm and compelled him to wait. Bolivar's intuition did not betray him. Victory lay ahead. The Spanish government had observed with anxiety the rekindling of rebellion in its colonial domain. Argentina and Venezuela were, in its opinion, the focal points of the Revolution. Spain had already decided as early as 1818 to send a new expeditionary force, but did not feel strong enough to carry out this policy alone. The King appealed to the conservative elements of the Holy Alliance. Prussia and Austria remained indifferent, but the Czar put a whole fleet at his disposal. However, when the ships of Alexander I arrived in Cádiz in February, 1818, they proved to be in

10 Cartas: Vol. II. pp. 131-32 of January 11, 1820.
11 Cartas: Vol. II. p. 146. O'Leary: Doc. Vol. XVII. p. 52.
12 Cartas: Vol. II. p. 136. O'Leary: Doc. Vol. XVI. p. 527.

the nature of floating Potemkin villages. They were not sea-
worthy and were returned to their sender.[13]

Meanwhile, the troops that were already assembled and
quartered in Cádiz waited for a whole year to embark. An
unoccupied army concentrated in one place is always a danger
to the peace of a state. The army felt maltreated; the officers
complained of the low and irregular pay; the soldiers complained of the food and quarters. In the officers' corps secret
organizations on the order of the Italian Carbonari were
founded. The men heard of the terrors of the South American
Revolution—that no one had returned from the previous expeditionary force; that yellow fever, the war, and the tropics had
swallowed them.

On January 1, 1820, with the cry, "Constitution and Freedom!" the Spanish army rebelled. Led by Colonels Riego and
Quiroga, they demanded the reëstablishment of the Constitution of 1812. The movement spread rapidly over the entire
country and infected the rest of the Spanish army. The King
relented and declared his readiness to reconstitute the state and
confirm it. On May 9 he took an oath on the Constitution.
Quiroga and Riego were promoted to field marshals, the liberal
politicos were recalled from prison or exile, and the Cortez
resumed its sittings. The most important factor for South
American independence in all these events was the disbanding
of the expeditionary forces.

The demobilization of the invasion army was an occurrence
of unprecedented importance for the victory of freedom in the
Western Hemisphere. On March 20 the first reports of events
in Spain reached the American continent. The official papers
in Caracas tried to minimize the situation and spoke of the
rebellion as without significance. Later, definite orders came
from Madrid. Morillo was instructed to publish the Constitution and to reëstablish peace by fraternal conciliation.[14]

13 F. Luckwaldt: Das Zeitalter der Restauration. Propyaenweltgeschichte. Vol.
VII. pp. 449 ff. W. S. Robertson: Russia and the South American Independence.
Hisp. Am. Rev. May, 1941.
14 Larrazabal: Vol. II. p. 31. Restrepo: H. d. R. C. Vol. III. pp. 45 ff.

Everything within the Spanish General's nature revolted against such a step—his pride, his military acumen, his political convictions. Nevertheless, he was obliged to resign himself to the circumstances, and the new statutes were solemnly proclaimed in Caracas. By the publication of the Constitution, Morillo became powerless. He had received orders from the King and now considered himself legally barred from command. However deeply this measure pierced his self love, he had yet a graver calamity to face. The royal ministry urged an end to the war that was ruining Spain. Morillo received the assignment to form a commission which was to treat with the heads of the Revolution. When he read these instructions, he gave vent to his indignation. "They have gone crazy in Madrid," he cried. "They ask me to demean myself by dealing with the very men against whom I fought. Everything is lost. I shall obey, but from now on, one need not count on the subjugation of these provinces."[15] Morillo was right. For Spain, it was the beginning of the end; for South America the end of the beginning.

Before all the ramifications of the events overseas had reached the shores of America, Bolivar had again set out. From Angostura he hurried to the Apure, where he consulted with Páez. From there he went to the Army of the North, which still lay in the region of Cucutá. A few weeks later he went to Bogotá where he arrived on March 4. Just one of his countless journeys would furnish enough material for the entire life of any man of the twentieth century, remarks Rourke.[16]

The President of Colombia came in triumph to Bogotá, but he was still as poor as any of his soldiers. His uniform was shabby and worn, and he was even without a change of underclothes. Friends provided these necessities the day after his arrival. In spite of his personal poverty, however, he took care of the widows and orphans and signed his pay over to them

15 Larrazabal: Vol. II. p. 32. Restrepo: H. d. R. C. Vol. III. p. 48. Díaz: *op. cit.* p. 239.
16 Rourke: *op. cit.* p. 234.

when no state funds were available.[17] The purpose of his trip
to Bogotá was to present himself as President to the Colombians.

The union with Santander turned out just as Bolivar had
wished. The Vice-President promised him every support that
New Granada was able to give. "Between you and me," said
Bolivar, "there is a fair exchange. You send me goods, and I
send you hope."

From Bogotá he returned to the Army of the North. The
plan to invade the coast was ready for execution. Montilla
and Brion pushed up from the sea to Río Hacha and Santa
Marta. A second fighting force was to move down from the
Magdalena River and wipe out the rest of the Royalists. At the
same time a division was ordered south to prepare the campaign
against Ecuador. By the end of March the three operations
whose common aim was the complete liberation of the Colombian center were well under way.[18] It was at this time that
the first reports of the Spanish revolution arrived in Bolivar's
headquarters. "What a mad stroke of fate," he cried. "The news
from Spain could not be better. It has decided our fate, for it
is now certain that no more troops will come to America. And
thus the fight turns in our favor."[19]

Bolivar decided to make the peace an easy one for Spain.
The Spanish had everything to lose in America and nothing
more to gain. In the North American Senate, Henry Clay had
proposed recognition of Colombia. England stepped more and
more out of its reserve and paved the way for diplomatic relations with Bolivar's government. The world seemed to decide
in favor of American freedom and against the Iberian monarchy. Bolivar thought the moment had come for an understanding with Spain.[20]

Two different activities filled the months of May to November, 1820. At the front the war ebbed and flowed; behind the

17 Groot: Vol. IV. p. 87.
18 O'Leary: Doc. Vol. XVII. p. 69.
19 Cartas: Vol. II. pp. 156-57.
20 Cartas: Vol. II. pp. 161, 194-95. Cartas Santander: Vol. I. p. 112. Restrepo:
H. d. R. C. Vol. III. pp. 86-87.

scenes the first negotiations began between the mother country and the rebellious daughter colonies.

Bolivar considered the diplomatic decisions more important at this time than the military ones, but it was natural that he did not neglect the war on this account. The conflict continued to zigzag and showed how well-founded Bolivar's distrust of the Republican army had been. In the south the Patriots were overrun by the Monarchists and were thrown back. The Spanish Colonel Calzada pushed deep into the already liberated provinces. Bogotá was his objective, though he never reached it. He did, however, succeed in surprising the Patriots at Popayán, and pushed on through the valley of the Cauca to the north. The Republicans then counterattacked and threw him back to Popayán.[21]

The spread of Republican influence was also slowed at the Atlantic coast. The erstwhile Viceroy, Samanó, who had found refuge in Panama, overcame his fears and attempted a reconquest of the lost land. He sent a crack force into the provinces of Antioquía and Choco. Although none of these undertakings had any decisive results, they blocked the Patriots and stiffened the situation. Bolivar now also felt the obligations which grew out of his liberation of New Granada. His greatest need was for commanding officers. "With four men we keep one hundred thousand square miles occupied, but we have as yet no factory that can turn out generals."[22]

Bolivar had intended to help the invasion of the coast from the interior, but the kindling of Monarchist resistance blocked his plans. The invasion troops had to make their way alone into the heart of the country. Here, too, the dreams of the Liberator were not entirely fulfilled. Montilla had appeared at the door of Río Hacha on March 12 with the Irish, and when the Spaniards refused to heed his orders to surrender, had landed. He wanted to liberate Santa Marta and Maracaibo. But the Irish mutinied, demanded better food and clothing,

21 Restrepo: H. d. R. C. Vol. III. pp. 17 ff.
22 Cartas: Vol. II. p. 229.

and asked to be brought to a British colony because they were tired of serving a state that did not fulfill its obligations.[23] Montilla's attempts to quell the rebellious mercenaries were unsuccessful, and finally he decided to do without them rather than have their rebellion infect the Americans. He gave orders to evacuate Río Hacha, but affairs did not move fast enough for the Irish. They got drunk and set fire to the city, took the ships in port by storm, and set sail for Jamaica. Bolivar's plan was frustrated for the time being. Nevertheless, he congratulated Montilla on his conduct and wrote him, "Nothing that you tell me about the Irish legion surprises me. One may expect anything of henchmen who will not kill without pay. They are like courtesans who do not give themselves before they get their money."[24]

Bolivar received the news of the failure of his plans with equanimity. If he could not play a military card, he still had a diplomatic trump up his sleeve. Morillo had, in obedience to the royal command, formed a council of pacification, a *junta de pacificación,* with its seat in Caracas. The council sent a circular to the leaders of the rebels—Páez, Bermúdez, Montilla, and many others—in which Morillo made known his desire to come to an agreement with them. He proposed an armistice for a month, during which the final treaty was to be concluded.[25]

If Morillo had hoped to create dissension in the camp of the Patriots, if he had counted on having one accept and the other reject his proposals, he was to be disappointed. Bolivar's political order survived its first test. Páez' answer was characteristic. He referred the Spaniard to the President of the Republic to whom he was subordinate.[26] Even an attempt by Morillo to deal with the Congress of Angostura made no headway. Morillo admitted that the key to any understanding lay with Bolivar. All further steps depended on the attitude of the President of the Republic.

23 O'Leary: Doc. Vol. XVII. pp. 82, 126, 128. Arch. Santander: Vol. IV. p. 211.
24 Cartas: Vol. II. p. 229. Larrazabal: Vol. II. pp. 26-27.
25 O'Leary: Doc. Vol. XVII. p. 303. Arch. Santander: Vol. V. p. 83.
26 O'Leary: Doc. Vol. XVII. p. 304. Páez: Autobiografía. p. 244. E. Restrepo Tirado: Preliminares del armisticio de 1820. B. d. H. Bogotá. Vol. XVI. p. 166.

Bolivar knew that any agreement initiated by the Crown would be, by its very origin, a definite advantage to the Republic.[27] His real goal had always been peace, but if this were unattainable, then he would accept an armistice which would include the recognition of the newly created state. Therefore, when Morillo's letter reached Bolivar, he answered La Torre, through whom it was sent: "With the utmost satisfaction, I accept, for the army stationed here, an armistice which you propose in the name of the commanding general for the duration of a month. . . . I regret that the delegates of the Spanish government made so many detours before they found their way to my headquarters." If, he continued, the Spanish delegates had come to arrange for peace and friendship with the Colombian government and were ready to acknowledge this state as an independent republic, then they would be warmly received. But if they had any other purpose in mind, he would refuse to see them.[28] Bolivar had already begun to feel the climactic effects of his actions. Mass desertions began in the Spanish army. Belief in Bolivar's victory was becoming stronger among the people of South America with each day.

Relying on these fortunate circumstances, Bolivar wrote to Morillo. He sent him the fundamental law of the Republic. This statute was the only basis, he informed the Spaniard, on which he could negotiate. Morillo's representatives had no power to accept the statute, but they were willing to deal with Bolivar as the President of a sovereign state. This concession gratified Bolivar so much that, contrary to his wont, he wrote to Santander in his own hand describing the event.[29] The negotiations that followed were, however, very long drawn out. The recognition of Colombian independence was too much for Morillo to accept without considerable deliberation. Bolivar continued to exhort the men in the Spanish camps, sometimes with conciliatory words, sometimes with threats. Meanwhile,

27 Cartas: Vol. II. p. 214. O'Leary: Doc. Vol. XVII. p. 232.
28 Cartas: Vol. II. pp. 213, 222, 232. O'Leary: Doc. Vol. XVII. pp. 260-61. Rodríguez Villa: Vol. IV. pp. 230-32. Restrepo: H. d. R. C. Vol. III. p. 50.
29 Cartas: Vol. II. p. 236. Rodríguez Villa: Vol. IV. p. 207.

he did not veer from his original determination: the armistice
should be concluded, not between the armies, but between two
sovereign states. July and August passed in anticipation.

Bolivar realized that a treaty of peace with Spain would be
very unlikely to accord the Republic an extension of territory,
and he wisely utilized this period of waiting in an effort to
expand his territorial boundaries. In September he took a trip
to the coast.[30] His ambition was to conquer Cartagena, Santa
Marta, and Maracaibo. He tried to win the Spanish officers by
offering them promotions in the Republican army, and even
went to the length of offering them money. This attempt at
bribery is surprising, and is incompatible with Bolivar's character. The Spaniards spurned his offers, however, and by the
middle of September he was again at his headquarters near
Cucutá.

Meanwhile, negotiations for the armistice made little progress. They seemed to move at the tempo of a peasant dance—
one step forward and two steps back. At first the two view-
points were so divergent that it seemed hopeless to try to reconcile them. Morillo's representatives had no power to recognize
Colombia's independence, even a de facto independence. Bolivar demanded that the Spanish evacuate the most important
ports, but reiterated his readiness to reach an agreement. "Meanwhile," so runs his letter, "we go on with the war."[31] Bolivar
wanted to show Morillo that Colombia had less interest in
peace than did Spain. With this in mind, he decided to make
a surprise attack on the border provinces of Trujillo and Mérida.
He took command of this expedition himself. This march over
barren country was an arduous one. A few troop divisions were
forced to detour; others were delayed while waiting for supplies. The journey was made in short stages and the element
of surprise was almost entirely lacking, but Bolivar's plans were

30 Cartas: Vol. II. p. 246. O'Leary: Doc. Vol. XVII. p. 404. Arch. Santander:
Vol. V. p. 121. Lecuna: Guerra en 1820. Vol. XXIV. No. 95. B. d. H. Caracas.
p. 306.
31 Cartas: Vol. II. pp. 258-9. O'Leary: Doc. Vol. XVII. p. 406.

carried out; he took Mérida on October 2 and Trujillo on October 7.[32]

The impression made on Morillo by these successes was heightened by the simultaneous triumph of the Republican forces on the Atlantic coast. The Magdalena River was freed, and Santa Marta was taken by Montilla. In Venezuela desertions from the royal banner became more numerous.[33] Influential local leaders put themselves at the service of the Liberator, and every breeze seemed to drive Bolivar nearer to his goal, a goal which he saw within his reach at the beginning of November. He sent Morillo a second carefully considered proposal for a six months' armistice.[34] Morillo answered with a counterproposal, but for the first time he appointed a deputation to deliver his reply to Bolivar. Thus negotiations approached a more formal and significant phase.

Morillo now moved closer to Bolivar, and near Trujillo he took his stand opposite the Patriots. With him came an army that at least equalled Bolivar's. The situation of the Liberator was becoming critical. He could not risk a battle, nor could he show weakness if he was to achieve an armistice. He slowly moved back to a more favorable position where he could make a successful stand if Morillo pushed any further.[35] During this entire period the two commanders exchanged notes that are among the most remarkable in history's annals. They explained the reasons for their moves to each other; both protested their wish for a speedy reconciliation. Bolivar demanded that Morillo halt his advance, and the Spaniard explained that he moved only to protect Maracaibo. Here and there the language of the notes rises to emphatic threats. "If your Excellency," writes Bolivar on November 13, "continues to push forward, and by so doing, believes that you can dictate the conditions of the

32 Proclamas: p. 251. Restrepo: H. d. R. C. Vol. III. p. 72. O'Leary: Doc. Vol. XVII. p. 493.
33 Restrepo: H. d. R. C. Vol. III. p. 60. Proclamas: pp. 251-52. Rodríguez Villa: Vol. IV. pp. 244-45.
34 Cartas: Vol. II. p. 266.
35 O'Leary: Doc. Vol. XVII. p. 557. Lecuna: Guerra en 1820. Vol. XXIV. p. 319.

armistice, I assure you that I shall never accept them, and that Your Excellency will be held responsible before mankind and your own country for the continuation of this bloody conflict." He was even more audacious in his personal interviews. When one of Morillo's representatives demanded that he return to Cucutá, he replied, "When Morillo goes to Cádiz."[36]

Both Morillo and Bolivar were prepared for the failure of their negotiations, but both tried to prevent any miscarriage of their plans. Morillo wanted an armistice because he considered the cause of Spain as lost, Bolivar because the advantages of a respite from fighting seemed inestimable. Affairs seemed to be heading toward a speedy agreement. Final talks began on November 21. Both parties made concessions in the matter of boundaries. On November 25 an armistice was signed which was designed to last for six months and which included the entire territory of the Colombian Republic. Each of the warring factions was to retain possession of those areas it held at the time. In Venezuela the boundaries were carefully laid out. Deputations were to lay down the lines in New Granada. Both parties to the agreement wanted to work for the humanization of warfare as well as a reconciliation between their countries, keeping in mind the possibility of a fresh outbreak of hostilities. A second agreement regulated the exchange of prisoners of war, burial of the dead, and the treatment of civilians. The agreement was an attempt to make war less barbarous. The opening words speak of the governments of Colombia and Spain, and prove in this that Bolivar had achieved his main purpose, the recognition of Colombia as a sovereign power.[37]

On November 27, Bolivar and Morillo ratified their agreement. The time of terror and destruction was over. In the very town, Trujillo, and in the selfsame house in which, seven years earlier, Bolivar had entered upon the war to extinction, he now called for its conclusion.

Morillo had expressed a wish to meet the Liberator person-

36 Cartas: Vol. II. pp. 276, 280. O'Leary: Doc. Vol. XVII. pp. 556, 558, 568.
37 O'Leary: Doc. Vol. XVII. pp. 575 ff.

ally, and Bolivar gladly agreed. Halfway between their lines, they encountered each other at the little village of Santa Ana. Morillo appeared at the appointed place on the morning of November 27, accompanied by a squadron of Hussars and fifty of his staff officers. He was in dress uniform with all his medals and decorations pinned to his tunic, and the highest ranking officers of the army surrounded him. Soon thereafter, Bolivar's aide, O'Leary, arrived to announce that the Liberator was on his way. Bolivar came without his troops, accompanied by only ten officers. "I thought my body guard was small," said Morillo, "to venture so far forward, but my old enemy has surpassed me in magnanimity." He sent his Hussars away. Then he saw Bolivar ride forward. "What!" he cried, "that little man in the blue coat and campaign hat sitting on a mule . . . that is Bolivar?" He had scarcely recovered from his astonishment when the little man stopped. Both dismounted and embraced. A meal had been prepared and Morillo invited Bolivar to dine.

The scene that now took place has the sound and color of a medieval tale. The spirit of chivalry burned brightly on both sides. Each tried to outdo the other in generosity. They spoke of the ten years of war, of heroism, of constancy, and of sacrifices made by both. Each hoped that hostilities were over forever. If any questions should arise over certain points in the armistice agreement, a court of arbitration was to clear them up. Morillo suggested erecting a monument on the very spot where he first embraced Bolivar, believing that this would be a monument to the tolerance and good intentions of both nations. Bolivar was delighted with the idea, and a large boulder was forthwith rolled out to the spot. Then came the time for toasts. Once again the scene was like the courts of Toledo or Mainz. Bolivar's speech was short. "I drink," said he, "to the heroic constancy of the fighters of both armies . . . to their loyalty, their sacrifice, and their courage, which are without equal; to the noble men who defended liberty through all their trials, and to those who died gloriously in defense of their country and their government; to the wounded of both armies,

who proved their fearlessness, their worth, and their character.
Eternal hatred upon those who lust for blood and who shed it
unjustly." Morillo, La Torre, and Correa followed his example,
giving brief but friendly speeches. Nightfall finally put an end
to the expression of these generous sentiments, and the two
generals, who had so often robbed each other of sleep, spent
the night under the same roof and in the same room. In the
morning Morillo accompanied the Liberator to the same place
where they had first met each other. They embraced again,
repeated their promises, and parted amid cheers for both Colombians and Spaniards. This was the meeting of Santa Ana, an
event as moving as one of the battles which they had but now
agreed to forego.[38]

It would be unjust to Bolivar to relate the events of November, 1820, as though they were melodramatic theatricals. Few
occurrences illuminate the complicated and cryptic soul of the
Liberator, with its mixture of calculation and drama, of generosity and persuasiveness, as did the meeting of Santa Ana. It
had been Bolivar's aim to win Morillo over to his own cause.
In his own words: "During the entire course of my public life,
I have never revealed more policy or shown more diplomatic
ruse than on that important occasion. And in this, I can say
it without vanity, I think I surpassed Morillo, as I surpassed
him in almost all military operations. I went to this meeting
with complete superiority to the Spanish General. I went armed
from top to toe with politics and diplomacy, with the semblance
of utmost frankness and good will, confidence and friendship.
. . . The armistice of six months there concluded, which was
so greatly criticized, was for me a mere pretext to let the world
see that Colombia negotiated with Spain on an equal footing
. . . as power to power. It was likewise a pretext for the important treaty concerning the legalization of peace . . . which
put an end to the horrible butchery, the murder of the defeated,
. . . the armistice was favorable for the Republicans, but

38 O'Leary: Memorias. Vol. II. pp. 56 ff. Proclamas: p. 253. Blanco: Doc. Vol.
VII. p. 471.

disastrous for Spain. But there is still more to be said. The armistice also tricked Morillo into returning to Spain and handing over his command to General La Torre, who was less able, less active, and less of a soldier than the Count of Cartagena. Let the dolts and my enemies say what they will about these negotiations. The results are in my favor. Never was a diplomatic comedy played better than that of the day and night of Santa Ana."[39]

This frank admission contains everything that can be said about the armistice. Morillo was actually bewitched by Bolivar's personality. Later he wrote to him as a friend and admitted that the Liberator's frankness had deeply affected him. Against the wish of all those who still cherished the hope of saving the King's cause in America, Morillo gave up his command. His successor, La Torre, was indeed less active and less able. He was also married to a relative of Bolivar and had already been half won over to the cause of a free America.[40] Who today can doubt that November 27 was a triumph comparable with the speech at Angostura or the battle of Boyacá? Curiously enough, however, this was not a popular victory, and there are few of Bolivar's decisions that have been so thoroughly criticized. It was said that the armistice was as bad as ten defeats, and the deputies at Angostura were quite displeased with it. "The great authorities of Angostura," wrote Bolivar, "think, that because they are on the Orinoco, they are on the Thames. And although they belong to the race of the *manaures,* they think they are all Pitts."[41]

To the advantages which Bolivar had enumerated, we must add some others. The agreement of Santa Ana gave him time to complete the arming of his forces. Every interruption was welcome to people who had endured ten weary years of war, and the Republic was credited with having brought them this measure of peace. From the standpoint of the monarchy, it

39 D. d. B. pp. 322-24. J. Basdevant analyzes the treaties from the point of view of international law in, B. d. H. Bogotá. Vol. XII. pp. 37 ff.
40 Cartas: Vol. II. p. 297.
41 Cartas: Vol. II. p. 263. Urdaneta: Memorias. p. 184.

had been an irremediable mistake to treat with Bolivar either as an excellency or as a president. With the armistice, the mother country lost the greater part of that moral strength which had hitherto supported her in the fight against independence.

The Liberator took care that the men with whom he had sat at table and under one roof were treated henceforth with respect by the Republican newspapers. Nevertheless, he interpreted the treaty more or less as he chose, sometimes, indeed, in a highly personal and questionable manner. He suggested that Santander withhold immediate publication of the armistice. Any excuse could be used, he said—the messengers might fall ill, the sheets be lost, etc. In this way he hoped to gain time to build up his positions in the south, and eventually to liberate Quito.[42]

Who can criticize the machiavellianism of these instructions? All great statesmen have used such methods. Here the freedom of an entire continent was at stake. Thus the year 1820 ended with a rich harvest. If it was not a year of decision, like 1817 or 1819, it had nonetheless brought Bolivar nearer to his goal.

The Liberator prepared for the last battle, at the end of which no Spaniard should remain on South American soil. After the battle of Boyacá, Páez had begged Bolivar to save heroic Venezuela, and Bolivar had replied, "You tell me that it is time to save Venezuela, and I tell you that now is the time to save South America!"[43]

42 Cartas: Vol. II. p. 290.
43 B. d. H. Caracas. Vol. XXIII. No. 92. p. 612.

CHAPTER 23

The Liberation of Venezuela

For the first time in ten years Colombia's guns were silent. The armistice, however, did not bring relaxation. There could be no rest for Bolivar so long as the final decision was merely pending. He had a respite of six months during which he could prepare for the ultimate decision. The agreement with Spain comprised a number of unknown factors. No one knew whether war or peace would ensue; and Bolivar was undecided, in the case of continued conflict, as to his point of attack.

One of the first documents Bolivar dictated after drawing up the agreement of Santa Ana was the outline of a new campaign. He had gone from the border into the interior, and at the beginning of January, 1821, we find him in Bogotá. Here he drew up his plan of operations. If the armistice ended without bringing peace, all his forces were to march on Venezuela and take Caracas. This was his first aim.[1]

At the same time, however, reports came that a move toward the south promised success. We remember San Martín's march. He had crossed the Andes and established freedom in Chile, and now he came to liberate Peru. San Martín's movements had surprising repercussions. The Spanish Viceroy in Lima found himself in an embarrassing position. Whole troop divisions of the Spanish went over to the Patriots. Entire provinces refused

---

1 O'Leary: Memorias. Vol. II. p. 64. Larrazabal: Vol. II. p. 65. O'Leary: Doc. Vol. XVIII. pp. 5, 6, 7. Lecuna: Campaña de Carabobo. B. d. H. Caracas. Vol. XXIV. No. 96. p. 422.

obedience. One of the most far-reaching results of San Martín's expedition was the rebellion of Guayaquil. The port of Ecuador had rebelled against the colonial authorities when it heard that the Argentinian General was approaching and had declared its independence.

For Bolivar this news was of especial importance. Indeed, it seemed so significant that for a moment he even thought of going south himself. According to the fundamental laws of Greater Colombia, Ecuador formed the third department of the new state. Declaration of the independence of Guayaquil made the completion of Bolivar's plans easier. He commissioned one of his generals to congratulate the government council of Guayaquil on the uprising and to offer Colombia's support for the future.[2]

There were certain decisions facing the new government of Guayaquil. Should it unite with Colombia or with Peru? Or should it create an independent state? The control of the port was vital to Colombia, and Bolivar wanted to prevent San Martín from acquiring it. A swift annexation of Guayaquil would come close to being a victory over his Argentinian rival, who was engaged in liberating the peoples of the south as was Bolivar those in the north. It would also be a step toward the creation of that domain in the Andes region which Bolivar was already envisaging.[3]

The time was not ripe, however, for the execution of this grandiose scheme. Urgent problems kept Bolivar in the north; he, therefore, gave up his plan to go to Ecuador at this time, sending, instead, General Sucre as his representative to Guayaquil to promote the annexation of this province to Colombia.[4]

Bolivar remained in Bogotá to hasten negotiations with Spain. He hoped to turn the armistice into a peace, and he appointed executors to carry on the negotiations in Madrid. He turned to La Torre; he wrote to Morillo and begged him

2 O'Leary: Doc. Vol. XVIII. pp. 15, 18. Cartas: Vol. II. p. 294.
3 Cartas: Vol. II. pp. 290, 295, 297, 298.
4 O'Leary: Doc. Vol. XVIII. pp. 19, 31. Proclamas: p. 255.

to use his influence; finally, he appealed to the King himself.[5] In a letter which obviously did not come from the heart, he congratulated Ferdinand on the creation of the constitutional monarchy and tried to convince him of the necessity of recognizing Colombia's independence.

Bolivar was prepared to make great concessions. He seemed quite willing to sacrifice the independence of Panama and Ecuador. He even agreed to guarantee Spain's position in Mexico if Colombia's recognition was acknowledged.[6] Let us consider whether this attitude was a surrender of his idea of continental solidarity.

Bolivar thought that the independence of the hemisphere was preordained. He fully believed that no promises to Spain could long retard liberty, and he was convinced that the recognition of Colombia would mean tremendous opportunities. The whole plan was a machiavellian inspiration designed to confuse the Spanish front. But it was not too well thought out, and showed that, as a statesman, Bolivar had never overcome a certain dilettantism. One thing, however, is certain; Bolivar was, during those first weeks of 1821, sincere in his wish to keep his agreement with Spain. All his letters confirm this.

The National Assembly of Greater Colombia was to convene during the first months of the year, and this event was of great importance to Bolivar. He left Bogotá to be present at the opening. On the way he received the surprising news that Maracaibo had revolted against Spain, and this unexpected event gave Bolivar's plans a new impetus. With characteristic speed he threw himself into the new project.

Among the leaders of the independence movement was General Rafael Urdaneta. Born in Maracaibo, he had been dissatisfied with an armistice that had left his country in Spanish hands. While Bolivar had been in Bogotá, Urdaneta had undertaken to assure a victory for the Revolution in Maracaibo.

5 Cartas: Vol. II. pp. 303, 305. Blanco: Doc. Vol. VII. p. 479. O'Leary: Doc. Vol. XVIII. p. 41.
6 Cartas: Vol. II. p. 302. O'Leary: Doc. Vol. XVIII. pp. 38-43. See also, C. Villanueva: Ferdinando VII y los nuevos Estados. Paris, 1912. p. 33.

He had evolved a plan that prepared for the liberation of this
all-important city and on January 28 Maracaibo was occupied
according to Urdaneta's instructions and upon his sole responsibility.[7] Bolivar had not only opposed Urdaneta's plans; he
had definitely refused to support them. This had been a drama
cast with divided roles. Urdaneta had been obliged to act independently in order that Bolivar should not be burdened with
a broken treaty. The armistice was, however, impaired. Bolivar
had now to decide whether he would cling to his policy of
agreement or whether he would support Urdaneta. He knew
that the uprising in Maracaibo would invite a break with Spain.
But he could not afford to exercise a delaying policy. Urdaneta
had, after all, acted in the true spirit of independence and he
had achieved a goal whose importance none knew better than
the Liberator. Bolivar congratulated both Urdaneta and himself on Maracaibo's annexation. He let the leaders of the army
know at once of the event and advised them to prepare for
the resumption of hostilities.[8]

It is certain that he acted against the letter of the agreement,
but the shirt was nearer to the body than the coat. Possession
of Maracaibo bound Venezuela and New Granada closer together, and a new intact province was opened to the Liberator.
The position of La Torre was considerably affected by the event.
In a military way this loss was not so palpable to the Spanish
army, but the moral damage was of importance, for Maracaibo
had been the citadel of the Monarchists since 1810. The Spanish Marshal sent an immediate protest against the occupation.
Bolivar's reply was sophistic. He stated that a case of this kind
had not been provided for in the treaty of Santa Ana, and he
proposed a court of arbitration to La Torre. The Spaniard refused and demanded the return of the province.[9] Letters went
back and forth between headquarters. Bolivar's position had
grown stronger through the spontaneous uprisings in Guaya-

7 Urdaneta: Memorias. pp. 191-92. Blanco: Doc. Vol. VII. pp. 524, 535. Restrepo: H. d. R. C. Vol. III. p. 107.
8 O'Leary: Doc. Vol. XVIII. pp. 65, 67-74.
9 Cartas: Vol. II. pp. 314 ff. Blanco: Doc. Vol. VII. pp. 557, 561.

quil and Maracaibo. When La Torre again offered an armistice, Bolivar demanded more favorable terms which he knew the Spaniard could not grant. In March he made a final attempt to force the enemy to accept peace. "It is my duty," he wrote to La Torre, "to bring about peace or to fight."

La Torre, of course, had no authority to sign a peace with Colombia. He confined himself, therefore, to informing Bolivar that the armistice would end on April 28. In an appeal to the Americans he blamed Bolivar for rekindling the flames of war. Bolivar answered immediately. He placed the responsibility on Spain. This war, he said, will be a holy war. We are fighting only to disarm the enemy, not to destroy him. All are Colombians to us, even the enemy, if they want to be Colombians.[10]

Even though the armistice had lasted only five and not six months, it had been advantageous to Bolivar. His army was more closely knit and was under better leadership than it had been during the previous year. The Spanish had sacrificed their military authority in the person of Morillo. With each new day they felt the ground melting under their feet.[11] Resumption of the fight could mean only one thing—the final liberation of Venezuela.

Bolivar had nursed the idea of this campaign since August, 1820. It was a question of uniting the three Armies of the West, those of Páez, Urdaneta, and his own and of seeking out the enemy simultaneously. At the same time the Army in the East was to attack Caracas and thus force the Spaniards to split their forces. Thereafter, the destruction of the enemy in a single battle like that of Boyacá would be an easy matter.[12] The difficulty of carrying out this plan lay in the great distance which separated the armies, in the problem of approaching the enemy unapprehended and above all in the problem of supplies. All these regions were denuded to the last blade of grass, and

10 Proclamas: pp. 256-57, 258, 259. Blanco: Doc. Vol. VII. pp. 567, 583.
11 Cartas: Vol. II. p. 243. Larrazabal: Vol. II. p. 74.
12 O'Leary: Doc. Vol. XVII. p. 373. A. Santana: La Campaña de Carabobo. Caracas, 1921. Lecuna: Campaña de Carabobo. p. 438.

the question of feeding a large army was a serious one. Bolivar had long ago advised Páez to acquire all the cattle available.[13] He was determined to solve the difficulties of feeding despite all resistance, despite the hostility of the civilians, and despite defiance and rebellion. Bolivar instructed Bermúdez, Commander-in-Chief of the Army of the East, to attack Caracas. Bermúdez was to assume no responsibility for the result of this undertaking; he was merely to follow Bolivar's instructions and make the attack.[14]

On the morning of April 28 the campaign began, and the Patriot armies began to move forward. Bolivar notified Páez concerning the place, the time, and the manner of their juncture. All hasty action against the enemy was to be avoided. Bolivar carried out his plan even though he was completely ignorant of the intentions of the Spanish. The Royal army had slowly drawn back to the northwest and had occupied positions from which it could block Bolivar's way to Caracas. La Torre, however, had not counted on the fact that the capital would also be atacked from the east, yet that was exactly what occurred. Bermúdez fulfilled his part of the program and occupied Caracas on May 13.[15] La Torre sent his representative, Morales, to detain Bermúdez, who retired before the stronger Spanish forces and gave up the city. But he had done what had been expected of him, and the evasion maneuver had succeeded; he had prevented La Torre from meeting Bolivar on his march to the north. Meanwhile, Bolivar developed his central idea, namely, the unification of the three Armies of the West.[16]

He reached the town of San Carlos on June 5. Here he wanted to meet Páez and Urdaneta. The march of these divisions had been slower than Bolivar had expected. Urdaneta's division, coming from Maracaibo, had to cross a difficult ter-

13 O'Leary: Doc. Vol. XVIII. p. 21. J. A. Páez: Archivo, 1818-1820. Bogotá, 1939. p. 336.
14 O'Leary: Doc. Vol. XVIII. p. 181. Blanco: Doc. Vol. VII. p. 592.
15 Díaz: Recuerdos. pp. 252-53. O'Leary: Doc. Vol. XVIII. pp. 286-89. Blanco: Doc. Vol. VII. p. 595.
16 Santana: pp. 89 ff. See also, Bolivar's letter of May 25, 1821, in Cartas inéditas de Bolívar. B. d. H. Bogotá. Vol. XVIII. p. 784.

rain. Their leader fell ill and gave up his command. Finally on June 19, after a march of six hundred kilometers lasting thirty-two days, Urdaneta's division met Bolivar.

Páez had been in San Carlos for a week. He, too, had been en route for almost a month and had covered four hundred fifty kilometers. With the consolidation of the three armies Bolivar had solved the most difficult problem of the campaign. La Torre had not known how to isolate the Republican armies and thus defeat them singly. As had been the case two years earlier, Bolivar's accomplishment lay in his ability to gain superior positions where he ran no risk of losing the final encounter. It was essential that one single victory should give him the unconditional surrender of Venezuela.[17]

Bolivar knew on June 15 that the Spaniards had withdrawn to the plains of Carabobo. There was dissension in the Spanish camp between the Commander-in-Chief, La Torre, and his representative, Morales, who sought the command for himself. This jealousy led to a sequence of errors. La Torre reacted to the slight evasion tactics of Bolivar with exaggerated violence. Bolivar had studied his opponents well in Santa Ana, and he knew how La Torre would respond to every one of his actions. Consequently, Bolivar played with La Torre as he chose during the short campaign. La Torre was secretly convinced of his eventual defeat. His army had shrunk and he now controlled only the territory immediately occupied.[18] He continued to fight only because honor and personal courage demanded it. After the consolidation the Patriot army had been organized into three divisions: Páez led the advance guard; the second division was under Sedeño, and Colonel Plaza commanded the reserves. Bolivar's entire army came to sixty-five hundred men. For the first time his army was numerically superior to the Spaniards, since La Torre's forces numbered only five thousand.[19]

La Torre chose the plains of Carabobo as the place where

17 Lecuna: Campaña de Carabobo. p. 472.
18 Santana: p. 104. Torres Lanza: Vol. V. pp. 159, 199.
19 O'Leary: Memorias. Vol. II. p. 82. Santana: p. 162. Blanco: Doc. Vol. VII. pp. 634 ff.

he would head off Bolivar, because the road to Valencia went
through these plains and Valencia was the gateway to Caracas.
On the morning of June 24, the Patriots took the hills of Buena
Vista, one mile from Carabobo. The morning fog had lifted
and Bolivar saw the enemy army in battle formation. Six
infantry columns and three cavalry regiments had moved up
and occupied the plains and the surrounding hills. The Royal
artillery was so scattered that their gunfire could sweep the
main roads which lead through the plains of Carabobo.[20] It
was clear that La Torre was prepared for an attack in the
center or on the left wing. Under such conditions a frontal
attack was out of the question. As at Boyacá, Bolivar used
surprise tactics. He had two of his divisions move up so that
the Spanish would be led to think that their center would be
assaulted. Meanwhile, he ordered Páez to surround La Torre's
right wing, which was the weakest, and to attack the enemy
from the rear.

Páez began operations at eleven in the morning. The terrain was difficult, the path so narrow that men could scarcely
march two abreast. Sometimes the Patriots had to cut their
way through the underbrush with machete knives. La Torre
realized too late that he would be attacked in the right wing.
His whole battle order was upset, and his reserves had to constitute the advance guard.[21] La Torre first led one regiment and
then two others against the approaching Patriots. The latter
were for the moment in a critical spot. The battalion, the Braves
of the Apure, retired, and the British Legion stepped into the
breach. They advanced with flying colors as though they were
on the parade ground. Their officers fell, one after the other—
seventeen in fifteen minutes—but the troops carried on imper-
turbably. Bolivar, who directed the battle from a hill, sent reinforcements from the second division. Infantry columns took
the Spanish positions by storm and then pushed on into the
plains. Both sides now put their cavalry into action, but Páez'

20 For the battle of Carabobo, see, O'Leary: Doc. Vol. XVIII. pp. 337, 349-55.
O'Leary: Memorias. Vol. II. pp. 80 ff. Cartas: Vol. II. p. 358.
21 Santana: p. 113. Páez: Autobiografía. pp. 253 ff.

riders scored the victory. Two Spanish regiments were blasted apart. A third surrendered when it was completely surrounded. What was left of the Spaniards, the artillery and two infantry regiments, attempted to retire to Valencia, but now the second and third divisions which Bolivar had held back hurled their whole strength at the retreating army. The Republicans sustained a serious loss when the leader of the third division, Colonel Plaza, died in battle, but they were encouraged by the surrender of one of the Spanish divisions. La Torre and Morales fled to Valencia with the single regiment that still held out. Meanwhile Bolivar had ridden into the plains himself. He tried to block the Spanish retreat by again flinging his riders into the battle. All officers of the Patriot army took part in this attack. General Sedeño rode alone against an entire formation of Spanish infantrymen, and died. When Bolivar realized that the pursuit had neither plan nor coherence, he threw himself in the midst of his men. At the top of his voice he cried, "Order! Discipline! Remember the Battle of Semen!" His words had the desired effect and the Republican troops became more orderly. Finally, the Spanish gave up their artillery and escaped their pursuers by retreating through Valencia to Puerto Cabello. Only four hundred remained of an army that had numbered five thousand.[22] The enemy had been destroyed in a victory as complete as that of Boyacá. Just as La Puerta had twice been disastrous for Bolivar, so Carabobo had twice brought him good luck. His losses had not been excessive, but in a battle lasting no more than an hour he had sacrificed some of his best officers. Páez, who had contributed so much to his victory, remained unhurt, but his aide and bodyguard, El Negro Primero, was mortally wounded. While the battle had been still in progress, this brave man had ridden to the rear. Páez looked at him with some surprise and asked if he were afraid. "No, my General," replied El Negro Primero, "I came to bid

22 O'Leary: Doc. Vol. XVIII. pp. 361, 368. See also, Duarte Level: *op. cit.* pp. 340 ff. Hasbrouck: pp. 233 ff. Manuel E. Rosales: La Batalla de Carabobo. Caracas, 1911.

you farewell," and bleeding from two deep wounds, he fell
from his horse.

Bolivar arrived in Valencia on the very evening of the
battle. His country was open to him. The Spanish garrison
of La Guayra tried in vain to fight through to Puerto Cabello,
and their leader finally agreed to the honorable surrender that
Bolivar offered him. Within a short time the scattered guerrilla
troops of the Monarchists who roamed the provinces of Coro
and Calabozo were also destroyed. All Venezuela had been
conquered for the Republic, and only Puerto Cabello and Cumaná continued for a time to resist.

Bolivar's entrance into Caracas was like his 1813 march of
triumph. Although he arrived at night, great crowds of people
gathered in front of his house to see him. It was midnight
before he could escape their embraces and felicitations. This
time he did not rest on his laurels. He made only the most
necessary decisions himself, and then called Soublette, whom he
entrusted with the government of Venezuela.

Bolivar's stay in Caracas was short. He no longer belonged
to Venezuela alone. He was President of Colombia and soon
perhaps would be the Liberator of South America, a man who
dreamed of going as far as the Amazon and La Plata
rivers.[23] Halfway between Caracas and Valencia was the estate
of San Mateo, and Bolivar remained there for several days,
giving himself up to rest and the inspirations of his phantasy.
The houses in which he had once lived were in ruins. Of the
hundreds of slaves who formerly planted sugar cane in this
region, he found only three, whom he immediately set free.
While he roamed the fields of San Mateo, he had the idea, or
rather the wish, to give up his power—either to flee or to live
here quietly and in seclusion as he had done before 1809. But
before he could seriously contemplate such a life there were
still many matters to be settled. Quito, at least, had to be liberated and the Republic established. "I hope before six months
have passed to return from Quito, and then to settle in San

23 Cartas: Vol. II. p. 379.

Mateo without either profession or office, for I am weary of
commanding and carrying responsibility."[24] This desire was
the leading motif of countless public and private utterances of
Bolivar during this and the following year. Their immediate
occasion was the meeting of the National Assembly in 1821
and the coming presidential election. The order that had thus
far existed was only an interregnum and could not be expected
to continue indefinitely. While Bolivar devoted himself to the
conduct of the war, Roscio had been named as his representative. Roscio, however, died in Cucutá shortly after he had
assumed office. Bolivar now named General Anzuola in his
place, but he, too, survived his appointment by only a few
weeks.

Among the prisoners whom the Spanish Revolution of 1820
had freed from the dungeons was General Antonio Nariño.[25]
He had just returned from Europe and Bolivar's choice fell on
him. For many reasons he seemed the desirable person to fill
the office of vice-president. He was a Granadian and a martyr
to liberty. He had spent a great part of his life in Spanish
prisons. Moreover, he shared Bolivar's political convictions. He
was a Centralist and an adherent of strong state rule. Under
Nariño's leadership the national assembly of nineteen free
provinces of Colombia united in Cucutá on May 6, 1821.

The first problem that occupied Parliament was the union
of New Granada and Venezuela and the formation of their
future government. The union of the two countries aroused
no resistance. It was unanimously accepted and proclaimed
in a solemn manifesto. The question as to the form of government was not so easy to solve. During the discussions all the
old ideological passions flared again; some wanted a state of
union, others a union of states. Only after a heated debate did
the idea of a state-union triumph.[26]

24 Cartas: Vol. II. p. 400.
25 O'Leary: Doc. Vol. XVIII. pp. 166, 226. Blanco: Doc. Vol. VII. p. 571.
Larrazabal: Vol. II. p. 79. R. Cortazar: Congreso de Cucutá: Libro de Actas.
Bogotá, 1923.
26 O'Leary: Doc. Vol. XVIII. pp. 236, 438-39. Blanco: Vol. VII. pp. 587 ff.,
604-05. Restrepo: H. d. R. C. Vol. III. pp. 145-46. Groot: Vol. IV. p. 158.

Bolivar awaited the parliamentary discussions with skepticism. He knew they were necessary if a democratic Republic on a grand scale was to be created, but he feared the pettyfogging and hair-splitting procedure of the Parliamentarians. The ideas which he had propounded in his speech of Angostura had a very cool reception. He was unwilling to see the formulation of a second constitution which would be incompatible with Colombia's true condition.[27] Bolivar desired a constitution commensurate with the future greatness of the Republic he had founded, but he was apprehensive lest the representatives could not keep pace with his deeds. Bolivar knew that he was exposed to calumny, that his enemies begrudged him the admiration of both the people and the army, and he was sensitive to open hostility and even to criticism. He had neither the strong nerves of Oxenstierna nor the scorn of Frederick the Great. He suffered indescribably under the suspicion of any fifth rate writer in a provincial newspaper.[28] He had already written to Santander in September, 1820, "The intrigues of the legislators have troubled me very much and have convinced me of the impossibility of keeping our equilibrium here. It will be a miracle if we can even salvage our naked lives from this Revolution. I am determined to give up my powers on the very day that Colombia's Congress convenes." When the opening of Congress was at hand he wrote to the Vice-President, "As far as I am concerned, you may rest assured that I shall not accept the presidency: first, because I am tired of giving orders; second, because I am tired of being accused of ambition; third, because the world would think that there is no one in the country but myself who is fit for this office; fourth, because I am only really good as a soldier; fifth, because the government will always be orphaned as it has been right along, because I am never in a position actually to carry out my functions. And, finally, I shall resist acceptance of the office, and if I am forced, I shall desert."[29] The coming years were to test the reliability of these words.

27 Cartas: Vol. II. p. 180.
28 O'Leary: Memorias. Vol. II. p. 95.
29 Cartas: Vol. II. p. 325.

PLATE III

AERIAL VIEW OF THE MAGDALENA VALLEY

Much of the lower Magdalena Country is bogland, which turns into vast lagoons during
the semi-annual rainy season

PLATE IV

ANTONIO JOSE DE SUCRE

His friends, however, were not satisfied, and he was obliged to keep telling them over and over again: "I am tired . . . of ruling this Republic of ingrates. I am tired of being called a usurper, tyrant, and despot. And I am even more tired of filling an office that is contrary to my nature. On the other hand, I believe that in order to administer the State, one should have certain knowledge which I do not possess and which I loathe. You may know that I have never looked at a bill, nor do I want to know what is spent in my house. Nor am I fitted for diplomacy because I am too naive, too often violent. I know diplomacy only by name. I do not understand anything, but I have a natural affinity for freedom and decent laws."[30] These letters, even though they are somewhat exaggerated and self-satisfied, are incomparable documents of the real Bolivar. When Congress convened in May, Bolivar immediately sent in his resignation which Congress as immediately repudiated. The members appealed to his patriotism, and Bolivar relented provisionally when the news of the victory of Carabobo arrived. The event heightened not only Bolivar's fame but also his political prestige. Congress confirmed the appointments he had suggested and agreed to all his provisos.

Bolivar had begun his inspection of Venezuela and had found it in a hopeless condition of exhaustion. "I believe that before peace is signed, I cannot desert this mad city or these people possessed by the Devil. This is chaos. Nothing can be done because the good people have disappeared and the bad ones have multiplied. Venezuela offers the spectacle of a people suddenly awakened from a great lethargy, and no one knows what its condition is or what should be done. . . . Everything is in a state of ferment and no men can be found for anything."[31]

From Maracaibo he wrote again to his friends in Cucutá in an attempt to prevent his final election as President. "I am determined to be a great example of Republicanism so that this act shall serve as a model for others. It is not advisable to have the government in the hands of the most dangerous man . . .

30 Cartas: Vol. II. p. 337, of May 21, 1821.
31 Cartas: Vol. II. pp. 365-66. O'Leary: Vol. XVIII. pp. 450-51.

it is not advisable that the commander-in-chief of the army should administer justice, for a general conflict is sure to arise against this individual, and when he falls the whole government will fall."[32] Here he showed amazing perspicacity about his own fate and that of the Colombian Republic. He wrote to the Minister of Finance on the same day, "I know what I can do, my friend, and where I can be useful. Be assured that I am only good to fight . . . or at least to march with the soldiers, and to prevent others from leading who are worse than myself. Everything else is still the illusion of my friends. Because they saw me steer a ship in a storm, they think I should be admiral of a fleet. . . . They tell me that history will say great things about me. I believe that it will think nothing was greater than my renunciation of power and my complete dedication to the arms which could save my country. History will say, 'Bolivar took over the government to liberate his countrymen, and when they were free he left them so that they would be ruled by law and not by his will.' This is my answer."[33] The words have the ring of sincerity. On the other hand, Bolivar did not always act according to his own inner knowledge; moreover, his resignation was not entirely an act of selfless renunciation. Bolivar simply preferred the glory of the Liberator to that of President. There were still other lands to free, and he felt that he had no time to lose. General Iturbide had liberated Mexico in June, 1821, and the independence of Central America had therewith become a reality. San Martín was in Lima and threatened to precede Bolivar in Ecuador.

Meanwhile, Congress had unanimously elected Bolivar President of the Republic. The members of the National Assembly had sent him urgent summons, and on September 22 he arrived in Cucutá. Once again, in a letter to the President of Parliament, he insisted that he felt incapable of ruling the Republic, that he was a soldier and nothing more. If, nevertheless, Congress insisted on its decision, he would accept the presidency for the duration of the war on condition that he be

32 Cartas: Vol. II. pp. 389 ff.
33 Cartas: Vol. II. p. 391.

permitted to complete the campaign. Parliament maintained its stand, and Bolivar took the oath of office on October 3, 1821, in the presence of the members.[34]

There was one cogent motive in Bolivar's conditional acceptance of the presidency. The form of government which the Republic had assumed corresponded only in small part with the ideas Bolivar had expressed three years before. The Constitution of Cucutá was liberal. It provided for a house of representatives elected for four years and a senate elected for eight years. The executive powers were in the hands of a president elected for four years with but a single reëlection possibility. Below him were a vice-president and a cabinet consisting of five secretaries of state and one member of the supreme court. In general, the legislative branch of the government in the Constitution of Cucutá was omnipotent, while the executive branch had little real power. The president was to be given extraordinary powers only during a war emergency or in case of internal rebellion.[35]

The government was constituted as a central power and the old orders of colonial days were rescinded. Instead of the great departments of Venezuela, New Granada, and Ecuador, smaller provinces were created. The offices of the regional vice-presidents were eliminated and in their stead were intendents. Venezuela was divided into three provinces and New Granada into four. This was undoubtedly a step forward toward the idea of the Greater Colombian Republic, but the fundamental spirit of unity which should have breathed life into this scheme was lacking. Under the new Constitution men continued to feel as Venezuelans or as Granadians. Since Ecuador's inclusion in the Republic had been decided upon, the capital was transferred to Bogotá. This created a storm of protest among the delegates from Venezuela. Actually, Bogotá lies halfway between Venezuela and Ecuador.

Among the numerous liberal measures, freedom of the

34 Proclamas: pp. 266-67.
35 The text of the constitution in, Blanco: Doc. Vol. VIII. pp. 25 ff. O'Leary: Memorias. Vol. II. pp. 102 ff.

press, tolerance, education, etc., was one for which Bolivar felt
personally responsible. It concerned the emancipation of the
slaves. Bolivar had not asked Congress to wipe out slavery
because he did not want to incur the resentment of the big
landowners. But he now demanded that at least the sons of
slaves should be declared free. He asked for this measure as a
reward for the victory of Carabobo, and Congress granted his
request.[36]

The Constitution of Cucutá was not what Bolivar had
hoped for Colombia. It, nevertheless, represented a gain when
compared with the plans which the Revolutionists had made at
the beginning of the war. No one could expect a perfect result
to be obtained from a group of men who had no legal experience and little knowledge of politics or administration. Bolivar,
however, saw only the weaknesses, but he was careful not to
speak of them in public. An imperfect constitution was better
than none. He did, nevertheless, confess his disappointment to
his friends. As the bells of Cucutá announced the promulgation
of the Constitution, he said, "They are Colombia's death
knell."[37]

Bolivar was prepared to have his ideas disregarded because
he knew that he would not be present to lead the government.
A special law empowered him to continue the campaign, leaving the reins of government in the hands of the vice-president.[38]
At first Bolivar wanted Nariño appointed to this position, but
Nariño did not understand how to curry favor with the Parliamentarians. Bolivar finally proposed Santander, and the
twenty-nine year old lad was actually entrusted with the administration of the state. This choice was fateful, but inevitable.
Santander was then the only one who could keep the war
against the Spaniards in progress and could, at the same time,
operate the confused administration. If, in later years, San-

36 O'Leary: Doc. Vol. XVIII. p. 387. Proclamas: p. 264. Blanco: Doc. Vol.
VII. p. 666. Restrepo: H. d. R. C. Vol. III. p. 149, 153.
37 O'Leary: Memorias. Vol. II. p. 101. Blanco: Doc. Vol. VIII. p. 129. Restrepo: H. d. R. C. Vol. III. p. 153. Proclamas: pp. 267-68.
38 O'Leary: Doc. Vol. XVIII. pp. 523, 546. Blanco: Doc. Vol. VIII. p. 148.

tander did not measure up to Bolivar's expectations, Bolivar had only himself to thank, for he alone had made the choice and he alone had arranged political and military affairs in this manner. Bolivar preferred to harvest the glory of the Liberator, instead of doing the tedious work of the administrator. In the first place, he was a soldier; moreover, the Spaniards were still on American soil. But it was not for these reasons alone that Bolivar turned his back on administrative activity. He did it because he doubted whether Colombia could ever become a living organism. Already he could see the negative forces that were nipping its growing energies in the bud.

Bolivar thought of the officers who had fought with him. "You have no idea of the spirit which animates our military leaders. They are not the same men you know. They are men you do not know, men who have fought for a long time . . . who believe that they have greatly merited and who are now humiliated, miserable, and hopeless of ever gathering in the fruits of their labors. They are Llaneros, determined and ignorant, men who have never considered themselves the equals of others who know more and make a better appearance than they. I, myself, who have always been their leader, do not yet know of how much they are capable. I treat them with the greatest consideration, yet even this consideration is not enough to give them the confidence and frankness which should exist among comrades and compatriots. We find ourselves at the edge of an abyss, or rather on top of a volcano that may soon erupt. I fear peace more than war. And herewith I give you an idea of what I do not and cannot say."[39]

Who can doubt that Bolivar was here giving a portrait of Páez? Here is the picture of that inferiority complex which had turned into presumptuousness, the shepherd and the hunter who regarded the state as he did the plains of the Apure, as his personal pasture wherein he could graze at will. Yet Bolivar could not ignore these men. He was dependent on them, and as a reward for their deeds, Páez, Bermúdez, and Mariño were

39 Cartas: Vol. II. p. 348.

appointed as intendents and commanders in Venezuela. The characteristics and the attitudes of these men were what Bolivar expected of his fellow countrymen, but the Granadians were no better; they were merely different. They were not riders and hunters, but lawyers and ideologists. Bolivar feared their objections and influence no less. "In the end," he wrote to Santander, "the literati will do so much that they will be outlawed by the Colombian Republic as Plato outlawed the poets of his Republic. These gentlemen think that their opinion is the will of the people, without realizing that in Colombia the people are in the army . . . for it is the people that decide, the people that work, the people that possess the power to do. All others are those who, with more or less patriotism, and more or less evil intent, just vegetate. Their only right is to remain passive citizens. We shall have to develop this policy, which certainly does not conform to that of Rousseau, so that these gentlemen will not ruin us."[40] The literati of Bogotá, the men of the highlands, who wore warm woolen clothing and who sat around the braziers in their houses, what did they know of the waters of the Orinoco, of the fishermen of Maracaibo, of the sources of the Magdalena, or the deserts of Colombia—of all the wild and terrible contrasts so familiar to the fighting forces? "Does it not seem to you, my dear Santander, that these legislators, who are more ignorant than evil and more presumptuous than ambitious, will lead us into anarchy and tyranny and finally to destruction? If it is not the Llaneros who will bring about our ruin, then it will be the gentle philosophers of Colombia." These men, he continued, think of themselves as people like Lykurg or Franklin or Camilo Torres. They want to create republics like the Greek, the Roman, or the North American. But, he asked, what do they achieve? They build a Greek structure on a Gothic foundation, and they build it at the edge of a volcano.

Bolivar's problem was a problem for every Colombian statesman, and in this belief Bolivar left the thankless job of the

40 Cartas: Vol. II. pp. 354-55, of June 13, 1821.

presidency to other men. "Neither you nor I shall, in our old age, see that sincere harmony which should exist in the big family of a state."[41] He foresaw that one day the dissident forces would blast unity apart, just as he foresaw almost everything that happened. As Sucre said, Bolivar's prescience was almost incredible. The future seemed to hold no secrets from him, but this very knowledge was for him what the foreknowledge of death is for most people. They are aware of the inevitability of death, but they prefer to let this knowledge sleep.

In the end, therefore, it seemed better to Bolivar to remain a soldier and to liberate more and more countries, than to be an administrator whom any ingrate could revile. Was this decision, however, a contradiction of principles, nay, even a real guilt in Bolivar's mental processes? What logic lay in the establishment of a free state if no one could undertake the responsibility of guiding it? In the not too distant future Bolivar was to realize that he could not escape this schism, but unfortunately the day of realization would come too late.

Temporarily his meteoric path still led him toward the stars. With all his pessimism, he was more irresistible than ever . . . victorious, generous, and wasteful as never before. Sometimes he did not have enough money to buy a hammock, but when he heard of a friend's need, he sent a servant with silver and jewels. When he learned that Camilo Torres' widow was in need, he had an annual stipend of one thousand pesos set aside for her from his own income.[42] He gave these orders in Bogotá, for he was now definitely on his way to the south. What still needed to be done in the north he left to his deputies. He set out to fulfill his promise to the people of Quito. "The clang of your chains has challenged the army of liberty. It is marching on to Ecuador. Can you still doubt of your own freedom?"[43]

41 Cartas: Vol. II. p. 339.
42 Cartas: Vol. II. p. 410.
43 Proclamas: p. 268.

CHAPTER 24

The Chosen Son

$\mathcal{A}$t the threshold of the year 1822, a change took place in the life of Simon Bolivar. He had stepped into the sphere of continental decisions, and his area of activity henceforth was to be the entire southwestern hemisphere. The continental idea had been the deciding factor in all his plans and aspirations ever since he had written the letter from Jamaica. But what had then been a vision, and what for the present continued to be a vision, nevertheless now neared reality. The destruction of a world empire had been a beginning. Now the liberated Americans were to be united in a new order of justice and self-government.

Immediately after the liberation of Venezuela, Bolivar turned to O'Higgins in Chile and to San Martín in Lima. In that verbose rhetoric which was then the official language of the South American free states, he told them that his army would break the chains of enslaved nations wherever they should be found.[1] He invited the admiral of the Chilean fleet, Lord Cochrane, to sail to Panama and to lead the Colombian soldiers south to the arena of new conflicts.[2] The details of a common campaign, however, significant though they might be as long as Spanish forces fought on South American soil, were not his only consideration. Bolivar now worked to call

1 See Bolivar's letters to San Martín, Cartas: Vol. II. pp. 380, 382, and B. d. H. Caracas. Vol. XXV. No. 97. p. 38.
2 Cartas: Vol. II. pp. 380, 381. B. d. H. Caracas. Vol. XXVI. No. 102. p. 108.

444

to life that international organism in which the people of South America were to find majestic representation before the world.

He named two emissaries extraordinary — extraordinary, because there could be no official representatives as yet — to pave the way for his ideas in both the north and the south. Miguel Santamaría was sent to Mexico and Joaquín Mosquera, to Peru, Chile, and Buenos Aires. The instructions Bolivar gave to Mosquera contained the program of his continental policy.[3] At this moment nothing seemed so important as the formation of an American league. But this federation was not to meet simply in accordance with the principles of an ordinary alliance for offence or defense. With the liberation of man as its goal, it was to be more closely bound than the Holy Alliance, whose policies had been directed against the freedom of the world. Bolivar wanted an alliance of sister nations wherein each would exercise its own sovereignty, but in which all would unite against any attacks from without. A congress of authorized ministers was to be called to promote common interests and to suppress all conflicts between the nations as they arose.[4]

Bolivar had long ago chosen Panama as the haven for the American federation. While he was still trying to lay its foundations, he also prepared for the building of the Panama Canal. Instructions to his deputy, Mosquera, bore on other matters than the federation. They contained the general basis for the formation of the South American states. All republics were to retain the territorial status which they had had at the outbreak of the independence movement in 1810. Only where they had voluntarily decided on greater unity, as in Colombia, would new boundaries be respected by the other American nations. Bolivar's international idea was clearly expressed in these proposals. It was his intention to build a league of South American free states around the nucleus of the Greater Colombian Republic.

3 F. J. Urrutia: El ideal internacional de Bolívar in Simón Bolívar. Madrid, 1914. pp. 199 ff. Restrepo: H. d. R. C. Vol. III. p. 162.
4 O'Leary: Doc. Vol. XIX. pp. 124, 170. Blanco: Doc. Vol. VIII. p. 70.

These were new and ambitious ideas in whose realization few men other than Bolivar believed at the beginning of the nineteenth century. Such novel propositions, unprecedented by example or tradition in the history of the modern world, were not likely to be realized merely by dispatching diplomatic delegations. Bolivar believed that in the last analysis only he, at the head of his army, could impose such ideas. One of the problems that endangered the union of the South American peoples was the question of governmental form. Bolivar was a republican, and he was convinced that the republic was the proper governmental form for South America. He knew, however, that not all men thought as he did, for monarchistic tradition was deeply rooted in the hearts and habits of the continent. Many men held that a compromise between independence and monarchism was a possible, even a desirable, solution. San Martín had but recently made a suggestion to the Peruvian Viceroy that Peru be made into a constitutional monarchy.[5] Similar movements were under way in Mexico, where some persons spoke of calling a Bourbon prince to the throne. A monarchy either to the south or the north would, in Bolivar's opinion, be a serious threat to Colombia.

Bolivar apprised his representatives in Bogotá and Caracas of this danger, and asked them to defend the Colombian idea of state against the gathering storm. What to him seemed even more important, however, was the final expulsion of the Spaniards from the continent and the mutual rapprochment of the South American peoples, and his decision to accomplish this end spurred Bolivar's resolution to go beyond the borders of Colombia in 1822 and to begin the political shaping of the continent.

Bolivar was inclined to identify his existence with an historic constellation wherein he alone was destined to create the South American federation of states, and he did not wish anyone to precede him in attempting to form such a union. Occasionally he betrayed this presumption in his diplo-

5 Restrepo: H. d. R. C. Vol. III. pp. 122 ff. O'Leary: Doc. Vol. XVIII. p. 517.

matic correspondence. If he wrote to San Martín, "After the welfare of Colombia, nothing concerns me so much as the success of your arms," he was actually more sincere than many statesmen might be.[6] Yes, San Martín's success did concern him. Certainly it was not unwelcome as long as it contributed to America's freedom, but Bolivar was deeply interested in winning the final victory himself. As he was preparing his expedition to the south, he said to Santander, "Be careful, my friend, that you have four to five thousand men for me, so that Peru yields me two victories like Boyacá and Carabobo. I do not wish to go if glory does not follow me. . . . I do not wish to lose the fruits of eleven years through one defeat, and I do not wish San Martín to see me other than I deserve to be seen, namely as the chosen son."[7]

Bolivar really considered himself the chosen son of fate, and he took care that no one should lift the star of fame from his brow. Originally Bolivar had planned to attack Panama after the liberation of Venezuela. From there he wanted to lead his expeditionary corps along the Pacific coast to Guayaquil by boat.[8] But the fear that San Martín might be quicker than he, that Peru might be liberated, and that Ecuador might possibly be annexed to Peru made him turn toward the south.

General Montilla and young Padilla had captured Cartagena, and Bolivar now ordered Montilla to undertake the campaign against Panama. Here, too, the course of events came to the aid of the Patriots when the population of the Isthmus rose against Spain. On November 28, 1821, a council consisting of officials, army officers, and clergy met and declared Panama independent, and announced its desire to unite with Colombia. The Republic had increased its domain without bloodshed. It now totalled eight departments, the most recent addition being of the greatest strategic importance.

Bolivar could have reached out toward the Caribbean from

6 Cartas: Vol. II. p. 380.
7 Cartas: Vol. II. p. 374. The expression "hijo predilecto" was first applied by Santander in praise of Bolivar.
8 Cartas: Vol. II. p. 406. O'Leary: Doc. Vol. XVIII. pp. 568, 578, 586.

Panama, since a thrust toward Cuba or Puerto Rico had now
become possible. Nevertheless, he continued to look to the
south. An encounter with San Martín was inevitable, and,
under the circumstances, it was necessary for Bolivar to take
both a military and a legal position. Preparations to assure this
position had long been under way. There was no one in the
army whom Bolivar trusted more nor whom he considered
better fitted to solve the problems about to be faced than General Sucre, who at the beginning of the year had been sent to
Guayaquil.

A few months before Sucre had gone south, Bolivar's adjutant, O'Leary, had seen him at headquarters and had asked
the Liberator, "Who is that poor rider?" Bolivar replied, "That
is one of the best officers in the army. He combines Soublette's
professional knowledge with the kindliness of Briceño, the
talent of Santander with the energy of Salom. Strange as it
may seem, people do not know or even suspect his abilities. I
am determined to draw him into the light, and I am convinced
that some day he will be my rival." [9]

Antonio José Sucre de Alcalá was born in the eastern part
of Venezuela. The family originally came from Flanders and
belonged to the Walloon nobility.[10] In keeping with the position of his family, young Sucre had received a good education
at the University of Caracas, and at sixteen he had joined the
Republican army. He fought under Miranda and after the
collapse of 1812 retired to his paternal home in Cumaná, where
he remained but briefly. During the Spanish persecution he
fled to Trinidad, coming back to the mainland with Mariño in
1813. Even at this time he was known as one of the bravest
men in the Republican army. He had undergone all the catastrophes of the Patriots with as imperturbable a demeanor as
Bolivar himself. In 1815 he went to Cartagena and helped the
besieged city defend itself against Morillo. He had escaped the

9 O'Leary: Memorias. Vol. II. p. 67. Lecuna: La question de Guayaquil y la
campaña de Pichincha. B. d. H. Caracas. Vol. XXV. No. 100. p. 336.
    10 M. Vegas del Castillo: Sobre la Genealogía del Mariscal Sucre. Rev. Belga,
June, 1944. Primeras armas de Sucre. B. d. H. Caracas. Vol. V. No. 20. p. 825.

wrath of the conquering Spaniards by fleeing across the Caribbean, but a storm in which most of his companions had been drowned wrecked his ship. Fortunately Sucre was a good swimmer; he had clung to a trunk for twenty hours and had finally been picked up half dead from exposure and thirst. Since that year the twenty-one year old lad had been in the front ranks of the Republican staff. In Bolivar's opinion he was even at that time the soul of the army.[11]

Sucre was short and slender, with a wide-arched brow, black hair, and brown eyes that held a gentle, thoughtful expression. His face revealed more the courtier than the warrior, more the philosopher than the officer, but his personality combined these characteristics. Dignity without affectation, loyalty without subservience, made up his nature. Tactful and sincere, trusting but realistic, he surpassed Páez, Mariño, and Bermúdez in every way. Sucre was a self-contained man who was out of sympathy with the exhibitionism of his tropical companions-in-arms. Like most introverts he was sensitive and easily hurt, and an exaggerated, almost childish sensitivity was his most outstanding weakness.

He was destined to win the two greatest victories for the Republic. Bolivar called him the Man of War, just as he had called Santander the Man of Law, but Sucre was more than a good warrior, for he also knew how to advise. As a general one might compare him with those great imperturbables, Washington, Moltke, and Foch. Without any feeling of rivalry, without jealousy or moodiness, he did what fell to him to do with sagacity, courage, and skill. "Sucre," said Bolivar, "is in all things a nobleman. He has the best organized mind in Colombia. He is systematic and capable of great ideas. He is the best general of the Republic and its first statesman. His principles are excellent and sound, his morals above reproach. He

---

11 L. Villanueva: Vida de Sucre. Caracas, 1945. E. López Contreras: Sucre. Caracas, 1945. J. A. Cova: Sucre. Caracas, 1938. A. Jaureguy: Sucre. La Paz, 1928. G. A. Otero: El Hombre del Tiempo Heróico. La Paz, 1925. J. Oropesa: Sucre. Santiago de Chile, 1937. M. Ancizar: Sucre. Bogotá, 1895. G. Sherwell: A. J. de Sucre. Caracas, 1924.

has a great and strong soul. He understands how to convince
men and how to lead them. . . . He is the bravest of the brave,
the truest of the true, friend of law and order, enemy of anarchy
and a true liberal. . . ."[12] Bolivar saw in him his successor,
although he realized that Sucre was not popular. The relationship between these two men in a world of ingratitude and
disloyalty was really exceptional, and, aside from occasional
moments of doubt, it remained free from all dross. Bolivar did
not begrudge him his fame, and Sucre asked only for the friendship of the Liberator as a reward for his efforts. His pliable,
receptive personality took up Bolivar's ideas and made them
his own, and his porous, almost feminine temperament, permeated with the inspirations of the greater man, found satisfaction
in being the executor of these ideas. Sucre was the only one
who completely understood Bolivar's American concepts, the
only one who would have been capable of carrying the torch
after the Liberator's death.

The assignment Bolivar had given Sucre in the south would
have been worthy of the Liberator. His mission was to support
the revolution in Guayaquil and to complete the annexation of
Ecuador to Colombia. When Sucre arrived at his destination,
he saw that Bolivar had sent him into a jungle. The impenetrable landscape spread before him, and he realized that neither
politically nor militarily was a way open to him.[13]

The revolutionists of Guayaquil had, in their first enthusiasm, hoped to penetrate inland and to be able to take the
capital, Quito, but the Spanish governor, Aymerich, was at his
post. He had completely destroyed the army that had advanced
from the coast in November, 1820. Only with great effort had
the Patriots maintained their position. Such was the situation
when Sucre arrived in the south with one thousand men.[14]

The military situation caused great anxiety, but the political

12 D. d. B. p. 238. Cartas: Vol. IV. p. 264.
13 De la Rosa: Firmas. pp. 170, 180, 222. O'Leary: Doc. Vol. XVIII, and XIX
passim. Arch. Santander. Vol. VI. p. 81.
14 N. Rincón: El Libertador Simón Bolívar en la campaña de Pasto. Pasto, 1922.
pp. 25, 38. R. Negret: La campaña del Sur y la Batalla de Bombona. Bogotá, 1922.

situation was labyrinthine and tortuous. The Monarchists were
not Sucre's only enemies; the inhabitants of Guayaquil and
the rulers of Peru also endangered the success of his mission.
The annexation to Colombia was not popular, since some
wanted the full independence of the city and others were more
inclined toward a union with Peru. Moreover, San Martín,
who was ruling in Lima at this time, regarded the latter solutions with approval. He had sent two of his co-workers to the
port to make propaganda for the annexation of Peru.[15]

The Patriots of Guayaquil knew that they could not hold
out without Bolivar's help. They grasped the outstretched
hand of Colombia in the hope of being able to let it go when
the storm was over, but Bolivar was determined to throttle the
lust for independence in a fraternal embrace. Sucre moved
cautiously over the quicksands of this situation. In May, 1821,
he signed a pact of friendship with the government council of
Guayaquil which assured him the support of his troops and
gave him the title of Commander-in-Chief of the Colombian
Aide Corps. The question of annexation was not mentioned,
and the wisdom of this omission was soon demonstrated.[16] The
Monarchists in Guayaquil were by no means without power,
and in July the adherents of Spain made an attempt at an uprising. The movement collapsed, but Sucre's position was not
greatly improved. With traitors at his back, rivals at his side,
and enemies before him, he had hardly a chance to draw his
breath.

In order to advance toward Quito, which like Bogotá, lies
twenty-six hundred meters above sea level, Sucre would have
had to risk a march across the Cordilleras, but he lacked the
equipment for such an adventure, not even possessing horse-
shoes to save his horses. He concluded, therefore, that it would
be wiser to leave the offensive to his opponent. Aymerich met
the situation by making the daring descent into the hot coastal

15 O'Leary: Doc. Vol. XIX. p. 57. See also, Arch. Santander: Vol. VI. p. 336.
Restrepo: H. d. R. C. Vol. III. p. 177. Mitre: San Martín. Vol. III. p. 582.
16 O'Leary: Doc. Vol. XIX. pp. 40, 42, 44. Blanco: Doc. Vol. VII. p. 581.

regions. He sent three thousand men in two divisions to march
on Guayaquil by separate roads. Sucre saw through the Spanish
plan. His forces scarcely equalled one half of the Royalists, but
with a swift, bold stroke, he defeated one division of Aymerich
and forced the other to retreat.[17] He believed he could now
achieve victory, and he let himself be persuaded into a hasty
march against Quito. The Spaniards, however, forced him to
do battle and turned the Colombian victories into a complete
rout. Sucre escaped with only one hundred men. Spain could
have made an easy conquest of Guayaquil at this time, but
though she did not lack courage for such an undertaking, she
did lack initiative. Two months passed before she decided to
take the offensive.

Meanwhile, Sucre had filled his gaps with the first men
available. He did not want to risk a battle; even to resist a
siege he felt was beyond his power. In Bolivar's school he had
learned that that man only is defeated who accepts defeat. When
the Monarchists offered him an armistice on November 21 he
signed it, and in this manner saved his position in Guayaquil.[18]

It was obvious that the Spaniards also drew some advantage
from the armistice. Despite revolution and constitutional monarchy, despite grave losses and serious defeats, the Spaniards
were not reconciled to the fact that their overseas domain was
now supported by single, isolated columns. Again and again
dauntless men, prototypes of the early conquerors like Cortez
and Pizarro, went across the ocean to gain possession of
America for the second time in behalf of His Catholic Majesty.
To the generation of imperturbables belonged General Juan
de la Cruz Murgéon, who had just been appointed Governor
of New Granada on the assumption that he would be able to
gain control over the lands that came under his title.

Murgéon had first gone to Panama, and had equipped an
army with which he landed in Ecuador at the end of 1821. He

17 De la Rosa: Firmas. p. 262. Arch. Santander: Vol. VII. p. 111. Restrepo:
H. d. R. C. Vol. III. pp. 171-72.
18 O'Leary: Memorias. Vol. II. p. 119. O'Leary: Doc. Vol. XVIII. p. 602,
Vol. XIX. p. 83. Arch. Santander. Vol. VII. p. 236. De la Rosa: Firmas. pp. 308-10.

crossed the Cordilleras by side trails with one thousand men, reaching Quito on December 24. Here he learned that Panama had deserted the cause of Spain, and he realized that with this event the Spanish colonies on the Pacific coast were cut off from all reinforcements from the mother country. Murgéon survived this failure of his great hopes by only a few months and his loss was felt, but the troops which he had led to Aymerich increased the Royal army to the extent that Quito could now be held against Sucre's forces. In the north the mountain passes of Pasto formed a barrier on which, ever since the outbreak of the revolution, every attack of the Patriots had been shattered. Thus little Ecuador was like a fortress which made the walls of the Andes unassailable. Bolivar set out for the south on December 13, 1821, with the intention of breaking through this impasse.[19]

Students of European history may at this point feel tempted to evaluate the campaign with a shrug of the shoulders. They may say, "Oh, another war without weapons and without soldiers!" But only he who takes into consideration the small number of fighters and then multiplies them by the miles they covered, by the hazards of nature, and by the failure of industry to produce equipment, will have a true concept of Bolivar's deeds. The main stem of the army which Bolivar led to the south, called the Guardia Colombiana, after the Napoleonic guard, once more marched the hundreds of kilometers from the Atlantic coast to the southern edge of Colombia.

Bolivar had chosen the capital of the Cauca Valley, Cali, as his headquarters. From this point he could reach the Pacific near Buenaventura or he could march inland via Popayán to Pasto. His first idea was to join Sucre in Guayaquil, and he had instructed Sucre to transport ships to Buenaventura for two thousand men.[20] Bolivar was ready to depart and had already written to the politicians of Guayaquil that Colombia

19 O'Leary: Doc. Vol. XIX. p. 111. Cartas Santander: Vol. I. p. 151. Lecuna: Campaña de Bombona. B. d. H. Caracas. Vol. XXV. No. 99. p. 215.
20 Cartas: Vol. III. p. 3. Proclamas: p. 270. Arch. Santander. Vol. VII. p. 256.

was unwilling to give up the fruits of her sacrifices, and that he would never give his consent to a union between Guayaquil and any other state than Colombia. But Bolivar was obliged to give up this first plan when he learned that a Spanish fleet was on the Pacific coast. He knew that his convoy could be destroyed by such a fleet and that he would run the danger of falling into enemy hands.[21] He decided with a heavy heart to abandon the idea of invading Ecuador from the sea; only the land route remained, and over this an evil star had hung since the first days of the revolution.

Pasto is the only large town between Popayán and Quito, and the entire region is called by the same name. Pasto was the Vendée of the South American revolution.[22] It was an inland country without communications or trade, and here a tough, stubborn, and fanatic race of men had developed. The clergy wielded complete power over the people, and had encouraged the growth of many primitive and outworn superstitions. The inhabitants of Pasto believed that the King of Spain and God were one person and that the Republic was the work of the devil. For ten years the Pastoans had fought for their King with a sacrificial passion not to be found in any other region of South America. They were the first to arm and the last to lay down their arms; neither terror nor cruelty was able to bend their stubborn will. Bolivar had to break their determined resistance and he dreaded the task. "Our cavalry will arrive without horses; our belongings will be lost. We shall need bread; cattle will be scarce, for the exhausted animals will get lost on the way. There will be innumerable diseases, because the rainy season is the worst time. Desertions will not cease as we have already learned. Then there are the enemy's advantages . . . he has four thousand men, a number I cannot raise, and these four thousand men will be well rested and in favorable position. I see clearly that we must fight the impossible, for I can alter neither the nature of this land nor that of these weak people."[23]

21 Cartas: Vol. III. p. 7. O'Leary: Doc. Vol. XIX. p. 122.
22 A. Galindo: Las Batallas decisivas de la Libertad. Bogotá, 1936. p. 342.
23 Cartas: Vol. III. p. 8.

The decision to march against Pasto robbed Bolivar of many a night's sleep, and he sought various diplomatic expedients to avoid the hazardous campaign. He tried to win over the fanatical bishop of Popayán, who had fled to Pasto, by telling him that the ruling party in Spain had become enemies of the church and haters of the priests. "Everything has changed," he wrote, "and you also must change." The prelate ignored his message.[24] Even more fantastic was another ruse of Bolivar. He instructed Santander to forge documents and newspaper articles which were to state that the mother country had finally acknowledged Colombian independence. By means of these papers he hoped to influence the Spanish commandant in Pasto and to convince him that it would be wise to give Ecuador over to Bolivar without a struggle.[25] Santander manufactured the desired documents with a skill that did honor to his stylistic abilities, but the Spanish officer had been washed by many waters, and he read the forgeries with scorn. "All is not gold that glitters," was his caustic message to Bolivar. The idea of surrender never occurred to him.

Finally, after a month of waiting, Bolivar had no recourse but to attack Pasto. Possibly the resistance of the people might have been broken down, but nature herself seemed to conspire to impede Bolivar. The difficulties he had overcome in the past appeared slight compared with those that loomed ahead. This war would be fought in a mountainous region where the snow-covered crests rose to a height of six thousand meters. On their slopes rushing streams had dug their beds deep into the narrow gulleys. Naked, steep rock walls, slippery paths, and a deadly climate changing from extreme heat to cold made Pasto an almost impregnable town. The territory over which Bolivar had to fight reached from Cali to Guayaquil, and in the center, at a height of eighteen hundred meters lay the plains of Pasto. Two treacherous streams with powerful falls cut through this country, in the north the Juanambu and in the south the Guai-

24 Cartas: Vol. III. p. 17.
25 Cartas: Vol. III. pp. 10-13, 24-25. These falsifications were so well executed that they were published as authentic in O'Leary's documents. Vol. XIX. p. 144.

tara. On the plateau of Pasto runs the only road that leads from
Popayán to Quito, and Bolivar could not avoid it. Even today
it is the most important connection between Colombia and Ecuador. The modern traveller who must spend an entire day on
the journey from Popayán to Pasto, proceeding from one abyss
to another, can measure the hazards which Bolivar had to overcome a century ago.

The Spaniards knew that their positions were unassailable,
and their leader had promised to destroy the Patriots and to
humble Bolivar. Don Basilio García had been fighting for
twelve years against American freedom. He had risen from the
ranks and his enemies said that he had once been a galley slave.
He was a brave officer who knew every nook and cranny of this
terrain, and since December, reckoning on an attack by Bolivar, he had entrenched himself in the hills that overlook Pasto.[26]

Bolivar went south at the beginning of March with three
thousand men, crossing the valley of Patia, which is known for
its murderous climate. With thirty men falling ill each day,
the ordeal of a month's march became a serious matter. Spanish guerrilla troops drove away the cattle and burned the farms
in advance of the Patriots, and then remained to harass Bolivar's rear guard. He lost almost one thousand men and begged
urgently for reinforcements.[27] On March 29 he crossed the
Juanambu, and while the army was recovering from the hardships of the past weeks, Bolivar himself assumed charge of
reconnaissance.[28]

The Royalists, who had offered little resistance to Bolivar's
crossing of the Juanambu, kept the hills above the Guitara
occupied by eighteen hundred men. Although their position was unassailable, Bolivar, nevertheless, decided to force
a crossing. If he did not make this attempt he would be obliged
to admit defeat and to retreat. He declared that the position

26 Rincón: *op. cit.* p. 26. López: Recuerdos. pp. 18 ff. Larrazabal: Vol. II. p.
121.
27 Arch. Santander: Vol. VIII. p. 3. Rincón: *op. cit.* p. 143. Restrepo: H. d.
R. C. Vol. III. p. 190.
28 López: Recuerdos. p. 64. Larrazabal: Vol. II. p. 119. Rincón: p. 144.

of the enemy was extraordinary, but maintained that his forces could not remain in position nor could they withdraw. He vowed that his army would and should win.[29]

The battle fought on April 7 has gone down in history as the Battle of Bombona. The day was far advanced when Bolivar gave orders to attack. General Valdés was to surround the left wing of the Spaniards by climbing the rocks and hills which protected their position. Meanwhile, the main section of the army under General Torres was to attack the Spanish center without delay. It was past noon, and there was no time for either rest or food. Torres, however, misunderstanding Bolivar's orders, allowed his men to halt and relax. Bolivar, in an excess of rage at this apparent insubordination, demanded that Torres give up his command. The accused General dismounted, broke his sword in two, and cried, "Liberator, if I am not worthy to serve my country as a general, I can at least serve her as a grenadier." The impetuous Bolivar immediately embraced him and returned him to rank.[30]

The battle began toward two-thirty o'clock, when only about four hours of daylight remained, since night in the tropics begins at six. The Spaniards defended the hills with guns and rifle fire, and the losses of the Patriots became terrific. Torres and many of the high-ranking Republican officers were fatally wounded. Bolivar, watching his battalion attack, remarked proudly, "How well my people go into battle!" but a comrade replied, "Yes, but they do not return."[31] The battle was one of the bloodiest of the war. After three hours Bolivar saw that the encirclement of the enemy had succeeded, and he hurled his troops once again at the enemy's center. The Spaniards did not give way. Night had fallen and neither side could continue fighting between the rocks and crevasses that made up the battlefield.

29 Larrazabal: Vol. II. p. 123.
30 Larrazabal: Vol. II. p. 123. Rincón: p. 148. Lecuna: Campaña de Bombona. *passim*.
31 O'Leary: Doc. Vol. XIX. pp. 236, 241. O'Leary: Memorias. Vol. II. pp. 135 ff. Rincón: p. 149.

The Battle of Bombona gave no victory to either side, but if one is to place the advantage, it lay with the Spaniards. Bolivar's losses were many times greater than those of García. He had sacrificed one-third of his men and he had not come one step nearer his goal. On the following day the Spanish Colonel sent him two Colombian flags which had been taken during the battle. In his message to Bolivar, he said that he did not want to keep the trophies of an enemy whom he could destroy but whom he could not conquer. In the same letter he suggested that Bolivar withdraw to Popayán since he had failed to take Pasto. Bolivar construed this gesture of the Spaniard as an attempt to come to an understanding, and he began negotiations in the hope of gaining time. García and Bolivar each considered himself the victor, and each attempted to deceive the other about his weaknesses. Neither, however, believed in his enemy's assurances. Both knew only too well that the strong need no words to win. Nine days after the Battle of Bombona, Bolivar renounced the idea of taking Pasto. Pasto had proved to him that it would not be taken.[32]

Bolivar did not escape censure for having attempted the impossible on April 7. The first Colombian historian has termed the Battle of Bombona an occasion of useless bloodshed.[33] As a single action it was unsuccessful, but in any comprehensive view of the campaign it is clear that it had a definite value. Bolivar had planned a double move: while he was pushing across the mountains into Quito, Sucre was to march inland from the sea. Both arms of the prong were then to meet in Quito. As we have noted, Bolivar was checked at Pasto, but he had drawn the best part of the Spanish troops upon himself. Even now García felt compelled to watch his movements closely. Under these circumstances Sucre's offensive was considerably facilitated.

After a year of misfortune, General Sucre was finally to come into luck, the kind of luck indicated by Moltke when he

---

32 Cartas: Vol. III. pp. 33-34. O'Leary: Memorias. Vol. II. p. 139.
33 Restrepo: H. d. R. C. Vol. III. p. 217. Rincón: p. 177.

said that only a capable man could enjoy it for any length of time. Sucre had long since prepared for the coöperation of the Argentine-Peruvian soldiers in the liberation of Quito. At the beginning of 1822, about one thousand men had come to him from neighboring Peru, and this division under Colonel Santa Cruz had joined Sucre's army in February. With this additional strength Sucre crossed the Cordilleras in April, and with each day his army had pushed closer toward the capital of Ecuador.[34] The Spaniards thought their position secure, but Sucre resorted to a military ruse and his surprise maneuver was successful. On May 16 the snowy peaks that guard Quito loomed before the eyes of his army. He now stood at the Spaniard's back between Pasto and Quito and only four miles from the capital. The enemy waited confidently for Sucre to attack from the south, but on the morning of May 24 the Republican soldiers descended the back of Mt. Pichincha and advanced on Quito from the north. The Spaniards rushed to defend themselves, and at ten-thirty the battle for the liberation of Ecuador began. Colombians, Argentinians, and the soldiers of the British Legion fought with equal courage. Victory for the Republican forces was finally decided by a storm attack led by Colonel Córdoba at the head of the Magdalena regiment.[35]

On the following day Sucre entered the capital. The victory of Pichincha was as complete as Boyacá and Carabobo. Governor Aymerich surrendered himself and his country to the twenty-seven-year-old Republican officer. The capitulation included the capture of eleven hundred men and their equipment, but more important than any other consideration was the liberation of Ecuadorian soil as far as Pasto.

Pasto itself was no longer able to resist. The inhabitants were still fanatically determined to fight and die, or to commit suicide rather than allow Bolivar to enter their city. The authorities, however, realized that Pasto lay between two

34 O'Leary: Doc. Vol. XIX. p. 282. Documentos relativos a la campaña del Sur, dirigida por el general Sucre. Blanco: Doc. Vol. VIII. p. 272. Arch. Santander: Vol. VIII. pp. 174 ff. Mitre: San Martín. Vol. III. p. 559.
35 O'Leary: Memorias. Vol. II. p. 142. Blanco: Doc. Vol. VIII. pp. 407 ff. Lecuna: B. d. H. Caracas. Vol. XXV. No. 100. p. 385.

fires, and for this reason García decided on May 28 to surrender the city to Bolivar. The latter was still in ignorance of the victory of Pichincha, and García was wise enough to keep silent about Sucre's triumph until he had secured the best possible terms from the Republicans. On June 6 the surrender was concluded, promising safety to all Monarchists and even offering the friendship of the Liberator to García.[36] Bolivar marched into Pasto on June 8. He conducted himself at the meeting with Don Basilio as though García was a crusader, returning him his sword and marshal's staff and inviting him to his quarters. Only then did Bolivar learn that Quito had been liberated. He was delighted with the news of Sucre's triumph, but his joy was not unclouded, for he felt that fate had robbed him of his victor's laurels. He wrote to Santander in an attack of jealousy, "You must understand that it was by my request that García surrendered, for here no one knew anything about Sucre's battle, nor could we have known. For this reason I do not want Sucre to be given credit for the capitulation of García. In the first place Sucre has had enough fame; secondly, it is true, very true, that the capitulation had been decided upon without knowledge of Sucre's activities. It seems to me that it would be proper to write something about this in the State papers in which both our deeds are recorded. Sucre had a larger number of troops and a smaller number of enemies than I. The land was very favorable because of its people and because of the character of the terrain. We, on the other hand, found ourselves in a veritable hell and fought with the Devil. The victory of Bombona is greater than that of Pichincha. The losses in each were equal and the characters of the enemy leaders were not. General Sucre did not carry away any greater glory on the day of battle than I, and the surrender he received was not more complete than mine. . . . I believe that with a little tact one could honor my division very greatly without detracting from Sucre's."[37] But Bolivar did not yield for long to this

36 O'Leary: Doc. Vol. XIX. pp. 264, 269, 298. Rincón: *op. cit.* p. 215.
37 Cartas: Vol. III. pp. 37-38.

attack of jealousy. He recognized South America's debt to Sucre, and was prepared to reward Sucre with the government of the liberated land.

With that fervor of activity which characterized him, Bolivar had already gone on to new problems. He wanted to pacify Pasto, to incorporate Quito into the Republic, and to discuss the problem of Guayaquil with San Martín. The pacification of Quito was the most important issue at the moment. Bolivar paid heed to the fanatic faith of the Pastoans by ostentatiously attending the Te Deum which was being sung in the cathedral to celebrate the victory. He next turned to the Bishop of Popayán, a man who had done his utmost to incite this region and who had now offered his resignation. Bolivar, in a letter which is a masterpiece of diplomatic art glistening with holy oil, refused to consider the Bishop's sacrifice. What! he remonstrated, the eminent shepherd would desert the flock which the Lord Himself had entrusted to him? And for political reasons? Who, then, was to tend the vineyards? A bishop's duty was not to resign, but to wait until the papal chair should recognize Colombia as a sovereign state. In this manner Bolivar dealt with his erstwhile enemies and won their sympathies. In the case of the Bishop of Popayán, Colombia lost an opponent and the Liberator gained an admirer.[38] The stubborn people of Pasto were not so easily taken in. Bolivar's appeals had little effect. Their submission was only outward.

Bolivar now advanced on Quito by short stages, arriving on June 16. Here he encountered an entirely different atmosphere. Everyone, from the poorest Indian to the heads of the Creole aristocracy, rushed to the streets to welcome him. The public squares were decorated with triumphal arches, the houses with flowers and flags; bells rang out and rockets were sent up. Bolivar embraced Sucre, congratulated the men, saw deputations, and listened to speeches. In short, he relived all the intoxication of the victory which had accompanied his army for three years.[39]

38 Cartas: Vol. III. pp. 39-41.
39 O'Leary: Doc. Vol. XIX. p. 310.

While the Liberator was riding slowly through the city, someone threw him a laurel wreath from a balcony. Bolivar caught
it, and looking up, met a pair of glowing eyes. On that same
night, at a ball given in his honor, he met Manuela Saenz de
Thorne, she who had thrown the morning's wreath. This
meeting, however, belongs to another chapter.

The governmental form of Ecuador had long occupied
Bolivar's thoughts. One law in particular isolated the regions
which Bolivar had conquered from the sphere of parliamentary
power.[40] He had been given administrative authority to deal
with these lands as he saw fit. Bolivar did not want to divide
Ecuador into provinces because he thought such a division
would encourage separatism. He created, instead, a large department, Quito, and appointed General Sucre as president.[41] In
vain did the all too modest man protest that he lacked the gift
to rule. Bolivar knew better, and he knew that the masses
would worship Sucre. Bolivar's emotional condition, after so
many triumphs, is revealed in a letter to Santander: "You already know what a liberated capital is like, to which one must
give Colombian laws, in which many people and many Patriots
live, etc., etc., in other words, I have no time for anything. I
do not lack moments in which to write, but the thoughts of
what to do with such a great and beautiful country are too
numerous. What shall we do to keep the good will of the
people, to win Guayaquil, and to preserve harmony with
Peru?"[42]

Guayaquil had now become Bolivar's foremost problem. He
had received the message that the town was ready to accept
the Colombian Constitution, and he was eager to forge the steel
while it was still hot and while the enthusiasm over Bombona
and Pichincha still ran high. He was, however, undecided
as to whether such an annexation might be construed as a
hostile act against Peru. He was obliged to remember that Peru
had just given aid in the liberation of Ecuador.

40 Blanco: Doc. Vol. VIII. p. 148.
41 Cartas: Vol. III. pp. 43-44.
42 Cartas: Vol. III. pp. 45-46.

The tension between Peru and Colombia had increased dangerously during the campaign, and San Martín had once come very close to declaring war on Colombia. What would be the outcome if Bolivar now grasped at Guayaquil?[43] Despite all objections, Bolivar decided on a policy of boldness. Those who were favorably inclined were allowed to work for the annexation of Guayaquil. Bolivar, for his part, endeavored to win public opinion, but, anticipating the necessity of more vigorous measures, he began to send troops to the coast.[44] At the beginning of July he set out on the journey himself. The way led through one of the most glorious landscapes in the world. The contrast between the peaks of the Andes, with their crown of eternal snow, and the lushness of tropical nature inspired Bolivar. Nevertheless, the legend that he climbed Mt. Chimborazo in one day has no basis in fact. He would have had to be a demigod to have accomplished such a feat. Bolivar was never on Mt. Chimborazo, and the hymn he is said to have composed there is a forgery, and a poor forgery at that.[45]

Bolivar arrived in Guayaquil on July 11. He now faced one of the most fateful decisions of his life. He had completed the creation of the Colombian Republic in six months, but was he to be content with this achievement? Would Guayaquil be the last gable in that edifice whose foundation he had laid so long ago? His first great ambition had been the creation of the

43 De la Rosa: Firmas. pp. 362, 380 ff. Mitre: San Martín. Vol. III. p. 596. Lecuna: Question de Guayaquil. Vol. XXV. p. 358.

44 Cartas: Vol. III. pp. 52-53. A. M. Candiotti: Una Comunicación del Libertador. B. d. H. Bogotá. Vol. XXVIII. p. 107.

45 O'Leary: Memorias. Vol. II. p. 146. *Mi delirio sobre el Chimborazo* is considered by many South Americans as one of the great poetic compositions of the Liberator. Even Lecuna: Proclamas. p. 280, has included it in his collection. However there is no proof that Bolivar ever climbed Mount Chimborazo; neither he nor any one of his friends or aides mention such a feat. Bolivar could, of course, have written the "delirio" without having been on Mount Chimborazo, but the hymn differs completely from all his other productions. The style, vocabulary, and ideas are not Bolivar's, but those of an imitator. Moreover, the "delirio" was published after his death in Proclamas: Caracas, 1842, which makes its authenticity even more doubtful. Recently, in the Boletín de la Academia de Quito, No. 66, 1945, a manuscript which is claimed to be the original text of the "delirio" was published. However, the handwriting is not Bolivar's, nor does it belong to one of his secretaries, as Mr. Lecuna told me. See also, B. Sanin Cano: Letras Colombianas. México, 1944, p. 45.

Colombian state. This dream had been fulfilled on the fields of Bombona and Pichincha. If he now went to Guayaquil, it was because a higher destiny beckoned him. It was his desire to carry the banner of freedom to Lima and Potosí, and then to found the South American league. From this aspiration he drew the strength to lead his army through the continent like another Alexander.[46] Guayaquil in itself was not of paramount importance, but Bolivar knew that here he would meet San Martín. For two years the shadow of the Argentinian had fallen across his path, and Bolivar was now prepared to meet the man. He was determined to remain what he had hitherto been—fate's chosen son. His journey to Guayaquil signified that Colombia no longer satisfied him. The stage set for his coming performances was the wider stage of the South American continent.

46 Mitre: San Martín. Vol. IV. pp. 52 ff.

CHAPTER 25

The Guayaquil Meeting

*T*he middle of the year 1822 constituted the zenith of the South American Revolution. This was the solemn and portentous moment when the movements from the north and the south came together. Freedom had blazed a trail from the Caribbean Sea to the southern border of Ecuador. It had spread northward from the La Plata to the confines of Peru. Flowing inland from the shores of the Atlantic, both revolutionary currents had crossed the Andes and had finally met at the Pacific. Their forces had joined in Ecuador, and the threads of their fate had become intertwined in Guayaquil. The meeting with San Martín was the final step in a series of events that had mounted toward this occasion for twelve years.[1]

From Mexico to Cape Horn, Spanish America had liberated itself from the mother country. Only in isolated instances did the remnants of the Spanish army continue their useless fight against the Independents, and there now remained but one state to be liberated—the viceroyal kingdom of Peru. The conquest of this realm was Bolívar's present aim, and the Argentine-Chilean troops under San Martín were already on the ground. Peru was to be the point of juncture of that mighty movement which had liberated a continent. Peru was also the dividing line where the Colombian and Argentinian demands for hegemony were to be clarified.[2]

1 Mitre: San Martín. Vol. III. p. 542.
2 Mitre: San Martín. Chap. III. pp. 576-77. Groot: Vol. IV. p. 263.

The Argentinians had contributed to the liberation of Ecuador, and Bolivar acknowledged this obligation on the day he entered Quito in a letter to San Martín. "I feel the greatest satisfaction in announcing to Your Excellency that Colombia's war is ended, and that her army is ready to march on to wherever its brothers call, especially to the land of our southern neighbor."[3] San Martín replied that the victories of Bombona and Pichincha had sealed the union of Colombia and Peru, and that there remained only one battlefield in South America, namely, Peru.[4]

Bolivar made a sincere effort to establish closer relations with Colombia's sister nations. The Colombian ambassador at Lima, Joaquín Mosquera, made a perpetual agreement with San Martín's government, the general principles of which presented no difficulties. The attempt to draw Guayaquil into the territory of the Colombian Republic, however, evoked the protests of the Peruvian minister. Peru wanted this port for herself, and hence suggested that Guayaquil be offered a choice of nationality. The Colombian foreign minister neither could nor would consent to such a proposition, for Bolivar's instructions on this point were clear and explicit.[5] At first this thorny problem was circumvented when both sides agreed that a later special covenant should regulate the borders between the two states.

In the dispute over Guayaquil which ensued, San Martín subscribed to the principle of nonintervention in the hope of gaining the port for Peru. Bolivar, on the other hand, proposed that Colombia should intervene. He made no secret of his attitude, writing to San Martín, "I do not believe with Your Excellency that the voice of a province must be heard before national sovereignty can be established, for not any one part, but the people as a whole deliberate these matters freely and lawfully in general assembly." Bolivar did not promise San Martín a

3 Cartas: Vol. III. p. 42.
4 Mitre: San Martín. Vol. III. p. 576. O'Leary: Doc. Vol. XIX. p. 335.
5 O'Leary: Doc. Vol. XIX. p. 324. Blanco: Doc. Vol. VIII. p. 453. Restrepo:
H. d. R. C. Vol. III. p. 224.

plebiscite, but he agreed that the people were to be asked for their opinion. Moreover, he expected definite results from the personal meeting with San Martín which now merely awaited the convenience of both men. "The interests of a small province cannot halt the majestic gait of South America. I look forward eagerly to the discussions which Your Excellency has deigned to suggest."[6]

Bolivar made certain preparations for this encounter, first, in his effort to put an end to anarchy in Guayaquil. The advocates of an independent Guayaquil were basing their hopes on the Argentinian division which had fought at Pichincha. The division's purpose in coming to Quito had not been the liberation of Quito alone, and if the division could have returned to Guayaquil in time, it would have taken all the Separatists under its protection. The Peruvian fleet was also on its way to Guayaquil.[7] Bolivar, however, apprehended San Martín's real intentions and succeeded in frustrating them by holding the Argentinian troops before Quito and by sending the Colombian army to Guayaquil. He arrived at the port himself almost simultaneously with his army.

A state of indescribable chaos reigned in the city. The streets were crowded with the followers of all three parties, as each man tried to outshout the opposition, and cries of "Long live independence!" mingled with cheers for Peru and Colombia. The Council of Guayaquil had no intention of giving up its designs for independence, but Bolivar left no doubt that from now on he would steer the course of events. In his customary manner he made an appeal to the masses, declaring that all provinces of the south were under the aegis of freedom and Colombian law. "You alone find yourselves in a false and ambiguous position. You are threatened with anarchy. I bring you salvation." He was, he told them, convinced that they wished to be Colombians, but he promised them a plebiscite so

---

6 Cartas: Vol. III. pp. 50-52. Bolivar's letter is the answer to a note of San Martín of March 3, 1822. See, Lecuna: B. d. H. Caracas. Vol. XXV. p. 488.

7 O'Leary: Memorias. Vol. II. p. 150. C. Destruge: Guayaquil en la Campaña Libertadora del Perú. Guayaquil, 1924.

that the world might have proof that every Colombian loved his country and her laws. He asked for a general vote to sanction the incorporation of Guayaquil in the Colombian Republic.[8]

This decisive vote was not to take place until the end of July, but it was clear to everyone that it would merely constitute an approval of a *fait accompli*. Meanwhile, the spirit of controversy became more tense with each passing day. In front of Bolivar's house the flag of Guayaquil was torn down by his followers, and the Colombian colors hoisted. The mob cheered Bolivar, and the ships that lay in the harbor fired salutes. The members of the City Council, fearing that their lives and their estates were endangered, fled in terror before the excited masses. Bolivar disapproved of these excesses in public, but in private he encouraged them, knowing that the moment when he should exploit this anarchy and confusion would give him control of the situation. At the opportune time he announced to the Council that he would have to assume all civil and military powers in order to prevent greater evils, but that this step would in no way influence the freedom of the people.[9]

In this manner the annexation of Guayaquil was accomplished, and Bolivar declared himself dictator of the controversial province. He had entered the city on July 12; on the twenty-fourth he celebrated his thirty-ninth birthday. One day later General San Martín arrived on a Chilean warship.

The meeting between Bolivar and San Martín has always fired the imagination of the South American people. Not only was it a meeting between the two greatest men of the South American Revolution wherein each could take the other's measure, but it became the proving ground for the question of Peru's national obligations. The meeting at Guayaquil has often inspired comparisons which, in the manner of Plutarch, present the lives of these men as both harmonious and discordant. Such descriptions are both fascinating and mislead-

8 Proclamas: p. 275.
9 O'Leary: Memorias. Vol. II. p. 156. O'Leary: Doc. Vol. XIX. pp. 347 ff.

ing. Their natures were essentially different, and the true and only parallel between them lies in the directive force of their life's work.[10]

San Martín and Bolivar, Buenos Aires and Caracas, are the focal points of that great ellipse that circumscribes the South American Revolution. A short sketch of San Martín's career will facilitate an understanding of the sense and content of their meeting.[11]

San Martín was born on February 25, 1778, in Japeguy, a little town that belonged to the viceregal kingdom of the La Plata. His father belonged to the high officialdom of the colonial government. San Martín was taken to Spain when he was still a small boy and there remained for twenty-seven years. His childhood, his youth, his military and political training he owed to Europe and to Spain, but we feel no doubt that he cherished a memory and a secret love for America.[12]

In Spain, San Martín entered the Royal Academy for the education of nobility. He became a cadet and at an early age was appointed adjutant to General Solano. In an undistinguished campaign against Portugal he had his trial by fire, and later ascended the ladder of military promotions by gradual steps. The occupation of Spain by Napoleon furnished him with one of the great impressions of his life. He had watched how the excited mob had killed his commanding officer and had dragged him through the streets, and the memory of this cruel scene never left San Martín. He was even then a convinced liberal, but he also scorned the masses and their impulses. In spite of this apparent conflict in his ideals, San Martín fought for the freedom of the Spanish people against French imperial-

10 Mitre: San Martín. Vol. III. p. 603. Blanco: Doc. Vol. VIII. p. 495. Vol. XIV. p. 491. O'Leary: Memorias. Vol. II. p. 168. Larrazabal: Vol. II. p. 151.

11 J. P. Otero: Historia de San Martín. Buenos Aires, 1932. See, Bibliographie in Vol. IV. E. García del Real: San Martín. Madrid, 1932. R. Azpurúa: Biografía de hombres notables de Hispanoamérica. Vol. I. Caracas, 1877. J. M. Gutiérrez: San Martín. Buenos Aires, 1863. R. Vicuña MacKenna: El general San Martín. Santiago, 1902. D. F. Sarmiento: Obras completas. Paris, 1909. Vol. III. pp. 297 ff. W. Dietrich: Belgrano y San Martín. Santiago, 1943. San Martín: Correspondencia. Museo hist. nacional. Buenos Aires. 1910-1911.

12 M. Leguizamón: La casa natal de San Martín. Buenos Aires, 1925.

ism; and when, in the Battle of Bailén, he distinguished himself, he was promoted to Lieutenant-Colonel. However, when news arrived that the moment for independence had flared up in his native country of Argentina, he decided to leave the Spanish service.

The Argentinian writer, Sarmiento, calls attention to the surprising fact that many of the South American Revolutionists received their first political training in Spain—Miranda, Bolivar, San Martín, Belgrano, to mention but a few. More than four hundred South Americans were living in Spain at that time, distributed among the army, the schools, the courts, and trade. The report of the outbreak of revolution filled them with jubilation, and they began at once to organize secret societies. There was a Free Mason Lodge, with all the forms and trappings of the order, called *La Logia de Lautaro,* or the Society of Lautaro. Its influence on the Argentinian Revolution cannot be ignored. In contrast to Bolivar, who ridiculed lodges even though he was himself a mason, San Martín had always taken these organizations seriously and had followed their instructions with care, although he preferred to have his membership remain a secret.[13] He decided to go to America and travelled to Argentina by way of England. Arriving in Buenos Aires in March, 1812, he offered his services to the Revolution.

San Martín was assigned the organization of the mounted grenadiers, and trained his army, man for man and officer for officer, with all the patience, discipline, and toughness he had learned in the armies of Europe. An early victory of his troops at San Lorenzo showed the effectiveness of thorough military training.[14] San Martín, however, was not interested in individual victories; his ideas were directed toward the liberation of South America, and he wanted to direct operations from a base in Buenos Aires as Bolivar had done from Caracas. He

13 M. F. Paz Soldán: Historia del Perú Independiente. Lima, 1868. Vol. I. p. 227. Blanco: Doc. Vol. III. p. 603. E. Gouchon La Masonería y la Independencia de América. Valparaíso, 1927. R. A. Zuñiga: La Logia Lautaro y la Independencia. Buenos Aires, 1922. B. Oviedo Martínez: La Logia Lautariana. B. d. H. Caracas. Vol. XII. No. 48. p. 436.

14 C. Smith: San Martín hasta el paso de los Andes. Buenos Aires, 1928.

had evolved the design for a continental campaign, and he carried out his plans in the face of all opposition. San Martín believed that the key to liberty lay in Peru. To understand the logic of his thinking, one need only compare certain salient points of the situation. The Spaniards had feebly defended the lands of the La Plata because of their slight economic importance. In an age that knew no grand scale overseas transports, the products of the pampas were of little value. On the other hand, the precious metals of Peru represented even then the vital element of Spanish economy. With a thorough comprehension of the situation, San Martín foresaw that Spain would defend Peru to the bitter end.

San Martín was obliged to cross the Andes to reach Peru; but, like Bolivar, he was a man of creative ability, and in a country whose people and whose customs were unknown to him, he set about raising an army that would have met even Wellington's standards. He settled in the province of Mendoza and there pitched a permanent camp, the fort of Tucumán, where he hoped he could make a successful stand against any Spanish attacks. The purpose of this defense was to raise an army behind the rifle pits of his camp capable of carrying out his plans for a continental campaign. His idea was to have "a small, disciplined army in Mendoza, to go to Chile and there to clean out the Spaniards and establish a friendly, stable government which would rout all anarchy." He wanted then to send the army overseas to Peru to take Lima. "Be assured," he wrote to a friend in 1814, "the war will not end until we are in Lima." This program and this prophecy he himself fulfilled.[15]

Unmoved by the intrigues and instability of the Argentinian government, San Martín made his plans. Slowly, war materiel was collected, and day after day he studied the terrain over which he was to attempt his ascent of the Andes. Spanish reaction had triumphed in Chile, just as it had under Morillo in New Granada, and San Martín admitted frankly that Chile

15 Mitre: San Martín. Vol. I. pp. 286-87. Mitre: Historia de Belgrano. Paris, 1887. Vol. II. p. 288.

would have to be reconquered, because no enemy of freedom could be tolerated on the borders of Argentina. He also prepared psychologically for the liberation of Chile. Numerous emigrants who had split up into different parties had fled to his camp, and among them San Martín favored a man who greatly appealed to his authoritarian temperament, Bernardo O'Higgins, a future leader of Chile.[16]

San Martín kept the government at Buenos Aires informed of his plans and at the same time misled the Spaniards by false rumors. When he began in the early days of 1817 to cross the Andes, the Royalists were under the impression that he had been beaten and his army destroyed. Actually he commanded a force of eight thousand men. "If the Spanish do not know in which direction I am headed, we shall get to Santiago by February 15." On February 15, San Martín entered the capital of Chile.

The difficulties San Martín had to overcome were possibly even greater than those of Bolivar in 1819, but his army was better equipped than the Liberator's had been. Nevertheless, the mountains between Argentina and Chile are higher and more hazardous than those in the north. The pass through which San Martín went lies fifty-three hundred meters high. In addition, he was far more dependent on the government than Bolivar had been. He was already on the march when an order forbidding the expedition reached him, but San Martín decided to ignore this governmental veto, although he knew that to do so was risking his neck.

On February 4 he began the descent into the valleys of Chile. It had taken him twenty days to cross the Andes. Fortunately, the Spaniards had missed their opportunity of defending the passes, and they finally risked battle when all the advantages were on the Argentinian side. The battle of Chacabuco brought San Martín the triumph on which he had counted. Three days later he entered Santiago de Chile.

16 D. Barros Arana: Historia general de Chile. Santiago, 1884-1902. Vol. XII. pp. 5-154. B. O'Higgins: Memorias. Santiago, 1844. Galindo: *op. cit.* pp. 374 ff.

In contrast to Bolivar, San Martín asked nothing for himself. His plans for the conquered territory specified an alliance of independent states; he was not interested in a Greater Argentinian Republic. Chile was constituted an independent state, and Bernardo O'Higgins, under the title of Director-in-Chief, assumed the office of president.[17]

Spanish rule in Chile, however, was only shaken, not eliminated. The leader of the Monarchists had concentrated his forces in the south, and in the spring of 1818 he made a counter-attack and succeeded in inflicting a heavy defeat on the united Argentine-Chilean army. It was a night battle and resulted in the wholesale flight of all Patriots, including San Martín and O'Higgins. But again the Spaniards failed to follow up their victory, and the delay gave San Martín time and space in which to recoup his losses in men and materiel. At the end of a month a new Patriot army faced the Spaniards on the plains of Maipú. Here, on May 15, 1818, the independence of Chile was won for all time.[18]

San Martín did not indulge in a theatrical enjoyment of his success. After Maipú he merely said, "We have won the action completely." Compared to Bolivar, he was restrained and little inclined to the dramatic. For San Martín there was only one virtue—that of being true to oneself. "Be what you must or you will be nothing," was his life's motto. He did not look back after he had liberated Chile. Argentina was suffering a confusion of conflicting elements, but it never occurred to San Martín to use his army to settle the anarchy of his country. When the political officials failed him, he had his command confirmed by the generals of his army. This was a daring step, for those who hailed him today could depose him tomorrow. But San Martín did not hesitate and began his preparations for the voyage to Peru without delay.

The liberation of Peru posed a new problem for San Martín

17 Mitre: San Martín. Vol. II. pp. 20 ff., 79 ff. A. García Gamba: Memorias para la historia de las armas españolas en el Perú. Madrid, 1916. Vol. I. pp. 359 ff. D. Amunátegui: El nacimiento de la República de Chile. Santiago, 1930.
18 B. Vicuña MacKenna: La Batalla de Maipú. Santiago, 1918.

because it demanded the creation of a fleet. Without Patriot warships, Spanish power in the Pacific would remain invincible. The organization of the Chilean fleet became the task of Lord Cochrane, who had entered the Chilean service in 1819. His courage, his talent, and his experience were unquestionable. No less, of course, were his delusions of grandeur and the greed which soon made him one of the most hated men on San Martín's staff.[19]

On August 23, 1820, the young fleet with forty-five hundred men set sail for Peru. "We are on our way to the last destination of our independence," wrote San Martín.

The moment seemed propitious. The Revolution in Spain had shocked the Monarchistic spirit even of Lima. Viceroy Pezuela had had the liberal constitution read in public and had declared his willingness to make contact with the leaders of the independence movement. The first of these significant conferences in which the Spaniards and Argentinians discussed the future of South America took place in Miraflores in September, 1820. San Martín demanded recognition of Peruvian independence, and in exchange offered the establishment of constitutional monarchy with a Spanish prince as king. This proposition had the support of a number of people, but the idea of Peruvian independence was repugnant to the Spanish Viceroy. Negotiations were, therefore, abrogated and hostilities resumed.[20]

San Martín wanted to incite the inhabitants of the Peruvian highlands to rebellion, and, at the same time, to besiege Lima. In this manner the Viceroy, finding himself bereft of help, might agree to capitulate. Pezuela was indeed in a ticklish position. The spirit of rebellion had spread among the people and had finally affected the Royal army. The Spanish officers deposed Pezuela and on their own responsibility appointed a new viceroy, General La Serna. La Serna travelled over the

19 Blanco: Doc. Vol. VI. pp. 746-48. Rivas Vicuña: Vol. IV. p. 382. G. Bulnes: Historia de la expedición libertadora del Perú. Santiago, 1888. Th. Cochrane: Memorias. Paris, 1863. E. Bunster: Lord Cochrane. Santiago, 1943.
20 C. A. Villanueva: Bolívar y San Martín. Paris, 1911. p. 168. Larrazabal: Vol. II. p. 156.

same road upon which his predecessor had failed. He paved
the way for negotiations with San Martín, and again San
Martín demanded a proclamation of Peruvian independence
and the establishment of a new regency council which would
clear the decks for monarchy. The discussions were prolonged,
but no decisions were reached.[21]

Meanwhile, La Serna had decided to exploit the resistance
against independence in the interior of the country. He left a
strong garrison in the fort of El Callao and concentrated his
army in the Sierra Mountains. Thus the capital was delivered
up, and San Martín was able to enter Lima on July 9, 1821.
Of course Peru was not yet liberated, since the Royal army
remained undefeated in the Sierras and could descend to the
coast at any time to drive the Argentinians into the sea. Even
though San Martín achieved another triumph in September,
1821, with the surrender of El Callao, his position in Peru continued treacherous. Operations were at a standstill. All that he
accomplished was to balance the scales and to establish an
equilibrium between European and American arms.

After his entrance into Lima, San Martín proclaimed and
pledged the independence of Peru. He assumed the title of
Protector of Peruvian Freedom, a title which was characteristic
of his temperament. Bolivar was the *Libertador;* San Martín,
the Protector. He defined his powers in provisional statutes,
and these were followed by a series of liberal measures. Nevertheless, the political situation remained precarious. San Martín
did not succeed in consolidating independence.

The Cabinet of the Protector was composed of Argentinians,
Peruvians, and Colombians—men who represented the most
varied purposes and heritages. Each held disparate ideas and
opinions about the future of an independent Peru.[22] It was
San Martín's constitutional program, however, that met with
the greatest opposition. The State Council had voted to send
a delegation to Europe to persuade a German prince to accept

21 Mitre: San Martín. Vol. II. p. 652. Restrepo: H. d. R. C. Vol. III. p. 121.
22 Paz Soldán: Vol. I. pp. 199-204.

the American imperial crown, but this decision was far from
pleasing to the Peruvians. Perhaps they were not entirely sure
of just what they did want, but they were certain it was not a
monarchy.[23]

Naturally, political hatred once kindled involved the person
of San Martín. He was rumored to have designs on the crown
himself. This suspicion was as unjust as it was unfounded, but
it contributed to undermining his prestige. Even San Martín's
companions-at-arms now thought it would be necessary either
to kill or to depose him in order to put an end to the war with
Spain. Their conclusions crystallized in the form of a conspiracy, but although San Martín learned of the plot he scorned
any idea of punishing the traitors. His heart, nevertheless,
was lacerated by so much ingratitude, disappointment, and
treachery.[24]

In the meantime, while high-ranking officers were losing
confidence in their leader, the army was disintegrating. Yellow
fever and desertion decimated the ranks, and the physical and
moral climate of Peru combined to destroy all discipline. Lima
was a sensual and lustful city, and none of the South American
armies had withstood its snares. The Protector saw what was
happening around him only too well, but he lacked the decisive-
ness to create order by drastic measures. Thus, at the beginning
of 1822, we find San Martín at an impasse. Liberation of Peru
was impossible without help from outside, and help from without meant help from Bolivar. San Martín felt that he had a
right to count on assistance from the Liberator, since he himself
had aided Colombia. As early as January, 1822, he had made
an attempt to meet Bolivar on the coast of Ecuador, but had
turned back on learning that Bolivar was in the interior. Now
in July, 1822, the moment seemed to have arrived. He assumed
that Bolivar was still in Quito, and he decided to visit him there
after he should have, with apparent inadvertence, annexed

23 Mitre: San Martín. Vol. III. pp. 138 ff. E. de la Cruz: La entrevista de Guayaquil, in Simón Bolívar. Madrid, 1914. pp. 268 ff.
    24 Paz Soldán: Vol. I. p. 225.

Guayaquil to Peru.[25] If he could bring off this coup and also persuade Bolivar to support him, he would have killed two birds with one stone and would thus have reëstablished his prestige. San Martín frankly admitted the advantages he hoped to gain from a meeting with Bolivar. "I shall meet the Liberator of Colombia. The common interests of Peru and Colombia, the effective conclusion of the war we are waging, and the stability of the political form toward which America is rapidly approaching, make our meeting necessary. The sequence of events has made us, to a great extent, responsible for this noble undertaking." In plain English these words meant that San Martín wanted to discuss Guayaquil, the war in Peru, and the problems of state government. He saw himself and his rival as the arbitrators of South America.[26]

At that time, however, the two men were diametrically opposed to each other, and San Martín courted disaster when he failed to recognize this fact. Bolivar was the liberator of three nations and the President of Greater Colombia. Moreover, he was no longer in Quito, but on the coast. He had solved the matter of Guayaquil as Alexander had cut the Gordian knot. How could San Martín, who had no roots in Argentina, who could not defeat the Spaniards in Peru, whose arms had begun to disintegrate, possibly have believed that he could deal with Bolivar as an equal? If San Martín had been a statesman, he would have known that he was going to Guayaquil without a single trump up his sleeve. But he was not a politician; he was a military man; and he viewed political problems with the eyes of a layman. So he came to Guayaquil without plan or preparation and without any exact idea of what he wanted to accomplish.

At the first report of the advent of the Protector, Bolivar sent one of his aides on board to welcome him, and on July 26,

25 O'Leary: Doc. Vol. XIX. p. 335. C. Destruge: La entrevista de Bolívar y San Martín, Guayaquil, 1918, pp. 44-45, thinks that San Martín had already pursued this plan on his first trip.
26 Mitre: San Martín. Vol. III. p. 610.

San Martín set foot on Ecuadorian soil.[27] All who were opposed to Bolivar's rule in Guayaquil took this opportunity to hail San Martín. He was escorted to the house which Bolivar had furnished and in which the Liberator awaited him. The Protector and the Liberator embraced for the first and the last time in their lives. Following the introductions and receptions, the delegations retired, the ladies departed, the officers went to their posts, and Bolivar and San Martín remained alone except for a secretary. Behind closed doors began the memorable discussions on which depended the fate of America.[28] San Martín's program comprised four points; first, the question of Guayaquil; second, his projected demand for restitution from the Colombian President for the losses the Argentinian division suffered during the campaign against Quito; third, his request for Bolivar's definite promise of reinforcements for the liberation of Peru; and fourth, his design to persuade the Liberator to accept his monarchistic plans.[29]

Bolivar could only surmise what intentions had brought the Argentinian to Guayaquil. But, in any case, he had nothing to fear, as his own position was secure. On the question of Guayaquil, San Martín had hoped to anticipate Bolivar, but he was powerless in face of the *fait accompli* of Bolivar's dictatorship. He, therefore, declared that he did not wish to discuss the

27 The meeting of Guayaquil is probably the most discussed topic in South American history. The controversial literature dealing with this problem constitutes a veritable ocean of passion and ink. A good survey, with which I agree on many points, may be found in Lecuna: Cuestión de Guayaquil. B. d. H. Caracas. Vol. XXVI. No. 101. pp. 3 ff. See also Rivas Vicuña: La democracia colombiana y la conferencia de Guayaquil. B. d. H. Caracas. Vol. XIX. no. 73. p. 113. H. D. Barbagelata: Bolívar y San Martín. Paris, 1911. J. E. Guastavino: San Martín y Bolívar. Buenos Aires, 1913. The most surprising contribution was E. Marmol: La entrevista de Guayaquil, Buenos Aires, 1940, that pretended to offer some unpublished letters of Bolivar, later proved by Lecuna to be forgeries. D. Carbonell: Escuelas de Historia en América. pp. 224 ff.

28 Neither J. Espejo: San Martín y Bolívar, Buenos Aires, 1873, nor T. C. Mosquera, Blanco: Doc. Vol. XII. p. 753, are very reliable. Mosquera claims to have attended the conferences between Bolivar and San Martín, which is very unlikely. However, we think it possible that Bolivar himself told Mosquera some of the facts he presents, because certain expressions have a ring of true Bolivarian spirit. See also, Mitre: San Martín. Vol. III. p. 622. Restrepo: H. d. R. C. Vol. III. p. 227.

29 Our principal source is the secret report written by Bolivar's secretary, General Pérez. Cartas: Vol. III. p. 61. J. M. Goenaga: La entrevista de Guayaquil. Bogotá, 1911. Cruz: *op. cit.* p. 262.

matter further and that he had no desire to interfere in affairs
that were not his concern. Any confusion on the subject he
laid at the doors of the inconsistent inhabitants of Guayaquil.
In a word, he realized how useless it was even to mention Peru's
desire for annexation. Bolivar played the sincere democrat,
explaining to San Martín that he was willing to grant him
his wish for a popular vote, but assured him that the vote would
certainly favor Colombia.[30] The discussions then veered to military affairs. San Martín asked Bolivar to make up the losses
that his troops had endured in Ecuador and requested an expeditionary corps for the liberation of Peru. Bolivar agreed, promising to send a Colombian division of four battalions. In all he
offered to place eighteen hundred men at San Martín's disposal.
The Protector was deeply disappointed. He declared that with
such meagre help Peru could not possibly be liberated, and suggested that if Bolivar did not want to entrust his Colombian
troops to him, Bolivar should come to Peru himself to fight the
last battle for independence. Only if the entire Colombian army
went to Peru, he said, could victory be won.

Bolivar refused this demand, hiding behind the pretext that
as President he could not leave the country without the permission of Congress. This certainly was only an excuse, as Congress would surely have given him permission. But Bolivar
had other reasons which he did not reveal to San Martín. He
could not strip Colombia of all troops at this time. Páez was
still fighting for the possession of Puerto Cabello; Pasto still
defied its conquerors; Guayaquil was a cauldron of rebellion.
If Bolivar had plunged head over heels into the Peruvian adventure, he would have risked the hard-won unity of Colombia.
Bolivar could not put his army at San Martín's disposal for the
simple reason that he needed it himself. San Martín could not
fathom the reasons for this refusal, which seemed to him to be
motivated by personal ambition only. He believed that Bolivar
was obsessed by a lust for power, and that he wanted to command, and to reap the fame of liberation. San Martín had an

30 Cartas: Vol. III. p. 61. Nos. 1, 2.

objective nature and fame meant little to him. He made the
Liberator a generous offer when he declared his willingness
to serve with his army under Bolivar's leadership.[31] When
Bolivar refused his offer, San Martín thought that he had failed
to convince Bolivar of his sincerity. He concluded that he,
himself, stood in the way of Colombia's active participation in
the liberation of Peru. This was a bitter realization, and it
required all his soldier's self-control not to display his con-
sternation during the first moment. But San Martín misinterpreted Bolivar's intentions. It must be admitted that the Liberator was selfish and that he wanted fame for himself, but these
were not his exclusive motives. San Martín's subordination
under Bolivar's command was both illogical and impossible.
Even if the older and professional officer had subjected himself
to the instructions of the younger, his army would not have
been willing to comply, and in every crisis Bolivar would have
had to fear an uprising of Argentinian troops and the proclamation of San Martín as commander.

Nevertheless, the Protector continued to protest his good
intentions, saying that Bolivar could ask what he wished of
Peru, even to a friendly settlement of the border question.
Bolivar thanked him, but he thought it wiser not to ask for
definite promises from San Martín. Bolivar knew that the
Argentinian's power had been undermined and that a political
earthquake was due in Lima.[32]

31 See San Martín's letter to Bolivar, of August 29, 1822. Mitre: San Martín.
Vol. III. pp. 644-45. This letter was first published in G. Lafond de Lurcy: Voyages
dans les deux Ameriques. 1844. Vol. II. p. 138. Lecuna: En defensa de Bolivar.
B. d. H. Caracas. Vol. XXIII. No. 91, declares it to be a forgery. However, Sarmiento: op. cit. Vol. II. p. 371, declares that he read the letter during a session of the
Institut de France attended by San Martín. In other words, San Martín publicly
confirmed the authenticity of the letter. Another letter of San Martín to Miller,
Goenaga: op. cit. pp. 18-19, confirms also the letter of August 29, 1822. Both documents give, of course, only San Martín's opinion, while Bolivar's ideas are revealed
in the secret report and in his letters to Sucre and Santander. I intend to deal with
the whole problem in a monograph. J. Arocha Moreno: El Libertador y el General
San Martín. San José, 1941.
32 Cartas: Vol. III. p. 62. No. 5. Mosquera reports that Bolivar informed San
Martín of the coming revolution in Lima, which is hardly possible. Considering the
great distance between Lima and Guayaquil and the small amount of maritime
traffic we cannot assume that Bolivar was better informed about the Peruvian situation than San Martín.

San Martín did not conceal his disappointment. He complained of the burden of responsibility and, above all, about his Argentinian companions-at-arms who had deserted him in Lima. He wanted to withdraw to Mendoza, and he assured Bolivar that before he had taken his departure from Lima, he had left a sealed note containing his resignation from the Protectorate. He stated that he would not accept reëlection as Protector, and that he would give up his command without waiting for the end of the war.

San Martín had one ambition, the foundation of the future government, and he announced his belief that the only solution for the state was his proposal to summon a European prince to wear the crown. At this point the discussion became violent and passionate. Bolivar said frankly that he did not want a monarchy either for Colombia or for America. European princes would be an alien element in the midst of the American people. He did, however, wish to establish a measure of permanency, and had, therefore, suggested that the presidency should be for life and that the senate should be hereditary. He knew that he could not inflict a superannuated system like monarchy on his continent. He had no desire, as Waldo Frank has said, to spare America any of her birth pangs, and he had no fears as he realized that a new race was about to be born. "We must not stem the progress of mankind with measures which are alien to the virginal soil of America." He was determined, he said, to resist the importation of princes.[33]

San Martín tried to make it clear that the rule of a foreign prince was only an idea for the future, but Bolivar declared that such a plan would be undesirable at any time. He suspected that San Martín had designs on the crown, but in this he completely misjudged San Martín, who was without personal ambition. He even resented the obligations of command, and he championed the idea of American monarchy because he con-

---

33 Mosquera: *op. cit.* Cartas: Vol. III. pp. 61-62. "Diré que no quiere ser rey, pero que tampoco quiere la democracia, y si el que venga un príncipe de Europa a reinar en el Perú. Esto último yo creo que es pro forma." See, Goenaga: *op. cit.* pp. 18-19.

sidered it the ideal solution. Even the problem of the form of government did not bring these men any closer together. The only question on which they did agree was the federation of the South American states, perhaps because this still lay in the distant future. San Martín proposed a Colombia-Peru union which he hoped would strengthen his authority. Such were the matters which the Liberator and the Protector discussed in their lengthy meetings of July 26 and 27.

On the night of July 27 a ball was given for San Martín. Bolivar, as usual at affairs of this kind, thoroughly enjoyed himself. San Martín remained cool and aloof and seemed depressed. At one o'clock in the morning he called his aides and told them he wanted to leave because he could not stand the noise. His luggage was already on board, and, unobserved, he left the hall, went to his ship, and set sail from the port. The next morning he arose early, still immersed in his thoughtful mood. After walking up and down the deck for a long time, he said to his staff, "The Liberator had anticipated us," and later, "The Liberator is not the man we imagined him to be."[34] These were the words of defeat, and San Martín was truly defeated, not so much by Bolivar as by circumstances. During the period of his trip to Guayaquil, revolution had broken out in Lima, directed against one of his closest collaborators, Bernardo Monteagudo. The Marquis of Torre Tagle, whom San Martín had appointed as executive, had sacrificed Monteagudo in order to save himself. This was the situation that greeted San Martín when he returned to Lima on August 20. He entertained no illusions. He saw that the Peruvians were no longer friendly to him, that he had left the government in the hands of weak and incompetent men, and that he had alienated the army. His hopes for the meeting with Bolivar had betrayed him. He felt that he was no longer needed and that his presence perhaps even delayed the advent of independence, so he decided to do America one last service. He resigned and announced his decision to leave Peru. He could have fought to maintain

34 Mitre: San Martín. Vol. III. pp. 623, 649 ff. Blanco: Doc. Vol. VIII. p. 482.

his power, but such an idea never occurred to him. He bade America a silent farewell; no resounding words, either of bitterness or of self-praise accompanied his departure. "I am tired of being called a tyrant . . . of having people say that I want to be King, Emperor, or even the devil."[35] San Martín went first to Buenos Aires and then to Brussels. On one later occasion, in 1829, he was again offered command of the Argentinian army, but resisted the temptation to accept. Retiring and unobtrusive, he lived in Boulogne in self-inflicted exile until his death in 1850, a great soldier and a great character, taciturn, proud, stoic, and selfless.

One wonders whether his resignation was the result of his meeting with Bolivar. Was it true that there was not room enough for both men in South America? Close friends of the two leaders said that neither was satisfied with the discussions; both preserved before the eyes of the world an impenetrable silence about all that had happened during their conferences.[36] Bolivar, who on other occasions laid great store by the power of public opinion, let this chance to dramatize his meeting with San Martín pass. He sent his foreign minister in Bogotá a secret report and dispatched a few letters to the closest of his co-workers, like Santander and Sucre, on the content and range of the discussions. San Martín said publicly that he had had the good fortune to embrace the Liberator of Colombia. His real feelings were of a different nature.[37] The taciturn, hard soldier and the tropical visionary never appreciated each other's real character. Bolivar spoke of San Martín with a suggestion of contempt. He considered him a lucky general, not a great man, and he thought that his reputation depended more on a semblance of success than on real merit. "His character seems to me very soldierly, active, mobile, and energetic," he wrote Santander. "He has ideas such as you like, but he is not receptive enough for the sublime either in ideas or in deeds."[38] The

35 García del Real: *op. cit.* p. 242.
36 Restrepo: H. d. R. C. Vol. III. p. 228.
37 Larrazabal: Vol. II. p. 161.
38 Cartas: Vol. III. pp. 59, 103.

whole incident faded out of Bolivar's consciousness, and he never spoke of this meeting with San Martín to any of his confidants in later years.

Naturally, San Martín was keenly disappointed. He found in Bolivar an extraordinary superficiality and inconsistency in principle, and a puerile vanity. He saw a man whose will to power was the controlling passion.[39] San Martín tried to minimize the importance of the conference, to have it known that nothing more than Colombia's help had been discussed, but his own letters gainsay this. In Guayaquil the fate of these two men had been decided, and with it the future of America. The discussions at Guayaquil had ended with the triumph of Colombian demands over those of Argentina and Chile.

Colombian hegemony did not last long, however. Bolivar, who dreamed of going to the La Plata, the Amazon, and to Cuba, got only as far as Bolivia. Perhaps the very idea of hegemony was a mistake. Today, after 125 years, the people of South America live in an atmosphere of mutual recognition and respect. The good-neighbor policy and Pan-American solidarity have extinguished the desire for a hegemony.

In one respect—that is, in his defense of the Republican idea against the monarchistic dreams of San Martín—history has unconditionally approved Bolivar. Thinking of San Martín's desires, Bolivar wrote, "According to Voltaire, the first king was a happy soldier, by whom he doubtless meant the good Nimrod. I am very much afraid that the four crimson sticks, which we call a throne, cost more blood than tears and cause more unrest than peace. Some believe it is easy to wear a crown and that all will bow before it. I believe that the era of monarchies is past and that thrones will never come back into fashion unless the corruption of mankind drowns the love of liberty. You will tell me that there are thrones and altars all over the world. But I tell you that these superannuated monuments are already jeopardized by the gunpowder of modern

39 Mitre: San Martín. Vol. III. p. 641.

ideas."[40] As a matter of fact, monarchy could not gain ground in Latin America. The few attempts that were made during the nineteenth century to transplant it to the western world ended in a sea of blood and tears.

Bolivar was not satisfied with San Martín, but he was eminently pleased with himself. "Thank God . . . I have achieved some important things with much luck and some fame . . . first, the freedom of the south; second, the annexation to Colombia of Guayaquil, Quito, and the other provinces; third, the friendship of San Martín and Peru. Now all I need is to bring my treasure to safety and to hide it in a deep cavern, so that no one can steal it. In other words, all I need now is to retire and to die. By God, I wish for nothing more. It is the first time that I have had nothing left to wish for and the first time that I have been satisfied with my lot."[41] He was happy and revelled in his happiness.

He wanted first of all to rest and to enjoy contentment. He foresaw that he would have to liberate Peru, but he preferred to postpone this undertaking. He had not taken seriously San Martín's assurance that he was tired of his command, and he anticipated being summoned only when the Protector had suffered a new defeat. When the news of San Martín's retirement came he received it coldly. "All in all . . . Peru has lost a good general and a benefactor."[42] This was his final word on the subject of San Martín. He saw no reason to have the occasion proclaimed as a victory, and even less to shed tears. Genius is egocentric.

The way to Peru was now open to Bolivar. When and where he would set forth on it could be determined only by military prescience and statesmanship. Bolivar planned to liberate Peru with a large army, but he could not afford to extemporize on this last campaign. He wanted to step in only if the men whom San Martín had left behind could not master the situation. He gave assurances of his willingness

40 Cartas: Vol. III. pp. 97-98, of September 26, 1822.
41 Cartas: Vol. III. p. 60.
42 Cartas: Vol. III. p. 103.

to help, but he acted with restraint, feeling that they should try their own luck. As after Carabobo and Boyacá, he was not inclined to any hasty action, knowing that the higher he climbed the lower he could fall. This consciousness retarded his steps.[43]

The international situation at this time was promising. The United States had just recognized Colombia's independence. The Monroe Doctrine removed the western hemisphere from the sphere of European influence, and Spain protested in vain against its restrictions. The age of colonial imperialism in America was over. The Holy Alliance was robbed of every possibility of intervention, and England, which had good reason to fear that it would be surpassed by the United States, finally considered factual recognition of the South American states. Legal recognition was bound to follow.[44] The knowledge of this situation strengthened Bolivar's determination to take his time. He thought day and night about the means with which to accomplish the liberation of Peru, but he did not permit himself to be rushed into things from which he might have been obliged to withdraw. In long letters to Santander, Bolivar instructed him to have money, arms, and men ready, and in the meantime he worked untiringly on the incorporation of the south, which was still only partially completed. After San Martín's departure Guayaquil had voted for annexation, but in Bolivar's own words, the area resembled Chimborazo. It was outwardly cool, but inwardly it burned with the fire of rebellion. The difficulties were tremendous, and Bolivar himself was obliged to take the organization in hand. "In four days," he wrote, "one cannot win the hearts of men, and only by winning them can one acquire a solid basis for power."[45]

43 Cartas: Vol. III. p. 110. See also the important document in, O'Leary: Doc. Vol. XIX. p. 370, in which Bolivar offered to send four thousand men to the Peruvian government besides the eighteen hundred that had already departed.

44 Blanco: Doc. Vol. VIII. pp. 279, 320, 328, 335, 363, 376. O'Leary: Doc. Vol. XIX. p. 256. Webster: op. cit. Vol. I. pp. 14-15. W. R. Manning: Diplomatic Correspondence of the United States concerning the Independence of the Latin American Nations. New York, 1925. W. S. Robertson: Hispanic American Relations with the United States. New York, 1923.

45 Cartas: Vol. III. p. 66.

Santander now begged for Bolivar's return to Bogotá, and at the same time his compatriots called him to Caracas. To the latter Bolivar explained his new and imposing position in these words: "I know better than any one else what rights the national soil may demand from its sons. You may believe me, cruel uncertainties are constantly tearing at me. . . . A prophetic instinct brings distant and uncertain evils closer, and I savor them with the bitterness of the son who sees his own mother's womb destroyed. . . . But realize this . . . I now belong not only to the Colombian family, nor even to that of Bolivar. Nor do I belong to Caracas. I belong to the whole nation . . . the people of the south have at their back Peru who hopes to tempt them, and there is still the Royal army which would like to conquer them by force." Bolivar could not desert the south without being untrue to himself.[46]

Bolivar was not quite so definite in his reply to Santander. The latter had called him to Bogotá in order that he might use his influence with Congress, and Bolivar did not underestimate the importance of this summons. The reasons which Santander advanced were good, but Bolivar's reasons for remaining in the south were better. He wanted under no circumstances to assume the burdens of the presidency, and he repeated all the arguments which he had already advanced in Cucutá. He wanted to fight the Spaniards and not his fellow citizens. When Santander pointed out to him that from now on everything would have to be done according to the letter of the Constitution, Bolivar was indignant. "I shall not keep the presidency if I am not given those extraordinary powers which Congress has voted me. I am convinced that Colombia can only be kept in order and well-being by absolute power. Colombia needs an army of occupation which will keep it free."[47] These were dangerous words, words which Bolivar might have hesitated to utter upon mature reflection. But he did not want to lose the fruits of his labors in disunity and dissension or through lack of patriotism on the part of the Parliamentarians.

46 Cartas: Vol. III. p. 91.
47 Cartas: Vol. III. p. 121.

When Bolivar learned that there was some thought of changing the Constitution by loosening the federal bonds of union,
he accepted it as a personal challenge. "The Constitution of
Colombia," he stated, "was decreed sacrosanct for a period of
ten years. It shall not be altered with impunity while I live,
nor while the army of the liberators is under my command."
He was even more outspoken in an official letter to Santander.
"Your Excellency knows, and all Colombia knows, that I have
dedicated my life to the safety, the freedom, and the fortunes
of Colombia. My policy was always for stability, for strength,
and for true liberty. . . . Your Excellency knows that I have
taken an oath on the Constitution and that I have become its
sponsor. The Constitution is unalterable for ten years. . . .
The sovereignty of the people is not entirely unlimited, for justice is its foundation and complete effectiveness its purpose.
. . . How can the representatives of the people think themselves entitled to a constant change in the social structure?"[48]
He himself, he added, would recognize no law that acted
against these sworn principles. He would rather leave Colombia than condone the destruction of the achievements of the
army of liberation.

Under the impact of this appeal, the voices that had sung
the siren song of a federated Colombia were silenced. One
must consider the full weight of all the obstacles to understand
the nature of the decision at Guayaquil. It would have been
irresponsible and careless of Bolivar to have left his country
when it was threatened with strife and dissension. "This country offers a thousand advantages for the future. But it is like
a virgin, who, once having lost her purity and virginity, can
never regain them."[49]

Delay was thus the hour's need. The moment of happiness
he had tasted in Guayaquil was gone by the end of 1822. "Believe me, I have rarely felt so much anxiety as now. I spend

48 Proclamas: p. 277, of December 31, 1822. Cartas: Vol. III. p. 130. Blanco:
Doc. Vol. VIII. p. 317.
    49 Cartas: Vol. III. p. 119.

sleepless nights trying to guess where Colombia's ship, whose course I steer, may be wrecked. I am deeply grieved that our work, after so much effort, disintegrates in our hands."[50] Bolivar would not admit that his work was all for naught, that he, like San Martín, could ever be called a good soldier but a poor statesman. Justice and strength were needed. Like some medieval king, he travelled from one province to another . . . from Guayaquil to Cuenca, from Cuenca to Quito, from Quito to Pasto.

Finally, Bolivar, too, began to feel the effects of twelve years of war. He had grown gray, and the fatigue of constant effort visited him. His senses became less alert. But he gave little importance to his own condition. He was prepared to exhaust his energies, all of himself, in the pursuit of his life's ambition. He, therefore, made the south his headquarters and awaited the moment when fate should summon him anew.

50 Cartas: Vol. III. p. 109.

CHAPTER 26

Interlude

The last strains of the *allegro majestoso* were still lingering on the air when a new movement in the symphony of Bolivar's life began. The vigorous and beautiful notes of the *scherzo con brio* are heard, and now it is a woman who conducts the music. For the first time in his life Bolivar meets a human being who means more to him than a pleasant adventure terminating in a hasty embrace. Manuela Sáenz aroused Bolivar's interest on the occasion when she threw him a laurel wreath on his march into Quito. His wooing was as direct as her response.

Manuela Sáenz de Thorne was twenty-five years old in 1822. She seems to have made some effort to conceal her origin. "My country," she once said, "is America. I was born beneath the Equator."[1] She was indeed a child of the tropical sun, of unrestrained growth and insatiable appetites. Today, however, we know that Manuela was born in Quito in 1797, and we are inclined to wonder why she made a secret of the fact.[2] It is true that her origin is darkened by the cloud of illegitimacy.[3] Her father, Simón Sáenz de Vergara, a Spanish nobleman, had come to Quito to seek his fortune and had married a woman of rank who bore him four children. Some time later Simón had become infatuated with a beautiful Ecuadorian of Spanish descent, María de Aispuru, and Manuela was one of the results.[4]

1 A. Miramon: La vida ardiente de Manuela Sáenz. Bogotá, 1944. p. 11. J. M. Cordovez Moure: Reminiscencias. Bogotá, 1900. Series IV. p. 70.

2 H. Moncayo: El Quito colonial y el de le época libertadora. El Comercio de Quito. August 1934. L. A. Cuervo: Notas historias. Bogotá, 1925.

3 A. Rumazo González: Manuela Sáenz. Cali, 1944.

4 Rumazo: p. 29. B. d. H. Quito. Vol. XXII. p. 231.

Such incidents were regarded with complete equanimity in Quito.[5] Manuela was a product of this society. No one blamed her father for her birth, but the child was aware that the circumstances of her upbringing were not entirely conventional. She saw little of her half brothers and her half sister, who were cold and unfriendly toward her, and she was sensitive to the animosity she met in her father's house. As companions she was given two Negresses, who became devoted to her. These intimates of her early life were good-humored and whimsical, and knew all the gossip of the town. Like most girls of their race, they matured early, and because of their environment soon became sensuous and dissolute. Manuela unconsciously absorbed licentiousness in her daily life.

Manuela's childhood was passed during the early years of the Revolution. With others she had fled to the country to escape the city's confusion. At this time she learned the few arts practiced by the Creoles, embroidery and the making of confections, but she also learned to ride, to throw a spear, and to shoot. Her character was a strange mixture of masculine and feminine traits. The thinly veiled scorn to which she was so often exposed developed in her the desire to distinguish herself in some way, to draw the attention of her fellows, and to excel in some field. She possessed an inferiority complex which necessitated some compensation. Her desire to be the center of attraction was soon fulfilled, for nature had endowed her in a brilliant way for this role. She was very attractive, and she was well aware of this fact. She was especially fond of animals, and with the instincts of a natural courtesan, preferred cats.

However, in the Catholic world there is an excellent means of disciplining coquettish young girls, and when Manuela was seventeen she was entered at the convent of Santa Catarina.[6] Once a month she was permitted to go to her mother's house

5 F. González Suarez: Historia general del Ecuador. Quito, 1890. Vol. IV. p. 286. Vol. V. p. 495.
6 Rumazo: pp. 75 ff.

and to attend mass outside the convent. She needed but one of
these occasions to start a love affair with a young officer. Her
love of uniforms, formed perhaps at this time, was to be preserved throughout her life—probably as an expression of her
vehement desire to show off. The young officer sent letters to
her by her Negresses, and Manuela answered them. Finally,
the impulsive and erotic girl defied convention and eloped with
him, but it is said that this first lover soon deserted her.[7] The
family took her back to the convent, but everyone was resigned
to the fact that she neither could nor would remain there.

Under the circumstances, it seemed best to marry her off as
quickly as possible. The problem of finding a husband was not,
however, a simple one. Among the South Americans of her
class a seduced girl was looked upon as degraded. Only a foreigner might overlook her misstep. At length, however, she
was betrothed to an English physician who lived in Quito, one
James Thorne. Manuela was twenty years old at this time and
her husband was forty. Doubtless she was pleased with her
marriage for it opened the doors of the world to her, but the
union was far from satisfactory, since Manuela never cherished
any feeling for Dr. Thorne but one of friendly compassion.
The unfortunate man loved her more dearly every day, adoring
her with a passion which neither time nor her variable moods
nor her faithlessness could destroy. The student of miscegena-
tion in South America is familiar with this phenomenon; cases
where the slow Anglo-Saxon temperament becomes a slave
to the caprices, the whims, and the inconsistencies of tropical
eroticism are not rare. According to a French physiologist,
love is a question of the epidermis, but the differences between
Manuela and Doctor Thorne included many other factors—
temperament, manners, heritage, outlook on life. She was
passionate and insatiable; he was slow, methodical, and good-
natured. Manuela expressed her attitude in cruelly frank
fashion. "As a husband you are clumsy. The monotonous
life is reserved for your nation. You practice love without feel-

7 J. B. Boussingault: Memoires. Paris, 1892-1903.

ing pleasure . . . conversation without grace. You walk with
measured tread, you greet stiffly. You rise and sit down with
care. You jest without laughter. I laugh at myself and at all
your British seriousness."[8] One can easily understand that the
pedantic Anglo-Saxon, who was more jealous of his flirtatious
wife than any Portuguese, must have seemed like a tyrant to
this Latin imp. Thorne made the mistake all jealous people
make—he sought the reason for her faithlessness, not in her
or in himself, but in circumstances and other people. Perhaps
a change of cities or scenes, a trip and new impressions would
change her. Manuela seized on the idea of a trip with the greatest enthusiasm, for nothing is so unbearable to a South American as any kind of consistent existence. Even the simple people,
the peasants and day laborers, wander from place to place,
exchanging one boredom for another, as they say. Dr. Thorne
with Manuela and the two Negresses moved to Lima.

During the three years they spent there, Manuela witnessed
the conquest of Lima by San Martín and the rebellion of Peru.
The ladies of Lima took an active part in the political movement. Their *salons* were centers of intrigue and conspiracy.
Another Ecuadorian, Rosita Campuzano from Guayaquil, was
the uncrowned queen of both the elegant and the political
world. She became San Martín's mistress, but secretly, since
the Protector was averse to scandal. Manuela made friends with
Rosita and soon the two were inseparable.[9]

In Lima, Manuela's friend was called La Protectora. Manuela
hoped for a similar destiny, and used all her wiles to achieve
her ambition. Fate played into her hands. Within a brief time
she was to overmatch her companion and to become La Libertadora. Meanwhile, she enjoyed the intoxication of many festivities. San Martín had created an order, the Order of the Sun,
which was bestowed on men and women who had distinguished
themselves in the service of Peruvian independence. Manuela

8 O'Leary: Memorias. Vol. III. pp. 305-7.
9 R. Palma: Bolívar en las tradiciones Peruanas. Barcelona, 1930. p. 89. C.
Hispano: Historia secreta de Bolivar. p. 198.

was named Dame of the Order of the Sun, and wore the red
and white ribbon of the Order with great pride.

Meanwhile, the unhappy Dr. Thorne came no closer to his
goal. Lima was a veritable purgatory to him, but with the
stubbornness of his race he clung to his resolve to win his wife's
affection. Ironically enough, Manuela's thoughts strayed further and further from him with each day. At the time of this
impasse in the Thornes' married life, Manuela's father came
to Lima on business. Manuela expressed the wish to see her
friends and relatives in Quito again, and Dr. Thorne agreed
that she should return with her father. She arrived in Quito
at the same time that Sucre's victorious army entered the city.
On the night when she was introduced to Bolivar, she appeared
to him, as to all men, to be the most beautiful woman he had
ever met. Her slightly oval face was the color of pearls; her
large black eyes were passionate and full of promise; she wore
her rich, dark hair loosely; her voice was gentle and charming;
her hands and feet were small like those of most Creoles. She
was really Manuela, *la Bella,* as Bolivar called her. But she was
also *la amable loca,* the charming fool who was in fresh trouble
every day. She delighted in wearing men's clothes; she took
part in battles and street fights, rode with the men, and slapped
bourgeois decency and good manners in the face whenever it
pleased her to do so. She was the complete mixture of Amazon
and Hetare, the ideal woman for a fighter like Bolivar.[10]

Yet Manuela's charms worked slowly. At first she was
hardly more than a passing adventure, variable and exchange-
able whenever more alluring prospects arose. When Bolivar
was in Guayaquil he met Joaquina Garaycoa, whom he called
La Gloriosa, and to whom he soon wrote the tenderest of letters.[11] "*La Gloriosa* is right to love me . . . for I love her
devotedly and gratefully." He thought of Joaquina on his journeys and he told her the story of his life. "The Church has

10 Rumazo: pp. 224-25.
11 Cartas: Vol. III. p. 120. See, J. B. Perez y Soto: B. d. H. Caracas. Vol.
XXIII. No. 92. p. 519.

conquered me. I live in a convent. The nuns send me my meals and the canon sends refreshments. The *Te Deum* is my song and spiritual prayer my slumber. I meditate on the beauties with which Providence has endowed Guayaquil. My life is wholly spiritual, and when you see me again I shall be angelic." And later, *"La Gloriosa* lives in my heart." The lovely girl addressed him as, "my dear sweet friend," and called him *"Mi Glorioso."* She identified herself with him and signed his name. This was half in jest and half in earnest . . . pretended adoration on his part, imaginary surrender on hers.[12] During this time he was also receiving letters from Manuela in which she declared that she was unutterably bored without him.[13] Had Bolivar recounted his amorous adventures, he would have found no one woman who could have been both friend and mistress, no one who could have so identified herself with the man and his great cause as did Manuela. She worshipped him, but she had enough wit to laugh at both herself and him whenever the great man seemed amusing to her. She became his secretary and soon thereafter, the guardian of his secrets. Bolivar entrusted his records to her.[14]

The affair was a scandal in South American society. Manuela's husband entreated her even after many years to return to him, but her reply was a vehement protest. "No, no, no! Man, for God's sake . . . my dear sir, you are excellent, you are inimitable. You may believe that I shall never tell you of your shortcomings. But, my friend, it is no small matter that I leave you for General Bolivar . . . do you seriously believe that if I am chosen by him and possess his heart that I would choose even to be the wife of the Father, Son, or the Holy Ghost, or of all three? I know very well that I cannot be united with him under the laws of honor, as you call them. Do you

12 V. Lecuna: Papeles de Manuela Sáenz. B. d. H. Caracas. Vol. XXVIII. No. 112, and F. L. Borja: Epistolaria de Manuela Sáenz. B. d. H. Caracas. Vol. XXIX. No. 116. See also, B. d. H. Caracas. Vol. XVI. No. 62. Cartas de mujeres. pp. 335, 339, 341.
13 Cartas de mujeres: p. 332.
14 Some of Bolivar's letters were written by Manuela at Bolivar's dictation.

believe that I feel less or more honored because he is my lover and not my husband? Oh, I do not live for the prejudices of society, which were invented only that we might torture each other."[15] There is something Goethian about this letter . . . something that resembles Claerchen's voice and that of George Sand. But fully to understand Manuela one must read the end of this letter. "Let us do something else. We shall marry again when we get to heaven . . . but not on this earth. In our heavenly home we shall lead angelic lives, entirely spiritual, for here on earth as a man you are very clumsy. There everything will be quite British. But enough of jesting. Seriously and without laughing, and with all the conscientiousness, truth, and purity of an English woman, I say that I will not marry you again."

Manuela's love for Bolivar, the passion that Bolivar felt for her, were no idyll of a bourgeois era. Here were neither rules nor binding agreements nor even much loyalty. In the long intervals when they lived apart, Bolivar occasionally forgot her. Then she became distraught and wrote to his aide for an explanation. "The General no longer thinks of me. In nineteen days he has scarcely written twice. What is wrong?" She would then do something that was beyond all reason.[16] Sometimes it was not the separation, but Bolivar's insatiable hunger for adventure that aroused her jealousy. The story runs that she once found a diamond bracelet in his bed. It was not hers, and she threw herself on Bolivar and tore his face with her nails. With the help of two aides he fought her off, but Manuela had so disfigured him that he could not appear in public for a week. "The General has a heavy cold."

Neither gave up anything for the other. The beautiful Manuela was, on her part, not unreceptive to the charms of novelty. It was natural that in her position as *maitresse de titre,* she should arouse the gossip and curiosity of the army. Some, like Sucre, liked her very much; others, like Córdoba, detested

15 O'Leary: Memorias. Vol. III. pp. 505-07.
16 Cartas de mujeres: p. 332.

her. Many envied her; many desired her, and the *Chronique Scandaleuse* made a Messalina of her. Her love for animals caused her to be accused of some amazing depravities. Her free and easy way with the officers was interpreted as shamelessness.

Their love was like a long thunderstorm—violent, loud with passionate utterances, still with angry silences. Manuela to Bolivar: "I am very angry and very ill. How true it is that long absences kill love and increase great passions. You had a little love for me and the long separation killed it. But I, who had a great passion for you, have kept it to preserve my peace and happiness. And it endures and will endure as long as Manuela lives."[17] Bolivar to Manuela: "I think of you and your fate every moment. Yes, I adore you, more today than ever."[18]

At times Bolivar was overcome by remorse, but never for very long, and his repentance for having snatched her out of her marriage was never entirely sincere. Sometimes he tried to convince himself that their renunciation of each other might compensate for their guilt, but he was scarcely out of her presence before he would beg for news of her and would be consumed with impatience at any delay. Occasionally she would threaten to leave him, either honestly or out of coquettishness. At such times Bolivar became desperate and implored her to stay. "Wait, on any condition, do you hear? Do you understand? If not, then you are an ingrate, unfaithful, and more, an enemy." To this communication he signed no name, merely adding a confession, "Your lover."[19] A little later he wrote, "My adored one, your answer is not clear about that terrible trip to London!!!??? Is this possible, my dear? Don't give me mysterious riddles to solve. Tell the truth and that you don't want to go anywhere. Answer what I recently asked you, so that I know your intentions definitely and surely. You want to see me . . . at least with your eyes. I want to see you, to

17 Cartas de mujeres: p. 334.
18 Cartas: Vol. IV. p. 315. Vol. V. p. 180.
19 Cartas: Vol. V. p. 267.

see you again . . . to touch you, feel you, taste you, to join myself with you in every sense. You don't love as much as I do? Well, that is the realest and most honest thing you can say. Learn to love and don't go away, not even with God Himself. To the only woman . . . Your Own." [20]

Manuela would not have been a woman if she had not made him swear that he loved no other. Bolivar wrote to her, "My enchanting Manuela, your letter delighted me. Everything in you is love. I, too, am suffering from this searing fever, which consumes us like two children. In my old age, I suffer from a sickness I should long since have forgotten. Only you keep me in this condition. You beg me to tell you that I love no one else but you. No, I do not love anyone, nor shall I love anyone. The shrine you inhabit will not be desecrated by any other idol or image . . . were it God Himself. You have made me into a worshipper of beauty . . . specifically of Manuela. Believe me I love you, and shall love only you and nobody else but you. Don't kill yourself. Live for me and for yourself. Live to console the unfortunate ones, and your lover, who pines for you." [21]

Manuela's tenderness, her whims, her passionate partisanship, even her follies, became a necessity to him. When political disappointments began to darken his heart, when he became ever more lonely, he could not do without her. Of the many hundreds of letters the passionate and faithless lover sent to his fiery and inconstant mistress, scarcely more than a handful have come down to us. It is sufficient to know that in all the errors and confusions of his life this was the only emotion that ever had room in his being, and Manuela was the only woman who understood how to supply his intense nature with fresh energy, how to discipline his inconstancy with suspense, and how to give relaxation to the still passionate spirit of this harassed and aging man.

Manuela's infatuation finally became a real love—consider-

20 Cartas: Vol. VI. p. 3.
21 Cartas: Vol. VI. p. 80.

ate, unselfish, and sacrificing. The conquest of Bolivar had been her triumph over a society in which she had no status, and she had been insatiable in her enjoyment of this love which seemed to establish her superiority. Exhibitionist that she was, she never missed an opportunity of being seen with Bolivar, and when alone with him their days and nights were spent in passionate embraces. Malicious tongues dealt harshly with her sexual temperament; she was called a nymphomaniac, and many other more diabolic things were said of her. No one knows the truth of these matters, but two things are certain; she was sterile and she was insatiable. Bolivar was indifferent to the first fact; the second was familiar to him. He, too, was sexually insatiable, but in his case, the consummation of their passion exhausted a body already strained by the hardships of ten years of war. Manuela, however, emerged from these torrid encounters refreshed and glowing. Bolivar's mother had died of a hemorrhage, and the Liberator had inherited her predisposition to tuberculosis. The first signs of the disease manifested themselves in the early days of his association with Manuela, and a year later he suffered his first breakdown. The violence of his love for her may have hastened the outbreak of his illness, but it is probable that the course of Bolivar's destiny was preordained, that, lacking Manuela, another woman, or many other women, would have wrought the same havoc in his burning and lustful nature. In any case, Bolivar's meeting with Manuela constituted a turning point in his life. Her name signifies the beginning of his physical decadence.

His sexual passion for Manuela by no means exhausted the content of their long relationship. This woman, more than any other person, gave herself unconditionally to Bolivar. She returned his affection with a thousand evidences of the strength of her attachment to him, and, although this love was the answer to her deepest ambition and the completion of her being, she was obliged to pay for her gratification in no small coin. The condemnation of society was only a beginning.[22]

22 Rumazo: pp. 254-55.

Years of poverty and exile were to follow. She was incapable
of calculation, and, once having broken with her husband, she
disdained to accept money or gifts from him. At Bolivar's
death she was driven out of Greater Colombia, and after many
bitter experiences, finally found a kind of refuge in the little
Peruvian port of Paita, where she made a living from the sale
of sweets. "What have I to do with politics?" she wrote four
years after the Liberator's death. "I loved Bolivar and I honor
him in death. Therefore, I am banished."[23] Garibaldi, whose
wanderings brought him to the Peruvian coast in 1854, thought
her the most amiable matron he had ever met.[24] For us she
remains what she was for Bolivar, the one and only Manuela,
his companion on the great Odyssey of American independence.

Throughout the fall of 1822 Bolivar was making preparations to leave for Peru. The countryside was enchanting. The
palm trees in the breeze, the mangoes with their sweet fruit,
the orange trees—all nature in the luxuriance of her growth
seemed to invite the prolongation of his stormy happiness. But
behind the green walls of this paradise lay a world in flames.
Pasto had again rebelled, and Sucre had been assigned to
subdue the region. But the fanatical inhabitants of this hill
country resisted him, and with the cry, "Long live Ferdinand
VII!" they had attacked the Patriots and had thrown Sucre
back. He had, however, returned with greater fighting forces
and had defeated the Pastoans, imposing a terrible judgment
on the province, which Bolivar confirmed.[25] All who had
taken part in the rebellion were drafted into the army and their
property was confiscated. The pro-Spanish clergy was driven
out, and even sterner measures followed. Thousands, many of
whom died on the way, were brought to Quito and thrown
into prison. Some declared a hunger strike; others committed
suicide. Even with severe measures Bolivar could not control
the province, and after six months resistance flared up for the

23 Rumazo: p. 273.
24 Rumazo: p. 283.
25 Larrazabal: Vol. II. p. 172. Lecuna: El Gobierno del Perú llama al Libertador. B. d. H. Caracas. Vol. XXVI. No. 103. p. 180.

PLATE V

BUST OF SANTANDER ON THE GROUNDS OF THE CHAPEL ROSARIO

PLATE VI

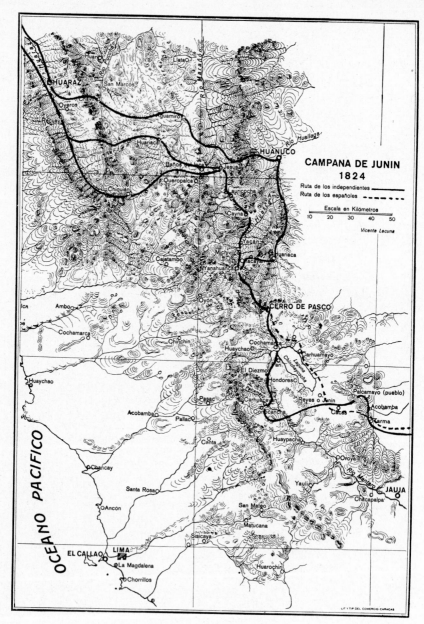

CAMPANA DE JUNIN
1824
Ruta de los independientes ————
Ruta de los españoles ▬ ▬ ▬ ▬

Escala en Kilómetros
10   20   30   40   50

Vicente Lecuna

MAP—CAMPAIGN OF 1824

third time.[26] This opposition could achieve importance only
if it were to be supported by the other side, that is, if the
Monarchists of Colombia should extend their hands to the
Spaniards in Peru. Thus this problem also involved the Peruvian question.

San Martín's resignation had plunged Peru in chaos. The
Peruvian Congress appointed a triumvirate to carry on the
government, but the new leaders were not united among themselves and made war upon each other, both openly and in
secret. They agreed on only one thing, their dislike of
Colombia.

When Bolivar offered to send them help, Parliament and
the government refused, stating that they wanted arms, but
no troops. The Colombian division which Bolivar had sent
to Lima, as he had agreed to do, was received with hatred and
envy. The newspapers published calumnies against the men
and their officers, and the government declared its open opposition. Finally the Commandant was obliged to give orders
for their return to Guayaquil. With nothing but the maledic-
tions of the Peruvians for their pains, they arrived in port in
January, 1823.[27]

Peru remained in a state of great confusion. The Argentinian army was demoralized, its leaders disconcerted and disappointed, while the Royal army maintained its stable position in
the Sierras. Laws passed by Parliament only increased the fever
that was consuming the country. The credit system was
disorganized and trade paralyzed by the introduction of paper
money. The government hoped in vain for a victory that would
restore its prestige. As was to be expected under the circumstances, the Peruvian army was decisively beaten by the Spaniards in January, 1823, at Torata and Moquehua.[28]

26 Cartas: Vol. III. p. 131. O'Leary: Doc. Vol. XX. p. 86.
27 O'Leary: Memorias. Vol. II. p. 178. Restrepo: H. d. R. C. Vol. III. p. 297.
Cartas: Vol. III. p. 138. O'Leary: Doc. Vol. XIX. pp. 390, 394, 395, 397, 401. Paz
Soldán. Vol. I. 2. pp. 12, 54.
28 O'Leary: Memorias. Vol. II. p. 180. L. Alayza Paz Soldán: Unanúe, San
Martín y Bolívar. Lima, 1934.

Finally, the garrison of Lima sent an ultimatum demanding the appointment of a new government with a man at its head in whom they could have confidence, and on February 27 Riva Agüero was appointed president. His first act of government was to send a minister extraordinary to Guayaquil to ask Bolívar for a new expeditionary force to liberate Peru.[29] Bolívar received General Portocarrero in March and repeated his readiness to give assistance. "Colombia will fulfill its obligations in Peru. It will lead its soldiers to Potosi and these braves will return to their country with the sole satisfaction of having contributed toward the destruction of the last tyrants of the New World. Colombia does not covet one single grain of Peruvian soil."[30] Bolívar had now concluded, after much hesitation, that he himself would be obliged to conduct the liberation of Peru.

For many weeks Bolívar had seriously considered whether it would not be better to leave Peru to its fate. Would it not be wiser to make peace with Spain and concentrate all his forces on the consolidation of Colombia? Chile and Argentina were engaged in civil wars, and he knew that the bacillus of disintegration could easily infect Colombia. Perhaps it would be better to leave the Spaniards in Peru for the time being, and thus draw a safety belt around his beloved Colombia. "The clamorers want new and weak governments which will make revolutions and still more revolutions. Not I. I do not want a weak government. I would rather die on the ruins of Colombia fighting for its principles and its unity."[31]

Bolívar thought that a strong government in Colombia might be easy to achieve if he used Spanish rule in Peru as a kind of moat between the Colombian citadel of freedom and the still existing anarchy in the southern part of the continent. This train of thought, which was not without Machiavellianism, arouses our interest, not because Bolívar pursued his idea,

29 Blanco: Doc. Vol. VIII. p. 603. O'Leary: Doc. Vol. XIX. p. 458. G. Bulnes: Bolívar en el Perú. Madrid, 1919. Vol. I. p. 127.
30 Proclamas: p. 282. Bulnes: Vol. I. p. 133.
31 Cartas: Vol. III. p. 133.

but because he finally gave it up. A European statesman—a Bismarck, a Disraeli, even a Cavour—would certainly have acted on these projected principles of Bolivar's, for they were directly in line with the dictates of statesmanship and national selfishness of the times. But Bolivar was no calculating politician of the Old World, but a visionary of the New. He was not only President of Colombia; he was the torchbearer of American freedom, and felt deeply the law of continental solidarity. Therefore, he could not ignore the Peruvian demands as they were transmitted to him through the delegates of Riva Agüero.

To be sure, Bolivar did not rush his decisions. As long as even a semblance of danger hovered over Colombia, he would not leave his country. When he received word on April 30, 1823, that the Spaniard, Morales, had gained more ground in Venezuela, he moved on to the north. This was four days after the President of Peru had begged him to come to Lima to assume command. On the way he received a special message from Bogotá with the information that Morales had again withdrawn. Bolivar returned to Guayaquil.

Personal motives also caused him, time and time again, to postpone the decision to go to Peru. He did not want his undertaking to be misinterpreted. He wrote to Riva Agüero, "I have the secret fear that my enemies will regard my trip to Lima with envy. There was only one Bonaparte, and our America has already had three Caesars. My three colleagues San Martín, O'Higgins, and Iturbide have already suffered an ill fate because they did not love freedom. And I do not wish even a faint suspicion to make me appear like them. The desire to end the war in America drives me to Peru, and the love of my reputation holds me back at the same time. I hesitate and decide nothing. . . . Nevertheless, I am inclined to think that, if it is destined to do so, my love for my country will triumph."[32]

Bolivar's country was America; nevertheless he delayed

32 Cartas: Vol. III. p. 164. Vol. X. p. 421.

action until all the conditions he considered contingent to
success were met. Gradually all his stipulations were fulfilled.
In northern Colombia the Spanish army was defeated, and in
Bogotá, Parliament confirmed the Constitution and the unity
of the Republic which was so near to Bolivar's heart. Moreover, the pleas which came from Lima became more urgent
every week.[33] Bolivar had promised the Peruvians an army
of six thousand men, which they had agreed to transport to
Lima. One division was already on the ships, and a second
was preparing to sail. At the same time the Peruvians renewed
their appeals to Bolivar to take charge of the campaign himself.
Bolivar replied that he was ready to come if the Colombian
Congress would give its consent.[34] Congress, however, hesitated, and Bolivar could not yet make up his mind to embark
on this adventure on his own responsibility. It seemed best to
send a pilot ahead to measure the depth of the Peruvian waters.
Bolivar chose Sucre for this assignment. He named him ambassador extraordinary to the government of Lima and gave
him command of the Colombian troops on Peruvian soil. Sucre
was to prepare the plan of campaign and to coördinate the
forces of the two nations. In this manner did Bolivar send out
the Prophet in order that the Messiah could follow. Sucre left
Guayaquil in the middle of April.[35] Soon fresh delegations
came from Lima begging again that Bolivar should take command, but he wanted to see what Sucre could do alone. He
was in constant communication with his General, and sent him
detailed instructions from week to week. Three months passed
thus—May, June, and July of 1823, and only at the end of
this period was Bolivar convinced that Peru could not be liberated without him.

At length, in August the Congress of Bogotá issued its
permission for Bolivar to take command in Lima. He had
already composed a letter to Santander in which he had said

33 O'Leary: Doc. Vol. XIX. p. 462. O'Leary: Doc. Vol. XX. p. 138.
34 Cartas: Vol. III. pp. 155, 156. O'Leary: Memorias. Vol. II. p. 199.
35 Cartas: Vol. III. p. 162. Blanco: Doc. Vol. VIII. p. 684. Arch. Santander:
Vol. IX. p. 278.

that he would go to Peru without waiting for Congress' permission. When the awaited news came on August 3, he tore up this letter and in feverish haste gave his last instructions. He set sail for Lima on August 6.[36] His ship neared the Peruvian coast on September 1, more than a year after San Martín had urged him to take command, but his delay had been consistent with his diplomatic beliefs. He came now, not at the invitation of one man, himself a stranger in Peru, but at the behest of the president of the state, Parliament, the officers, and the army.

As Bolivar's ship slowly neared the harbor, he thought of the strange fortunes of this land he wanted to liberate. Its treasure had become its doom. The curse of gold hung over it. The barren coast stretched before his eyes, and the lonely hills rose from the sea. They seemed a symbol of what he knew awaited him,—civil war, weakness, and treason on all sides. Gold had decimated the land and poisoned its people morally and politically. As he thought of these things, a feeling of rage and contempt arose in Bolivar. The Peruvians had sent a delegation to welcome him. He received the deputation with a sharpness previously unknown in him. "You may count on me," he said, "only if you do away with your malpractices and institute reforms in all branches of the government where venality and decadence appear."[37]

36 O'Leary: Memorias. Vol. II. p. 206. O'Leary's description of Bolivar's departure is not quite exact, see O'Leary: Doc. Vol. XX. p. 243.
37 Larrazabal: Vol. II. p. 205.

CHAPTER 27 ———————————

Junin and Ayachuco

*B*olivar stepped out upon the shore of Lima in September, 1823. Ten years of bloody and tenacious conflict had been rewarded by the independence of three countries. The struggle which awaited him was to be even more pitiless and savage. It lay there before him—the land of wonders, the envy of thousands of adventurers, the fountain from which gold and silver had for three centuries flowed into Europe. As long as Castile held the country, the New World could only dream of freedom. Let us consider why Peru remained deaf to the call of liberty.

Geographically Peru was a part of the Andes mass stretching from Venezuela down to Tierra del Fuego. Its composition may be comprehended in a brief survey.[1] A narrow coastal strip, not more than 140 kilometers wide, extends from north to south. This coastal region is almost entirely desert, a plain in which there is almost no rainfall and where only the cactus blooms. It is traversed by a few streams that come down from the mountains. These streams irrigate small areas, where tropical vegetation thrives, small oases in the monotony of the desert. In these more fortunate zones lie the harbor cities of El Callao, Trujillo, Pisco, and Huacha, which control communications with the real country, the Sierra. In some places the Andes push to the very edge of the sea and at others they retreat inland. This mountainous country, with its noble crests of eternal snow,

---

1 Blanco: Doc. Vol. VIII. p. 565. A. Fuentes Rabe: Geografía militar del Perú. Santiago, 1917.

with its bizarre rock formations—confusing, chaotic, impenetrable—is the real Peru. Its capital, Lima, is the *Fata Morgana* of glamor and luxury, but in the mountain regions where once the ancient Inca culture had flourished, the heartbeat of reality is felt.

A country thus constituted posed incredible problems to Bolivar. Nothing that he had done before could serve as precedent for what he must do now. Possession of the Sierras was requisite for the control of Peru. The Spaniards were in the Sierras, and were still, therefore, the rulers of the kingdom three years after San Martín had proclaimed the independence of Peru. The operation of an army in this country was a serious and perplexing question.[2] Two solutions, however, were possible: the road through the mountains could be used, though it would be a slow and fatiguing march; or the troops could be transported by water from port to port. Although this was still the age of the sailing vessel, an army could be moved five times as fast by sea as by land, and it was for this reason that San Martín had raised a fleet. With it he had hoped to take possession of the harbors and to starve out the armies scattered throughout the mountains. We know that this plan failed because control of the sea represented only one aspect of the problem. Conquest of the Sierras alone could complete what the blockade had begun, and the Argentinian had recoiled from this undertaking.

After San Martín's resignation the insubstantial structure of Peruvian independence had collapsed like a house of cards. Bolivar knew what to expect. "Peruvian affairs have reached a peak of anarchy. Only the enemy army is well organized, united, strong, energetic, and capable. The Patriot army is lost. Seven warlike powers fight each other under the flags of Peru, Chile, Colombia, Buenos Aires, the Government, Parliament, and Guayaquil."[3]

2 Cortes Vargas: Participación de Colombia en la Libertad del Perú. Bogotá, 1924. Vol. I. p. 7.
3 O'Leary: La emancipación del Perú, 1821-1830, Correspondencia d. General Heres con el Libertador. Madrid, 1919. Cartas: Vol. 10. p. 430. O'Leary: Memorias. Vol. II. p. 200.

It is true that Sucre had been sent ahead to reconnoiter and
to create order, and he had indeed been active in Peru since
the beginning of May, but his presence had only proved the
general disintegration.[4] Sucre had first devoted himself to the
task of improving living conditions among the Colombian divisions. If the fight was to be brought out of the lethargy of a
sit-down war, he had to raise an army of six thousand men and
lead it to the arteries of the Spanish positions. Sucre and General Santa Cruz, who was in command of the native troops,
agreed that such a plan should be put into operation.

The execution of this stratagem was, however, frustrated by
the anarchy of the country. Within a short time Sucre was
enmeshed in a web of unrestrained party politics which threatened to strangle Peru. Government and Parliament struggled
for leadership and each sought support from the Colombian
reinforcements in Peru.[5] Each contestant wanted Sucre to take
command, but Sucre was firm in his refusal, feeling that such
a position was not compatible with the office of Colombian
ambassador. However, the situation darkened and soon developed into an emergency when the Spaniards left their quarters
and set out to conquer Lima. By mid-June, 1823, General
Canterac stood at the gates of Lima, and Sucre was now obliged
to take charge. He gave up the capital and withdrew with the
army to the harbor fort of El Callao.

Unfortunately, the President and Parliament had also fled to
El Callao, and here each maintained a position of resolute and
active opposition. Sucre realized that it was only a matter of
time before the army would also become involved, and he tried
to save the situation by threatening to leave. Finally he proposed that the civil authorities seek other quarters to the north
in the port of Trujillo, where the hostile groups could settle
their disputes with greater freedom. His suggestion was accepted, and the Parliamentarians went to Trujillo, but before

4 López Contreras: Sucre. p. 77. O'Leary: Doc. Vol. XX. p. 25.
5 Villanueva: Sucre. p. 240. Paz Soldán: Vol. I., 2. pp. 89 ff. Lecuna: B. d. H.
Caracas. Vol. XXVI. No. 103. pp. 231 ff.

they left they impeached President Riva Agüero and appointed Sucre commander-in-chief of Peru.

The frenzied conflict was continued in Trujillo. Parliament insisted on its rights and the President on his powers. Finally the latter convened Parliament on July 19 and then routed it by force of arms. The majority of Parliament retired to Lima, which the Spanish had again evacuated. Riva Agüero was declared a traitor, and a counterpresident, the Marquis de Torre Tagle, was elected.[6]

Thus, besides the seven powers which Bolivar had expected, there were also two presidents. With all his tact, Sucre still could not save the corrupt and demoralized country from self-destruction. But he had fulfilled his mission; he had proved that Bolivar and his army were needed to drive the Spaniards out of Peru. While Sucre awaited the arrival of the Liberator, he was free to act as general; and, following General Santa Cruz, he went south with the Colombian division, thus becoming dependent on Santa Cruz' movements and decisions. His fate now lay in the hands of this General.

Such was the situation encountered by Bolivar upon his arrival. From the first moment he became engulfed in a turbulent sea of difficulties. He had been prepared to deal with disparate groups; actually their number was legion. The most difficult feature of this situation lay in the lack of any semblance of unity among these groups. That fusion of elements which, in an earlier state, had worked for the liberation of Peru was destroyed; the atoms acted against, instead of with each other. There were no less than four armies—the Peruvian, Argentinian, Chilean, and Colombian—each one obeying a different authority, while the fleet, under the British naval officer, Guise, worked independently. In addition, the Peruvian Parliament, the deposed President in Trujillo, the new President in Lima, presented a completely dislocated political scene.

It is interesting to note that the spirit of anarchy and insubordination had perfectly logical causes. The independence

6 O'Leary: Doc. Vol. XX. pp. 148, 149, 150. Villanueva: Sucre. p. 264.

movement in Peru had not originated there, but had been
imposed from without. The great mass of the people, Indians
by blood and tradition, remained lethargic and indifferent to
the political situation, while the Creole upper class vacillated.
When circumstances seemed to favor the cause of freedom they
followed it; when the barometer of the new cause dropped,
they quickly turned and, elusive as mercury, followed the
Spaniards.

Bolivar had encountered every kind of opposition in his
twelve years of revolutionary battles. Incompetence, envy,
jealousy, and rebellion met him at every turn of the road.
It cannot be said, however, that any one of the Colombian
revolutionaries was ever disloyal to the cause, and in this distinction lay the root of Peru's cancer; treason and the inclination to play up to Spain vitiated any endeavor to encourage
a spirit of independence. Bolivar was aware that his presence
even increased the pre-disposition toward Spain. "I shall always
be the foreigner to most people and I shall always arouse jealousy and distrust in these gentlemen. . . . I have already regretted that I came here."[7]

At first, however, conditions seemed propitious. President
Torre Tagle had welcomed Bolivar as a saviour on his arrival
in Lima and the people had cheered him. Parliament appointed
him arbitrator of all internal dissensions, and welcomed him
at a solemn conclave on September 13. The National Assembly
gave him highest military authority in Peru and endowed him
with all the powers the situation demanded. Bolivar promised
victory and freedom, but assured them that he did not covet
political powers.[8] He was wise to make this assertion because
the Peruvians were suspicious of the Liberator just as they had
been of the Protector. Yet despite all his assurances to the
contrary, Bolivar's position was that of a military dictator.
Torre Tagle remained chief of the civil government, but he

7 Cartas: Vol. III. p. 240. Lecuna: Decomposición del Perú. B. d. H. Caracas.
Vol. XXVI. No. 104. p. 271.
8 Proclamas: pp. 285-86. Larrazabal: Vol. II. p. 210. Blanco: Doc. Vol. IX.
p. 84.

was well aware that his wings had been clipped, and he began
to work against Bolivar.

Nevertheless, these days were the honeymoon of the Peruvian adventure. "Congress and the Peruvian people believe that
I hold the thread of the Cretan labyrinth, and that I would
proceed with it like Theseus. . . . Lima is a large pleasant city
which once was rich. It seems very patriotic. The men seem
loyal to me and say they are ready to make sacrifices. The
ladies are pleasant and very pretty. There is a ball being given
today where I shall see them all." And a few weeks later, "I am
more delighted with Lima every day. So far, I have got along
very well with everyone. The men respect me and the women
love me. That is all very nice. They hold many pleasures for
those who can pay for them. . . . Naturally I lack for nothing.
The food is excellent, the theatre fair but adorned by beautiful
eyes . . . carriages, horses, excursions, bull-fights, Te Deums
. . . nothing is lacking but money."[9]

The carnival atmosphere of these first weeks did not last
long. After all, Bolivar had not come to Peru to take excursions and make gallant acquaintances. The first test demonstrated the real gravity of affairs. "Spaniards and anarchy
threaten this nation with death. Peru is split into two zones . . .
the southern one is in the war with the outside, the northern
one is torn by civil war. Only Lima, plundered and devastated
as it is, has a legal government, but debts are all she may call
her own."[10] He saw that he must act swiftly. He got in touch
with the Peruvian army; he wrote to Admiral Guise; he sought
a loan in England; he begged Chile for reinforcements. But
as long as anarchy existed he may as well have spoken to the
wind and written in the sands. Since Congress had given him
authority above that of the two presidents, Bolivar now set out
to consolidate the Peruvian state. At first he did not attempt
to use force. Wooing, persuasion, consideration of justifiable

9 Cartas: Vol. III. pp. 237-38, 253. See, R. Proctor: Narrative of a Journey.
London, 1825. p. 246.
10 Cartas: Vol. III. pp. 235, 242.

sensitivities and unjustifiable vanities—these were his first
methods.

His wanderings were like a march through the swamps. It
was of utmost importance that he learn to distinguish between
the fatal quicksands and the occasional areas of firm ground.
He waded knee-deep in the mire, and he remained unflinching
and undeterred.

The axioms of his policy were clear, and he did not hesitate
to hammer them into the Peruvians. At one of the many celebrations held for him in Lima, he drank to the good angel of
America which had led San Martín from the La Plata to the
coast of Peru, but he ended with the hope that the people of
America would never consent to the erection of a throne on this
soil. He hoped for the complete abjuration of all monarchistic
desires and all thought of compromise with the Spanish
crown.[11] Peru could become a republic only when the many
hostile parties became reconciled and when they united to
acclaim the new ideal of state.

Bolivar first approached the rebellious ex-President, Riva
Agüero, but this Peruvian who, only a few months previously,
had begged Bolivar to save his country, had now become his
sworn enemy.[12] Calling Bolivar a tyrant and a usurper, he tried
to draw the army to his side. Unfortunately, an alarming number of officers of the army and navy allowed themselves to be
misled by him. For Bolivar the most dangerous circumstance
was Admiral Guise's favorable attitude toward Riva Agüero.
An uprising of the fleet would at this moment have been the
end of the Peruvian undertaking, for if Bolivar could not count
on Colombian reinforcements, only possible by sea, he was
indeed lost.[13]

Two things now occurred which made Bolivar's position
even more precarious. The Peruvian army under Santa Cruz
had landed in a southern port, whence it was to go to High Peru.

11 Proclamas: pp. 284-85. See, Blanco: Doc. Vol. IX. p. 79.
12 O'Leary: Memorias. Vol. II. p. 232.
13 O'Leary: Memorias. Vol. II. p. 233.

These five thousand men, however, had scattered to the four winds without having engaged in a single battle; and Sucre, who had wanted to join this army, was forced to return to Lima without having scored a single success. Sucre's men were the only troops on which Bolivar could count.[14] The second blow was hardly less catastrophic. Bolivar had proof that Riva Agüero had begun negotiations with Spain after having refused the intercessions of the Liberator. It was Riva Agüero's intention to unite the Spanish and the Peruvian armies in an effort to oust the alien—that is, Bolivar.[15] Bolivar's reaction was instantaneous. He wrote to Santander, "I need six thousand experienced troops and weapons and everything, but everything, needed as equipment. . . . For Colombia's welfare, I shall brave the storm. If I am supported, I can do anything."[16] Months were to elapse, however, before his cry was heard in Bogotá. A simple letter required weeks to go between Peru and Colombia. How much more time would be needed to transport the troops! Could Bolivar risk the delay while Riva Agüero was carrying out his attempt? The army of the south no longer existed; the fleet was undependable. If the ex-President could now unite with the Royal army in the north, Bolivar would be caught in a trap and there would be nothing left for him to do but flee.

Bolivar begged Sucre to take over the action against Riva Agüero, but Sucre refused, saying he did not wish to become embroiled in a civil war. Finally, Bolivar took command himself, and set out to find Riva Agüero at his headquarters. He collected about four thousand men to oppose Agüero's three thousand. Bolivar had to prevent Riva Agüero's men from joining the Royal army, and he wanted to separate them from their traitorous leader. Chance came to his aid. Among Riva Agüero's officers was one Colonel La Fuente, who had travelled

14 Cartas: Vol. III. pp. 259-61. Villanueva: Sucre. p. 281. O'Leary: Doc. Vol. XX. pp. 372-81, 435 ff.
15 Cortes Vargas: Vol. I. p. 224. Paz Soldán: Vol. I., 2. pp. 177 ff.
16 Cartas: Vol. III. pp. 260-61. P. Pruvonena: (Riva Agüero) Memorias y Documentos. Paris, 1858.

back and forth between Lima and Trujillo on several attempts
at intercession. Bolivar had submitted to him several proofs
of Riva Agüero's treachery, and the Colonel had been greatly
impressed. La Fuente called his comrades together, revealed
the President's treason, and begged them to rise against him.
Riva Agüero was captured on November 5 and the Liberator
permitted him to sail for Europe. In this manner Bolivar was
rid of a deserter and at the same time avoided becoming engaged in a civil war. Now that he was in the north, he remained
there, choosing first Cajamarca, then Trujillo, as his headquarters. These provinces were well selected for the creation of a
new army, the raising of which Bolivar thought about day and
night.

Meanwhile, it was an open secret that only Bolivar and
Colombia were still promoting Peru's cause. Argentina had
quietly withdrawn her support when she had made a temporary
agreement with Spain which was to be followed by a final
peace. The Argentinian troops, meanwhile, remained in Peru,
and their upkeep was now Bolivar's concern. Chile provided
him with an even keener disappointment. A free Peru was
vital to Chile's independence, and the Chilean government had
promised aid to Peru on condition that Bolivar should take
command himself. The Chilean soldiers had left from Valparaíso on October 15, but when their commander had received
orders from Bolivar to sail to the port of El Callao, he had
returned immediately, and the Chilean government had approved his ignoble act. Bolivar saw each day more clearly that
he was alone in this struggle. "Chileans and Argentinians can
no longer be relied on. And these Peruvians are the most miserable kind of people for this war."[17] Thus he described the
situation. Peru could count only on Bolivar, and Bolivar only
on Colombia. More letters were sent to Guayaquil and Bogotá;
new demands were made of Santander. "In the midst of the
Andes, breathing the pestilential air called the *sorroche,* above
the snow, and with llamas at my side, I write you this letter.

17 Cartas: Vol. III. p. 309.

It will surely be frozen if the condor does not carry it away and warm it in the sun."[18] His hopes might also have died in the deadly atmosphere of treachery, but he pulled himself together and warmed himself in the sun of his conviction that America's freedom was inevitable. "These Peruvians are not fit to be soldiers. They flee like chamois. Here we can count only on the Colombians. Send me the old guard . . . for with it we are invincible."

It was now demonstrated how right Bolivar had been to insist on the incorporation of Guayaquil. Without this port, direct communication with the Colombian arsenal would have been impossible. Even so, the problem that awaited Bolivar was almost superhuman. Sucre, who was not easily discouraged, wrote at this time, "I don't know whether I may congratulate myself on his Excellency's arrival in Peru. Resistance and endless difficulties will arise that may endanger the reputation which the Father of Colombia has achieved by dint of so much work and effort during these thirteen years."[19] Bolivar was not deeply concerned about his reputation, but he did not view the situation less pessimistically than Sucre. "If I go north, the south will disintegrate; if I go south, the north will revolt."[20] The outcome remained unpredictable. From intercepted letters, Bolivar knew that the Spaniards had sent a fresh squadron to the Pacific, and he was well aware that an enemy fleet could cut the artery between Peru and Colombia. His next step was, therefore, to assure himself of the loyalty of the Peruvian armada. On his own responsibility Admiral Guise had blockaded the Peruvian coast in order to cut Bolivar off from his supplies. Bolivar now succeeded in persuading Guise to rescind this order, and finally to acknowledge the government in Lima as the rightful representative of Peruvian sovereignty.[21]

It was this very government, however, that gave Bolivar fresh

18 Cartas: Vol. III. p. 293.
19 O'Leary: Doc. Vol. XX. p. 453.
20 O'Leary: Memorias. Vol. II. p. 240.
21 Cartas: Vol. III. pp. 311, 313. O'Leary: Doc. Vol. XXL. pp. 32, 132, 136, 167-76, 178, 182.

concern. Shocking reports came out of Lima. People were weary of war. They were sick of making sacrifice after sacrifice. They despaired of achieving independence for their country. Why should they continue to fight when perhaps they could, with Argentina's intervention, make peace with Spain? Bolivar could form only an approximate idea of the direction of events, but he sensed the danger and was determined not to watch it with folded hands. "I believe that if the government does not adopt stringent measures against the Royalists and the Rebels, Peru will fall a victim to her own leniency." He considered going to Lima himself, and meanwhile it was arranged that Sucre should take command. The disorders, bad as they were, evoked but an occasional sigh from Bolivar. "Providence only with her omnipotent finger can create order out of this chaos." He was dependent on a few men who, like himself, recognized that this was to be the last round between despotism and liberty in South America. He wrote imploringly to Sucre. "I beg of you, my dear General, help me with all your might to carry out this plan. If you do not, I shall have no one who can support me spiritually. On the contrary, there is an uprooting of things, of men and of principles, which disconcerts me at every turn. Sometimes I lose courage. Only patriotism gives me back my energy."[22] Bolivar knew that he could rely on Sucre to reorganize the army while he himself would search out any new traitor in Lima who might sell the country to the Spaniards.

Bolivar set out at the end of December. He still seemed like a machine of inexhaustible energies, but the strain of the last months had taken its toll of him. On January 1, 1824, his ship reached the little harbor of Pativilca, thirty miles north of Lima, and here the Liberator collapsed and was carried ashore. Almost unconscious and wracked by a high fever, he fought for his life for seven days. In a small deserted village, without doctor or medicine, his iron will resisted the disease which had already been undermining his constitution for years. It was diagnosed as a gastric fever common in the tropics. More

22 Cartas: Vol. III. p. 302.

likely, however, it was the first attack of tuberculosis. After two weeks his temperature began to fall, but he was exhausted, his body emaciated, his arms and legs painfully thin. When his men beheld him leaving his hut for the first time to get fresh air, they had difficulty in restraining their tears.[23] He wrote to Santander, "You would not recognize me, for I am very spent and very old." It was two months before he could think of resuming his travels—two months in which he tried to direct the course of the Peruvian revolution from Pativilca. The amazing toughness of the man is shown in his correspondence. Bolivar fell ill on January 1; on January 7 he had already begun to dictate again. His first letter was addressed to President Torre Tagle. He put on paper what he had planned to say personally.

At the time of Bolivar's collapse in Pativilca, an Argentinian delegate visiting the capital proposed Peru's admission to the peace parleys with Spain. The government favored the suggestion and Parliament did not disapprove.[24] When Bolivar was informed of the circumstances, he took the attitude that negotiations with the representatives of His Catholic Majesty were harmless enough so long as they were based on the principle of Peruvian independence. Very likely he believed that the maneuver of Santa Ana would be repeated. An armistice would of course be welcome, because he hoped within six months to be joined by eight thousand Colombians. Much, however, depended on the manner in which these discussions were carried on. As a ruse of war they were excellent; as a symptom of weakness they would be ruinous.[25]

Bolivar begged Torre Tagle to extricate himself from his ambiguous and vacillating position. "Believe me, the country will not be saved in this way. My own was liberated because we had unity and discipline. . . . You cannot imagine what this war for liberty can be and can cost. We endured the war to

23 Blanco: Doc. Vol. IX. pp. 343-45. Letter of J. Mosquero to J. M. Restrepo.
24 O'Leary: Memorias. Vol. II. p. 245. Bulnes: Vol. II. p. 133. Cortes Vargas: Vol. I. pp. 272-73.
25 Cartas: Vol. IV. pp. 14-19. O'Leary: Doc. Vol. XXI. pp. 273, 287.

extinction for fourteen years, and you complain about four years of dark bread."[26] In spite of Bolivar's protest Torre Tagle sent a representative to Spanish headquarters. He, too, was now willing to gamble away his country for a mess of pottage.[27]

The Marquis was a typical example of Peruvian aristocracy —well-brought up, indecisive, extravagant, susceptible to every fleeting impression, and as variable as an April day. He had gone through all phases of politics with chameleon-like alterations. When treason was the fashion in Peru he became a traitor. Like his predecessor, he feared the Liberator would remove the power from his weak hands. It seemed more bearable to share his authority with the Spaniards than with the Colombians. The coarseness of the Colombian officers had repelled not only Torre Tagle; it had aroused the ire of his wife. It was said in Lima that the lady influenced her weak Marquis to betray Bolivar in revenge for the instance when the Liberator's Secretary-General had thrown her lax morals in her face. However this may be, it is certain that Torre Tagle preferred to come to an understanding with the old master rather than to take orders from the new. He offered to surrender the fort of El Callao to La Serna and to place the Peruvian cavalry at his disposal.[28]

While Bolivar was on his sickbed and while Torre Tagle stood ready to open the gates of Lima to the Spanish, the garrison at El Callao revolted. The government had grossly neglected these troops, and poor food and inadequate pay had driven them to insurrection. Even under these circumstances the rebels could have been held to the side of independence; their demands were only for back pay and for repatriation, since most of them were Argentinians and Chileans. The government, however, missed this last chance, perhaps out of weakness, perhaps because the loss of El Callao had already been foreseen by Torre Tagle and he saw in it an opportunity to

26 Cartas: Vol. IV. pp. 3-7, 20.
27 Bulnes: Vol. II. p. 133. Cortes Vargas: Vol. I. p. 272.
28 O'Leary: Memorias. Vol. II. p. 250.

disguise his treachery.[29] On February 10 the inevitable happened. The Royal flag was hoisted over the fort and the Spanish prisoners set free. They made immediate contact with the viceroy, and Lima was lost. The only authority left in the capital was Parliament, and in a last desperate effort Congress resigned and Bolivar was named Dictator of Peru with unrestricted powers.[30] The Spaniards occupied Lima on February 12, 1824. Anarchy had finally destroyed itself, but had not the idea of a free Peru perished too? All who regarded the situation impartially believed that Peru was lost. Those who had access to Bolivar's intimate thoughts advised him not to accept the role of Dictator. Even Sucre counselled him to withdraw.[31]

Bolivar, however, refused to heed these warnings. He, too, saw the dangers, but beyond them he visioned victory. The complete collapse of the Peruvian state resembled the many catastrophes of his life—1812, 1814, 1815, 1816, and 1818. He was experienced in meeting the storms of a violent fate. Moreover, he now possessed what had not previously been his: namely, the fortress, Colombia, on which he could lean for support. The gravity of the situation was, nonetheless, clearly recognized by him. "This country is afflicted by a moral pestilence. In the five months that I have been here, I have experienced five phenomena of evil. The first was the loss of the army of Santa Cruz; the second, Riva Agüero's war with us and his treason; the third was the desertion of the Chileans; the fourth, the uprising of the Peruvian fleet; and the fifth, the insurrection of the garrison of El Callao."[32] "Every scoundrel wants to be supreme. Every scoundrel defends his own petty possessions with fire and blood."

The drama of this egoistic anarchism filled him with repugnance and pain. "The sorrow I feel is so ghastly that I

29 O'Leary: Doc. Vol. XXI. p. 448. For the events in El Callao, see, Blanco: Doc. Vol. IX. pp. 203, 205, 216. Cortes Vargas: Vol. I. p. 289.
30 O'Leary: Memorias. Vol. II. p. 246.
31 O'Leary: Memorias. Vol. II. p. 247. Arch. Santander: Vol. XI. p. 312. "El Libertador no desconfia porque su alma grande es superior a todos los peligros; pero también aseguro a Usted que es el único que confía." Mosquera to Santander.
32 Cartas: Vol. IV. p. 79.

don't want to see or to eat with anyone. The presence of people irks me. I live among the trees of this miserable place on the coast of Peru, and I have become a misanthrope overnight. But you must realize that . . . this is not the result of any physical ills or any great personal sorrow. This revulsion against people and society comes from deep thought and from the most inescapable conviction that I ever had. My age is that of ambition. Rousseau said that ambition guides men when they are forty years old. But my ambition has died. Notice the change in human affairs. At all times the work of man has been perishable, but today it is like the seed that dies even before it germinates. On all sides I hear the sounds of disaster. My era is that of catastrophe. Everything comes to life and perishes before my eyes as though struck by lightning. Everything passes, and should I flatter myself that I stood firm in the midst of these upheavals, in the midst of so many ruins and the moral revolution of the cosmos? No, no, my friends; that cannot be. And since death does not care to take me under his protective wing, I must hurry to hide my head in the mists of forgetfulness and silence, before the hail and lightning which make the heavens tremble, strike me and turn me to dust . . . to ashes . . . to nothingness. It would be madness to watch the storm and refuse to seek shelter. . . . Everything is felled to the ground, struck by the ruthlessness of disaster. And am I still to remain erect? That cannot be. I, too, must fall." [33]

But this eloquent outpouring of his poetic pessimism gave him only personal relief. It was his private philosophy, but he did not permit it to interfere with his political convictions or prevent him from doing his duty. At this time, and while he was still burdened with a feeling of discouragement and despair, one of the most memorable events of his life occurred. The Colombian ambassador to Peru, Joaquín Mosquera, was on his way back to Bogotá and wanted to make his report in person to the Liberator. He found him in Pativilca, in his garden,

33 Cartas: Vol. IV. pp. 37-38.

sitting on a tumble-down bench . . . emaciated, his head bound up in a kerchief. Bolivar looked so much like a dying man that Mosquera had trouble hiding his tears. He foresaw the annihilation of the Colombian army. "What will you do, my General?" he asked in a trembling voice. The weary eyes of the Liberator lighted up, and in a decisive voice, he retorted, "Triumph!" And this was no play to the galleries. In a sober, technical manner, and with a calm voice, he explained to Mosquera just how and why he would triumph. "In three months I shall have an army for the attack. I shall climb the Cordilleras and defeat the Spanish." Mosquera was deeply moved. The sun was sinking into the sea as they parted, and he could not escape the impression that it was the sun of Peru. The calm vista of the desert, the silence of the sea, all nature seemed portentous. He feared he was never to see Bolivar again. The Liberator, lying on the ground, too tired and too ill to rise, gave Mosquera a last message. "Tell our comrades how you left me lying on this inhospitable shore, where I fight with broken arms to achieve the independence of Peru and the safety of Colombia."[34] This message to Colombia was urgent, because Bolivar needed soldiers, and he knew he would meet with resistance from the politicians.

Bolivar was not overwhelmed by the situation, since he knew its political importance was relatively small. The differences that rose between him and Santander were of a graver nature. Bolivar still maintained his old confidence in Santander, but his correspondence with him had only one motif—an *adagio,* as he called it. "If I am sent troops, freedom will follow." He asked too much of Santander, and when his wishes were not carried out to the letter, he became impatient and insulting. Santander was willing to serve him and to serve the great cause, but personal envy hampered his accomplishments. "The Liberator thinks I am God and can say, 'Let it be done!' and it will be done. So he asks pitilessly for arms and men, and the worst of it is Don Simon gets all the acclaim, while the

34 Blanco: Doc. Vol. IX. p. 344. Cartas: Vol. IV. pp. 26-27.

Peruvians fail to recognize the efforts of the Colombian government."[35] He hid behind the letter of the Constitution in order
to reduce or slow up Bolivar's demands. "There is no law that
empowers me to assist Peru, and without such a law I can do
nothing." At another time he wrote, "Nothing was so painful
to me as your official letter in which you blame this government
for the Peruvian ills because it regards your demands with
indifference. I am honorable, General . . . and my conduct
deserves from no one, and least of all from you, such an unjust
and deliberate accusation. . . . I rule Colombia, not Peru. The
laws that were given me by which to rule this republic have
nothing to do with Peru, and their character does not change
because Colombia's president commands an army on foreign
soil. . . . Either there are laws or there are none. If there are
none, why do we deceive people with phantasms? And if there
are, they must be kept and obeyed."[36] Fundamentally both men
were right. Colombia's inner security depended on the organic
growth of constitutional life which Santander defended: external security depended on the independence of Peru, for which
Bolivar was fighting.

In the end they came to understand each other. Santander
pushed an authorizing law through Congress which assured
Peru help from Colombia, and for his part, Bolivar recognized
the logic of Santander's position. "I believe," he wrote him,
"we should, for the benefit of our mutual understanding, let
bygones be bygones." The bills which today are in the Colombian archives tell in restrained terms the extent to which
Santander carried out Bolivar's program.

Bolivar's appointment as Dictator left him free to erect a new
state over the ruins of Peruvian sovereignty. "I am determined
to leave nothing undone, even if I have to pawn my soul, to
save this country." "The fate of His Excellency," says an official document, "and that of the army under his command, is
unalterable. . . . It means triumph or die in Peru."[37] Among

35 Cartas Santander: Vol. I. p. 243.
36 Cartas Santander: Vol. I. p. 219.
37 O'Leary: Doc. Vol. XXII. p. 193.

the adverse reports Bolivar also received a comforting message: Puerto Cabello and its commandant had capitulated to Páez. Thus Colombia was safe and free, and the treason of seven Peruvian presidents was balanced. It was obvious that if Bolivar could survive the moment of crisis, he could collect new forces. The enemy resorted to all kinds of ruses to get rid of him. Murder was common, and Bolivar discovered a plot in his own vicinity. He was not afraid for his own person, but he wrote to Sucre, "I suggest that you use some caution, and take care not to walk out alone, for the fashion of the day is a bit dangerous for those who have anything to lose." [38]

Bolivar was reminded of the year 1813-1814. "Let us turn a deaf ear to the cries of all. . . . War lives on despotism and is not waged with God's love. Leave nothing undone. Be terrible and adamant. Discipline the forces under your command . . . if there are no guns there are spears." [39] He reduced the government to a one-man cabinet, and set up a *gobierno ambulante,* or mobile government, as he had once done on the Orinoco. [40] Peru's affairs were now in the hands of one minister, the Peruvian Sánchez Carrión, a man who had distinguished himself by his great ability and his patriotism. The problem of state finances was of paramount importance. Most of the desertions from the army had been occasioned by the poor pay. Bolivar now reduced the pay to one-fourth, but he made sure that the men really got it. He took a similar stand in regard to the state officials. [41] Since he was receiving no more help from the other South American nations, he invited them to participate at least in the cost of the undertaking. Until they agreed, however, he had to live from hand to mouth. Under the circumstances he did not hesitate to take a daring but logical step. Peru was the silver treasury of the world; its churches were bursting with

38 Cartas: Vol. IV. p. 93.
39 Cartas: Vol. IV. pp. 75, 123.
40 Cartas: Vol. IV. p. 100.
41 O'Leary: Memorias. Vol. II. p. 252. O'Leary: Doc. Vol. XXII. pp. 9, 156. Blanco: Vol. IX. p. 245.

costly hand-wrought vessels. Bolivar confiscated this wealth and paid his soldiers.[42]

Such methodical and sometimes ruthless measures pleased neither the self-seeking nor the vacillating, and Bolivar's opponents, with Torre Tagle at their head, used the ensuing criticism to decry him as a new Napoleon who would annex Peru to Colombia. Bolivar answered them. "I would have preferred not to go to Peru. I would even have preferred failure to the terrible title of Dictator. But Colombia was involved in your fate and I could do nothing else. In the name of Colombia and in the sacred name of the Army of Liberation, I promise you that my authority will not exceed the time necessary to prepare for victory." [43]

Victory? It seemed unattainably remote. To understand the audacity of Bolivar's proclamation, one must compare his position with that of the Spaniards. Bolivar controlled but a single province; his enemies controlled the rest of the country. They had about twelve thousand men in the mountains, and in addition, the capture of Lima and El Callao had once again opened the sea routes to them. Without delay the Spanish set sail, confident in the belief that they had at last come within reach of their goal—the destruction of Bolivar.[44]

Toward the end of 1823 the short-lived age of liberalism in Spain came to an end. The revolutionary era was brought to a conclusion by the French weapons of the Duke of Angoulême; and Ferdinand, once more absolute king of his realm, was bent on becoming absolute monarch in his colonies. Spanish authorities in Peru congratulated each other on this change, for no constitutional law could now obstruct their ambitions. Bolivar, too, was glad that the Spanish had cast aside the mask of honest democracy they had so briefly assumed. The conquest

42 Cartas: Vol. IV. pp. 110, 113. O'Leary: Doc. Vol. XXI. pp. 446, 528. Vol. XXII. p. 171. F. Olivas Escudero: Apuntes para la Historia de Ayacucho. Ayacucho, 1924. p. 156.
43 Proclamas: p. 288-89.
44 See the opinion of the Spanish historian, Torrente, in Blanco: Doc. Vol. IX. p. 212.

of Peru was, nevertheless, fraught with difficulties. He needed a base of operations, materiel, and time.

First, Bolivar organized his staff. Sucre was given command of the allied army, while Bolivar, as dictator, retained leadership of the campaign. The Peruvians were instructed to pitch their camps in the north and the Colombians were moved nearer to the mountains; in this manner the Peruvians were prevented from going over to the enemy and the Colombians from deserting. Immediate action was out of the question, and although Sucre favored an offensive, Bolivar convinced him that defense was the only possible solution. "We are the executors of South America. We must conserve our strength. The secret of this war consists in maintaining the army. For my part, land, cattle, horses, peasants, even money can be forfeited if only we preserve our raw material and the morale of the army. . . . I expect much of time. . . . What matters to us after all, is to keep intact at any cost. Then the year shall not end without our reaching Potosí."[45]

Trujillo, Bolivar's headquarters since March, was converted into an arsenal. The women made uniforms; ponchos and blankets were commandeered from the natives and assigned to the army.[46] All the available metal in the vicinity was collected to make the canteens for the troops on their marches. Tin was necessary for soldering the seams of these utensils, and it was finally furnished through a combination of luck and ingenuity. Bolivar tore his trousers one day on a nail in his chair, and on examining the cause of his mishap, he discovered that the nail was made of tin. From that moment no article with tin nails was left intact in Trujillo.[47]

Another matter of great importance was the shoeing of horses and mules. These animals walk the desert sands unshod, but crossing the Sierras was a different matter. Bolivar gave exact instructions as to how the hoofs of the horses could be toughened, how the shoes were to look, just what kind of nails

45 Cartas: Vol. IV. pp. 62-65, 92-94. Bulnes: Vol. II. pp. 201-07.
46 Cartas: Vol. III. p. 231. Cortés Vargas: Vol. II. p. 55.
47 Cartas: Vol. IV. p. 111. O'Leary: Memorias. Vol. II. p. 256.

were to be used, the fodder that should be procured, and other details *ad infinitum*.

The element of surprise in the coming campaign would not be very important, since both sides knew each other's positions too well. Consequently, it was Bolivar's plan to delay matters and to subject the troops to an intensive training that would prepare them for mountain fighting. When Bolivar wanted to make a surprise attack, as in 1819, he did not consider whether the troops were adequately clothed, whether the horses might collapse, or whether the men might suffer from change of climate. Now, however, faced by the possibility of a long campaign, he paid scrupulous attention to every detail. Besides his service horse, each cavalryman was furnished with a mule to carry arms and munitions. Ten thousand beef cattle formed the reserve supplies, in addition to the corn and oats for the horses. The soldiers practiced mountain marches as a precaution against coming down with mountain sickness. Bolivar had shelters prepared with food and water ready, where the troops could bivouac.[48]

Bolivar could not possibly supervise the execution of all these orders himself, but he had an excellent substitute in Sucre, who was his equal in all the military arts and who surpassed him in method. Sucre not only trained the soldiers: he rode into the mountains to familiarize himself with the roads; he made maps; he organized the bivouacs; in a word, he was indefatigable. He was for Bolivar what Gneisenau had been for Bluecher . . . the well-ordered brain that missed no detail.[49] The new army consisted of Colombian reserves under young Colonel Córdoba, while the Peruvian division was under the command of Marshall La Mar. The Argentinian General Necochea, and the British Miller had salvaged a Hussar regiment from the collapse of Lima, and the cavalry was assigned to them.[50] By April the army numbered almost ten thousand

48 Cartas: Vol. IV. p. 130. Cortés Vargas: Vol. II. p. 143.
49 O'Leary: Doc. Vol. I. p. 154. O'Leary: Doc. Vols. XXI, and XXII. *passim*.
50 Miller: Memorias. Vol. II. pp. 90-97. Bulnes: Vol. II. pp. 226-28.

men, and they presented a remarkable spectacle. General Miller told a friend, "I assure you that the Colombian infantry, as well as cavalry, could hold a parade in St. James Park and would attract attention." And another foreign observer said, "I don't know where Bolivar got so much money, so many horses, mules, and everything else necessary to equip a large army from this depleted country. The genius of the great Bolivar is truly prodigious." [51]

Let us now assess the strength of the Spanish in Peru. Possession of the highlands, which also took in the territories of today's Bolivia, called Alto-Peru in colonial days, was their greatest asset. The visitor to this strange land receives a first impression of tremendous confusion. The mountains, torn by volcanic outbursts, drop perpendicularly to the sea. Their snow-covered crests seem insurmountable. Narrow trails, barely wide enough for a single mule, connect the lonely valleys. Here and there are plateaus, but they are not as extensive as those of Quito and Bogotá. The population is almost entirely pure-blooded Indian.[52] Everything is reminiscent of past Inca glory, and at every step one meets the large blocks of their architecture. The Indians had surrendered to the Spaniards, as once they had surrendered to the Incas, and with the same fatalistic unconcern as they would one day receive the armies of independence. They changed uniforms, but who can say what went on in the hearts of these inert and taciturn people? They knew that it was their fate to serve.

Viceroy La Serna's headquarters were at Cuzco, erstwhile capital of the Incas.[53] His army, consisting of almost twelve thousand men, was made up of natives, best suited for fighting in regions lying three or four thousand meters above sea level. A homogeneous staff of Spanish officers, whose best brains were General Canterac and Valdés, commanded the army. The Spanish lines extended from Cuzco to the south, and comprised

51 Bulnes: Vol. II. p. 222.
52 Bulnes: Vol. II. p. 193.
53 Bulnes: Vol. I. pp. 78-79.

all of Bolivia; to the north they reached the fertile valleys of the Jauja. Here the Spanish army under Canterac was prepared to attack the Patriots if the latter should venture to make the ascent.[54] From Jauja the Spanish could also push down to the coast at La Serna's command. Fortunately, the command did not come, and Bolivar was saved. Rebellion in La Serna's ranks had delayed him, and the consequent loss of time and opportunity was irrevocable.

We have seen how Bolivar had to combat treachery. It was only logical that the army of the Monarchists should be similarly afflicted. In upper Peru, General Pedro Antonio de Olañeta with his army of four thousand men rebelled against the authority of the viceroy. Olañeta had ruled with great independence in upper Peru, and it would seem that his position aroused in him the desire to withdraw from the patronage of the Viceroy. He defied La Serna's power for personal reasons, but his courage did not go so far as to infringe on the three hundred-year-old rule of the Spanish crown. Olañeta made a military disturbance, filled the government positions with men of his clan, and assumed the pompous title of Governor of the Provinces of the La Plata. The Viceroy had to bring the rebel Olañeta into line, and a clash between the two Royal Armies was imminent. Olañeta was no admirer of American freedom. On the contrary, he was an absolutist. Unconsciously, however, he did Bolivar a great service. His defection prevented the concentration of Spanish fighting forces during those critical months when Bolivar was stricken.[55]

When the news of Olañeta's insurrection reached him, Bolivar had fan-fares blown. "The Spanish now also suffer the influence of the evil star of Peru. The Pizarro's and Almagros fought each other. La Serna fought Pezuela. Riva Agüero fought with Congress, Torre Tagle with Riva Agüero, and Torre Tagle with his fatherland. Now Olañeta is fighting with

54 Cortés Vargas: Vol. II. p. 100.
55 Cartas: Vol. IV. p. 125. Bulnes: Vol. II. 1. p. 191. García Gamba: Memorias. Vol. II. *passim.*

La Serna, and therefore we have time to fall in line in the Palestra, armed from head to foot." [56] Naturally Bolivar construed events to suit his purpose. He wrote to Olañeta as though the latter were fighting for the good cause and offered him his friendship. From Olañeta he received assurances of like sentiments—sentiments that obligated neither. The news of Olañeta's insurrection, however, gave Bolivar courage for the leap. "Since receiving word of the quarrel between La Serna and Olañeta I have decided to begin my campaign against Jauja in the month of May." [57]

The great Cordilleras of the Andes, the backbone of South America, fork into three parallel mountain ranges at the entrance to Peru—the East, Central, and West Cordilleras. They join at a point called Pasco. They diverge again and form the highland of Jauja, which lay in the path of Bolivar's advance. He gave orders to march forward on June 15. "I am possessed by the demon of war and am about to end this fight one way or another. . . . America's genius and my fate have gone to my head."

To march forward meant to ascend. The army had to cross the West Cordilleras, whose passes lie four and five thousand meters high. The hazards of such an undertaking were such that British officers like Miller and O'Connor thought no European soldier could survive, but the long-suffering nature and toughness of the Indians were known to be remarkable.[58] Bolivar was undecided as to whether he should bring the three divisions of his army up on separate roads or bring them to their destination together. Both plans had disadvantages. He finally decided to have them march by separate routes. Although they would not be able to assist each other on the way, the danger that a great part of the army might perish in one battle was thus minimized.

General Miller has given a graphic description of the sol-

56 Cartas: Vol. IV. p. 148.
57 Cartas: Vol. IV. p. 129. O'Leary: Doc. Vol. XXII. p. 227.
58 Burdett O'Connor: Memorias. p. 117. Miller: Memorias. Vol. II. pp. 130-32.

diers' obedience and submission on this march. Many times cries that rose to the hills were heard coming from the depths of a mountain stream asking whether the right road had been chosen. Trumpet notes from soldiers on the higher slopes gave them assurance, but many times both sides lost their directions. The repeated sound of the horns, the distant voices of the offi-cers and men, the neighing of horses, the whining of mules—the cries of men and beasts in need of rest, made a strange and terrible concert that echoed in the lofty solitudes through the dark of the night.[59] Mountain sickness, increased by the radia-tions of the minerals, attacked whole battalions. The army might have been lost, but Sucre had taken care that provisions were constantly brought up by hordes of tireless Indians who were used to roaming the hills.

By July 15 the three divisions had crossed the Andes and had penetrated into the Sierras. The first part of the plan had been accomplished. Without maps, in unfamiliar country, Boli-var and his companions had succeeded in the daring under-taking of leading the army to Pasco.

On August 2, Bolivar reviewed a parade of six thousand Colombians and three thousand Peruvians. Sucre thought it the finest army that had ever fought in America, and Bolivar looked upon it with pride. It was his work, and he had literally created it out of nothing, in spite of the antagonism of men, in spite of adverse circumstances, even in spite of the advice of his friends. This was the appeal that he made to the soldiers. "You will complete the greatest task that heaven has ever assigned to men: that of saving a whole world from slavery. Soldiers, the enemy you are about to destroy boasts of the triumphs of fourteen years. They are worthy of measuring their arms with yours, which have shone in a thousand battles. Soldiers, Peru and all of America expects peace at your hands . . . peace, the daughter of victory. Even a liberal Europe looks with pleasure upon you, for the freedom of the New World is the hope of

59 Miller: Memorias. Vol. II. pp. 132-37. See also, H. Paulding in Blanco: Doc. Vol. IX. pp. 308 ff.

the universe." [60] This is the most impressive speech Bolivar ever made. Just how deeply his spirit had penetrated into coming events, the unhappy children of the twentieth century now know—they who have watched the self-destruction of Europe and for whom the liberty of America is the hope of the universe.

Meanwhile, the Spanish camp had got wind of Bolivar's forward march. Canterac undertook a reconnaissance tour to learn for himself whether it was true that the Liberator had begun operations. Bolivar marched on Jauja in the hope of attacking the enemy from the rear, and on the afternoon of August 6 the two armies met.[61] Canterac's main objective was the protection of Jauja, for this was the base of his operations. He, therefore, drew back when he beheld the Patriot army, but Bolivar was afraid of losing this opportunity to match forces with the enemy and decided to force a battle. He rode ahead with the cavalry, which was commanded by Necochea, and confronted Canterac on the Plains of Junín at five in the afternoon.[62]

Perhaps Bolivar displayed a lack of caution in precipitating this battle. It has been said that he wanted to liberate Peru on the 7th of August in commemoration of that glorious day when he had liberated Colombia. In any case, the encounter took place on terrain unfavorable to Bolivar's army. Canterac saw that he had the advantage and attacked Bolivar's center and left flank.[63] The Colombians waited quietly, their long spears in their hands, according to the tactics the Llaneros had developed in the Plains. The clash, when it came, was terrific. Necochea was wounded seven times, captured, and released. Not a single shot was fired during the entire engagement. Sabers and spears alone were used, and the air rang with the clash of steel on steel. Almost all the Republican generals took part in the engagement.

60 Proclamas: pp. 289-90.
61 García Gamba: Memorias. Vol. II. p. 256. Cortés Vargas: Vol. II. p. 128. Paz Soldán: Vol. I. 2. p. 253.
62 Bulnes: Vol. II. p. 249. See, O. F. Braun's report of the battle, in B. d. H. Bogotá. Vol. XXVI. p. 903. Miller: Vol. II. p. 144.
63 O'Leary: Memorias. Vol. II. pp. 268-70. Blanco: Doc. Vol. IX. p. 346.

At first Canterac did have the advantage; the Patriots were obliged to draw back and in so doing lost their formation. The Spaniards, on the other hand, pushed too deeply into the Republican lines, and when the Peruvian Hussar regiment took the offensive, the recoil was so strong that the Spanish victory was suddenly turned to defeat. Canterac said himself that his eleven squadrons began to flee without his being able to fathom the reason.[64] The fight lasted only one and a half hours. The plains were covered with dead and wounded, and riderless horses ran distractedly among them. The Patriots pursued the Spaniards with their long spears and pushed them back to their point of departure, where they sought refuge behind the infantry. The Royalists lost 400 men, the Republicans 120.

The brilliant skirmish of Junín, as Bolivar called it, had repercussions far outweighing its military importance. Self-confidence was transferred from the Royal army to Bolivar's forces. Panic seized Canterac's men and they left the plains of Junín that same night in wild disorder, thus preparing the way for the final success of the Republican arms four months later. Bolivar described the battle of Junín as follows: "The genius of America led us, and fortune smiled on us. It is not yet a year since I set out from Lima to take fifteen provinces that were in the hands of the renegades, and to liberate more than twenty that were in the hands of the oppressor. All this I have achieved without having to fire a single shot."[65]

In brief, Bolivar had taken the fertile highlands of Jauja and thus cut off the source of supplies of the Spanish north army. He and his army were firmly entrenched in the Sierras, but Junín had not been a decisive battle because the enemy army had not been destroyed. Moreover, the flight of Canterac had been so precipitate that the Liberator had little prospect of catching him. The Spaniards withdrew to the central point of their lines. They stopped first in Cuzco, where they joined

64 O'Leary: Memorias. Vol. II. p. 272. Lecuna: La Batalla de Junín. B. d. H. Caracas. Vol. XIX. No. 76. p. 534.
65 Cartas: Vol. IV. p. 195.

PLATE VII

BUST OF BOLIVAR IN THE PARK AT VILLA DEL ROSARIO

In the chapel here, almost completely destroyed by earthquake in 1870, the republic's first constitution was written in 1821

PLATE VIII

HOUSE WHERE SIMON BOLIVAR DIED

the soldiers of the viceroy, and then went on to collect all their forces in preparation for the final test.

Bolivar also wanted to enlarge his army. New troop divisions had arrived from Colombia, but many others were still scattered through the conquered regions. Sucre, officially commander-in-chief of the army, was commissioned to bring the lost, stranded, and convalescent back to headquarters. He undertook the mission and carried it out conscientiously, but when he had done so he aired his grievances. Despite his great gifts he was as sensitive as a mimosa. He had conceived the notion that Bolivar wanted to get rid of him, that the mission had made him ridiculous in the eyes of his colleagues, and he begged to retire. Bolivar's answer was unhesitating: "I reply to your letter that Escalona brought to me, with an expression of Rousseau's. . . . This is the only thing that you have done in your life without talent. I think you are entirely lacking in judgment if you think that I wanted to insult you. I myself wanted to carry out the assignment I gave you, but because I thought that you with your remarkable energy would be better able to do it, I entrusted it to you as a proof of my esteem, and not to humiliate you. . . . This sensitiveness, this listening to the gossip of little men, is unworthy of you. Glory consists in being great and useful." He left Sucre to reconsider, and Sucre withdrew his resignation.[66]

The months of August and September were spent in freshening the troops. The rainy season had set in and in the Sierras the rain falls with the force of tropical cloudbursts. Little streams swell into waterfalls which sweep tree trunks and rocks along in their path.[67] Under these conditions the campaign seemed to come to a temporary halt, and Bolivar decided that his best plan was to encamp the soldiers during this period. He, as well as Sucre, overestimated the effects of the battle of Junín when he assumed that the Spanish army would long remain under the cloud of its defeat. Bolivar fully believed that

66 Cartas: Vol. IV. pp. 179-81.
67 Bulnes: Vol. II. pp. 260-61.

the fatal battle for Peru would be fought only at the beginning
of the following year.[68] The urge to action overcame him, however, and he sought a new field of activity.

Lima and El Callao had been in the hands of the Royalists
since February. Bolivar knew that if he could liberate the capital, the cause of independence would thereby receive a great
impetus.[69] Appointing Sucre anew commander-in-chief of
the army and giving him permission to take either a defensive
or an offensive position as he saw fit, Bolivar set out for the
coast on October 7. In his capacity as Dictator, he organized the
country through which he travelled. Governors and judges
were appointed, education reëstablished, and state property
guaranteed.

On October 24, as he was riding through the province of
Jauja, he received a strange letter from the Colombian government. Bolivar's constitutional position was unusual, since he
was at the same time President of Colombia and Dictator of
Peru. In October, 1821, an enabling act had given him command of the Colombian forces, and by virtue of his position as
Dictator of Peru, he was also at the head of the Peruvian army.
The Colombian Parliament now reversed its decision and rescinded Bolivar's powers at the moment when he needed them
most.[70] Santander, Vice-President and Bolivar's deputy, endeavored to give the impression that Congress had taken this
ill-advised decision on its own initiative, but indications are that
he was the wirepuller. As the reader remembers, Santander
and Bolivar had differed on various occasions, and it seems
likely that the Vice-President now revenged himself by showing the Liberator that laws and the Constitution could also
exercise a definite power. His attitude was, of course, preposterous. To send troops to Bolivar for the liberation of Peru

68 Cartas: Vol. IV. p. 195. O'Leary: Doc. Vol. I. p. 182. Bulnes: Vol. II. p. 264.
69 Bulnes: Vol. II. p. 265. The idea, broached by Galindo, *op. cit.*, that Bolivar
went to Lima so that the blame of a defeat would not fall upon him, is absurd. Such
an attitude would be out of keeping with Bolívar's whole character.
70 Blanco: Doc. Vol. IX. pp. 410-11.

and then to challenge his right to command them was taking an utterly untenable position.[71]

Bolivar was more disillusioned than indignant. "Happy they who die before they see the end of this bloody drama. However sad our death may be, it will be gayer than this life." He wrote these words under the first impact of his deep disappointment. His political position was, however, unassailable. The decision of Congress was a blow to his pride but he endured it, not without bitterness, but without inveighing against it. He instructed Sucre immediately to inform the army of the decisions of the Colombian Parliament, but he ordered him to make sure that neither discipline nor routine suffered thereby. Sucre was put in command, no longer as Bolivar's deputy, but with full powers to act.[72]

It was natural that the army should protest. Sucre sent the Liberator a petition signed by all the officers, in which they begged him to resume command.[73] Bolivar did not accede to this request; he did not even send the petition to Bogotá. His reaction was simply to curtail his correspondence with Santander, whom both he and Sucre held responsible. Other than this the parliamentary action had only negligible consequences. Bolivar remained Dictator of Peru.

By the beginning of December, Lima was again in Bolivar's hands. He reinstated the constitutional government and appointed ministers and judges, but his first concern was for the war. He wanted to raise an army that would be equal to Sucre's, for he expected the Spaniards to seek him out on the coast. Therefore, he let Sucre know that for the time being he could not send him any help. But Bolivar was mistaken; events did not fall as he had expected.[74]

Bolivar had warned Sucre to be very circumspect. He was to keep the army together and to remain close to the enemy

71 O'Leary: Memorias. Vol. II. p. 291. Lecuna: El Ejército Libertador y la ley del 28 de Julio. B. d. H. Caracas. Vol. XXVIII. No. 109. pp. 3 ff.
72 O'Leary: Memorias. Vol. II. p. 292.
73 O'Leary: Doc. Vol. XXII. pp. 541-42.
74 Cartas: Vol. IV. p. 215.

no matter what direction the latter should take. He was prepared for a war of position, since nothing seemed to indicate a
Spanish offensive. A month passed in outpost skirmishes. Then
suddenly on November 1 Sucre received the news that the
Spanish and all their forces were on the march.[75] La Serna had
united all the Spanish troops, and three divisions of infantry,
cavalry, and artillery, comprising some ninety-three hundred men, were advancing on Sucre. La Serna planned to
surround the Colombian general and push him to the north,
and La Serna hoped that Sucre would be utterly baffled when he
should find the road to Jauja blocked and contact with Bolivar
cut off. As a matter of fact, there were some days of anxiety in
the Patriot camp, but if La Serna thought that this maneuver
would discourage Sucre, he was doomed to disappointment.
Sucre said, "Wherever the enemy may be we shall destroy him.
I have unbounded confidence in this army." Bolivar went even
farther. He wrote to Sucre that the Spanish move seemed excellent because it forced his men to fight with desperate courage
in order to escape the trap.

It is well-nigh impossible to describe the movements of the
two armies. Any detailed account of their marches and countermarches would split the framework of Bolivar's life history.
To escape from La Serna's encirclement Sucre began a thirty
day retreat across a hundred miles of territory. The Viceroy
rushed his advance in an effort to overtake Sucre. It was like
a game of hide and seek, but La Serna was too eager. He
exhausted his soldiers with endless marches over a terrain of
mountains and rivers. Bolivar, who was watching the campaign from a distance, wrote to Sucre, "The axiom of the
Marshal of Saxony is being fulfilled. Feet spared Peru; feet
saved Peru; and feet will again cause Peru to be lost. Fixed
ideas always avenge themselves. Since we cannot fly like our
enemies, we reserve our energies. Sooner or later they will stop,
and we shall defeat them."[76] The month of November passed

75 Cortés Vargas: Vol. II. pp. 172-73. Vol. III. p. 83.
76 Bulnes: Vol. II. p. 304. O'Leary: Memorias. Vol. II. pp. 305 ff. Villanueva:
Sucre. p. 351.

in marches. From the first of December on, the armies were almost parallel to each other. Sucre was eager to force the issue, but he believed that Bolivar's instructions did not permit him to engage in a battle. Then he received a letter from the Liberator telling him to take the offensive whenever he should decide the moment was auspicious. From that moment on it was merely a question of choosing the time and the place.[77]

The viceroy, on the other hand, thought that Sucre was in a trap. He ordered the natives of the surrounding villages to arm so that they would be able to kill the defeated Republicans as they fled. It was precisely the situation for which Bolivar had wished. His men had to win victory on the battlefield if they did not want to fall into the hands of the Indians, who, like vultures, lay in wait for their prey.

On December 8 the two armies came face to face. The field on which Peru's freedom was to be decided is called Ayacucho, said to mean Corner of the Dead. It is a small plain lying thirty-four hundred meters high. The Royal forces were separated from the Republicans by deep and hazardous ditches. La Serna was hiding in a hill, a gunshot away. On the morning of December 9 he called his generals together and their decision was to risk a battle. At ten o'clock both armies stood ready. Sucre addressed his men in few words. "Upon your efforts depends the fate of South America." The soldiers replied with a cheer for the Liberator and the Republic. Sucre felt certain of victory, although his army was inferior to La Serna's. He had only 5,780 men.[78] Before the battle began, scenes reminiscent of the conflicts of the Middle Ages took place. In both armies there were friends and relatives whom coincidence or conviction had placed on opposite sides. They stepped out from their ranks and bade each other farewell.[79]

The lines of the Patriots were angled. The Colombian divi-

77 Paz Soldán: Vol. I., 2. pp. 271-72. Cortés Vargas: Vol. II. pp. 192-93. Bulnes: Vol. II. p. 296.
78 Lecuna: Batalla de Ayacucho. B. d. H. Caracas. Vol. XIII. No. 50. p. 207. Miller: Memorias. p. 173. López: Recuerdos. p. 140. García Gamba: Memorias. Vol. II. pp. 298 ff.
79 Larrazabal: Vol. II. pp. 267-68. Cortés Vargas: Vol. II. p. 245.

sion under Córdoba took the right wing; to the left were the
Peruvians under La Mar; Sucre had moved his cavalry up to
the center. The Spanish occupied the hills and were supported
with artillery. Both facts were favorable to them. The viceroy
wanted to attack Sucre's left wing and force him to retreat, then
to make a thrust at the enemy's center pushing it to the rear,
thus achieving victory. The Spanish right wing began the attack, driving back the Peruvians under La Mar. If Sucre had
now waited until the numerically superior enemy had carried
their drive on into the plains, he would have been lost. But he
had planned in advance to prevent such a contingency. La
Mar's division was reinforced and Sucre sent his right wing and
the cavalry ahead to meet the attack. Young Córdoba's heroism
won the battle. Dismounting, he addressed his men in a calm
voice. "Soldiers, march forward to triumph!"[80] Cheering Bolivar and without firing a single shot, the Colombians went forward, accompanied by two cavalry regiments. The Spaniards
tried in vain to stem the tide. Córdoba moved on inexorably
until he came within range, then gave the order to fire and to
attack with bayonets. Driven back and overrun, the viceroy
threw his center troops into the fray, but to no avail. The
Colombians drove on until the enemy had been forced back
behind its own entrenchments. Córdoba now met with almost
no resistance. He captured the Royal artillery, drove the frightened regiments of the Spanish reserves ahead of him, and led
his troops in triumph up the hill that formed the support of
the Spanish positions. Viceroy La Serna was taken prisoner.

General Canterac now appeared and offered Sucre his surrender. "Although the enemy's position was such that he had
to agree to unconditional surrender, I believed that it was worthy
of American generosity to render some honor to an enemy who
had survived in Peru for fourteen years. Therefore the capitulation took place on the battlefield. . . . It included the surrender of the Spanish army, plus the relinquishment of the
whole region of Peru which they had occupied, and the aban-

80 Bulnes: Vol. II. p. 323. Cortés Vargas: Vol. II. p. 293.

donment of all garrisons, all military supplies and the fort of El Callao, plus its equipment."[81]

The man who had laid the flag of Castile at America's feet was hardly thirty years old. Success had not spoiled Sucre. Not a word of boasting can be found in his letter to Bolivar announcing the results of Ayacucho. On the same day he had named Colonel Córdoba, who he said had won the battle, division-general. "If I have done wrong, please forgive me. I felt justified by your friendship, by justice, and by victory to do this. As reward, I beg that you preserve your friendship for me."[82]

It is said that Bolivar, when he received the news of Ayacucho, danced through the room intoxicated with joy, and cried, "Victory! Victory! Victory!" This time he felt no sense of rivalry for his pupil and companion-at-arms, and he appointed Sucre Marshal of Ayacucho. Bolivar had reached his goal; Peru was liberated, and with Peru, all of South America.

81 O'Leary: Memorias. Vol. II. p. 312. Cortés Vargas: Vol. III. pp. 119-21.
82 See Sucre's letter to Bolivar, O'Leary: Doc. Vol. I. p. 198.

CHAPTER 28 ⸻

Bolivia

$\mathcal{T}$he battle of Ayacucho gave Bolivar membership in that rare company of dreamers whose dreams have been realized. Even the defeated were impressed. General Canterac wrote to Bolivar, "As one who honors glorious deeds even in the face of personal defeat, I feel I must congratulate Your Excellency for having finished your assignments in Peru by the battle of Ayacucho." [1]

Were Bolivar's assignments really finished, however? He had still to deal with the remnants of Spanish rule in Peru. The capitulation of December 9 was rejected by the commander of El Callao, and Bolivar was obliged to besiege this stubborn garrison for more than a year. [2] He was able to use the small army at Lima as a check, but it was imperative that he re-establish peacetime conditions throughout Peru. The political future of the nation was still in question. Bolivar was its supreme Dictator, and he announced the convening of a national assembly to meet in Lima on February 10. "It is time for me to fulfill the promise I have given you, namely, the abolishment of dictatorship on the very day that victory decided your destiny." [3] "The day on which your Parliament convenes will be the day of my glory, the day on which my most ardent desires have been fulfilled, the day on which, once and for all, I resign my rule." [4]

---

1 O'Leary: Memorias. Vol. II. p. 323. See, Bolivar's answer to Canterac, Cartas: Vol. IV. p. 230.
2 Cartas: Vol. IV. p. 235. Larrazabal: Vol. II. p. 275. Blanco: Doc. Vol. IX. p. 513.
3 Proclamas: pp. 297-98. Larrazabal: Vol. II. p. 284.
4 Proclamas: p. 299. Cartas: Vol. IV. p. 237.

Was Bolivar sincere when he wrote these words, or was he again using a solemn formula beneath which were concealed his aspirations for supreme power? Very likely both were true. Bolivar habitually renounced a dictatorial power which, in point of fact, he considered his due.

The National Assembly met on February 10, one year after Bolivar's appointment as Dictator. He came before the Parliament to give a brief account of his deeds. "My administration," he said, "has been only a campaign. . . . The host of misfortunes gave us no choice but to defend ourselves." He had done all he could, continued Bolivar, but he had not been able to complete his plans for political reform. The National Congress would now be obliged to conclude this part of his program. The achievement of victory called for rule by law and not by dictatorship.

The deputies did not accept Bolivar's resignation. Very likely they never considered it more than a gesture. His address was followed by a concert of passionate speeches after the fashion of Latin American parliaments. In answer to their pleas Bolivar declared, "Today is the day of Peru, because today she is without a dictator." He said that he could not accept an office that would conflict with his conscience, but that he was willing to continue serving Peru with his sword and with his heart. His aim, he added, was the creation of that great federation in which Colombia and Peru would combine their forces.[5] Certainly no one will be surprised to learn that Bolivar was again entrusted with the supreme executive power, and that he remained Dictator of Peru for another year. Parliament was to meet again only in 1826.

Many proofs of confidence and gratitude followed Bolivar's reappointment. Medals were coined, monuments planned, inscriptions suggested. Congress proposed giving him one million pesos, but Bolivar refused to accept. In spite of the fact that he lived more lavishly in Lima than ever before, he still found no use for such gifts. His glory could not be measured in the coin

5 Proclamas: pp. 305-06.

of the realm. The offer was repeated, and Bolivar finally asked that the money be given to Caracas as a contribution toward its reconstruction.[6]

Thus Bolivar continued to be President of Colombia and Dictator of Peru. "Here they compare me with Mercury's staff which had the power to link in friendship all the serpents which might have devoured each other. Nobody gets along with anybody, but everyone gets along with me."[7] His extraordinary position of president-dictator was necessary if Bolivar was to reach the goal he had set for himself. "Every day I become more convinced that it is necessary to give our life a foundation of security."[8]

In what did Bolivar find this basis of security? The answer gives the key to all his planning during the next eighteen months. Security meant, first, the complete expulsion of the Spaniards from South American soil; second, the adoption of a final design for the political map of his continent, which included not only the definitive marking of boundaries, but the political birth of that enormous country of mountain plateaus, High Peru, on whose future Bolivar had placed the highest expectations; last, but not least, security meant that the final choice between the establishment of a monarchical or a republican government in South America must now be made, a question debated at Guayaquil and once more occupying an important place on the agenda. And ultimately the security of South America implied its incorporation in the system of international relations, its recognition by the nations of the world, and its appraisal by both friends and foes. Bolivar's last link in this chain of security, therefore, was the forging of a

6 Blanco: Doc. Vol. IX. pp. 579, 581. Larrazabal: Vol. II. pp. 292 ff. Cartas: Vol. IV. p. 273. Bolivar intended the money to be used for the moral reconstruction of Caracas, and called on the English educator, Lancaster, whom he had met in London in 1810, to organize education in Venezuela. Lancaster came to Caracas, but the Peruvian millions were actually never handed over, and Bolivar paid the expenses of Lancaster's contract out of his own pocket. See also, Cartas: Vol. VII. p. 44. See also, El Millón de pesos del Perú. B. d. H. Caracas. Vol. VIII. No. 31. p. 19.

7 Cartas: Vol. IV. p. 258.
8 Cartas: Vol. IV. p. 240.

bond of union between the liberated countries. He believed that the solution of this problem could be found in a federation of the South American states. In union they would acquire the strength of which their isolation deprived them. "I foresee civil war and disorder spreading from one part to another, from one country to another, and my native gods destroyed by internal fires . . . this idea occupies me day and night. . . . As the only remedy I return to my project of federation." [9] These motifs, like the themes of a sonata, were combined in Bolivar's plans for the security of his continent. The thought of them fills Bolivar's life in 1825-26, sometimes overlapping, sometimes hindering, but always vitalizing and enriching each other.

At this point the biographer of Bolivar must decide whether his narrative should follow a chronological order in which all of the Liberator's problems are described at once, since Bolivar tried to solve them simultaneously, or whether it should follow a more unified and basically logical order. The writer believes that the former procedure would only result in confusion. History involves more than the accumulation of facts. It includes understanding and interpretation, which alone have the power to waken source material from its deep sleep in books and archives. For this reason the complicated motives for Bolivar's action during these years have been separated in accordance with their interpretation and significance. In this manner the ideas which inspired his deeds and which make his life a great and memorable one become clearer and take on a more distinctive character.

After the battle of Ayacucho two remnants of Spanish rule remained on Peruvian soil, the harbor of El Callao and the army of Olañeta in High Peru. To take El Callao was a mere military task, but to conquer Olañeta's forces implied various political considerations of great importance. The solution of these problems lay in Sucre's hands. Seizure of the Peruvian territory in the Sierras and at the coastal area, was, after Ayacucho, a fairly simple matter. The few Peruvian troops that had escaped

9 Cartas: Vol. IV. p. 240.

the general surrender followed the example of the viceroy and gave themselves up.[10] Sucre entered Cuzco, the old Inca capital, on December 24, and here received Pizarro's ensign and the royal robe worn in ancient times by the founders of the Inca dynasty. Together they symbolized the renaissance that South America had experienced in its movement for independence.

Sucre was now at the very borderland of the High Peruvian mountain plateau where General Olañeta still maintained himself, and Sucre was obliged, in the absence of instructions from Bolivar for which he had urgently appealed, to take upon himself the entire responsibility for further action. He decided, as any capable officer would have done, to continue the war to its end. To halt his forces at the border of High Peru, where a Royal army confronted him, would have been utter folly. Moreover, his advance was not dangerous since it was little more than a mopping up operation to take possession of the entire mountain country. Sucre preferred, however, to come to an agreement with Olañeta if possible.[11] Bolivar held the same opinion and wrote to Olañeta from Lima, "The victory of Ayacucho will not let us forget what we owe you." [12]

Sucre was cautious, however, and refused to stake the gain of an entire country on the play of a single diplomatic card. While the letter to Olañeta was on its way, he began the occupation of High Peru in preparation for Olañeta's inevitable surrender, whether it came by force of arms or the power of persuasion. Bolivar approved Sucre's plan of procedure and wrote from Lima advising him to carry on negotiations with the enemy and at the same time to advance into their territory. He was of the opinion that Olañeta would not come to any quick agreement, and in the meantime he planned to arrive in person to conclude the final arrangements in High Peru.[13] However, Bolivar was delayed, and events reached a climax in

10 Lecuna: Documentos referentes a la creacion de Bolivia, 2 Vols. Caracas, 1924. Vol. I. pp. 11, 26.
11 Lecuna: Documentos. Vol. I. p. 39.
12 Cartas: Vol. IV. pp. 222, 236.
13 Cartas: Vol. IV. pp. 249, 250. Cartas Santander: Vol. II. pp. 22-23.

the mountains. Olañeta's headstrong disposition led him to attempt a suicidal resistance.[14] Sucre, in turn, issued a proclamation to the provinces of High Peru inviting them to come to the aid of the revolutionary army. In January, 1825, when Sucre had just begun his march, great sections of Olañeta's division had abandoned him, and the garrison of Cochabamba now joined the Patriots' cause and opened the gates of the city to Sucre. On February 20 he entered La Paz; by March 9 he had captured all the Spanish generals with the exception of Olañeta, who, though he had no chance of escape, preferred in true Iberian style, to consider the fifth act of his life as a *corrida de toros,* and to carry his fight to the bitter end. Finally, on April 13 came the expected encounter. The remainder of his division was dispersed and he, himself, fatally wounded. Sucre occupied Potosí.[15]

The battle in which Olañeta was killed was the last to be fought on the American mainland against Spanish troops. In twelve months' time an army of eighteen thousand men had been destroyed; the last support to which Spanish rule had desperately clung had crumbled, and the old regime had come to an ignominious end. The thirty-year-old Sucre, who brought all this about, seemed a giant to his contemporaries. Bolivar described him in glowing terms: "With one foot resting on the Pichincha and the other foot on the Potosí he looks down on the chains his sword has broken." [16] Sucre was, however, no titan, but a sensitive and often irritable human being, a man who was sometimes afraid of his own courage. His liberation of High Peru had been accomplished, just as that of Ecuador and Peru, according to the instructions of Bolivar.

At this juncture in the affairs of High Peru, Sucre was uncertain as to how he should proceed. The history of the country was a glorious one, a history which linked it to the revolutions of Caracas, Bogotá, Quito, and Buenos Aires. The first martyrs

14 Lecuna: Documentos. Vol. I. p. 59.
15 Lecuna: Documentos. Vol. I. p. 143. Blanco: Doc. Vol. IX. p. 721.
16 Larrazabal: Vol. II. p. 273.

of South American freedom had been killed in La Paz, and
Sucre had called this city the cradle of American independence.[17] To him it seemed out of the question to occupy such a
territory by force of arms. He believed it should be organized
as a free nation. During the long campaign of 1824 Bolivar
had frequently discussed his plans for national independence
in High Peru, and Sucre felt he was justified in establishing
the Liberator's ideas.[18] On February 9, 1825, therefore, he issued
his famous decree proclaiming High Peru an independent nation. A national assembly was called to settle the destiny of the
provinces and to decide on their form of government.[19]

Bolivar, however, was not inclined to favor this action of
Sucre's. He considered that the young general had exceeded
his mandate as commander of the army, since no political rights
had been conferred on him; and, further, he believed that the
proclamation of independence had been issued without taking
into account certain vital facts. Sucre, in declaring High Peru
an independent state, had violated one of the basic principles
of the American revolution, the principle of *uti possidetis* by
which each nation was to preserve the territorial status quo of
1810, the year when the movement for independence had been
inaugurated. High Peru had been a province of Peru until
1768, and since then had formed part of the Vice-Kingdom of
the La Plata. The future of these regions should, therefore, be
decided by Peru and Argentina together. A new state could
be erected in High Peru only with the consent of these two
neighbors. In consequence, Bolivar addressed a vehement admonition to Sucre. "You and the army at your command are
subordinate to me. Your province is only to carry out what I
order. Neither you nor I, nor the Peruvian or Colombian parliaments can break or violate the principles of public law which
we have recognized in America." [20]

17 Lecuna: Documentos. Vol. I. p. 121.
18 See, Sucre's letter to Santander of April 23, 1825. Lecuna: Documentos,
Vol. I. p. 183.
19 Lecuna: Documentos. Vol. I. pp. 94-95. O'Leary: Memorias. Vol. II.
pp. 381 ff.
20 Cartas: Vol. IV. pp. 263, 270.

Sucre supported his action with entirely valid arguments. He asserted that he had done only what Bolivar himself had planned to do. Moreover, he had been left without specific instructions from the Liberator. In any case, he added, the meeting of the national assembly could be delayed if Bolivar disapproved of the measures he had taken. It goes without saying that he concluded his defense with an offer of his resignation.[21] Bolivar's response was given with all the ardor of an older brother: "A high destiny is in store for you. I foresee that you will be the rival of my own glory. You have already won two campaigns, and in amiability, energy, and zeal for the common cause, you exceed me." Nevertheless, he added, for these very reasons Sucre should recognize his shortcomings and should refuse to be blinded by flattery.[22]

The real basis of the argument, however, was a question of "how" and not of "what"; of a means of accomplishing a result, not the result itself. Some time previously Bolivar had also planned the creation of a free state in the mountain region of Lake Titicaca, but he had no intention of allowing Sucre to carry this idea into effect. He was unwilling to see Sucre's military reputation enhanced by the glory of liberating an entire nation. As a result Bolivar himself, three months later, issued an order confirming Sucre's decree in all its essential points.[23]

The situation in Lima was by this time so stabilized that Bolivar's power could, with safety, be delegated to his assistants. He appointed a cabinet in which the minister, La Mar, Sánchez Carrión, and Colonel Heres were the leading figures. Bolivar left them a program which was a model of sagacity and political tact.[24] On April 10 he left Lima on a visit to those regions of Peru which he had not reached during the campaign. His journey took him through the coastal area and again became

21 Lecuna: Documentos. Vol. I. pp. 147, 151, 172.
22 Cartas: Vol. IV. pp. 316-19. J. M. Rey de Castro: Recuerdos del tiempo heroico. Guayaquil, 1883.
23 Lecuna: Documentos. Vol. I. pp. 91, 94, 180-81. Villanueva: Sucre. p. 436.
24 See the Text of the Instructions in, O'Leary: Memorias. Vol. II. p. 352. O'Leary: Doc. Vol. XXIII. pp. 159, 200, 227, 228.

something in the nature of a triumphal march. The inhabitants in their bright-colored ponchos ran into the streets, saluting him as their saviour and kissing his hands. Bolivar looked upon the magnificent monuments of the Inca period, but he saw at the same time the miserable living conditions of the Indians. He vowed to alleviate their unhappy lot in whatever way he was able. Occasionally the distances between cities would be too great to cover during a day's travel, and Bolivar was then housed in hastily constructed huts of wood and reeds. The Indians in the villages awaited his approach with great eagerness, their shacks illuminated by candles and torches. Bolivar accepted their devotion with gratitude. He listened to their complaints and immediately sent instructions to Lima giving information and ideas regarding the promotion of commerce, agriculture, and mining. Education in these areas had been sadly neglected and hygiene was unknown. Bolivar endeavored to improve conditions, giving short, precise orders. He had observed, as he rode through the Sierras, that the Indians hunted herds of llamas which were indispensable for their primitive existence, and he gave orders forbidding the llama's extermination, and outlined a project for taming and rearing these animals.[25]

Arriving in Arequipa in the middle of May, he proceeded exactly as Sucre had predicted; he called the deputies of High Peru together in a legislative assembly. He stipulated, however, that the deliberations of this body should be provisional pending the agreement of Peru and Argentina.[26] Bolivar's decree was a repetition of the very proclamation he had so severely criticized Sucre for making. No ill feeling between the two grew out of this incident, however, probably because Sucre, now fully vindicated, preferred to forget it.

From Arequipa, Bolivar proceeded to Cuzco. Travelling was difficult and he suffered from mountain sickness, but again and again he felt joyful and uplifted when the simple native

25 O'Leary: Memorias. Vol. II. pp. 360-63. Lecuna: Documentos. Vol. I. p. 263.
26 Lecuna: Documentos. Vol. I. pp. 220-21.

people greeted him with enthusiasm. His imagination soared in the presence of the vast and awesome natural beauty of the country, and his thoughts were inflamed as he considered the greatness of a history which seemed to speak directly to him.[27] He rode to the cathedral in Cuzco on a horse with a gilded saddle which the inhabitants of the city had presented to him, and he was there hailed as a father by the Indians, who, still swayed by the primitive instincts of the stone age, looked upon their rulers as gods and protectors. The ladies of the city crowned him with a crown adorned with pearls and diamonds.[28]

Bolivar next turned his steps toward High Peru. In one of the villages through which he passed, the mayor, José Domingo Choquehuanca, is said to have addressed him with these words: "You are the man of destiny. Nothing that has happened in the past bears any resemblance to your accomplishments. To imitate you, it would be necessary once again to liberate a world. You have created five republics, an achievement which, in its unprecedented demand for their development, shall lift your image to a height never yet reached by any human being. Your glory will grow with the centuries, as the shadows grow when the sun is setting." [29] This speech, found in almost every biography of Simon Bolivar, belongs to legend rather than to history, but it is noted here as a part of the Bolivarian myth which has grown to enormous proportions with the passing years.

While Bolivar was making his way toward High Peru, great events had transpired in that region. The National Assembly had convened in Chuquisaca on July 10. The deputies, calling upon Bolivar as the first-born son of the New World, implored

27 Cartas: Vol. V. p. 8. Restrepo: H. d. R. C. Vol. III. p. 471.
28 Larrazabal: Vol. II. p. 308.
29 Lecuna: Documentos. Vol. I. p. 276. For the personality of Choquehuanca, see, E. Posada: El discurso de Choquehuanca. Rev. Bol. April, 1935. p. 460. The oration was first published by F. Garcia Calderon, in 1879. I have serious doubts with regard to its authenticity. The assertion "habéis fundado cinco repúblicas" was unthinkable in 1825, since Venezuela, New Granada, and Ecuador, formed one state— Greater Colombia. Bolivar himself writes that he was called the father of three republics. (Cartas: Vol. V. p. 13) Therefore, Choquehuanca's speech in its now known form cannot be considered authentic.

his protection.[30] On August 6 they declared their independence in solemn convocation. It was their determination to form a free and sovereign nation, capable of administering its own affairs.

This youngest nation adopted the name Bolívar, later changed to Bolivia. The name of the Liberator, like the name of Alexander, was given to innumerable towns, but in Bolívar's case an additional glory was accorded him, that of having a whole nation commemorate his name. Bolívar sometimes remarked that the name Bolivia was more euphonious than the name Colombia.[31] Half in jest, half in earnest, he wrote, "I shall soon die, but the republic of Bolivia will endure until the end of time. Romulus founded a city which gave its name to an empire. I have not founded a city, but a state bears my name, a state made up of people who love freedom."[32] He was delighted when the deputies commissioned him to draw up a constitution for Bolivia. Free rein was given him in this project, the only restriction being that the instrument of government should be republican, representative, and centralistic in character.

Bolívar arrived in La Paz on August 18, 1825. After attending *Te Deum* in the cathedral, he went to a reception in the government palace. Here, too, a golden crown prepared by his admirers was awaiting him, and it is a fact that one of the clergy seriously desired to crown him.[33] Bolívar refused this final acknowledgment of his success, however. "The crown," he said, "is not due me." He turned it over to Sucre, who also refused this emblem of power. Sucre passed it on to Córdoba, and the crown finally remained in the hands of this young hero. In general, Bolívar, who had little interest in material things, distributed whatever gifts he received—golden spurs, precious saddles, etc.—among his comrades. Admiration, praise, adora-

30 O'Leary: Memorias. Vol. II. pp. 396-97. Lecuna: Documentos. Vol. I. p. 278. A. Arguedes: Hist. de Bolivia: Fundación de la República. Madrid.
31 D. d. B. p. 317.
32 Cartas: Vol. V. pp. 86-87. See also pp. 88 and 141.
33 Cartas: Vol. V. p. 75. See Arch. Santander: Vol. XIII. p. 175. E. Posada: Apostillas. p. 41.

tion were of more importance to him, and he thoroughly enjoyed these attributes of glory. He was delighted to hear himself hailed as the man of providence, and he did not find it difficult to believe himself all that his followers claimed him to be. Had he forgotten that words are of little importance and nowhere of less importance than in South America? Had he forgotten that the days of fiesta are but the dreams in the life of man, that they pass and are followed by the inevitable disappointments encountered in daily routine?

Leaving La Paz, Bolivar travelled southward to Potosí, a city which his vivid imagination had pictured in brilliant colors. On October 5 he entered the famous town whose silver mines had supported Spanish rule for three centuries. Even today the mint at Potosí, in the form of gigantic barrels, provokes our admiration. Behind the city rises the desert mountain peak of Potosí, which gave its name to the community. Bolivar and his staff climbed its desolate slopes, taking with them the flags of Colombia, Chile, Peru, and Argentina. Their act was a symbolic one, almost a rite, announcing the complete freedom of the South American nations. A dreamer stood there on the remote height—but a dreamer whose dreams had come true. In retrospect Bolivar visualized the bloody fights of fifteen years, that here had been concluded. While the standards of four nations floated in the wind, he conjured this recollection. "We come victorious from the Atlantic coast. In fifteen years of continuous and terrific strife, we have destroyed the edifice that tyranny erected during three centuries of usurpation and uninterrupted violence. . . . Standing here on this silver mountain of Potosí, whose rich veins were Spain's treasury for three hundred years, I must declare my belief that this material wealth is as nothing compared with the glory of bearing the ensign of freedom from the ardent shores of the Orinoco to plant it on the summit of a mountain which is the admiration and envy of the world." [34] Bolivar's theatrical display of eloquence veiled, as usual, a determined diplomatic purpose. He wanted to make

34 Proclamas: p. 314. L. Subieta Sagarnaga: Bolívar en Potosí, Potosí, 1925.

a striking and overwhelming manifestation of the unity of the
American people, not so much for its effect on the outside
world as on South America itself.

General Alvear and Doctor Díaz, acting as delegates from
Argentina, visited Bolivar in Potosí.[35] Their official commission was to congratulate the Liberator for the services he had
rendered to the New World. They were also authorized to
negotiate with Bolivar about any difficulties which might arise
in regard to Bolivia's boundaries. This diplomatic façade,
however, concealed a deeper purpose. Argentina wanted to
obtain Bolivar's assistance in her fight with Brazil for the
control of the La Plata River.[36] In 1822, Pedro I, a member
of the house of Braganza, had led a revolution which separated
Brazil from the crown of Portugal. The young emperor had
extended Brazil's claim to the eastern bank of the La Plata
and had incorporated Montevideo in his new empire. The
great majority of the inhabitants of Montevideo were not inclined to accept their new master and expressed a desire to
belong to the United Provinces of the La Plata, as Argentina
was then called. These circumstances placed Argentina in a
difficult position, however, for if she listened to the pleas of the
Montevideans she was certain to become involved in war with
Brazil; on the other hand, if she failed to assist Montevideo,
her mighty neighbor would assuredly expand to the La Plata.
In face of this issue the Argentine statesmen had conceived the
idea of utilizing Bolivar and his army as a means of intimidat-
ing Brazil and of forcing the restitution of Montevideo. They
relied on Bolivar's warrior instincts and on his insatiable desire
for glory. The idea was not entirely illogical. Certainly Bolivar
was not insensible to the additional fame he might acquire in
becoming the protector of Argentina. Moreover, he had many
reasons for looking upon Brazil with aversion. Brazil was an
empire, for one thing; and more, she had but recently infringed

35 Lecuna: Doc. Vol. I. p. 510. Larrazabal: Vol. II. p. 314.
36 Lecuna: Doc. Vol. I. pp. 510-11. Cartas: Vol. V. p. 108. Blanco: Doc. Vol.
IX. p. 731, Vol. X. p. 143.

on Bolivia's rights. These facts inclined Bolivar to listen sympathetically to the proposals for alliance which the Argentinians offered. Accordingly, he received the ambassadors, at first in secret meetings, to ascertain the extent of their aims. The Argentinians expressed their country's wish for closer relations with Colombia, going so far as to declare their willingness to place Argentina under a protectorate of the Liberator. Their plan was that Bolivar, with his army and his fleet, should come to the La Plata, and that all expenses for such an expedition should be met by the Argentinian government.[37]

Bolivar had ventured to enter upon these negotiations because he needed Argentina's good will for two major projects. The first was concerned with the establishment of an independent Bolivia, and the second, with the South American League of Nations.[38] Bolivar was desirous, therefore, of winning the benevolence of the Argentinian government, but he wanted to accomplish this end without committing himself to any venture he was neither able nor permitted to undertake. Nor was he to be drawn by flattery or an appeal to his ambitions. In any case, the Colombian government informed him that it did not approve of the Argentine adventure.[39]

On October 16 Bolivar, surrounded by the highest officers of his staff, met the delegation in ceremonial fashion. He delivered a challenging address in which he reprimanded the Brazilian emperor for his encroachment on Montevideo. He declared his willingness to ally himself with Argentina, and said he would even undertake to send part of his army to the Brazilian frontier, but not farther. He felt that he was justified in risking this much, and he knew he needed to go no further in the realization of his aims.[40] In May, 1825, Argentina had given Bolivar full power to settle boundary questions between

37 Lecuna: Doc. Vol. I. pp. 510-11, 513, 524.
38 Lecuna: Doc. Vol. I. p. 525.
39 Cartas: Vol. V. p. 65. Cartas Santander: Vol. II. p. 24.
40 Proclamas: p. 314. Cartas: Vol. V. p. 139. Decisive for Bolivar's attitude towards Brazil was the fact that England was opposed to a war between Argentina and Brazil. L. A. Herrera: La Mision de Lord Ponsonby a la Paz en 1828. Rev. del Inst. Hist. y Geog. del Uruguay. Vols. XIII, XIV, XV.

that country and Bolivia. Bolivar took this as a recognition of
Bolivia's independence by the government of Buenos Aires,
and at the moment he was content with this achievement. The
young state that should make his name immortal was his first
concern during these weeks.

As far as international law was concerned, Bolivia's affairs
were still in an ambiguous state; even her sovereignty could not
be considered a fact, but, says Vauvenargues, he who would accomplish great deeds must act as though he were immortal. The
statesman who desires to create a new political form must
disregard the insecurity of human reckoning and must act as
though he had eternity at his command. This Bolivar did. He
decided that he would remain in the country for a year, and he
was determined to effect its reorganization within that time.[41]

The administration of justice, shamefully neglected during
the colonial period, was his first concern. Local and appellate
courts were established. A new body of laws which would
incorporate liberal ideas was promised.[42] A sound economic
policy was instituted. This was a country whose peacetime
revenues were considerable because of the abundance of precious
minerals, but the lack of any systematic policy had resulted in
a confusion of receipts and expenditures. Bolivar established a
financial equilibrium. The state confiscated the abandoned
mines, abolished the Indian tribute, and suppressed the con-
sumer taxes which had supported the Spanish here and elsewhere.[43] Today Bolivia suffers from an incurable illness, her
lack of access to the sea, but Bolivar planned to avoid this situation when he assigned the harbor of Cobija to her and arranged
for its completion.[44]

The Indians were abysmally ignorant of even the rudiments
of hygiene. They buried their dead in the churches, and their
temples were filled with the odor of putrefaction. Bolivar

41 S. Pinilla: La creación de Bolivia. Biblioteca Ayacucho. Madrid. Cartas:
Vol. V. p. 94.
42 Lecuna: Doc. Vol. I. p. 444.
43 Lecuna: Doc. Vol. I. pp. 246, 276. Blanco: Doc. Vol. X. p. 11.
44 Lecuna: Doc. Vol. I. p. 465. O'Leary: Memorias. Vol. II. p. 447.

ordered the establishment of cemeteries. New roads were constructed, customs duties examined; the possibilities of agriculture and mining were taken under consideration. Even more
important was the question of education. Bolivia's population,
even today, is 85 per cent Indian or *mestizo*. A century ago
Bolivar found the native stock more backward than any he
had encountered. The Llanero of Venezuela was a barbarian,
but the Indian of Bolivia was a slave, who as far as all practical
purposes were concerned still lived a neolithic existence. During
Spanish rule he had lost all impulse toward progress or a higher
standard of living. The continued use of coca, a plant whose
leaves, mixed with lime, are chewed by the Indian, had exhausted a potentially vigorous race and had brought it to early
decay.

Bolivar decided to use part of the clerical revenues for education. The great number of orphans, who wandered everywhere
without care of any kind, were taken into asylums. Bolivar's
obsession with the problem of instruction is demonstrated by
the fact that he called on his own teacher, Simón Rodríguez, to
head the department of education. This man had returned to
South America after twenty-five years of aimless travel, and
Bolivar had learned of his presence in the country at the time
when he lay ill in Pativilca. He wrote to him, "Oh, my teacher,
my friend, my Robinson, you are in Colombia, you are in
Bogotá, and you have not told me!" He begged Rodríguez
to come to him.[45] "Instead of a mistress, I am in need of a
philosopher. For the present I prefer Socrates to Aspasia." He
instructed Santander to provide his former teacher with money,
adding, "This man might become very useful to me."[46] The
eccentric Rodríguez, who had lost all contact with the New
World, actually did come and undertook to teach the Indians
of High Peru. When Sucre inherited Bolivar's political position
at Lake Titicaca in the following year, he also fell heir to the
many instances of folly that characterized Rodríguez' activities.

45 Cartas: Vol. IV. p. 32.
46 Cartas: Vol. IV. p. 151.

More than once Sucre was at his wits' end to know what to do with this unpredictable creature. Finally he was obliged to sacrifice him to public protest against his insane acts.[47]

In addition to fundamental problems there were an infinite number of details that demanded Bolivar's attention. The last months of 1825 were spent in Chuquisaca, at that time the capital of Bolivia, where another national assembly was about to meet and to deliberate on problems of law and the constitution. Bolivar was not able to wait for its opening because of urgent problems in Peru which demanded his presence.[48]

February, 1826, saw him back in Lima. He had delegated his authority in Bolivia to Sucre—Sucre, who burned with impatience to quit the service and its duties and to return to the beautiful Marquesa de Solanda, who waited for him in Quito. He had repeatedly tendered his resignation, but had retracted it each time at the admonition of his master. "My friend," wrote Bolivar, "we must not give up our tasks as long as we can work nobly and justly. Let us become the founders and benefactors of three great nations. Let us be worthy of the fortune that has come to us. Let us show Europe that America has men capable of emulating the glory of the heroes of the ancient world. . . . A passive, inactive life is the image of death, is the loss of life. It is the anticipation of nothingness before its arrives." Sucre was pacified and accepted the government of Bolivia.[49]

Bolivar had left one problem unsolved when he took his departure for Peru at the beginning of the year; this was the problem of the constitution. Now in May, 1826, the National Assembly of Bolivia asked again for the governmental design he had promised them.[50]

Bolivar's responsibilities were greatly augmented by this assignment to outline a constitution for Bolivia. Since 1812

47 O'Leary: Memorias. Vol. II. pp. 350-51. For Simón Rodríguez' educational project, see, Lecuna: Doc. Vol. I. p. 409. O'Leary: Doc. Vol. I. pp. 332, 347, 348, 349, 354 ff.
48 Proclamas: p. 317.
49 Cartas: Vol. IV. p. 249.
50 Lecuna: Doc. Vol. II. pp. 163-64. Cartas: Vol. V. p. 254.

he had held precise and deeply rooted principles in regard to the constitution of an American republic. A strong state, an efficient executive with broad powers, the leadership of the intellectual and moral elite—these were the foundation stones of his program. Colombia, in 1821, had not adopted his ideas, but Bolivar had not concerned himself greatly over this defection. He had gone on to the conception of a great empire which he should build in the Andes, an empire half democratic, half feudal; half league and half federation.

At this moment of his career the organization of Bolivia brought the problem of state structure once more before his mind. It was a task he could not avoid, but he feared the responsibility it involved. He was torn between the desire to fulfill his promise and the fear of failure. His feelings are expressed in a letter to the poet, Olmedo. "Here I may be seen outlining the constitution for a newborn state. The road that leads to military glory is overlaid with the weapons of death, but the road that leads to wisdom is obscured by heavy fog. . . . I have travelled but a few steps on this peaceful path. The war, the destruction of our enemies, the freedom of my country, have demanded my entire attention. But this same love for America has forced me into a new career, and this love has, in part at least, dispelled any feeling of awe I might have had in exposing myself to the criticism of those who have grown grey in studying the science of government. Perhaps my example will inspire a similar courage in other Americans, to the end that we shall eventually possess our own models and shall not need to beg for them outside our world."[51] When Bolivar sent his constitution to the National Assembly in Chuquisaca, he included a presidential message which helps us today to understand the thoughts and feelings which moved him as he composed this bewildering and paradoxical document.

Bolivar believed that two evils threaten every free state—tyranny and anarchy. They constitute an ocean of oppression

51 Cartas: Vol. V. p. 335, of June 2, 1826.

out of which only a few happy islands of freedom emerge.[52]
In order to avoid these evils, Bolivar, in 1826, took an unre-
served stand on the side of authority. Abraham Lincoln's
famous words declare that democracy consists in the government of the people, by the people, and for the people. Bolivar's
constitution restricts the people, as far as possible, from exercising any influence on government; it emulates Napoleon's
consular government. However, Bolivar does not advocate
unrestricted rule in the hands of one man. He demands a
division of power, and in addition to Montesquieu's three
departments of government he enumerates a fourth, these
divisions being the elective, the legislative, the executive, and
the judicial.[53] Nevertheless, the basis of power remains with
the moral and intellectual elite.

The procedure for initial elections was complicated. Ten
citizens in each province were to appoint an elector. These
electors constituted a second electing body which finally appointed the representative of the people. In addition, this
electoral group was given the right to indicate the candidates
for the position of mayor in the cities and villages, and they also
nominated local justices and presented complaints. Bolivar
believed that these various stipulations constituted an approach
to the liberties of the federal system. In reality his constitution
admits no form of self-government.[54]

The legislative power was to be divided into three bodies:
tribunes, senators, and censors. At one time Miranda had advanced similar ideas, but they are also an expression of Bolivar's
most intimate political beliefs. The tribunes were to have the
initiative in proposing all measures relating to finance and were
to handle important issues such as war and peace. They were,
in fact, the supervisors of the administration. The senators
were to compile a code of law, supervise the courts, and control

52 Lecuna: Doc. Vol. II. pp. 311-12.
53 Belaunde: La Constitución Boliviana. B. d. H. Caracas. Vol. XI. No. 44.
p. 378. C. Ponce: Las Ideas del Libertador. Quito, 1936. J. Toro: Las Ideas del
Libertador. Quito, 1936. Bolivar's models were Napoleon's Consular Constitution
of 1799 and the Peruvian Constitution of 1823.
54 For Bolivar's models see Belaunde: op. cit. pp. 378-79.

religious worship. The censors, finally, were to be responsible for morals and were also to propose the members of the supreme court and the highest clerical authorities. The censors represented a moral power such as Bolivar had proposed in his speech at Angostura. They were to be elected for life, while the senators held office for eight years and the tribunes for four. The process of renewing these bodies was also extremely complicated. The citizens were only permitted to present a list of candidates, and from this list the members of each chamber chose those men they considered worthy of being their successors.

According to Bolivar the president should be the sun of this planetary system. This official was to be appointed for life and had the privilege of appointing his successor. Bolivar dared to call this design of government "the most sublime inspiration of republican ideas." Such an exaggeration has all the earmarks of a guilty conscience. These provisions, above enumerated, merely made Bolivia a monarchy without a monarch, with an elective kingship such as the Catholic church and the Holy Roman Empire possessed. The king-without-a-crown appointed the vice-president, who also held the office of prime minister and who would succeed the president in office. "According to such a procedure elections would be avoided, elections which are the greatest scourge of republics and which produce only anarchy."[55] Bolivar named Pétion as his precedent, but in reality his model was Napoleon.

As if this were not enough, Bolivar went on to demand that the vice-president be hereditary; in other words, that the power of the prime minister be concentrated in the hands of one family—an illogical and ridiculous stipulation and the weakest point in the Bolivian constitution. The other parts of the constitution do not need detailed analysis. Those paragraphs that deal with human rights are short and somewhat vague; those concerning administration are traditional; those which take up the administration of justice are open to question.

55 Lecuna: Doc. Vol. II. p. 317.

However, in spite of these defects in Bolivar's instrument of government, he had not entirely forgotten that his first appellation was that of Liberator, and in the chapters demanding the abolition of slavery he lived up to his title.[56] The constitution was to remain unchanged for ten years, no amendment being permitted until the expiration of that period.

The Bolivian Constitution, adopted in July, 1826, is the amazing product of political imagination and extravagance. The writer has found no proof that it was not entirely the child of Bolivar's own brain.

During all the fluctuating circumstances of Bolivar's life, we find that certain basic elements of his political thinking remained unaltered—nationalism, republicanism, unity of the state, an independent congress, efficiency in the executive power, and respect for cultural and religious forces. As Bolivar developed, these ideas remained unchanged, but they are combined in many different ways at different periods of his life. In the Bolivian Constitution there is a maximum of authority, stability, and security, but a minimum of spontaneity in the free expression of the people's will.

In order to be fair to Bolivar, however, we must bear in mind the character of the people for whom he designed this Constitution—a people considered to be the most backward in South America. One should on this account accord him an unbiased judgment. His reactionary ideas were introduced as checks against subversive movements and anarchistic desires. It must be admitted, however, that the provision for censors was absurd and as utopian in 1826 as in 1819. But it was not this mistake which doomed the Constitution; rather it was Bolivar's proposals for the unlimited power of the president and vice-president. Even if one were willing to accept the idea of a lifetime presidency, one would still find it impossible to justify his stand on the hereditary nature of the vice-presidency. Only in rare instances is the art of government inherited, and certainly these cases are far too limited in number to serve as the

56 Lecuna: Doc. Vol. II. pp. 318-19. Belaunde: *op. cit.* p. 388.

basis for a constitutional ruling. Bolivar's plan for an hereditary vice-president who would also occupy the post of prime
minister is so repugnant to all common sense that the student
is obliged to look further for an explanation of its essential
absurdity. Bolivar thought South America could be ruled
only through personal influence: "Laws have no value in the
eyes of our people who are ignorant of their meaning," he states,
and in consequence he believed it necessary to establish personal
influence in the form of an institution.[57] As he outlined his
idea of an hereditary vice-presidency, his mind dwelt on Sucre.
He wrote to him, "You must be convinced that a great destiny
awaits you. A crown has been offered to me that ill becomes my
head, but in consideration of the uncertainty of the future I plan
to place it on the temples of the man who won the victory
of Ayacucho."[58] It was for Sucre's sake, then, that Bolivar had
conceived the erroneous idea of an hereditary vice-presidency.
Later developments will show whether this attitude was an
indication of monarchical tendencies.

Bolivar's critics are not unanimous in their opinions concerning this Constitution. Those who are inclined to be severe
in their criticism believe the document to be a signpost on the
road to Bolivar's mental decay.[59] This writer is disposed to be
more lenient. It seems to him that Bolivar's unusual and illogical provisos are the results of an attempt to deal with difficult
circumstances by daring means.[60] His error lay in the fact that
these means were both contradictory and inadequate. Bolivar's
desire was to combine the virtues of all political systems; his
achievement was a combination of all their defects. He went
even further in his error; he became enamored of this child
conceived in the ecstacy of his political phantasy, and he came
to look upon it as a patent cure-all, a sure remedy for all ills.
"Everyone will consider this constitution as the ark of the

57 Villanueva: Imperio de los Andes. Paris, 1912. p. 286.
58 Cartas: Vol. V. p. 294.
59 Lozano: op. cit. p. 96. Belaunde: op. cit. p. 377. Gil Fortoul: Hist. p. 349.
J. R. Vejarano: Bolívar, Legislador., in Simón Bolívar. Madrid, 1914. p. 516.
60 E. Finot: Bolívar Pacifista. Rev. Bol. Vol. II. Nos. 19-20. p. 264.

covenant, as a transition between Europe and America, between soldier and civilian, between democracy and aristocracy, between imperialism and republicanism. Everyone tells me that this constitution will be the great instrument of our social reform."[61] This is not only an overstatement of his own achievement in the field of political thought, but also a demonstration of his failure to appreciate South America's fundamental problems. Bolivar had always identified freedom with independence, but he seems to have neglected the truth that freedom's realm holds sway over internal affairs as well. South America's determination to be free was coincidental with its determination to settle its own problems and to manage its own government. If Bolivar denied these unequivocal rights of independence, his denial was ultimately a repudiation of the basic truths of the entire movement and a frank and open declaration of the immaturity of the continent. He failed to perceive that the virus of democracy leads a life of its own and sooner or later infects a people with suspicion of all forms of monarchy or dictatorship. In brief, the Bolivian Constitution is one of Bolivar's greatest blunders.

The conclusion stated above does not infer that the creation of an independent Bolivia was also a mistake. On the contrary, it must be admitted today, after one hundred and twenty years of that state's existence, that it was by no means an artificial framework. Bolivia owes its existence to Bolivar's comprehension of a political necessity, not to his whims or his vanity. If today this republic seems anomalous because it is without access to the sea, we must remember that this circumstance was contrary to Bolivar's plan. Bolivar recognized that the enormous territory which is the republic of Bolivia was too important and had too potential a future to be governed from such remote centers as Lima or Buenos Aires.

Bolivar has been accused of acting from selfish and machiavellian motives in his establishment of an independent Bolivia. It has been said that he was unwilling to allow its wealth of

61 Cartas: Vol. V. p. 291., Vol. VI. p. 29.

precious minerals to fall into the hands of either Peru or Buenos Aires. This may indeed be a fair accusation, for such calculations were not alien to Bolivar and may well have influenced his decisions. Considered in this light, the creation of Bolivia becomes the last move in that great game begun at Guayaquil— that is, the organization of South America around Colombia as a center of gravity. It seems certain, however, that Bolivia would have become in time an independent republic even without Bolivar's interference. One should not forget that for Bolivar even Colombia was not the main issue. The idea of a South American federation came before any other interest, whether of Colombia, Chile, Argentina, or Bolivia. Bolivia was but one of the many pieces that the Liberator moved in his big game.

The creation of Bolivia and its Constitution concludes a strange chapter in Bolivar's life. These two events are the last heroic acts in his career as Liberator. Up to this point he had been inspired by a genuine desire for glory, but he now seems ambitious to ascend to the rank of a demigod whose mythical existence would give life to an entire nation. The contemplation of this final pinnacle of fame seems to have obscured some of Bolivar's finer faculties with a veil of impracticability. A great capacity for organization is linked with defective political thought. The Constitution of 1826 is an utopian plan whose ideals are those of the past, while the American league of nations is a design that is prophetic of the needs of the future.

The life of the Liberator reached its summit in Bolivia. Only a descending action could follow. The resignation of his political power alone could have prevented this decline. Resignation, however, was not in keeping with the character of Bolivar.

CHAPTER 29

Simon I?

$\mathcal{A}$fter a long, hot August day the sun at length sets, and the air for some time remains suffused with warmth and light. But this lingering splendor is only the afterglow of the dying day and foretells the coming of night. Bolivar's life in the year 1826 is like one of these memorable summer evenings, luxurious, serene, sumptuous, brilliant, but the presentiment of decline had invaded the atmosphere about him. For the first time in his life he was free of all the miserable details that had been necessary for the maintenance of a war machine. There were no more battles to fight. Bolivar now had time for reading and for meditation.

For most of humanity, philosophy is the result of tribulation. Bolivar differed from others in this respect: "I am more the philosopher when I am happy than when I am unhappy. If I am sad it is for others. Fate has lifted me to such a height that it would be difficult for me to be unhappy."[1] These are audacious words. Invulnerability is the possession of no man, whatever lofty height he may attain. Bolivar was a philosopher whether in fortunate or unfortunate circumstances, and the constant stream of contemplation that accompanies his acts gives added color and interest to his life. Liberator of South America though he was, he did not lose his sense of proportion, and when the poet, Olmedo, sent him some verses on the battle of Junín, a rhetorical outburst, Bolivar's reply was censorious.[2]

1 Cartas: Vol. IV. p. 199.
2 V. M. Rendón: Olmedo. Paris, 1904.

"You have extolled us to such a degree that we are cast down into an abyss of oblivion. You cover the weak reflection of our dubious virtues with an infinity of light. . . . If I were not so honest and you were not a poet, I could believe you wished to write a parody of the *Iliad* using the heroes of our miserable farce as characters. This is not my belief, however. You are a poet and you are aware, as was Bonaparte, that it is but one step from the sublime to the ridiculous."[3] The remainder of Bolivar's criticism is an illustration of his literary taste, though Bolivar himself admits that he is like the blind man who chastises an invisible culprit, since he had but a meager knowledge of his subject. The praise of the poets was not the only homage he received. The golden crowns were passed on to his younger companions, and he refused to accept the millions which the grateful Peruvians and Bolivians wanted to bestow upon him. He was, however, enchanted to hear the people attending mass sing the following verse:

> O, Lord, all good things come from thee.
> Thou hast given us Bolivar.
> Glory to Thee, great God!
> What a man is he, O, heaven,
> Who by thy hand with love and skill is crowned.
> The future he knows as well
> As though time did his voice obey.[4]

Bolivar's life was at this time really princely, although we must accept only as fairy tale exaggeration the reports that he ate from golden dishes with golden knives and forks. It is true that the inhabitants of Lima spoiled him, and equally true that he enjoyed it. Among the many gifts were an ostentatiously decorated uniform and a golden sword set with diamonds which the capital presented to him.[5] Bolivar lived outside the

3 Cartas: Vol. V. p. 7. O'Leary: Doc. Vol. IV. p. 381.
4 Restrepo: H. d. R. C. Vol. III. p. 471.
5 O'Leary: Memorias. Vol. II. pp. 448, 450. Blanco: Doc. Vol. X. p. 150.

city limits during this time, occupying a country house called La Magdalena. It became notorious as the seraglio of the Liberator, the place where Manuela, though the undisputed favorite, nevertheless shared the affections of the great man with many others. The reports are very likely exaggerated by envious gossip, but so much smoke argues some fire.[6] Without doubt Bolivar lived the life of a monarch at La Magdalena, but in minor matters he remained a moderate man. In his butler's records there is no item that indicates waste or extravagance.[7] It would be naive, however, to expect to find the whole truth displayed in an account book. Bolivar settled a pension of three thousand pesos on the Abbé de Pradt, and begged him to accept "the paltry sum."[8] Widows and orphans remained the recipients of his generosity. He lived as the patrician he had been born, a gentleman and a hero.

The echo of his achievements expanded toward the east and north. Byron was on the point of embarking for South America, for the country of Bolivar, as he expressed it, but learned that freedom had other, more accessible battlefields, and went to Greece instead.[9] Of more significance was the letter written to Bolivar by the old Marquis de Lafayette at the suggestion of George Washington's family. Washington's descendants sent Bolivar a gold medal once the property of the president, coined after the capitulation at Yorktown. "The second Washington of the New World" was the highest expression of their appreciation.[10] This recognition moved Bolivar deeply. He was a completely different man from that sedate and composed country gentleman of Virginia; he would never enjoy an old age spent in the peace of a Mount Vernon, but he felt that the letters and the gift from this great American's descendants had conferred on him a distinction he had craved for fifteen

6 R. Palma: Bolívar en las tradiciones peruanas. Barcelona, 1930.
7 L. Correa: B. d. H. Caracas. Vol. XI. No. 42. p. 145.
8 Cartas: Vol. V. pp. 258-60. M. Aguirre: Un ignorado archivo bolivariano. B. d. H. Caracas. Vol. XIX. No. 76. p. 514.
9 See Byron's letter of June 12, 1822. Blanco: Doc. Vol. VIII. p. 423. E. Posada: Apostillas. p. 3.
10 Larrazabal: Vol. II. p. 339. Blanco: Vol. X. p. 103.

years. "Washington hand in hand with Lafayette is the crown of all human rewards."[11]

The word "crown" appears now with suspicious frequency in Bolivar's letters. However, it is a word indicating more a tendency of his contemporaries than an attitude of Bolivar. The fear of anarchy had become general and was directed toward the arbitrary government of various leaders of the Revolution. An authoritarian regime seemed to be the only solution, but in nineteenth century politics authority and monarchy were synonymous; consequently, the decision between monarchy and republic was again up for discussion. Bolivar, as we know, favored authoritarian government, but was he now willing to return to the monarchistic ideal which he had so bitterly opposed four years previously? The answer to this question lies in a fine discrimination between the objective, or constitutional, problem and the psychological, or personal one.

Ambition was the governing passion of Bolivar's life. After the great days of Ayacucho and Junín he was obliged to decide which path led to greater glory. He had attained the name of Liberator on the battlefield, and it was only natural that the thought of war occurred to him now. "Everything goes wrong in Buenos Aires because of daily pressure from Brazil. It seems to me that we should go to the aid of these ungrateful and unfortunate people. The demon of fame will lead us down through Tierra del Fuego, but what do we risk? . . . I beg you to ask Congress in my name that I be allowed to follow my fate and that I be permitted to go where danger to America and the reputation of Colombia may lead me. . . . I am efficient only where peril and difficulties are combined. . . . If I were allowed to indulge in my diabolic disposition, I should in the end accomplish all the good I am capable of."[12] In this manner Bolivar projected a crusade to assist Argentina or to liberate Paraguay from dictatorship. He was enchanted with

11 Cartas: Vol. V. pp. 206, 252. C. Pereyra: Bolívar y Washington, *passim*. Otero d'Costa: Bolívar y Washington. B. d. H. Bogotá. Vol. XX. p. 254. O'Leary: Doc. Vol. XII. p. 168.
12 Cartas: Vol. V. pp. 88-89.

the title of Protector of America; and, desiring to extend its significance, he asked for permission to go southward for a few years. The idea of going north also occurred to him, since he occasionally contemplated carrying the war to Havana, Puerto Rico, and even to the Philippines. These outbursts of military ambition are of little importance from a political point of view, because Bolivar was not long forgetful of his real assignments, but they are significant as human manifestations and display an unsatisfied ambition for further heights of fame.

During these years Bolivar came more and more under the influence of Napoleonic theory. His public utterances on this subject were carefully guarded, but inferences are quite clear. An English admirer sent him a set of books once the property of the Emperor, and in acknowledging them, Bolivar referred to Napoleon as "the honor and the desperation of the human mind."[13] Bolivar often compared himself with Napoleon, and he reflected deeply on the great Corsican's career of splendor and misery.[14] Is it not understandable that he considered Napoleon his model in other respects? Was this not the moment for him to crown himself? Was an Andean empire not the epitome of all his dreams? Simon the First! Was this not the conclusion of his five great victories? The demand for authority that had arisen in South America would have found a natural satisfaction in such an empire, and its significance in an outside world would have been considerable. The foundation of an empire in the region of the Andes would have facilitated friendly relations with the European powers. The French foreign minister, Prince Polignac, had let it be understood that he was indifferent as to whether a European prince or an American general should bear the crown in South America. The statesmen of Europe were concerned only with the creation of an order similar to that which had existed on the continent since 1815.[15]

13 Cartas: Vol. IV. p. 208.
14 D. d. B. p. 198.
15 Cartas: Vol. IV. p. 280.

If dreams of an empire allured Bolivar, his only safe procedure was to conceal his ambition beneath a necessity to come to terms with the European powers. As events transpired even this became unnecessary, because the South Americans themselves offered him the crown. This unprecedented circumstance originated in Venezuela.

In northern Colombia the symptoms of anarchic disintegration multiplied daily. Veterans of the Patriot army and erstwhile soldiers of the Royalist forces threatened civilian life and order. Páez, who had command in Venezuela, held this danger in check. He rounded up the gangs of looters and robbers and confined them within camps. However, in spite of all he could do leaders and demagogues arose in all parts of the country to try their hand at uprisings and rebellions.[16] Páez and his friends observed the state of affairs with a great deal of apprehension. In the fall of 1825, Páez and a group of officers decided to discard the republican form of government and to create an empire after the Napoleonic fashion. Páez wrote to Bolivar in an attempt to explain the situation: "This country is similar to France on the day when the great Napoleon was in Egypt and was called upon by the most famous men of the Revolution to save France. You should become the Bonaparte of South America because 'this country is not the country of Washington.' "[17] Páez' letter was delivered to Bolivar by special envoy, and other confirmations of similar Caesarian tendencies reached the Liberator. His sister, María Antonia, who knew of this turn of events, wrote to him, however, in a different vein. "They send you now a commission to offer you the crown. Receive them as they deserve to be received, because the proposal is infamous. . . . Tell them always what you told them in Cumaná in 1814, that you will be the Liberator or nothing. This title is your real one; it has extolled your name among the great of the earth; it is the title that will now preserve your

16 Restrepo: Vol. III. H. d. R. C. p. 413. Arch. Santander: Vol. XII. p. 143.
17 Cartas: Vol. V. p. 243. Páez: Autobiografía. p. 485 denies that he ever wrote this letter. However, his authorship is proved.

reputation built at the cost of untold sacrifice. You should repudiate anyone who offers you a crown, because such a one is interested only in your downfall."[18]

Did such a dream ever nourish the heart of Bolivar? The writer is convinced that in this respect he was never tempted to follow in the steps of Napoleon. His reputation had always meant more to him than his power, and this reputation was based on the title of Liberator, rather than on the possible one of Emperor. Therefore, it seems natural that Bolivar answered Páez' appeal by saying he had received the message with surprise. "It seems to me that you are not impartial in your judgment of men and affairs. Colombia is not France, and I am not Napoleon. . . . Napoleon was great, unique, and extraordinarily ambitious. . . . I am not Napoleon, nor do I wish to be. Neither shall I emulate Caesar, and even less Iturbide. Such examples seem to me unworthy of my glory. The title of Liberator is beyond any reward ever offered to human pride. . . . And our population is not that of France. We resemble the French in nothing, nothing, nothing! The republic has raised this country (Colombia) to fame and prosperity; it has given us laws and freedom. . . . A throne would produce terror as much by its height as by its splendor. Equality would be obliterated, and the colored races, in the face of a new aristocracy, would feel that their rights had been entirely lost. . . . I confess frankly that this plan is inappropriate for you, for me, and for the country."[19]

Bolivar continued by saying that reform in Colombia should only be considered in 1831 because the Constitution of Cucuta had been accepted for a period of ten years. In no case should extreme changes be made at this time, since chaos would assuredly result. Bolivar doubted and was justified in doubting the loyalty of those who would make him emperor. These men had once been federalists, then constitutionalists; now they

18 B. d. H. Caracas. Vol. XVI. No. 62. p. 275. See, L. Aviles Pérez: Anotaciones sobre María Antonia Bolívar. B. d. H. Bogotá. Vol. XXIV. p. 88.
19 Cartas: Vol. V. pp. 239-41. L. Vallenilla Lanz: Críticas de Sinceridad y Exactitud. Caracas, 1921. See the chapter: Simón I., Rey de las Américas. p. 193.

were Bonapartists, and tomorrow they would be anarchists. Even if Bolivar had had blind faith in their words, he still would have been unable to agree with their ideas. "My enemies and my foolish friends have talked so much about this crown that I will be expelled from Colombia and America. They refuse to believe that I detest power as greatly as I love glory. Glory does not imply command, but the practice of great virtue. I wanted freedom and fame; I have achieved both. What else can I wish?"

Bolivar had indeed achieved the status of emperor, even though he wore no crown. He had no legitimate heirs; consequently, the usual incentive to dynastic ambition did not exist for him.[20] He lacked the family instinct that induced Napoleon to distribute his conquered crowns among the members of his clan. Bolivar's efforts were inclined toward educating his nephews to become good citizens rather than to be simply the relatives of the Liberator.[21] "Fortune," he wrote his sister, "has lifted me to the height of power, but I crave no more rights than those of the simplest citizen." He forbade María Antonia to interfere with politics, and ordered her to silence her sons or dismiss them from the house if they should presume to meddle in politics.[22]

Since there was a conspicuous lack of motive in making Colombia a monarchy, it would seem idle to accuse Bolivar of this ambition. His motto was ever "Liberator or nothing." The sincerity of his refusal is proved in the message to Santander accompanying his rejection of the crown: "I send you this letter openly, so that, after reading it, you may use any seal you wish and may then forward it to Páez."[23]

Constitutional decision and foreign interests were likewise

---

20 Cartas: Vol. V. p. 271. Sucre had the same opinion; see, Villanueva: Imperio de los Andes. p. 80. Bolivar had no legitimate heir. However in Potosí a natural son was born to him. See also, L. A. Cuervo: Un Hijo de Bolívar. B. d. H. Bogotá. Vol. XXIII. p. 469.
21 Cartas: Vol. V. p. 319.
22 Cartas: Vol. VI. p. 13.
23 Cartas: Vol. V. p. 248. For Santander's opinion see, Cartas Santander: Vol. II. p. 203.

involved in the idea of monarchy. Is it inconceivable that
Bolivar rejected the plan of monarchy as it implicated him,
but approved of it as a solution for South America's future?
Occasionally he made declarations in the presence of European
officers and diplomats that support this interpretation. Witness
his remarks to an English captain who visited him in March,
1825: "Of all countries, South America is perhaps the least
suited to a republican form of government, because the population consists of Indians and Negroes who are even more ignorant than the Spanish from whom we have liberated ourselves.
A country ruled by such a class is headed for certain disaster.
There is no way out except to ask England for help." He declared that he had never been an enemy of monarchy and
promised that if the British government should ever propose
the establishment of ably administered monarchic states in the
New World, he, Bolivar, would become their first advocate.
"I know," he went on to say, "that many people believe that I
desire to become king. This, however, is far from true. I shall
never accept the crown for myself, and when I see this country
happy and safe under a good and stable government, I shall
retire again to private life."[24] He spoke to French visitors on
the same subject, varying his remarks by flattering France
instead of praising England.[25]

The student of Bolivar must not be diverted by these typic-
ally Bolivarian subterfuges. The Liberator never intended to
wear a crown; no more did he intend to experiment with
monarchy in Latin America. The conversations reported above
were export goods intended for European consumption. Bolivar used this method to calm the conservative powers and to
win the favor and protection of Great Britain.[26] He assured his
older relatives that from now on the prodigal American son
would behave himself and would imitate his elders in all things.

24 Villanueva: Fernando VII y los Nuevos Estados. p. 259-61, and Cartas:
Vol. IV. pp. 292-93.
25 Villanueva: op. cit. pp. 248, 268, 270.
26 J. R. Vejarano: op. cit. p. 497. Belaunde: La Federación de los Andes.
B. d. H. Caracas. Vol. XII. No. 46. p. 211.

He was willing to follow any governmental plan—kingdom, restricted monarchy, anything, if he was but allowed to work out South American problems without foreign interference. Bolivar hoped in this manner to avoid the armed intervention of the Holy Alliance and at the same time to obtain the benevolence of the British Empire with its fleet, its commerce, and its capital.

The reader may feel that there is some inconsistency in the foregoing statement, since it has been maintained that the Liberator wished to install in Bolivia a government which was to all intents and purposes a monarchy, lacking only titles and a crown. It has also been asserted that the Bolivian Constitution contains the keys to Bolivar's most intimate political thoughts. He was not deaf to the demand for a stable rule nor was he blind to the justifiable desire to establish authority once again in the Western Hemisphere. His aim was to lay a secure foundation for the future, and he was obliged to find a practical solution for this difficult and pressing problem. If these colonial nations, accustomed as they were to obeying governmental orders, were not yet ready to practice democracy, if the blend of races was still too new for stability, Bolivar would design a governmental structure compatible both with his own political ideas and with the needs of the country—instead of an emperor, a life-time president; instead of an aristocratic class, a moral and intellectual elite. Despite the fact that Bolivar himself was a Creole aristocrat, he had not the slightest intention of perpetuating the prerogatives of his class. He did not consider the state a museum for the preservation of outworn privilege. The elite, who were to supplant the ancient aristocracy, were to be chosen on a basis of merit won during the war for independence. The victors in the battle for freedom were to be the first members of the new class—Sucre, Santander, Páez, Montilla, Soublette, and many others. Convinced that the Bolivar Constitution was the arcanum of political wisdom, Bolivar wanted to establish its principles instead of monarchy in the republics he had liberated. In a letter to Páez he wrote, "You will find here that all guarantees of stability and freedom, of equality and order, are united. If you and your friends agree to this proposal, it could be discussed and recommended to public opinion. Here is a service we can render the fatherland."[27] The offer of a crown had offended Bolivar because it assumed him to cherish a vulgar ambition, an ambition which visualized no other heights of fame than those attained by Alexander, Caesar, or Napoleon. "I will excel them all in unselfishness, since I cannot match them in action. My example may be useful to my country, since moderation in the first leader will impress every citizen, and my life will become a model. The people will adore me, and will consider me as the ark of their unity."[28] Here is Bolivar in his essence. He rejected the crown with the hope that his people might become educated in the spirit of true citizenship, but he did aspire to be the rainbow which should arch over the future existence of the South American nations.

The developments in Peru seemed to give foundation to this aspiration. With the capitulation of El Callao, Bolivar had concluded his assignments as Liberator and the moment had now come when he should fulfill his promise to return to Colombia with the army. The rewards of power, however, proved to be too enticing. Bolivar found little difficulty in resisting the proffer of a crown, but it was another matter to close his ears to the voices that claimed him to be unique and irreplaceable, as the man of destiny who should become the pivotal point of a great movement.

His residence in Lima became again the nerve center of the Peruvian state. But the horizon was not unclouded, and as early as 1826 a conspiracy against the Liberator was discovered. Two ministers of state and certain high Peruvian and Argentinian officials and officers were involved. Boliver crushed the incipient rebellion, but it would seem that the significance of the incident escaped him. He continued to be enchanted by

27 Cartas: Vol. V. p. 241.
28 Cartas: Vol. V. p. 224.

the richness, the luxury, and the lushness of Peruvian life. And so, while Bolivar gave himself up to the pleasures of the capital, opportunity knocked and moved on.[29]

The opening of the Peruvian Parliament, which had adjourned in 1825, was imminent, and everyone expected Bolivar to resign his dictatorship at this time. Finally, in March, sixty deputies came together, but a violent controversy arose concerning the powers of this new assembly. There was no official body to examine the election procedure nor to determine the right of title of the representatives. Bolivar and the government were of the opinion that the Peruvian Supreme Court, which was under their influence, should exercise this function. The deputies, on the other hand, maintained that the matter fell within their province.[30] Bolivar, as Dictator, imposed his interpretation, and his intervention disclosed the presence of alarming fissures in the unity of Peru. Bolivar's triumph was attributed more to the presence of Colombian bayonets in Lima than to the equity of his cause.

Criticism of the Liberator became widespread. Bolivar met it with a threat to abandon Peru. Lima society now became alarmed for fear anarchy might return. The city council, the corporations, the artisans' association began a pilgrimage to La Magdalena to implore Bolivar not to desert them. Forty-two deputies signed a petition for the adjournment of Parliament. The Minister of the Interior went even further, demanding a plebiscite to ascertain whether Peru would accept the Bolivian Constitution. The procedure was not only lawless; it constituted a *coup d'état*. But Bolivar was infatuated with his handiwork, and he counted on being elected President of Peru for life.[31] Bolivar's decision to impose his Constitution on Peru was one of his greatest mistakes, first, because he was obliged to spend more and more time in Peru, and second, because he

29 Restrepo: H. d. R. C. Vol. III. pp. 519-20. Paz Soldán: Vol. II. pp. 57 ff. J. Tamayo: La Gran Colombia. Bogotá, 1941. p. 196.
30 O'Leary: Memorias. Vol. II. pp. 491-92. Blanco: Doc. Vol. X. p. 200. See also, Proclamas: p. 317.
31 Cartas: Vol. V. p. 374. Blanco: Doc. Vol. X. p. 469.

was totally deceived about the trends of public opinion in the country. "My heart," he wrote to Santander, "is weak when it comes to those who love me. And, in truth, everyone loves me in Peru, at least they all protest with great cordiality that they do. It is certain that out of thousands scarcely one detests me, or rather, is afraid of me."[32]

Of thousands scarcely one! There were now many who raised their voices against the Liberator. Had he not sworn to resign his dictatorship? True, he was to be elected only as President, but a lifetime presidency seemed, in certain respects, worse than kingship, especially if that president were a foreigner, a Colombian backed only by the power of his guns. Independence was far from being complete so long as Bolivar ruled in Peru and six thousand Colombian soldiers, like locusts, laid waste the country. During these weeks Bolivar's popularity suffered a severe decline. A new conspiracy interrupted the establishment of internal peace, and this time his enemies had determined to kill him. For the second time Bolivar failed to recognize the warning that was implicit in this reverberation of violence.[33] With fatal ease his ministers persuaded him that the Constitution was opposed only by a handful of demagogues, and that he alone could give security and peace to Peru. They found little difficulty in getting Bolivar to accept the dignity of lifetime President of the republic.

Everything went according to plan. On August 16, 1826, the Bolivian Constitution was adopted for Peru and Bolivar was elected President. Hearing the result of the elections, he said proudly, "This constitution is the work of centuries, because in it I was successful in combining the theories of experience and the advice and opinion of wise men." This boast, unfortunately, contains scant truth. Nevertheless, Bolivar refused to accept the presidency because, he said, Colombia needed him. Again the Peruvians tried to induce him to remain; even the ladies of Lima took part in the procession of

32 Cartas: Vol. V. p. 269.
33 O'Leary: Memorias. Vol. II. p. 525. Cartas: Vol. VI. pp. 16, 19, 20-23, 25 ff.

appeal; certainly no one would miss Bolivar more than they. He addressed them as follows: "Ladies, silence is the only answer I can give to your enchanting words. They captivate not only my heart, but my conscience. When beauty speaks, who can resist? I have been a soldier in the service of beauty, for I have fought in the cause of liberty, and liberty is both beautiful and alluring." The ladies of Lima surrounded him; they were convinced he would stay. This episode gives some idea of the moral climate of Bolivar's life in 1826.[34]

Bolivar cannot escape the accusation that the all too human enjoyment of power caused him to lose irrevocable months in Peru, but it would be unjust to assign this as the only reason for his delay. There were other and more objective motives that made him remain. Bolivar was looking for a foundation of security, not only for the internal structure of the state, but for the relations between the liberated republics. He believed that the Federation of the Andes, which he now planned, might grow in unity if the constitutional bases of each of the republics were identical. Bolivia and Peru had already adopted the Bolivian Constitution, and Bolivar had sent the text of his political inspiration to Colombia in the hope that it might eventually replace the Constitution of Cucutá. He even went so far as to plan for the acceptance of his program by Argentina and Chile.

The plan which lay at the center of Bolivar's dreams was both lofty and fantastic. It had, assuredly, a certain greatness of perception. If the South American nations would consent to accept his constitution and would elect him as protector, then indeed the task of welding them in some form of international organization would be greatly facilitated. Simon the First, Emperor of the Andes, was not an irresistably tempting title for Bolivar, but Simon Bolivar, creator of three republics, President of the South American League of Nations, was perhaps the intimate and long contemplated goal of his ambitions.

34 Proclamas: p. 337. Larrazabal: Vol. II. p. 355.

At the time when Bolivar aspired to see his Constitution adopted in the north and south of the continent, a congress met in Panama. Here the delegates of the liberated republics were to discuss their common destiny. New horizons had opened, and America stood face to face with Europe; a league of free nations confronted the Holy Alliance. The Congress of Panama—its preparation, its history, and its failure—completes the portrait of Bolivar in the years 1825-26. The tragic greatness of his life becomes visible only in the light of his Pan-American vision.

CHAPTER 30

The South American
League of Nations

Foreign policy in South America originated at the time of the country's birth as a federation of free nations. The term, foreign policy, however, needs some limitation as applied to Latin America. It does not include the use of force to obtain territorial gains, nor does it imply enslavement of one nation by the other; it is not a policy of expansion and imperialism after the European fashion. If we omit the inherently selfish ambitions which exist in nearly all long-established foreign policies and visualize South America's policy as a result of the integration of the continent and its consequent capacity to deal with foreign nations, then we may say, in all truth, that South American foreign policy was born in 1826, and that Simon Bolivar fathered its birth.[1]

The problem of international relations was the third great theme of these years. It was a complicated problem and gave Bolivar a twofold assignment. He had first to construct a foundation for inter-American relations on the continent itself, but at the same time he had to present these republics to Europe and the United States as an integrated group.

How had the world reacted to Bolivar's achievements? The South American revolution had so far produced little interest among European statesmen, and certainly the Holy Alliance had not ventured to launch an interference. The South Ameri-

1 J. Pérez Concha: Bolívar, Internacionalista. Quito, 1939.

579

can war for independence differed from the North American revolution in that the Latin struggle had been exclusively between the mother country and its colonies. The fall of Napoleon had only indirectly influenced the course of events. Spain could not count on help from other conservative European countries, since they had neither fleets nor maritime bases in the Western Hemisphere.

England's attitude had been one of extreme caution. The Tory minister, Castlereagh, with England's interests in mind, supported the Holy Alliance, but England's interests in South America were still concerned with the conquest of foreign trade. As the movement for independence had prospered, Castlereagh became more and more inclined to favor the establishment of constitutional monarchies that would by their nature link the Latin Americans more tightly with Great Britain. He realized that a republican government would bring them closer to the United States. This was the situation when George Canning took charge of the English Foreign Office. Events in South America had not supported the overcautious policy of Castlereagh. South America had decided in favor of republican government. Moreover, Spain and Portugal had been overwhelmed by the revolutionary tide. The statesmen of the Holy Alliance met at the Congress of Verona in an attempt to dam the flood and to reëstablish the legitimate ruler in Spain by armed force. Their intervention, carried out by the French army under the Duc d'Angoulème, resulted in the reëstablishment of Ferdinand VII to an absolutist throne. England took no part in these events, and Canning expressed his disapproval of them.[2] He made an attempt to interest the United States in a common declaration against this continental policy in order to prevent interference in South America by the Holy Alliance. Canning had every expectation that the North American statesmen would be sympathetic to his plan, because at the time they were involved with Russia in difficulties over Alaska and

2 W. C. Temperley: Life of Canning. London, 1905. Temperley: The Latin American Policy of Canning. Am. Hist. Rev. Vol. XI. 1906.

would therefore favor a rebuke to any interference of the Holy Alliance in the Western Hemisphere.[3]

The North American diplomats were, however, quite capable of dealing with Canning's diplomatic schemes. The United States had already recognized the sovereignty of a majority of the South American republics and gave Canning to understand that they expected England to do likewise.[4] A common cause against the Holy Allance could be considered only after this step had been taken. Canning, however, was much too cautious to embark on such a procedure; he still feared to alienate Spain or any European power.

At this critical moment, President Monroe issued his famous message in which he forbade all non-American intervention in the Western Hemisphere.[5] Canning, realizing that the United States had anticipated him, made attempts to recover his position and did succeed in persuading France to forego the use of force against the South American nations.[6] Taking advantage of this concession, he represented himself as the foremost champion of South American freedom. And South America accepted this as Canning's real attitude. Even Bolivar believed him and thought of England as the only friend of South American independence among the selfish and reactionary European powers. Canning now recognized the young states as sovereign republics, first, Argentina and later, Colombia and Mexico.[7]

Meanwhile the Holy Alliance remained impotent. Prussia, Russia, and Austria protested to Canning, but the necessary means for action against South America were withheld. In this way circumstances had made Canning's *volte-face* not only an accomplished fact, but had given the occurrence an international importance. Canning clothed his change of attitude with all the attributes of a grand gesture when in 1826, he said, "I

3 G. Heinz: Die Beziehungen Russlands, Englands und Nordamerikas 1823. Berlin, 1911.
4 F. J. Urrutia: Páginas de Historia Diplomática. Bogotá, 1917. pp. 217-38.
5 Dexter Perkins: The Monroe Doctrine, 1823-26. London, 1927. Whitacker: *op. cit.*, pp. 428 ff., 464 ff.
6 Webster: *op. cit.*, Vol. I. p. 19.
7 Blanco: Doc. Vol. IX. p. 514.

called the New World into being to redress the balance of the Old." The reader may remember that these words were borrowed from Bolivar's letter from Jamaica, and they lead us back to the origin of our reflections.

What was Bolivar's position in the midst of diplomatic intrigue on both sides of the Atlantic? The movement for independence in the New World displays a trend that is quite lacking in previous revolutions; it is the trend toward solidarity that accompanied the struggles of the Western World, and Bolivar had become its mouthpiece. He was not without forerunners. The city councils of Buenos Aires, Caracas, and Bogotá had consulted with each other in 1810, when they first contemplated shedding the yoke of three hundred years of tyranny. These people were united in believing their undertaking to be of common interest. Miranda had shown the way, and Moreno in Buenos Aires, Martínez de Rosa in Chile, Cecilio del Valle in Guatemala, had responded to his idea of South American solidarity. But Simon Bolivar surpassed them all. "From the very beginning of the revolution I understood that if we could once establish free nations in South America, a federation among them would be the strongest form of union."[8] In 1812 the continental vision was already his; in 1813 he said to his soldiers: "America expects freedom and salvation from you."

The form of the federation was the next consideration. Bolivar in his Letter from Jamaica had rejected a South American superstate, whether republic or monarchy. However, he stressed the fact that the inhabitants of the continent had one origin, one language, one religion, and that they possessed customs and a code of morals in common. They could unite. Panama could become the Corinth of the New World, the theatre of a glorious congress which might bring together all the people of America.[9]

Three years later Bolivar addressed the director of the Ar-

[8] Cartas: Vol. IX. p. 430. See also, Boletín de la Unión Panamericana, May, 1942.

[9] Cartas: Vol. I. p. 202. F. Lozano y Lozano: El Congreso de Panamá. B. d. H. Bogotá. Vol. XVIII. p. 225. E. Finot: Bolívar Pacifista. New York, 1936.

gentine Republic as follows: "We shall put our greatest effort into making the South American covenant a reality—a reality which will melt all our republics into one body."[10] Treaties of alliance with Mexico, Guatemala, Peru, Chile, and Argentina would pave the way for the South American League of Nations.[11] It was Bolivar's intention to form a truly American League, a society of brotherly nations, a society whose federated strength would oppose the Holy Alliance.[12] Bolivar aimed at voluntary union in America as opposed to that union by conscription which the Holy Alliance imposed on small and defenseless nations. He was trying to realize the ideals proclaimed by the Abbé de Saint Pierre at the beginning of the eighteenth century and so admirably elucidated at a later date by Kant in his essay, *Vom Ewigen Frieden*.[13]

A few days prior to the battle of Ayacucho, Bolivar had sent a circular to the governments of Mexico, Guatemala, Argentina, and Chile. "After fifteen years of sacrifice," he wrote, "devoted to the guaranteeing of American freedom in a system of security which, both in war and in peace, might be the shield of our destiny, the time has now arrived when the interests and associations which unite the American republics should secure a firm foundation." Bolivar, therefore, suggested an assembly of plenipotentiaries to meet in Panama. "The day on which these plenipotentiaries shall exchange their credentials will be considered immortal in the history of America. When, after a hundred years has passed and posterity has made researches into the origin of our international law, it will remember these

10 Cartas: Vol. II. p. 20. A. F. Ponte: Simón Bolívar. Caracas, 1919. p. 220. F. Velarde: Congreso de Panamá en 1826. Panama, 1922. M. Oliveira Lima: La evolución histórica de la América Latina. Madrid, pp. 160-70.

11 Cartas: Vol. III. pp. 54, 58, 62, 63, 81, 108, 257. Blanco: Doc. Vol. IX. pp. 297, 305, 717.

12 Urrutia: El ideal Internacional de Bolívar. *op. cit.,* p. 202. R. Rivas: Bolívar Internacionalista. B. d. H. Bogotá. Vol. XXV. p. 664.

13 Pérez Concha: *op. cit.,* p. 113. Urrutia: La Evolución del Arbitraje en América. Madrid, 1920. It has sometimes been said that San Martín and his minister, Monteagudo, really originated the plan for a South American League of Nations. However, this is a misconception since San Martín in his famous proclamation of November 13, 1818, asked only for a treaty of alliance between Argentina, Chile and Perú, while Bolivar was aiming at a true League of the South American nations.

treaties that have fortified our destiny, and the treaties of the
straits of Panama will be recalled with respect."[14] When Bolivar
received satisfactory responses from the majority of the republics invited to attend the assembly, he believed the success of
his congress had been secured. His ardent imagination here
again anticipated a promise of future greatness to which, unconsciously, he himself gave reality. More than fifteen years previously he had foreseen the results of the war. He now foresaw
a century of international development.

Bolivar had, moreover, concrete reasons for recommending
and insisting on his plan for an American League of Nations.
It has been mentioned that he was still in fear of intervention
by the conservative powers of Europe. The Congress of Panama
would be the best means of blocking once and for all such attempts at interference. A new international organization would
confront an old one, their principles diametrically opposed.
"While in Europe everything is done for the sake of tyranny,
in America everything is done for the sake of freedom."[15]

At the suggestion of Santander, an invitation to the Congress
was extended to the United States and to those European nations who had interests to defend in the Western Hemisphere.
By this move, it has been said, Santander wrecked Bolivar's
plans, but the accusation is entirely unjust. Bolivar's failure
can be ascribed more truthfully to a duality of interests, and
these interests seem contradictory. At the time he was planning
his Pan-American league, he was also preparing a more limited
and imperialistic design—that is, the Federation of the Andes.[16]
This second vision was the idea of a federation of all the states
in the region of the Andes from Mexico to Cape Horn, and this
idea grew and strengthened in the Liberator's mind. "Mexico,
Guatemala, Colombia, Peru, Chile, and Bolivia might form a
glorious Federation. . . . Such a Federation would have the
advantage of being homogeneous, solid, and closed. The North

14 Cartas: Vol. IV. pp. 216-18, 266. The idea that a pan-American congress
should meet in Panama was first proposed by Miranda. Robertson: Life. Vol. I. p. 230.
15 Cartas: Vol. IV. pp. 267, 288.
16 Cartas: Vol. IV. pp. 308, 343.

Americans and the Haitians would be a foreign substance in our body."[17] It is obvious that Bolivar is at this point concentrating on a league of Hispanic American nations. The universal Pan-American league remained only as a kind of framework to give the Federation of the Andes some ideological dignity.

Bolivar continues by outlining another idea which may seem surprising and erratic in many respects. He suggests that this Federation of the Andes be placed under the protection of Great Britain, "the Mistress of the Nations," as he called her.[18] He hoped to conclude an alliance for offense and defense with England whereby England in recompense would take over the protection of the Andean republic.[19] Let us make an attempt to understand this bewildering idea. Are we to believe that Bolivar wanted to retreat to Miranda's concepts; had he shaken off Spanish rule only to take on British domination? The most heterogeneous considerations are mingled in Bolivar's plan for a British protectorate. England was for him the liberal country par excellence; its constitution had become Bolivar's model because its government was founded on freedom. Bolivar had no fear that England, even in the role of protector, would concern herself with the internal problems of South America. Of more importance was his feeling of certitude that only England could ever wage successful warfare against South America, a continent defended by two oceans. "England," wrote Bolivar, "moves along an ascending line. Woe to him who opposes her! They who have not already become her allies or have not linked their destiny with England's are indeed unfortunate. All America is not worth the British fleet. Even the Holy Alliance is helpless against an England that is supported by immense resources and liberal principles. An alliance with England would mean more to us than the battle of Ayacucho."[20]

To understand fully Bolivar's desire for a British protec-

17 Cartas: Vol. IV. p. 348.
18 Cartas: Vol. V. p. 13.
19 Cartas: Vol. V. p. 26.
20 Cartas: Vol. V. pp. 26-27, 204, 214, 215. Cartas Santander: Vol. II. pp. 74, 93.

torate in South America, we must appreciate his skeptical attitude toward the capacities of his people. He was convinced that they were too immature to defend themselves from outside aggression; moreover, he did not trust their democratic protestations. He was not afraid that a protectorate would at some future date endanger national sovereignty, for he said, ". . . in its shadow we would grow and become men; we could cultivate and strengthen ourselves and could finally present ourselves among the nations with that grade of civilization which is demanded of a great people."[21] This quotation sets the tone for Bolivar's political thinking during the years that followed Ayacucho. He was well aware that the mere fact of South American independence had not altered the atmosphere of colonial dependency which had for so many years governed the lives of the South American people.

Bolivar dreamed of founding a great nation that would be able to compete with others in both power and culture. To attain this end he believed it necessary to establish internal security through an authoritarian regime and to acquire stability among foreign powers by means of a protectorate. He did not minimize the dangers involved in such a plan, but he looked upon them as inevitable risks if the nations of the Andes aspired to educate themselves for a significant role in world affairs.

It does not appear that England gave Bolivar's appeal any consideration whatever. Great Britain had limited herself, during the nineteenth century, to economic penetration and conquest in South America. A protectorate would have been an expensive experiment doomed to certain failure because of the natural antagonism that would have been aroused in the United States.

While he contemplated the perspectives of this federation, Bolivar continued to urge forward the preparations for the Congress of Panama.[22] The program for this first Pan-American

21 Cartas: Vol. V. pp. 215-16.
22 Proclamas: p. 315: Un pensamiento sobre el Congreso de Panamá. R. Porras Barrenechea: El Congreso de Panamá. Lima, 1930.

conference is extant and includes the following points: The states of the New World would be united under a common international law. There should be a basis of equality in their mutual relationship. Any member of the League refusing to accept its resolutions should be expelled. The League was to hold the power of mediator and should arbitrate on all disputations arising among the members, as well as between a member and an outside power. When external aggression or internal anarchy threatened the existence of any member, the League was to give assistance. Racial discriminations were to be abolished. Every new attempt to initiate colonial experiments on South American soil should be rejected. Slave trade must be abolished. Any vestiges of Spanish power in the New World were to be liquidated. America should be open to British trade and should serve as an economic bridgehead between Europe and Asia. The British should be given the rights of South American citizens, and South Americans should emulate the British and embrace their moral code. It is clear from the foregoing stipulations that Bolivar was obsessed by his admiration for Great Britain.

It will not come as a surprise that the Congress of Panama did not fulfill Bolivar's expectations. In 1826 the United States was not willing to forbid the slave trade; and, of greater importance, it refused to agree to further revolutionary development in the Caribbean Sea. Neither Cuba nor Puerto Rico could shift its political position at this time because revolutionary activity in this area might jeopardize North American influence. President Adams' cabinet was aloof to Bolivar's project, but the President went so far as to appoint a representative to the Congress at Panama. Unfortunately, this envoy died en route, with the result that the United States did not participate in the deliberations at Panama.[23]

England's attitude was equally cool. The advantages Bolivar offered her were hers without the assumption of responsibility, and British policy never admitted obligation without defi-

23 Blanco: Doc. Vol. X. p. 227.

nite reward. Consequently, England sent only an observer to
the Congress. The South American republics were hesitant.
Chile was not hostile to Bolivar's plans, but internal exigencies
prevented her from taking an active part in Panama. Buenos
Aires and Brazil made excuses. In the end only a rump congress met. The first deputies to arrive were the Peruvians; six
months later the Colombians came; finally in June, 1826, the
representatives of Mexico and Guatemala turned up. On June
22, at the Franciscan monastery in Panama, the Pan-American
Congress was convened with due solemnity. Only four Latin
American republics had sent deputies. On July 15 the meetings
were adjourned.

The resolutions accepted by the Congress of Panama are as
follows: The four republics represented made an internal alliance treaty which was open to all American republics.[24] The
federation, thus constituted, should have an army and a navy
at its disposal supported by all the federated states. This armed
force was to be entrusted with the defense of all American
affairs. An assembly, representing the federated states, should
meet bi-annually, and in case of war, yearly. Because of Panama's pestilential climate, the location of later conferences was
to be moved to a Mexican village.[25] The above account is a
rough summation of the resolutions taken at the Congress of
Panama. A South American League of Nations had not been
established. Neither Argentina nor Chile nor Brazil agreed to
the resolutions, and the deputies from Bolivia arrived too late to
take part in the negotiations.

Bolivar, who was still in Lima, had refused to put any
pressure on the delegates in Panama, but he was profoundly
disappointed in the outcome of their deliberations.[26] The provisions for common defense seemed meager and unstable; he
considered the adoption of a Mexican location for League head-

24 See, Briceño's report in O'Leary: Memorias. Vol. II. p. 564. Blanco: Doc.
Vol. X. p. 432.
25 J. B. Lockey: Pan-americanism, its Beginnings. New York, 1920. The four
treaties signed in Panama, in Blanco: Doc. Vol. V. p. 499. V. Mendoza López: El
Congreso de Bolívar y el Panamericanismo. La Paz.
26 Cartas: Vol. V. p. 222. O'Leary: Memorias. Vol. II. p. 557.

quarters as a mistake, since it moved the federation farther away from his jurisdiction and brought it closer to Mexican control and into territory bordering the United States. He ordered a postponement of the ratification of the treaties, and in one of his grandiloquent metaphors compared himself to the Greek madman who attempted to plot the courses of ships sailing the high seas from a rocky base on the mainland.[27]

It was indeed true that the Congress of Panama was a failure, since its principal objective, the creation of a South American League, had not been achieved. However, its importance lies in the fact that Bolivar conceived this idea more than a century ago, and that he made a definite attempt to realize it. He was the first to advocate international arbitration in the Western Hemisphere and one of the first to demand abolishment of the slave trade. The common defense of the Hemisphere, another of his great concepts, was left for the twentieth century to carry out. Certain very real advances had been made; the Pan-American conferences became a permanent institution, and the idea of international courts gained more and more ground. Franklin D. Roosevelt's Good Neighbor Policy corresponds closely to the Liberator's most intimate wishes. The resolutions of Chapultepec and San Francisco were animated by the spirit which motivated Bolivar when he called the first Congress of Panama.

The blow to his hopes had not taken Bolivar entirely by surprise. Later, in an intimate conversation, he confessed, "I called the Congress of Panama in order to create a sensation. It was my ambition to bring the name of Colombia and the other South American republics to the attention of the whole world. . . . I never believed that an American League, comparable to the Holy Alliance formulated at the Congress of Vienna, would result from its deliberations."[28] He referred to the Congress as a vain boast, a *coup de théâtre,* but he had by no

---

27 Cartas: Vol. VI. pp. 68-69. Whitacker: *op. cit.,* p. 578. F. L. Reinhold: Hisp. Am. Hist. Rev. Vol. XVIII. pp. 342 ff.

28 D. d. B. pp. 318-19.

means lost faith in the principles which had inspired the convocation. He, nevertheless, saw with greater clarity the disparate interests which hindered international agreement in America. The republics had but one common possession—their independence. "I considered the Congress of the Straits as a theatrical performance, and like Solon, I believed the measures promulgated there to be snares for the weak and supports for the strong."[29]

Bolivar now concentrated his attention on his second trump card, the Federation of the Andes. Once more the emperor's crown was offered him. Influential interests in Peru attempted to convince him that the moment was propitious for the establishment of a great empire, stretching from the Orinoco to Potosí. Bolivar should be its emperor, since his presence would stabilize the country and appease the European powers. This party took as its watchword: "Bolivar or nothing."[30] As a matter of fact, Bolivar's position in 1826 was equal to that held by the Spanish king during the colonial period. He controlled Venezuela, Ecuador, New Granada, Panama, Peru, and Bolivia; his voice was powerful in Chile and Argentina, and even in Central America. In many ways it would have seemed wise to consolidate such a position. Nevertheless, Bolivar again refused, and instead of the proposed empire he urged his Federation of the Andes. This idea now usurps the place of his earlier interest in a South American League of Nations.

In 1815 Bolivar had held the opinion that an overexpanded state with borders far removed from a center of operations must, of its very nature, disintegrate into tyranny. A far-flung monarchy is difficult to maintain, he said, but a widespread republic cannot be maintained. Now, eleven years later, we find him defending an opposite viewpoint. His political vision had expanded to the dimensions of his military successes, and he seemed unwilling to relinquish the influence he had won over

29 Cartas: Vol. VI. p. 10.
30 O'Leary: Memorias. Vol. II. p. 505. O'Leary: Doc. Vol. X. pp. 144-66. Cartas: Vol. V. p. 288. Pérez Concha: op. cit., p. 5.

the continent.[31] The establishment of a Federation of the Andes now appeared to him in the light of a super victory, as a final solution for all the tormenting problems of the continent. Such was his illusion.

Bolivar's dream envisioned himself as Protector or President of the Federation; he was indifferent as to the exact title he should assume. Colombia, Peru, and Bolivia were to constitute the original membership of the Federation, but they were each to undergo a certain division. Colombia should again be partitioned into three states—Venezuela, Cundinamarca, and Ecuador. Peru and Bolivia together should also be divided into three states, thus integrating the Federation on the basis of six federated states. Bolivar explained his project in great detail in a letter to General Gutiérrez de la Fuente. "After long contemplation, we, that is, the men of sound judgment and I myself, have decided that the only remedy for the terrible evils [of anarchy] is to be found in a general federation between Bolivia, Peru, and Colombia. Such a federation should be a more closely knit union than that of the United States. It should be directed by a president and a vice-president. The Bolivian Constitution should form the basis of its government, since this constitution is adaptable to both the federation and individual states if certain modifications are made. The purpose of the federation is to establish as complete a unity as is possible under a federated government. The government of the individual states must remain in the hands of the vice-presidents and the two chambers in all matters pertaining to religion, justice, civil administration, and economy, that is in all things which do not concern foreign affairs or war. . . . The Liberator, as supreme ruler, would visit the member states at least once a year. The capital should be located at a central point of the federated states. . . . This federation should adopt any name; the name does not matter . . . but it would have one flag, one army, and would be one nation."[32]

31 Belaunde: La Federación de los Andes. *op. cit.*, p. 205.
32 Cartas: Vol. V. p. 296.

A few days later Bolivar wrote to Santander, "Here we have great plans in hand regarding the constitution and federation of Bolivia, Peru, and Colombia."[33] But he was already abandoning the idea of federation and in its place he proposed union —the Union of the Andes. It goes without saying that he was to be life-president of his projected empire-republic, with Sucre as his successor. The founding of the German Empire comes to mind, with Colombia in the role of Prussia, but Bolivar was not Bismarck and from the beginning his plans were doomed to failure.

The movement for independence had never reached a point of universal acceptance in South America as it had in North America. The thirteen colonies in the north had proclaimed their liberty with one voice in the Declaration of Independence; in the south each state had come to its decision separately. Bolivar underestimated the significance of this fact, or possibly he preferred to ignore it. Ten years previously he had described with great eloquence the many variations in the South American states; now, in 1826, he demands that a unified nation be formed from these same disparate states.

Bolivar's co-workers were more skeptical than he. Santander considered union between Colombia and Peru as utopian and absurd. Sucre was doubtful whether such a giant republic would be of benefit to the liberated nations. He could not feel certain that they would submit themselves to one government.[34] But Bolivar would not listen to any objections; he was still enthralled with his idea and saw in the Federation of the Andes the culminating glory of his whole life. The reader may recall the words, "Let us look for a foundation of security," which began this chapter of Bolivar's life. The Federation of the Andes was for him the answer to his quest. It incorporated a new political and geographical order after his own wishes; moreover, it would embrace the Bolivian Constitution and would regulate

33 Cartas: Vol. V. pp. 292, 367. Cartas: Vol. VI. p. 59.
34 Belaunde: Federación de los Andes. p. 207. For Sucre's opinion about the Federation see, O'Leary: Doc. Vol. I. pp. 374, 422.

interstate relations. Finally, it might even include security against external enemies—the Holy Alliance or Brazil. Confident in this belief, Bolivar felt that he might eventually challenge the United States and carry the fight for freedom to Cuba and Puerto Rico.[35]

A strange mixture of personal ambition, desire for internal stability and external prestige lay at the bottom of Bolivar's hybrid idea. He dreamed of one mighty nation in South America that would parallel the achievement of the United States and would be capable of competing with this northern power in authority and importance. He cultivated this dream, however, in spite of his inner knowledge that the metal of the South American soul was unable to support such an ideal. He was aware that geographical barriers, racial and national prejudices, separated the new states—but lately dependent colonies— from one another. But Bolivar refused to admit this truth, hoping, perhaps, that the South Americans might possibly be united by authoritarian pressure.

Bolivar's idea of dictatorship was illuminated by an educational motive, somewhat like certain of Fichte's ideas, both magnificent and delirious. Like Disraeli, Bolivar was not primarily a statesman. He was an artist and a poet who tried to breathe life into American clay. Like Schiller, he thought, "this century is not mature enough for my ideal; I live a citizen of times to come," with the difference that Bolivar was not content to wait for the actors of the future to take up their parts. He wished to stage his magnificent drama under the pressing illusion that these participants in South America's destiny were even now in the wings, waiting eagerly for their cues. With a total disregard for the basic obstinacy of the South American, Bolivar demanded his right to realize his dream. But human beings are not lightly disregarded, and certainly not the South Americans. They were indifferent to Bolivar's idea of federation; they cared nothing for his Bolivian Constitution,

35 O'Leary: Doc. Vol. XXIV. p. 8. Cartas: Vol. VI. pp. 54-55. J. M. Yepes: El Congreso de Panamá. Bogotá, 1930.

and they were vociferous in their disapproval of his dalliance with a British protectorate. They had fought and bled and died for independence. This was their goal and they had reached it. Liberty, to them, meant self-determination, and they viewed a Federation of the Andes as a complete negation of all their efforts toward freedom. They had no intention of submitting themselves to an imperialistic regime.

Bolivar's great conception was doomed to failure, and his political thinking became tragic and hopeless. No one thought or planned as he did in terms of continents. And even while the architecture of his Andean Federation rose clear and splendid in his mind's eye, the very foundations of its structure began to tremble. The earth opened and devoured both workers and scaffolding. Colombia was on fire from one end to the other.

Part IV

MAN OF SORROWS

CHAPTER 31

Páez and Santander

*A*s long as the liberators congregate around me Colombia will remain united; afterward there will be civil war."[1] Two years after Bolivar had made this statement the event he had predicted came to pass. Colombia's disintegration emerged from a latent into an acute stage. The immediate cause of conflict was a disagreement between Páez, military commander of Venezuela, and Santander, head of the civil administration of the Republic.

Greater Colombia's political structure had been no more than a temporary affair, a kind of breastwork behind which Bolivar fought his last battles against Spain. The state created during this period of emergency embraced regions of the utmost variety: the ardent plains of the Orinoco and the high plateaus of Bogotá and Quito; the coastal areas of two oceans and the gigantic block of the Andes. The three great divisions had no common economic policy, their interests were conflicting, and they were separated by great distances. Their provinces had been devastated by war, and although it was not reasonable, it was only natural that the young Republic should be blamed for the accumulation of misery. The liberal administration, hardly more than an improvisation, had no time for reforms, and was, therefore, hampered by innumerable abuses dating from the colonial period.

The following circumstances amply demonstrate the coun-

1 Cartas: Vol. IV. p. 121.

try's condition. Under Spanish rule a very considerable textile industry had developed in New Granada and Ecuador, protected by the Spanish ban on the importation of foreign goods. When the Republic adopted a policy of free trade, the country was immediately inundated with French and English products. The native factories went into bankruptcy, and the invested capital was lost. Agriculture suffered from lack of roads and means of transportation. In the coastal regions North American flour was cheaper than Colombian flour.[2] Moreover, the financial administration of the young state was notably weak and inefficient; smuggling, embezzlement, and fraud were daily occurrences, with the result that the whole fiscal network had become entangled. In place of the customary duties, a general tax on the entire population had been imposed and had produced both opposition and financial stagnation. Loans made by foreign nations were wasted. Any semblance of harmony between the three federated states was purely superficial. These people had lived without economic exchange or intellectual intercourse for three hundred years; consequently, each unit of the colonial administration had felt itself independent and self-sufficient.[3]

Most Europeans thought of the South Americans as one people; the disparities between Colombians, Venezuelans, and Ecuadorians seemed to them no greater than the difference between Austrians, Bavarians, and Swiss. But the undercurrent of local idiosyncrasies and misunderstanding which acted as a barrier between the South American countries had cut deep into the primitive nature of these people, and the common experience of a struggle for independence had failed to bridge the dark stream. There was some truth in the Colombian saying that Venezuela was a barracks, Colombia a university, and Ecuador a monastery. In Caracas the soldier was important; in Bogotá, the lawyer; in Quito, the priest. The

2 O'Leary: Memorias. Vol. II. p. 582.
3 E. Caballero Calderón: Un Continente sin Bautizar. Rev. d. l. Indias. August, 1945.

latter presented no danger to the formative state, but the lawyers and writers of Colombia, the officers and Llaneros of Venezuela, displayed an open and avowed antagonism. Bolivar was well aware of these obstacles to union, and he knew quite accurately what to expect. "I swear with the utmost sincerity," he wrote to Santander, "that I fear my beloved fatherland more than all the rest of America. I believe myself more capable of ruling the New World than of ruling Venezuela."[4]

An influential party in Venezuela had been working toward the dissolution of unity in Greater Colombia. Caracas, Bogotá's rival, had as early as 1821 protested against the Colombian union. The Venezuelan group made its ideas public in addresses and newspapers, but the Colombian politicians gave no heed to the growing animosity, continuing to press their demands for unity.[5]

"Before the advent of revolution everything is endeavor," runs one of Goethe's aphorisms, "but afterward everything is the assertion of prerogatives." The incident of Colonel Infante is a case in point. Infante, a Venezuelan and the hero of countless battles, had come to Bogotá in 1819. The transition to civil life, however, did not agree with him, and it was not long before he had taken on the habits and appearance of a boor. He became involved in a quarrel over a girl and killed a Colombian lieutenant. The trial which followed took on political importance because of Infante's rank. The Supreme Court of Bogotá sentenced him to death, and Santander, although he had the power to commute the sentence to life imprisonment, confirmed the decision.[6] We may assume that the sentence was just, but there was little wisdom in demanding the death penalty. Possibly Santander was moved by his legal conscience, or it may be that he was influenced by his hatred for the Venezuelan military spirit—a hatred which many Venezuelans believed responsible for a widespread persecution.

4 Cartas: Vol. IV. p. 322.
5 O'Leary: Memorias. Vol. II. p. 586. Baralt: Vol. II. pp. 91 ff.
6 P. M. Ibáñez: El coronel Leonardo Infante. B. d. H. Bogotá. Vol. III. No. 26. O'Leary: Memorias. Vol. II. p. 593. Blanco: Doc. Vol. IX. p. 627.

That the latter idea had motivated Santander in his action was
the opinion of one of the justices, Miguel Peña, a Venezuelan,
and he had consequently refused to sign the majority decision.
For a long time Bolivar had realized that an unfriendly Peña
would constitute a real danger, and he implored Santander to
pacify Peña and to keep him occupied in Bogotá. But Bolivar's
warning was rejected by Santander, and Peña was accused of
violating the law. Peña, though president of the Supreme
Court, had an unenviable record blackened with many shady
dealings, and he considered it the part of wisdom to evade
his trial.[7] He, therefore, fled to Venezuela and refused a summons to return to Bogotá. It was a foregone conclusion that
he now dedicated himself to the easy task of increasing the
discord between Colombia and Venezuela.

Conditions in Venezuela in 1826 have already been noted.
Numerous insurgent bands roamed the country, fomenting
rebellion and disregarding public authority. Páez had exerted
every effort to keep matters in hand, but at the end of 1825
he had felt obliged to call on the militia to enforce some
measure of control. But the civil governor, Intendant Escalona,
refused to obey his orders, declaring that Páez had exceeded
his authority in drafting the militia.[8] He sent a memorandum
of his complaint to the central government in Bogotá, and
in March, Páez was accused by the Colombian Parliament of
violating the Constitution, and he was ordered to present himself at the capital.[9]

Páez agreed to come to Bogotá to answer the government's
charge, but he was enraged at being treated like any common
soldier. He was a man of primitive emotions, and the accusation had, to use his own words, penetrated his heart like a
dagger.[10] Vulnerable to insult and by nature susceptible to

7 Restrepo: H. d. R. C. Vol. III. p. 485. Cartas de Santander: Vol. II. pp. 16-17.
See, Arch. Santander: Vol. XII. p. 302. O'Leary: Doc. Vol. II. p. 256.
    8 Blanco: Doc. Vol. IX. p. 611. O'Leary: Doc. Vol. XXIV. pp. 100 ff.
    9 Restrepo: H. d. R. C. Vol. III. p. 484. O'Leary: Memorias. Vol. II. p. 607.
Cartas Santander: Vol. II. p. 93.
    10 O'Leary: Memorias. Vol. II. pp. 614-15. Restrepo: H. d. R. C. Vol. III.
p. 498. Larrazabal: Vol. II. p. 345.

flattery, Páez was open to the insinuations of false friends, whose speaker was, in this case, Dr. Peña. How was it that Páez gave his consent to a summons from Bogotá which might bring him a death like that of Colonel Infante? Would it not be a wiser plan to destroy the unpopular union with New Granada and himself take the leadership of the Venezuelans? He was the hero of the plains, the Lion of the Apure, and he should hold the reins of power. Peña's words awoke a popular echo. The city council of Valencia issued a declaration stating that all the inhabitants had full confidence in the leadership of General Páez. Other cities followed Valencia's example. Their action constituted a revolt against the central government. On May 16 Venezuela made Páez its civil and military chief. Certain cautious and discreet citizens of the country were strongly opposed to open rebellion and wrote to Bolivar demanding that he return and accelerate the reform of the Constitution.[11] Even Santander now urged the Liberator's return from Lima. "Your presence," he wrote, "is absolutely necessary."

The quarrel between Santander and Páez was a phenomenon not unusual in the history of revolutions. Páez represented the attitude of the seasoned soldier, the man who had fought and suffered, the man who for years had been free from the restrictions of a civil order. He naturally looked upon the state as his to dispose of. Santander, on the other hand, had lived within the limits of a society controlled by civil law, and although he owed his rise to the revolution, he now wanted to conclude the chaotic period and to seal it with a return to legalized authority. In this manner the dissension became a contest between military force and civil law. Santander's central government should have crushed the uprising, but it had neither money nor arms for such an undertaking. Moreover, no one cared to take Paez' measure; he was still remembered as the fearless and ruthless soldier of the revolution.[12] This

11 Blanco: Doc. Vol. X. pp. 436, 526. Cartas Santander: Vol. II. p. 219. O'Leary: Doc. Vol. VIII. p. 181.
12 Cartas Santander: Vol. II. pp. 220, 242. Blanco: Doc. Vol. X. p. 409.

situation, coupled with the incompetence and vacillation of the
Bogotá government, gave free rein to the seditionists. New
fires broke out in many parts of the country.[13]

Bolivar could not pretend to be surprised at the course events
had taken. His friends had warned him many times of the
danger in which Colombia stood and had begged him to return
to Venezuela with the army to establish law and order. And
Bolivar had given his promise: "I offer to keep Colombia at
peace with the help of the victorious army of Ayacucho."[14] He
endeavored to pacify Páez and advised him to obey Parliament
with little hope that Páez would accept his advice. And indeed
he saw quite clearly how things were shaping up. "If the
gentlemen of Congress choose to compel Páez to come to
Bogotá, and if he refuses to obey, it is not I who am responsible
for the blunder. If the Constitution and the laws made by
Congress ruin the Republic, it is not I who am responsible. If
the army is restless because it is poorly paid and is rewarded
only by ingratitude, again it is not I who am responsible. Nor
am I responsible if the colored people rebel and destroy everything because the government is too weak to exercise control."[15]
Was it, however, possible for Bolivar to disclaim all responsibility, and like Pontius Pilate, wash his hands and say, "I am
innocent"?

Bolivar's error lay in his failure to return to Colombia. After
the battle of Ayacucho, most certainly after the establishment
of Bolivia, the importance of an early return to Colombia
should have been apparent to him. If he believed that Greater
Colombia would survive as long as the hosts of liberators
considered him their leader, then clearly his place was in the
presidential palace at Bogotá. But Bolivar ignored these evident truths and remained in Lima, where the pleasures of
power and the fascinating dream of a Federation of the Andes

13 Restrepo: H. d. R. C. Vol. III. p. 539. Acuerdos d. Consejo d. Gobierno
d. l. República d. Colombia, 1825-27. Bogotá, 1942. pp. 201 ff. Páez: Autobiografía.
pp. 368, 452.
14 Cartas: Vol. V. p. 100.
15 Cartas: Vol. V. p. 349.

overcame his better judgment. Many circumstances were responsible for Bolivar's apparent blindness. He was not an administrator; in the moment of emergency he became master of the situation, but he disliked red tape and abominated desk work. He omits few opportunities to acquaint us with this trait of his character. Bolivar did not have the capacity of Frederick the Great to return to civilian affairs after seven years of war and dedicate himself for the rest of his life to reconstruction and administration. Talleyrand's reflection on the time and patience required to transform the leaves of the mulberry plant into silk held no appeal for his hasty and impetuous nature. Opposition irritated him to the point of madness. "I am not capable of playing on such a complicated keyboard. I would break it," he once confessed.[16]

Bolivar was now accustomed to dictatorial power. Since 1813 he had exercised his authority with almost no hindrance, and in Lima his position assumed the attributes and prerogatives of a sultanate. A constitutional presidency, with its train of carping ministers, critical officials, presumptuous deputies, and an omnipresent public, did not attract him. He stayed in Lima, where his word was law. But his self-indulgence was fatal. Had he used his influence in Colombia, the final rupture between Santander and Páez might have been avoided.

O'Leary, Bolivar's aide, was commissioned to go to Bogotá and Caracas, and to reveal Bolivar's intimate ideas for Colombia's future to the two antagonists. Copies of the Bolivian Constitution, that miraculous cure-all for political ills, accompanied O'Leary. "God grant we could apply this Constitution in Columbia when we attempt reform."[17] While O'Leary was on his way, Páez established headquarters in Caracas. The officials and the army took an oath on his new "disorder," and Páez swore to accept no further orders from Bogotá. Three provinces—Caracas, Carabobo, and Apure—sided with him,

16 Cartas: Vol. V. p. 368.
17 Cartas: Vol. V. p. 327. Cartas Santander: Vol. II. p. 62. Restrepo: H. d. R. C. Vol. III. p. 525.

but the others remained loyal to the legal authorities. In the meantime Páez had written to Bolivar giving his own account of events. He blamed Santander for all that had happened, describing his rival as both quarrelsome and adroit. He asked Bolivar to act as arbiter and to settle the dispute.[18]

In other parts of Colombia the cries for help became more and more pressing. Urdaneta and Briceño lent their voices to the general appeal. Finally, Bolivar made his long-postponed decision and on September 3, 1826, he left the Peruvian capital. "Colombia," he said in his farewell address, "calls on me and I obey."[19] Colombia had been calling on him for many weeks, but her anxious voice had gone unheeded.

Bolivar left the Peruvian government in the hands of men he considered reliable. The larger part of the Colombian army remained in Peru and Bolivia, an ill-advised measure as Bolivar must have known, because of the enmity his soldiers provoked. He returned to Colombia without an army, confident of the magical influence of his name. An apprehension of his own negligence must have troubled him, however, for on reaching Colombian soil in Guayaquil he offered his countrymen what he called "the olive branch of peace." "There is only one person responsible for your quarrel, and that is I. I have returned too late. Two allied republics, the daughters of our victories, delayed me and enchanted me with infinite gratitude and immortal rewards."[20]

The cry of rebellion uttered in the north had already been echoed in Guayaquil. The Separatists of this section who, since 1823, had been forced to restrain their discontent and resentment, now made public demonstration against the Colombian Republic, openly damning the power that had held them in check. From one end of the state to the other society was disunited; in Quito, Bolivar heard complaints against the unpopu-

18 Cartas de Páez: B. d. H. Caracas. Vol. XV. No. 60. pp. 249, 262. Páez: Autobiografía. p. 378. O'Leary: Memorias. Vol. II. p. 631. Restrepo: H. d. R. C. Vol. III. p. 503.
19 Proclamas: p. 338.
20 Proclamas: p. 340. Cartas: Vol. VI. p. 93.

lar tax system; he learned of the dissatisfaction of the army, and he saw the authorities of the republic in undisguised conflict.[21] Bolivar's partisans told him that the people wanted monarchy, but he answered that he was circumscribed by the Bolivian Constitution. It was not his ambition to become a kingmaker, but to elevate himself to the role of arbiter, from which lofty position he could deal, like another Solomon, with all the struggling and disunited groups.[22] He bestowed offices and titles as though he were still Colombia's all-powerful dictator, while as a matter of fact and according to the Colombian Constitution he was merely a victorious general who had returned to his fatherland. Bolivar expected Colombia to confirm his assumption of authority; the dictatorship was essential to the success of his projected constitutional reform.[23]

Everything now depended on Bolivar's diplomacy in presenting the platform of his constitutional reform. According to the statutes of 1821, the Constitution of Cucutá was inviolable for a period of ten years. But Bolivar considered this Constitution too weak and too liberal, and he wrote Santander that the Páez rebellion could never be crushed under the laws then in force.[24] Santander protested against making any change, suspecting Bolivar of planning a new period of dictatorship. He declared that any alteration of the existing governmental form would be unconstitutional. As a matter of fact Bolivar publicly rejected the title of Dictator. "I do not want to hear the word 'Dictator,'" he said, but the letters written by the Liberator on his way from Lima to Bogotá furnish ample evidence that he was fascinated with the idea of again becoming Dictator of Colombia.

An apparent change in tone now takes place in the correspondence between Santander and Bolivar. Bolivar's letters become cutting and aggressive. Santander had made the incau-

21 Blanco: Doc. Vol. X. p. 568. O'Leary: Doc. Vol. IV. pp. 451 ff. O'Leary: Memorias. Vol. II. pp. 642-43.
22 Cartas: Vol. VI. pp. 28-30, 61.
23 Cartas: Vol. VI. pp. 67, 68, 70, 75. Larrazabal: Vol. II. p. 364. Restrepo: H. d. R. C. Vol. III. p. 549.
24 Cartas: Vol. VI. p. 76. Blanco: Doc. Vol. X. pp. 629, 630, 667.

tious and undiplomatic suggestion that Bolivar should not trouble himself with governmental problems on his return to Bogotá. He suggested that Bolivar should lead the army to Venezuela and restore peace and order there.[25] Such a move would have placed Bolivar, as a general, under the command of Santander, and Bolivar was far too clever to be led into such a trap. Santander had told Bolivar that he feared losing his power, and the Liberator was quite unlikely to forget this confession. He began to criticize Santander's accomplishments openly. Colombia's ills, he said, did not stem from the war for independence, but from iniquitous laws. The Republic was exhausted because the capital sucked the blood from the body politic. The waste of foreign loans was ascribed to Santander; and, unfortunately for Santander, there were others who held this opinion. The foreign loans were, however, but one stone in the intricate mosaic. The real problem was to locate and suppress the causes of discord in Colombia.

"We must make a new social contract; the people must redeem their sovereignty"—these words became Bolivar's motto.[26] He thought an appeal to public opinion might bring the acceptance of the Bolivian Constitution—an absurd and fatuous attitude, since it would mean tearing down the old house simply in order to build a new one. Had Bolivar forgotten that four years previously he had sworn to defend the Constitution of Cucutá with the army of liberators? Santander warned him that the Bolivian Constitution would never be popular, but Bolivar rose to angry heights of indignation at Santander's opposition. He issued threats to resign and leave the country. "I have no desire to preside over Colombia's obsequies."[27]

The reception granted him on his trip through Quito, Pasto, and Popayán made Bolivar think that the catastrophe could still be averted. His unbounded confidence in Colombia's

25 Cartas Santander: Vol. II. p. 258.
26 Cartas: Vol. VI. pp. 82, 91.
27 Cartas: Vol. VI. p. 98.

future leapt over all obstacles. But he was no longer the old Bolivar; illness and hardship had consumed his body. He who had in former years ridden horseback for hours on end, now showed the effects of his journey. To Manuela, whom he had left in Lima, he wrote, "I am so tired with all this travel and with all the troubles of your country that I have no time to write you long accounts in small letters as you wish me to do."[28] On November 14 he finally arrived in Bogotá.

The reception accorded the Liberator was somewhat different from the ceremonious farewell of five years ago. Bolivar had spent the intervening years in the south, and they were long years—too long for the tropics, where men are easily aroused and as easily forget. As he entered the city, he was greeted by a delegation, and in a speech of greeting the spokesman referred to the violated laws. Bolivar rose angrily in his stirrups to answer. "This day," he cried, "is a day set aside for the glory of the army; talk of it and not of the broken Constitution." He turned his horse and left the group, confounded and hurt. A chill rain fell, and although the city had been decorated in his honor, few people were gathered to greet him. Billboards with the inscription: *Viva la constitución* were everywhere, and he realized that Santander's anti propaganda had been efficient. Almost alone Bolivar rode on through the city.[29] The official ceremonies, however, proceeded without further incident. Bolivar and Santander agreed to maintain the Constitution without change. Bolivar was to take over the executive power; and, supported by Article 128 of the Constitution, was to assume the special authority granted in emergencies such as civil war and rebellion.

On November 16 Bolivar received the foreign diplomats and assured them of his continued adherence to liberal ideas. In a proclamation addressed to the Colombians he professed his profound aversion to assuming the responsibilities of a ruler.

28 Cartas: Vol. VI. p. 80.
29 J. Posada Gutiérrez: Memorias histórico-políticas. 2nd edition. Bogotá, 1929. Vol. I. p. 43. Restrepo: H. d. R. C. Vol. III. p. 555. Blanco: Doc. Vol. X. p. 700. O'Leary: Doc. Vol. VII. p. 559.

"As a simple soldier, as a true republican, and as an armed citizen, I wish to defend the most beautiful trophy of independence, the rights of my compatriots."[30] But disintegration was by now far advanced, and his words found scant response. Bolivar's sincerity was doubted less by Santander himself than by his friends and co-workers. These men, versed in jurisprudence and possessed of cultured backgrounds, considered themselves the guardians of the Constitution. The silence they had maintained during the colonial period had changed to a noisy eloquence; they imitated the Jacobins and the Girondists, and were even a bit ridiculous as they pronounced their views in lofty phrases amid the bigotry and narrowness of Colombian life. But the Sotos, the Azueros—be their names what they were—definitely were looking for trouble. A memorandum presented to Bolivar, written by Azuero, but signed by hundreds of liberals, contained the following sentence: "Bolivar shall be great and the fatherland shall be free." This statement did indeed present the issue, but it remained to be seen whether the two sentiments were compatible.[31]

During Bolivar's short stay in Bogotá, events seemed propitious for his success in reconciling the two factions. The English minister to Bogotá, Campbell, wrote to Canning, "General Bolivar is mild and extremely gentlemanly in manner and appearance, but very animated in conversation on subjects of interest to him. He possesses the entire confidence of all classes, and his moral influence is unbounded, as is likewise his complete ascendancy over the men of most talent in the capital." Bolivar organized the cabinet on a better basis; he looked after the administration of justice and finance, and cut superfluous expenses and salaries. This was but the work of days, almost of hours. He was at the same time preparing to leave for Venezuela, where he planned to wrest the military power from Páez' hands. During his absence Santander was to take charge in

30 Proclamas: p. 344.
31 Acevedo Latorre: Colaboradores de Santander. Bogotá, 1943. F. Lozano y Lozano y G. Hernández de Alba: Documentos sobre V. Azuero. Bogotá, 1944.

Bogotá. This concession to Santander was by no means the only one he had been obliged to make during these days.[32]

Bolivar explained his Federation of the Andes to his cabinet and received the opposition of Santander and his colleagues with a feigned acceptance. He pretended to come to terms with Santander's party, but he was merely concealing his intentions.[33] At the very time he made important concessions to Santander, he was writing flattering letters to Páez. He called him one of the pillars of the Republic, and promised him that he would do whatever lay in his power for Venezuela. Last, but not least, he presented him with gifts.[34] The writer believes that Bolivar's ambiguous policy was designed to lure the vain and primitive Páez into his camp by means of flattery and a show of generosity, and in this manner to facilitate a voluntary submission, while at the same time he furnished himself with a rearguard to protect him from the liberals of Bogotá by entering into a fake appeasement with Santander.

The end of November saw him in the saddle and on his way to subdue the rebellion in Venezuela. This country was in a state of tremendous confusion. Sentiment among the Venezuelans had not gone over completely to the side of Páez, and men like Arismendi and Bermúdez had remained loyal to the central government. However, Páez was still master of vast regions, and Bolivar's envoy, O'Leary, had failed to break his stubborn spirit.

At a meeting in Caracas, the Separatists had declared the dissolution of Colombia a fact. Páez had gone still further by calling a national assembly to provide Venezuela with a new constitution. But once again fortune favored Bolivar; Puerto Cabello turned away from Páez' solicitations and declared its loyalty to the idea of Greater Colombia.[35] Briceño Méndez, the husband of a niece of Bolivar and one of the

---

32 Blanco: Doc. Vol. X. p. 724. Webster: Vol. I. p. 425.
33 J. J. Guerra: La Convención de Ocaña. Bogotá, 1908. p. 99.
34 Cartas: Vol. VI. p. 99. See also, Cartas Inéditas. B. d. H. Bogotá. Vol. XVIII. p. 787.
35 Blanco: Doc. Vol. XI. pp. 7, 16. Restrepo: H. d. R. C. Vol. III. p. 573.

Liberator's most ardent partisans, took command of the fortress, and Páez besieged the harbor in vain. The resistance of Puerto Cabello proved fatal to the Llanero. The news of Puerto Cabello's resistance was delivered to Bolivar when he was on his way to the coast. His tone toward Páez suddenly changed; any resolution of Páez' so-called national assembly, he declared, would automatically become null and void. "My enemies," wrote Bolivar, "are sent to their ruin according to the will of Providence, but my friends, such as Sucre, ascend." Páez would have to decide on which side he cared to place himself.[36]

During his trip from the interior to Maracaibo on the Atlantic coast, Bolivar made complete preparation for open war against the rebels. An army was drafted; money and food supplies were collected. Bolivar's determination was answered by Páez' vacillation. The latter now appealed to the Liberator to intercede between him and the central government, but he omitted giving Bolivar his presidential title, merely addressing him as a native of Venezuela. This repudiation of his authority infuriated Bolivar. "I returned from Peru in order to avert the crime of civil war . . . and you now call upon me as a simple citizen without legal authority? This is not possible. . . . There is no legal authority in Venezuela but mine." The voice of the nation, he continued, unanimously demanded Bolivar and reform. No one could wrest the reins of government from his hands. Yet he continued to offer Páez his friendship. Bolivar was inspired by his desire to avoid civil war, and he dictated one of the most moving letters of his life. But it was addressed to a deaf audience. Páez was not the man to listen to the admonitions of unselfish patriotism. As Bolivar's secretary sealed the letter, he glanced up. "Pearls before swine," he remarked.[37]

On his arrival in Maracaibo, Bolivar issued another proclamation to his fellow countrymen begging them to relinquish their fratricidal war. He promised that a reform of the Constitution

36 Cartas: Vol. VI. pp. 117, 127.
37 Cartas: Vol. VI. pp. 132-34, 136. Larrazabal: Vol. II. p. 375.

would be initiated without delay. Bolivar wasted no time in
Maracaibo, and in a few days pushed on across the burning
earth of Coro toward Puerto Cabello, where he assumed that
he would meet Páez. He questioned whether he should conquer him by force. Certainly he was strong enough to do so,
and he was, moreover, perhaps the only man who had no fear
of an encounter with the Llanero. But this was not the year
1817, and Páez was not Piar. Bolivar spent a sleepless night
over his problem, and then decided that he would not drive
Páez into a corner. On January 1 he issued a general amnesty.
No persecution or punishment of any kind should be visited
upon the rebels; no one should lose either his job or his fortune.
Páez would continue to head the civil and military power, and
the title of supreme leader in Venezuela should be bestowed
upon him. In recognition of this generosity, Bolivar asked
Páez to accept his authority as President and Liberator and to
promise obedience to all future orders.[38]

Bolivar's decree facilitated the reconciliation, but it was only
too obvious that he had paid an excessive price for his accomplishment. His concessions not only exonerated the rebels but
gave his approval to the rebellion. Páez had hardly expected
such a magnanimous attitude, and he speedily acknowledged
Bolivar's authority and abandoned his national assembly. Civil
war had been avoided, and it is not difficult to understand
Bolivar's satisfaction with a peace so expeditiously arranged.
His gratification, however, caused him to lose his balance. After
having, only short days before, insisted that Páez recognize his
presidential dignity, he now went to the other extreme and
indulged in extravagant praises of the rebel's merits. He called
Páez the saviour of the republic, the one who had preserved
the ship of state from catastrophe. He declared that the nation
was deeply indebted to Páez.[39] It is problematical whether
Bolivar spoke from a sense of boundless gratitude or from a

38 See the decree in Blanco: Doc. Vol. XI. pp. 74-75.
39 Blanco: Doc. Vol. XI. p. 79. Restrepo: H. d. R. C. Vol. III. p. 589. Larrazabal: Vol. II. p. 382.

feeling of impotence; certain it is that his words were fatal to the political structure he was endeavoring to preserve. Their correspondence was followed by a meeting of reconciliation. Páez, suspicious to the last moment, came attended by his bodyguard, but the Liberator came alone and embraced Páez. Together they entered Valencia and a week later appeared in Caracas. The capital honored Bolivar with the traditional pageantry—the arch of triumph, palms, garlands, addresses, and celebrations. Bolivar would not have been a South American if he had not enjoyed the pomp.[40] Believing he should make some gesture to contribute to the general festivities, he presented Páez with his sword in a solemn scene. Páez thanked him in the manner of a medieval Spanish vassal. My fellow countrymen, he said, Bolivar's sword is in my hands. For him and for you I shall march with it to eternity. All too soon he was to forget his dramatic oath.[41]

The political and social carnival set in motion by Bolivar's arrival in Caracas lasted for two months. Bolivar went from one ball to another; he rejoiced in again seeing his sisters, his old nurse, Hipolita, and his nephews and nieces, one of whom he married to an officer in his forces, much to her chagrin. And all during this time he cherished the illusion that the Republic had been saved and that he and Páez had accomplished this miracle.[42] His attitude toward Páez constituted, in fact, a reward for disobedience and disloyalty, and was one of the greatest enigmas of Bolivar's career. It demands explanation.

Bolivar had never felt any special sympathy toward Páez. "My friend, General Páez," he was wont to say, "is the vainest and most ambitious man in the world. He knows only his own nothingness, and the pride of ignorance makes him blind. He will always be a tool in the hands of his advisers."[43] He con-

40 Cartas: Vol. VI. p. 205. Larrazabal: Vol. II. pp. 386-88. See, La Entrada Triunfal del Libertador en Caracas 1827. B. d. H. Caracas. Vol. X. No. 38. p. 144.
41 Larrazabal: Vol. II. pp. 390-91. Páez: Autobiografía. p. 478.
42 Cartas: Vol. VI. p. 160.
43 D. d. B. p. 241.

sidered Páez to be the most dangerous man in Colombia. He was influenced neither by a sense of comradeship because of his campaign intimacy with Páez, nor was he biased by the fact that they were both Venezuelans. His decision to absolve Páez and to raise him to an heroic level was motivated entirely by a political conception, a conception which proved to be one of his greatest political mistakes.

Bolivar had returned to Colombia to prevent a civil war, and he had reached this first stage without too great an effort. He now intended to realize his deepest obsession, the Federation of the Andes. The general concept of the Andean Federation, however, was based on the idea that Colombia should be divided into three states. The Colombian unity as created by the Constitution of Cucutá, therefore, presented an obstacle to Bolivar's plans. This being the case, any movement jeopardizing the Constitution, such as Páez' rebellion, was viewed by Bolivar as more of a help than a hindrance to his plans. Páez had declared the Constitution of 1821 null and void, but this was also an end which Bolivar wished to achieve. For this very reason he was careful to avoid a demand that Páez submit to the Constitution, contenting himself with Páez' acknowledgement of his personal superiority. He wrote to Páez saying, "I can't divide the republic, but I would like to do so for Venezuela's sake. And this division shall take place when the national assembly meets, if it is the desire of Venezuela." He told Páez that he need not yield to the constitutional authorities if he would simply recognize the personal authority of the Liberator. Characteristically, he concluded, "My only thought now is the great federation between Peru, Bolivia, and Colombia."[44]

His letter to Páez explains his attitude—an attitude for which he has frequently been reproached, but which few have really comprehended. His program in 1827 still included prevention of civil war, the convocation of a national assembly, the partition of Greater Colombia into three states which would adopt the Bolivian Constitution; and, finally, as a crowning achieve-

44 Cartas: Vol. VI. p. 181. See, O'Leary: Doc. Vol. V. p. 447.

ment, the Federation of the Andes. This dream of greatness induced Bolivar to believe that Páez would involuntarily become his partisan. But Bolivar did not realize his remote and glorious dream, and by his policy he endangered what had already been gained—the Republic of Greater Colombia.

Bolivar was convinced that a far better arrangement would take the place of the 1821 Constitution, and he therefore insisted on preserving his own power and position. When Páez' officers become presumptuous, he put them in their places. "Here," he said, "there is no other authority and no other power besides mine. Among my companions I am the sun. If they shine it is because of the light I lend them."[45] He flatly rejected any plans for reform which were not compatible with his Federation of the Andes.

For some time it did indeed appear as though Bolivar's intuition had been right. "Bolivia has elected Sucre president and has signed an alliance with Peru and Colombia. Peru has appointed me as president and has adopted the Bolivian Constitution. The entire south is willing to ally itself with Colombia, and the Colombian people wish what I wish because they have confidence in me, knowing that I have always had their welfare at heart."[46] Such was Bolivar's mirage of unanimous accord.

But deep in the Liberator's consciousness lay the knowledge that the unity to which he aspired and which seemed almost within his reach would last no longer than he, perhaps not so long. The revolutions would continue and only God or time could check them. This realization brought him to the moving confession, "They will say of me that I liberated the New World, but they will not say that I have improved the happiness or stability of one single nation in America."[47] In truth, happiness and stability seemed beyond the grasp of the New World. Bolivar had changed his course and had decided in favor of

45 Cartas: Vol. VI. p. 191. Proclamas: p. 347. Larrazabal: Vol. II. p. 384.
46 Cartas: Vol. VI. p. 223. Blanco: Doc. Vol. XI. p. 25.
47 Cartas: Vol. VI. p. 203.

Venezuela against New Granada and Ecuador. The inevitable reactions from other parts of the country came without delay. The Colombian center, Bogotá and New Granada, answered with a vehement protestation against the new trend. Bolivar had become reconciled with Páez, but only at the price of finding himself face to face with a stronger and more intelligent foe. Santander and Bolivar now enter upon their tragic dissension.

These two men had no trait in common, and their friendship, begun in 1819, was possible only because they had been separated by great distances. During the seven years they had worked together, Santander had administered Colombia and had helped Bolivar to win his victories. It is difficult to say whether the Venezuelan criticisms leveled at Santander were just. Had he really neglected the eastern part of Colombia in order to favor his native country? Was he unjust; did he enrich himself at the expense of the state? Today no unequivocal answer can be given to these questions. Certain it is that he had committed serious blunders from the very outset of the quarrel with Páez. His general attitude was not at fault, for the defense of the Constitution was incumbent upon him, and he undertook the vindication of the government with a noble perception of its significance. However, he did not meet Páez' accusations in Parliament with any clear justification of his actions, and he irritated Páez still further by petty administrative regulations.

Bolivar had at first contemplated acting as mediator between the two rivals, but the accumulation of administrative abuses which he encountered in every department of the republic gave him many misapprehensions in regard to Santander. He drew Santander's attention to the ruined state finances, pointing out such abuses as the unduly large number of public employees. To his friends Bolivar was still more outspoken, and sternly criticized Santander's greed and dishonesty.

Santander agreed to institute the reforms demanded by Bolivar, but he had been insulted by the Liberator's accusations and asked what basis there was for the impeachment of his administration. Bolivar admitted that so far he had received no official denunciation of Santander, but that the disruption of the nation was only too obvious. "The Republic offers a spectacle of general misery; there are neither public nor private means available. Public confidence, love for law, respect for state officials have vanished. The dissatisfaction is general. I don't know who is responsible for this development, but the results are clear and palpable."[48] This was a definite charge against Santander, and the Vice-President took it as such. His correspondence with Bolivar continued and they called each other friends, but a certain mocking hollowness echoed in the sound of the intimate names. Santander, a past master in hypocrisy, still feigned in public the old admiration for the Liberator, but with his friends in Bogotá he maintained a different attitude. He criticized Bolivar's actions; he condemned his constitutional, or rather unconstitutional, ideas, declaring them to be but a thin veil to cover ambitions for dictatorship. The liberals in Bogotá looked upon Santander as their natural leader and gave him every encouragement. They formed groups whose aim was to obstruct Bolivar's policy in every way. Finally, the dissension between the two great men reached the newspapers, a majority of which were liberal, and soon the Federation of the Andes and the idea of a lifetime presidency became the subject of excoriating attacks. Santander's followers, sometimes called faithful Constitutionalists, sometimes Republicans, and sometimes Patriots, now began to demand separation from Venezuela. A *coup d'état* was even attempted. It was suppressed by Santander, but it gave him assurance that he would be supported in his opposition to the Liberator. He now made every effort to sabotage Bolivar's plans; he delayed answering his letters, etc., but continued to act the part of innocence.

Bolivar's reconciliation with Páez had aroused Santander's

48 Cartas: Vol. VI. p. 157. T. T. Guerra: La convención de Ocaña, Bogotá, 1908, p. 140.

deep and bitter resentment, for the appointment of Páez as head of the Venezuelan government had removed a vast territory from the sphere of Santander's administrative power. Bolivar's unwarranted praise of his rival, Páez, in calling him the saviour of the republic, had wounded Santander sorely. He considered himself a victim of his sense of duty and his legal conscience.

In Caracas, on the other hand, Bolivar listened to the voices of Santander's enemies, and allowed himself to be persuaded that the Vice-President had been disloyal to him. He wrote, "I can no longer rely on him; I have confidence neither in his heart nor in his morals."[49] Thus in March, 1827, he renounced his friendship with Santander and declared he would refuse to receive further letters from him. Santander's answer was given in a long, dignified communication, its handwriting as calm and steady as ever.[50] In April the rupture between the two leading figures of Greater Colombia was complete and the affair had become common knowledge.

The general state of affairs was chaotic in the extreme. Santander and his friends advocated the separation of New Granada and Venezuela. Páez had similar aims, but his motives were different. The picture was further darkened by events in Peru. The Colombian division quartered in Lima mutinied against its Venezuelan officers.[51] Obeying the orders of their New Granadian chief of staff, Colonel Bustamente, they arrested the officers of Venezuelan descent, asserting that they did so in an effort to defend the Constitution against dictatorial tendencies. The division then left Lima and sailed for Colombia.[52] With the departure of the army Bolivar's work in Peru fell apart. The Bolivian Constitution was abrogated and a new president elected. Nor was this the extent of the disruption. The Peruvians were determined to annex Guayaquil and eventually to separate Ecuador from Greater Colombia. They counted on

49 Cartas: Vol. VI. p. 223.
50 Cartas Santander: Vol. III. pp. 123-25.
51 Larrazabal: Vol. II. pp. 396-97.
52 Blanco: Doc. Vol. XI. pp. 73, 103, 105, 107, 199, 226, 340.

Bustamente and his division as auxiliary forces to gain their objective. In view of these events it became evident that a violent reaction had taken place not only against the Liberator himself, but also against his work and his general political conception.

When Santander received the news of Bustamente's mutiny, he had the bells rung in celebration of the event, and he went out on the streets to receive the applause of the cheering masses. He was, of course, thought to be the instigator of the rebellion. Whether this was true or not is hard to say, but the incident placed Santander in an extremely ambiguous position. He had condemned Páez' revolution and in the same breath had approved Bustamente's mutiny.

Bolivar felt more grief than anger when he learned of the rebellion of the third division. Colombia, he said, has only lost an army, but Peru will be engulfed in anarchy. For a moment he considered going to Lima to punish the traitors like an avenging demigod. However, he realized that it was impossible for him to leave Colombia in a period of such acute danger.[53]

In February, 1827, Bolivar once more resigned the presidency of the Republic with no other idea in mind than to be asked to continue in office. He had his resignation published, but it failed to convince his enemies as signally as it now fails to convince us, and the conflict over the future of Colombia continued.[54] Santander and his friends had dropped their pretense, and in a newly founded newspaper they demanded Bolivar's removal from the presidency. Bolivar disdained entering a verbal battle, believing that his name was still a powerful talisman. In the face of stiffening opposition, however, he realized that more drastic measures would be necessary and that he could no longer build on the foundations of a past glory.

During the first six months of 1827, he stayed in Caracas, where he tried to reorganize the shattered administration. Conditions in the country were in an unbelievable state of disinte-

53 Cartas: Vol. VI. pp. 266, 272. Guerra: p. 154.
54 Proclamas: p. 348.

gration. Soldiers and officials were literally dying of starvation; the treasury was empty and national credit exhausted. Bolivar fell to work as he had in the old days—indefatigable, tenacious, and energetic, he occupied himself with customs duties, education, hospitals, and the miserable conditions of the slaves. But there was little hope that he could cure Colombia's illness; the disease was organic and he could not expect to heal it with analgetics. "We Americans, brought up with a system of slavery, don't understand living according to simple laws or liberal principles. I am determined to do my utmost. To save my country I once declared the war to extinction . . . to save it again I shall fight the rebels even if I must die by their daggers." [55]

Did Bolivar have in mind the reëstablishment of a rule of terror? His friends urged him to return to Bogotá and to fill the office of president, which had again been conferred upon him. Both the English and the American ministers spoke and wrote in the same vein.[56] But if Bolivar were to leave Caracas now, Venezuela would again become submerged in chaos. "I never come to the end of my suffering. What I establish with my hands others trample underfoot." [57] It was but natural that he was disinclined to live in Bogotá after his rupture with Santander, and he delayed his voyage for several weeks. His decision was finally taken when he learned that Bustamente had invaded the region of Guayaquil. This circumstance presaged the daily possibility of war between Colombia and Peru.

Bolivar said goodbye to a Caracas that he was never to see again and announced his intention of returning to Bogotá. "Your enemies threaten Colombia with destruction; it is my duty to save her." [58] He added that he would go down to Guayaquil and preserve the existence of the Republic. Bolivar knew that he would again be obliged to fight on two fronts; he would have to defend the territory of the republic and at the same time

55 Cartas: Vol. VI. pp. 241, 251.
56 Cartas: Vol. VI. pp. 275-77. Manning: Vol. II. p. 1310. Blanco: Doc. Vol. XI. p. 240.
57 Cartas: Vol. VI. pp. 295-96.
58 Proclamas: pp. 350-52.

settle his dispute with Santander. The Vice-President resorted
to audacious measures now that Bolivar was actually approaching the capital. He induced the garrison of Bogotá to send a
petition to the government demanding the maintenance of the
Constitution. But Bolivar met this threat with a similar action.
The garrisons of Maracaibo and Cartagena demanded the Bolivian Constitution. Both sides were sowing the wind; both sides
were to reap the whirlwind.

Santander and his partisans now became greatly alarmed at
the prospect of Bolivar's return. Their spokesman, Azuero, required the New Granadians to decline the Colombian union in
a formal announcement. They were prepared to risk anything,
even revolution, to keep Bolivar out of Bogotá. Their attempt
at rebellion failed largely because of the cabinet's cautious and
prudent behaviour. Bolivar's enemies, however, refused to withdraw. They declared that Bolivar was coming to Bogotá, as
Morillo had come, to shed the blood of the Patriots, that if he
was on a peaceful errand he would dismiss his army and enter
the city unaccompanied by military power. Santander wrote to
Bolivar warning him that the government could not support
an army, that his soldiers would die of hunger, and that their
presence in the city would be both scandalous and superfluous.[59]
Bolivar was unmoved and ordered his men to march on to the
interior. Santander then declared his action to be a breach of
the Constitution; it was a case of Bonaparte returning from
Egypt. Bolivar turned to Parliament, saying that under the
present circumstances he could not consent to any alteration in
the size of his army. If Parliament should order any reduction
of his military force he would refuse to accept the presidency.[60]

This was the first time that Bolivar had admitted officially
that he was planning to take possession of the executive power.
Two weeks later the Colombian Congress met in the church of
Santo Domingo in Bogotá. Bolivar rode into the city on horse-

[59] Blanco: Doc. Vol. XI. p. 515.
[60] Proclamas: pp. 354-57. Cartas: Vol. VII. p. 14. Acuerdos d. Consejo:
op. cit., p. 257.

back, entering as usual at the northern gate and riding southward. The populace received him coldly. Those who had made
bets that he would not take the oath on the Constitution lost
their money. He joined the session of Congress and was sworn
into office. His speech was brief; he described the victorious
drive of the years following 1819, a drive that had now led them
to the brink of civil war. His political program was summed
up in a few words—the convocation of the National Assembly.[61]

The National Assembly, or as Bolivar called it, the Great
Convention, should, he said, decide upon the necessary reforms,
more specifically the requisite alterations in the structure of the
Constitution. In spite of disintegration and anarchy, he declared, Colombia would emerge from her afflictions a united
nation.

Santander had made every possible effort before Bolivar arrived to prevent him from taking over the executive power,
but the prestige of the Liberator had proved too great and
Santander was obliged to accept his defeat with what equanimity he could muster. He awaited Bolivar in the presidential
mansion; they embraced and exchanged elaborate greetings.[62]
Who was taken in by this display of friendliness? Bolivar was
ready to forgive, but Santander could not forget. Bolivar sent
word to his enemies who were in hiding outside the city that
they might safely return to Bogotá; they had nothing to fear.
His heart had neither hatred nor a desire for vengeance. He
hoped he could reconcile them as he had reconciled Páez.
However, in both instances he was utterly deceived.

Certain grave changes had been made in the panorama of
public affairs since he had left Lima in 1826. At that time he
had believed that his mere presence would suffice to restore
harmony between the warring factions of the Colombian family. The collapse of the Bolivian system in Peru had destroyed,
at a single blow, any illusions he had cherished for a Federation

61 Posada Gutiérrez: Vol. I. p. 107. Proclamas: pp. 357-58. Blanco: Doc. Vol.
XI. p. 536.
62 Larrazabal: Vol. II. p. 409.

of the Andes. The Peruvians had already begun to violate the Colombian frontier. How long would it be before Bolivia was also lured into the camp of the enemy? Bolivar's expectations had been based on a fallacy; none of his calculations had proved correct.

Anyone who meditates on the fateful year of 1826-27 must face the question of Bolivar's action. Could he have followed another course; was another road open to him? This writer feels that Bolivar was neither wise nor adroit in his methods. In the first place he prolonged his stay in Peru beyond all reason; second, he made a grave error in leaving the army in Peru when he needed it in Colombia to quell Páez' rebellion. In the third instance, he refused to face certain undeniably serious matters with a fearless judgment—he knew that Páez was no saviour of the Republic, and he must have known that his reconciliation with him was neither honest nor courageous. Moreover, it should have been apparent to Bolivar, had he been willing to admit it, that the Federation of the Andes was considered no more than a fantastic dream in the north as well as in the south, and that it was looked upon with contempt and derision. The Bolivian Constitution was admittedly unpopular in Colombia, and in spite of Bolivar's saying, "Throw it in the fire if you don't want it—I don't have an author's vanity," he clung obstinately to his Constitution.[63] And it was this last consideration, his political program, that more than anything else estranged the great majority of the liberal party, suspicious as they were of every ideology that even faintly suggested monarchy or dictatorship.

A second question is only logical. Could the disintegration of Colombia have been avoided? In this case there is only one possible answer: under the circumstances the downfall of Greater Colombia might have been delayed, but not circumvented. One is inclined to wonder whether Bolivar did not recognize the inevitability of his country's fate, or whether he preferred to close his eyes to the approaching catastrophe. He

63 Cartas: Vol. VI. p. 303.

had written to Santander, "The origin of our existence is impure. All that has preceded us is covered by the dark cloak of crime. With this mixture of blood, with these moral elements, it is impossible to make laws for heroes or to lay down principles for men." [64]

Bolivar had said on many occasions that South America could be ruled only by an astute despot, but that he did not want to take over such an assignment. But if this were the case why did he not sacrifice himself to his belief; or why did he not follow San Martín's example and retire into voluntary exile? The answer lies deep within the Liberator's own personality. For sixteen years he had fought against insuperable difficulties. Defeat, hardship, exile, had failed to thwart his indomitable will. With the same invincible tenacity he now clung to the crumbling columns of the Colombian Republic. His glory was at stake, and he could not bear to relinquish any part of it. He could allow no human being to destroy his vision of a future greatness for South America. If Bolivar had resigned in 1827, he would have spared himself infinite bitterness of spirit, but his nature would never have suffered a retirement from active participation in his country's history; he did not have the makings of a gentleman of leisure. Personal happiness is not a concomitant of historical greatness, and Bolivar now began his *via crucis*.

64 Cartas: Vol. VI. p. 11.

CHAPTER 32

The Night of September 25

In 1827 Bogotá was a small town sleeping beneath the protection of the Cordilleras. In its narrow streets dwelt some twenty thousand people. Here, at the center of the city in the hollow between two towering peaks, stands the cottage presented to Bolivar by the city in 1820. Today this small dwelling is still called *La quinta Bolivar,* because here the Liberator spent whatever time he could spare from governmental affairs, which were dealt with in the presidential mansion.[1] A high wall surrounding the property gives access to the house through a beautiful portal opening on a drive of stately cypresses. It is a one-story house in the colonial style, with a red tile roof and a surrounding veranda. The rooms are floored in brick; the ceilings are low, and the windows open on a view of century old cedars, wild roses, and masses of honeysuckle. Here the city noises are distant and faint, and the house gains thereby a sense of rural isolation. The four rooms—library, parlor, dining-room, and bedroom, furnished in the style of the Empire in mahogany and unadorned—are warm and colorful. On cold evenings heat was furnished by fireplaces or open charcoal braziers. On the slope above the house is a modest pavilion, added by Bolivar, and called *El Mirador* because it affords a magnificent view of the mountains. Beside the pavilion is a swimming pool where Bolivar, even at twenty-six hundred meters, had his daily

1 Cartas: Vol. VII. p. 9.

cold water bath. Manuela's dressing table is still to be seen in the little room beside the pool.[2]

Manuela had stayed on in Lima. While Peru mutinied and Bustamente betrayed Colombia, Manuela had fought against the inevitable. She had gone into the army quarters disguised as a man, a pistol in one hand, money in the other, and had implored the soldiers to remain faithful to Bolivar. But neither words nor money were of any avail. The Peruvian Minister of War ordered her imprisonment, but she escaped by boat to Colombia.[3] General Córdoba, of Ayacucho fame, sailed on the same vessel. These two held a deep hatred for each other— Córdoba because he detested Manuela's extravagances, and Manuela because she believed Córdoba guilty of disloyalty to Bolivar, a suspicion not without good foundation. By way of Quito, Manuela finally reached Bogotá. Bolivar had longed for her presence. "The ice of my years," he wrote, "melts under your kindness and graciousness. Your love resuscitates a life that was perishing. I cannot be without you. I cannot voluntarily renounce Manuela. . . . come, come, come!"[4]

She lived with Bolivar in his *quinta* or in the presidential palace of San Carlos. The *quinta* is still a place of touching beauty. Those who have walked under its old trees or have sat on the stone benches while the sun sets and the moon slowly rises behind the mountains have felt in touch with Bolivar's life, the life of an aristocrat who moved restlessly through the continent and whose sense of beauty speaks in so many places. Manuela found her friend greatly changed. He was no longer the brilliant conqueror who had left her in Lima. As he paced up and down in his blue uniform with the silver braid, she noticed how thin he was. His hair was sparse, and had receded further from the high, narrow forehead. His eyes, once so full of emotion, were sombre and regained their old expression only

2 J. Otero Muñoz: En la Quinta de Bolívar. Conferencias de la Academia. Bogotá, 1935.
3 L. A. Cuervo: Apuntes historiales. Bogotá, 1925. p. 195. Palma: *op. cit.*, p. 107.
4 Cartas: Vol. VII. p. 377.

in fleeting moments. Manuela cared for him as he slowly recovered from the fatigue of his long journey from Caracas.
She made no secret of her love for the Liberator, appearing in
public with him whenever she could. Bogotá society was still
bounded by its provincial horizons, and it was considered a
scandal that the President should live openly with his mistress.
The people of Bogotá were no more virtuous than anyone else,
but they allowed a certain respect for the conventions to conceal
their weaknesses. Manuela was a foreigner, and Bogotá was
hostile to aliens; moreover, Manuela went out of her way to
excite public disfavor. An exhibitionist by nature, she went
out on horseback in men's clothing and committed one folly
after another. When the Bogotans were polite they called her
the foreigner; in other moods they gave her much more unfriendly names.[5] A mistress in the palace and soldiers in the
streets! What was this independence achieved at such sacrifice?
So went the talk from house to house. But Manuela had become indispensable to the aging President. She sometimes
irritated him by appearing at the parties to which she had not
been summoned, but her care, her tenderness, gave his trembling heart an ardor that he could not find elsewhere.[6] Sitting
in his little pavilion overlooking the city, everything seemed
calm and peaceful, but from the borders of Ecuador to the
Atlantic Ocean the whole country seethed with rebellion.

Bolivar concerned himself first with the defense of the south
against Peruvian ambitions. After he had taken possession of
the presidential office he issued a proclamation to the inhabitants of Guayaquil imploring them to remain loyal to Greater
Colombia. "You are not the ones responsible," said Bolivar;
"the people can never be responsible. The pernicious and
erroneous ideas come from the leaders; it is they who bring
about the public calamities."[7] Who were these leaders working
toward the separation of Guayaquil and Colombia? In the first

5 Rumazo: p. 211.
6 See, Manuela's letter to Bolivar. B. d. H. Caracas. Vol. XVI, p. 334.
7 Proclamas: pp. 358-59.

place, there was the rebel, Bustamente, to whom a considerable money reward had been promised by Peru if he were successful in his enterprise. His plan had been to occupy the whole of southern Colombia and to annex it to Peru, and he had set forth with the third division to consummate this objective.[8] However, news of his intentions preceded his arrival in the endangered territories, and a group of officers living in Guayaquil and devoted to Bolivar and his Greater Colombian ideas improvised a defense and attempted to separate the third division from its treacherous leader. The troops were stubborn, however, and declared they would fight Bolivar's dictatorship. They rightly counted on the lack of unity among the inhabitants of Guayaquil. A revolution ousted the local authorities and gave General La Mar, a Peruvian by birth, charge of the civil and military administration. In the meantime Bustamente had penetrated deep into Ecuadorian territory. Ecuador seemed lost to Greater Colombia and was rescued only by the energy of General Flores.

Flores was born in Venezuela and had fought for independence since the days of the Spanish terror. The triumph of freedom had brought him to the south, and he had ascended to important positions in Ecuador. Bolivar described him in the following words: "Few men in Colombia surpass General Flores in astuteness and cleverness in both war and politics. He has a natural talent developed by study and reflection. Moreover, he is extremely courageous and also has the ability to charm people. He is generous and knows when to spend. But his ambition exceeds all his other virtues or defects; it is the motive for all his actions. . . . Flores will play an important part in this country." [9] In the critical situation described above Flores used his influence to get in touch with certain officers of the third division. He explained the full implications of Bustamente's project; and, appealing to their patriotism, managed to gain their support. Bustamente and forty of his friends

---

8 Restrepo: H. d. R. C. Vol. IV. pp. 27-28. Larrazabal: Vol. II. p. 399.
9 D. d. B. p. 167. See, O'Leary: Doc. Vol. IV. *passim.*

SIMON BOLIVAR

were arrested and turned over to Flores. Only the harbor of
Guayaquil insisted on continuing the rebellion.

Flores was commissioned to bring the rebellious city back
to obedience. Utmost confusion reigned in both camps, and
the situation was further complicated by a daily shift in parties,
commanders, and spheres of influence. However, as soon as
Bolivar had taken over the presidency the south recognized that
the tide of war was turning, and at the end of September, 1827,
Flores entered Guayaquil at the head of a reliable army. The
traitors fled across the nearby Peruvian border and Flores declared Guayaquil again under Colombian law. It was Bolivar's
first success as President, and he took it as a sign that he might
succeed in holding Colombia together. "I am concentrating
all my plans, all my glory, to the end that Colombia may, united,
present herself before the great convention. I have scarcely six
months to win this national victory." [10]

Before he had come to Bogotá, he had said that he could
save Colombia only if he were allowed to exercise an unlimited
power.[11] Then he had submitted to the Constitution, and affairs seemed easier than he had expected. He retained the
secretaries of state with whom Santander had coöperated for
so long, and the mere presence of the Liberator seemed to allay
the antagonisms of the various parties.[12] Congress expressed
its confidence in him; his decrees issued in Venezuela were approved, and he obtained the prerogative to make military
appointments without the sanction of Congress. Further, his
plan for an administrative reform was accepted.

But it was clear that in everything he did Bolivar was trying
to advance the interests of his own party. In his journeys up
and down the continent he had been persuaded that the masses
would side with him. He counted on the army to balance the
influence of the lawyers and writers, and also, for the first time
in his political career, he gave some thought to the support of

10 Cartas: Vol. VII. pp. 31, 59.
11 Cartas: Vol. VII. p. 14.
12 Restrepo: H. d. R. C. Vol. IV. p. 62. Guerra: p. 234.

the clergy. He invited the ecclesiastical dignitaries to his table; he celebrated the saints of the fatherland and the shepherds that guarded the Colombian flock. In a series of decrees favorable to the position of the church he confirmed this new approach.[13] His motive was obvious; he was endeavoring to establish an alliance of all conservative forces.[14] From the first day of his return to Bogotá, Bolivar's correspondence was dedicated to the establishment of this alliance. His refrain is forever the same: the destiny of Colombia will be decided by the great convention; if this chance is neglected everything will be lost. It was, therefore, necessary to select the deputies with the greatest of care. Only moderate men of firm purpose and pure hearts should represent the country.[15]

It was but natural that his enemies also realized the issues at stake. Santander wrote using almost the same words: "It is important that only patriots are elected who have been proven and who are incorruptible and very liberal." [16] The difference between the two statements lay in the principles which were back of them. Bolivar wished Greater Colombia to be united under a conservative regime; Santander looked for the separation of New Granada from the sister republic in order to construct a liberal state. However, the disparity between the two leaders extended further than the difference in these objective attitudes toward state policies would seem to indicate; an incident of a personal nature soon aggravated their conflict. It has already been mentioned that the foreign loans were squandered during Bolivar's absence from Bogotá. Money had never been a source of temptation to Bolivar. Even during these years when his personal fortune was almost exhausted, he fulfilled his obligations with great punctuality, preferring to pay the expenses he had incurred as President out of his own pocket rather than allow national prestige to suffer. He could not understand officials who would enrich themselves at the expense

13 Proclamas: p. 359. Blanco: Doc. Vol. XII. pp. 693, 697, 721.
14 R. Botero Saldarriaga: El Presidente Libertador. Bogotá, 1928.
15 Cartas: Vol. VII. pp. 28, 29, 30, 31, 33, 34, 40.
16 Cartas Santander: Vol. III. p. 127. Arch. Santander: Vol. XVII. p. 223.

of the community. He suspected Santander of misuse of the loans and impulsively expressed his suspicion in casual remarks. Santander demanded an investigation, and Bolivar passed this request on to Congress. After heated debates Congress appointed a commission to inquire into the matter, but no clear-cut decision was ever reached. The affair was fatal, however, as far as the relations between the two were concerned. Their enmity had now expanded into the field of personal accusation, and any reconciliation seemed out of the question.

Santander now became the accepted leader of the opposition, a place which he held with the skill of experience. He knew how to approach these people and he quickly made himself popular. He drank chicha with them, went into the towns and villages, promised everything to everybody, and in general prepared for the elections with rare demogogic talent.[17] He was determined to wrest the administration of Congress from Bolivar's control. And, unfortunately, Bolivar's markedly contradictory attitude during this time lent him great support.

As has been said, Bolivar attached much importance to the great convention, but he felt, nevertheless, that his reputation would not permit his taking part in the election proceedings. He had no wish to be accused of using the executive power to further his personal interests, and with this thought in mind he ordered the government officials to refrain from interfering with or influencing the voting.[18] Only the greatest naïveté could have made him believe that his enemies would give him credit for his objective action. On the contrary, they asserted that he was planning a military dictatorship which would make Morillo's rule appear a mild affair. Bolivar also rejected with indignation the suggestion that he present himself before the National Assembly to influence their deliberations. He felt certain that he should not attend their debates, and he seemed sometimes to have a premonition that his efforts would be in vain. "I have no desire to commit myself to doing anything;

17 Cartas: Vol. VII. p. 122.
18 Cartas: Vol. VII. p. 58. D. d. B. p. 150.

since nothing will last, it is senseless to work."[19] Torn by conflicting emotions, he lost any firm basis for belief or hope. The
tone of his letters veers from one extreme to another; sometimes
confident and at other times despairing, they show the depression of a man who fights the inevitable. "I can't improve things
because I have no power to do so. I can't step over the barriers
of a constitution which I must uphold. I cannot change the
laws that complicate our governmental system, and finally, I
am not God that I can change men and matters. . . . Colombia
and America are lost for one generation." [20] At another time
Bolivar writes: "The influence of civilization gives our people
indigestion, so that what should nourish us, ruins us."

These many contradictory reflections did not cause him to
influence the elections, however, and for the truth of this statement we have not only Bolivar's word, but the testimony of
the Secretary of the Interior.[21] Santander's ultimate victory,
nonetheless, enraged Bolivar. He wrote, "Santander is the
idol of this people." He went on to say that his enemies had
arranged a fraudulent election, a childish accusation, since
Bolivar was himself in power. If he had really believed that the
great convention would make the final decision in regard to
Colombia's future, he should have tried to win the election by
securing a majority for his own party. Supported by the mayors
and the priests, he could have decided the outcome of the elections. If he looked upon such practices with scorn and refused
to use them himself, he was in no position to complain that
his enemies took advantage of obvious subterfuges to attain
their own ends.

With the results of the elections against him, Bolivar could
do nothing but let the convention run its course. Since he had
made it the focal point of his program, he could not now take
a stand against it. In his public addresses, therefore, he avoided
the question of the Constitution and simply expressed his hopes

19 Cartas: Vol. VII. pp. 71, 80, 86.
20 Cartas: Vol. VII. pp. 114-15.
21 Restrepo: H. d. R. C. Vol. IV. pp. 82-83.

for the unity of the nation. In the meantime, he concentrated his energies on practical problems.

Although the south remained temporarily calm, the rebellion had smouldered in Venezuela ever since the day when Bolivar had left Caracas. Gangs pretending to fight for the king of Spain ravaged the plains. Other lawless groups looted the environs of Caracas. Arms and money were supplied to them from nearby Puerto Rico by the Spaniards, and there were rumors that Morales with twelve thousand men was preparing to invade Venezuela. Bolivar was seriously concerned about these reports, as well he might be, for even the rumor of a Spanish landing in Venezuela would be sufficient to rekindle the flames of civil war so recently and so indefinitely extinguished.[22] Páez, military commander of Venezuela, acted with energy and promptitude; the insurgent leaders were shot and their followers pardoned. But these measures failed to stamp out the rebellion and Páez seemed unable to control the situation. The uprisings spread to the Orinoco, then to Barinas, to Coro, to Guayana, and at length to Cumaná.[23] Páez and the other Venezuelan generals did their best to keep these rebels separated in order to deal with them one by one. Nevertheless, no one could contemplate the Venezuela of these days with any show of equanimity, and least of all Bolivar. He thought his presence in Venezuela might serve to pacify the province, and he made plans to leave Colombia. No longer was he expecting great things of the national convention. "My enemies have succeeded in making me unpopular," he said, and consequently he threw himself into the Venezuelan project with great energy. Under the circumstances his decision to go to Caracas appears more in the nature of an escape than a program.

When Bolivar was ready to leave, he again made use of Article 128—that is, he claimed the prerogatives due him in an emergency. He was determined this time, however, not to relinquish his power to the vice-president, still nominally Santander, and he seemed intent on reserving the dictatorial power to him-

22 Cartas: Vol. VII. p. 57. Botero: p. 83.
23 Blanco: Doc. Vol. XI. p. 619. Cartas: Vol. VII. pp. 67, 77, 85, 119.

self and on using it during his journey. Santander's name was not even mentioned in the decree, and this omission was a new wound to the vice-president's already lacerated feelings.[24] Bolivar appointed Soublette to be his general secretary and reinforced the Bogotá cabinet with one of his most loyal supporters, Urdaneta.

On February 20, 1828, Bolivar issued a decree establishing special courts for cases of high treason in order to safeguard the republic from conspirators.[25] Such measures were interpreted by his enemies solely as preparations for an imminent dictatorship. One Bogotá newspaper published vehement denunciations of Bolivar's sinister plans, and his officers answered by burning the edition. On the following day the newspaper appeared with the headlines *El incombustible*. Bolivar regarded these events as symptomatic of the approaching deluge. On March 13, he declared the public order disturbed, a statement tantamount to the proclamation of martial law. Drastic decisions regarding the state budget followed, and although Bolivar's purpose was to take any measures to cancel the deficit, his fellow-countrymen saw only the iron hand of governmental power, and raised a great outcry over their oppressions.

Such were the circumstances as the President left the city for Venezuela.[26] While en route he learned that the danger of a Spanish invasion had been averted and that peace had been restored. He could have returned to Bogotá, but two events induced him not to do so: The first was Admiral Padilla's attempted rebellion; the second was the opening of the national convention in Ocaña. Padilla's uprising had taken place in Cartagena; the great convention was in conference near the Magdalena Valley. Bolivar, therefore, chose a spot from which he could assume control if circumstances demanded his intervention. For more than three months he made his headquarters in Bucaramanga.

Padilla, a mulatto, had distinguished himself in battles with

24 Guerra: pp. 244-45.
25 Restrepo: H. d. R. C. Vol. IV. pp. 84-85. Botero: pp. 84-85. O'Leary: Doc. Vol. XXVI. pp. 25, 27.
26 Proclamas: p. 375. Cartas: Vol. VII. pp. 180, 185.

the Spanish fleet. He was different from the other officers in that he espoused liberal ideas and was a partisan of Santander. He was a man of passionate impulses. Once, when gambling, he had observed that his partner was using loaded dice, and he had transfixed the cheater's hand to the table with his dagger.[27] He now took a vigorous stand for Santander. His attempts to overthrow the authorities in Cartagena lasted but seven days when he was himself overthrown by Mariano Montilla, the commander of Cartagena. For inexplicable reasons, possibly because he believed that Santander would protect him, he fled to the interior. At Ocaña, together with some of the liberal deputies of the convention, he planned another rebellion against Bolivar. Returning to Cartagena, he was arrested at once by Montilla and was sent to Bogotá for trial. Padilla himself was little more than an adventurer, but his rebellion was important in that it proved the serious intention of the liberal party to take power by force in case the Ocaña deliberations did not bring the results they desired.

The National Assembly, or as it is called in Colombian history, the Convention of Ocaña, had opened in solemn convocation on April 2, 1828, in the church of St. Francis. The first speech, by Dr. Soto, showed unconcealed hatred for Bolivar, but the election of Castillo y Rada, a former minister of Bolivar, as President of the Convention was a triumph for the Liberator.[28] Bolivar's party was comparatively small: Santander's held the advantage, and a third group, called the Independents, among whom were many friends of Bolivar, planned to act according to circumstances. Bolivar may have made a mistake in refusing to attend the conferences of Ocaña, for he could easily have influenced this undecided group, but he continued to limit his activities and addressed the Convention only in a written message.

Bolivar's message was purely critical in tone, and a bitter

27 Otero d'Costa: Vida del Almirante Padilla. Manizales. Posada: Apostillas. p. 374. J. P. Urueta: Vida de Padilla. Cartagena, 1889.
28 Guerra: pp. 268-79. Blanco: Doc. Vol. XII. *passim.*

disappointment appears in its wording.[29] Colombia, he wrote, once the creator of her own existence, is exhausted. Though Santander's name is not mentioned, the message is a direct accusation of him and his administration. Bolivar points out that it was Santander who had directed the state and who had encouraged everyone to think of his rights but never of his duties. The government was poorly organized; it did not correspond to Colombian reality. Parliament had absorbed all the power, but its laws were neither integrated nor coherent. The government, instead of being a center of force, was lethargic and indifferent. Special powers were needed for every action; it was alternately a poisoned source and a devastating flood. The security of civilians had no police protection. Agriculture was ruined; the few industries had perished; commerce with the exterior failed to supply the necessities of existence. The army, once the pride and model of South America, was disintegrating. This interior dissolution had culminated in Colombia's domestic and foreign bankruptcy. Peru, which could not exist without Colombia, had dared to challenge Colombia. Only a powerful government could resolve this chaos, and the country, longing for its resurrection, prayed for a strong and efficient government. "Without force there is no virtue; without virtue the state dies. Anarchy destroys freedom, but unity preserves it. Give us inexorable laws." Thus ends Bolivar's message to the legislators of Ocaña.

These grim words, directed toward men who for the most part had been members of the Colombian Parliament since 1821, served only to increase the distrust with which Bolivar's intentions were viewed. Santander's adherents attempted to sabotage the reading of the message, but although their opposition was stiff, they were defeated.[30] During the first sessions, the Convention was overwhelmed with a flood of petitions from the army, the city councils, and the provincial authorities demanding constitutional reform as outlined in Bolivar's message.

29 Proclamas: p. 360.
30 Guerra: pp. 282, 288.

Santander and his friends, however, gave them no consideration, believing them to have been written to order at the Liberator's request.[31]

From the first day of the Convention it was obvious that the National Assembly was to be a duel between Bolivar and Santander. For example, Bolivar counted on the support of the Venezuelan representatives, among whom was the notorious Dr. Peña, but Santander was quick to raise objections. He demanded Dr. Peña's expulsion on the ground that Peña had not cleared himself of the embezzlement charge. From Bucaramanga, Bolivar tried to force Peña's admission but failed.[32]

The reform of the Constitution was the one and only problem on the agenda at Ocaña. Discussion began with the proposition of a Venezuelan deputy to dissolve Colombia's unity in a loose federation. The rejection of this idea was one of Bolivar's few triumphs at Ocaña. The Convention next decided on the reforms to be made in the Constitution and appointed a committee of both parties to elaborate the text of the revision. The committee members failed to coöperate, however, with the result that each group presented its own project for reform.[33]

Santander's party asked for a division of the Republic into twenty departments; they wanted the upper house restricted and the lower house strengthened. Article 128, granting dictatorial powers in cases of emergency, was to be deleted.

Bolivar's party, on the other hand, asked for a strong and efficient government. The president should have the veto power, and the right to appoint and dismiss state officials. Article 128 should be preserved. In debating these two propositions, the Ocaña delegates took a resolution which the writer thinks unique in the history of parliamentary procedure. It was decided to discuss the two projects at the same time. The result was exactly what the reader would anticipate. Both groups flew

31 J. S. Rodríguez: La Convención de Ocaña. Memoria relativa a la convención. B. d. H. Caracas. Vol. XVII. No. 66. pp. 139, 150. Guerra: p. 297. Posada Gutiérrez: Vol. I, p. 137. A. Urdaneta: La Convención de Ocaña. Caracas, 1900.
32 Proclamas: pp. 377-79. Cartas: Vol. VII. p. 184, 206-07. D. d. B. p. 190.
33 Guerra: pp. 321-402. Posada Gutiérrez. Vol. I. p. 139.

into passionate vituperation; insults were hurled; the words liar and traitor hissed across the aisles of the church of St. Francis. Every hope of compromise vanished.

In the meantime, Bolivar waited in Bucaramanga, in his customary state of impatience, for the results of the Convention. He wrote letters to all points of the compass; he sent his aides to Ocaña for frequent reports. And he vacillated. From time to time he thought of going to Ocaña himself to exert his influence on the meetings. He delayed doing so only because he expected the Convention to urge him to come. Much to his chagrin, however, the Convention seemed to feel no need for his presence and the invitation did not arrive. Santander was only too well aware of the radiation of Bolivar's personality. He frankly confessed that he himself had frequently approached the Liberator in a mood of hatred and revenge, only to find that in Bolivar's presence his enmity had dissolved and a feeling of admiration for this extraordinary man, the creator of the fatherland, had taken its place.[34] If Santander, the lawyer and logician, reacted in this manner, how much chance had the average deputy with his weak resources to defend himself against Bolivar's personal influence? So Bolivar remained in Bucaramanga like a wild beast in a cage. He dispatched his daily affairs, rode horseback, played cards, and indulged in reminiscences of the glorious days of the war. Bolivar's life during these months is reflected in the diary of his aide, Peru de la Croix. At the arrival of bad news Bolivar would lock himself in his room and give in utterly to his feeling of depression. He refused to attend festive balls, although he had always had a reputation as a passionate dancer; instead, he turned to the services of the church, realizing that he might in this manner gain important advantages from the Catholic clergy. His indifference to his old pastimes included his attitude toward women; he was indifferent toward all but Manuela, who wrote faithfully and who occupied his mind to a limited extent. Only here and there, as in the letter to the poet, Olmedo, do we get a glimpse

34 Cartas: Vol. VII. p. 292.

of his old literary force. "I have returned to my old position of being a poor devil. My whole taste has become common, averse to power and glory. I have finally returned to my former being, to what the French call a *vaurien*. Yes, my dear friend, I have been converted to the ways of heaven. I am repentant for my worldly behavior. I am tired of imitating Alexander, and instead I look for Diogenes to steal forth from his jar, or his barrel, or his house. One can get saturated with everything in this world . . . it is time for other heroes to take the stage and to play their rôles, because my part is over. You know that fortune, like any female, loves change, and since my mistress is tired of me, I myself repent of her."[35]

Even in his melancholy, however, Bolivar maintains his position as one of the most remarkable men of his century. He sketches a human character with a few simple strokes; his candid snapshots of Colombia's officers and statesmen are lifelike in their perfection; his historical judgment remains independent and philosophical.

The tension created by the events in Ocaña kept Bolivar awake at night and ruined both his temper and his appetite. He was humiliated by the attacks made on him by Santander, Azuero, and Soto. How was it possible for these men to delude themselves into believing that he was fighting against Colombia's disintegration from motives of personal ambition? "What do I need Colombia for? Even her ruins will testify to my glory. The Colombians will appear before the eyes of posterity covered with ignominy, not I. . . . My love has been for the fatherland; my only ambition freedom. Those who impute something different to me don't know me." And again, "The wretched creatures! Even the air they breathe they owe to me —and they dare to suspect me!"[36] It was despair that induced Bolivar to utter these famous words about the ingratitude and instability of America.[37] And surely there was both instability

35 Cartas: Vol. VII. p. 321.
36 Cartas: Vol. VII. pp. 223, 237.
37 Cartas: Vol. VII. p. 295.

and ingratitude, but what else could he have expected from
countries that were still in the formative state? Bolivar's rage
caused him to be, if not ungrateful, at least unjust. He accused
his followers of lacking his own fanatical zeal, of being too
moderate in their support of a great cause. He wrote, "Man
is the son of fear, and the slave and the criminal are doubly so."[38]
But the fault did not lie with the Ocaña deputies. They were a
minority and hardly capable of inspiring fear in their adversaries.

When, at length, the projected constitution came up for
debate, Bolivar urged an inflexible stand. Better, he said, to
defend the Republic by arms than to compromise. He brought
all his old tricks into play, including the threatened resignation,
but they had no effect. The two parties faced each other alienated and implacable; a solution acceptable to both was inconceivable. The fanatics were already searching for a speedier
and more effective way out; Bolivar was informed that Santander and his friends had commissioned an officer to come
to Bucaramanga and kill him, but he made light of the warning,
saying that Santander was really not as bad as that.[39]

Santander, on the other hand, could not feel confident of his
own safety. Bolivar broadcast his opinion that the army would
never submit to Santander's plans even though he should triumph in Ocaña. Santander finally demanded personal protection and asked for a passport to go abroad, but instead of
facilitating his departure, Bolivar took this opportunity to make
Santander aware of his power.[40] And so the mistakes accumu-
lated, a mountain of errors that explain the failure of the National Assembly.

Bolivar's party had followed his instructions, and when it
became obvious that Santander's constitution would be accepted,
the Bolivaristes boycotted the meetings. On June 6 this group
withdrew unequivocally from the sessions, placing the blame

38 Cartas: Vol. VII. pp. 212, 215. D. d. B. pp. 148, 333. See, Castillo y Rada:
Memorias: Publicado por E. Rodríguez Piñeros. Bogotá, 1914.
39 D. d. B. pp. 171-73.
40 Arch. Santander: Vol. XVII. p. 281. Forero: p. 187. Cartas: Vol. VII.
p. 224.

for the frustration of the Convention squarely on Santander and his friends.[41] Their absence deprived the Ocaña assembly of a quorum, which by constitutional law indicated an interregnum, since the Constitution of Cucutá was no longer valid and no new instrument of government had been accepted. This was the situation according to Bolivar, who stated that Colombia was lacking both a parliament and a constitution.

Event now followed event with startling rapidity. The rump parliament of Ocaña decided to set the revolution in motion. Secret plans were made and the deputies sworn in. Santander was chosen as leader, and certain members went so far as to demand Bolivar's death.[42] But again Bolivar had anticipated his enemies. When he had learned that his minority planned to wreck the convention, he had written to his adherents in Bogotá to make preparations for the emergency and to decide upon what measure should be taken.

On June 13 the governor of Cundinamarca called for a popular meeting to be held on the plaza in Bogotá. This meeting resolved to retract the commissions of the Ocaña deputies, to disavow any decisions made by the Convention, and to put all power in Bolivar's hands. The Council of Ministers agreed with these resolutions, and many communities expressed their approval.[43] The whole procedure was highly arbitrary, but it sufficed for Bolivar. He received the call to assume dictatorship when he was already on his way from Bucaramanga to Bogotá. Smiling, he remarked, "Now the bull is out, and we shall see who has guts." On June 24 he entered Bogotá to the cheers of the multitude. "The whole nation recognizes my authority."[44]

Bolivar went at once to the cathedral, wishing to remove himself from any contact with Santander's liberals and freemasons. There on the great plaza, in the presence of the local and national authorities—the Cabinet, the Supreme Court, the

41 Blanco: Doc. Vol. XII. p. 600. R. Rivas: Castillo y Rada. Rev. del Rosario. No. 291. Botero: pp. 107-08.
42 Restrepo: H. d. R. C. Vol. IV. p. 102.
43 Blanco: Doc. Vol. XII. pp. 623-25.
44 Cartas: Vol. VII. pp. 323, 325, 333. D. d. B. p. 398. O'Leary: Doc. Vol. VII. p. 453.

Governor and his officials—Bolivar took over the power of the chief executive. He received the congratulations of his friends and colleagues and declared that he would always be the defender of public rights and freedoms, but that whenever the people desired he would renounce his power and return it to the nation.[45] There followed a banquet at the palace at which Bolivar gave a toast to the commonwealth of Colombia. "The good of the republic does not consist in hateful dictatorship. . . . Dictatorship is glorious when it seals the abyss of revolution, but woe to a people that accustoms itself to live under dictatorial rule."[46]

What were Bolivar's intentions? He himself had coined the phrase "hateful dictatorship." His dictatorial power was based on the army and on that part of the bureaucracy that was devoted to him. All the high-ranking generals, Urdaneta, Mariño, Páez, Soublette, Arismendi, Flores, Córdoba, Montilla, Bermúdez, and Salóm, assured him of their loyalty. Santander's name alone was missing from this roster of the great names of the revolution. Bolivar, however, wanted to be assured of the consent of the people. "It is necessary that the good patriots make every effort to get the sanction of the people for the latest events. . . . For I do not want to rule against the will of the people."[47] These popular manifestations poured in according to Bolivar's orders.

Bolivar's program might be defined as democratic Caesarism. He outlined his commission in the "Organic Decree" of August 27, wherein he baptized the new regime.[48] The decree was an enabling act giving the dictator full power to reorganize the state. Bolivar did not take the title of dictator, however; he was called instead the President-Liberator. A state council was to look out for the preservation of civil rights. On January 2, 1830, a new national assembly should meet and draw up a

45 Proclamas: pp. 379-84.
46 Larrazabal: Vol. II. p. 440.
47 Cartas: Vol. VIII. pp. 28-29.
48 Blanco: Doc. Vol. XIII. p. 13. Cartas: Vol. VIII. pp. 27, 30, 31, 36-37.
C. Parra Pérez: La Dictadura de Bolívar. Cultura Venezolana. April, May, 1924.

constitution. In the meantime, Bolivar wished to devote all his
energies to the restoration and development of national economy. The Organic Decree was accompanied by a proclamation
to the Colombians which includes this strange sentence: "Let
us equally deplore the nation that obeys a single man, and the
man who alone holds power."[49] Exactly four weeks later Bolivar was the victim of his own prophetic vision. The dictatorship
was indeed hateful. One group hated dictatorial rule as such;
another group despised the Bolivaristes, and still another was
antagonistic to the Liberator himself. The people of Bogotá
had no sympathy with the army—especially an army whose
ranking officers were in many cases foreigners. They abhorred
a military dictatorship, and they detested Manuela.

And Manuela was an easy target for gossip. She invited a
group of her friends to the *quinta* one day when the battalion
grenadiers were on guard. An effigy which she had fashioned
of rags and on which she had pinned the label, "Francisco de
Paula Santander dies for treason," was propped against the
garden wall. In the presence of her guests she called the guard
and ordered him to fire. One officer refused to obey, but another
was called and executed her command.[50] General Córdoba,
hearing of the incident, sent a protest to Bolivar, who answered
that he was only too well aware of the fanaticism of his friend,
that he had tried to break away from Manuela in vain. Córdoba
was right, he continued, and he promised to send Manuela away.
It was fortunate for Bolivar that he was no more successful in
banishing her this time than he had been before.[51] Certain authors, such as Ludwig, think that Bolivar should have done in
all seriousness what Manuela did in jest. Such an attitude
signifies a basic misunderstanding of the situation. Deprived
of his official position though he was, Santander was still a
power. In spite of the fact that he had not been given office
or authority in the Organic Decree, Santander remained in
Bogotá and quite naturally became the head of a projected

49 Proclamas: pp. 385-86.
50 Rumazo: *op. cit.*, pp. 214-15. The event took place in July, 1828, not in
March, as Rumazo assumes. See, Cartas: Vol. VII. p. 376.
51 Posada: Córdoba. p. 246. Cartas: Vol. VII. pp. 375-76.

conspiracy against Bolivar. The new motto of these liberals was: "There is no liberty as long as the Liberator lives."

The members of the conspiracy represented various interests.[52] There were young writers like Vargas Tejada—men who had experienced the impact of the revolution in their childhood and who now attempted to defend its issue; adventurers, like the mysterious Dr. Arganil, who had been driven to the shores of America by the waves of the French Revolution and who now, for obscure and incomprehensible reasons, became involved in the plot; isolated individuals, like the French Horment, said to be a spy in Spanish pay; like Florentino González and Mariano Ospina, whose sense of justice was offended by the dictatorship.[53] Moreover, there were certain powerful voices such as Colonel Guerra, chief of staff, and Major Carujo, who promised the rebellion immediate success. The direction of the revolution was put in the hands of a committee of seven. Santander was still considered the legal vice-president and would assume the presidency as soon as Bolivar had been liquidated. It was of vital importance, therefore, to initiate action by the seizure of Bolivar and his ministers. Their plan was to make the arrests on Bolivar's saint day, the day of St. Simon, when they would be protected by the general confusion of the festivities.[54]

The original plan was changed, however, and it was decided to have Bolivar murdered under cover of a masked ball. It is uncertain how Bolivar escaped the trap. It has been said that Manuela saved him, but the writer considers this extremely dubious; others say that Santander protected him, a still more doubtful supposition. In spite of such sinister occurrences Bolivar continued to believe in his invulnerability. He did not dream that anyone would dare to lay hands on him, and on all occasions he appeared without arms or bodyguard.[55] His min-

52 L. Vargas Tejada: Recuerdos históricos. Biblioteca popular. Bogotá. Cordovez Moure: *op. cit.*, p. 47.
53 A. Miramón: Los Septembrinos. Bogotá, 1939.
54 F. Gonzales: Memorias. Buenos Aires, 1933. p. 135.
55 Restrepo: H. d. R. C. Vol. IV. pp. 115-16. Groot: Vol. V. pp. 248-49. Blanco: Doc. Vol. XIII. pp. 64 ff. García Ortiz: Estudios. p. 239. O'Leary: Memorias. Vol. III. p. 300.

isters were more skeptical, and it seems likely that they were
more or less aware of the revolutionary plots that smouldered
underground, and probably it was they who convinced Bolivar
that Santander should be exiled. On September 5, without
warning, Bolivar announced, "Santander will leave the country
in one way or the other," and a few days later the erstwhile
vice-president was appointed minister to Washington. This promotion was obviously an honorable exile which was designed
to deprive the opposition of its leader.[56] After some hesitation
Santander accepted the post, but continued his anti-Bolivar
agitation. He remained in Bogotá, closely informed as to the
progress of the conspiracy, but outwardly ignorant of its existence. He even delayed the outbreak of the rebellion, not from
any desire to protect Bolivar, but because he considered the
plans not fully matured. He neither rejected the idea of revolution nor, on the other hand, did he notify the authorities of the
imminent danger. He thought to appear like a god descending
from a cloud if the rebellion should succeed; he would come
at the call of the people, but with hands unsmirched by blood—
for he was the Man of Law.

Events took a totally unsuspected turn, however. On September 25, Captain Triana returned to his barracks completely
drunk. Meeting a comrade, Lieutenant Salazar, he began to
curse Bolivar violently, shouting that the moment had come
to drown tyranny in streams of blood. Salazar reported the
incident and Triana was arrested, but the conspiracy could now
no longer be considered a secret. When Colonel Guerra learned
of the affair and realized that the plot had been exposed, he
commissioned his aide, Major Carujo, to inform the other conspirators. They were now forced to act with great speed, for
they had but a few hours before the knowledge of their plans
would become general. At seven thirty in the evening the conspirators met at the house of Vargas Tejada and decided to
strike that same night. Three groups were formed; the first
should seize Bolivar at any cost; the second should take the bar-

56 Restrepo: H. d. R. C. Vol. IV. p. 115. O'Leary: Memorias. Vol. III. p. 297.

racks; and the third was to hold itself in readiness for any eventuality. At midnight the first group closed in on the palace of San Carlos.

Bolivar had spent the evening at the palace.[57] He was not well and had sent for Manuela, who arrived, fortunately for the coming exigency, in high boots to protect herself from the dampness. Bolivar was taking a foot bath, and he told her of Triana's arrest, but said he thought any immediate danger had been averted. Manuela read to him until he fell asleep. Meanwhile, the conspirators had overcome the portal guards and now, torch in hand, were making their ascent of the staircase, cheering the Constitution as they came. Ybarra, Bolivar's aide, was encountered and left behind wounded. At length they reached the door of Bolivar's bedroom. Manuela, still awake, heard the unwonted noise, and thought immediately of the rumors of rebellion that had run through Bogotá for weeks. Hastily she wakened Bolivar, who seized pistol and sword prepared to face the invaders. Manuela, however, kept her head. Did he intend to fight for his life in a nightshirt? The idea was preposterous; he must dress at once. As Bolivar obeyed, the thought came to Manuela that only a few days before he had remarked upon the ease with which he could escape through the window, and she now reminded him of this possibility. "You are right," said Bolivar, and having drawn on Manuela's boots he opened the window. She drew him back while she made certain that the streets were deserted. Meanwhile, the group outside were hammering on the door, threatening to break the bolt if they were not admitted. Bolivar jumped to the ground, about nine feet below, and Manuela saw him run northward. Go to the barracks, she cried. Then she turned and opened the door. The conspirators rushed in, and seizing her, shouted for Bolivar. To gain time and to distract their attention from the open window, she told them that Bolivar was in the conference room. "And

57 The principal source for the events of September 25 is the long report that Manuela wrote on O'Leary's request in 1850. O'Leary: Memorias. Vol. III. pp. 301 ff.

the window?" "I opened it to see what the noise was about." They did not believe her, but were undecided as to what they should do next. Manuela counted the seconds; with every passing moment Bolivar was increasing the distance between himself and his would-be assassins. The men were frantic and ran up and down the room in their agitation. If Bolivar escaped they were doomed. One crazed conspirator tried to kill Manuela, but Horment saved her, saying "We are not here to murder women."

The dishevelled bed and the open window were, however, clear evidence, and when Manuela merely reiterated the statement that Bolivar was in the conference room, they demanded that she lead them there. In the corridor the wounded Ybarra cried to her, "Is the Liberator dead?" and dropping all pretense, Manuela answered, "No, he is alive." Then she knelt and bandaged Ybarra's wound with her handkerchief. The knowledge of their failure was now clear to the plotters, but when Bolivar's aide, Fergusson, came down the street and, in spite of Manuela's warning from the window, entered the palace, Carujo killed him with one shot. Shortly after this incident they gave up and fled. When, several minutes later, Urdaneta and Herrán arrived and asked Manuela where Bolivar was, she had difficulty in restraining her smile. In the midst of all her confusion and excitement it seemed amusing to her that anyone would expect her to know where he was.

Bolivar had met one of his servants on his flight from the palace, and together they had raced for the bridge of San Agustín. They saw soldiers going and coming and heard shots, so Bolivar decided to hide under the arch of the bridge, and here for hours of fateful uncertainty he stood in the water waiting for what might come. Finally, his servant ventured out to reconnoiter and met a band of soldiers who cheered Bolivar. This gave the Liberator sufficient confidence to leave the bridge. Covered with mud and soaked to the bone, he made a dash for the barracks.

The assault on the barracks had also been a failure. Although the conspirators had succeeded in liberating Admiral Padilla, they had not achieved their principal goal because the regiments had remained loyal to the Liberator. Urdaneta, who had been informed of the attempted *coup d'état* had taken command and ordered the arrest of the conspirators. By dawn all was over; the rebellion had been crushed.

On arriving at the barracks, Bolivar had asked for a dry uniform and a horse and had then ridden on to the great square. The entire garrison was drawn up and all the generals were gathered. In a hoarse, sepulchral voice, Bolivar thanked them for their faithfulness and then ordered the prosecution of the traitors. When Santander and Padilla would have congratulated him, he cut them with contempt. Then he returned to the palace, and embracing Manuela, he said, "This night you have been the liberatress of the Liberator."

Manuela was herself ill and had a high fever, but Bolivar did not observe her nervous state. He was in an almost delirious condition. Changing his clothes, he tried to compose himself for a few moments' rest, but the tension of the last hours still claimed him. He asked Manuela to tell him what had happened during the night, but interrupted her answer with, "Don't tell me anything!" Almost at once the question would be repeated, but again he would silence her. Thus passed the tragic morning of September 26.

In the meantime, the conspirators had been captured and brought to the palace, where Bolivar waited to hear their depositions. Colonel Crofton was prevented from strangling young Horment by the Liberator himself, who then ordered dry clothing for his would-be murderer. General Paris, turning to the conspirators, said, "And this is the man you would kill!" "Not the man, but his system," responded Horment.

What were Bolivar's reactions to this serious attempt upon his life, an attempt that had exposed a deep-seated repugnance toward his ideas and toward himself as their protagonist? He expressed his determination to pardon the criminals and then to resign. If the people had turned from him, if they misunderstood the nature of his sacrifice in trying to save Colombia, there was no alternative.[58] He summoned Castillo y Rada, president of the state council who, on his arrival, found Bolivar apparently controlled and firm. Bolivar explained that he had meditated over the events of the previous night and could find but one answer to the problem—his resignation. He asked Castillo y Rada to convoke the cabinet and prepare the resolution. He planned, moreover, to issue a general amnesty to the conspirators. Their names he did not even wish to know.

Bolivar's renunciatory mood met with concerted opposition from his generals. Urdaneta, Córdoba, and many others protested that the army had proven its loyalty to the Liberator and that he could not desert it now. His resignation, they said, would constitute an approval of the murderous attempt. They repudiated the idea of surrender and declared that the mutiny should be crushed and the conspirators suffocated in their own blood.

Again Bolivar yielded. He remained in office as the President-Liberator. The investigation was begun without delay under special procedure.[59] A court of four judges and four officers was appointed, and on September 30 the first death penalty was delivered. In order to hasten the liquidation of the conspiracy, Urdaneta had taken charge of the investigation, and, relying on the decree of February 20, took over all the prerogatives of both state attorney and judge. Córdoba, meanwhile, took charge of the Ministry of War, although his attitude on the night of September 25 had not been above suspicion. Urdaneta lost no time, and on October 2 Admiral Padilla was shot; other executions followed closely.

On September 26 Santander had been remanded for trial, charged with participation in the plot. Bolivar was convinced that Santander was the master mind of the conspiracy, and although the Vice-President denied the accusation, he was forced to admit his cognizance of the affair and that he had

58 O'Leary: Memorias. *op. cit.* Botero: p. 164.
59 Cartas: Vol. VIII. pp. 64 ff. Blanco: Doc. Vol. XIII. pp. 99 ff. Groot: Vol. V. p. 255.

given advice to the conspirators. It was true that he had only sharpened the arrow and had allowed others to pull the bow-string, but Santander was a general of the Republic, an ambassador to the United States, and as a state official it should have been his first duty to expose any threat to the Republic at the first hint of danger. Santander was, therefore, sentenced to death.[60]

Bolivar submitted the verdict to the Ministers' Council for approval. The ministers agreed that Santander's sentence was just, but they knew, too, that his execution might form the basis of violent reaction, while imprisonment or exile might produce a favorable impression. Their reasonable attitude enraged Bolivar; why had Piar and Padilla paid with their lives for insurrection if Santander was to escape the penalty?[61] Finally, however, he accepted the decision, and Santander was sent into exile. Outwardly Bolivar was the victor in this fundamental struggle between the two leaders, but he later confessed, "It was our ruin that we did not come to terms with Santander," and in many ways it was indeed but a Phyrric victory.[62] The shadow of the erstwhile Vice-President pursued Bolivar from one end of the Republic to the other, and in the final analysis it was Santander who could claim the victory, not because he returned to Bogotá as President after Bolivar's death, but because he represented a political principle that was closer to reality than Bolivar's dream of greatness.

Public opinion in Europe and North America was that Bolivar had pardoned Santander out of mere weakness. This underrated the Liberator. He had, in reality, sacrificed his passion for revenge and his desire to be rid of his greatest enemy to his greater ambition of preserving the Colombian Republic. Shortly afterward, a general amnesty for those conspirators who had fled from retributive justice was recommended by the min-

60 Cartas: Vol. VIII. pp. 95, 99. Arch. Santander: Vol. XVIII. pp. 11 ff. E. Ortega Ricaurte: Documentos sobre el proceso de la conspiracion del 25. de septiembre. Bogotá, 1942.
61 Cartas: Vol. VIII. p. 117. Blanco: Doc. Vol. XIII. p. 192.
62 Cartas: Vol. IX. p. 289.

isters and granted by Bolivar. However, those deputies who were known to be Bolivar's personal enemies were sent away, the lodges of the freemasons were abolished, and education was reorganized along conservative lines. Slowly the country returned to normal.

But the heart of Bolivar had been mortally wounded. The night of September 25 had sounded his death knell as far as his aspirations and ambitions were concerned. However much he reflected on that fatal night's events, he still could not comprehend that he, the creator of Colombia, had escaped death at the hands of his countrymen by inches only. What would have become of the Republic had his enemies succeeded? Civil war, bloodshed, and anarchy would have overwhelmed the state in a general conflagration. This nightmare pursued Bolivar; in his dreams he saw the fateful weapons of his enemies raised against him; he felt the steel entering his flesh. To his intimates he cried in agony, "They have destroyed my heart."[63] To the physical decay that had begun in Lima, or perhaps previously, was added the deep melancholy of his knowledge that his great effort had been in vain. America was ungrateful for his life's sacrifice, and he could bear no more. "For I am not a saint, and I have no desire to suffer martyrdom."[64] In spite of everything, however, he did not abandon his command, but remained on the bridge in a desperate effort to bring the Colombian vessel into port.

63 Restrepo: H. d. R. C. Vol. IV. p. 119. Larrazabal: Vol. II. p. 454.
64 Cartas: Vol. VIII. pp. 93, 116.

CHAPTER 33
_____

Disintegration of Greater Colombia

$\mathcal{T}$he events of the night of September 25 resulted in a political success for the Liberator. Every frustrated attempt to overthrow a regime in the end strengthens the government against which it is directed. Accordingly, Bolivar's dictatorship became more powerful than ever. He had been profoundly shaken by the occurrences of that memorable night; his thoughts were sombre and his heart was deeply wounded. That he never gave any descriptive account of the affair is illuminating in itself. But his enemies were, at least for the time being, silenced. The feeling of horror that swept the country when the news of the attempt on his life was received surrounded Bolivar's government with moral prestige. He had acquired the support that enabled him to maintain his position for a year and a half longer.

Whatever Bolivar's enemies or his critics may say about his dictatorship, they cannot maintain that he ruled merely because he was obsessed by a love of power.[1] He refused to relinquish his authority because he had a mission to fulfill—the preservation of Colombian unity. The existence of the Republic was threatened from without as well as from within. Peru, liberated at the expense of Colombian blood, challenged her dearly won victory.

1 Cartas: Vol. VIII. p. 168. Groot: Vol. V. p. 367. Tamayo: *op. cit., passim.* Lleras y Ruda: Historia de la Gran Colombia. Bogotá, 1896. Abreu y Lima: Resumen histórico de la Ultima Dictadura del Libertador Simón Bolívar. Ed. by Carbonell. Río de Janeiro, 1922.

The overthrow of Peruvian politics affected the personal accomplishment of Bolivar in the south of the continent, that is, the erection of the Bolivian state. Here, in 1826, Sucre had been elected President for life. The young marshal had taken the precaution of accepting the election with certain reservations. He promised to serve Bolivia only until 1828, the year when the first parliament should meet.[2] Sucre's government was a model of political foresight; it was patterned on the outline Bolivar had drawn up during his rapid inspection tour of the country in 1825, and it endeavored to animate this backward country with liberal ideas.

Sucre's administration gave little occasion for reproach, though it must be admitted that his excessive integrity and purity of motive bordered on weakness.[3] An attempt was made on his life by a certain Matos only a few months after Sucre's election to the presidency. The man was caught and sentenced to death, but Sucre, moved by the mother's pleas, not only commuted his sentence to exile, but supplied him with two hundred pesos out of his own pocket. Such leniency was an out and out reward for political murder, and it is not surprising that considerable advantage was taken of Sucre's attitude.

Peru had never given up hope of annexing Bolivia, depending for success on the unreliability of the Colombian division quartered in Bolivia. Secret agents sought to influence the army, and a Peruvian force under General Gamarra moved menacingly toward the Bolivian frontier. Rumor has it that personal motives entered into the conflict; Gamarra accused Bolivar of courting his wife, a circumstance sometimes irritating to husbands, and he no doubt desired some measure of revenge.[4] Whether this be true or not, rebellion broke out in Bolivia at Christmas, 1827. Sucre, however, managed to subdue the insurgents, and in spite of certain proof of Gamarra's responsibility, he endeavored to convince the Peruvian general

2 Restrepo: H. d. R. C. Vol. IV. p. 8.
3 Villanueva: Sucre. p. 443. J. M. Rey de Castro: *op. cit.*, pp. 216 ff.
4 See, Sucre's letter, in C. Hispano: Bolívar y la posteridad. Bogotá, 1928. p. 136.

that neither he nor Bolivar had hostile intentions toward Peru. His conciliatory words had no effect, and Gamarra continued his agitation. On April 18 the Chuquisaca garrison mutinied, and Sucre, on his way through the city, was attacked and wounded in the arm. Unable to resist his attackers, he was taken prisoner. Meanwhile, under the flimsy pretext that they moved to protect Sucre's life, the Peruvians crossed the Bolivian border. Bolivia was forced to sign an agreement whereby all foreigners—that is, all Colombians—should be expelled from the country.[5]

Sucre was, according to the letter of the agreement, a foreigner. Hampered by his wound, he had delegated all political affairs to his representative and was ready and willing to go. He refused, however, to capitulate to pure force and to leave as a fugitive the country he had liberated. It was not until August 3, at the convening of Congress, that he resigned his power. His last message to the Bolivian Parliament is notable for its dignity and its scrupulous sense of honor. "The Constitution," said Sucre, "declares me inviolable; I do not bear any responsibility for the acts of government. However, I ask to be deprived of this privilege and to have my conduct examined. If a single violation of the laws, committed before April 18, can be found, or if the houses think the cabinet should be accused, I shall return from Colombia and submit myself to the sentence. I demand this reward with so much greater right, since I solemnly declare that I, myself, ruled during my administration. Whatever good or evil has been done, I am responsible for it."[6] In September, 1828, his arm still paralyzed from his wound, Sucre arrived in Quito, where he took up his residence.

Bolivar considered Sucre's treatment at the hands of the Bolivians an insult to Colombia.[7] Tension increased dangerously when the Peruvian government became openly hostile towards its northern neighbor. The Peruvian minister in Bogotá repudi-

5 López Contreras: Sucre. p. 101. Villanueva: Sucre. p. 456.
6 Lecuna: Doc. Vol. II. p. 616. O'Leary: Doc. Vol. I. p. 496.
7 Cartas: Vol. VII. pp. 174, 175, 345. See, Sucre's letter to Bolivar. Blanco: Doc. Vol. XIII. p. 54.

ated the treaties and obligations agreed upon between the two
governments during the heroic years of 1823 and 1824. He
was suspected of the masked provocation of Bolivar's enemies in
Bogotá, and the Colombian government finally returned his
credentials and broke diplomatic relations with Lima. Other
incidents aggravated the situation, with the result that Peru
believed Colombia was preparing to declare war. She, therefore,
mobilized her own forces, and her president, General La Mar,
took command of the army. Bolivar issued a message in which
he characterized the Peruvians as being both faithless and treacherous, and he called upon the Colombians of the South to
mobilize and hold themselves in readiness for his arrival. "My
presence among you shall be the signal for battle."[8]

This address of Bolivar was in many respects an unusual
one. Not only did his manifesto offend all rules of international
courtesy, but it also threatened the Peruvians with a war for
which Colombia had no desire. Peru's answer was a presidential
pamphlet directed against Sucre and Bolivar. The latter would
now have resorted to war, but his cabinet resisted the idea and
he gave in to their wishes. Adjutant O'Leary was, therefore,
sent to Lima to pave the way to compromise, a commission
wherein he achieved no results whatever. The Peruvian government refused to grant him safe conduct and he never even
reached Lima. The Peruvians went even further and denied
Bolivar both presidential title and honor, referring to him in
their proclamations only as "the General." Finally, open hostilities were begun.[9]

The Peruvian fleet blockaded Colombia's Pacific ports, and
La Mar waited with four thousand men at the Ecuadorian border. In view of the gravity of the situation Bolivar named Sucre
as his personal representative, and Sucre hesitatingly accepted.
After eighteen years of almost constant service in the public
cause, Sucre felt justified in his desire to live his own life. But
Bolivar persuaded him that fame was of more importance than

8 Proclamas: p. 384. Cartas: Vol. VII. pp. 344-45.
9 Cartas: Vol. VIII. pp. 4, 8. Restrepo: H. d. R. C. Vol. IV. pp. 136-37.

personal happiness, and he finally accepted full charge of the southern theatre of war.[10]

Bolivar knew that this was an unpopular war. In the bitter tone that marks the letters of his last years he wrote, "These nations do not offer the basis for heroic deeds."[11] He accommodated his actions to the *raison d'état,* which ordained that he should remain in Bogotá and continue the work of internal consolidation. A true picture of his mind during these months, as revealed in his correspondence, shows the havoc wrought by disillusionment and frustration. Recollections of the fatal September night are frequent, and the grief and anger they occasioned made him often unjust to his fellow countrymen. But it was still rare for Bolivar to refuse any demand made of him. His natural generosity breaks through the crust of his bitterness in such words as: "My dear friend, I wish I had a great fortune that I might share it with every Colombian. But I have no possessions. I have only a heart to love them and a sword to defend them."[12]

Bolivar relied on Sucre's ability to solve the Peruvian conflict until the time he received word that two of the commanding officers of the South had set up a rebellion against the government. He knew the character of these men, Colonel López and Colonel Obando, only too well. To Perú de la Croix he had said, "López is an evil doer without decency or honor, a ridiculous boaster and bluffer, inflated and full of vanity. . . . Without talent, without military spirit, without courage and knowledge of war, he thinks himself able to command and conduct an army. But all his knowledge is nothing but deceit, disloyalty, and treason. In a word, he is a scoundrel." Obando was still more of a rascal. "He is a murderer . . . a daring and cruel robber, a repulsive henchman, a blood-thirsty tiger, who is not satisfied with all the Colombian blood he has already shed . . . they dishonor and disgrace the army to which they

10 Cartas: Vol. VIII. pp. 84, 98.
11 Cartas: Vol. VIII. pp. 84, 92.
12 Cartas: Vol. VIII. p. 121.

belong and the ensign they bear."[13] In truth, López and Obando were the pirates of the revolution; civil war had become a habit with them. It is very unlikely that their enterprise was motivated by any political idea, but they entrenched themselves behind the pretext of fighting for the Constitution of 1821.

López and Obando dominated the Cauca Valley and could penetrate into Ecuador over Pasto, thus establishing contact with the Peruvian army.[14] It was this danger which impelled Bolivar to act. He again changed the list of his co-workers; once more Urdaneta became the leading figure in the cabinet. A series of administrative measures followed, intended to guarantee the stability of the republic while Bolivar was on campaign. Not all of these measures corresponded strictly to the ideal of a free state, but they did include the decree calling for a new national assembly on January 2, 1830. Finally, Bolivar delegated affairs to the ministerial council and departed for the South.[15]

Never before had Bolivar felt so acutely the hardships of travel. He could endure riding on horseback for no more than two hours at a time. Exhausted in body and distressed in mind, he realized how short a time was left him. Córdoba had been sent ahead to conduct the military part of the undertaking; he conquered Popayán and began a guerrilla warfare against the rebels. Bolivar, following closely after Córdoba, offered them an amnesty if they would lay down their arms.[16] When Obando realized that the assistance he had expected from the Peruvians would not arrive in time to protect him from Bolivar, he saved his skin by signing an agreement with the Liberator's deputy.[17] Bolivar has been severely criticized for this palliative measure, and, as a matter of fact, it is difficult to understand why he spared men whom he had characterized as rascals and hench-

---

13 D. d. B. p. 251.
14 See, Obando's letter to La Mar in O'Leary: Memorias. Vol. III. p. 391. Cartas: Vol. VIII. pp. 146, 173, 178.
15 Cartas: Vol. VIII. pp. 180, 183. Blanco: Doc. Vol. XIII. p. 290.
16 Cartas: Vol. VIII. pp. 218, 220. Blanco: Doc. Vol. XIII. p. 366.
17 I. H. López: Memorias. Bogotá, 1942. Vol. II. pp. 14, 42. Posado Gutiérrez. Vol. I. p. 221

men and at the same time demanded that the idealistic conspirators of Bogotá pay with their lives. The monstrous Obando remained master of the regions of Pasto, free to devise other crimes.

If Bolivar had known that the danger of a Peruvian invasion had already been averted, his conduct toward the rebels might well have been less generous. Three days after signing the agreement with López and Obando, and as he was entering the city of Pasto, he learned that Sucre had, for the third time, proven himself to be the best general of the Colombian army. Sucre's first intention had been to avoid a fratricidal war at all costs. It seemed infamous to him that Peru and Colombia should be in arms against each other only five years after the battle of Ayacucho. His attempts to come to terms with Peru, however, were failures. President La Mar rejected all proposals, and the war became inevitable.

At the outset the Peruvians seemed to hold the advantage with a few moderate successes; they occupied Guayaquil, and were confident that their army of eighty-four hundred men would beat the Colombians. Sucre had only six thousand men, but his military talent equalized the numeric inferiority. A thirty day campaign in which he completely outwitted La Mar was successfully concluded by the battle of Tarqui—a conclusion deserving to rank with Pichincha and Ayacucho. Sucre was opposed to further bloodshed; moreover, the battle of Tarqui had restored Colombian prestige, and Sucre accordingly offered La Mar an honorable surrender. The treaty of Girón, signed on February 28, awarded modest reparations to Colombia and guaranteed her territorial integrity.

Bolivar hastened to Quito to congratulate Sucre, but when they met he was so overcome by emotion that his voice failed him. Twice he attempted to express his gratitude and twice his voice was drowned in tears. Finally he embraced Sucre in silence. Here was a man who had also endured the ingratitude of South America and whose heart had not been shattered.[18]

18 Larrazabal: Vol. II. p. 474.

In spite of success and an amicable treaty, however, Bolivar continued to mistrust the Peruvians, and events justified his premonitions. La Mar had instructed his second in command to ignore the provisions of the treaty of Girón and under no circumstances to return Guayaquil to Colombia. Because of this breach of faith, Bolivar decided to remain in the South until Colombian rights had been restored in full. He set up his headquarters on the coast and made preparations to besiege Guayaquil.[19] His efforts were superfluous, however, and the port was taken without the firing of a single shot. A revolution in Lima deposed La Mar, and the newly elected President of Peru hastened to inform Bolivar that the country would never forget the extraordinary services Colombia had rendered her. The treaty of Girón was ratified and Guayaquil was occupied by the Colombian army.

The campaign of 1829 marks the end of Bolivar's military career; victory was his, but a victory without glory. He had fought for Colombia's integrity and he had fought to preserve it, but whether it would survive his own lifetime was problematical. Bolivar was worn out, and his death was not far off. In Guayaquil a serious illness attacked him, which he believed to be a gastric fever but which keener observers noted as the progress of his pulmonary disease.

It was to be expected that the Diadochos were already scheming to divide Alexander's realm among themselves. General Córdoba planned to depose the sick Liberator, then to separate New Granada from Venezuela, leaving Ecuador independent. He hoped that his countrymen would side with him. It is needless to add that he reserved the high command to himself.[20] Córdoba was without physical fear. His courage at Pichincha and Ayacucho had been responsible for decisive action. His was a type of courage, occasionally encountered among South Americans, which faces the elements as though they were pow-

19 Proclamas: p. 389. Cartas: Vol. VIII. p. 299.
20 T. Mosquera: Memorias sobre la Vida del General Bolívar. Bogotá, 1940. pp. 659, 660, 663. Posada Gutiérrez: Vol. I. p. 232. Páez: Autobiografia. p. 711.

erless to harm human beings. Córdoba was insensitive to the imponderables, believing that his personal participation in any cause would insure victory. He had gone to the South with Bolivar and here, simple and primitive as he was, had become ensnared in politics. He became increasingly aware that the Liberator did not trust him; he heard rumors that Bolivar planned to become an emperor; he saw certain letters, listened to slander, and finally, temperamentally averse to logical thought, lost his head, returned to his home province, Antioquía, and with three hundred volunteers initiated a movement to overthrow Bolivar.

Bolivar saw no reason for apprehension. He had tried to appease Córdoba and had planned to send him to Europe on a diplomatic mission. Circumstances now forbade such a compromise, and he issued decisive orders.[21] Urdaneta undertook to deal with the foolhardy general, sending O'Leary to suppress the revolt. The latter invaded the Antioquian Mountains and on October 17 met and defeated Córdoba. The wounded rebel general dragged himself to a hut which was serving as a campaign hospital, and here the Irishman, Hand, one of O'Leary's legionnaires, found him and killed him in cold blood. Hand said later that he had merely obeyed orders from above, and some historians accuse Bolivar of the cowardly act, but there is no basis of proof for the charge.[22]

Córdoba's rebellion was easily crushed, but a feeling of sorrow swept the nation. With the execution of Padilla, the exile of Santander, and the murder of Córdoba, it seemed as though the revolution, like Saturn, was devouring its own young. Each day the ingratitude of South America demanded a fresh victim; Córdoba would not be the last. Bolivar, however, wasted no time in mourning the loss of Córdoba, who had never occupied a place in his heart. Córdoba was himself of little importance in comparison with the great mass of South Americans and their tragic unpreparedness.

21 Cartas: Vol. IX. pp. 56, 146, 150, 166. See, Córdoba's Proclamation. Blanco: Doc. Vol. XIII. p. 633.
22 Urdaneta: Memorias. p. 377. Botero: Córdoba. Bogotá, 1927.

During the upheaval of this year, Bolivar's emotions were those of despair, disgust, and a resultant melancholy; these feelings are manifest in all he thought or wrote about himself and about Colombia. "As for me, I despair of my own power, and I wait only to see the national assembly united so that I may separate myself from the ungrateful and the perfidious. They will receive their punishment from others as ambitious as they themselves are."[23] Every day gave him a new reason to complain of the "devilish ideas" that were agitating South America. "The perspectives of South America depress and sadden me; this earth is condemned."[24] "Ingratitude has destroyed me and has deprived my mind of all resources. I am determined to abandon Colombia and to die of sorrow and misery in a foreign country. . . . My grief has no bounds. Slander strangles me as the serpents strangled Laocoon."[25] I cannot stand it any longer; I am tired; I have had enough,—such is the tenor of his letters day after day. "During twenty years of work I have done what I could. Who has the right to demand more of me? And who shall demand that I must die on the cross. . . . Even on the cross, I could at least come to the end of my torments. Jesus Christ endured this human life for thirty-three years. I have passed forty-six, and the worst of it is that I have spent these years without being a god who is above suffering. I cannot bear more. I cannot bear more; a hundred times a day my heart tells me so."[26]

The attacks of his illness became more frequent; his fatigue increased. "I resemble an old man of sixty." Illness, however, was not the only element with which his depressed spirits were obliged to contend. As we have seen, Bolivar's whole life had been governed by his two conflicting interests—personal ambition and the ideal of liberty. In the person of the Liberator the two tendencies were combined without loss of merit or dignity. He had led the people to independence, and he alone knew

23 Cartas: Vol. VIII. p. 279.
24 Cartas: Vol. IX. pp. 20, 79.
25 Cartas: Vol. IX. p. 246.
26 Cartas: Vol. IX. pp. 108, 115.

the path by which they might advance toward a future greatness. But what if they did not wish to take this path? What
if they should resist, and instead of joining their forces in a
great empire should elect to become independent nations . . .
ah, then indeed were they faithless and ungrateful. . . . Such
were Bolivar's reflections, and it took no great effort to
convince himself that the South American nations both resented
and resisted his political ideas.

Bolivar looked upon himself as the Liberator, but for many
of his fellow countrymen he was now merely the President, or
worse, the Dictator, the usurper.[27] "I a usurper? . . . I cannot
bear the idea and the horror it causes in me is so great that I
would prefer rather to see the decline of Colombia."[28] Bolivar's
character and work were similarly estimated in other parts of
the world. In Europe, Benjamin Constant severely criticized
Bolivar for espousing dictatorship. When Bolivar first learned
of Constant's attitude, he made a definite effort to have the accusation refuted.[29] Later, however, he began to feel certain that
he would not be able to prevail over his critics, that he was not
going to receive justice from the living, and that only posterity
would correctly evaluate his merits. In a premonitary mood he
wrote the proud words, "My name belongs already to history,
and there I shall have justice. Do not, therefore, take the trouble
to defend me from this accusation by means of which Benjamin
Constant tries to stain my reputation. He would judge me
differently if he could know the events of our history more
accurately. My patriotism is on a par with that of Camillus.
I love freedom no less than Washington, and no one can dispute that I have the honor to have humiliated the Spanish lion
from the Orinoco to Potosí." In the same vein he also wrote,
"A general calm, an absolute indifference, has taken possession
of me and dominates me completely."[30]

27 J. V. Castro Silva: La tristeza de Bolívar. Bogotá, 1935.
28 Cartas: Vol. IX. p. 22.
29 Cartas: Vol. IX. pp. 31, 40-41. M. Aguirre: Una celebre polémica francesa
de 1829. B. d. H. Caracas. Vol. XX. No. 79. p. 357. Blanco: Doc. Vol. XIII.
p. 352.
30 Cartas: Vol. IX. pp. 33, 121.

At another time Bolivar said, "We have tried all systems, and nothing has proved effective. Mexico has fallen; Guatemala is destroyed; there are new revolutions in Chile. In Buenos Aires they have killed the president. Bolivia has had three presidents in two days, and two of them have been murdered."[31] "There is no end to it; right and duty are not respected. America is in a turmoil, a chaos of passions, difficulties, and disorders." But had not Bolivar himself, five years previously, called this America the hope of the universe, the promised land? Yes, but, he answered, his belief had been a chimera; wishes had deceived them all, just as they deceive children. In such a mood Bolivar wrote the deeply affecting monologue which he called *A View of Spanish America*. Here we find the famous words, "There is neither faith nor truth in America, whether it be among men or among nations. Treaties are mere scraps of paper, constitutions are books, elections are battles, freedom is anarchy, and life is a torture. This is our situation, and if we do not change it, it were better that we should die."[32]

Was it possible that he still cherished a hope that America might change? Indeed, he would not have been Bolivar had he given up his hope of preserving Colombia. This hope was stronger, more urgent than life; no grief, however deep, could shatter it completely. He thought constantly of Colombia's future, and his first aim was to present her intact to the National Assembly. He declared that he would submit to the free decision of the people; his reputation as the Liberator demanded that he do so, but he did not believe that Colombia's problems would derive any real solution from constitutional discussions. "I am disappointed in constitutions, and even though they are in vogue today, their failures are the same."

Bolivar had decided to conclude his dictatorship on January 2, 1830, and his resolution was a sincere one. The events of the preceding year in Ocaña must not be repeated. The choice of a future leader for the republic should be made freely and peace-

31 Cartas: Vol. VIII. pp. 277, 279.
32 Blanco: Doc. Vol. XIII. p. 496.

fully by the legislative assembly. His attitude toward these practical matters of governmental action did not, however, preclude his continuous attempt to devise some means of saving the republic from disintegration. That such a disintegration was probable, he knew, but he would have embraced any means to avert it.

He returned to his former plan of establishing foreign protection, and again thought that Great Britain should accept the trust. America, he wrote to his ministers, needs a peacemaker. The most powerful nation of the world should protect the young states of South America from devouring each other.[33] At other moments he considered the possibility of imposing the Bolivian Constitution and of appointing Sucre as his successor to carry out a program he knew only too well he himself would not live to complete. Among the many speculations that flashed like lightning through his mind is one that claims our interest. In a letter to O'Leary he outlined a new and in many ways a revolutionary project. "Would it not be better for Colombia and for me . . . that a new president should be elected and that I should remain only as generalissimo? I would go around the government as a bull runs around a herd of cows. . . . I would hasten through the provinces, I would avert rebellions. . . . My mobility would be admirable. I could be everywhere that necessity or danger should call me. . . . Colombia would gain much by this plan, and I should gain glory, freedom, and happiness."[34] Bolivar's proposal seems fantastic, but at an earlier date it might have been a feasible plan. An essential requirement would have been the establishment of a perfect harmony between Bolivar, as generalissimo, and the government. Given such conditions, the Liberator might have gone from town to town, like a medieval emperor, adjusting, improving, encouraging. Such a position would have been compatible with the semifeudal character of Colombian society and economy; it might have been of some help in bridging the great distances

33 Restrepo: H. d. R. C. Vol. IV. p. 211. See also, Cartas: Vol. VIII. p. 305.
34 Cartas: Vol. IX. pp. 91-92.

that prevented the centralization of the country; in a word, it might have helped to develop a national spirit in Colombia. Had Bolivar thought of this solution in 1825 he might have averted, or at least postponed, the disintegration of his work. Now, in 1829, the patient was too far advanced in illness to apply the remedy.

Meanwhile, the Colombian ministers were contemplating another way out. If Colombia could not be maintained as a republic, she could be converted into a monarchy.[35] Bolivar's prestige in Europe was considerable. He was appreciated not only as a great military genius, but also as a warrant for the peaceful reorganization of the liberated continent. The Swedish king, Bernadotte, said: "There are many analogies between Bolivar and me. We both owe our rise to our swords and our merits; we are both beloved by our people; we are faithful to the cause of liberty, distinguishing ourselves from Napoleon in this matter." Many voices in France and England also were raised in admiration of Bolivar.[36]

Early in 1829 the French government had sent M. de Bresson as Minister Extraordinary to study conditions in the South American republics as a basis for the possible establishment of diplomatic relations between these new born states and the France of Charles X. De Bresson, who was accompanied by the Duc de Montebello, son of Marshal Lannes, set up a mission which soon became the focal point of a great political intrigue. Its aim was the creation of a constitutional monarchy whose king should be a Bourbon prince. The Colombian cabinet, which was willing to embark on any adventure promising a solution for the country's crisis, approved the French plans, and there is no doubt that the upper classes and the clergy were also favorably inclined. Urdaneta became the principal advocate of this unfortunate scheme.

Urdaneta apparently expected to award the crown to Bolivar,

35 L. A. Cuervo: La Monarquía en Colombia. B. d. H. Bogotá. Vol. X. p. 289. Larrazabal: Vol. II. pp. 493 ff. Groot: Vol. V. p. 302. Restrepo: H. d. R. C. Vol. IV. pp. 202 ff. Botero: pp. 221 ff.
36 Larrazabal: Vol. II. pp. 490-91.

a plan that had small likelihood of success in view of the Liberator's manifest aversion to monarchic rule. Urdaneta, however, felt justified in his intentions because of Bolivar's expressed despair over the anarchical conditions in America. Moreover, the Liberator had instructed the cabinet to obtain foreign protection, and his ministers were of the opinion that a monarchy would, by contrast, be a minor evil. Meanwhile, the original plans had been somewhat altered. It was now believed best to continue Bolivar in the presidency until the end of his life and then to select a French prince who should rule as King of Colombia. In June, 1829, an assembly of high officers, state officials, and clergy, meeting in Bogotá, approved the project, and agreed to prepare public opinion for the new program. Venezuelan leaders were also apprised of the contemplated action.[37]

Bolivar, thousands of miles from Bogotá, ill and tortured by grief, now learned that his ministers considered his plan of creating a protectorate as impracticable, and that instead they proposed to institute monarchical rule as a check against anarchy. He wrote his secretary of state that monarchy had not the slightest chance of success in America. No European prince would embark on such a maelstrom of passions without specific guarantees, and conditions in South America cancelled the possibility of any guarantee. The country was too poor to sustain a royal court; the lower classes would be violently averse to a new aristocracy, the inevitable accompaniment of the new rule, and the upper classes would regard such innovaters with envy and malice. There would, moreover, be certain opposition from abroad. England would never consent to the expansion of Bourbon power, and both the United States and the other South American republics would oppose monarchy for ideological reasons. Bolivar wished to veto the whole affair unless England and France gave their full approval. He added that he was not motivated by personal ambition, and that if the plan promised Colombia's salvation, he would be the first to hail it.[38]

37 Restrepo: H. d. R. C. Vol. IV. pp. 203-05.
38 Cartas: Vol. IX. pp. 21-22.

It is clear that Bolivar's convictions had not changed, nor can he be reproached with concealing his disapproval. His illness and his remoteness from the scene of these affairs, both of which prevented close communication with his ministers, alone prevented his immediate rejection of the monarchical scheme. The unavoidable silence of delayed intelligence was taken for consent by his ministers, and the Colombian representatives in Paris and London were instructed to approach the French and English governments with regard to the establishment of a monarchy on American soil. This precipitation of the monarchical scheme for Colombia produced only the results foreseen by Bolivar—external confusion and internal strife. The American ambassador, Mr. Harrison, took the opportunity to interfere in Colombia's innermost political problems. He wrote Bolivar long letters in which he advised him how to rule the Republic using the United States as a model. Harrison was seeking to establish some connection with the enemies of Bolivar, and it is said that he was the real instigator of the Córdoba rebellion. Colombia finally demanded his withdrawal, even making threats to expel him. President Jackson acceded to the Colombian request and sent another ambassador to Bogotá.[39]

The English response to the plan of monarchy involved much greater peril for the Republic than Harrison's bungling attempts at interference, because the English were more dexterous in their manoeuvres. Only the extreme naïveté of the Colombian ministers can account for their artless belief that England would for a moment tolerate any fresh attempt by France to gain a stronghold in the Western Hemisphere. England did not employ Harrison's ingenuous stratagems, but resorted instead to ruse and intrigue. That Colombia had labored under a permanent crisis since 1827 was clearly understood, and it was quite obvious that the disintegration of the Republic

39 Cartas: Vol. IX. p. 192. Restrepo: H. d. R. C. Vol. IV. pp. 218-20. H. Montgomery: The Life of W. H. Harrison. New York, 1857. H. R. Lemly: Simón Bolívar. Boston, 1923. p. 433.

would automatically liquidate the whole scheme. On April 9,
1829, the British Vice-Admiral, Fleming, commander of all
British forces in the Caribbean, arrived in La Guayra, where he
was given an ostentatious reception by Páez. To all appearances
Fleming's mission was an open attempt to strengthen the Venezuelan secessionists in their desire to dissolve the Colombian
union. Moreover, the British Foreign Minister informed the
cabinet in Bogotá that his government recommended the election of a Spanish prince to the proposed Colombian throne.
Lord Aberdeen knew, of course, that such a suggestion was
entirely unacceptable to both Bolivar and his cabinet.[40]

In the meantime the Venezuelans proceeded to use Urdaneta's monarchical proposition as a pretext for their own rebellion against the unity of Greater Colombia. Páez had, from the
beginning, entertained the Urdaneta plan with a great display
of caution, declaring that he could neither accept nor reject it
until he should know what attitude Bolivar would take. No
one knew Bolivar's ideas about monarchy better than Páez,
because he had been the one to receive Bolivar's famous refusal
in 1825, but Páez adopted the rôle of innocence and sent one of
his officers, Colonel Austria, to Bolivar, ostensibly to learn the
Liberator's views about the future government of Colombia.
Austria met Bolivar in the South after the latter had set forth
on the return trip to Bogotá. The journey had been fatiguing
in the extreme. The rains had washed out the roads, and Bolivar's exhausted frame could scarcely meet the strain it was
obliged to bear. But illness and the hazards of travel could not
delay him, and at the end of November, from Popayán, he gave
his final opinion on the plan of a Colombian monarchy. He
instructed the ministers to break off all negotiations on the
subject, informing them that only Congress could sanction decisions concerning problems of national sovereignty.[41] Bolivar
explained to Colonel Austria that any monarchical experiment

40 Blanco: Doc. Vol. XIII. pp. 499, 536. O'Leary: Doc. Vol. II. p. 283. Restrepo:
H. d. R. C. Vol. IV. pp. 250-51. Gil Fortoul: Hist. pp. 466-67. Botero: p. 254.
41 Cartas: Vol. IX. p. 195. Restrepo: H. d. R. C. Vol. IV. p. 244.

would encounter insurmountable obstacles. He, Bolivar, would not accept the crown even if the entire state of Colombia came to offer it to him. He was, nevertheless, willing to make any sacrifice to insure the preservation of unity, even to serving under Páez if the latter should be elected president. "I assure you," he wrote to Páez, "that I am most willing to serve under your command if you should become the head of the state."[42] This letter is dated December 15, and we are given a clear picture of the Colombian Republic, with its great distances, its lack of roads and means of communication, when we learn that at the time this message was sent events had taken place that made its content untenable—events of which Boliver was for some time ignorant.

Páez had taken no avowed stand against the monarchistic scheme, but stealthily he took advantage of the rumor of Bolivar's coronation to disparage the Liberator in the eyes of his countrymen. The moment seemed opportune for Páez' own plans. Bolivar was far away; New Granada still trembled from the shock of Córdoba's rebellion; and so it was that Páez decided to take the risk and separate Venezuela from Greater Colombia.

The fall of 1829 saw the events of 1826 repeated. Venezuela became the stage of a separatist revolution directed against the person of the Liberator. A triumvirate, composed of Páez, Soublette, and Peña, guided the rebellion. These were the men in whom Bolivar had placed his trust; he had heaped praises on them with the sole idea that they would be his co-workers in the great undertaking of preserving the national unity. The revolution in Venezuela put the stamp of doom on all Bolivar's plans as a statesman and on all his hopes as a human being.

A consistent program of vilification and calumny initiated the Venezuelan rebellion. On the walls of houses appeared insulting inscriptions denouncing Bolivar. The next step was taken when the city councils of Valencia, Calabozo, and Caracas refused to obey the Liberator's orders and demanded that he

42 Cartas: Vol. IX. p. 216.

be forbidden to cross the Venezuelan borders. He was proclaimed a tyrant, a hypocrite, a man of vaulting ambition whose name should be obliterated.[43] Páez should assume leadership, for he held the people's confidence. At this point Páez dropped his pretense, and by taking an oath constituting Venezuela an independent state, he gave his approval to the perfidy of Bolivar's erstwhile supporters. This act of public defiance was followed by a personal challenge. Páez wrote Bolivar that he was ready to defend Venezuelan sovereignty by arms. If the Liberator cared to oppose him, guerrilla warfare would flame up just as it had fifteen years ago. He went so far as to threaten, in a veiled manner, that Venezuela might again become the prey of the Spaniards.[44] Bolivar's grief and disillusion upon learning of Páez' infamous conduct were indescribable. "I have never suffered so much," he cries, "and I long for the moment when this life, now become so ignominious, may end."[45] Bolivar blamed the ministers and their monarchistic intrigue for the catastrophe. Urdaneta especially irritated him, and during these weeks Bolivar withdrew from him entirely.

The cabinet refused to bear the onus of events and resigned. It would seem that Bolivar and his ministers were equally deluded by the illusion that the Colombian Republic might still be saved. The cabinet would rescue the state by means of a dangerous operation, the introduction of monarchy; Bolivar would preserve the Republic by embalming it in the stagnating bonds of a protectorate. When Bolivar returned to Bogotá early in 1830 he chose a new cabinet. He was not ready even yet to admit that the game was up, and prepared himself once more to attempt the impossible with the new legislative assembly. On January 15 he entered the capital for the last time. The streets were adorned in festival array, but the crowd was silent; they seemed to feel that they were attending the obsequies of the Republic. When, at last, Bolivar rode by, everyone was shocked by his ill and exhausted appearance. Pale, with sunken

43 Blanco: Doc. Vol. XIII. pp. 714 ff., 722, 723. Vol. XIV. pp. 12 ff.
44 See, Páez' letter to Bolivar in Blanco: Doc. Vol. XIV. pp. 29, 54.
45 Cartas: Vol. IX. p. 227.

eyes and scarcely audible voice, he gave unmistakable evidence of the imminence of death.[46]

The new Congress, Colombia's third constitutional assembly in ten years, has been called *el admirable* because its sixty-seven deputies numbered many patriotic and honest names among them. Bolivar attended the election of the president when Parliament opened on January 20. Sucre's election was pleasing to Bolivar, and he congratulated the deputies on their decision, calling the marshal the most worthy general of the Republic. This estimate of Sucre was entirely just, but Urdaneta, nevertheless, felt a deep resentment.

Sucre delivered Bolivar's message to Congress after the Liberator had retired. The former President said, in brief, that it had been his ambition to present the Republic intact to the National Assembly; the rebellion in the South had been crushed and the war with Peru ended. The Venezuelan mutiny had overthrown his calculations, but he, nevertheless, expected the National Assembly to prepare a constitution for the entire Republic, and he promised to accept it. "Believe me, a new president is necessary to the Republic. The nation wants to know whether I shall ever cease to rule." The language of Bolivar's message is more measured, more moderate, than the expressions of his earlier years. He avoided any display of his profound pessimism and deep melancholy, except in the last paragraph. The account of his dictatorship is followed by these words: "Citizens, I blush to admit that independence is the one good that we have achieved at the expense of everything else."[47] The situation in South America in 1830 cannot be defined more exactly.

In another proclamation issued on the same day, Bolivar addressed the Colombians: "Today I have ceased to rule. Listen to my last words. At the moment when my political career comes to an end, I implore and demand in the name of Colombia that you remain united."

46 Posada Gutiérrez: Vol. I. p. 340.
47 Proclamas: p. 398.

Parliament did not accept Bolivar's resignation, but on this occasion it was motivated by practical considerations only. Congress made it clear that the principles of the Constitution must first be promulgated, that until these fundamentals were accepted, Colombia's destiny depended on individual men. Bolivar, they said, had committed himself to the presidency until the time when the new constitution should be formulated and a new president should be elected. Bolivar was, in other words, not indispensable, but he filled a temporary need.[48]

Bolivar still believed that he could persuade Páez and Soublette to accept peaceful submission, and he asked Parliament to give him permission to meet Páez at the frontier. Remembering Bolivar's mistakes of 1827, the deputies refused the request, giving the diplomatic excuse that the president should remain in the capital while the constitution was still under consideration. In this way Bolivar was spared the disgrace of having his proffered hand rejected by Páez.

In the meantime the effort to establish an independent state had made rapid progress in Venezuela. Páez had called a constitutional assembly to meet in April and did not, under the circumstances, wish to involve himself in premature negotiations with New Granada on any matters except the problem of boundaries.

The work of the constitutional assembly in Bogotá was conditioned by Páez' attitude. The new Constitution was inspired by liberal principles somewhat like the principles which underlay the Cucutá Constitution of 1821. Two basic problems, however, bore heavily on all decisions regarding the future of Colombia: would the assembly adhere to the idea of Greater Colombia after the secession of Venezuela, since it might appear that they were drawing up a constitution for a state in the process of disintegration; and, secondly, whom should they choose to lead the nation in this new era? Both problems were of profound importance to Bolivar, but he realized that it would be impossible for him to continue in office. Recognizing the

48 Blanco: Doc. Vol. XIV. p. 123.

imminence of a physical and psychological collapse, he asked for a temporary retirement. Permission was granted and Bolivar was allowed to choose his successor.

On March 1, after naming General Caicedo as Acting President, Bolivar dropped the reins of government never to seize them again and withdrew to a farm near Bogotá. Although the attacks of his mortal illness increased and although he knew that he lacked the strength to guide the affairs of the nation, he was again and again to feel the magical attraction of politics. About the middle of March news indicating the complete decline of the Republic reached Bogotá. A regiment, quartered in the coastal region, had deserted, and its commanding officer had placed himself under Páez' command. Bolivar's first thought was to take up his office again, believing that his dictatorship would avert greater calamity. He did not realize that he lacked support for this venture, that his colleagues of 1828 were now estranged from him and his views. He was still confident that Urdaneta, Herrán, París, and Castillo y Rada would follow his lead; accordingly, he invited them to a conference at his place of retirement.[49] This memorable meeting took place on the twentieth of March. Bolivar proposed that he should assume authority and declare war on the Venezuelan secessionists. The gentlemen ventured to say that such a war would be unpopular; the separation of Venezuela was a fact and should be accepted as such. It was quite clear that the majority was opposed to the plan. Up to this moment Urdaneta had remained silent, and Bolivar now turned to him for an expression of his opinion. But this was Urdaneta's opportunity to take his revenge. He had never forgotten that Bolivar had called Sucre the most worthy of all the generals, and he also resented Bolivar's accusation that he, Urdaneta, was responsible for the chaotic state of the Republic. He gave Bolivar a vehement and cruel answer. The separation from Venezuela, he said, had been consummated as early as 1827, when Bolivar himself had sounded the death knell of the Republic by pardoning Páez.

49 Cartas: Vol. IX. p. 252. Restrepo: H. d. R. C. Vol. IV. p. 299.

Bolivar could not refute the accusation; moreover, he was without support from his former friends. Castillo y Rada, after excusing himself from the meeting, had sent a letter which the Liberator now read, his voice trembling with fury as he apprehended its contents. Renounce the power forever, his former prime minister advised; the separation from Venezuela is a fact; the war you contemplate would be unpopular; the issue must be faced, and an independent government for New Granada must be constituted—a government without Bolivar! In his rage Bolivar heaped accusations and reproaches on his erstwhile co-workers. They would have him desert the wheel of state—but he would not go; he would stay in spite of them, in spite of everything! The meeting broke up without having reached any decision. Returning to Bogotá through the fog and rain, the politicians felt that they had been in attendance at the agony of a great man.[50]

There were many who feared that Bolivar might attempt to seize dictatorship even without political reassurances, relying entirely upon the army. Those who entertained this fear wanted Bolivar to leave the country; they would have considered his death a dispensation of Providence. Insulting references to the Liberator appeared in the press; in Bogotá slanderous remarks again spread from house to house, from street corner to street corner. The government was, however, on the watch, and was prepared to deal with any attempt to attack him.

By this time the government recognized the futility of any effort to stem the general current of opinion and decided to embark upon the peaceful dissolution of Greater Colombia. Congress debated a suggestion that New Granada voluntarily reject the Greater Colombian idea, and the government adopted this solution, declaring that the promulgated Constitution should be valid only for the provinces of New Granada. The funeral bell had sounded for Bolivar's political dream.

It was only logical that the question of the Liberator's succession in the presidency should likewise be solved in an anti-

50 Posada Gutiérrez: Vol. II. p. 38.

Colombian, or rather, an anti-Bolivarian fashion. For the last
time Bolivar tried to impose his own name for the presidency.
All the high officials and politicians were summoned to a meeting that should proclaim him the national candidate. In order
to maintain an appearance of impartiality Bolivar refrained
from attending the meeting and confidently awaited the commission in his country house. But the delegation which brought
him the report brought his crushing defeat. Not only had the
meeting refused to proclaim him President, but it had also
deemed it wise to inform him that his continued residence in
the capital of New Granada was a threat to domestic peace.
The painful message was delivered by old friends of Bolivar—
Caicedo, Herrán, Baralt—but Bolivar treated them as enemies,
personally interested in his dismissal. He completely lost control of himself, but the delegation was not intimidated. Finally,
Bolivar asked what his position would be after he had declined
the presidency, and they answered that he would always be the
first citizen of Colombia.[51]

Slowly Bolivar recovered his self-control, and his wrath gave
way to a melancholic resignation. A moving report of one of
these last days in his political death struggle was written by his
friend, Colonel Posada Gutiérrez: "One afternoon we went for
a walk across the beautiful meadow of the estate. Bolivar's gait
was slow and weary; his voice was scarcely audible; only with
difficulty could he make himself understood. We walked along
the banks of a brook that wound through the silent landscape.
With folded arms Bolivar contemplated the current, image of
human life. 'How much time,' he said, 'it takes for this water
to mix with the infinite ocean, even as man in the decomposition of the grave mixes with the earth from which he comes—
some part evaporates like human glory. . . .' And suddenly,
with his hands pressing his temples, he cried in a trembling
voice, 'My glory, my glory! Why do they destroy it? Why
do they calumniate me?' "[52]

51 Cartas: Vol. IX. pp. 254-55. Restrepo: H. d. R. C. Vol. IV. p. 309. Posada
Gutiérrez: Vol. II. p. 51.
52 Posada Gutiérrez: Vol. I. p. 370.

On April 27 he said farewell to his countrymen. "The common good of the fatherland demands my separation from the country that has given me life in order that my presence may not prove a hindrance to the well-being of my compatriots." On May 4 his political fate was sealed. The Constitution had been accepted, and Congress proceeded with the election of a president. Not a single vote was cast for Bolivar; even his choice of a successor was passed over, Joaquín Mosquera being elected. Santander had triumphed over Bolivar in Bogotá, as Páez had triumphed in Caracas.

Everyone was aware that Bolivar was to be exiled. The order was embellished with courteous words and was even accompanied by a pension, but it was exile, nevertheless. The few days left to Bolivar in Bogotá were days of excitement. On learning of his resignation, one part of the army mutinied and marched toward Venezuela, and the students of the capital blamed Bolivar for the event. There was some fear that a repetition of September 25 might be attempted. Bolivar's last night in Bogotá was a sleepless one. The head of the government and the ministers remained with him to prevent any attack. On the morning of May 8, accompanied by his ministers, his officers, the diplomats, and many foreigners, Bolivar took his departure from Bogotá. As the cavalcade disappeared in the mists of the high plateau, the English minister said, "He is gone, the gentleman of Colombia!"[53]

Two letters reflect the emotions of this hour of farewell; the first is from Bolivar to Manuela. "My beloved one, I am glad to tell you that I feel well, but I am filled with your grief and my own over our separation. My beloved, I love you very much, and I shall love you much more if you will now be more reasonable than ever before. Be careful what you do, or you may ruin yourself, and that means both of us. I am always your devoted lover, Bolivar."[54]

53 Larrazabal: Vol. II. p. 540. Posada Gutiérrez: Vol. II. pp. 66, 73. P. M. Ibañez: Crónicas de Bogotá. Bogotá, 1891. p. 311.
54 Cartas: Vol. IX. p. 265.

The second letter is from Sucre to Bolivar. "When I came to your house to accompany you, you had already departed. Perhaps this was just as well, since I was spared the pain of a bitter farewell. In this hour, my heart oppressed, I do not know what to say to you. Words cannot express the feeling of my soul, but you know my emotions, for you have known me a long time. And you know that it was not your power that inspired the warmest feeling in me, but your friendship. I shall always preserve that friendship whatever destiny awaits us, and I flatter myself that you will keep the opinion you have had of me. I shall endeavor to be worthy of it under every circumstance. Adieu, my general. Receive as a token of friendship these tears shed for your absence. Be happy wherever you may be, and wherever you are you may count on your faithful and devoted, Sucre."[55] Bolivar, already on his way to exile, answered, "If it gave you pain to write to me, what shall I say, who leave not only my friends, but my country . . .?" The night of tragedy began to cast its shadows over these two great heroes of South American liberty.

With the culmination of Bolivar's career as a statesman, it seems necessary to say a last word about his political achievements. Bolivar gave up political action at the moment when he realized that he could no longer serve his ideas of political greatness. His resignation and the disintegration of Greater Colombia coincide and condition each other. Bolivar's rule was never aimed at the satisfaction of selfish desire, nor did it pander to a hollow lust for power. He had hoped to carry out a political conception, and when he saw that he had failed, he surrendered —with hesitation and reluctantly it is true, but without resorting to the force which was at his disposal. This is the great difference between Bolivar and Napoleon and between Bolivar and all the dictators of the twentieth century. It is useless to deny that he was ambitious and authoritarian, but even from a democratic standpoint he can be reproached only for an intention to remain in power against the will of the people, but not for

55 Cartas: Vol. IX. p. 268.

the realization of this intention. One can make this statement in regard to few great statesmen of world history.

Bolivar failed as a politician because his ideas did not coincide with the most deep-seated instincts and desires of the nations liberated by him. He had intended to lead Hispano-America out of the war as it had entered the war, a united and solid whole. From this desire had sprung his projects of a Greater Colombia, a League of South American nations, a Federation of the Andes. Knowing that the masses of the continent were politically too immature to comprehend his conception, he had tried to train them by means of an educational dictatorship.[56] He was republican only as far as form was concerned; he did not accept the essential significance of the concept. Ultimately it was his belief that only a military and authoritarian regime could give stability to South America, and his dream of a South American superstate demanded this stability. But the South American nations agreed to ideas of federation and league only so long as the emergency of war required them. Temperamentally they found such ideas unbearable. These are the deep lying reasons for Bolivar's downfall, and to have a clear picture of this period of disintegration it is necessary to understand them.

It has been pointed out that the immense distances, the many difficulties encountered in the tropics, were obstacles to the creation of such a realm as Bolivar envisioned. Other observers remind us of the lack of common economic interests and a trained bureaucracy. These facts are indisputable, but they do not constitute the decisive factor in Bolivar's failure. The final reason for the disintegration of the Liberator's various forms of union was the people's refusal to be organized in any supernational entity. The decomposition of the Spanish Empire was followed closely by the awakening of South American nationalism, and Bolivar's lack of success is directly attributable to this fact. The South American nations were averse to any kind

56 A. Miyares: El Libertador como Político. B. d. H. Caracas. Vol. XIV. No. 53. p. 14.

of political organization that might interfere with their individual interests or rights. Bolivar thought they would hold together as a conglomerate, but the relationship of Argentina, Chile, Peru, New Granada, and the others was scarcely more than an agglomerate.

Paradoxical as it may seem, this decisive trend toward nationalism is an inheritance of Spanish rule. Each of the new South American republics had been an administrative unit from the sixteenth to the eighteenth century, and nothing gives more force to the rise of nationalism than a common destiny experienced under one public administration. The histories of Germany, Switzerland, and Austria bear out this statement. In these countries the same language, the same racial background, and often the same religion prevailed, but each felt itself to be a national entity. In South America, similarly, the hammer of Spanish administration had forged nationalities whose inclinations were inward rather than outward. Bolivar attempted to disregard these inherent truths. He believed he could disregard the Spanish inheritance in this field as he had disregarded it in so many others, but the tendencies of the popular will resisted all his efforts and finally strangled his dream of greatness.

It may well be that South America visualized its destiny more clearly than Bolivar. Historical greatness does not consist in territorial expansion, a fact borne out in the case of the Scandinavian nations, which also refused to form a political bloc. South America paralleled this attitude; the nations of the south Western Hemisphere cultivate their individual lives with a certain jealous love, but on the whole have remained free from aversions or territorial appetites in regard to their neighbors, and today there is even a feeling of solidarity among them which, including the United States in its scope, links them all in the bonds of a common destiny. They have returned to Bolivar's idea of an American league, or better, they have taken more progressive steps toward this end. Bolivar's ideas have undergone a metamorphosis; in a truly dialectical process, they have become converted and today embrace all the South

American nations as equal and sovereign states. Bolivar tried to omit this intermediary phase, an omission which resulted in the frustration of his entire plan.

As for the internal organization of the state, very much the same criticism may be made. Bolivar's superstate declined because his constitutional ideas were not in harmony with the claims and pretensions of the social groups that pressed forward to gain their share of power. Bolivar considered the revolution concluded when he assumed the supreme title of President; these groups, however, were unprepared and averse to any conclusion which presented them with an inelastic solution like the Bolivian Constitution.

The two tendencies which were in conflict in South America during the nineteenth century are today still in open battle for the domination of the continent. On one side there is *caudillisimo* or the personal leadership of talented or merely brutal men; on the other side is the desire to introduce a well-regulated constitutional life according to legal norms. Páez and Santander were the embodiments of these two tendencies, and neither could find Bolivar's projects acceptable; each would have preferred anarchy to Bolivar's conception of order and stability. Thus for the span of a century South America became the continent of permanent revolution, the continent of pronunciamentos and rebellions, where little groups disputed among themselves for the leading position in the state. Bolivar had foreseen this development. His diagnosis had been correct, but the remedies he produced were not effective. Today, 118 years after his death, the process has not been terminated. South American democracy continues in a state of ferment.

Bolivar's frustration as a statesman derives from the wide discrepancy between his plans and South American reality. All his ideas were based on the power of his personal prestige; they would become untenable at his death. Only if he had resolved to ignore Rousseau and follow Napoleon might he have succeeded in founding an empire. The glory of the Liberator, however, remained for him a higher reward than the title of Emperor.

The dilemma of Bolivar's life continued to be what it had been since the days of his adolescence in Paris. A contemporary French writer formulated it in these words: *L'empire de la liberté, ou la liberté de l'empire.*[57] So it was in the days of Colombia's disintegration, and so it had been since the day when he had first seen Napoleon. Twenty-six years after he had resolved to win glory through freedom, he was obliged to acknowledge that there was but one way for him to preserve his reputation as Liberator—the way of resignation and dispassionate forbearance.

57 J. M. Aguirre: *op. cit.*, p. 357.

Death and Transfiguration

*A*fter eleven years as President, Bolivar retired to private life a poor man. Before he left Bogotá he sold his silver, his horses, and some of his jewels for seventeen thousand pesos, a sum representing only a part of his former annual income.[1] The copper mines of Aroa were all that remained, and as things went in Venezuela, Bolivar feared that his titles to even these last possessions would not be recognized by the new government. "They say that my ownership of the property is not legal, and that for a man in my position there are no laws; in other words they consider me a canaille. I don't need anything for myself, or at least very little, for I am accustomed to a military life. However, the honor of my country and my position alike oblige me to appear decently, especially since it is known that I was born to wealth."[2] Bolivar wrote these words while he was resting in a little village on one of the first days of his strenuous voyage. He was still undecided whether to go to Europe or to find refuge in the Antilles. His material situation bordered on indigence if compared to his former affluent state, but, as a matter of fact, he was far from being a beggar. Parliament had granted him a yearly pension of thirty thousand pesos for life, and he travelled accompanied by aides and servants.[3]

1 Posada Gutiérrez: Vol. II. p. 71.
2 Cartas: Vol. IX. p. 209. Lecuna: Papeles. Vol. II. pp. 153, 157. Cartas: Vol. IX. p. 263.
3 J. I. Méndez: El Ocaso de Bolívar. Santa Marta, 1927. p. 42.

681

His journey led him down through the Magdalena Valley to the burning plains of Mariquita, where he remained for a few days to recover from the fatigue of his long ride. As was his custom in better days, he bathed regularly in the fresh cold springs. Reminded by one of his officers that Alexander had died after taking a bath, Bolivar smiling replied, "When Alexander went into a cold bath, all flushed, he was at the peak of his glory. Such a danger does not exist for me. Besides, some attribute his death to Antipater, who poisoned him as Santander tried to murder me."[4]

In the meantime a ship had been prepared for Bolivar; a tent protected him from the parching heat, and a second boat with provisions followed at a distance. Bolivar stood at the bow of the ship, hat in hand, and waved goodbye to his friends. The river rapidly bore him away toward the Atlantic coast.

His state of health on arrival at Turbaco on May 25 was lamentable, and the heat of the coast only aggravated his illness. He went from Turbaco to Cartagena, where he hoped to board an English ship. The commander of Cartagena implored him not to abandon Colombia, asking him if he wanted to live like a beggar abroad. "If I don't die during the voyage, the British will not let me die of hunger. Besides Colombia wanted it this way."[5] Circumstances prevented his departure, however; one boat had no space for him; another planned a route that did not coincide with his wishes. And so it was that he stayed in Cartagena for a few weeks.[6]

The downfall of the Republic became more certain from day to day. The plains of Casanare had withdrawn from New Granada and had joined Venezuela; in the South the cunning Flores had proclaimed the independence of Ecuador. The state of complete anarchy, prophesied by Bolivar, had arrived, the breach of all the legal and international principles that had, until this moment, been valid in South America. On May 13

4 Posada Gutiérrez: Vol. II. p. 92
5 Posada Gutiérrez: Vol. II. p. 189.
6 Méndez: pp. 54-55. Groot: Vol. V. p. 376.

the independence of Ecuador was decided; on June 4 Sucre was murdered.[7]

The news that the Marshal of Ayacucho had been slain in the Berrecuos Mountains reached Bolivar on the night of July 1, as he sat alone, meditating on the frustration of his hopes. Sucre had been President of Congress, but he had had no further ambitions. He wanted to serve the state only as long as he knew what course the ship was taking. As early as 1829 he had written to Bolivar, "I do not refuse to serve the state, but I wish to know the system and the aim. For a long time we have been without both, and I am too tired and too ill to work at hazard." His proposal in Congress that for the next four years no commanding general should be elected president or vice-president was a clear demonstration of his self-abnegation. His ideas were liberal; he was generous and good, and it would seem that he was hated and pursued only because of his virtues. There were only too many rascals and scoundrels to whom a man like Sucre was a thorn in the flesh.[8] His talents were so brilliant, his merits so undeniable, that sooner or later he would be chosen as president. Bolivar's enemies were not through when they had accomplished his exile; they were still faced with the necessity of destroying the heir.

The plot against Sucre's life was planned carefully and in cold blood. The assassins knew that he would hurry from Bogotá to Quito by the shortest route, and Obando, the commander of Pasto, laid the trap along this way. The murderers were so sure of the success of their plans that four days before they struck one Bogotá newspaper actually published the following sentence: "Perhaps Obando does to Sucre what we have not done to Bolivar."[9] The rumor of an impending attack on Sucre spread through the country, and his friends warned him of the approaching danger, advising him to choose another road

7 Restrepo: H. d. R. C. Vol. IV. p. 333. Blanco: Doc. Vol. XIV. p. 235.

8 Larrazabal: Vol. II. p. 548. See, N. A. González: El Asesinato del gran Mariscal de Ayacucho. Bogotá, 1908.

9 El Democrata. Bogotá, June 1, 1830. E. Posada: El crimen de Berruecos. B. d. H. Bogotá. Vol. XXX. p. 326.

to Quito. But Sucre only laughed; he could not imagine that anyone had murderous designs on him. On a distant mountain path in the midsts of the forests of Pasto he was shot on June 4. For one whole day his body lay in the mud: then, without ceremonies, he was buried at a hidden spot.

No satisfactory explanation of this crime has ever been found. It has been said that the murderer had personal motives; others hold that Sucre's wife was responsible. But none of these explanations stands a critical test. Sucre's assassination was a political act, and the demagogues of Bogotá, the generals, Flores and Obando, and the groups of bravos serving as instruments for the more powerful men behind the curtain, were directly responsible.[10]

On hearing the news, Bolivar cried, "My God, they have shed the blood of Abel!" And so it was; Cain had risen and had slain his gentle brother. On that same night, ignorant of Flores' guilt, Bolivar wrote to him: "It is impossible to live in a country where the most famous generals are cruelly and barbarously murdered, the very men to whom America owes its freedom. . . . I believe that the purpose of the crime was to deprive the fatherland of my successor. . . . I can no longer serve under such a country; I shall go to Venezuela."[11]

But Venezuela was no better. In his native country all the hatred of vicious demagogy turned against the Liberator himself. Not only was an attempt made to strip him of his property, but the National Assembly, in session at Caracas since May, indulged in outright slander and vituperation. The dissolution of Colombia was decided, and the deputies informed New Granada that they would consider an alliance only after Bolivar had been expelled from the realm. In a final cruel and unwarranted measure the National Assembly proscribed him and declared him outlawed wherever he might be.[12] Bolivar would

10 Martínez Delgado: Sucre. Bogotá, 1945. López Contreras: Sucre. p. 107. J. B. Pérez y Soto: El crimen de Berruecos. Vols. I-IV. Rome, 1924-26.
    11 Cartas: Vol. IX. pp. 279, 281.
    12 Anales de Venezuela. Vols. VI, VII. Caracas, 1891. Blanco: Doc. Vol. XIV. p. 184. D. Carbonell: 1830. Paris, 1931. p. 47.

have learned of the ignominious resolutions early enough, but the secretary for the interior in Bogotá took great pleasure in communicating them to Bolivar by official letter. It was Dr. Azuero, whom he had offended in 1819 and had sent into exile after September 25, who now took his revenge. According to Keyserling, South America is the world at the third day of creation, and the scorpion belongs to the general picture of hatred and persecution.[13]

Bolivar did not stoop to answer Azuero, but the resolutions of Caracas were all he needed to give up the fight definitely. "I cannot live among murderers and rebels. I have no honor among such scum and no tranquility under their menace."[14] There was no relief from the grief that corroded his heart. It was nothing to him that the people of Quito invited him to take up his residence there; it was of no consequence that Bolivia offered him the post of ambassador to the Vatican. The words of his sister fell on deaf ears when she wrote from Caracas that the whole nation called for him, that the clergy sided with him and claimed the Liberator, Simon Bolivar, as their father. María Antonia wrote at the same time that the persecution was intense, that she was in fear of death, and that many believed the family of the Liberator should be exterminated root and branch. There was indeed no consolation for him. Even a sudden turn of politics left him cold; he was by now, like the dead, inaccessible to both good and evil.

For the last time the seducer approached him, tempting him with offers to return to politics. In June a group of Venezuelan officers had asked him to work for the preservation of unity in Colombia, and a little later they offered him the presidency. In Bogotá there remained an influential group which based all its hopes on the return of the Liberator. Manuela was behind this move. Bolivar had implored her to be cautious, but he might as well have asked the Magdalena River to be cautious.

13 Méndez: pp. 68 ff. Los últimos días del Libertador. B. d. H. Caracas. Vol. XXV. No. 100. p. 290.
14 Cartas: Vol. IX. p. 321.

When the government demanded that she return the Bolivar archives which she held in her possession, she refused and asked to see the law that had outlawed the Liberator. She fomented scandals; she distributed leaflets glorifying Bolivar.[15] In this way public opinion was gradually prepared for the counter-revolution which should return Bolivar to the palace.

Urdaneta became the head of the plot, and the regiment of El Callao, composed of veterans from Junín and Ayacucho, rose against the government in Bogotá. The resistance of the government was ineffectual, and the surrender to the counterrevolution was inevitable. On September 5 the President and Vice-President resigned, and a commission was immediately sent to Bolivar in Cartagena asking him to return and take charge of the presidency.[16] His friends overwhelmed him with letters; the ambassadors of England, the United States, and Brazil declared publicly that the Liberator alone could save Colombia. In Cartagena the military and political leaders appointed Bolivar chief of the army. He was promised complete freedom to take any measures necessary to maintain order in the Republic. But Bolivar resisted the temptation. He was, he said, still ready to serve his country, but the spasmodic movement in his favor formed no basis for his return to the presidency.[17] All such action was marked with the stigma of anarchy against which he had always fought. Urdaneta, who now urged his return, had but five months previously opposed his continuance in office. Bolivar expected nothing of a constructive nature to come from these uprisings, nothing for himself and nothing for the Republic. "I am old, ill, tired, disappointed, grieved, calumniated, and badly paid. Believe me I have never looked upon uprisings with friendly eyes, and during these last days I have even repented of those we undertook against the Spaniards"—a terrible confession which is saved for later comment. "All my reasoning comes to the same conclusion; I have no hope of

15 Rumazo: pp. 250-51. E. Posada: B. d. H. Bogotá. Vol. XVII. p. 237.
16 Restrepo: H. d. R. C. Vol. IV. p. 367.
17 Proclamas: p. 406.

saving the fatherland. This feeling, or rather, this conviction, strangles my wishes and surrenders me to desperation. I am of the opinion that everything is lost forever. . . . If it were only a case of making a sacrifice, even were it my happiness, or my life, or my honor, believe me, I should not hesitate. But I am convinced that such a sacrifice would be useless, for to change a world is beyond a poor man's power, and since I am incapable of establishing the happiness of my country, I refuse to rule it. Moreover, the tyrants of my country have expelled and outlawed me; thus I have no country to which I could render sacrifices."[18]

For the first time in his life Bolivar was definitely resigned. Nothing had meaning; all was futile. Perhaps the whole movement for independence had been premature. Sometimes his grief swept him into overstatements, as when he said he was sorry he had ever undertaken the liberation of South America. Miranda had died in a Spanish prison; San Martín was in exile; Sucre lay murdered; he himself, on this burning and sterile coast, was outlawed and waiting for death. Of what avail had been the twenty years of war and revolution? "We have ploughed the sea" was his bitter conclusion.[19]

It is more than likely that a premonition of his approaching collapse was primarily responsible for Bolivar's tragic resignation. The inroads of his disease had become more marked since the middle of October, and in spite of the heat of the equatorial sun, he went wrapped in wool from head to foot and the least movement cost him great effort. He now demanded a physician, but since he still refused to take any remedies, there was little hope for improvement in his condition. The courtesy and exquisite amiability that had characterized him in better

18 Cartas: Vol. IX. pp. 323-27 of September 25, 1830.
19 Groot: Vol. V. p. 368. With the following words Bolivar concluded his political career: "La América es ingobernable. Los que han servido a la Revolución han arrado en el mar. La única cosa que se puede hacer en América es emigrar. Estos países caerán infaliblemente en manos de la multitud desenfrenada para después pasar a los tiranuelos casi imperceptibles de todos las colores y razas, devorados por los crímenes y extinguidos por la ferocidad. Los Europeos tal vez no se dignarán conquistarlos. So fuera posible que una parte del mundo volviera al caos primitivo, éste sería el último período de América.

times continued to distinguish him throughout these weeks in Barranquilla. But his cough was continuous, his voice slow, his walk uncertain. Occasionally he tried to revive his natural vigor by taking wine or some other stimulant, but the ensuing exhaustion cancelled any strength he might have gained.[20] In spite of his prostration, he continued his correspondence. He advised Urdaneta, he admonished others to be obedient and conciliatory, but his words were written with daily diminishing force. "I would inspire pity even in my enemies. I am only a living skeleton."

By the irony of fate, Bolivar found his last refuge in the house of a Spaniard. Joaquín de Mier, an admirer of the Liberator, offered him his hacienda, San Pedro Alejandrín, in the neighborhood of Santa Marta, for residence, and at the beginning of December, Bolivar embarked on his journey to this last sanctuary. It almost seems that destiny herself had arranged the final scene of Bolivar's life with the hand of a great artist. The setting of Santa Marta was perfect. There was a small bay, with sapphire blue waters, protected by mountains; and along the shore tall palms bent to the will of the December breeze. The old Spanish forts still watched over the harbor, and high up through the cover of clouds could occasionally be seen the white and shining peaks of the Sierra Nevada.

Bolivar arrived at this refuge on December 1 and met here the French physician, Dr. Reverend, who attended him until the end. Bolivar was carried from the ship. He was no longer able to walk; his voice was husky, and his general state betrayed the presence of death. Dr. Reverend diagnosed his illness as an advanced stage of tuberculosis and recognized that there was no hope of a cure. Dr. Night, who also saw Bolivar upon his arrival, agreed with Dr. Reverend's opinion.[21]

20 Diario de Barranquilla. B. d. H. Caracas. Vol. XXVI. No. 103. p. 258. Carbonell: 1830. p. 167.

21 A. P. Reverend: La última Enfermedad, los últimos Momentos y los Funerales de Simón Bolívar. Paris, 1866. F. Bolívar: Los últimos Días del Libertador. B. d. H. Caracas. Vol. XXV. No. 100. p. 298. There has been a heated controversy in regard to Bolivar's mortal illness. Some historians accuse Reverend for the responsibility of

On December 7 Bolivar journeyed to San Pedro Alejandrín, some miles distant from Santa Marta. The hacienda was a small one where sugar cane was cultivated. Simple white buildings, with modest rooms and rural furniture, were set in the midst of a magnificent garden. The tamarinds of San Pedro Alejandrín are extraordinarily beautiful, but it is unlikely that Bolivar was able to enjoy them. Each day made it clearer that his end was near.

Bolivar still gave evidence of his innate sensitivity. One of his friends who enjoyed smoking a pipe was asked to sit farther and farther away from the bed. A little hurt, the officer finally said, "My general, the odor of tobacco never irritated you when it came from Manuela." "Ah, then . . ." answered Bolivar sadly. He objected also to the smell of hospital and drugs that clung to his doctor and the apothecary, drugs that he obstinately refused to take. Dr. Reverend soon saw that remedies were useless and did not prescribe them any longer. Bolivar asked him why he had come to America. "For the sake of liberty," answered the Frenchman. "And have you found it here?" "Certainly, Your Excellency." "Oh, then you have been more fortunate than I. You should return to your beautiful France where the glorious tricolor flutters. In this country you can't live; there are too many scoundrels." At another time he talked of going to France with Dr. Reverend—to France, where liberty again prevailed.[22]

The moments of exhaustion grew to hours, and symptoms of the fatal euphoria of consumptives became evident. In his delirious dreams Bolivar spoke of his recovery. His nephew, Ferdinand Bolivar, informed Montilla of the advance of the disease, and sent for musicians to entertain him. On December 10 the bishop of Santa Marta visited him and admonished him to put his house in order. Bolivar realized at last that he was

---

his death. However, agreeing with Lópes de Mesa and Carbonell, I can see no reason for questioning Reverend's diagnosis. R. Chacón: La última Enfermedad del Libertador. Caracas, 1883. and F. Gnecco Mozo: El médico del Libertador. B. d. H. Bogotá. Vol. XVIII. p. 741. attack Reverend's diagnosis.

22 Reverend: pp. 28, 29.

lost and drew up his will. He provided lavishly for his butler, who had served him for many years; Sucre's sword, a gift from the marshal, was returned to the latter's heirs; the golden medal received from Bolivia was to be returned to the republic that bore his name. All papers that might have been harmful to Urdaneta and his government were ordered burned. The bulk of his fortune was left to his sisters and their children. He expressed the desire to be buried in Caracas.[23] Finally he confessed and received the last sacrament. The significance of this last act has been frequently discussed, but since no one except the priest attended Bolivar's confession, it would be daring to venture a judgment. One can only say that Bolivar died in the rites and ceremonies of the Catholic church as he had lived by them.[24]

There remained but one thing to do—he must say farewell to Colombia. Perhaps his last words, spoken from his death bed, might put an end to the fratricidal war. On December 11 he wrote General Briceño, "I write these lines in the last moments of my life, to ask you for the only proof of friendship and estimation that you can still give me. I ask you to reconcile yourself sincerely with General Urdaneta and to join him in supporting the present government of Colombia. My heart assures me that you will not deny me this last honor. Only by sacrificing our personal feelings can we protect our friends and Colombia from the horrors of anarchy." This letter breathes the magnanimity that was an inherent part of Bolivar's nature and requires no comment. Those writers who recount that Bolivar also said during these last days that Jesus Christ, Don Quixote, and he were the three greatest fools of history seem to ignore the discrepancy between his last serious thoughts and the melodramatic nonsense of such a remark. Bolivar's mind was at this time tuned to affairs of greater import.[25]

In his room were Generals Montilla and Silva; the Spaniard,

23 Cartas: Vol. IX. p. 411. See also, the letter of Bolivar's aide, Wilson. B. d. H. Caracas. Vol. XV. No. 57. p. 38.

24 N. E. Navarro: Anales de la Universidad de Venezuela. November, December, 1930.

25 Cartas: Vol. IX. pp. 410-11. The inventor of this poor story was probably R. Palma: *op. cit.* The account is certainly not veracious, because Bolivar uses the

De Mier; his nephew, Ferdinand; and Dr. Reverend. Propped up in bed, Bolivar asked his secretary to read his last message:

"Colombians, You have witnessed my efforts to establish Liberty where formerly Tyranny prevailed. I have labored unselfishly, sacrificing both my fortune and my tranquillity. When I became convinced that you distrusted the integrity of my intentions, I renounced my power. My enemies have abused your credulity and trampled upon that which I held most sacred—my reputation and my love of liberty. I have been sacrificed to my persecutors; they have brought me to the brink of the grave. I forgive them.

"At this moment of my departure from among you, my heart tells me that I should express my last wishes. I aspire to no other glory than the consolidation of Colombia. Everyone should work for the inestimable benefits of unity. . . . Colombians, my last wishes are for the happiness of my country. If my death can contribute anything toward the reconciliation of the parties or the unification of the country, I shall go to my grave in peace."[26]

Bolivar's moving farewell brought tears to his friends, but he had not finished. "To my grave," he repeated, "this is where they have brought me, but I forgive them. I wish to God I could have the consolation that they will remain united." In these last words of Bolivar the picture of the hero is completed. Here the Liberator wins his victory over all selfish ambition, and here we see the restoration of those great ideals for which the war for independence had been fought. The proclamation of San Pedro Alejandrín sounds the final resolving chords in the symphony of his life.

His physical agony was drawn out for seven more days. In his delirium he spoke of his exile: "Let us go; bring my luggage on board. They do not want us in this country. Let us go." The ship that was to bear him away lay waiting in the harbor—

name of Don Quixote exclusively in a contemptible sense. See the whole Diario de Bucamaranga and his letters.

26 Proclamas: p. 407.

it was the ship of the dead. On December 17, 1830, at one
o'clock, he embarked on his final journey to a land of glory—
a glory that has grown as the shadows grow when the sun is
declining.

* * *

Bolivar was forty-seven years old when he died, a short life
when measured by the average age of man. Every life, however,
has its external and its internal span, a visible and an invisible
measure of time. The experiences of Bolivar's internal time
would crowd a century of ordinary existence. Few great men
of action have known twenty years of ceaseless activity. "I am
like the sun; I throw my rays in all directions," he said of himself.[27] So it was that the blaze of his life was extinguished more
rapidly than are those fires which smoulder endlessly. But
Bolivar, even as Raphael and Mozart, did not die young; he
died, as Zarathustra might have said, at the right time.

On December 18 Bolivar's body was sent to Santa Marta
for embalming. His shirt was torn and shabby, and General
Silva supplied one of his own in order that the Liberator of
South America should not be buried in rags. The funeral was
held in the cathedral of Santa Marta.

Only a few received the news of Bolivar's death with sorrow.
Manuela had been very confident, even in November. "The
liberals may as well give up hope," she wrote to an English
friend, "because the Liberator is immortal. He will never die
even if they should burn him. And at that, aren't they really
lucky??? Just think if he should die??? The wretched liberals. Everyone would choose the Liberator as his saint. Even
I, if I were to be so remiss as to survive him, even I would make
him my saint, and despair would perhaps drive me to all manner of rash attempts."*

When the news of his death finally came, she said she
wished to die like Cleopatra from the bite of a snake, but she
survived this desire to live a long life full of privations and

27 Cartas: Vol. X. p. 422.
* Unpublished letter, written in Guaduas, November 24, 1830.

persecutions. "I loved the Liberator when he was alive," she said, "now that he is dead, I worship him."[28]

His old comrades, O'Leary, Wilson, Perú de la Croix, and a few Colombians felt as Manuela did, but in Venezuela a persistent hatred clouded Bolívar's memory for many years. On January 21, 1831, the governor of Maracaibo reported to the minister of the interior that Bolivar, "the spirit of evil, the author of all misfortunes, the oppressor of the fatherland," had died. Twelve years passed before the family dared transport his body to Caracas. Then the dead Bolivar was finally granted the honors denied to the living man. He was brought by convoy to La Guayra, and his old comrades carried the catafalque through the streets of Caracas. The same men whose political hatred and stubbornness had poisoned his last days now indulged in high praise of his merits.[29]

New Granada had asked to keep Bolivar's heart, and in a little urn it was interred at Santa Marta. At the beginning of this century, however, historians searched for the urn in vain.[30] The incident is a symbol of that process whereby Bolivar has entered the realms of myth. His heart is not underground, confined within walls of clay; it lives and beats in every South American breast.

After Bolivar's death a transfiguration took place which may be called unique in modern history. Provinces and cities adopted his name; the public squares were adorned with monuments to his glory; he became more than a hero—a demigod or superman. Books are full of appreciation for his achievements; at celebrations in his honor, in newspapers, through loudspeakers, in churches, schools, meetings of parliament, the name of Bolivar is exalted and glorified. Even the poorest peon, who can neither read nor write—and there are still millions of them

28 Rumazo: pp. 267, 273. The legend of the beautiful Anne Lenoir who spent eighteen years waiting for Bolivar only finally to attend his funeral is another story told by Rourke: *op. cit.*, p. 358. There is absolutely no proof for it. L. A. Cuervo: Amores de Bolívar. Bogotá, 1913.

29 I. S. Alderson: Los Funerales de Bolívar. B. d. H. Caracas. Vol. XI. No. 41. p. 49.

30 Méndez: pp. 212-13.

in South America—associates something great and overwhelming with the name of Bolivar; to the ignorant soul it signifies the essence of his native soil, the destiny of the continent, and the freedom of its inhabitants. This glorification of Bolivar is exclusively lyrical and rhetorical. There is probably not one poet or writer in South America who has not composed an ode, or an essay, or an oration on the subject of the country's greatest hero. He is the foremost theme of all South American literature, from Rodó to Valencia, from Gabriela Mistral to Neruda. And it would be both foolish and undiscerning to mock this hero worship. These nations are still in the process of crystallization and the Bolivarian myth is an essential element in their development.

It is, nonetheless, quite comprehensible that even in his own continent Bolivar is more loved than understood, more extolled than analyzed. In North America and in Europe, moreover, he is scarcely known. Thirty years ago he was little more than a name in both the Old and the New World, and his figure during the nineteenth century remained in the background. Only a few recognized his greatness; Wellington; Byron; Humboldt; and Goethe, who pinned the recorded dates of Bolivar's biography on the door of his bedroom. In Paris people wore hats á la Bolivar, and a few French romanticists dedicated poems to him.[31] His life remained overshadowed, first by Napoleon and later by Cavour, Bismarck, Lincoln, and Disraeli. Neither Macaulay nor Ranke, neither Burckhardt nor Taine mentions his accomplishments, and a man of the importance of Seeley writes that the South Americans created several republics "in a moment of distraction." The only exception to this general sciolism is the great work of the German, Gervinus, *The History of the Nineteenth Century.*

Europe's blindness to Bolivar's historical greatness may be construed in several ways. In the first place, it may be explained by the failure of Bolivar's political plans. As a result of this

31 L. A. Cuervo: Notas Históricas. pp. 24-25, 68. R. Paredas Urdaneta: Simón Bolívar. Hamburg, 1930.

failure South America reverted to a chaotic condition, and
Europe came to consider the country merely as a source of raw
material. In the second place, Bolivar's complex personality
defied any exact interpretation of his character. Where was his
niche; into what category did he fit?

Bolivar was an aristocrat who had discarded class consciousness, a revolutionist who aspired to authoritarian power, a
champion of national sovereignty and self-determination who
nevertheless considered the people too immature to realize such
a concept, the liberator of a continent who repented of his
achievement, a man of action, an artist, writer, sociologist who
vacillated in his decisions like a true opportunist. Romanticist
and realist, visionary and diplomat, active and contemplative
at the same time, Bolivar is indeed not easy to catalog. Even
as a warrior Bolivar cannot be measured with discrimination.
Certain critics aver that he cannot be considered a great general
because he never encountered an adversary worthy of his steel.[32]
Such a low opinion of the Spanish generals may not be just,
but certain it is that Bolivar does not merit comparison with
Caesar or Frederick, with Napoleon or von Moltke. The history
of war would be the same if Bolivar had never fought a single
battle, yet who but Bolivar could have overcome the gigantic
difficulties of nature, of space, and of the particular people he
dealt with? He was the one man that South America needed
for the establishment of her independence. Bolivar's statement
about the war is equally true of his own personality: "This war
is like the polishing of a diamond which becomes harder and
more brilliant with every cut. . . . Really, as a theatrical spectacle there is nothing more magnificent."[33]

In contemplating Bolivar's life and in searching for parallels,
one soon becomes aware that very few comparisons fit the case.
Bolivar and Washington? Bolivar and Napoleon? Bolivar and
Cromwell? All are untenable. There is, however, a surprising
analogy between Bolivar and Winston Churchill: They are

32 F. Lorraine Petre: Simón Bolívar. New York, 1910. p. 439. See also Blanco
Fombona in Simón Bolívar. Madrid, 1914. p. 370.

33 Cartas: Vol. X. p. 422.

both the men of difficulties, of world historical emergency. Both are from old and noble families accustomed to command, and warfare is in their blood. Both are officers, yet amateurs as far as strategy is concerned; nevertheless, both were recipients of those profound intuitions that so often surpass the knowledge and wisdom of experts. Both faced desperate circumstances with unshakable belief in victory. Both at the outset of their careers committed far-reaching blunders; Churchill as well as Bolivar learned the art of victory from defeat. Both are masters of the word and artists by nature. The famous speeches of Churchill after Dunkirk are very like the orations delivered by Bolivar in Casacoima, Angostura, and Pativilca. However, a world separates the Anglo-Saxon from the Creole, the disciplined parliamentarian from the fanatical leader of tropical nations. One fought to maintain an empire, the other to destroy one from whose ruins a free continent should rise. And here we come to the last reason for the neglect that Bolivar has suffered in the nineteenth century. Bolivar's century thought in terms of nations and nationalities, but Bolivar did not believe the national concept was the last step in historical development. He thought in continents; and though by external chronology he belongs to the nineteenth century, by internal chronology he is a citizen of the twentieth. The combination of democracy and authority, the creation of huge regional blocks, the idea of a league of free nations—these are all conceptions of our times. Is it, then, surprising that any clear perception of his amazing prevision should have come so late? A century after his death the world began to understand that he had been the champion of coöperation and Pan-American solidarity.

Finally, the principle of a league of nations, which has influenced the political thought of the world since 1918, is a confirmation of Bolivar's internationalism. This institution, imperfect in 1919 as it still is, nevertheless represents an ideal essential to the welfare of humanity, granted that mankind still preserves the hope of survival. Bolivar was one of the first to proclaim the ideal of a commonwealth of nations. In Geneva the league deputies recognized that the Liberator of South America could no longer be considered only as an American personality; he had become a universal figure, a founder of our world.

The modern critic will probably raise one objection to Bolivar's policies—his blindness to the economic factors of life. It is true that his economic understanding was strictly limited; he never saw clearly that political independence must be followed by economic and social revolution if the process is to be complete. However, Bolivar shares this blindness with most of the men of his age and in this respect he is certainly a man of the nineteenth century.

Since historical evolution has moved from east to west and since America has become the stage of all future decisions, the figure of Simon Bolivar has emerged from the darkness of benevolent ignorance into the footlights of history. "America," said Bolivar in 1823, "is not a problem; neither is it a fact. It is the highest and most irrefutable assignment of destiny."[34] For us, who recognize the historic power in these words, Bolivar needs neither legend nor stylistic gaud. His weakness, his errors, his contradictions, cannot be denied. Bolivar was both great and tragic. To ignore his faults would result either in a diminution of his grandeur or the fossilization of his character.

Bolivar's destiny parallels that of all great men of history who have helped humanity to advance—men who have had a deep and inherent knowledge of the anxieties of their fellowmen and who have known how to give a voice to the silent needs of the masses. The more conscious the twentieth century becomes of its mission, the more will it consider Bolivar as one of the founders of its destiny. This world is one, and America's freedom is still, as Bolivar said at Junín, its hope and its salvation.

We conclude the story of the life of Simon Bolivar with the words of an hitherto unpublished document that well deserves

34 Cartas: Vol. X. p. 435.

to be called his political will. It dates from 1829.[35] "I love my country, and I think I understand it. . . . When Colombia was the prey of Spanish despotism, I ventured my life and my fortune for the victory of independence. I have gone even further. I have led the name of Colombia to the slopes of the Chimborazo and the Pichincha. . . . The dictatorship which I hold has not the omnipotence of tyranny which I abhor; it is a sacrifice which I offer to the public order. . . .

"This country will pass through all forms of government until the day dawns when the Anglo-Saxon race invades Hispano-America in a democratic fashion and one immense nation is formed that one day will conquer the American sea and will bring the wealth and civilization of Europe to this great continent. The destiny of America is deep and sublime, but before it is realized America will experience every stage of the medieval nations.

"I have achieved no other good than independence. That was my mission. The nations I have founded will, after prolonged and bitter agonies, go into an eclipse, but will later emerge as states of the one great republic, AMERICA."

35 El Pasatiempo. No. 16. December 6, 1851. Arch. Bolívar. Caracas.

ABBREVIATIONS

Abbreviations

Arch. .Archives
Doc. .Documents
Rev. .Revue, Review, Revista
Hist. .Historisch, Historical, Historico

Arch. Miranda . . . . Archivo del General Miranda. Edited by V. Dávila. Caracas, 1930 ff. 63 vols. in 3 series.

Arch. Santander . . . . Archivo Santander. Edited by the Academia de la Historia. Bogotá, 1913 ff. Vols. I-XXIV.

Blanco Doc. . . . . Documentos para la Historia de la Vida Pública del Libertador. Edited by José Felix Blanco. Caracas, 1875-77. Vols. I-XIV.

Baralt . . . . R. M. Baralt y Díaz: Resumen de la Historia de Venezuela. Brugge, 1939. 2 vols.

B. d. H. Caracas. . . . . Boletín de la Academia Nacional de la Historia. Caracas.

B. d. H. Bogotá . . . . Boletín de la Historia y Antigüedades de la Academia de Bogotá.

B. d. H. Quito . . . . .Boletín de Historia de la Academia de Quito.

Bulnes . . . . G. Bulnes: Bolívar en el Perú. Madrid, 1919. 2 vols.

Cartas .Cartas del Libertador. Edited by Vicente Lecuna. Caracas, 1929. Vols. I-X.

Cartas Santander . . . . Cartas de Santander. Edited by Vicente Lecuna. Caracas, 1942. Vols. I-III.

Cortes Vargas . . . . .Cortes Vargas: Participación de Colombia en la Libertad del Perú. Bogotá, 1924. Vols. I-III.

Cuervo Marques . . . . .L. Cuervo Marques: Participación de la Gran Brêtaña y de los Estados Unidos en la Independencia. Bogotá, 1935. Vol. I.

De la Rosa: Firmas . . . . .A. de la Rosa: Firmas del Ciclo Heroico. Lima, 1938.

D. d. B. . . . . .Diario de Bucaramanga. Edited by N. E. Navarro. Caracas, 1935.

Forero: Santander . . . . J. M. Forero: El General Santander. Bogotá, 1937.

Gil Fortoul . . . . .J. Gil Fortoul: Historia Constitucional de Venezuela. Berlín, 1907. Vol. I.

Groot .J. M. Groot: Historia ecclesiástica y civil de Nueva Granada. Bogotá, 1893. Vols. I-V.

Hisp. Am. Hist. Rev. . . . . .The Hispanic American Historical Review.

Hispano: Libro . . . . .C. Hispano: El Libro de Oro del Libertador. Paris, 1925.

Larrazabal ....F. Larrazabal: Vida y Correspondencia General del Libertador Simón Bolívar. New York, 1901. 2 vols.

Lecuna: Adolescencia ....V. Lecuna: Adolescencia y Juventud de Bolívar. B. d. H. Caracas. Vol. XIII. No. 52.

Lecuna: Los Cayos ....V. Lecuna: La Expedición de los Cayos. B. d. H. Caracas. Vol. XIX. No. 75. Vol. XX.

Lecuna: Guerra ....V. Lecuna: La Guerra a Muerte. B. d. H. Caracas. Vols. XVII, XVIII.

Lecuna: Papeles ....V. Lecuna: Papeles de Bolívar. Caracas, 1917.

Lévene: H. d. A. ....R. Lévene: Historia de América. Buenos Aires, 1940. Vols. I-VII.

Libro de Actas ....Libro de Actas del Congreso de Angostura. Edited by R. Cortazar. Bogotá, 1921.

Libro Nac. ....El Libro Nacional de los Venezolanos. Caracas, 1911.

Mancini ....J. Mancini: Bolívar y la Emancipación de las Colonias Españolas. Paris, 1930.

Mitre: San Martín ....B. Mitre: Historia de San Martín y de la Emancipación Suramericana. Buenos Aires, 1890. Vols. I-IV.

O'Leary: Doc. ....D. O'Leary: Memorias. Caracas, 1883. Vols. I-XXVI. These volumes contain the letters to Bolivar and the official reports to and from Bolivar.

O'Leary: Memorias ....D. O'Leary: Memorias. Caracas, 1883. Vols. I-III. These volumes contain the statements which O'Leary devoted to the life of Bolivar.

Parra Pérez: Bayona ....C. Parra Pérez: Bayona y la política de Napoleón en América. Caracas, 1939.

Parra Pérez: Miranda ....C. Parra Pérez: Miranda et la Révolution Française. Paris, 1925.

Parra Pérez: Primera República.C. Parra Pérez: Historia de la Primera República de Venezuela. Caracas, 1939. 2 vols.

Paz Soldán ....M. T. Paz Soldán: Historia del Perú Independiente. Lima, 1868-74. Vol. I, 1, I, 2, Vol. II.

Pereyra: Juventud ....C. Pereyra: La Juventud Legendaria de Bolívar. Madrid, 1932.

Posada Gutiérrez ....J. Posada Gutiérrez: Memorias histórico-políticas. Bogotá, 1929. Vols. I-III.

Proclamas ....Proclamas y Discursos del Libertador. Edited by V. Lecuna. Caracas, 1939.

Reverend ....A. P. Reverend: La Ultima Enfermedad, los Ultimos Momentos y los Funerales de Simón Bolívar. Paris, 1866.

Rev. Bol. ....Revista Bolivariana. Bogotá.

Rev. Hisp. ....Revue Hispanique. Paris.

Restrepo H. d. R. C. ....J. M. Restreo: Historia de la Revolución de la República de Colombia. Besancón, 1858. Vols. I-IV.

Rivas Vicuña ....F. Rivas Vicuña: Las Guerras de Bolívar. Bogotá, 1934. Vols. I-IV.

Robertson: Miranda ....W. Robertson: Francisco de Miranda. Bogotá, 1918. Spanish translation.

Robertson: Life ....W. Robertson: The Life of Miranda. Chapel Hill, 1929. 2 vols.

Rodríguez Villa ....Rodríguez Villa: Biografía de Pablo Morillo. Madrid, 1908-10. Vols. I-IV.

Rourke ....Thomas Rourke: Man of Glory: Simón Bolívar. New York, 1939.

Torres Lanza ....P. Torres Lanza: Independencia de América. Fuentes para estudio. Vols. I-VI. Madrid, 1912.

Vejarano: Origenes ....J. R. Vejarano: Orígenes de la Independencia Suramericana. Bogotá, 1925.

Villanueva: Sucre ....L. Villanueva: Vida de Sucre. Caracas, 1945.

Webster ....C. K. Webster: Britain and the Independence of Latin America. Oxford, 1938. 2 vols.

Yanes: Relación ....F. J. Yanes: Relación Documentada de los Principales Sucesos Ocurridos en Venezuela. Caracas, 1943. 2 vols.

The books which are undated in the Notes are published without dates.

BIBLIOGRAPHY

Bibliography

For a Complete Bibliography See—

1. Bibliography of the Liberator, Simón Bolívar. Compiled in the Columbus Memorial Library of the Pan American Union. Washington, D. C., 1933.
2. Catálogo de la Exposición de Libros Bolivarianos. Compiled by Biblioteca Nacional. Caracas, 1943.
3. E. Planchart: Bibliografía de J. A. de Sucre. 2 vols. Caracas, 1946. Typewritten manuscript.
4. Santiago Key Ayala. Series hemero-bibliográficas, primera serie bolivariana. Caracas, 1933.
5. M. S. Sánchez . . . Bibliografía de índices bibliográficos relativos a Venezuela. Cambridge, Massachusetts, 1940.

SELECTIVE BIBLIOGRAPHY

The following works represent only a partial list of the complete bibliography on Simón Bolívar and the South American Independence. An exhaustive bibliography would comprise a volume. The present list, selected on a practical basis, is designed to give directives for further study to both layman and scholar, and has been compiled through the author's careful evaluation of each title submitted here for reference.

This enumeration does not include all the works used in the notes. Especially have books dealing with background material and specific problems been excluded. The notes and the bibliography are in this way complementary, and must be so understood by those readers who would make a further study of the subject.

The editions listed in the notes are in every case those used for reference. The editions listed in the bibliography are those most accessible in the United States.

Bibliographical Aids

Catálogo de la Exposición de Libros Bolivarianos. Caracas, 1943. Biblioteca Nacional.

Key Ayala, S.: Series hemero-bibliográficas. Caracas, 1933.

Sánchez, Alonzo B.: Fuentes de la historia española e hispano-americana. Madrid, 1927.

Sánchez, M. S.: Anuario bibliográfico de Venezuela. Caracas, 1917.

707

Sánchez, M. S.: Bibliografía de índices bibliográficos relativos a Venezuela. Cambridge, Massachusetts, 1940.

Unión Panamericana: Bibliography of the Liberator Simón Bolívar. Washington, D. C., 1933.

Manuscripts

Archivo del Libertador. Caracas. Casa Bolívar.

Archivo nacional de Colombia. Bogotá.

Archivo nacional de Venezuela. Caracas.

Colección de documentos para la historia del Libertador. Collected by V. Lecuna. Typewritten manuscript. Biblioteca Bolivariana. Caracas. Academia de Historia. 20 vols.

Documents and Letters

Acuerdos d. Consejo de Gobierno de la República de Colombia, 1825-1827. Bogotá, 1942.

Aguirre, M.: Un ignorado archivo bolivariano. Bol. d. la Academia de Historia. Caracas, Vol. 19.

Archivo de Miranda. Caracas, 1936-1946. 15 vols.

Archivo Santander. Publicación hecha por una comisión de la Academia nacional de Historia. Bogotá, 1913. Vols. 1-25.

Blanco, José Felix (ed).: Documentos para la historia de la vida pública del libertador de Colombia, Perú y Bolivia. Caracas, 1875-1878. Vol. 14.

Bolívar, Simón: Bolívar pintado por si mismo, recopilación de documentos, notas y prólogo de R. Blanco-Fombona. Buenos Aires, 1913.

Bolívar, Simón: Cartas de Bolívar, 1799-1822. Prólogo de José Enrique Rodó y notas de R. Blanco-Fombona. Paris, 1912.

Bolívar, Simón: Cartas de Bolívar, 1823, 1824, 1825. Notas de R. Blanco-Fombona. Madrid, 1921.

Bolívar, Simón: Cartas de Bolívar, 1825-1827. Notas de R. Blanco-Fombona. Madrid, Editorial-America, 1922 (?).

Bolívar, Simón: Cartas del Libertador corregidas conforme a los originales. Ed. by V. Lecuna. Caracas, 1929-30. 10 vols.

Bolívar, Simón: Papeles de Bolívar, publicados por Vicente Lecuna. Caracas, 1917.

Bolívar y Santander: Correspondencia, 1819-1820. Bogotá, 1940.

Calvo, C.: Anales históricos de la revolución en la América Latina. Paris, 1864-1867. 4 vols.

Camacho, S.: Sucre: Cartas al Libertador. New York, 1883.

Cartas de Santander. Ed. by V. Lecuna. Caracas, 1942. 3 vols.

Colección de Decretos leyes de las cortes de España. México, 1829.

Colección de Documentos relativos a la vida pública del libertador de Colombia y del Perú, Simón Bolívar; para servir a la historia de la independencia de Suramérica. Caracas, 1826-1833.

Collection of documents and letters for the history of Bolivar. Published by V. Lecuna and others in Bol. de la Academia de Historia, Caracas. Vols. 13, 15, 16, 17, 18, 19, 20, 21, 23, 24, 25, 26, 27, 28, 29.

Colombia: Acuerdos del consejo de gobierno, 1821-1824. Bogotá, 1940.

Colombia: Codificación de todas las leyes de Colombia desde 1821. Bogotá, 1924.

Colección de los decretos expedidos por S. E. el Libertador, presidente de Colombia desde . . . 1826 hasta . . . 1827. Caracas, 1828.

Congreso constituyente de Venezuela, 1811. Caracas, 1911.

Congreso de Angostura. Libro de actas. Published by R. Cortazar y L. A. Cuervo. Bogotá, 1921.

Congreso de Cucutá: libro de actas. publicado por R. Cortazar y L. A. Cuervo. . . . Bogotá, Imprenta nacional, 1923.

Congreso de 1823; actas, publicadas por R. Cortazar y L. A. Cuervo. . . . Bogotá, Imprenta nacional, 1926.

Congreso de 1824; Senado, actas, publicadas por R. Cortazar y L. A. Cuervo. . . . Bogotá, 1931.

Corrales, M. E.: Documentos para la historia de la provincia de Cartagena de las Indias. Bogotá, 1883.

Cuervo, Rufino: Epistolario. Bogotá, 1918.

Diario de Bucaramanga. Ed. by N. E. Navarro. Caracas, 1935.

Documentos en honor del Gran Mariscal de Ayacucho. Caracas, 1890.

Documentos históricos del Perú. Edited by M. Odriozola. Lima, 1875. 6 vols.

Documentos para los anales de Venezuela desde el movimiento separatista de la unión Colombiana hasta nuestros días. Caracas, 1889-1909. 7 vols.

España, archivo general de Indias, Sevilla. Independencia de América, fuentes para su estudio. Ed. by P. Torres Lanza. Madrid, 1912. 6 vols.

Lecuna, V.: Documentos referentes a la creación de Bolivia. Caracas, 1924. 2 vols.

Lozano y Lozano, F. y Hernández de Alba, G.: Documentos sobre V. Azuero. Bogotá, 1924.

Manning, W. R.: Diplomatic correspondence of the United States concerning the Independence of the Latin American Nations. New York, 1925. 3 vols.

Marquez, M., Santander: Documentos históricos sobre la muerte del Libertador, Simón Bolívar. Barranquilla, 1930.

O'Higgins, B.: Epistolario, 1798-1823. Santiago, 1916.

O'Leary, Daniel Florencio: Memorias del General O'Leary. Caracas, 1879-1888. 32 vols.

Ortega Ricaurte, E.: Documentos sobre la conspiración del 25 de Septiembre. Bogotá, 1942.

Páez, J. A.: Archivo 1818-1820. Bogotá, 1939.

Perú de la Croix, Louis: Diario de Bucaramanga; o, Vida pública y privada del Libertador Simón Bolívar. Paris, 1912.

Porras Barrenechea, R.: El congreso de Panamá. Lima, 1930.

Proceso de Nariño. Ed. by J. M. Pérez Sarmiento. Cádiz, 1914.

Proclamas de Bolívar, Sucre, Santander, y Padilla. Bogotá, 1878. 1 vol.

Proclamas y Discursos de Libertador. Ed. by V. Lecuna. Caracas, 1939.

Rosas, A. E. de la: Firmas del ciclo heroico. Documentos inéditos para la historia de América. Lima, 1938.

San Martín: Documentos del archivo. Buenos Aires, 1911. 11 vols.

San Martín, José de: Su correspondencia 1823-1850. 3rd ed. Madrid, 1911.

Webster, C. K.: Britain and the Independence of Latin America. Oxford, 1938. 2 vols.

Contemporary Works and Memoirs

Abreu y Lima, J. J. de: Resumen histórico de la última dictadura del Libertador Simón Bolívar. Río de Janeiro, 1922.

Adlercreutz, F. Th.: La cartera del conde de Adlercreutz. Introducción y notas de C. Parra Pérez. Paris, 1928.

Antepara, J. M.: South American Emancipation. London, 1810.

Aranda y Ponte, F.: Obras. Caracas, 1858.

Austria, J. de: Bosquejo de la historia militar de Venezuela. Caracas, 1855-57.

Bolívar, Fernando S.: Recuerdos y reminiscencias del primer tercio de la vida de Rivolba. Paris, 1873.

Boussingault, J. B.: Memoires. Paris, 1903.

Briceño Méndez, P.: Relación histórica. Caracas, 1933.

Caballero, J. M.: En la Independencia. Bogotá, 1902.

Castillo y Rada: Memorias. Published by E. Rodríguez Piñeros. Bogotá, 1914.

Cochrane, Th.: Narrative of services in the liberation of Chile, Perú, and Brazil. London, 1859.

Díaz, José Domingo: Recuerdos sobre la Rebelión de Caracas. Madrid, 1829.

Ducoudray-Holstein, H. Lafayette Villaume: Memoirs of Simón Bolívar. London, 1830. 2 vols.

Ensayo sobre la conducta del general Bolívar. Lima, 1827.

Espejo, Jeronimo: Recuerdos históricos. San Martín y Bolívar; entrevista de Guayaquil (1822). Buenos Aires, 1873.

Espinosa, José María: Memorias de un Abanderado. (Nueva Granada 1810-1819.) Madrid, 1920.

Exposición de los sentimientos de los funcionarios públicos . . . y demás habitantes de la ciudad de Bogotá. Bogotá, 1826.

Flintner, G. D.: A history of the Revolution of Caracas. London, 1819.

Fray Nicolás de Vich: Víctimas de la anárquica ferocidad. 1818.

García del Río, J.: Meditaciones colombianas. Caracas, 1830.

García Gamba, General: Memorias del General García Gamba. Madrid, 1846.

González, Florentino: Los conjurados del 25 de septiembre. Bogotá, 1853.

González, Florentino: Memorias. Buenos Aires, 1933.

Guido, Th.: San Martín y la gran epopeya. Buenos Aires, 1928.

Guzmán, A. L.: Ojeada del proyecto de constitución que el Libertador ha presentado a la república de Bolívar. Lima, 1826.

Heredia y Mieses, José Francisco: Memorias del regente Heredia. Madrid, 1916.

Hippisley, G.: Narrative of the expedition to the rivers Orinoco and Apure in South America. London, 1819.

Lafond de Lurcy, Gabriel: Voyages dans l'Amerique Espagnole pendant les guerres de l'independence. Paris, 1844.

Lander, T.: Reflexiones sobre el poder vitalicio. Caracas, 1826.

López, J. H.: Memorias. Bogotá, 1942.

López, Manuel Antonio: Recuerdos históricos de la guerra de la independencia. Colombia y el Perú. 1819-1826. 2nd ed. Bogotá, 1889.

López, Vicente Fidel: El conflicto y la entrevista de Guayaquil expuesta al tenor de los documentos que la explican. Buenos Aires, 1884.

Mahoney, William D.: Campaigns and cruises in Venezuela and New Granada and in the Pacific Ocean; from 1817 to 1830. London, 1831. 3 vols.

Miller, John: Memorias de General Miller al servicio de la República del Perú. . . . Traducción por el General Torrijos. Madrid, 1910. 2 vols.

Morillo y Morillo, P.: Memoires. Paris, 1826.

Mosquera, Tomas Cipriano de: Memorias sobre la vida del Libertador Simón Bolívar. Part 1. New York, 1853.

Mosquera, T.: Memorias sobre la vida del general Bolívar. Bogotá, 1940.

Obando, A.: Autobiografía. Bol. d. la Academia de Historia. Bogotá. Vol. 8.

O'Connor, F. B.: Independencia americana, recuerdos. Madrid, 1915 (?).

Páez, José Antonio: Autobiografía. New York, 1865.

Palacio Fajardo, M.: Esquisse de la revolución de l'Amerique espagnole. Paris, 1817.

Paulding, H.: A sketch of Bolívar in his camp. New York, 1834.

Posada Gutiérrez, Joaquín: Memorias histórico-políticas. 2nd ed. Bogotá. Imprenta Nacional. 1929. 4 vols.

Poudenx, H., et F. Mayer: Memoire pour servir a l'histoire de la revolution . . . de Caracas. Paris, 1815.

Pradt, Dominique de Fourt de: Congrès de Panamá. Paris, 1825.

Pruvonena, P.: Memorias y documentos para la historia de la independencia del Perú y causas del mal éxito que ha tenido ésta. Paris, 1858. 2 vols.

Rafter, M.: Memoirs of Gregor McGregor. London, 1820.

Recollections of a Service of three years during the war of extermination in the republics of Venezuela and Colombia. By an officer of the British navy. London, 1818. 2 vols.

Restrepo, Jose Manuel: Historia de la revolución de la república de Colombia. Besanzón, 1858. 4 vols.

Reverend, Alejandro Próspero: La última enfermedad, los últimos momentos y los funerales de Simón Bolívar, Libertador de Colombia y del Perú, por su médico de cabecera. Paris, 1866.

Richard, K.: Briefe aus Kolumbien. Leipzig, 1822.

Rodríguez, Simón: Defensa de Bolívar. Caracas, 1916.

Rodríguez, Simón: El Libertador del medio día de América. Arequipa, 1830.

Sánchez, Carión: Memorias. Lima, 1825.

Santander, Francisco de P.: Historia de sus desavenencias con el Libertador. Bogotá.

Segur, F. de: Memoirs et Souvenirs. Paris, 1827. Vol. I.

Sevilla, Rafael: Memorias de un oficial del ejército español; campañas contra Bolívar y los separatistas de América. Madrid, 1916.

Stevenson, William Bennet: Memorias . . . sobre las campañas de San Martín y Cochrane en el Perú; versión castellana de Luis de Terán. . . . Madrid, 1917.

Torrente, Mariano: Historia de la revolución hispano-americana. Madrid, 1829. 3 vols.

Torre Tagle, Marques de: Manifesto. Lima, 1824.

Urdaneta, Rafael: Memorias del General Rafael Urdaneta. Madrid, 1916.

Urquinaona y Pardo, P. de: Memorias. Madrid, 1917.

Vargas Tejada, L.: Recuerdos Históricos. Biblioteca Popular. Bogotá (?).

Walton, W.: Outline of the Revolution in Spanish America. New York, 1817.

Travelbooks

Adam, W. J.: Journal of voyages to Margarita, Trinidad, and Maturin, etc. Dublin, 1824.

Andrews, J.: Journey from Buenos Aires to Potosí. London, 1827.

Brackenridge, H. M.: Voyage to South America. London, 1820.

Camacho, S.: Recuerdos de Santa Marta. Caracas, 1844.

Chesterton, George Laval: A Narrative of the proceedings in Venezuela in South America in the years 1819 and 1820. London, 1820.

Cochrane, Charles Stuart: Journal of a residence and travels in Colombia during the years 1823 and 1824. London, 1825.

Duane, W.: A visit to Colombia in 1822-1823. Philadelphia, 1826.

Hackett, J.: Narrative of the expedition which sailed from England in 1817, to join the South American Patriots. London, 1818.

Haigh, S.: Sketches of Buenos Aires, Chile, and Peru. London, 1831.

Howell, J.: The Life of Alexander Alexander. London, 1830.

Mollien, G. Th.: Voyage dans la republique de Colombia en 1823. Paris, 1825.

Niles, John Milton: History of South America and Mexico; comprising their discovery, geography, politics, commerce and revolutions. Hartford, 1838. 2 vols.

Proctor, R.: Narrative of a journey across the cordillera of the Andes . . . in 1823-24. London, 1825.

General Historical Works on South American Independence

Acosta de Samper, Soledad: Época de la independencia. Bogotá, 1909-10.

Altamira, R.: Historia de España y de la civilización española. Barcelona, 1900. 4 vols.

Altamira, R.: Resumen histórico de la independencia de la América española. Buenos Aires, 1910.

André, Marius: El fin del imperio español en América. Barcelona, 1922.

Arrubla y Henao: Historia de Colombia. Bogotá, 1929.

Azpurua, R.: Biografías de hombres notables de Hispano América. Caracas, 1877.

Baralt, R. M., and R. Díaz: Resumen de la Historia de Venezuela. Brugge, 1939. 2 vols.

Barbagelata, H. D.: Histoire de l'Amerique espagnole. Paris, 1936.

Barros Arana, D.: Historia general de Chile. Vols. XII-XIII. Santiago de Chile, 1887.

Becker, Jeronimo: La independencia de América (su reconocimiento por España). Madrid, 1922.

Benedetti, Carlos: Historia de Colombia. 2nd ed. Lima, 1887.

Benzo, E.: La libertad de América. Madrid, 1929.

Bingham, Hiram: The journal of an expedition across Venezuela and Colombia, 1906, 1907. New Haven, Yale University Press, 1909.

Blanco, Eduardo: Venezuela heróica; cuadros históricos. Caracas, 1883.

Briceño, Mariano de: Historia de la Isla de Margarita. Caracas, 1885.

Bulnes, Gonzalo: Historia de la expedición libertadora del Perú (1817-1822). Santiago, 1887-88. 2 vols.

Calle, M. J.: Leyendas del tiempo heróico. Guayaquil, 1905.

Camacho, J. M.: Compendio de la historia de Bolivia. La Paz, 1927.

Carlyle, Th.: El doctor Francia. Buenos Aires, 1905. (Spanish translation.)

Cleven, Nels Andrew Nelson: Readings in Hispanic American history. Boston, 1927.

Coroleu, José: América. Historia de su colonización, dominación e independencia. Barcelona, 1896. 4 vols.

Corredor, Rubén: La Gran Colombia. Mérida, 1930.

Cortés, José Domingo: Diccionario biografía americano. 2nd ed. Paris, 1876.

Cortés, José Domingo, ed.: Galería de hombres célebres de Bolivia. Santiago, 1869.

Crichfield, George W.: American supremacy; the rise and progress of the Latin American republics and their relations to the United States under the Monroe Doctrine. New York, 1908. 2 vols.

Cuervo Marques, L.: Independencia de las colonias hispano-americanas. Participación de la Gran Brêtaña y de los Estados Unidos. Bogotá, 1935. 2 vols.

Daniels, Margarette: Makers of South America. New York, 1916.

Delgado, C.: 1815. Cartagena, 1916.

Destruge, Camilo: Historia de la revolución de octubre y campaña libertadora de 1820-22. Guayaquil, 1920.

Dousdebes, P. J.: Trayectoria militar de Santander. Bucaramanga, 1935.

Edwards, W.: British foreign policy, 1815-1933. London, 1934.

Forero, M. J.: Santander. Bogotá, 1937.

García, H. M.: La gran Colombia. Caracas, 1925.

García Calderón, F.: Ideas e impresiones. Madrid, 1919.

García Calderón, Francisco: La creación de un continente. Paris.

García Calderón, Francisco: Les democraties latines de l'Amerique. Paris, 1914.

García Chuecos, H.: Don Fernando de Peñalver. Caracas, 1941.

García Chuecos, H.: La capitanía general de Venezuela. Caracas, 1945.

Gervinus, J. J.: Geschichte des XIX Jahrhunderts. Leipzig, 1858. Vol. 3.

González, E. G.: Dentro de la Cosiata. Caracas, 1907.

González, E. G.: Historia de Venezuela . . . hasta 1830. Caracas, 1930.

González, Eloy G.: La ración del boa. Caracas, 1908.

González, F.: Santander. Bogotá, 1940.

González, Nicolás Augusto: Cuestión histórica; el asesinato del Gran Mariscal de Ayacucho. 2nd ed. Quito, 1906. 4 vols.

González Suárez, F.: Historia general del Ecuador. Quito, 1890. 7 vols.

Graham, Robert Bontine C.: José Antonio Páez. London, 1929.

Griffin, Ch.: La opinión pública norte americana y la independencia de Hispano-América. Caracas, 1941.

Groot, José Manuel; Historia eclesiástica y civil de Nueva Granada, escrita sobre documentos auténticos. 2nd ed. Bogotá, 1889-93. 5 vols.

Guerra, J. J.: La convención de Ocaña. Bogotá, 1908.

Guzmán, Antonio Leocadio: La guerra a muerte. Caracas, 1876.

Harrison, M. H.: San Martín. Buenos Aires, 1943.

Heres, Tomás de: Historia de la independencia americana; la emancipación del Perú. Madrid, 1919.

Herrera, L. A.: La revolución francesa y Sudamérica. Paris, 1910.

Humbert, Jules: Histoire de la Colombie et du Venezuela des origenes jusqu'a nos jours. Paris, 1920.

James, Herman Gerlach, and Percy A. Martin: The republics of Latin America; their history, governments and economic conditions. New York and London, 1923.

Jane, L. C.: Libertad y despotismo en la América española. Buenos Aires, 1932. (Spanish translation.)

Jauregui Rosquellas, A.: Antonio José de Sucre. La Paz, 1928.

La Fuente y Valera: Historia general de España. Barcelona, 1922. Vols. 16 and 17,

Lallement, G.: Histoire de la Colombia. Paris, 1826.

Levéne, R.: Historia de América. Buenos Aires, 1940. Vols. I-VII.

Lockey, Joseph Byrne: Pan-Americanism; its beginnings. New York, 1920.

López Contreras, Eleazar: El Callao histórico. Caracas, 1926.

López Contreras, E.: Sucre. Caracas, 1945.

Mitre, B.: Historia de San Martín y de la emancipación sudamericana. Buenos Aires, 1889. 4 vols.

Moses, Bernard: The intellectual background of the revolution in South America, 1810-1824. New York, 1926.

Oliveira Lima, M. de: La evolución histórica de la América Latina. Madrid.

Oliveira Lima, M. de: Pan-Americanismo (Monroe-Bolívar-Roosevelt). Río de Janeiro, 1907.

Oliveira Lima, M. de: The evolution of Brazil compared with that of Spanish and Anglo-Saxon America. Stanford University, 1914.

Otero, J. P.: San Martín. Buenos Aires, 1932. 4 vols.

Parks, E. T.: Colombia and the United States. Durham, 1935.

Parra Pérez, C.: Historia de la primera República de Venezuela. Caracas, 1939. 2 vols.

Parra Pérez, C.: Miranda et la revolution française. Paris, 1925.

Paxon, F. L.: The independence of South American republics. Philadelphia, 1903.

Paz Soldán, Mariano Felipe: Historia del Perú independiente . . . Segundo período, 1822-27. Lima, 1870-74. 2 vols.

Pereyra, C.: Historia de la América Española. Madrid, 1920-26. 8 vols.

Pereyra, C.: Humboldt en América. Madrid, 1917.

Pinilla, Sabino: La creación de Bolivia; prólogo y notas de Alcides Arguedas. Madrid, 1917.

Posada, E.: La patria boba. Bogotá, 1902.

Posada, E.: Provincias unidas de la Nueva Granada, 1811-1816. Bogotá, 1924.

Rippy, J. Fred: Rivalry of the United States and Great Britain over Latin America. Baltimore, 1929.

Rivas, R.: Relaciones internacionales entre Colombia y los Estados Unidos. Bogotá, 1915.

Rivas Groot, J. M.: Páginas de la historia de Colombia. Bogotá, 1907.

Robertson, W. Spence: Francisco de Miranda y la revolución de América Española. Bogotá, 1918. (Spanish translation.)

Robertson, William Spence: History of the Latin American Nations. New York, 1922.

Robertson, W. S.: Rise of the Spanish American Republics. London, New York, 1928.

Robertson, W. S.: The Life of Miranda. Chapel Hill, 1929. 2 vols.

Rodríguez Villa, Antonio: El teniente general Don Pablo Morillo. Madrid, 1908-10. 4 vols.

Rojas, Aristides: Leyendas históricas de Venezuela. 1st series. Caracas, 1890.

Rojas, R.: El santo de la espada. Buenos Aires, 1940.

Rueda Vargas, T.: Visiones de la historia colombiana. Bogotá, 1933.

Samper, José Maria: Apuntamientos para la historia política y social de la Nueva Granada desde 1810. Bogotá, 1853.

Siegfried, André: L'Amerique Latine. Paris, 1934.

Tavera Acosta, Bartolomé: Anales de Guayana. Ciudad Bolívar, 1913-14. 2 vols.

Tavera Acosta, B.: Historia de Carúpano. Caracas, 1930.

Tamayo, J.: La Gran Colombia. Bogotá, 1941.

Terán, J. B.: El nacimiento de la América Española. Tucumán, 1927.

Urdaneta, Amenodoro: La convención de Ocaña. Caracas, 1900.

Urrutia, F. J.: La evolución del principio de arbitraje en América. Madrid, 1920.

Urrutia, F. J.: Los Estados Unidos de América y las repúblicas hispano-americanas. Madrid, 1918.

Urrutia, F. J.: Páginas de historia diplomática. Bogotá, 1917.

Valenilla, Lanz, L.: Disgregación e integración. Caracas, 1930.

Valenilla, Lanz, L.: La guerra civil de la independencia. Caracas, 1911.

Vega, José de la: La federación en Colombia (1810-1812). Madrid, 1912.

Vicuña, Mackenna, B.: La revolución de la independencia del Perú. Lima, 1860.

Villanueva, Laureano: Vida de Don Antonio José de Sucre, Gran Mariscal de Ayacucho. Paris.

Whitacker, A.: The United States and the Independence of Latin America. Baltimore, 1941.

Williams, Mary W.: The people and politics of Latin America. Boston, 1945.

Zea, Francisco Antonio: Colombia. London, 1822. 2 vols.

Works on Bolivar and His Times

Agosto Méndez, J. M.: Libro del Centenario de Angostura. Ciudad Bolívar, 1920.

Aguirre Elorriaga, M.: El abate de Pradt en la emancipación hispano americana. Rome, 1941.

Alamo Ybarra, Carlos: La constitution de Bolívar pour la republique qui porte son nom. Genève, 1922.

Alayza Paz Soldán, L.: Unanue, San Martín y Bolívar. Lima, 1934.

Alcance al Diario de Bucaramanga. Caracas, 1912.

Aldao, C.: Miranda y los orígenes de la independencia americana. Buenos Aires, 1928.

Alessio, Giovanni d': Bolívar. Rome, 1932.

Alfaro, R. J.: Carabobo. Panamá, 1921.

Amunategui, M. L.: Vida de Andres Bello. Santiago, 1882.

Andrade Coello, A.: Motivos Nacionales. Quito, 1911.

André, Marius: Bolívar y la democracia. Barcelona, 1924.

Angell, H.: Simón Bolívar. New York, 1930.

Antología Bolivariana. Bogotá, 1938.

Antuña, José G.: Bolívar símbolo de América; el Libertador, el legislador, el apóstol. Montevideo, 1932.

Antuña, J. J.: Nuevas páginas Bolivarianas. Montevideo, 1942.

Aragón, A.: Popayán. A la memoria del Libertador. Popayán, 1930.

Arboleda, G.: Historia contemporánea de Colombia. 2d ed. Cali, 1935.

Arcaya, P. M.: Estudios sobre personajes y hechos de la historia venezolana. Caracas, 1911.

Arcaya, P. M.: Influencia del elemento venezolano en la independencia de la América Latina. Caracas, 1916.

Arce, L. A. de: Bonaparte y Bolívar. La Habana, 1940.

Arguedas, Alcides: Historia de Bolivia. Madrid.

Arias Argáez, D.: El Canónigo don José Cortés y Madariaga. Bogotá, 1938.

Arocha Moreno, J.: Bolívar juzgado por el general San Martín. Caracas, 1930.

Arocha, M.: Iconografía del Libertador. Quito, 1943.

Arrocha Graell, C.: El Libertador en Guayaquil. Panamá, 1926.

Baraya, José María: Biografías militares e historia militar del país en medio siglo. Bogotá, 1874.

Barbegelata, Hugo David: Bolívar y San Martín. Paris, 1911.

Barrera, Isaac J.: Simón Bolívar, Libertador y creador de pueblos. Quito, 1930.

Bates, Lindon Wallace: The path of the conquistadores. London, 1912.

Bayo, Ciro: Bolívar y sus tenientes: San Martín y sus aliados. Madrid, 1929.

Bayo, Ciro: Examen de próceres americanos (los libertadores). Madrid, 1916.

Becerra, Ricardo: Vida de Don Francisco de Miranda. Madrid. 2 vols.

Belaunde, V. A.: Bolívar and the political thought of the Spanish American revolution. Baltimore, 1938.

Bellegarde, Dantes: Pétion et Bolívar. (In Revue de l'Amerique Latine, Paris, December, 1924).

Bermúdez de Castro, L.: Boves. Madrid, 1934.

Bingham, Hiram: Simón Bolívar, the George Washington of South America. Washington, D. C. U. S. Gov't Print. Off., 1930.

Blanco-Fombona, R.: Mocedades de Bolívar. Buenos Aires, 1942.

Biographical sketch of the life and services of General William Henry Harrison, together with his letter to Simón Bolívar. Montpelier, Vermont, 1836.

Borges, Carlos: La casa de Bolívar. (Discurso pronunciado . . . en la inauguración de la casa natal del Libertador). Lima, 1929.

Botero Saldarriaga, R.: El Libertador presidente. Bogotá, 1928.

Briceño, Olga: Bolívar americano, Bolívar criollo, Bolívar Libertador. Madrid, 1934. 3 vols.

Bulnes, Gonzalo: Bolívar en el Perú; últimas campañas de la independencia del Perú. Madrid, Editorial-America, 1919. 2 vols.

Campano, L.: Biografía del Libertador, Simón Bolívar. Paris, 1868.

Carbonell, D.: 1830. Paris, 1931.

Carbonell, D.: Influencias que se ejercieron en Bolívar. Caracas, 1920.

Carbonell, D.: Psicopatología de Bolívar. Paris, 1916.

Carbonell, D.: Reflexiones históricas y conceptos de crítica. Río de Janeiro, 1922.

Chacón, Rodrigo: La última enfermedad y últimos momentos de Bolívar. Caracas, 1883.

Chaves Mata, José María: El Libertador, estudio. 2nd ed. Guayaquil, 1928.

Chiriboga, A. L.: Bolívar en el Ecuador. Quito, 1942.

Chiriboga Navarro, A. I.: Tarqui documentado. Quito, 1929.

Churión, Juan José: El humorismo del Libertador. Cien anécdotas. Caracas, 1916.

Clarens, J. P.: Bolívar, sa vie, son oeuvre. Bordeaux, 1884.

Colombia (Republic of Colombia, 1886-   ) Estado Mayor General: Campaña del ejército libertador colombiano en 1819. Bogotá, 1919.

Colombres Mármol, E.: San Martín y Bolívar en la entrevista de Guayaquil. Buenos Aires, 1940.

"Comité Simón Bolívar." Hamburg: Homenaje al Libertador en la ciudad libre y anseática de Hamburgo. Hamburg, 1926.

Congreso panamericano conmemorativo de Bolívar, 1826-1926. Panamá, 1927.

Conte Bermúdez, Héctor: La creación de Bolivia y la constitución boliviana en el istmo de Panamá, 1930.

Cordovez Moure, J. M.: Reminiscencias, series 1-7. Bogotá, 1900-1911.

Correa, Luis: Viaje stendhaliano. Caracas, 1940.

Cortés Vargas, C.: Participación de Colombia en la libertad del Perú. Bogotá, 1924. 3 vols.

Cova, J. A.: El superhombre, vida y obra del Libertador. Caracas, 1941.

Cova Maza, J. M.: Mocedades de Simón Bolívar. Barcelona, Ven., 1924.

Cruz, Ernesto de la; José Manuel Goenaga; Bartolomé Mitre; y Carlos A. Villanueva: La entrevista de Guayaquil (El Libertador y San Martín). Madrid.

Cruz, Ernesto de la: La entrevista de Guayaquil; ensayo histórico. Santiago, 1912.

Cuervo, L. A.: Amores de Bolívar. Bogotá, 1913.

Cuervo, L. A.: Apuntes historiales. Bogotá, 1925.

Dalencour, Francois: Alexandre Pétion devant l'humanité; Alexandre Pétion et Simón Bolívar; Haiti et l'Amerique Latine. Et Expedition de Bolívar par Marion ainé. Port au Prince, 1928.

Dávalos y Lisson, Pedro: Bolívar (1823-1827) Episodio de la independencia peruana. Barcelona, 1924.

Dávila, V.: Bolívar intelectual y galante. México, 1942.

Dávila, V.: Investigaciones históricas. Caracas, 1927.

Delgado, Luis H.: Bolívar, Perú y Bolivia. Lima, 1942.

Destruge, Camilo: Cuestión histórica; la entrevista de Bolívar y San Martín en Guayaquil. Guayaquil, 1918.

Dietrich, W.: Simón Bolívar. Hamburg, 1934.

Duarte Level, Lino: Cuadros de la Historia Civil y Militar de Venezuela. Madrid, Editorial-América.

Finot, E.: Bolívar pacifista. New York, 1936.

Forero, Manuel José: Los últimos días del Libertador; homenaje en el centenario de su muerte. Bogotá, 1930.

Francia, Felipe: Genealogía de la familia del Libertador. (In Gaceta de los Museos Nacionales, Caracas, 1912-1913, I.)

Galindo, Anibal: Batallas decisivas de la libertad. Paris, 1906.

García Calderón, Francisco: Bolívar (in Ideas e impresiones). Madrid, Editorial-América.

García Naranjo, N.: Simón Bolívar. San Antonio, Texas, 1931.

García Ortiz, L.: Estudios históricos. Bogotá, 1938.

Goenaga, José Manuel: La entrevista de Guayaquil. 2nd ed. Rome, 1915.

González, E. G.: Bolívar en la Argentina. Caracas, 1924.

González, F.: Mi Simón Bolívar. Manizales, 1930.

González, Juan Vicente: Biografía del general José Felix Ribas. Madrid, Editorial-América, 1918 (?).

Guastavino, Juan Estevan: San Martín y Bolívar. Buenos Aires, 1913.

Guzmán Blanco, Antonio: El Libertador de la América del Sur. London, 1885.

Hasbrouck, Alfred: Foreign legionaries in the liberation of Spanish South America. New York, 1928.

Hernández, C.: El estilo de Bolívar. Bogotá, 1945.

Hernández de Alba, Guillermo: La misión de Bolívar a Londres en 1810. Bogotá, 1930.

Herriot, E.: De Bolívar a Kellog. Valencia, 1928.

Hispano, C.: Bolívar y la posteridad. Bogotá, 1922.

Hispano, C.: El libro de oro de Bolívar. Paris, 1925.

Hispano, C.: Historia secreta de Bolívar. Bogotá, 1944.

Hispano, C.: Los cantores de Bolívar en el primer centenario de su muerte. Bogotá, 1930.

History of Simón Bolívar (The), Liberator of South America. London, 1876.

Ibañez, P. M.: Crónicas de Bogotá. Bogotá, 1913-23.

Irazabal, C.: Hacia la democracia. México, 1939.

Izpizua, S. de: La ascendencia vasca de Simón Bolívar, in Los vascos en América. Madrid, 1919. Vol. VI.

Jaramillo, A. P.: Estudios históricos. Quito, 1934.

Jiménez Arrechea, S.: Bolívar y la confederación americana. Cali, 1930.

Key Ayala, S.: La vida ejemplar de Simón Bolívar. Caracas, 1942.

Kienzl, F.: Bolívar, der Befreier. Berlin, 1935.

La conferencia de Guayaquil. Caracas, 1940.

Lafond, Georges y Gabriel Tersane: Bolívar et la liberation de l'Amerique du Sud; preface de M. Raymond-Poincaré. Paris, 1931.

Landaeta, Rosales M.: La batalla de Carabobo, 1821. Caracas, 1911.

Larrazabal, Felipe: Correspondencia general del Libertador Simón Bolívar. New York, 1865-66. 2 vols.

Latino, Simón: Vida de Bolívar para niños. Bogotá, 19—. 1 vol.

Lecuna, Vicente: En defensa de Bolívar, la entrevista de Guayaquil. Caracas, 1940.

Lecuna, V.: Historia de la casa de Bolívar. Caracas, 1924.

Lecuna, V.: La campaña de Bombona. Caracas, 1922.

Lecuna, V.: La campaña de Carabobo. Caracas, 1921.

Lecuna, V.: La campaña del Libertador en 1818. Caracas, 1939.

Lecuna, V.: La expedición de Los Cayos. Caracas, 1928.

Lecuna, V.: La liberación del Perú. Caracas, 1941.

Lemly, Henry Rowan: Bolívar, Liberator of Venezuela, Colombia, Perú, and Bolivia. Boston, 1928.

Lepervanche Parparcen, R.: Núñez de Cáceres y Bolívar. Caracas, 1939.

Loewenthal, M. von: Bolívar. San José de Costa Rica, 1941.

López Contreras, Eleazar: Bolívar conductor de tropas. Caracas, 1930.

Lozada, Jesús Rodolfo: Simón Bolívar, 1783-1830. Amberes, 1930.

Lozano y Lozano, Fabio: El maestro del Libertador. Paris, 1913.

Ludwig, E.: Bolívar. Buenos Aires, 1942.

Machado, José Eustaquio: El estandarte de Pizarro y la espada de Bolívar. Caracas, 1924.

Mancini, Jules: Bolívar et la emancipación des colonies espagnoles. Paris, 1912.

Marschal, Phyllis, and John Crane: The dauntless Liberator, Simón Bolívar. New York, 1933.

Martin, Percy Alvin: Simón Bolívar, the Liberator. Stanford University, 1931.

Martínez, Mariano R.: Simón Bolívar, íntimo. Paris, Buenos Aires, 1912.

Medina, P. A.: Campaña de Casanare, 1816-1819. Bogotá, 1916.

Méndez, José Ignacio: El ocaso de Bolívar. Santa Marta, 1927.

Mendoza, Cristobal: La junta de gobierno de Caracas y sus misiones diplomáticas en 1810. Caracas, 1936.

Mendoza López, V.: El Congreso de Bolívar y el pan-americanismo. Buenos Aires, 1926.

Mijares, A.: Hombres e ideas en América. Caracas, 1940.

Miramón, A.: La vida ardiente de Manuela Saenz. Bogotá, 1944.

Miramón, A.: Los Septembrinos. Bogotá, 1939.

Monsalve, José D.: El ideal político del Libertador Simón Bolívar. Bogotá, 1916.

Monsalve, José D.: Estudios sobre el Libertador Simón Bolívar. Bogotá, 1930.

Montalvo, Juan: Siete tratados. Paris, 1912.

Navarro, N. E.: La cristiana muerte del Libertador. Caracas, 1930.

Navarro, N. E.: La política religiosa del Libertador. Caracas, 1933.

Navarro, N. E.: Páginas de Perú de la Croix. Caracas, 1936.

Nucete-Sardi, José: El escritor y civilizador Simón Bolívar. Caracas, 1930.

Núñez Domínguez, José de J.: Bolívar y México; contribución al centenario de su muerte. México, 1930.

Olivas Escudero, F.: Apuntes para la historia de Ayacucho. Ayacucho, 1924.

Olmedo, José Joaquín: La Victoria de Junín. Canto a Bolívar. London, 1826.

Orjuela, L.: Ricaurte y sus impugnadores ante la crítica. Bogotá, 1922.

Ortega Paris: Bolívar. Bogotá, 19—(?).

Palma, Ricardo: Bolívar en las tradiciones peruanas. Madrid, 1930.

Paredes-Urdaneta, Rafael: Biografía de Simón Bolívar, el Libertador. Hamburg, 1930.

Parra-Pérez, C.: Bolívar contribución al estudio de sus ideas políticas. Paris, 1928.

Pereyra, Carlos: Bolívar y Washington; un paralelo imposible. Madrid, 1915.

Pereyra, Carlos: La juventud legendaria de Bolívar. Madrid, 1932.

Pérez Díaz, L. L.: Bolivianas, ensayos históricos. Caracas, 1933.

Pérez Díaz, L. L.: La batalla de Boyacá. Caracas, 1919.

Pérez y Soto, J. B.: Defensa de Bolívar. Lima, 1878.

Petre, Francis Loraine: Simón Bolívar "El Libertador." London, 1910.

Picón Febres, G.: Don Simón Rodríguez. Caracas, 1939.

Planas Suarez, S.: La doctrina Monroe y la doctrina de Bolívar. Habana, 1924.

Ponte, Andrés: Arbol genealógico del Libertador Simón Bolívar. Caracas, 1911.

Ponte, A. F.: Bolívar y otros ensayos. Caracas, 1919.

Ponte, A. F.: La revolución de Caracas y sus próceres. Caracas, 1918.

Pool, John de: La trilogía psíquica del Libertador.

Porras Troconis, G.: Gesta Bolivariana. Caracas, 1935.

Posada, Eduardo: Apostillas. Bogotá, 1926.

Posada, E.: Biografía de Córdoba. Bogotá, 1914.

Rendón, V. M.: Olmedo. Paris, 1904.

Rey de Castro, J. M.: Recuerdos del tiempo heróico. Guayaquil, 1883.

Rincón, Nemesiano: El Libertador Simón Bolívar en la campaña de Pasto, 1819-1822. Pasto, 1922.

Rivas Vicuña, Francisco: Las guerras de Bolívar. Bogotá, 1934. 4 vols.

Rojas, Marques de: Simón Bolívar. Paris, 1883.

Rourke, Th.: Man of Glory: Simón Bolívar. New York, 1939.

Rumazo, A.: Manuela Saenz. Cali, 1944.

Saavedra Galindo, J. M.: Colombia libertadora. Bogotá, 1924.

Saavedra Galindo, J. M.: El Libertador. Bogotá, 1931.

Salaverría, José María: Bolívar el Libertador. 1st ed. Madrid, 1930.

Samper, José María: El Libertador Simón Bolívar. Caracas, 1878.

Sánchez, Manuel Segundo: Apuntes para la iconografía del Libertador. Caracas, 1916.

Santana, Arturo: La campaña de Carabobo (1821). Caracas, 1921.

Santovenia y Echaide, E.: Bolívar y las antillas hispanas. Madrid, 1935.

Sañudo, José Rafael: Estudios sobre la vida de Bolívar. Pasto, 1925.

Sarmiento, Domingo Faustino: Bolívar y San Martín (1847). Entrevista de Sarmiento con San Martín en Gran Bourg. (In his Obras. Paris, 1889-1909, Vol. II; Vol. XXI.)

Schryver, Simon de: Esquisse de la vie de Bolívar. Brussels, 1899.

Sherwell, Guillermo: Simón Bolívar el Libertador, patriot, warrior, statesman, father of five nations. Washington, D. C., 1921.

Silva, J. Francisco V.: El Libertador Bolívar y el dean Funes en la política argentina. Madrid, Editorial-America, 1918 (?).

Simón Bolívar, Libertador de la América del Sur, por los más grande escritores americanos. Madrid, 1914.

Simón Bolívar y Andrés Bello: Correspondencia. Universidad de Chile, 1935.

Subieta, Sagarnaga L.: Bolívar en Potosí. Potosí, 1925.

Sucre, L. A.: Historial genealógico del Libertador. Caracas, 1930.

Urbaneja, Ricardo: Bolívar, su grandeza en la adversidad. Caracas, 1930.

Urdaneta, N.: Bolívar y Urdaneta. Caracas, 1941.

Uribe, Angel Manuel: El Libertador, su ayo y su capellán. Bogotá, 1884.

Urrutia, Francisco José: El ideal internacional de Bolívar. Quito, 1911.

Valdivieso Montaño, A.: José Tomás Boves. Caracas, 1931.

Vallenilla Lanz, L.: Centenario de Boyacá. Caracas, 1919.

Vallenilla Lanz, L.: Cesarismo democrático. Caracas, 1929.

Vallenilla Lanz, L.: Críticas de sinceridad y exactitud. Caracas, 1921.

Vasconcelos, J.: Bolivarismo y Monroismo. Santiago de Chile, 1935.

Vaucaire, Michel: Bolívar el Libertador. Paris, 1928.

Vejarano, Jorge Ricardo: Orígenes de la independencia sur-americana. Bogotá, 1925.

Velarde, F.: El congreso de Panamá en 1826. Panamá, 1922.

Velasco Ibarra, José María: Estudios varios. Quito, 1928.

Vicuña Mackenna, Benjamín: El almirante Don Manuel Blanco Encalada. Madrid, 1918.

Vilardell Arteaga, R.: Bolívar, Martí y la independencia de Cuba. Caracas, 1936.

Villanueva, Carlos A.: Bolívar y el general San Martín. Paris, 1912.

Villanueva, Carlos A.: Fernando VII y los nuevos estados. Paris, 1912.

Villanueva, Carlos A.: El imperio de los Andes. Paris.

Villanueva, Carlos A.: La santa alianza. Paris.

Villa Urrutia, Wenceslao Ramírez de: La reina María Luisa y Bolívar. Madrid, 1928 (?).

Vivanco, Carlos A.: La conjuracion del 25 de setiembre. Quito, 1929.

Waugh, Elizabeth: Simón Bolívar, a story of courage. New York, 1942.

Wendehake, José Rafael: The master of Bolívar. Colón, 1930.

Yanes, Fr. J.: Relación documentada de los últimos sucesos ocurridos en Venezuela. Ed. by V. Lecuna. Caracas, 1943. 2 vols.

Yepes, J. M.: El congreso de Panamá. Bogotá, 1930.

Ybarra, T. R.: Bolívar, the passionate warrior. New York, 1929.

Magazine and Newspaper Articles

Agosto Méndez, J. M.: El médico del Libertador. (In El Universal, Caracas, September 13, 1930.)

Alban, Mayor H. M.: La idea de Bolívar. (In El Comercio, Quito, July 24, 1930.)

Alfaro, Ricardo J.: Les derniers jours du Liberateur. (In Bulletin special de l'Union Panamericaine, 1931, pp. 13-29.)

Alfaro, Ricardo J.: The Panamericanism of Bolivar and that of today. (In Bulletin of the Panamerican Union, June, 1926, pp. 551-562.)

Alvarado, Lisandro: Leyendas históricas. 1st series. Los delitos políticos en la historia de Venezuela. (In El Cojo Ilustrado, Caracas, 1908, Nos. 65, 78, and 166.)

Andara, J. L.: The Bolívar Doctrine. (In Inter-America, New York, October, 1920, pp. 40-46.)

Andara, J. L.: La doctrina de Bolívar. (In Cultura Venezolana, Caracas, June, 1918, pp. 9-20.)

Arcaya, Pedro Manuel: Bolívar forjador de almas. (In Boletin de la Union Panamericana, December, 1930, pp. 1268-1269.)

Arias, Augusto: Bolívar y Sucre en el Tarqui. (In America, Quito, May, 1929, pp. 121-123.)

Arias, Harmodio: The international policy of Bolívar. (In Inter-America, New York, October, 1918, pp. 7-13.)

Barbagelata, H.: Pichincha y Sucre. (In Rev. d. l'Amerique Latine, 1922.)

Bermúdez, José Alejandro: La quinta de Bolívar en Bogotá. (In Boletín de la Academia Nacional de la Historia, Caracas, March, 1931, pp. 37-41.)

Boletín del Museo Bolivariano: Magdalena Vieja, Lima, Year 1, Nos. 1-2, September-October, 1928.

Boletines del Ejército Libertador de Venezuela, Boletines de 1813 y 1814. (In Boletín de la Academia Nacional de la Historia, Caracas, April 7, 1922, pp. 709-771.)

Bolívar as described by contemporaries. (In Bulletin of the Pan American Union, December, 1930, pp. 1332-1339.)

Bolívar et l'opinion Francaise. (La presse francaise au lendemain de la mort du liberateur.) (In Revue de l'Amerique Latine. Paris, December, 1924, pp. 555-572.)

Brandt, Carlos: La paz del mundo. La obra de Bolívar. (In Cuba Contemporánea, Havana, May, 1924, pp. 59-72.)

Brandt, Carlos: Universal peace, the work of Bolívar. (In Inter-America, New York, October, 1924, pp. 44-54.)

Carvajal, Angel León: Bolívar desde los puntos de vista jurídico, político y sociológico. (In Anales de la Universidad Central, Quito, October-December, 1930, to October-December, 1931.)

Castañeda, Francisco: El Congreso Americano. Antecedentes históricos. I. Proyectos de Valle y de Alberdi. (In Centro-America, Guatemala, October-December, 1916, Vol. VIII (4) pp. 581-591.)

Castro, Antonio N.: Campaña de Bolívar. (Part 1-2) Estudio crítico de las campañas de 1824, de la confederación Peru-Boliviana y del Pacífico hasta la Breña. (In Memorial del Ejército, Lima, June, 1920, pp. 620-629; July, 1920, pp. 643-649.)

Castro Silva, José Vicente: Oració fúnebre en memoria del Libertador. (In Diario Oficial, Bogotá, December 17, 1930, pp. 654-656.)

Coll, Pedro Emilio: Años de aprendizaje de Simón Bolívar. (In El Universal, Caracas, January 27, 1928.)

Corona de Bolívar. (Historical sketch.) (In Cromos, Bogotá, March 18, 1921.)

Correa, Luis: El Libertador en el Perú. (In Boletín de la Academia Nacional de la Historia, Caracas, April-June, 1928.)

Cromos, Bogotá, December 13, 1930, illus. (Special issue.)

Cuervo Marquez, Carlos: Bolívar en México. (In Boletín de la Academia Nacional de la Historia, Caracas, October-December, 1928.)

Cultura Venezolana. Caracas, December, 1930. (Special issue.)

El Comercio. Lima, December 16, 17, 18, 1930. (Special issues.)

El Comercio. Quito. (Articles published December 10-15 and 17, 1930, in commemoration of the centenary of the death of the Liberator.)

Correo de Orinoco. 1818-1821. Reprod. facsimile. Paris, 1939.

Frías, José D.: Las relaciones entre Augustín Iturbide y Simón Bolívar. (In Excelsior, México, D. F. September 27, 1921.)

Gaceta de Caracas, 1808-1818. Reproducción fotomecánica. Paris, 1939.

González, Eloy G.: Los abuelos del Libertador. (In Revista de la Sociedad Boliviana. Bogotá, January, 1927.)

Guimaraes, Argeu: Bolívar y el Brasíl. (In Boletín de la Academia Nacional de la Historia, Caracas, December 31, 1924, pp. 51-68.)

Gutiérrez, José Fulgencio: Bolívar y su obra. (In Estudio, órgano del Centro de Historia de Santander, Bucaramanga, July, 1931, pp. 3-22; August, 1931, pp. 59-78; October, 1931, pp. 107-147.)

Humbert, Jules: Les origenes et les ancêtres du Liberateur Simon Bolivar. Les Bolivar de Biscaye. (Extrait du Journal de la Societé des Americanistes de Paris, Nouvelle serie, Vol. IX, 1912, pp. 1-17.)

Lecuna, Vicente: Adolescencia y juventud de Bolívar. (In Boletín de la Academia Nacional de la Historia, Caracas, October-December, 1930, pp. 446-669.)

Lembcke, Jorge Bailey: La verdadera Manuelita Saenz. (In El Universal, Caracas, September 9, 1927.)

Leturia, Pedro: La acción diplomática de Bolívar ante la Santa Sede a la luz del Archivo vaticano. (In razon y Fe, Madrid, December, 1924, pp. 445-460; February, 1925, pp. 176-191.)

López de Mesa, L.: Simón Bolívar y la cultura ibero-americana. Rev. América, Vol. I, 1945.

Lozano y Lozano, Fabio: Bolívar antes de la revolución. (In revista de la Sociedad Boliviana, Bogotá, January, 1927.)

Lozano y Lozano, Fabio: Bolívar, el Congreso de Panamá y la solidaridad americana. (In Revista del Colegio Mayor de Nuestra Señora del Rosario, Bogotá, February 1, 1930, pp. 32-64.)

Martí, José Julian: Simón Bolívar. (In Revista de Derecho Internacional, Habana, December 31, 1930, pp. 212-219.)

Masur, Gerhard: Simón Bolívar y Alexander von Humboldt. (In Educación, Bogotá, marzo-abril, 1942.)

Méndez Pereira, Octavio: Bolívar orador, pensador, y apóstol. (In La Revista Nueva, Panamá, July, 1917, pp. 1-15.)

Mijares, Augusto: El Libertador como político. (In Boletín de la Academia Nacional de la Historia, Caracas, January-March, 1929, pp. 14-36.)

Naranjo, Enrique: Irish participation in Bolivar's campaigns. (In Bulletin of the Pan American Union, October, 1925, pp. 1015-1022.)

Pan American Union. Centenary of the death of the Liberator, Simón Bolívar, 1930. Clippings and speeches prepared by the Pan American Union. Washington, D. C., Pan American Union, 1931. 1 vol.

Panhorst, Dr.: Simón Bolívar und Alexander von Humboldt. "Ibero-Amerikanisches Archiv." Berlin, 1930.

Parra-Pérez, C.: Bolívar y Venezuela. (In Cultura Venezolana, Caracas, June, 1918, pp. 117-133.)

Parra-Pérez, C.: La dictadura de Bolívar. (In Cultura Venezolana, Caracas, April to June of 1924, pp. 5-29, 123-135.)

Planchart, Julio: Las cartas del Libertador. (In Boletín de la Unión Panamericana, December, 1930, pp. 1445-1459. Illus.)

Relaciones entre Agustín de Iturbide y Simón Bolívar. (In El Porvenir, Monterrey, N. L. México, September 16, 1924.)

Rippy, J. F.: Bolívar as viewed by contemporary diplomats of the United States. Hisp. Am. Hist. Rev., Vol. XV., p. 287.

Rippy, J. F.: The Bolívar centenary. I. Its significance. (In Bulletin of the Pan-American Union, October, 1930, pp. 993-995.)

Rivas, Raimundo: Bolívar as internationalist. (In Bulletin of the Pan-American Union, December, 1930, pp. 1266-1311. Illus.)

Shepherd, W. R.: Bolívar and the United States. Hisp. Am. Hist. Rev., Vol. I., No. 3, pp. 270 ff.

Vivanco, Carlos A.: Cronología de la vida del Libertador. (In Revista de la Sociedad Boliviana, Bogotá, January, 1927, to November, 1936.)

Waters, M.: Bolívar and the Church. Catholic Hist. Rev., December, 1934.

INDEX

Index

A

Agüero, Riva, 502, 503, 509, 512-514, 519, 528

Alto-Peru, *see* Bolivia

Angostura, Venezuela, 277, 297-299, 301, 304, 308, 310, 311, 312, 319, 328, 331, 333, 337, 340, 362, 363, 366, 397, 409, 410, 413; Congress at, 344-361, 386, 395, 398-401, 416, 423, 559

Antilles, 37, 68, 76, 80, 103, 197, 228, 246, 269, 270, 280, 409

Antioguía, New Granada, 387, 388-389

Anzoátegui, officer, 369, 370, 378, 382, 392

Apure River, 203, 305, 315, 317, 318, 325, 327, 328, 329-330, 333, 345-346, 361, 363, 364, 365, 369, 397, 409, 413, 441, 603

Aragua, Venezuela, 95, 223, 227

Aranda, Count, 22, 40

Arauca River, 203, 315, 318, 326, 363, 372, 373

Araure, battle of, 217-221, 230

Argentina, 244, 246, 253-254, 266, 342, 368, 411, 472, 473, 484, 502, 516, 546, 548, 551, 553, 563, 567, 577, 581, 582-583, 588, 590, 678. *See also* Buenos Aires, San Martín, La Plata.

Arismendi, Gen., 244, 277-278, 280, 287, 293, 299, 303, 304, 307, 324, 368, 397-401, 404, 609, 641

Aury, Louis, 274-275

Ayacucho, battle of, 537-540, 543, 544, 567, 583, 585, 602, 625, 657

Aymerich, Gov., 450-453, 459

Azuero, Vicente, 384, 608, 620, 638, 685

B

Barbados, 80, 228, 279

Barcelona, Venezuela, 183, 195, 227, 228, 292-295, 297, 298-299, 347

Barinas, Venezuela, 178-179, 312, 347, 366, 632

Barquisimeto, Venezuela, 136, 137, 216

Barrancas, New Granada, 162-163

Barranquilla, Venezuela, 241, 688

Barreiro, Col., 374, 378-382, 395, 404

Belgrano, Manuel, 254, 470

Bello, Andrés, 34, 84, 101

Berbeos, Juan Francisco de, 24-25

Bermúdez, Francisco, 194, 226, 228, 244, 246, 274, 275, 285-286, 290, 295-296, 299, 307-308, 311, 368, 416, 430, 441-442, 449, 609, 641

Blanco, minister, 306-307

Bogotá, New Granada, 10, 23, 26, 51, 156, 161-162, 239, 241, 245, 249, 366-367, 374, 380, 381, 390, 391, 395, 401, 402, 413-414, 425-427, 439, 443, 446, 451, 483, 487, 503, 504, 513, 514, 520, 527, 535, 545, 555, 582, 597-603, 605, 606, 608-609, 615-616, 619-620, 624-650, 666, 669, 672-675, 681, 683-686; liberation, 98, 236-237, 292, 383-384. *See also* Cundinamarca

Bolivar, Doña María, 28, 32, 33, 34

Bolivar, family, 28, 29

Bolivar, Juan de, 29

Bolivar, Juan Vicente, 30, 31, 84, 85, 96, 128

Bolivar, Juan Vicente, the elder, 28, 30, 31, 34, 38, 46

729

THE AUTHOR

Gerhard Masur: born, Berlin, Germany, 1901; Ph.D. University of Berlin, 1925; began work in history field by preparing reports on philosophy, and on European history between 1815 and 1871 for "Historische Zeitschrift"; lectured at International Congress of History, Oslo, Norway, 1928; taught medieval and modern history, University of Berlin, 1930-35; technical advisor to Minister of Education, Bogotá, Colombia, 1936-38; head of language department, Escuela Normal Superior, lecturer at Escuela Normal Superior, and Catholic University, Bogotá, Colombia, on European history, history of arts, history of literature, and history of philosophy, 1938-46; Rockefeller Foundation grant to finish present book begun in 1941, Caracas Archives, Library of Congress, 1945-46; visiting professor of history, Sweet Briar College, Virginia, 1947—; Author: *Rankes Begriff der Weltgeschichte,* Muenchen, 1926; *Friedrich Julius Stahl: Geschichte seines Lebens,* Berlin, 1930; *Goethe, la ley de su vida,* Bogotá, Colombia, 1939; numerous studies and essays published in Germany and Colombia.